SOCIAL INTERACTION

SOCIAL INTERACTION

Process and Products

Muzafer Sherif

With a new introduction by Augustine Brannigan

ALDINETRANSACTION
A Division of Transaction Publishers
New Brunswick (U.S.A.) and London (U.K.)

Second printing 2009
New material this edition copyright © 2006 by Transaction Publishers.
Copyright © 1967 by Muzafer Sherif.

Library of Congress Catalog Number: 2005053648
ISBN: 978-0-202-30788-6
Printed in the United States of America

Library of Congress Cataloging-in-Publication Data

Sherif, Muzafer, 1905-
    Social interaction process and products / Muzafer Sherif ; with an introduction by Augustine Brannigan.
        p. cm.
    Originally published: Chicago : Aldine Pub. Co., 1967.
    Includes bibliographical references and index.
    ISBN 0-202-30788-3 (alk. paper)
    1. Social psychology. I. Brannigan, Augustine, 1949- II. Title.

HM1033.S49   2005
302—dc22   2005053648

CONTENTS

Introduction to AldineTransaction Edition   ix

Introduction   1

Part I: INTERDISCIPLINARY RELATIONS AND METHODOLOGY

1   If Basic Research Is To Have Bearing on Actualities   29

2   Social Psychology, Anthropology, and
    the "Behavioral Sciences"   40

3   Social Psychology: Problems and Trends in
    Interdisciplinary Relationships   48

4   The "Institutional" vs. "Behavioral" Controversy
    in Social Science, with Special Reference
    to Political Science, *with Bertram Koslin*   98

5   Analysis of the Social Situation   117

Part II: EXPERIMENTAL MODELS FOR SOCIAL INTERACTION

6   Some Social Factors in Perception: The Orientation   125

7   Formation of Social Norms:
    The Experimental Paradigm   136

8   Differential Influence:
    Process underlying Social Attitude   149

9   The Psychology of Slogans   154

10 Conformity-Deviation, Norms, and Group Relations,
    with Carolyn W. Sherif   164

11 A Study in Ego Functioning: Elimination of
    Stable Anchorages in Individual and Group Relations,
    with O. J. Harvey   190

Part III: THE SELF AND REFERENCE GROUPS

12 The Self and Reference Groups: Meeting Ground
    of Individual and Group Approaches   223

13 The Problem of Inconsistency in Intergroup Relations   240

14 The Adolescent in His Group in Its Setting,
    with Carolyn W. Sherif
    A. Theoretical Approach and Methodology Required   247
    B. Research Procedures and Findings   275

Part IV: CONCEPTS, ATTITUDES, AND EGO-INVOLVEMENT

15 Some Social-Psychological Aspects
    of Conceptual Functioning   313

16 Some Needed Concepts in the Study of Attitudes:
    Latitudes of Acceptance, Rejection,
    and Noncommitment   330

17 The Social Judgment-Involvement Approach
    to Attitude and Attitude Change,
    with Carolyn W. Sherif   342

18 The Own Categories Procedure in Attitude Research,
    with Carolyn W. Sherif   353

Part V: EXPERIMENTAL AND FIELD RESEARCH: MAN IN IN-GROUP
        AND INTERGROUP RELATIONS

19 The Necessity of Considering Current Issues
    as Part and Parcel of Persistent Major Problems   369

20 Integrating Field Work and Laboratory
    in Small Group Research   374

21 Experimental Study of Intergroup Relations   392

22 Approach, Hypotheses, and General Design
    of Intergroup Experiments   424

23 Superordinate Goals in the Reduction
    of Intergroup Conflict   445

24 Creative Alternatives to a Deadly Showdown   455

25 Conflict and Cooperation between Functionally
Related Groups, *with Carolyn W. Sherif*   464

Works Cited   475

Index   499

INTRODUCTION TO THE ALDINETRANSACTION EDITION

A YOUNG TURK JOINS THE US ACADEMY

Muzafer Sherif (1906-1988) was one of the twentieth century's most original and productive pioneers in the field of American social psychology. He wrote some twenty-four books and sixty journal articles and chapters. *Social Interaction: Process and Products* was one of the last books he published and remains a classic volume that showcases his most enduring contributions. Sherif was born in Odemis, Izmir, Turkey. He earned a B. A. at the Izmir International College in 1926, and his first M. A. at the University of Istanbul in 1928. In the following year he traveled to the United States where he took his second M. A. at Harvard University in 1932. En route back to Turkey, he stopped in Berlin where he attended a course of lectures by Wolfgang Köhlers on gestalt psychology. In Germany, he also observed first hand the devastating effects of the Great Depression and the frightening rise of fascism in its wake. For his doctoral work Sherif switched to Columbia University where he found Gardner Murphy's political liberalism more consistent with his own socialist leanings. He presented his doctoral thesis, *A Study of Some Social Factors in Perception* in 1935 under Murphy's supervision (Harvey 1989).

His thesis was based on his experimental studies of the "autokinetic effect" that he had initiated at the Gazi Institute (Ankara) where he had taught for a year before registering for his doctoral work at Columbia. The effect is the illusion of movement in a stationary point of light in a darkened environment. It was used as a device to illustrate how individuals and persons in groups who were asked to estimate the magnitude of movement evolve judgments based on their own prior decisions and on the information acquired from others. It became the lynchpin for his insights regarding norm formations, the shaping of attitudes and was extended to the analysis of political change through sloganeering and propaganda. In respect of the latter, Sherif wrote that his analysis pointed to the possibility of "welding together everyday actualities...with a conceptual scheme developed in laboratory research" (p. 154, this volume). This interchange between the identification of basic cognitive processes in the lab and the interpretation of pressing concerns in everyday life became a hallmark of his distinctive approach to social psychology. In his 1936 book, *The Psychology of Social Norms*, Sherif argued that the study of the autokinetic effect in the lab captured "in a simple way the

x   *Introduction to AldineTransaction Edition*

basic psychological process involved in the establishment of social norms" (1936: 105-106). When confronted by an ambiguous stimulus, people borrow information from those in their environment and evolve "frames of reference" to define the stimulus. Such frames of reference become the psychological basis for "stereotypes, fashions, conventions, customs and values" (ibid). The key concept, frames of reference, reflected Sherif's grasp of the emerging importance of gestalt psychology.

In 1937, Sherif returned to Turkey. Initially he rejoined the Gazi Institute but moved to Ankara University in 1939 where he translated many important works of American psychologists. During this period Sherif became involved with socialist causes and wrote social commentaries for the newspapers. He was a critic of the Turkish government's political sympathies with the Nazi regime. In 1943 he published a book in Turkish on *Race Psychology*. It explicitly contested the Nazi doctrine of inherent racial differences and criticized the linkage of racism and fascism (Asliturk and Cherry 2003). For Sherif putative differences in ethnic, racial or cultural groups originated in the collective frames of reference that structured the identities, norms and attitudes of individuals. As a result of his political activism he was detained in 1944 without trial by Turkish authorities and held in solitary confinement for four months. He was only freed after the intervention of the U. S. State Department acting at the behest of his former professors and graduate students, and returned to America in 1945 where he joined the faculty at Princeton as a fellow of the U. S. State Department. In 1945 his book, *The Changing World*, a collation of previous newspaper articles appeared in Turkish co-authored with a Marxist scholar, Behice Boran (Alsiturk and Cherry 2003). In 1947 Sherif became a Rockefeller Research Fellow at Yale. There he collaborated with Hadley Cantril on *The Psychology of Ego-Involvements* (1947). This book borrowed significantly from Marxist concepts such as historical materialism and it praised the developments of equality in the Soviet Union. "In a socialist organization where all means of production and exchange are owned and operated by the state, the possibility exists for each worker…to identify himself with purposes and aspirations of the whole society" (Sherif and Cantril 1947: 375). At Yale, Sherif also met and married his wife, Carolyn Wood Sherif (1912-1982), who initially worked for him as a research assistant and who later became his collaborator and a innovative scholar in her own right.

In 1949 Sherif acquired a tenured position in psychology at the University of Oklahoma where he remained until 1966. In subsequent years he was a visiting professor at the University of Texas and the University of Washington before becoming a Professor of Sociology at Pennsylvania State. In 1967 he was awarded the prestigious Kurt Lewin Memorial Award, one of many tokens of recognition of his accomplishments.

Although we celebrate the work of Dr. Sherif in this volume, one of the things that history has not credited appropriately is the role that Carolyn Wood Sherif played in Muzafer's research. The current volume indicates that C. W. Sherif was a co-author on *some* of his achievements. Even after C. W. Sherif received her doctorate in 1961, the politics of the academy led many to treat her simply as a wife who typed his manuscripts and did not give her due credit for her academic accomplishments. Towards the end of her life she wrote that "a careful historian will recognize that both of us were involved in everything under the name of Sherif after 1945. In several instances where Muzafer asked me to appear as a co-author, instead of in a footnote or preface, I declined, a tendency that persisted into the 1960s. I would not do so again" (C. W. Sherif, 1983: 285-86). The record shows that Dr. Carolyn Sherif not only published nine books with Muzafer, but was senior author on two of them. Later in her career she became a prominent proponent of feminism in psychology, a cause that her husband supported whole-heartedly. In my view, C. W. Sherif was co-author or collaborator to one degree or another in the majority of the chapters that form this collection.

In the following discussion I highlight some of the elements in Muzafer's work that distinguished his thinking in terms of voice, vision and vicissitudes.

VOICE IN THE WORK OF MUZAFER SHERIF

The question of "voice" is that of the starting points from which a scholar speaks, his or her presuppositions and intellectual grounds. What were Sherif's? We find a clue in John Greenwood's history of social psychology in which he argues that at some point in the mid-twentieth century, social psychology began to atrophy when it lost its sense of "the social" in social psychology (2004). Psychologists drifted into cognitive analysis, behaviorism and divided the field into discrete, autonomous areas—personality, attitudes, conflict and conformity *et cetera*, all of which increasingly were tackled by sterile, experimental methods. Notably, Greenwood identifies Sherif as an *exception* to this trend. What distinguished Sherif was his recognition of the dialectical play between the elements that preoccupied psychologists—ego formation, personality, attitudes, stereotypes etc. on the one side, and the larger social and cultural context on the other. For Sherif, ego's affiliations, attitudes, norms and attractions were laid down in large part by the contingencies of society. In other words, the psychology of individuals, without entirely disavowing natural appetites, was essentially social. However, it was not fixed. It could vary by class and culture. In addition, individuals had the capacity to counter domineering group stereotypes often associated with social conflict by leadership and by learning how to restructure the group bonds and hence individual identities, making societies potentially more harmonious. This reflected Sherif's commitment to identifying questions of relevance in the areas of science and public policy.

Sherif had witnessed warfare when European armies attempted to invade Turkey during World War I, and had been exasperated by the needless death of numerous innocent civilians. At the end of war, Turkey was plunged into a civil war among the political factions struggling for power. For Sherif, the primary purpose of studying social psychology was to confront the darkest aspects of human societies, conflict and politically grounded misery. Social psychology became his life's work because it promised to overcome political conflict through scientific analysis of social interaction, and to identify morally informed public policies to alleviate conflict and suffering. His commitment to a socially relevant psychology was intensified by his own experience of arbitrary political oppression in his homeland during World War II.

The emancipatory interests in Sherif's voice appeared in various places in his work but no where more clearly than in *The Psychology of Social Norms* (1936: 201) where he wrote: "At the present, the peoples of many countries are members of more or less sharply defined social classes, the chief of which are the employing class and the working class. From this situation there have naturally arisen different norms of work and enjoyment associated with different standards of living of opposing social classes, even within the same country. These differences in the ways in which opposing classes regulate their lives inevitably bring about intense friction. This indicates that in order to eliminate such basic differences in the norms regulating the lives of human beings, the classes themselves must be eliminated. " Sound familiar?

I make a final point specifically in regard to Sherif's scientific voice. Where social psychology had become marked by sharp divisions and "either-or" dichotomies, Sherif recurrently advocated a more dialectical "both-and" perspective. He advocated the use of both experiments and field work, he advocated that the subject matter of social psychology was both historical and scientific, both scientific and humanistic, that both institutional and behavioral levels of analysis applied, that the field entailed analysis of both group dynamics and ego formations, and that human experiences were jointly determined by internal and external factors. Why? The study of social life should be structured by a keen sense of the issues of interest found in the life world, not by the a priori theories and instrumentalities of what he referred to as the "in-crowd" or the various paradigms. He thought that a discipline rigidly demarcated by such sharp epistemological boundaries fosters a proliferation of inconsequential publications, careerism and institutional isolation but it provides little by way of consensus about the decisive answers to the core questions, and fosters intellectual sectarianism where those in different schools simply omitted references to works of persons holding contrary views. Sherif's advocacy of conceptual inclusiveness was based on his view that the social condition of humanity was based more on a dynamic model of change where system components become re-defined over time as opposed to a hydraulic system based on equilibrium in which system components always returned to their natural status. Sherif's ideas reflected the old Marxian distinction between metaphysics (what we now call positivism) and dialectics.

VISION IN THE WORK OF MUZAFER SHERIF: FROM THE AUTOKINETIC EFFECT TO INTERGROUP CONFLICT

In my view there are two enduring moorings in the lifelong work of Sherif that I believe are interrelated. The first is his work on the autokinetic effect, the second the Robbers Cave group conflict study. Sherif shows that when confronted with an ambiguous stimulus, an optical illusion, observers reported estimates of movement similar to those who were naive subjects like themselves. These estimates converged. Estimates given by subjects observing alone were independent, varied from person to person and persisted from one session, indeed from one day, to another. In other variations of the experiment, Sherif used confederates of some prestige to influence the estimates of the naïve subjects. In some cases the experimenter himself suggested that the subjects were over and/or under-estimating the movement. The subjects tended to bring their estimates into line with the cues from the prestigious confederates and the experimenter. Sherif wrote that "our whole point is that the autokinetic effect can be utilized to show a general psychological tendency and not to reveal the concrete properties of norm-formation in actual life situations…our aim is to show a fundamental psychological tendency related to norm formation" (1936: 93-94). The experiment is an analogy to or metaphor for what occurs naturalistically. Even at the level of physical perception, what people see is colored by their social context. "We have used laboratory material of a sort which is not found commonly in actual social life, but which, nevertheless, demonstrated the psychological processes in such cases" (1935: 47). In other words, the experiment is an allegory that demonstrates a view of social processes that was held in advance of the empirical study, and the study itself was not the source of Sherif's vision but a stage for demonstrating it.

I believe the same argument can be made for his equally important "Robbers Cave Experiment," the study of inter-group conflict and its resolution. This work was undertaken with O. J. Harvey, B. J. White, W. R. Hood, and C. W. Sherif. There were actually three field experiments in 1949, 1953 and 1954, the last of which was held in Robbers Cave State Park in Oklahoma. The study was initially circulated as a technical report in 1954, reprinted informally by the University of Oklahoma bookstore in 1961 but only appeared with a copyright in 1988 with Wesleyan University Press. Unlike Sherif's earlier work, Sherif et al explicitly laid out the research program through a series of specific hypotheses, but the actual conduct of the experiments appears to have had significant ad hoc features arising from contingencies of the field work.

The first study (1949) brought together twenty-four well-adjusted ten- and eleven-year-old boys into an isolated camp setting for eighteen days. After a few days the boys were divided into two groups that participated separately in camp activities. The experimenters then created conflict situations where the two groups competed for rewards. The results suggest that the separate groups evolved distinct identities—the "Red Devils" versus the "Bull Dogs"—as well as internal role hierarchies, informal patterns of discipline to maintain loyalties, emotional attachments, etc. They also engaged in nasty conflicts involving food fights, theft and personal confrontations. Sherif et al. stress that the outcomes including personal animosities, and conflicts were not a property of the individuals, but the structure of segregation and competition created experimentally.

In the subsequent field studies, Sherif et al. introduced the idea of "superordinate goals" to show how inter-group conflict might be abated. As observed previously, individuals assigned to groups and given common tasks, challenges and interactional opportunities evolved group characteristics of role differentiation, group identification, common norms and in-group loyalties. The groups were put into competition. The resulting losers experienced friction and frustration. The sense of frustration resulted in inter-group enmity and hostility – again, not as a function of any individual's disposition, but due to the structural division between the groups and their competition for scarce resources. Attempts to abate conflict through opportunities to socialize did not have the desired effect. Then, a new condition was introduced. The experimenters created a water short-age and encouraged members of each group to help solve the problem, something they undertook with collective enthusiasm since they had an equal interest in restoring the supply. Likewise, when the camp supervisors announced that they could not secure the rental of some favorite films without the cooperation of each group, the boys responded positively, each group contributing to the rental costs for entertainment for the whole camp. Again, the identification of a superordinate goal created the social capital to transcend in-group loyalties and inter-group hostilities.

My point is that these complicated, and long-term field experiments, like the autokinetic effect, read now as allegories. In this volume Sherif moves from the account of the Robber Cave field studies to an analysis of the cold war and how superordinate goals may have a key role to play in securing world peace. So the lesson of the field studies is not limited to the conduct of delinquent boys, nor is it about adolescence. Sample sizes were small, there were no tests of significance or sophisticated scales. The lesson is about how social structures help to shape inter-group animosities in society generally, and how the observations from ma-nipulations undertaken in the field, in this case the identification of superordinate goals, may contribute to governance nationally and internationally. Were he alive today, Sherif would be encouraging people to think about this paradigm in the face of world terrorism. The finding that most of the recent individuals involved in terrorism individually were relatively decent chaps is entirely consistent with Sherif's belief that prejudice and inter-group hostility arises internally from groups facing inter-group frustration and humiliation. Are there superordiante goals to transcend such inter-group conflicts today?

VICISSITUDES IN THE WORK OF MUZAFER SHERIF

Sherif's last paper concerned the "crisis in social psychology" (1977). He noted that by the late 1960s and early 1970s that the discipline was experiencing a profound sense of crisis and disappointment. The paradox was that there was at the time a "sky-rocketing boom" in the number of publications, but no sense of breakthrough. Rodrigues and Levine (1999) convened a conference of social psychologists from the classical period who explored the same themes. Social psychology as a discipline failed in this period to develop a consensus on the important questions, failed to show evidence of incremental progress over time, became increasingly preoccupied with cognitive mechanisms and was incorrigi-bly fixated on the experimental method (Brannigan 2004). In 1967 Sherif noted that "substantial breakthroughs. . . are urgently needed". . ."yet, realistically, it cannot be claimed that the anticipated breakthroughs are in sight" (p. 10 this volume). He reviewed the two most productive areas of social psychology in the 1970s—small groups research and attitude change research. As for the small groups research, he noted: "This huge harvest looks impressive especially in technical surface, in the announced levels of significance of findings. Yet when we start to separate golden kernels from the chaff to store them for the future, it is quite a different story. It does not add up to much" (1977: 368-69). Likewise in his reference to the attitude change research he noted, "not much is needed to point to the scanty yield in spite of tremendously thriving output" (1977: 370).

What was the problem? For Sherif the scientific method in social psychology had created an emphasis on approaches that may have been fruitful in the natural sciences, but were less relevant in the social sciences. First he identified *reductionism*. Small group researchers wanted to reduce properties of groups to traits of individuals and to their personalities (leadership, independence etc), rather than focusing on the emergent properties of normative regulation, role coordination and group functions. The second problem was *ahistoricism*. Researchers approached groups devoid of any sense of the contingencies and context of groups in everyday life, and acted as though groups and group membership could be presupposed. This approach lacked "the specification of the terms of interdependence" (1967: 369) – the norms, values and motives that linked persons to groups. People join and leave groups under particular circumstances, necessitating an approach that puts the role of the group into the larger context of human life.

Sherif suggested that the discipline could benefit from two things. The first step to getting on more solid ground was the cultivation of a greater skepticism towards the efficacy of experimental methods; he cited Rosenthal's work on "experimenter effects" and Orne's studies of "demand characteristics. " Sherif specifically criticized the pseudo-scientific precision of approaches to attitude change in the lab that had little bearing on processes in everyday life, however ingenious the lab designs. In addition, he advocated cultural and comparative psychology—approaches that suggested much greater variability in how other societies organized human behavior compared with the Western, industrialized model, as well as environmental/ecological psychology which suggested how social structures varied in the face of challenges in the physical environment. Sherif's approach was to advocate greater eclecticism both in terms of methods and in terms of models of society.

However, his core remarks to facilitate a resolution of the crisis were put in the form of two specific questions. If social psychologists hoped to overcome the crisis identified in the 1970s, they would have to confront two fundamental questions. First, "what is the nature of the social system" in terms of its structure and functioning (p. 375)? Remarkably, the first question is about the macro level environment in which social action is situated, not the biological substrata. This signaled Sherif's belief that human nature, norms, motives, attitudes and emotions were tuned primarily to and by the social environment. The second question was: "what is the nature of the *human* psychological system" (p. 376)? Is human nature like a "physical equilibrium system" with prefixed settings for norms and attitudes? Or is it "transformed during development and concrete interchanges with the social environment" with potential shifts in value orientations regarding race, gender, class and occupation? Clearly, Sherif preferred the latter conception.

Reading between the lines one can see his dialectical and phenomenological presuppositions. On the dialectical side, societies are always changing, frequently in conflict, but in a constant struggle to achieve human aspirations. This element of his thinking was more vivid in his earlier writings, and indeed appears to have been muted after his settlement in Oklahoma. Asliturk and Cherry (2003) suggest this may have been a result of the McCarthyism of the early 1950s and Sherif's vulnerability as an immigrant alien. However, his historicist sensibilities survived. On the phenomenological side, his preoccupation with the world of everyday life, with embodiment, with the influence of the social in perception, motives, feelings and norms remains paramount, and this goes some way towards explaining his methodological eclecticism.

Augustine Brannigan

REFERENCES

Asliturk, E. and Cherry, F. 2003. "Muzafer Sherif: The interconnection of politics and profession," *History and Philosophy of Psychology Bulletin* 15(2): 11-16..

Brannigan A. 2004. *The Rise and Fall of Social Psychology*, New Brunswick NJ: AldineTransaction.

Greenwood, J. D. 2004. *The Disappearance of the Social in American Social Psychology*, New York: Cambridge University Press.

Harvey, O. J. 1989. "Muzafer Sherif," *American Psychologist* 44: 1325-26.

Rodrigues, A. and Levine R. V. (editors) 1999. *One Hundred Years of Experimental Social Psychology*, New York: Basic Books.

Sherif, C. W. 1983. "Carolyn Wood Sherif" pp. 279-93 in A. N. O'Connell and N. F. Russo (editors) *Models of achievement: Reflections of eminent women in psychology*, New York: Columbia University Press.

Sherif, M. 1936. *The Psychology of Social Norms*, New York: Harper.

_____ 1977. "Crisis in social psychology: Some remarks towards breaking through the crisis," *Personality and Social Psychology Bulletin* 3: 368-382.

Sherif, M and Cantril, H. 1947. *The Psychology of Ego-Involvements*, New York: Wiley.

INTRODUCTION

These selections from my work are grouped under five headings: (1) Interdisciplinary relations and methodology; (2) Experimental models for social interaction; (3) Self and reference groups; (4) Concepts, attitudes and ego-involvement; and (5) Man in in-group and intergroup relations.

The selections range from strict laboratory experiments to field studies carried out in natural settings; however, the conceptual tools and logic used in specific research units are the same. The same theoretical formulation and rationale operationalized in these research units are elaborated in the more generalized analysis of the social situations in which human interaction takes place (Part I). They are applied to a variety of specific controversial issues (for example, the "institutional"-vs.-"behavioral" controversy in political science and, for that matter, in contemporary social science in general). The same conceptual framework proved useful in the conception and design of research projects on man in his in-group and intergroup relations (Part V).

The key problems of human interaction and its impact on man are not covered by considering interaction only as a process at one point in time. The consequences of interaction are manifested in value-charged products, such as social norms and structure differentiation (statuses and roles). Unless we consider such products of interaction, we cannot account for the person's self-picture, which contributes to whatever consistency he may maintain in subsequent interaction episodes. The products of interaction are the basis for whatever stabilization or orderliness is achieved in subsequent interactions.

But products of interaction—roles, norms, attitudes—which do contribute to the consistency and orderliness of interaction among persons, are not immutable. They are products of interaction, but they are subject to change during further interaction. Thus the topic of *social change* and specification of conditions conducive to change are integral parts of the problem of social interaction. Hence my close concern from the very beginning of my work over such apparently diverse topics as norms, organization, sociocultural setting, collective interaction and social movements, on the sociological side; on the psychological side, I have

1

been equally concerned with motivational urges, deprivation and feelings of uncertainty, feelings of insecurity, feelings of frustration, and widespread unrest.

My early experiments with autokinesis were designed to demonstrate in step-by-step sequence the *stabilization* of reactions that participating individuals achieve through their interaction in fluid and unstable conditions (Selection 7). The individuals' convergence on a common norm over time, after starting from normlessness and erratic diversity, can best be expressed as the establishment of stability within the bounds of prevailing conditions. It is not accidental that the other research problems that occupied me at the same period were the strivings of people to change their lot through participating in collective interaction situations and social movements. Interaction in out-of-the-ordinary conditions is the most fertile ground for convergence on new values and for social change. This conceptualization is reflected well in "The Psychology of Slogans," which was published during that early period (Selection 9).

In brief, a rounded study of human interaction has to go beyond the study of a process at a point in time. It entails study of the products of interaction (structure and norms). It entails the problem of change and the specification of conditions conducive to change in both their psychological and sociological aspects. My research has been marked by a constant search for those interaction situations (wherever they may occur) that are conducive to stabilization of social relations and for those interaction situations (wherever they may occur) that are conducive to the change of stabilized, bureaucratized schemes of social relations and associated attitudes. This search for interaction conditions optimal for the study of stability and conditions optimal for the study of change in social relations is responsible, more than anything else, for the wide diversity of topics tackled over the years.

COMMON THREADS

Despite the wide diversity of topics and problems selected for investigation, a few threads are unmistakably common to all. The common threads lie in systematic orientation and basic principles that have served as consistent guides in formulating problems, whether the problems were theoretical or topical. The same orientation and principles have governed the manner in which each specific problem or study topic was approached. They have guided the formulation of hypotheses and dictated the research strategies. In fact, the choice of methods and techniques for the study of every topic (whether in the laboratory or under natural field conditions) falls within the domain of theoretical orientation and basic principles. Methodology, including the particular research design, is not merely a technical issue, independent of the delineation of the problem and the hypotheses derived from this delineation.

The common threads in theory and in research strategy, including the choice of variables, procedures, and techniques, are elaborated in my various works. They are responsible for whatever measure of coherence that may have been achieved in the selections presented in this book, and are specified especially in Part I. Their implications are followed throughout, as exemplified in "Integrating Field Work and Laboratory in Small Group Research" (Selection 20) and in both experimental and field studies of group and intergroup relations (Selections 21, 22, and 23). They are providing the guidelines for our ongoing projects, initiated in 1958, on adolescent groups in differentiated sociocultural settings in various cities (Selection 14).

Needless to say, what is presented in the way of systematic theoretical orientation, research strategies, and research technology did not drop from the blue. In all these matters I am indebted to many; these debts are acknowledged in appropriate places. I can only claim that I borrowed selectively from diverse theoretical and technical developments, and combined them into one work program. No theoretical orientation, no technical advance that moves solidly to the future is the single-handed creation of one man or one school in isolation. I learned my lesson well from reading such giants as Marx and Engels, Durkheim, William James, George Herbert Mead, Bartlett, Wertheimer, and Piaget: The first requisite in building anything worthwhile is close familiarity with the background and prevailing state of things. It is only through recognizing the background and accumulating developments in one's problem area that one can find his own bearings and proceed to the future on solid grounds.

Of course, a person immersed in a particular line of development, especially in a personally involving area like social psychology, cannot be impartial with regard to what he claims are the main features of his work. He is *in* it. What he attempts to achieve may be different from what he actually delivers. Despite the possibility of such an autistic evaluation, I may not be unrealistic in selecting as the salient characteristic of the social psychology presented here its insistence that research have a sure bearing on actualities (Selection 1). A closely related concern has been that the problem selected for investigation be significant, not trivial.

It requires a deliberate decision to insure that all of the wear and tear, the costly and time-consuming procedures, and the instrumental paraphernalia of research are focused on getting realistic answers to a significant problem in human relations. A fateful decision has to be made before research begins. It concerns what will come first; the problem itself, or some cherished commitment to a school of thought, with its addiction to a lingo, a set of procedures, and other instrumentalities currently *en vogue* with the "in crowd" who are supposed to have the "know-how."

The choice of a problem for study is not an idle matter. If the problem is significant and if it is clarified through sufficient familiarity with actualities, the *problem sets limits* in the choice of relevant variables, in the formulation of appropriate and plausible hypotheses, and (to no lesser degree) in the choice of an effective research design, procedures, and measurement techniques.

Most of the game is played already by the time it is decided what variables are crucial out of the many possible variables. The hypotheses stating certain alternatives from so many possible outcomes drastically limit the solutions that can be expected or even that are possible. For the same reasons, the choice of study procedures and techniques is no matter of mere technical refinement, even though technical refinement is ultimately one sure proof of the maturity of a discipline.

When human relations are themselves the topic of study, the procedures and techniques that the researcher introduces become parts of the stimulus conditions that affect interaction. If he is not aware of this fact, his research methods become unaccounted for variables, occasionally weighing as heavily as those he has deliberately introduced in the study design. Unfortunately for the researcher, the human person perceives, evaluates, and reacts in terms of all factors in the situation, not only those that the investigator intends for him to notice (see Sherif, 1936, Chapter 3; Sherif, 1966).

Perhaps neglect of the considerations just raised may be at least partly responsible for the fact that solid advances in social science have constituted only a minute fraction of the huge research output, some of which is technically impressive. One might declare therefore that, at this primitive stage of social science and the current state of human relations, the breakthroughs needed in social science lie less in technical refinement than in taking stock of what has piled up through our orthodox pursuit of the habitual grooves in theory and research of our respective disciplines and their "schools." If the breakthroughs needed could come merely from the technical refinement of models already developed in the more established disciplines, such as mathematics or physics, we might just as well relinquish our difficult task to a few mathematicians and physicists, keeping ourselves busy under their guidance to work here and there in building the edifice. Unfortunately, our task is much more difficult. The voluminous yet patchy output in research literature is ever forcing us to confront the problem of the isomorphism between theoretical models and the pattern of human interaction situations.

The alternative I have followed throughout my efforts in social psychology has been more modest, more primitive if you will, than building upon and refining a formal model borrowed from the more securely established sciences. I shied away from "premature formalization," and was equally wary of falling into the confusing welter of descriptive eclecticism that shoots off in all directions, lacking directive orientation. In actual work practice, my alternative choice has been to start with some *persistent* problem in human relations. The problems of what constitutes the human interaction situation, of norm formation, of differentiation and function of group organization, of the person's conformity and deviation, of attitude formation and change, and of intergroup relations are among these persistent problems. My initial step in research, therefore, has been to bring such a problem and its manifold aspects into focus.

STRATEGY AND OPERATIONAL INSTRUMENTALITIES

After bringing the persistent problem into focus, I made it a point *not* to plunge immediately into postulational or even definitional preoccupations, much less into the choice of techniques. First, I took pains to "waste" a great deal of time gaining familiarity with the actualities of the problem area by direct personal exposure to them and to those who dealt with the actualities in the course of their daily tasks. Obviously, this is what is referred to as a phenomenological approach.

But the world, especially the world of human relations, is not fully revealed in one person's direct experience. One person's experience is limited in scope and, of course, it is not immune to his particular brand of selectivity. We must check ourselves against the subjectivism of an unbridled and undisciplined kind of phenomenology. No matter how well trained the person may be, his direct experience is subject to the distortions of his own particular commitments, predilections, or vested interests. His experiences have to be checked against those of a wide variety of persons who have dealt with events in the problem area. Even this is not sufficient before one engages in building hypotheses and designs that will provide effective strategies in data collection.

At this stage, my practice has been to look into two sorts of literature. One consists of cases that reveal relevant events more or less independently across hitherto unrelated developments and across cultures. Thus, before getting to the hypotheses and design of the experiments on intergroup relations, I looked into cases of conflict and prejudice. The psychological literature then available was primarily devoted to ethnic and racial prejudice, studied chiefly through attitude scales and questionnaires in the 1930's and 1940's. It was not sufficient to cover the scope of the intergroup relations problem. Then we looked into cases of conflict in labor relations and conflict between nations, with special emphasis on the rise of new alignments and new conflicts in social movements. I tried to locate where the information acquired from personal observation intersected with the wide variety of cases of intergroup conflict reported in the available literature. The common properties identified at this intersection pointed to the hypotheses tested in several intergroup experiments (Part V).

The intersection of information had to be conceptualized. For this purpose, I turned to a second sort of literature. In search of working principles and operational strategies (procedures, techniques), I have not found the speculative literature on how sciences are built, the philosophy of science, or abstract discussions of methodology very helpful. We have found it more helpful to turn directly to the relevant research literature—laboratory or developmental studies in psychology and reports from social scientists who bothered to use empirical data in their theorizing.

In addition to familiarity with actualities, one needs a set of appropriate principles to guide the formulation of specific hypotheses. Unless we go beyond a "disciplined phenomenology" at this point, we have no basis for capturing from the flow of behavior those particular events that serve as reliable indicators of underlying psychological processes. The best basis for selecting such indicators is the recurrent findings in experimental and empirical studies of a problem area that have stood the test of time.

The principle of psychological selectivity, the principle that experience—and hence behavior—is jointly determined by factors both internal and external to the person, and the principles governing the relative contribution of external stimulus factors in structured and unstructured situations are among those that have guided me in formulating hunches and selecting what is and is not appropriate in research operations.

The set of principles that I have come to rely upon throughout the years is not derived so much from speculative systems but rather from verified findings reported by various authors. I have acknowledged the sources of such principles in appropriate contexts. These principles are not just a collection of unrelated, untried, or merely programmatic assumptions; they constitute a set with a coherent pattern. I have used them consistently in formulating research.

A word on the research strategy adopted throughout and the considerations observed in selecting research tools, techniques, and procedures: I have always regarded the instrumentalities for data collection (experimental set-up, procedures, techniques, observer, experimenter, apparatus, questionnaires, rating material, interview schedule, attitude scale) as *part and parcel of the interaction situation*. This conception of the research situation had the highest priority in my thinking from the beginning of my work. Its implications were observed in the experiments on norm formation, in which the individuals participating were not aware that they were mutually influencing one another toward a common norm. The implications of considering all procedures, techniques, and the subject-investigator relationship in the chores of data collection were incorporated in detail into the operations developed in our recent and current studies of group formation and functioning.

They prompted us to insist that methods of attitude measurement should be *indirect* or disguised in order to minimize and (hopefully) to eliminate the "demand character" of the research situation.

Guided by the conception that research instrumentalities are parts of the interaction situation (which has been amply verified in recent years), my practice has been to use the criterion of appropriateness to the demands of the problem in selecting procedures and techniques rather than their *refinement in the abstract* without regard to their consequences.

For example, in the study of groups, the formally more appealing procedure of obtaining reaction samples at prearranged time intervals with a fixed number of participants in each session is the *last* thing we should do if we are concerned with learning something about the workings of actual groups, of leader-follower relations as they occur, especially in tightly knit human groups.

Groups are not formed for the benefit of a technologist in social science. Human groups have degrees of secretiveness of their own. If not secrets, human groups have degrees of in-group exclusiveness that prompt them to freeze in various degrees when outsiders intrude or attempt to impose their presence, even without harmful intent. "Small-group" researchers are not exceptions in the matter of protective secrecy, precautions, or the propriety of exclusiveness or privacy, practiced by any human group. Of course, if we are satisfied with perpetuating the study of two or more individuals without established reciprocities as "group research," and if we are satisfied with restricting ourselves to eliciting responses to such matters as the desirability of good weather or the affirmation of the consensus on motherhood or God, the pre-arranged neat and symmetrical designs of data collection will continue to yield "clean" data that can be made to fit obligingly into the formal model to which we are committed.

When we accept in earnest the challenge of considering our methods and techniques as integral parts of the interaction situation in the study, when we follow the implications of this challenge to the point of insuring that only the variables stated in the problem design are operative, we are taking upon ourselves a whale of a job. Maintaining the naturalness of interaction is not an idle matter. It creates serious risks and additional tasks in data collection. Under these less artificial and less strait-jacketed conditions, it is very difficult and objectively risky to obtain and handle data. For one thing, there is the serious risk that the observer will be subjectively selective. This risk becomes serious especially when he reports, for example, on interaction episodes that he should *not* and indeed cannot record when the events are taking place, because he is not supposed to interrupt the natural flow of interaction.

In the face of these serious difficulties, we tried to avoid falling into expediency for the convenience of the researcher. It would be so easy to have tape recorders capture every word and cameras capture every move, thus obtaining neat data in measured sequence. But in this case, "neat" data so collected would be another heap of artifacts or orderly data on inconsequential matters.

Instead of paying such a price for tidy data, I have found it more worthwhile to find ways to check the reliability of the observer's reports. One is to use a *combination of methods*. In addition to observation, I have introduced, in inconspicuous and natural fashion, sociometric choices, independent raters, and ratings of performance as indicators of interpersonal relations (like-dislike). These combined techniques served as a check on the representativeness and reliability of the observer's reports on the open-ended conditions of natural interaction.

If we are sufficiently concerned that our findings have a bearing on actualities, we can impose upon ourselves the further task of moving back and forth in our research between the laboratory and the field while studying the same problem. Over the years this has proved to be an effective check on the validity of generalizations.

It seems to me that the difference between the strategy of allowing natural open-ended interaction situations (which at times yields patchy, unsymmetrical, and incomplete data that are hard to handle in the short run) and the strategy of neatly prearranged point-to-point subject interaction (which yields neat, symmetrical, well-arranged data) is not that the first is tender-minded and permissive while the second is hard-headed and rigorous. "Hard-headedness" in this case not infrequently amounts to bull-dozing over the very variables that were supposed to be the object of investigation in the first place. This kind of "tough-mindedness" may amount to being soft-headed and irresponsible.

Briefly then, this is the substance of the main threads that run through these 25 selections. The threads running through them all have unerringly guided my work through the years in both its theoretical aspect and its operational aspect. These common threads, I repeat for emphasis, are that: (1) research have a bearing on actualities; (2) it be on some significant persistent problem in human affairs; and (3) the research strategy and operations (procedures, methods, techniques) be deliberately selected in line with the master criterion of their appropriateness to the dictates of the problem at hand.

It was highly gratifying that my colleagues converged on these common threads when they had occasion to comment on my work. At the annual convention of the American Psychological Association in 1966, the Division of Social Psychology and Personality organized a symposium on my works. Upon the invitation of the symposium chairman, Dr. O. J. Harvey, colleagues sent their comments, and their common theme was my insistence that the research have a bearing on actualities and that the problem studied be significant.

My insistence on these common threads and my persistence in

repeating them are more than professional matters to me. They are rooted in my personal intellectual development. Otherwise, it would have been extremely difficult for me to follow them so consistently, even when expediency and the ups and downs of professional life and pressing financial considerations dictated that I follow other alternatives.

Because it is relevant, I will say something about this personal background. As an adolescent with a great deal of curiosity about things, I saw the effects of war: families who lost their men and dislocations of human beings. I saw hunger. I saw people killed on my side of national affiliation; I saw people killed on the other side. In fact, it was a miracle that I was not killed along with hundreds of other civilians who happened to be near one of the invasion points the day Izmir (Smyrna) was occupied by an army, with the blessings of the victorious Western colonial powers at the end of World War I.

It was the period of the final dissolution of the Ottoman Empire and the rise of nationalisms within the disintegrating empire. The rise of Turkish nationalism, which fascinated me as it did all other young-sters of my generation, resulted in the new Turkish Republic, born against great odds, against obstacles created by colonial powers. Having firsthand experience in the mystique of a rising nationalism has helped me greatly in studying and understanding the social movements that mold new nations in Africa and Asia.

I was profoundly affected as a young boy when I witnessed the serious business of transaction between human groups. It influenced me deeply to see each group with a selfless degree of comradeship within its bounds and a correspondingly intense degree of animosity, destruc-tiveness, and vindictiveness toward the detested outgroup—their behavior characterized by compassion and prejudice, heights of self-sacrifice, and bestial destructiveness. At that early age I decided to devote my life to studying and understanding the causes of these things. Of course, for some years I did not know how to go about it, but I started reading whatever I could lay my hands on about history and social problems. By the time I came to the United States for graduate study, I had firmly decided that my life's work would be social psychology. It had become a growing conviction with me that social psychology could make a major contribution to the discovery of the principles governing the workings of human relations. Through the years, my conviction re-garding my choice of social psychology has been strengthened.

Having chosen social psychology as my life's work through the impact of direct encounter with grim events in human relations and having spent years in search of appropriate strategies and techniques for their study, I believe that the most urgently needed scientific break-throughs have to be in the understanding and prediction of man's social relations such as they are: messy, contradictory, and fraught with con-flict, suffering, and agony.

"SCIENTIFIC AND HUMANISTIC"—
NOT "SCIENTIFIC VERSUS HUMANISTIC"

I am only one of a growing number of social psychologists who are committed in one form or another to the conviction that substantial breakthroughs in the study of man's social relations are urgently needed. Various proposals have been advanced for such substantial developments. Some have seen this potential thrust through models in the image of mathematics and physics, some through concerted interdisciplinary efforts with the social sciences, and some through highly complicated, tightly rigorous experimental and other designs. Plagued with practical problems that require immediate solutions—desegregation, juvenile delinquency, disadvantaged youth, attitude change in ideological confrontations, intergroup conflicts, and war—in recent years research funds have been made available at a geometrically accelerated pace by both the federal government and large foundations.

Yet, realistically, it cannot be claimed that the anticipated great breakthroughs are in sight. The transfer value of generalizations derived on the basis of high-powered inferences and impressively rigorous studies for solving the actualities of current problems is highly questionable in many instances. Dismayed with this state of what is considered the "scientific approach," with its "heartless" aloofness and its maladaptive rigor, one reaction has been a plea to depend on "the humanistic approach" for achieving insight into the human problems and their solution. A manifestation of this is the appearance of the society of humanistic psychology in the 1960's, which includes among its members some well-known psychologists and other scholars.

It seems to me that the "scientific" and the "humanistic" need not necessarily be opposed to one another. The "scientific" need not be heartless in selecting, in initiating its problems, in its concerns over the applications of its discoveries. And the "humanistic" need not be "soft-headed" and merely breast-beating. The humanistic orientation and objectives can be realistically implemented through analyses and instrumentalities that are only possible through the scientific approach. Other modes of dealing with human problems have been tried for centuries: the politician's, the general's, the theologian's, and those of authority figures in public life and academia. And where did they lead human destinies? Some of the central study problems of social psychology, for example, have also been persistent problems for humanists: among them the rise, functioning, resistance, and change of *valuation* or the normative process in man; the identification of the person; the widening horizons of this identification. The comprehensive treatment of such persistent problems awaits the concerted concentration of both the "scientist" and the "humanist."

The cause of dismay is not in the scientific approach per se. What is needed is more science, not less. The source of dismay lies in mal-adaptive use of methods and techniques, in uncritical, unimaginative use of models. It lies in insufficient initial familiarity with the domain of the problem area and in insufficient articulation of its properties that will lead to the selection of appropriate techniques and their refinement. Therefore, what is needed is more science and not less, even if we are initially prompted by humanistic concerns. The plea of "more science than less science" is not, however, another plea for the brave shiny world of technocracy. There is much more in the human organizational patterns than the hand-to-mouth efficiency of the technocrat.

THE METHODOLOGICAL NECESSITY OF
AN INTERDISCIPLINARY APPROACH

The choice of "Interdisciplinary Relations and Methodology" as a title for Part I (devoted to the approaches of theoretical guideposts and the methodological commitments suggested by these guideposts) is more than a matter of terminological preference.

The point is made in various connections that interdisciplinary borrowing is necessary if social psychology is ever to amount to any-thing. The social psychologist, whose task it is to study man's experience and behavior in relation to social stimulus situations, has to borrow his information on social stimulus situations from the sociologist, the anthro-pologist, the political scientist, and other social scientists. Social or-ganization, the norm system, language, and other aspects of nonmaterial and material culture that surround man are social stimuli that should be considered at their meaningful and patterned *level*. Reductionistic conceptions of sociocultural stimuli have led us into sterility and dead ends.

In some quarters, interdisciplinary give and take is interpreted as spreading oneself too thin. This interpretation is a hasty one and reflects a tone of superciliousness toward social science on the part of those who still consider it more prestigious to have psychology grounded in the camp of natural sciences. Psychology, including experimental psychology, has always been interdisciplinary. It has always borrowed from physics, chemistry, anatomy, and physiology. Borrowing from more established physical sciences was considered proper; it was the thing to do; it was done almost with an air of pride. But borrowing from sociology and anthropology, which are not so well established and do not have impressive gadgets, was viewed in a different light. The ortho-doxy of the establishment, on the whole, considered preoccupation with materials from social sciences detrimental to specialization in depth within psychology. The result was a social psychology lacking interest in and ill informed about the sociocultural stimulus situations. A social psychology that sorely neglected developing the needed framework concerning stimulus conditions (the setting) within which the interaction takes place was doomed to make no effective headway. There is much more to the pattern of the social stimulus situation than what catches the eye in a glance. The factors in the situation that *count* in shaping the behavior are not merely those that an experimenter explicitly presents to the respondent. These factors explicitly introduced by the researcher—instruction, forms to be filled in, apparatus, and so forth—are only *parts* of the situation.

Specification of the sets of factors in a situation should be the first task of the researcher. They cannot be taken for granted. The recent corrective against what was lost by neglecting the rounded account of the explicit and *implicit* factors in a social situation came in the currently flourishing movement referred to as the "social psychology of psychological experiment."

My research program was initiated with the specification of the stimulus conditions for social perception. This theoretical and methodological concern is well reflected in the discussions of "The Frame of Reference in Psychological Phenomena" (Chapter III) and "Stimulus Situations in Social Psychology" (Chapter IV) in my first book, *The Psychology of Social Norms* (1936; Torchbook edition, 1966). This concern over the proper analysis of the situation in which interaction takes place is apparent in all the selections, specifically Selection 5.

The examination of the state of things and trends in social psychology points unmistakably to this conclusion: the pattern of the human interaction situation is not embodied in this or that aspect of it. It is not a punctiform affair. There is much more to an interaction situation than even the sensitive recording devices can capture. The interaction situation involves a sociocultural *niveau*. It involves ingredients frequently taken for granted or *not* made explicit in the study designs. These should be specified. Such specification necessarily involves the patterned, the meaningful characteristics (properties) of the sociocultural ingredients in the situation.

The description of the sociocultural stimulus situation through reductionistic, unsystematic improvisations of the psychologists, as a rule, have yielded distorted, incomplete, ill-informed pictures of man's sociocultural surroundings. The social psychologist has no choice but to borrow his information from the social scientist and the anthropologist if he is not to remain forever ignorant about sociocultural setting, organizational pattern, value system, and related topics. This information is at least as essential to the social psychologist as what the psychologist was ever eager to learn from the physicist and other natural scientists about the nature of physical stimulus energies.

This borrowing of sociocultural information is one of the major interdisciplinary tasks of the social psychologist. The patterned properties of sociocultural objects have to be kept under consideration in the study of social judgment and social perception. The structural properties of the status and role reciprocities must be considered in the study of interaction in in-group and intergroup relations if we are to avoid falling again into the trap of collecting mutilated data.

This, in turn, has inescapable implications for the choice of research strategies, data collection procedures, and techniques. The patterned nature of sociocultural objects, the exact arrangements of these patterns, and the structural characteristics of roles and statuses make the use of certain strategies and techniques appropriate and the use of others inappropriate, no matter how desirable these latter may be in the abstract.

Devising research strategies and techniques appropriate to the patterned character of the social situation is only part of the picture. When it comes to selecting a model for research, the psychologist has been prone to select one ready-made, frequently from the physical sciences. However, sociocultural structures and events are *not* mere continuations of physical or biological events, even though they are not independent of them (see Selection 3). Therefore, a model extrapolated directly from a physical model is bound to omit characteristic features of human interaction. Surely this is simplistic unless we carefully test the *isomorphism* of the model with at least the essentials in the pattern of interaction situations.

BLINDERS DRAWN BY DICHOTOMIES

An inevitable aspect of culture is putting things and events into categories. One dominant and frequent case is putting things in *either-or* form—that is, putting things in dichotomies—with all the resulting consequences of partisan evaluations.

Some of the blinders standing in the way of functional analysis of interaction process and its products derive from time-honored dichotomies: individual vs. group, heredity vs. environment, behavioral vs. institutional, cognitive vs. behavioral, leadership vs. followership, federal power vs. state power.

In my research program I have taken a stand with regard to such dichotomies. Studying the processes involved, I have had to point out that, on both factual and theoretical grounds, these dichotomies are untenable. They lead to artificial categories that blind us to the implications of the interrelationship of the factors in the pattern or system. Thus I have argued against putting the relationship in terms of the laboratory-*versus*-field approaches. Instead, I have been making the plea for putting the relationship in the form of laboratory *and* field approaches for cross-checking the validity of generalizations. Again, in the matter of analysis, we have made the plea of institutional *and* behavioral analysis as opposed to the feud of institutional *versus* behavioral. But the plea for both institutional and behavioral, of course, does not obliterate the fact that these are different levels of analysis, requiring different units of analysis. Instead it proposes a *sequence* of analysis starting first with larger structures (see Selection 2 and Selection 3).

In the time-honored dichotomy of individual vs. group, which is a source of irreconcilable controversies, I found it erroneous to take sides as either a romantic individualist or a romantic group apologist. We adhere to the study of groups with their own properties and then study individuals as parts of the system. Thus it is feasible to consider groups as realities without falling into the individualistic trap and yet not obliterate the individual. Instead we start with the systemic properties of groups and carry the analysis to single individuals. This allows the study of the individual in as elaborate detail as desired, but within the appropriate setting of interaction. I shall illustrate the point when I deal with "Man in In-Group and Intergroup Relations" (Part V).

The same conception is applied to the leader-follower dichotomy. The leader too, no matter what his power, is not outside the collectivity. The leader is always a leader in relation to the collectivity and not outside it, even if he is a ruthless tyrant or an inspiring hero. Leadership studies started to make headway when leaders were studied in relation to followers and followers in relation to the patterned ties that bound them and the leader together.

INNER AND OUTER INFLUENCES JOINTLY CONSTITUTE THE FRAME OF REFERENCE OF BEHAVIOR

One vantage point achieved both in psychology and in sociology with seminal implications for theory and the actual conduct of research has been the interactionist position. The interactionist position (whatever its variations may be in the works of various authors) has served as a corrective to a dichotomy concerning the fundamental issue of the determinants of outlook and behavior of man. The crucial issue is the place of environment (culture, group, and so forth) and the place of individual psychodynamics (instinct, libido, personality traits, and so on) in shaping the person's outlook and behavior. The interactionist position holds that it is untenable to make one or the other set of factors supreme determinants in all cases.

An accumulating body of empirical and experimental facts from social science and psychology points to the generalization that experience and behavior are *jointly* determined by factors *external* as well as *internal* to the individual. The internal factors, especially the strong urges (for food, sex mate, and so on) and persistent self-related aspirations (for acceptance, recognition, the defense of one's self-respect, or moving up in the scheme of things), determine the *goal-directed, selective* nature of psychological activity. Behavior does not follow directly from external forces or stimulation impinging on the person, uninfluenced by his processing of the stimuli. Neither is behavior unaffected by the concrete situations and events surrounding him. Under specifiable conditions they take the upper hand. When the individual is confronted with situations which are compelling and sharply articulate (thus allowing little room for man's motive-directed selectivity to operate), the external things and events take the upper hand. A man working in an assembly line or the driver caught in the whirl of heavy traffic are but two examples from everyday life.

The proper frame of reference for analyzing behavior consists of the totality of external (stimulus) and internal factors and, especially, their relationships. The terms of the interactionist position that have guided my work for years are diagrammatically presented and discussed in Selection 3 (pp. 86–89).

The implications of the interactionist position in designing research strategies are far-reaching. Through spelling out the terms of this position, it has been possible to devise behavioral indicators of the person's likes or dislikes in interpersonal relations, high regard or depreciation of other persons in his own group, and his prejudice or identification with persons in various groups. The rationale for using simple behaviors as indicators of such complex psychological functions is that under specified conditions the whole person is reflected in his relatively simple perceptions, judgments, and categorizations.

For example, when two persons give judgments of an apparently neutral stimulus under conditions lacking objective structure, hence allowing alternatives in judgment, their judgments reveal the personal prestige that one has for the other, without arousing an awareness that their personal relationship is in question (Selection 8). Another example can be drawn from the more complicated area of identification with one's own group and prejudice against a detested rival group. The task in this case was a relatively simple one, estimating performance on the basis of brief visual inspection. Here the over- or under-estimation of performance proved to mirror the person's positive or negative regard for the group in question (Selections 21, 22, and 23).

Another fruitful area for applying the terms of the interactionist position in research has been the development of behavioral indicators of attitudes on complex social issues and of their change. Under appropriate conditions, it has been demonstrated experimentally that commitments and rejections of the person on such issues can be detected without his being aware of revealing them, through the manner in which he categorizes relevant stimulus items (Selections 16, 17, and 18).

Such developments in our work and the work of others have been possible by eliminating the blinders imposed by conceiving of cognition and motivation as two distinct processes. In view of such evidence it seems to me that positing a primarily cognitive or motivational or behavioral psychology is a lingering relic of faculty psychology.

PERSONAL CONSISTENCY, SELF, AND REFERENCE GROUPS

The characteristic consistency of the human person from day to day and from situation to situation has been one of the central, yet one of the toughest, problems in psychology. The fragmentary accounts of the various psychological functions in isolation (judgment, perception, learning, thinking) and fragmentary accounts of separate human motives (hunger, sex, acquisitiveness, curiosity, aggression, dominance) did not add up to account for the whole person with the consistent characteristics which are the hallmarks of his uniqueness. If personal uniqueness is to be studied operationally, it must be in terms of the consistency the individual reveals in different situations and at different times. In view of the dismay aroused by the patchy, disjointed picture of the human person, the search for integrative concepts and principles came to the focus of concern in an irrevocable way.

The achievement and sustenance of characteristic consistency by the person is a considerable feat. As a rule, the person strives to keep his characteristic consistency intact despite the ups and downs of situations surrounding him, especially in the complex flux of modern life. Generally, he achieves his characteristic consistency fairly well in spite of the bombardment of exhortations, messages, and communications conflicting with the main supports of his consistency.

Recently the prevalent mode of theoretical accounting for the maintenance or restoration of personal consistency in the face of disrupting forces from outside, or from his own strong urges of the moment that tend to derange it, has been some variant of an equilibrium model, whether formulated in terms of balance-imbalance, consonance-dissonance, or congruity-incongruity. These models, on the whole, have been in terms of physical models, energy systems, or hydraulic leveling. Systematic accounts of such models have not paid sufficient attention to the special substantive properties of the psychological system of the human adult as developed in any culture. In the human adult, the maintenance of stability (balance) or restoring stability after onslaughts of disruptive factors is *on special terms*. Not just any kind or level of stability will do. The human person has set for himself definite levels for attainment and goals for achievement in matters of significance to him. The levels and goals in different matters are *not* the same. Operatonally they can be ranked as to their relative importance for him. Yet they are all components of his self-image. In the human adult, maintaining and restoring stability is in terms of the self image. Therefore, a theory of the self system is needed before we can deal adequately with maintaining consistent stability and restoring it upon disruption by the demands of situations.

Perhaps this explains why some of the leading theorists—from William James, James Mark Baldwin, and George H. Mead to Jean

Piaget—have focused on a theory of self. Because of the same considerations, a developmental account of self (ego) has been central to my own work from the beginning (Selections 12, 13, and 14). It was central as well in grappling with problems of attitude change, which after all involves disruption of whatever consistency or stability has been achieved on the issues at hand.

Ultimately, one of the basic cornerstones of an adequate theory of human motivation will be a theory of self system. For whatever motive (hunger, sex, acquiring the good things of life) is aroused at the time, the claims of the self system in that respect are also aroused. In short, involvement of the self (ego) in directing psychological activity goes with the arousal of every motive, including the bodily ones. Thus ego-involvement gives the directionality, the selectivity to psychological processing in almost all cases of motivated behavior, not only in matters that are explicitly recognized as concerns and commitments of the self system (social ties, acceptance, prestige, identification, self-esteem).

Ordinarily, human beings do not satisfy their hunger, thirst, or sexual appetites in just any way. They satisfy, postpone, or deny them on terms defined by the self system. This is why the channels and the means of satisfying even biological needs vary so greatly from culture to culture and time to time. In this sense, one can justifiably say that satisfaction of biological urges is accompanied also by gratification of the self of the person. Thus, eating becomes an adventure of finding the place, the dish, and the companionship that satisfy oneself and impress one's friends. Efforts in satisfying sexual urges become a game of sport and conquest.

The self system is not, however, a unitary structure cut from whole cloth, even though its components are interrelated; nor does it emerge full blown and as an immutably fixed structure. At times its components (attitudes, identifications, commitments) contradict one another. Because they are components of an interrelated self system, such contradictions become the source of inner conflicts, with all of the wear and tear and unfortunate psychological consequences. Cases of marginality and contradictory roles from one situation to the next are examples. In treating these out-of-phase and contradictory commitments, the conceptual analysis provided by the reference group formulation is proving effective.

Reference groups are groups or sets of people with whom the person identifies himself or to whom he aspires to belong. Thus the definition of reference groups is social psychological, that is, the definition is made from the point of view of the individual relative to groups, whether he actually belongs to them or not. It is not coincidental that reference group problems, with their attendant contradictions of identifications and values, are especially prevalent in highly complex, "casually patterned" Western societies with diverse groups pursuing different values and vested interests. Nor is it coincidental that the conflict of generations with the attendant personal and social problems is prevalent in societies in the state of transition (in one way or another) like the United States (Selection 14) or in new nations in the process of transforming themselves from tribalism. Reference groups or sets are the source of the person's directive attitudes and strivings in relation to others. Although they may not correspond exactly to the groups in which the person is physically located, they provide for the social psychologist a means for linking the person's self picture with concrete actualities as he has experienced and conceived them.

MEASUREMENT OF ATTITUDES IN
THE SELF SYSTEM AND THEIR CHANGE

One of the remarkable features of human psychological functioning with consequences that are not always a blessing is that man classifies or categorizes objects; his reactions to them reflect these categorizations. The concepts of his language consist of a classificatory scheme that the individual utilizes as a rule (Selection 15). When the domain of objects is emotionally neutral, he discriminates them according to the gradations of their objective properties as well as his language allows.

However, when the domain is one that touches on the person's commitments and identifications, his categorization of events in that domain becomes an evaluative process, whether he is conscious of it or not. Certain categories of objects represent what he is attached to, what he puts on a pedestal in his scheme of things. Objects falling outside of these are judged according to their closeness or remoteness to what he has enshrined on the pedestal. Those that resemble what is on the pedestal are seen favorably, but those that diverge or contradict are detestable and even obnoxious to him.

What is expressed here in everyday language depicts the pattern of an attitude more effectively than considering only what is on the pedestal, neglecting the proximity or divergence of other things in that domain. Therefore, terms were coined to translate these notions into research operations: latitude of acceptance, latitude of rejection, and latitude of noncommitment. Noncommitment here refers to those cases where the individual is still straddling the fence or prefers neither to accept nor to reject, for reasons of his own.

Categorizations as "on the pedestal" or close to it and as detestable are the stuff of which self systems are made. As components of his self (ego) system, they define aspects of his personal stability. His consistency consists largely of their maintenance against the onslaughts of disruptive words, deeds, messages, communications in person-to-person exchange or in speeches emanating from mass media of communication.

The assessment of attitudes and their change become important in the social sciences because groups with competing vested interests, rival ways of life, and conflicting ideologies have come into sharper confrontation with one another in a shrinking world. Old ways of life and ideologies which had their day in the past and the new emerging ones are in a deadly struggle to have the tide of future on their side, and each party is all set out to win the outlook and the hearts of men for its camp.

The topic would not have major importance if attitudes were not the stuff of which the person's self system is made. However, the components of the self system do differ in their rank in the person's scheme of things, as noted earlier. For one person, his politics may be a life-or-death matter, for another it is his religion, and for a third, his business. It is in this highest echelon of personal concern that his consistency reigns supreme. Other attitudes move him to a lesser extent, according to their rank in his scheme. In other words, he is more one thing than he is other things, and he is other things in gradations. Thus, exhortations and information will affect his stability or disrupt it proportional to the priority of his ego-involvement in the matter at issue.

It follows, therefore, that degree of ego-involvement is a major consideration in the study of attitude change (Selection 17). Analysis of the pattern of an attitude in terms of latitudes of acceptance, rejection, and noncommitment, instead of the traditional single score or average, provides the basis for assessing relative involvement as well as how discrepant he will perceive a message relative to his stand or commitment. The predictions as to change or resistance to change as a result of being exposed to a partisan communication follow from this analysis on more solid theoretical and empirical grounds (Selections 17 and 18).

MAN IN IN-GROUP AND INTERGROUP RELATIONS

MAN IN IN-GROUP RELATIONS

One of the great developments in both social psychology and all social science has been the study of groups as the context of leader-follower relations, attitude formation and change, and the urgent problems of segregation and prejudice, as well as other vital issues of human relations. This too is as it should be. Traditional studies of man's behavior that conceived his action in isolation have fallen far short in explaining his motives, aspirations, frustrations, and gratifications. When one considers that man's claims for success in every sphere of living, his concerns for prestige and recognition, his desires to improve his lot, his claims for the good things of life, including the desired residence and the desired sexual mate, are all relative to other people, it is surprising that this development did not flourish earlier. Resistance to orthodoxy dies slowly.

The tasks of daily living as well as the pursuit of significant plans and goals take place in a context in which success depends on how a person fares in his dealings with his fellows. This traffic among men is not haphazard and fortuitous. It falls into a pattern of reciprocities consisting of mutual expectations, role relations, and power arrangements.

If we have learned anything from empirical and experimental research in social science, it is that human interaction in a pattern of reciprocities is not the same as the behavior of the same individual in isolation. As a rule, the actual behavior of the person is not what he *might* have done in isolation, but what he does as affected, modified, and even transformed within a pattern of reciprocities, in which he has a particular place. In brief, the pattern in which interaction takes place and behavior occurs has *differential effects* (Selections 1, 3, 5, 6, 7, and 20).

The human group is the paradigm that embodies the pattern of reciprocities in which man channels the conduct of his affairs. Therefore, it is more and more evident that the proper context for studying human motivation—in fact, the emergence of the self system, its functioning and change—is the human group (the family, neighborhood church, precinct political organization, labor union local, social club, fraternal organization, and so on).

The most essential and ubiquitous reciprocities of the pattern that is a human group are the role and status differentiations among individuals. These organizational (role-status) reciprocities and expected modes of outlook and behaviors derived from the norm repertory of the group are not transitory. They are products of interaction occurring over time, as individuals come into traffic with one another pursuing concerns for living, for pleasure, and for making a place for themselves in the sun. However, the mounting literature that passes under the name of "group research" has not always taken cognizance of these essential earmarks of groups or their developmental history. A great deal of what passes as "group research" can hardly be considered group research at all because the essential properties of a group are lacking in their conception and design.

In initiating a series of studies on groups, I was particularly attentive to the task of extracting these minimum essential properties of a human group, especially from the research of sociologists (Selection 20). In line with the earlier emphasis on the kind of methodology required in social psychology, a combination of methods and techniques was selected and developed as appropriate for the study of interaction in human groups. These are summarized in Selection 14 and presented in detail in our *Reference Groups* (1964).

What I want to dwell upon here is not the procedural details, although they have absorbed a great deal of time. In an introduction like this, it is more important to dwell upon the particular place of the groups singled out for intensive study within the sociocultural setting of which they are parts.

Small groups are not closed systems. Therefore, they have to be located within the setting where they arise and function, taking note of the ecological characteristics and value orientations prevalent within these settings. As a consequence, the intensive study of the outlooks and behaviors of particular group members (which is the focus for social-psychological analysis) has to be framed within the ecological character and value orientations of their settings.

What are required, then, are a research strategy, design, and combination of techniques to study the attitude and behavior of the individual as a member within the pattern of group relations and within the ecological and value framework of the setting. Obviously a research program is needed that focuses on (1) attitude and behavior of individual members as they interact with each other and with outsiders (utilizing methods and techniques that do not clutter the flow of interaction to the point of deflecting it); (2) the values and goals prevalent in the setting to provide a framework or a *baseline* within which the attitudes and aspirations of group members under study can be assessed in a meaningful way; and (3) the analysis of the sociocultural and ecological setting, with particular attention to indices of socioeconomic rank, family status, and ethnic composition as developed by social scientists (Selection 14).

Devising procedures and methods adapted to the natural flow of interaction process among group members has proved highly trying and arduous. It requires infinite patience from the researcher, who is forced to postpone judgment and wait for data collection until rapport with the group has reached the point where his procedures are not seen as intervention into their private affairs. This is in striking contrast to the "neat" research where the researcher suits himself as to the time and manner of data collection and uses the techniques that are convenient for him and respectable in his colleagues' eyes. For groups have secrets of their own; they move about and do things among themselves. They do things which they would not engage in were they aware that any outsider knew what was going on. This exclusiveness and secretiveness of groups is not a monopoly of what is called anti-social groups or gangs. As a rule, it is true for any group in following its schemes and designs, including a political organization, a business firm, a ladies' club, or a family.

Since 1958 our concentration has been on adolescent natural groups studied within this multifaceted design. The generality of group formation at this age level, in a society itself in transition, with the associated problems of adult-youth conflict in values and aspirations, provides a unique opportunity to study the essentials of group functioning. Several dozen groups, each studied intensively for periods of six months to a year, have provided ample basis to verify certain hunches about group formation and functioning derived from social science literature and to clarify several persistent theoretical issues. I shall restrict myself to one such persistent issue and follow its implications a bit.

It pertains to the time-honored but still prevalent dichotomy between the individual or personality approach, on the one hand, and the group approach on the other. Let us evaluate this dichotomy in the light of generalizations that are amply verified: Whenever a number of individuals interact with some common concerns, they do develop a group organization regulating their relationships and norms regulating their outlook and actions in matters of mutual concern. That is, the rise of an organization with differentiated roles and power relations is an invariant product of human interaction over a time span.

However, *who* occupies what position and what role within a particular group pattern is very much the contribution of unique characteristics or qualities of particular individuals. These unique personal qualities and resources that contribute to a particular person's achievement of a particular role are not traits or resources in the abstract, but they contribute as they are relevant or in demand in the particular interaction situations. This is a concrete illustration that individual concerns, aspirations, and activities have to be studied within the pattern of group reciprocities and that this pattern provides a context within which unique personal contributions can be realistically assessed. If the implication of this generalization is followed, findings about groups and findings about unique individual qualities support one another for constructing an integrated account of human behavior, rather than causing fruitless controversies about either a group approach or a personality approach in the study of human outlook and behavior.

Even though small groups are the context in which the individual moves and forms many directive characteristics of his self image, we must go beyond the immediate boundaries of these reference groups to grasp fully the sources of his attitudes and aspirations. Broadening the picture is necessary because small groups are not self-contained, closed systems. In the extensive data we collected through procedures for assessing self-radius and goals of youngsters, the sources of aspirations and the person's success picture (for good or evil) are found embedded in the reference idols and reference sets extolled in the larger cultural setting, of which the small groups are parts.

At this point the empirical or experimental researcher on small groups, even with all of his sophistication in technique and design, can ill afford to gloss over the ideology dominant in the setting. Otherwise practical prescriptions based on findings within the confines of small groups, such as changing attitudes and directions by working with in-group members, will prove to have little transfer value. No doubt this is why a number of well-intentioned action programs concentrating on small juvenile groups, for example, yield such meagre returns with little transfer value, as the grim picture of the statistics in several spheres of juvenile life is depicting year after year.

MAN IN INTERGROUP RELATIONS

Let me repeat what almost everybody knows today: No problem is as vital and urgent as that of intergroup relations. In fact, the fate of the human race may hinge on how they are handled.

Both the theoretical formulation of this vital problem area and practical handling of prevailing states of tension and conflict in issues of civil rights, and national and international relations require more than hand-to-mouth solutions. What is required is a realistic *theory of conflict* to establish first the conditions conducive to the rise of intergroup tensions. Only on the basis of a realistic theory of conflict can we hope to conceptualize the states of friendship and enmity, cooperation and competition between groups, pointing toward the direction for effective solutions to the problems they pose.

In attacking these problems, we looked first at literature for cases of intergroup hostility involving diverse groups, to extract the common conditions invariably associated with hostility. This survey provided leads to formulate plausible hypotheses and procedures to test them experimentally.

The major lesson we learned is that good will or prejudice, hostility or alliance between human groups cannot be extrapolated on the basis of similar states in person-to-person relations of individuals that are not related to their identifications as members of different groups. Those theories that posit instinctive aggressiveness or dominance or individually evolved frustrations unrelated to the directions and practices of the group context have missed the limiting factor that determines the relations of group to group. Nor can these positive or negative states of intergroup relations be posited on the basis of prevailing practices within the confines of the in-groups in question. At times intergroup hostility and vindictiveness may be proportional to the degree of in-group solidarity (cohesiveness) and cooperation. In-group democracy need not necessarily imply democracy toward out-groups.

Thus, in Selections 19 through 25, we persist in dwelling on the generalizations derived from the survey and supported by a series of experiments that psychological functioning, including motivational strivings, in interpersonal contexts cannot be carried by analogy to explain interaction situations within groups and that those operative within group boundaries need not be analogous to relations between groups. The limiting condition determining states of prejudice or good will, cooperation or competition, hostility or conflict is the nature of relations between groups. If a group is seen by another group, rightly or wrongly, as an obstacle to its schemes and designs or as a potential prey to be subordinated to the service of its own ends or as an enemy whose defeat is required for its own victory, then a state of envy, competition, or hostility will arise with all of their attendant emotions, feelings of prejudice and unfavorable stereotypes, which are used in turn to justify the group's course of action.

This formulation was tested in large-scale experiments and verified. Groups were formed from scratch. The experimental conditions were designed to test the generalization that a group organization with its peculiar set of norms is an invariant product of interaction over time among individuals with common concerns. The use of a combination of methods (observation, ratings, sociometric choices, variations in judgment) proved to be effective in cross-checking the validity of findings. The naturalness of the interaction situations was preserved, and the subjects were not aware of the constant observation (Selections 20, 21, and 22). Intergroup conflict, in turn, was created by introducing a series of competitive and mutually frustrating situations, in which the victory of one group signalled defeat for the other.

Having verified in experiments the formulation in regard to the rise of intergroup conflict through the introduction of its necessary and sufficient conditions, the next step was to proceed to the reduction of prevailing tension and hostility between groups. The theory of conflict, if valid, should provide corollaries in regard to the conditions that will transform the state of competition and hostility to that of understanding, good will, and even friendship.

In planning the design of the experiments, several measures proposed by various authors or practiced by various action programs were evaluated for experimental testing. These include opening avenues of communication through person-to-person contacts, dissemination of information, exchange of persons, meetings of leaders, and emotional catharsis. It became painfully evident, when we reached the stage of reducing conflict, that favorable information about the detested enemy fell on deaf ears and aroused a whole bill of counter arguments asserting the wicked nature of the "other side." Meetings of leaders at this stage to negotiate their difficulties were simply out of bounds. Any leader who would seriously consider negotiation was suspect by his own group. A series of *contact* situations was attempted involving activities that would have been pleasant for each group alone or in the absence of mutual distrust. These contact situations, which could have been pleasant for their duration at least, served as occasions for the exchange of invectives and even incipient outbreaks of hostile acts.

The interaction condition between groups that was effective in reducing tension was suggested by the formulation on the nature of conflict. As the rise of intergroup prejudice, distrust, and hostility is produced by the groups pursuing mutually incompatible goals, where the victory of one means defeat and frustration for the other, so transformation of the existing state of tension into understanding, a willingness to live and let live, and eventually to cooperation and harmony is contingent upon the appearance of mutually compatible goals that are felt with a sense of urgency by all parties in the intergroup system. This corollary formulation suggested the introduction of *superordinate goals,* which are urgently shared by the parties involved but which cannot be realized by the efforts and resources of any single party to conflict, and require joint efforts of all caught in the predicament.

As should be evident from this analysis and the experimental results, superordinate goals cannot be introduced artificially through exhortations or appeals to good will. They have to arise through conditions that engulf all the groups. Thus, one such condition in the experiments was a shortage of water that affected friend and foe alike (Selections 23 and 24).

We have taken great pains to note in our writings that conditions effective in reduction of intergroup conflict (that is, concerted actions directed toward superordinate goals) are not an alternative to other measures proposed (dissemination of information, meetings of leaders, exchange of persons). Superordinate goals provide the necessary *motivational base* that prepares the ground for these and other specific measures to become effective. Once groups in a state of tension engage in activities, separately or jointly, toward superordinate goals that are urgently felt, specific measures proposed for the reduction of intergroup conflict do become effective, singly or in combination. Thus favorable information about the out group no longer falls on deaf ears. They are no longer intolerant to face-to-face contacts between their members and those of other groups. They cease to be adamant to their leaders' meeting. In moving toward understanding and the development of procedures that are binding to all parties in the intergroup system, the groups cannot impose upon one another the rules practiced within the exclusive bounds of their own in-groups. The rules that are not divisive nor a source of renewed bickering emerge as superordinate to the in-group norms and practices (Selection 25).

Our research program in the area of intergroup relations envisages planned experiments of a wider scope than two opposing groups as in the previous experiments. A dozen groups, created experimentally, who make alignments and counter-alignments in blocs, and then move toward conditions that engulf them all is a more adequate paradigm of intergroup relations today. We predict that, through their interaction in time, they will evolve superordinate goals implemented by organizational devices and superordinate rules binding for all (Selection 25).

PART I

INTERDISCIPLINARY
RELATIONS
AND METHODOLOGY

ONE

IF BASIC RESEARCH IS TO HAVE BEARING ON ACTUALITIES . . .

My title is somewhat unorthodox. Therefore, I shall start with a few words of explanation.

Logically, "if" should not be in the title. Of course, what is called *basic research* should have bearing on the domain of events it attempts to investigate and predict. What is called *applied* should be application of some principles or generalizations that are solidly based on research findings. In fact, the justification for calling research *basic* is that its findings are the basis for generalization. Logically and in practice, what is called basic and what is called applied should be closely related aspects of the scientific process.

Ironically, the "if" has to be included in the title because there are strong trends in behavioral science toward divorcing the "basic" and the "applied." Professional meetings and professional journals can almost convince a person that there is a cold war between those engaged in basic research and those in applied fields—when they are not ignoring each other completely. At times, it appears that the twain will never meet.

On the one hand, some psychologists and social scientists in applied fields move ahead to secure data or to settle this or that practical problem, without great concern over how their prescriptions are related to what people are doing as basic research. On the other hand, some representatives of what is called basic or pure research tend toward aloofness from events outside of their laboratory or research center. On both sides, therefore, the essential interplay between basic research and application is blocked. Applied effort ceases to be the application of anything related to scientific study and becomes hand-to-mouth improvisation. Basic research is deprived of feedback from events in real life and stops trying to make predictions about actualities. Yet, in the long run, the interdependence of what is basic and what is applied is essential to the progress of any science.

Invited address to the fourth annual Psi Chi Day, Pennsylvania State University, April 2, 1966.

The stakes are high in the controversy: whether behavioral science is to develop to a point where its theory has predictive value. By this time, you probably recognize that the question I am raising is the much neglected problem of the *validity* of research findings and generalizations based on them. On the whole, the all important problem of validity has been put on the shelf, despite pious lip service to the contrary. The problem of validity has been merged with the criterion of reliability, to the point where we are in danger of being *reliably wrong* in our generalizations and predictions. This is why it is important for us to raise the question of how basic research can have bearing on actualities.

In the rest of this paper, I shall try to make what I have said so far more concrete and then suggest some pointers for insuring that basic research is both reliable and valid. Let me begin by considering representative practices in what is called applied research.

A few years ago, I was in a large Washington hotel during the national convention of candy wholesalers. In addition to the free candy bars left at their doors each night, the other hotel guests were offered copies of the association's official publication. The issue included elaborate analyses of survey data on the public's taste in candy, on preferred color of the wrappings, and on the kind of people who consume the most candy. The quantity of data and the sophistication of the analyses far exceeded those of research typically reported in psychological journals. Yet all the sophisticated analyses yielded were the facts that some people consume more candy than others and prefer certain packages to others. This may be useful information for some immediate commercial purpose. But the "why's," the "how's," and the consequences of these preferences remained almost untouched.

Much of today's research into public opinion and consumer preference has precisely this nature. Nothing is applied except some trappings of the trade—cookbook rules for asking questions that are not "leading," established sampling methods, and data processing by computers—which convince almost everyone that something scientific is going on. Unfortunately, the use of these tools does not guarantee that the product will have anything to do with behavioral science or its application.

This state of applied activities is not confined to survey research. Some clinicians are convinced that the effectiveness of clinical practice rests entirely upon the personality of the therapist. By their definition, clinical practice is not application of anything based on research. And, I should add, social psychologists are not exempt from the tendency to rush into application—for example, on such matters as leadership and productivity—with little concern over what they are applying.

The claim of behavioral science to a place under the scientific sun must rest on conduct of basic research, not on ventures into practical affairs of the moment. The development of any science presumes research activities that are more than dated studies of immediate practical concerns. Louis Pasteur's studies for the French wine makers would not be remembered outside the wine industry if he had confined his interest only to spoiling wine or, for that matter, if bacteria flourished only in such a spirited environment.

What is the distinctive character of research defined as "basic"? Formally, it starts with a *problem* for study that defines the domain of events to be investigated, including the essential independent variables. The problem defines the domain of study in a generalized way. The concepts used to define the problem are generalizations representing the major variables and are based on initial familiarity with the problem area at hand and prior research findings. Units of analysis, appropriate to the variables in question, are defined. Measurement techniques are selected to secure indicators of these variables. A plan or design is formulated to include the major variables, controlling some and varying others in the combinations necessary to eliminate alternative explanations of the results. Data are collected by procedures that can be communicated to others and reproduced by them. Finally, statistical analysis and inference are used to evaluate the data.

Clearly, basic research involves abstraction from actualities at every step. There can be no escape from the abstraction process, nor should there be. In abstraction lies the power of science to predict a great variety of apparently discrete and unrelated events. Our question here is what *kind* of abstractions give this power. Abstraction becomes a game if divorced from actualities; it becomes abstraction for its own sake or for the impression it may make on one's colleagues in the profession. In this case, abstraction becomes inner gymnastics for a select group of people who are "in" on the secret and exclusive lingo.

The history of psychology includes many graveyards filled with abstractions that were insulated from actualities. Let me give a few examples, necessarily in short-cut and somewhat dramatized form. Here are some generalizations that have been proposed seriously on the basis of what is called basic research.

Frustration always leads to aggression. Among other things, this generalization was used to explain why poor white southerners indulged in lynching Negroes. Unless "frustration" is a completely abstract concept, it does not explain why the even more deprived Negroes seldom behaved aggressively toward whites during the same period.

People change their attitudes more in response to a communication opposite to their own than to a view nearer their own stand, particularly when the matter is of considerable personal importance to them. If this generalization bears on actualities, it is very difficult to see why, for example, we find no mass defections from liberal groups to the Ku Klux Klan nor from White Citizens Councils to the civil rights groups.

Judgments of value statements are not influenced by the attitudes of persons doing the judging. This assumption was considered basic to scaling attitudes by the method of equal-appearing intervals. In fact, judgment *is* influenced by relevant attitudes, as shown, for example, by judgments made by civil rights workers and by white supremacists of a moderate position on the desegregation issue. To the civil rights worker, a moderate position is pro-segregation; to the white supremacist, it is support for the desegregation movement. For the civil rights worker, the pace of desegregation is too slow; for the white supremacist, the pace is too fast.

I have deliberately chosen examples from social psychology. They could have been selected with equal ease from other research areas in behavioral science. What is called "pure" research has at times been so pure that it omitted essential independent variables that operate in real life and hence had very little bearing on events outside of the particular laboratory. We must ask, therefore, how pure we want to be. Do we want to be so pure that our generalizations are violated every day by events in life going on around us? Is basic research to be merely a stunt to impress those who are part of the "in crowd"? Can we afford to refuse the feedback from actualities?

When basic research becomes aloof from the correctives that can be derived from such feedback, the risk we take is a risk to basic research itself. We do not have to think that behavioral science has a *duty* to participate in the solution of social problems or even to insure the future of its application. Without close familiarity with actualities at the outset, basic research risks leaving out some of the essential variables or of taking them so much for granted that they are never included in theory.

In recent years, more researchers have become seriously concerned about the state of affairs that tends to produce artifacts instead of valid results and generalizations. Among the correctives in this respect is the experimental orientation represented under the title, "the social psychology of the psychological experiment." This movement is among those shaking the complacent assumption that the only variables that count in shaping the response are those immediately salient to the naked eye.

Some researchers have only recently discovered variables that would have been essential in their study designs had they not been indoctrinated to view the laboratory as an insulated environment, free of influences that pervade the simplest social situation. Evidence is rolling in to show that the laboratory, too, is a social situation, no matter how circumscribed the set-up is. The important variables need not be confined to those the experimenter happens to choose and writes up in his procedures, without due regard to the laboratory situation, his own role in it, and others who may be there.

Martin Orne of the University of Pennsylvania has shown that the laboratory experiment has potent "demand characteristics" involving differential authority and responsibility for experimenter and subjects.

Like any people in any social situation, research subjects have expectations about the laboratory and about the experimenter. Experiments by J. D. Frank and by Orne have shown that research subjects will engage without question in boring and meaningless activities (such as adding random numbers and systematically destroying each sheet of addition) to the point of boring the experimenter.

Subjects have considerable faith in the experimenter as a responsible person and place value upon their own contribution to the scientific effort. Thus, most of Orne's subjects who were instructed to simulate hypnosis quite willingly reached for a poisonous snake, plunged their hand into a bowl of acid, and threw the acid at the experimenter when instructed to do so. Stevenson and his co-workers succeeded in having adult subjects perform the ridiculous task of placing marbles into holes at rates beyond their endurance to maintain—simply because it was an experiment. Over 80 per cent of Stanley Milgram's subjects administered a level of shock labeled highly dangerous, merely because they had been paid as subjects and the experimenter ordered them to do so.

It should not be thought, however, that the research subject is merely reacting passively to the experimenter's instructions. On the contrary, as persons in any social situation will do, subjects try to appraise what the researcher is up to, and they differ in the accuracy of their assessments. As Stevenson and his co-workers have shown, a task that may appear to the experimenter as extremely simple may become highly complex for the subject who has an overly sophisticated hunch about the purpose of the procedures. Dahlke and his students have recently shown that the spread of affective value from an emotionally toned word to a neutral word in paired-associate learning occurred only among those subjects who correctly sized up the experimenter's intent and also desired to appear as a "good subject" in his eyes. Those who did not catch on to the basis for pairing, and those who were annoyed at the idea of conforming to his intent, did not increase their ratings of the affective value of neutral words.

Milgram's research, referred to earlier, demonstrates clearly the complexity of variables in a laboratory situation. The level of shock administered by subjects and the proportion of subjects refusing to administer high levels decreased with the distance between the subjects, according to whether the experimenter was physically present or communicating by telephone and even according to whether the experiment was performed in the Yale laboratory or in an office building in Bridgeport.

Finally, the experimenter himself and his own hypotheses about the outcome undeniably affect the results he obtains, as Rosenthal has shown in a series of experiments. A few years ago, Rosenthal thought that the solution to this problem was to randomize assignment of experimenters, none of whom knew the correct hypothesis. This suggestion has been discarded in his recent writing, because even uninformed experimenters seem to develop their own hunches, right or wrong.

There are, of course, some ways to circumvent these problems of experimenter bias and of the demand character of research situations. We have been incorporating the most obvious of these into our research since 1947: the use of a combination of independent measures obtained by different techniques to minimize bias and the development of research designs that do not alert the subject to the fact that his behavior is being studied.

The studies of the psychological experiment as a social situation, of which there are a good many, point to a larger lesson that should concern us seriously when we define problems for research. These show that it is impossible to escape actualities, even in the laboratory. Actualities, in fact, constitute the backdrop or context for the operation of those variables that the investigator has singled out for experimental manipulation. True, the context of the laboratory represents actualities of a particular kind, not necessarily representative of many other social contexts. However, the logical conclusion is that our definition of research problems, concepts, and research designs must include specification of the variables in this context, not arbitrarily isolated from it. This is an enormous task, but necessary if findings and generalizations based on them are to have points of contact with actualities outside of the laboratory.

The prevailing intellectual heritage has provided a ready-made escape route from this huge task. Following the models of earlier work in chemistry and physiology, some psychologists concluded that the essence of science was to reduce complex phenomena to their simplest units and that efforts should be concentrated on study of these elemental units. It was further assumed, of course, that the elements would be combined, but meanwhile, *basic* research meant study of the simplest possible units of analysis. This was the model for the great founders of experimental psychology, including Wundt and Titchener with their "mental chemistry" model, and for the early behaviorists with their model of a punctiform stimulus and response, as Arthur Melton (a behavioristic psychologist himself) aptly characterized it.

There need be no quarrel at all with those who wish to make it their life work to study the nerve synapse rather than the nervous system, visual discrimination rather than perception of the visual field, or the learning of words rather than sentences. It must be emphasized, however, that in each of these cases, the simpler unit is in no sense more basic than the more complex, if our aim is prediction of behavior in the actualities of a social context. The properties of a pattern are as real as the elements whose relationships compose the pattern, as shown by experimental work by Gestalt psychologists, by Bartlett, and by Helson, among others. What is basic is defined by the problem at hand, not necessarily by what is arbitrarily chosen as elemental.

In his recent revision of *A Textbook of Psychology,* the experimentalist Donald Hebb made the point so clearly that I shall quote him at some length. Near the end of a book offered as a basic text without a single chapter on an applied topic, Hebb discussed the same problem of what are to be considered *basic* units of analysis, in relation to psychology and physiology.

It seems on occasion to be thought that neurological entities are somehow more substantial, more "real," than psychological entities: that the study of nerve impulses is a more scientific affair than the study of anxiety or motivation. This is entirely mistaken. It may be that the "probable error" of a psychological conception is larger than that of the neural conceptions of anatomy and physiology; our conceptions, that is, may need more revision and sharpening, but they are not less related to reality. The wood is as real as the trees; a shower of rain as much an entity as the drops that compose it. There must be different levels of analysis in natural science, from the microscopic (or submicroscopic) to the large-scale macroscopic. At any given level, "reality" consists of the unanalyzed units whose existence is taken for granted as the basis for analyzing the next higher level of complexity. Otherwise we should have to deny the reality of the raindrop as well as of the shower, for the drop is "only" a group of molecules, and such reasoning would lead us to the ultimate conclusion that the only fit objects for scientific discourse are the subatomic particles of nuclear physics—this page would not exist as an entity, nor would the student who is now reading it (Hebb, 1966, pp. 319–20).

If Hebb's conclusion is correct—and I have been supporting such a view strongly for years—then our task is to consider how those behavioral scientists who are interested in human perception, learning, problem-solving, and decision-making in social contexts can select units of analysis and design research that do have a bearing on the actualities of human behavior and human relations. There is no escape from the first step.

The concern at the outset should be close familiarity with the events in the problem area as well as with techniques for studying them. Ironically, the need for close familiarity and accurate description of actualities is sometimes recognized more clearly by people in the more established sciences than by those in behavioral science. For example, in one of the basic texts in college mathematics, Allendoerfer and Oakley (1959) state the first principle of model building as follows:

The first step in the study of any branch of science is that of observing nature. When enough facts have been collected, the scientist begins to organize them into some pattern (p. 19).

The plea for the importance of first-hand familiarity through observation and description as the first step is not new. Among those who have emphasized its importance in psychology is Robert MacLeod of Cornell's laboratory, who called for a "disciplined phenomenology" at the outset to achieve familiarity with the problem area together with the acquisition of technical skills needed for the conduct of research.

In the training of young behavioral scientists, it should go without saying that the study of the history of and theories in psychology, the essentials of physiology, research findings in the major problem areas, laboratory techniques, research design, and statistical inference are fundamental—and let us not forget computer programming. But where can familiarity be gained with the social context of behavior and the variables that compose it? The sensible answer is to turn to those disciplines that concentrate upon various aspects of the social context—upon its pattern of role relationships, its patterns of organization and authority, its social norms and values that compose so much of what is called culture, its language system, its distribution of political power, and so forth. It has been demonstrated time and again that the individual does not leave the effects of these social contexts in the coatroom before he enters the laboratory as a subject. In other words, the sensible way to train young behavioral scientists to grapple with the variables of the social context is to include in the training program, in addition to the fundamentals mentioned before, the study of sociology, anthropology, linguistics, political science, and other social sciences required by their particular research interests.

The social field is not a haphazard collection of stimulation. It has order and patterned relationships that cannot be described adequately in terms of the characteristics of individuals functioning within it. This order and these relationships are the principal focus for the social sciences. If it seems a large order to require the study of social sciences by students of psychology, then let me remind you that we have chosen a field whose problems are much more difficult and complex than those of physics, chemistry, or biology. When Einstein was asked why man's understanding of human behavior lagged so far behind that of his physical environment, he is reported to have replied that the problems of physics are much simpler than those of human behavior.

What I have just proposed about the desirability of familiarity by behavioral scientists (including experimentalists) with findings in social science on culture and social organization will have beneficial effects for selecting significant problems and fruitful, testable hypotheses in basic research, at least in the areas related to human relations. Some of the experiments that forged the frontiers in our field demonstrate the fruitfulness of such familiarity. Thus, it was Sir Frederic Bartlett, of Cambridge University, whose familiarity with African cultures enabled him to inaugurate the experimental research on perceiving and remembering without a break between laboratory findings and the actualities of these processes in various cultures. Thus, one cannot help finding in Jean Piaget's research of enduring value on the development of moral judgment in the child that the problems he raised were sharpened by his familiarity with the work of French sociologists. Again, it was a professor of both psychology and sociology, Theodore Newcomb of the University of Michigan, who contributed the well-known Bennington study that is still a landmark in the study of attitude and attitude change.

Let me share with you the benefits gained in our own experimental research program through preoccupation with the findings of social science. Whatever may be substantial in this research owes a great deal to initial study of the sociological and anthropological literature. It started from the lessons learned in this regard from such great works as those by Bartlett and Piaget that were just mentioned.

This is not the place to trace the interconnections between the findings in social science and the research problems and designs in even a part of our research program. Therefore, I shall simply list a few of the studies, then make the point more concrete through one with which many of you may be familiar. As we shall see, the problem for the experiments on the formation of social norms utilizing the autokinetic phenomenon was derived directly from sociological literature (see Selection 6). A subsequent study on experimentally produced insecurity and its effects on judgment was based on accounts reporting greatly increased variability of response when individuals face a crisis situation or a state of normlessness in which familiar anchorages are lacking (Selection 11). The projects on attitude and attitude change, which included psychophysical experiments as well as studies of social judgment, were formulated with close attention to the literature on reference groups, the varying ranges of behavior deemed acceptable within them, and the anchoring effects of reference group ties in assessing communication (Selections 12 and 17). Familiarity with findings on the properties of the human group and of interaction between groups provided the basis for specifying the experimental conditions in our experiments on the formation and change of intergroup attitudes and stereotypes among initially like-minded individuals (Selections 20 and 23). Our current research on attitude and behavior and their modification—utilizing a combination of methods that include observation, survey methods, and laboratory-type techniques—could not have been initiated without familiarity with the independent variables and methods for assessing them from the works of such sociologists as William Foote Whyte, Eshref Shevky, Wendell Bell, and others (Selections 14a and 14b).

I shall take the liberty of making the point more concrete through considering the experiments on group norms and their effects on individual response, partly because I trust that they may be more familiar and also because the results have been replicated in several score experiments in various laboratories since they were carried out in the middle 1930s.

As you may remember, the essentials of the laboratory set-up were individuals, alone and together, judging the extent of apparent movement of the autokinetic light in a totally dark laboratory. Over time, the differing judgments by individuals converged toward a common range. Subsequently, the individuals maintained this norm for response when they faced the same situation alone; that is, their response was henceforth regulated by the common norm established while interacting with others in this highly unstructured situation.

These experiments were designed to demonstrate an important characteristic of human behavior in any culture: its regulation in accordance with norms established in social interaction. The conception of the research did not arise within the confines of the laboratory, though the precision and rigor of the laboratory were utilized. It did not arise from the study of vision itself, although vision was involved. (In fact, other sense modalities could have been utilized, as subsequent experiments with auditory and thermal stimulation showed.) The problem and hypotheses were formulated on the basis of leads derived from sociological accounts of norm formation and its psychological effects. Specifically, the work of Emile Durkheim, the French sociologist, produced the fundamental idea that new norms arise when people interact in ambiguous and fluid situations where the alternatives for behavior are increased to include those not ordinarily available when life proceeds in the compelling grooves of daily routine. Similarly, a reading of small group studies by Chicago sociologists like Clifford Shaw and Frederic Thrasher revealed that individuals interacting in situations that lacked stable yardsticks for behavior do form their own guides for conduct, which become binding for them over time.

In short, the formulation of the problem of norm formation and the hypotheses thus derived determined the development of an experimental design and a laboratory set-up for studying them. Certainly all that had been gained in graduate study of psychology and research methods became very handy then, but it was not essential in choosing a problem and formulating hypotheses with a bearing on some actualities of social life. Of course, the experiment was only a model or paradigm of norm formation in real life. Any research, and especially laboratory experiments, is necessarily an abstract and even a stripped-down model of the events it studies. It would be unmanageable to study even the simplest event in the laboratory in all of the richness with which it actually occurs.

However, if we want to do research that will yield valid results, the experimental design must include the *essential* variables of the events in question. When the problem concerns behavior in a social context, the essential variables can seldom be extracted by chopping off little bits and pieces from the pattern of the event. What is basic to valid study lies, rather, in those variables that constitute the main properties of the pattern. In extracting these variables, both close familiarity with the domain of the problem area and the researcher's ingenuity are required.

However, the scientific process cannot stop when the researcher completes the experiment, if he is concerned over the validity of the findings. He must then return to actualities to check his generalizations and to insure that they are capable of predicting events in real life. I doubt very much that the experiments on norm formation would be remembered today if it had not been shown time and again that convergence toward common guides for behavior does occur under conditions represented in the experiment, both in experimental studies of groups and in studies of natural groups whose members face a choice of alternatives in unstructured situations. Consequently, such research findings do have implications for actualities, including the problems of conformity and nonconformity in social life, the bounds placed on what is considered desirable and undesirable by individuals, and the ceilings placed on individual aspirations through membership in different groups. At this point, basic research activities and applied work become interrelated parts of scientific process, instead of a source of controversy for members of different camps.

T W O

SOCIAL PSYCHOLOGY, ANTHROPOLOGY, AND
THE "BEHAVIORAL SCIENCES"

When a social psychologist takes stock of the background of problems he studies experimentally and of related factual evidence, he cannot help realizing how much material he has borrowed from related social sciences, especially from anthropology and sociology. For example, it is a matter of historical fact that social-psychological investigations of "social perception," norm formation and functioning in human groups, problems of linguistic functioning, and of interpersonal and group relations in given socio-cultural settings could not have made effective headway without reliance on the rich findings and generalizations of social scientists working in these areas.

In the experimentation on social perception, which has been flourishing for two decades, one of the stock references is to the anthropologist Malinowski (1927), who observed that the perception of similarity or difference is, to a significant extent, a function of cultural norms. For example, the finding or not finding of similarity between human faces is influenced by norms related to kinship demarcations. Likewise, the anthropological finding that distance and time localizations are shaped by the socio-cultural conditions of the society was full of psychological implications (for example, Goldenweiser, 1926; Radcliffe-Brown, 1922).

In the middle thirties experimentation on the formation of social norms drew from sociologist Emile Durkheim's analysis (1915) of *representations collective*, or cultural norms, which rise in collective interaction situations that lie largely outside the humdrum of daily routine.

The generalization, nearly four decades ago, by Edward Sapir (1921) and other linguists that linguistic concepts have a great deal to do with the way the individual categorizes experience and the stimulus

From *Southwestern Social Science Quarterly* (September, 1959), 40, 105–112. Reprinted by permission.

world around him is even now stimulating experimentation on judgment and discriminative processes, some of them utilizing subjects with different languages and cultural backgrounds.

There is reason to think that experimentation in social psychology will continue to benefit from the work by anthropologists and sociologists on related problems. For example, interpersonal relations is the topic of much experimental work today. The study of interpersonal relations in modern society will gain in perspective if the full implications of a generalization, noted by anthropologists for years, are developed. This generalization is exemplified by R. H. Lowie's statement (1925, p. 80) that "a native may be at a complete loss how to treat a stranger who falls outside the established rubrics." Who can say that this is not true, for any one of us, even now? When we meet a new person, we have an itch to find out his station in life, to what ethnic, religious, social, and economic classification he belongs, before we stabilize our interpersonal relationship with him. This generalization is also related, of course, to the insightful discussions by Charles H. Cooley and George H. Mead on interpersonal relations and ego development in the interaction process.

These examples contribute to a realistic assessment of the place of experimentation in social psychology. The point was well made by Gardner Murphy (1937) when he asserted that experimentation should come not as the first step in the research plan but only after an adequate grounding in the problem area (Chap. 1). In social psychology, this adequate grounding always includes knowledge of the socio-cultural setting.

During the last two decades, the exchange of notes between psychology and anthropology, sociology, and other social sciences has become increasingly frequent. It is not unusual to encounter psychologists at anthropology or sociology meetings, or anthropologists and sociologists at psychological conferences. Especially since the Second World War, there have been numerous opportunities in the form of conferences, research projects, and programs of instruction for people in the various social sciences and in psychology to meet, talk, and, less frequently perhaps, actually to work together. This elbow-rubbing among members of various disciplines has had a broadening effect on the whole. On a number of occasions, the mingling of the various disciplines has resulted in serious discussions on the interdependence of the social disciplines in seeking solutions to central problems of common interest to all of them.

In psychology, the impact of anthropology has trickled through to even the introductory texts. The current undergraduate textbook includes cautions—at one point or another—on the danger of universalizing research findings from a single culture and offers some colorful examples of contrasting behavior in different cultures. At a more sophisticated level, the trend toward interdependence of the social disciplines has made it decidedly unfashionable in psychology to adopt a frankly "individualistic" approach. On the other hand, in the social sciences, the popularity of a "rubber stamp" theory, or in Homans' terminology, a "Social Mold Theory," of cultural determination has diminished (Homans, 1950, p. 317).

Nowadays, it is granted that the general effect of interdisciplinary activities has been healthy. In the long run, our aim is to understand the concrete "flesh and blood" individual in his relations with other individuals, as a member of groups which are related to other groups and larger organizations, and to understand the products of man's interaction with other men. In pursuing this aim, psychology, anthropology, sociology, history, economics, political science and archeology each has a distinct contribution to make.

The dream of an integration of interdisciplinary efforts is embodied most prominently today in the phrase "behavioral sciences." In recent years, the trend flourishing under the banner of "behavioral sciences" has been strengthened by the support of important research foundations.

A danger in the trend subsumed under the rubric "behavioral sciences" is that one discipline may assimilate others, either because of its numerical or financial superiority or because of the awe aroused by its techniques. The topic is, of course, a controversial one. The emphasis on "behavioral sciences" has been used opportunely by some social scientists, including anthropologists, in their efforts to divorce themselves from the grandiose theorizing and reification of culture which was sometimes advanced without due concern for the validation of theory through demonstrable empirical and experimental facts.

But current research and writing seem to indicate that there is more to the trend labeled "behavioral sciences" than the efforts of some social scientists to free themselves from the speculations of the past. The general picture that emerges is one with a greater emphasis on individual behavior, on research data consisting of items of the behavior of single individuals—somewhat to the neglect of comparable emphasis and comparable data on the organizational patterns among individuals, their institutions, value or norm systems, and technology. There are even cases in which culture is defined, operationally, in strictly individual terms. Then culture is seen only within the confines of specific interpersonal relations, or in the unique personality traits of informants, or in the responses of a selected number of individuals to psychological questionnaires and projective tests.

Carried to its extreme, the trend known as "behavioral sciences" would lead to the absorption of the social sciences by an all-embracing science of individual behavior—which would, of course, be some kind of psychology. If this should happen, one regrettable consequence would be its effect on the development of psychology itself. In the past, psychology has benefited from the healthy correctives of anthropology and sociology. On the whole, these correctives have not stemmed from the "psychological" theorizing of anthropologists and sociologists but from their investigations of the value or norm systems in different societies, of language systems, of the organizational patterns of various groups, and of contrasting modes of living. It was the impressiveness of anthropological *findings* that led psychologists to begin to look for principles of behavior that could eventually accommodate cultural variations in behavior.

I suspect that until recent years the type of psychology that traveled most comfortably under the "behavioral sciences" label was some derivative of the behavioristic learning theories. The fact that such theories have undergone some mixture with psychoanalytic conceptions may make them more palatable to those social scientists who have also been influenced by psychoanalytic thinking.

A note of caution and misgiving may be in order. Those social scientists who want to be counted primarily as "behavioral scientists" may be cutting the ground from under their own feet. In the human sciences, there are, after all, certain ecological problems. If too many people try to kick the same ball, someone is bound to be crowded out. It would be unfortunate, I think, if the pursuit of the study of human groups and societies, their organization, division of labor, their material achievements, language, and system of values or norms were relegated to the background. Certainly that would not be an answer to the call made by Edward Sapir for the study of "tangible problems of behavior rather than selected problems set by recognized disciplines" (Mandelbaum, 1949, p. 513). Sapir desired the development of a "genuinely social" psychology. But he did not see this development as the primary task of anthropology. In fact, he hoped for the development of social psychology so that the socio-cultural investigator could be "free to study the rationale of group forms, group functions, group changes, and group interrelationships from a . . . cultural point of view" (1921, p. 364).

The development of a genuinely social psychology is, in no small part, dependent upon the socio-cultural investigator doing just what Sapir conceived as his most important task. Social psychology cannot be separated from psychology in general, in the sense that its unit of study is also the individual and that its concepts also deal with the experience and behavior of the individual. But a science of psychology is not possible without relating experience and behavior to the preceding and current stimulating conditions in which the individual functions, and the most significant aspects of those stimulus conditions are socio-cultural.

The conception of "stimulus situation" that has functional value in social psychology deals with objects and situations in their contextual or patterned relationships (Sherif and Sherif, 1956, Chaps. 1 and 2). The experimental work stemming from F. C. Bartlett of Cambridge

University, from *Gestalt* psychologists, and from psychologists investigating reference scales in judgment has demonstrated that the psychological significance of a stimulus item is dependent upon the functional system or frame of reference of which it is a part. Furthermore, the experience of meaning of social stimuli is immediate, in the sense that it occurs prior to the differentiation of particular elements or cues. There is a *psychological* basis for approaching social stimulus situations on a meaningful level, in terms of their patterning and properties studied by the social sciences.

However, certain distinctions survive in the claims of some sociologists and some cultural anthropologists which impede the social psychologist's attempts to utilize their treatments of social stimulus situations. For example, because of their respective historical developments and interests, an assumption arose that anthropology is primarily concerned with the study of "culture" and sociology with "society" and social systems. When the social psychologist examines representative studies, he finds it difficult at times to decide whether a study is anthropological or sociological in these traditional terms. Is not the study of kinship, for example, a study of social organization? Durkheim's analysis of religious forms is claimed by both disciplines; and the Middletown studies of the Lynds or the Yankee City studies by Warner and his associates can be classified with equal justification as sociology or anthropology. In fact, both sociology and anthropology seem to be concerned with social systems and with their cultural products. In this respect, I am inclined to agree with Kluckhohn's critical comments in *Toward a General Theory of Action,* on the conceptual distinction made in that volume between "cultural resources" as "non-social," on the one hand, and individual actors and "collectivities" as "social objects," on the other (Parsons and Shils, pp. 26–27). From the point of view of social-psychological inquiry, such a distinction is of questionable merit, both as a classificatory device and as a research tool.

If the social psychologist is to achieve an adequate grasp of social stimulus situations, he cannot help finding some truth in the dictum "you shall know man by his works." The notion is basic to the technique of content analysis, which is used to formulate generalizations about groups through the analysis of the frequencies with which given value categories are found in the work of man in given cultural settings. Content analysis has come to the foreground as a perfectly acceptable scientific technique.

On the other hand, the attempt to boil down patterned cultural products and patterns of social organization to items of individual behavior, which is called "reductionism," is still strong in psychology and in the larger trend subsumed under the label "behavioral sciences." Yet, the legitimacy of the subject matters of the various social disciplines needs no defense. To deny their legitimacy leads to the untenable solipsism that everything is psychology, including physics and chemistry. From the point of view of social psychology, the reduction of social stimulus agents to individual terms amounts to omitting crucial factors which enter into the shaping of the individual's mentality, his perspectives, and his behavior.

To be sure, if there were no human beings to interact, there would be no culture, no social organization, no value systems, no means of communication, no means of transportation, no means of production. But once such products come into existence and accumulate, they become stimulating conditions for the individual. Man makes machines; we can also say that machines, in turn, make man. Man creates social organization; we can also say it is social organization that recasts man. Man is in the beginning of these things, but his products are not man himself. His products become the subject matters of study in their own right; and they can be, and they are, studied at their own level in a meaningful way without reference to single individuals.

Even though the growing individual does not always detect the items of his culture in the highly tangible way that he literally bumps into material objects, still all of that culture is initially external to him. The "exteriority" of social values or norms—a fact upon which Emile Durkheim so rightly insisted—can be demonstrated unmistakably through the consequences of their observance or their nonobservance by an individual member of any human group. The insistence that the products of man's social life can be studied in their own right need not lead to a metaphysical enthusiasm for supraindividual properties, however. At this time, it is necessary to distinguish the study of the products of social interaction from the study of the experience and behavior of individuals. In doing so, I take issue with Durkheim, whose conception of "exteriority" was just praised.

Traditionally, it was considered that there were two sorts of psychologies: one dealing with individualistic processes in elementaristic terms, which called for no emerging properties in experience and behavior, and one dealing with group and collective processes, in which emerging properties were recognized. The dichotomy is a false one. When an individual faces a real and vital problem situation with which he has no established ways of coping, but which must be solved, his behavior does exhibit emergent properties. When two or more individuals interact in a problem situation without established norms, they produce new modes of behavior and new norms. The psychology of the emergence of social norms is embedded in the basic psychology of the individuals.

This brings us to a brief discussion of the contributions that social psychology can make most effectively. The exteriority of socio-cultural products does not imply their mechanistic imprint on the individual. On the contrary, the fact of exteriority may serve as a base line for the more adequate study of the active part played by the individual in achieving norm-regulated behavior and in participating in the formation of new socio-cultural products.

In ordinary times, individual variations in behavior occur within a *range of tolerable behavior,* defined by the values or norms of the individuals' group. Individual variations within this range provide data on the unique individualities of members occupying given positions within the range of conformity. Behavior exhibited outside the range of tolerable behavior is nonconformist in that respect. In short, the definition of the social organization and norm system of a group provides a base line which is essential to an understanding of individual behavior in that respect, whether it be conforming or nonconforming. However, the description of the socio-cultural products is not in itself psychology. The socio-cultural setting becomes psychologically meaningful relative to a reacting individual, who comes with his particular endowment, his past history, his personally experienced desires and aspirations toward certain goals, his preoccupations with being a part of groups that in his eyes have value, with achieving some role and status in them and with improving that status. The psychologist is interested in the perceiving, the judging, the learning, the remembering, the actions of the individual within his socio-cultural setting.

In the process of becoming a member, and a "good" member, of his groups, the individual forms social attitudes toward significant aspects of his socio-cultural setting. The coercive presence of other group members toward conformity is supplanted, in time, by his own inner promptings. In fact, those attitudes which define his place in the scheme of things and his reference groups become parts of a psychological system of relatedness to his environment, which social psychologists study in terms of the individual's "ego" or "self." The disruption of this relatedness to his environment is correlated for the individual with a sense of insecurity, loss of stable moorings, and demonstrated behavioral consequences. Psychologically, these facts are significant in understanding behavior during periods of social change and the tendencies toward stabilization of new socio-cultural forms.

It is obvious in this discussion that the social sciences and social psychology are approaching related problems, or even the same problems, at two different levels of analysis, each employing appropriate units of analysis. Various problems of social systems and socio-cultural products are studied by anthropologists, sociologists, and other social scientists. Their units of analysis need not be the behavior of the individual; more appropriately they may pertain to the patterned aspects of man's interaction, his social organization, his productive and distributive relationships, his technological products and relations, his music and art forms, his language systems, his kinship systems, his values, and so on. The social psychologist, on the other hand, is studying the smallest unit of a functioning social system—the human individual. In order to study his experience and behavior, the social psychologist must learn about the conditions in which he functions. Here he has to turn to those social scientists who are studying man's social environment in a meaningful way on its own level.

This conception of the social disciplines working at their own level of analysis and of psychologists working at a level of analysis concerned with individual experience and behavior provides a method for the cross-disciplinary checking of results. If a generalization reached at one level of analysis is valid, it is not contradicted by valid generalizations reached at the other level. For example, the sociologist's generalization that the collective action of a group has properties peculiar to the group level should be supported by the psychologist's findings concerning the behavior of individual members. In fact, this support is found in psychological research showing the differential experience and behavior of individuals performing tasks in a group setting.

For the foregoing reasons, at least this social psychologist is apprehensive of the currently flourishing trends toward reductionism in the social sciences. This reductionism will deprive social psychology of much-needed checks and of the correctives stemming from the study of socio-cultural phenomena at their own level of analysis.

THREE

SOCIAL PSYCHOLOGY: PROBLEMS AND TRENDS IN INTERDISCIPLINARY RELATIONSHIPS

INTRODUCTION

The topic of social psychology in relation to cognate social disciplines is so broad that it is necessary to delimit the task undertaken here at the outset. The first task of this chapter will be to define social psychology. This definition will point to the distinctive concepts of social psychology vis-à-vis the concepts of other social disciplines. The units of analysis implied in the definition have direct bearing on effective interdisciplinary efforts. Then the present formative state of social psychology will be discussed.

Following this general discussion, a few illustrative topics which have preoccupied social psychologists, sociologists, and cultural anthropologists alike will be summarized. Both divergence and convergence will be noted.

Finally, general trends of convergence in social psychology that appear to be most promising will be presented briefly. Interdisciplinary contributions to these developing trends will be indicated.

SOCIAL PSYCHOLOGY AND INTERDISCIPLINARY EFFORTS

Interdisciplinary attacks on problem areas of mutual concern to sociologists, cultural anthropologists, and psychologists date at least to the turn of this century (Hallowell, 1954, p. 173). During the twenties and especially the thirties, collaboration by these disciplines was encouraged by institutionalization and financial support (Kluckhohn and Murray, 1948; Zetterberg, 1956). Since World War II, interdisciplinary conferences, large-scale interdisciplinary research projects supported

Carolyn W. Sherif collaborated in writing this chapter. B. J. White, W. R. Hood, and Lawrence La Fave assisted in surveying the literature.
From *Psychology: A Study of a Science*, Vol. 6, edited by S. Koch. Copyright © 1963 by McGraw-Hill, Inc. Used by permission of McGraw-Hill Book Company and the editor.

by government, business, or foundations, and even interdisciplinary academic units have become commonplace. Today social psychologists have more and more traffic with sociologists and anthropologists, as well as with psychiatrists, social workers, and others in applied fields of endeavor.

It is not always clear to participants in interdisciplinary efforts what distinguishes the various disciplines other than preferences for distinctive terminology. Certainly the topics of interest do not serve as a clear-cut basis. Yet it is precisely when social psychologists attempt interdisciplinary collaboration that a clear conception of their discipline becomes most essential.

What distinguishes social psychology from cognate social disciplines? What are its appropriate and most productive relations with sociology and anthropology? An answer to the first question implies at least the directions that the second will take. Accordingly our first task is to arrive at an adequate characterization of social psychology.

DEVELOPMENTS IN DEFINING SOCIAL PSYCHOLOGY

In 1908 two books on social psychology appeared, the earliest formal textbooks in the field. One author, the sociologist Edward A. Ross (1908), set social psychology squarely upon the study of collective behavior. The psychologist William McDougall (1908) conceived with equal vigor a social psychology focused on the individual as the main determinant of social life.

In social psychology, it seems, the textbook has been the most frequent and influential vehicle for systematic efforts. Although formal definitions do not impart the full viewpoint and contents, substantial differences in definition usually reflect variations in both. Following social psychology's double debut, some fifteen texts accumulated by 1930. The definitions differed considerably. We find social psychology defined as "the science of the motives of people living in social relations" (Williams, 1922); as "the science which studies the behavior of the individual in so far as his behavior stimulates other individuals, or is itself a reaction to their behavior" (F. H. Allport, 1924); as "essentially group psychology" (Dunlap, 1925); as "the study of the individual as he develops cultural behavior equipment" (Kantor, 1929); as dealing "with those human characteristics that make political life inevitable" (Murchison, 1927).

Under the circumstances it was not surprising that social psychology became chary in committing itself. Thus, Cottrell and Gallagher stated that "one of the most clearly marked trends in social psychology" during the subsequent decade (1930–1940) "has been the consistent refusal by social psychologists to define and limit their subject with any exactness" (1941, p. 3).

Between 1940 and 1960, more than two dozen textbooks on social psychology were published in the United States, excluding readings and handbooks. Differences in formal definition persist, along with variations in content (Asch, 1952; Doob, 1952; Krech and Crutchfield, 1948; Queener, 1951). However, since 1940, definitions in texts tend to cluster around a few points of emphasis rather than many. All include the terms "individual" or "behavior" (referring to an individual) in contrast to its neglect in some earlier definitions. Most authors (e.g., Hartley and Hartley, 1952; Klineberg, 1954; Newcomb, 1950; Sargent, 1950; and Young, 1956) include the term "interaction" either in formal definition or subsequent elaboration.

About one-third of the definitions since 1940 specifically mention groups and social institutions as principal stimulating influences in social psychology (e.g., Bonner, 1953; Faris, 1952; La Pierre and Farnsworth, 1949; Lindesmith and Strauss, 1956). Approximately another third do not mention groups in formal definition, but treat groups in the text (e.g., Newcomb, 1950; Queener, 1951). Only about a fifth of the formal definitions designate stimulating conditions broadly enough to include other individuals, groups, institutions, and other cultural and technological products (e.g., Asch, 1952; Bird, 1940; Sherif, 1948), although most authors do include many, if not all, of these as social-stimulus conditions in their texts.

A DEFINITION OF SOCIAL PSYCHOLOGY

Taking account of the converging definitions of our discipline, an adequate characterization of social psychology includes the conception that it is an integral part of psychology (otherwise the designation "social *psychology*" has very little meaning). The characterization must also indicate that its specialization is *social*.

If psychological notions were ancillary to analysis of social organization and its cultural products, the area could be designated "psychological sociology" or "psychological ethnology," as the case might be. In stating that the individual is the unit of analysis in social psychology, there is no implication that psychology is more central or more established than other disciplines. The insistence here is on clarification of the appropriate level of analysis in social psychology and hence the nature of its conceptual tools. Its concepts or "principles" need not bear the trademark of any of today's competing schools of psychology. I refer to concepts and generalizations that have been or will be established on the basis of demonstrated validity, regardless of special preferences of any school. Admittedly a rounded psychology is far from an accomplished fact, especially in areas of closest concern to man's social relations—motivation, learning, conceptual functioning, and other processes traditionally termed "higher mental processes" (cf. Koch, 1956).

It seems to me that the following definition satisfies the above requirements and offers a clear basis for fruitful give and take with the social sciences: *Social psychology is the scientific study of the experience and behavior of individuals in relation to social-stimulus situations.*

Consideration of the main terms of this definition will provide smoother passage to problems of social psychology–social science relationships. Social psychology is termed a "scientific study" to stress the fact that its empirical data are obtained through reproducible and verifiable procedures and that it aims at achieving a consistent and communicable set of concepts and definitions, so that any hypothesis or generalization advanced can be tested by anyone with adequate training.

As noted above, the concepts of social psychology are necessarily in terms of "experience and behavior of the individual," that is, his judging, perceiving, imagining, learning, remembering, thinking, behaving, or acting. It is the individual who judges, discriminates, perceives, learns, remembers, and thinks. The unit of analysis in social psychology, as in all psychology, is the individual, whether he is alone, participating in interpersonal, in-group, or intergroup relations, or acting in the frenzy of a mob situation.

The psychological activity of the individual, from simplest judgment through more complex activities of problem solving and thinking in social situations, is not solely an outcome of external-stimulus agents (social or nonsocial), nor is it an outcome solely of internal impulses (motives, attitudes, ego-involvements). Ordinarily, psychological activity (perception, learning, memory, and so on) is a product of interrelated factors coming both from the external field of stimulation and from internal influences.

Therefore, it becomes meaningless to take sides as culture-group (environment) determinists or as "instinct," "need," or individual determinists. For this reason, the definition of social psychology stated that experience and behavior are studied "in relation to" social-stimulus situations, rather than "as determined by" social-stimulus situations. The direction of influences linking individual and social setting is not one way, but reciprocal.

SOCIAL-STIMULUS SITUATIONS

Now we come to the final words in the definition, namely, "social-stimulus situations." Here I use "stimulus situations" as a generic term for factors which at a given time are external to the individual, the skin being the usual limit for externality. Although the ambiguity of the word "stimulus" increases by the year, a distinction between internal and external factors is analytically necessary in social psychology, particularly in dealing with problems of socialization and conformity. Of course, certain external objects may become internal through swallowing or subcutaneous insult; but extraceptive, introceptive, and proprioceptive impulses can be designated as such without using the stimulus symbol. Conceiving stimulus situations as external to the individual, it seems to me that sound conceptions of the properties of social-stimulus situations will go a long way toward building a social psychology commensurate with the activities of the individual in the actualities of his social setting. Furthermore, it will provide guideposts for delimiting the focus of social psychology vis-à-vis cognate social disciplines and an explicit rationale for their interdisciplinary relationship.

For that matter, the general problem of stimulus properties is one of the basic problems for all psychology. Until fairly recently, highly influential behavioristic schools of psychology made no systematic issue of the properties of stimulus objects and situations confronting the individual. This neglect almost amounted to assuming that cues or stimuli had absolute values for the reacting individual, irrespective of the relations of the stimuli in the particular conditions. It was sometimes assumed that only a designated set of elements, and not others surrounding them, were stimulating agents.

A description of the above state of affairs was recently made by Melton (1956):

Finally, I wish to mention a specific characteristic of our contemporary S-R theory that, it seems to me, must be overcome if progress is to be made. I refer to the assumption throughout much theory and experimentation, especially on the simpler forms of learning in the rat and in human conditioning, that the stimulus is a simple punctiform affair, something that can be dealt with as though it occurred without context, as though it were the stimulation of a single receptor. The comment is certainly not new. It has been made by the critics of S-R theories of behavior since the first such theory was formulated. But it is also one to which some dominant S-R theories have not adjusted adaptively. We have had Hull's principle of afferent neural interaction stated, but nothing much has been done about it either experimentally or through revision of theory (p. 28).

The conception of stimulus situation that has functional significance in social psychology deals with objects and situations in their contextual relationships. Writers in the social sciences have consistently stressed the desirability of conceptualizing the social field in such terms. For example, sociologists like Durkheim (1938) and W. I. Thomas (1918) and social philosophers like George H. Mead (1934) were groping in this direction, each in his way.

In the experimental work of gestalt psychologists and of psychologists investigating judgment, it became evident that relations among various items, even in simple judgment and perception situations, are as important as the component items themselves. The psychological significance of any item cannot be determined independently of others which constitute a functional system, variously called a "whole" or a "reference scale" as the case might be (Koffka, 1935; Köhler, 1929; Volkmann, 1951; Wertheimer, 1939; Wever and Zener, 1928).

Emphasis on the relationships of parts within patterned wholes becomes indispensable in characterization of social-stimulus situations for purposes of social-psychological analysis. The individual experiences and reacts to social objects, persons, groups, cultural items (furniture, tools, words, music, and so on) in terms of meaningful relations prevailing in the characteristic patterning of these stimulus agents. It has been demonstrated that experience of meaning of social stimuli is prior to singling out particular elements or associations (Cantril, 1932; Tolman, 1917). There is a psychological basis, therefore, for approaching social-stimulus situations on a meaningful level, in terms of their patterning and properties studied by social science.

In writing social psychology books, some authors centered upon interpersonal relations as the primary concern of social psychology, to the neglect of social structures within which interpersonal relations ordinarily function. Naturally, students of culture found little of relevance to their work. Other authors elaborated on social groups and organizations to the neglect of interpersonal relations. Some authors were fixated on culture and its effects. The products offered as social psychology with primary emphasis on a single variety of social-stimulus situations resembled the well-known descriptions of the elephant examined by the blind men, as Sargent has noted (1950, Chap. 1). To be sure, experience and behavior do not follow altogether different principles in different stimulus situations. However, the validity of such basic principles can be established only by testing them in the gamut of stimulus situations, from interpersonal to intergroup and cultural.

Recognizing the importance of the properties and varieties of social-stimulus situations, a social psychologist is confronted with some distinctions which were historically important in the development of social science and which still survive in the claims of some sociologists and cultural anthropologists. Traditionally, those investigators called "anthropologists" were concerned with cultures and peoples who were considered distant, primitive, bizarre, and esoteric. On the whole, sociologists traditionally dealt with contemporary societies. Because of their respective historical developments and preoccupations, an assumption arose that anthropology is primarily concerned with the study of culture and sociology with society or social systems.

When we examine representative studies of a given people, we find that they could be presented either as sociology or as anthropology if we did not know that the author calls himself a sociologist or anthropologist. One of the anthropologist's interests has been kinship systems. Is not the study of kinship exactly a study in social organization? Durkheim's analysis of religious forms (1915) is claimed both by sociologists and anthropologists. The Lynds' Middletown study (1937) or the Yankee City studies by Warner and his associates (e.g., Warner and Lunt, 1941) can be classified with equal justification as sociology or anthropology. Both sociology and anthropology are concerned with social structure or systems and with their cultural products (value systems, institutions, etc.). Cultural products such as values or norms are products of a group. The set of norms pertaining to status and role arrangements in the groups is at least partly accountable for the perpetuation of its social system or organization. Such considerations raise a question as to the usefulness of categorizing these aspects of the situation in which a person ("actor") is behaving as (1) "non-social, that is, physical objects or accumulated cultural resources, or (2) social objects, that is, individual actors and collectivities" (Parsons and Shils, 1951, p. 5; cf. Kluckhohn's comment in the same volume, pp. 26–27).

Following the above rationale, we may list the varieties of social-stimulus situations in the following general categories:

1. Other people
   a. Other individuals—represented in interpersonal relations.
   b. Groups—represented in the individual's (a) intragroup (in-group) relations and (b) intergroup relations.
   c. Collective interaction situations—represented by fluid and critical situations which need not be identical with in-group or intergroup relations of more stable times.

2. Cultural products—products of human interaction in the past or present.
   a. Material culture.
   b. Nonmaterial culture.

Needless to say, the varieties of social-stimulus situations listed above are not mutually exclusive. At times, the individual is confronted with representatives of all of them on a single occasion. For example, a wedding ceremony, a political convention, or a protest rally may involve most of them. I shall comment on each variety. A more extensive discussion of each variety is available (Sherif and Sherif, 1956, pp. 11–28).

Other Individuals as Stimuli. To be sure, interpersonal relations in which two or more individuals serve as stimuli for each other are examples *par excellence* of day-to-day social interactions. The motivational claims of individuals are in relation to one another (for bodily care, for companionship, for a sense of belongingness, for proving one's worth, for recognition, for love, and so on). Development of one's notion of himself as a human individual is unthinkable apart from his relations with other individuals. However, ordinarily, reciprocal personal expectations as friends, as companions, as parent and offspring, as husband and wife, as sweethearts, as business partners, as employer and employee and even as equals in given capacities take place within more or less stabilized organizational patterns and sets of values (norms) of a given sociocultural setting.

Groups as Stimulus Situations. As a stimulus situation for an individual, a group (e.g., a clique, gang, club, or labor or management organization) has unmistakable structural properties. These structural properties are represented by a particular pattern of status and role relations which is reflected even in the intimacy of interpersonal contacts of the individual members. It is the implications of these structural properties for the reciprocal expectations and behaviors of individual members that brought the study of groups irrevocably to the foreground. A group—conceived as a delineated social unit in which individual members occupy identifiable positions and roles and share a set of values—is a concept at the sociological level of analysis. Since all groups within differentiated societies are functionally related to other groups and are parts of larger organizational structures, relations between groups are likewise ubiquitous and consequential as social-stimulus situations.

Collective Interaction Situations. Collective interaction (represented by rallies, crowds, mobs) cannot be properly classified as interpersonal interaction. For one thing, the number of individuals involved is greater than the usual scope of face-to-face relations. Likewise, it is difficult to subsume collective interaction under group situations. At least initially, a collective-interaction situation lacks stabilized, orderly status and role delineations embracing all participating individuals. It should be noted, however, that closely knit nuclei composed of a smaller number of individuals may be mainly responsible for initiating and influencing the course of events in such collectivities.

Collective-interaction situations usually take place under conditions of crisis, fluidity, or out-of-the-ordinary events. At times, the "cake of custom" is shattered and new values or norms arise in the form of short-cut formulations, dicta, and slogans (Blumer, 1946; Durkheim, 1915; Hughes, 1946; Le Bon, 1897). Out-of-the-ordinary type of behavior and emergent products of collective-interaction situations have been described dramatically by various authors (e.g., Chapman and Eckstein, 1954; LeBon, 1897; Ross, 1908). Such occasions give rise to accentuated expression of motives and frustrations on the one hand. On the other, they also produce emergent types of behavior which are conducive at times to the stabilization of new social values and new patterns of human relationships. For these reasons, collective-interaction situations should provide fertile soil for point cultivation by social psychologists and social scientists.

The two varieties of stimulus situations yet to be discussed pertain to parts of culture as stimulus situations. I have deliberately chosen the wording "parts of culture" rather than the generic term "culture." Especially in modern societies, no one individual is confronted with the whole of a culture even during the course of an entire lifetime. His acquaintance with culture is confined to his experience.

The topic is a controversial one. Some students today are busily engaged in defining culture, primarily in individual and psychodynamic terms, in an effort to divorce themselves from the grand theorizing and reifications of "Culture" by past anthropological systematizers. It is easy to swing too far in the opposite direction. Then culture is seen only within the confines of discrete interpersonal relations or in the unique personality characteristics of informants or a select number of "natives" responding to psychological questionnaires and projective tests. These psychological data can, of course, be valuable. But they become valuable when viewed in terms of the more fundamental problem of what constitutes sociocultural stimulus situations for the individual.

If all the social objects that the individual utilized in his day-to-day activities were *mediated* only through other persons, if his conception of them were molded *only* by the words and example of other individuals, then it might be possible to study cultural stimulus situations only in terms of interpersonal and group contacts. However, the individual is confronted from birth on with furniture, buildings, tools, melodies, means of transportation, and mass communication. Such man-made structures do exert an unmistakable influence in shaping his scales of magnitude, his sense of appropriate proportions, his notion of the tempo of events—whether or not they are mediated through other individuals.

Social psychology must be concerned with the socialization process through which the infant becomes in time an individual member of a particular sociocultural setting. Adequate analysis of this process requires a clear conceptual distinction between the sociocultural situations he faces and his particular psychological processes and products at a given time. Without this conceptual distinction, the historical error of attributing social attitudes and traits to an unfolding and fixed "human nature" is repeated over and over. Defining culture as the "man-made part of the environment" (Herskovits, 1949) permits specification and analysis of the sociocultural setting of the newly born member of a society.

To be sure, if there were no human beings to interact, there would be no culture, no social organization, no value system, no means of communication, transportation, or production, and no technology. But once such products come into existence and accumulate through generations they take their appropriate places as stimulus conditions, setting certain limits and forming the basis for perspectives of human beings. It is man who made machines; we can also say that machines, in turn, make man. It is man who created social organization; we can also say that it is social organization that recasts man. Man is in the beginning of things, but his products are not man himself. His products (social organization, technology, language, etc.) become subject matters in their own right, and these subject matters can be and are studied on their own level in a meaningful way without reference to single individuals. Thus economics is a discipline in its own right, and so are ethnology, linguistics, archaeology, and musicology. To think otherwise would lead us to an untenable solipsism which would assert that everything is psychology, including physics and chemistry.

Reduction of social-stimulus agents to only psychological terms—leaving out their material setting and the value or norm system which regulates even man's most intimate relationships—would mean omitting crucial factors which enter into shaping the individual's mentality and behavior. The perspectives and the reference scales which the individual forms during his encounters with man-made parts of his surroundings and the categorizing effects of the structure of his language are among the significant components of the bounds of his mentality. The "sociology of knowledge" has called attention to these components in an impressive way (e.g., Manheim, 1936).

Against this background, parts of culture can be discussed as social-stimulus situations under the two remaining headings.

Parts of Material Culture as Stimulus Situations. Products of human interaction and labor are parts of the material culture. Furniture, dwellings, facilities for cooking and sleeping, plumbing, streets, playgrounds, means of transportation (oxcart, car, train, bus, boat, plane), means of communication (books, newspapers, radio, television), and other technical products (machines) used in producing means of livelihood are parts of material culture.

Man's works reveal a great deal about his designs for living, his attainments, his standards of living, his modes of thinking, and his tastes. The foreigner who enters New York Harbor and takes a taxi to a hotel does not need to be told of the riches and industrial might of the United States. The skyline of the city, the shop windows, the density of traffic, the unceasing hustle and bustle are more eloquent than any words. Through archaeological findings we learn a great deal about the modes of living, thinking, and feeling in extinct societies.

Our notions of space and time, our standards of living, the radius of our psychological world—all are influenced by the material culture which confronts us. On the whole, this area is sadly neglected in social-psychological works. Yet items of material culture are stimulus situations, and some of the individual's significant reference scales can be effectively studied in relation to them. He uses such reference scales in appraising, for example, what is "too primitive" to bear or what is "splendid" beyond his wildest dreams. We learn from the historian Webb (1936) that the introduction of barbed-wire fencing had an appreciable effect on the development of agricultural activities, social organizations, and individual attitudes on the American Great Plains (pp. 270–318).

Or, to take one more example, we learn from the anthropologist Lang (1946) that the work of Chinese youngsters in industrial plants appreciably affected the pattern of role relations of the traditional Chinese family (p. 206).

Several decades ago, the anthropologist Sapir (1949) called attention to the effects of technological changes on human relations:

> Every profound change in the flow of civilization, particularly every change in its economic bases, tends to bring about an unsettling and readjustment of culture values. Old culture forms, habitual types of reaction, tend to persist through the force of inertia. The maladjustment of these habitual reactions to their new civilizational environment brings with it a measure of spiritual disharmony, which the more sensitive individuals feel eventually as a fundamental lack of culture. Sometimes the maladjustment corrects itself with great rapidity, at other times it may persist for generations, as in the case of America, where a chronic state of cultural maladjustment has for so long a period reduced much of our higher life to sterile externality (pp. 317–318).

The point of emphasis here is not akin to the unbridled technological determinism advocated some time ago by the exponents of "technocracy." Material culture seldom, if ever, affects social relations singlehandedly. Its effects have to be considered in conjunction with other parts of the social setting as these are related to the motivational directions and goals of the people involved. As Quincy Wright (1949) stated: "The effect of a particular technological invention or importation upon a particular social order depends upon the way in which it is utilized, and that utilization is in large measure influenced by the values and culture of the social order" (p. 177).

The study of the effects of material culture, though often neglected, has decided advantages as a problem area for interdisciplinary cooperation between social scientist and psychologist. Items of material culture are suitable for quantitative specification, and they can be studied with considerable precision as stimulus conditions (independent variables) in relation to reference scales or perspectives which the individual forms internally and utilizes in his judgments and appraisals, along the lines suggested by Volkmann (1936, pp. 288–294).

Items of Nonmaterial Culture as Stimulus Situations. Material culture is not all of the man-made part of the individual's environment. Even from birth, he is confronted with lullabies and feeding and sleeping schedules which change according to medical and nonmedical vogues. In a few years, the infant learns that he is a boy or a girl; that certain toys are appropriate for boys, certain others for girls; that certain qualities (e.g., being brave or coy) and certain activities are more appropriate for a boy or a girl. A little later he internalizes certain regularities shaping his role expectations and behavior. These are only a few of the items of nonmaterial culture that a child in any group faces.

Since he is initially rather mercurial in his goal-directedness, and since his conceptual and motor capacities are not fully developed, it takes years to internalize these social items. This internalization is not merely a "stamping" process involving rewards and coercive measures applied by grown-ups. It includes active processes involving the individual's particular selectivity and gradually his strivings to become like others and do what others are doing. Such strivings emerge as the child's conceptual capacities develop, as he interacts with others, and as he acquires a grasp of the language system. The crucial importance of language is only hinted at here; as several authors have emphasized, language is not merely another item of culture, but rather the scaffolding and vehicle for the formation and perpetuation of culture (Lindesmith and Strauss, 1956; Mead, 1934; Sapir, 1949).

The would-be member of a society is literally immersed in items of nonmaterial culture. They include a language system, social organization, religion and its organization, art forms, music forms, schedules regulating vital activities, conceptions of man and the world around him. One ubiquitous area of nonmaterial culture is a system of values or norms which includes items pertinent to every important phase of his interpersonal, social, religious, educational, and work activities.

Some parts of nonmaterial culture are fairly concrete in perceptual form and sequence (e.g., nursery rhythms, regularity of daily activities, authority of parents in the family group). Some are more abstract (e.g., sentence structure of the particular language; notions of past and future, of town, state, and nation, of the values and organization of school, church, and profession).

The growing individual does not immediately detect all the items in his nonmaterial culture in the tangible way that he recognizes items of material culture, which he can literally bump into. Nevertheless, all items of the nonmaterial culture are initially external to him. As Emile Durkheim (1938) so rightly insisted, the exteriority of social values or norms can be unmistakably demonstrated through the consequences of observance or nonobservance of these norms by an individual member of a group. Reactions of fellow members to deviation *beyond the range of acceptable behavior* (within which individual variations are permissible) are one of the best indexes of the external reality of a social value or norm (e.g., Durkheim, 1938; Freedman *et al.*, 1952; Shaw, 1930). Reactions to deviation tend to become standardized in a group, depending on the nature and severity of deviation. Once a social norm is clearly established, even the leader is not outside the demands of members to behave within the latitude of acceptable behavior which it defines (e.g., Whyte, 1943, pp. 262ff.).

Insistence on recognizing the external reality of social products is not an idle issue, nor is it overenthusiasm for supra-individual group properties. Traditionally, two sorts of psychology were recognized—one dealing with individualistic processes in elementaristic terms which allowed for no emergent properties in experience and behavior, the other dealing with group or collective processes in which emergences were recognized. Here we part company with Durkheim, whose exteriority criterion of group norms was cited above.

There are not two sorts of psychology—one for individual processes and one for collective processes. The psychology of the emergence of social norms as products of interaction among individuals is embedded in the basic psychology of the individual, and this basic psychology is the same in all cultures. Whenever the individual faces a stimulus situation where clear alternatives for established modes of action are lacking, his reactions tend toward stabilization, revealing emergent properties (e.g., Sherif, 1936). The weighty evidence from child psychology (Merei, 1949; Piaget, 1932) and research on clique and gang formations (e.g., Thrasher, 1927; Whyte, 1943) warrants this conclusion: whenever individuals interact without established or adequate norms to deal with a problem situation with strong appeal value to them, they produce new values or norms for behavior.

The external reality of social products is stressed here to delineate the nature of concepts and facts appropriate for analysis at the sociological level and at the psychological level. Clear delineation of the nature of our data and concepts can bring order to the confusing mixture that is prevalent today in both social psychology and cognate disciplines. This does not place the sociologist (or anthropologist) and the psychologist in sealed and separated compartments. On the contrary, it makes interdisciplinary give-and-take a necessity.

I will illustrate the delineation of sociological and psychological analysis briefly by discussing the concepts of social norm and social attitude. *Social norm* is a sociological concept denoting expected or even ideal modes of behavior inferred from similarities of behavior by group members and from their reactions to deviation (Freedman *et al.*, 1952). Social attitudes are formed by the individual in relation to social norms. *Social attitude* is a psychological concept inferred from the individual's characteristic modes of response to relevant situations (Campbell, 1950; Sherif and Cantril, 1947). The term "internalization" or "interiorization," used widely by social psychologists in discussing social norms, is symptomatic of the stage of development in social psychology. The term implies that a social attitude is formed in relation to a social norm, or that a social item (e.g., social norm) is learned.

Recognition of the exteriority of social norms does not imply that there is a mechanical imprint of these norms on the individual. It does not obliterate the individual's active part in forming norm-regulated behavior. On the contrary, exteriority provides a baseline which facilitates more adequate study of the psychological problems. Here the baseline is the range of acceptable behavior in terms of the "expected" or "ideal," as defined by the value or norm. Limits can be established by observing the points at which deviation elicits correctives from the identified members of the group. Within the latitude of acceptance variations provide data concerning the unique individualities of members who are within the range of conformity. Individuals exhibiting behavior outside the latitude of acceptable behavior in a given respect are the nonconformists in that respect.

Once the relative positions of individuals within and without the latitude of acceptable behavior are established, we can proceed to the comparison of personality characteristics of conformist and nonconformist individuals as intensively as we wish. Conformity and nonconformity are not absolute qualities. The very terms are relative to a baseline which is defined by the norm, independently of the behavior of any particular individual.

In the process of becoming a "good" member of the groups in his sociocultural setting, the individual forms social attitudes in relation to parts of the sociocultural setting. These social attitudes enter into the patterning of his experience and behavior as regulating factors in relevant matters. The constant presence of coercive pressures from other group members and the threat of correctives are supplanted in most instances by his own inner promptings. In fact, as he forms attitudes relative to central values of his group (defining the belongingness and status of members), these attitudes become part of a functioning system of relatedness to his environment which is termed "ego" or "self." Thus the central values of his group become the individual's own personal values. (For example, the individual says, "I am an American," or "I am a college man," or "I am white," with all that these statements imply.)

SOME PROBLEMS OF INTERDISCIPLINARY APPROACHES

Since social psychology studies experience and behavior in relation to social-stimulus situations, it necessarily becomes dependent upon cognate social disciplines for an understanding of its stimulus situations. On the other hand, when sociologists and anthropologists become interested in change and conflict, invention and diffusion, assimilation and acculturation, enculturation and role changes, they inevitably encounter some of the central problems in social psychology (e.g., Murdock, 1954; E. Sapir, 1949). The interdependence of the social disciplines in seeking solutions of many central problems has been seriously discussed in numerous interdisciplinary conferences (e.g., Gillin, 1954; Hulett and Stagner, 1956; Miller, 1950; Rohrer and Sherif,

1951; Sargent and Smith, 1949; Sherif and Wilson, 1953). As one result, both traditionally individualistic psychological approaches and the rubber-stamp tradition of cultural determinism have become somewhat passé.

Despite the current fashion of "behavioral science," dreams of interdisciplinary integration are far from realized. Too frequently, it is assumed that each contributor represents a unified discipline, and that his approach and conceptual tools are "the" approach and concepts of psychology, sociology, or anthropology, as the case might be. At times, interdisciplinary contact results in wholesale borrowing of concepts to be sprinkled through one's writing at random or tacked onto one's research report as a friendly gesture.

Progress toward a genuinely interdisciplinary approach may be materially speeded through recognizing the levels of analysis of the various disciplines (Asch, 1952; Sherif and Sherif, 1948). The social sciences (sociology, anthropology, economics, etc.) and social psychology are approaching related problems at two different levels, each employing appropriate units of analysis. Various problems of the social system are studied by historians, economists, sociologists, anthropologists, linguists, and others of the traditional social sciences. Their units of analysis are not individual man, but man's social organization, his productive and distributive relationships, his technological products and relations, his music and art forms, his language systems, his kinships systems, his values, and so on. The unit of analysis employed requires appropriate concepts for handling relevant variables.

The human individual is the smallest unit of this functioning social system, and he himself is also a functioning system. The scientist who studies his experience and behavior necessarily turns to those investigating various aspects of the individual system—the biochemist, the geneticist, and the physiologist. He also needs to know the conditions in which the individual functions. If he is a social psychologist, this means learning about social-stimulus situations faced by the individual; he must turn to the sociologist, anthropologist, linguist, historian, economist, and others studying man's social environment. But what he learns from them is not social psychology. Social-psychological analysis must be made in terms of the individual's functioning in relation to these social-stimulus situations. Thus many of the most useful concepts in social psychology are relational terms.

The direction of influences between individual and individual and between individual and groups and their products (culture) is reciprocal. The process is interaction rather than simple reaction. The social psychologist may find himself concerned with regularities and patterns of interaction which the sociologist may not have investigated. When the social psychologist investigates these regularities, he is working at the sociological level of analysis. Likewise, when the sociologist or anthropologist becomes preoccupied with the component parts of the social organization (individuals), he is working on a psychological level.

CROSS-DISCIPLINARY CHECKING

While the notion of levels is no panacea, its consistent utilization would help to eliminate a number of obstacles to effective interdisciplinary cooperation. Such practice provides invaluable checks on the validity of findings and conclusions. If a generalization reached at one level of analysis is valid, it is not contradicted by valid generalizations reached at another level. For example, the sociologist's generalization (of several decades' standing) that collective action of a group has properties peculiar to the group level (Durkheim, 1915; Hiller, 1928; Thrasher, 1927) should be supported by psychologists' findings concerning individuals when participating as members of a group. This support may be found in psychological research over several decades concerning differential experience and behavior by the individual performing tasks in a social setting (e.g., Allport, 1924; Dashiell, 1935; Kelley and Thibaut, 1954).

On the other hand, a psychologist may conclude that human social patterns in aggression or dominance relations, for example, are basically like the pecking order of domestic fowl or dominance relations in sub-human primates. Scientists familiar with properties of human social organization can document in detail the significant differences between them—differences traceable to differing capacities and underlying processes in the respective species (Schneirla, 1953, pp. 70–73). As Schneirla (1946, 1952) has suggested, if the comparative psychologist were equally concerned with differences and similarities produced by evolutionary processes, he could contribute to the genuinely comparative study of life to the mutual benefit of all disciplines. But if the differences are not taken into account, his contribution is likely to be a caricature of human behavior and human social organization.

SEQUENCE OF ANALYSIS

A sequence of study appropriate for problems of interdisciplinary concern derives from the concept of levels of analysis. An observation by the anthropologist Malinowski (1922) is pertinent. When Malinowski wrote about a rather complicated system of exchange called "Kula" among island groups in the Western Pacific, he commented that individuals participate effectively in the complex exchange relationships without ever grasping the nature of the "total outline" of the system itself. The individuals involved

. . . know their own motives, know the purpose of individual actions and rules which apply to them; but . . . not even the most intelligent native has any clear idea of the Kula as a big, organized social construction. . . . If you were to ask him what the Kula is, he would answer by giving a few details, most likely by giving his personal experience and subjective views of the Kula. . . .

For the integral picture does not exist in his mind; he is in it, and cannot see the whole from the outside (p. 83).

If a social psychologist were to study the behavior of single individuals in these Pacific islands without knowing about the Kula as an organized system of relationships, he would be likely to draw erroneous conclusions. True, if he were genuinely concerned with a functional analysis of these behaviors, he would start observing the interactions of the individuals in pertinent activities and eventually arrive at an over-all description of the Kula system, as Malinowski did. But if he persisted in a strictly individual approach to this behavior without first relating it to the patterned relationships of the Kula system, he would have little basis for distinguishing individual variations, individual contributions, or innovations. In short, a primary task in social psychology is learning the properties and functioning of social organizations with their culture patterns. Once the social-stimulus situations are studied, the social psychologist is prepared to investigate individual functioning in relation to them.

Suppose his problem concerns suicide, that individual act of self-destruction which Durkheim (1951) so eloquently incorporated into the realm of the "socially determined." If he looked for a careful ecological analysis of a city, such as a recent investigation in London (Saintsbury, 1955), he would find that areas of social isolation, mobility, and "disorganization" contribute significantly to suicide statistics. He would also find that the incidence of this individual act, like most individual acts, is not determined entirely by these over-all sociocultural conditions. In the study noted, at least a quarter of the suicides could not be attributed readily to such conditions. The social psychologist would want to investigate both samples, the sample of individuals who had not been affected by these grossly defined social conditions, and the sample of individuals who seemed to have been significantly affected by them. He would need to frame his analysis within over-all sociocultural conditions to grasp the interrelationships of immediate environmental factors, unique personal characteristics, and variations in life history from birth onward. If such a sequential analysis seems inordinately demanding for the social psychologist, one can only reflect that this is the required task if he wants his social psychology to be *social.*

SOCIAL PSYCHOLOGY IS STILL IN A FORMATIVE STAGE

The integration of findings from psychological and sociocultural levels necessary for an integrated social-psychological theory is still far from attainment. This conclusion will surprise no one whose enthusiasm has not blurred his perspective. As a scientific discipline, social psychology is still in its formative stage.

In handling the current flood of research data, the social psychologist faces a plethora of contradictory and overlapping concepts. Turning to sociology and anthropology for help, he finds disciplines which themselves lack unity in approach and conceptual tools. For example, sociology may seem topically compartmentalized (into urban and rural, theory and social problems, crime and marriage, etc.). To borrow a phrase from the sociologist Becker (1956), it may seem to be devoted to "self-inflicted shortsightedness." In anthropology, he finds statements of conceptual unity (Murdock, 1954), but contradictory approaches to important problems (Bidney, 1949) and serious doubts about the reliability of many empirical findings in the field (e.g., Kluckhohn, 1949; Lewis, 1952).

From the turn of the century, some social psychologists have had their training in and are identified with academic departments of sociology; some have developed in departments of psychology. In terms of this classification, roughly a third of the textbooks in the field since 1908 were written by sociologists and about two-thirds by psychologists. Courses are taught today in departments of both sociology and psychology.

While little can be said here about the general character of sociology and psychology, reference to important trends which influenced social psychology is necessary. During the first decades of this century, some sociologists became seriously concerned with problems of individual functioning, notably in the area of motivation.

Alongside the domain of "bare existence" in which "structuralists" of the time moved so elegantly (e.g., Titchener, 1929), the rise of behaviorism in psychology brought a further trend away from those problems of individual functioning which most interested sociologists. By the 1920's, the predominant trend in psychology, despite McDougall and despite Freud, concerned reflexes, habits, and performance. Motivational problems were touched lightly or motivational concepts were translated into behavioristic terminology, e.g., "pre-potent reflexes" (Allport, 1924). Sociological concern with motivational problems continued. This is reflected in a comparison between the page references to twelve motivational concepts in the indexes of five introductory psychology texts (Carr, 1925; Griffith, 1923; Leary, 1928; Moore, 1922; Perrin and Klein, 1926) and five introductory sociology texts published in the 1920's (Dow, 1922; Hart, 1927; Lumley, 1928; Ross, 1923; Ward, 1928). The concepts are *drive, emotion, Four Wishes, instinct, interest, libido, motive, sentiments, will to power, attitudes, self, prejudice.* "Drive" was not included in any of the sociology texts. "Four Wishes," "libido," "sentiments," and "prejudice" were omitted from all the psychology texts. The psychology texts had an average of 32 page references per book to these concepts, while the sociology texts averaged 61 page references per book.

Thus, in this period, social psychology proceeded along two

different paths (Bernard, 1942; Faris, 1945; Karpf, 1932; Reuter, 1940). On the one hand, there were the interactionists such as James Mark Baldwin, John Dewey, the sociologist C. H. Cooley, G. H. Mead, W. I. Thomas, Ellsworth Faris; on the other hand, there was a general tide of behaviorism in academic psychology as epitomized in the 1920's by F. H. Allport's text (1924). It is well to note that each discipline was influenced to some extent by the other, even though the differences between the two approaches can be termed "fundamental" and "irreconcilable" (Reuter, 1940). The 1927 *Sourcebook for Social Psychology*, edited by the sociologist Kimball Young, included six chapters on "Psychological Foundations of Social Behavior" with selections written predominantly by psychologists. And Murphy and Murphy's first *Experimental Social Psychology* in 1931, summarizing research largely from the psychological laboratory, defined social psychology as the study of "interaction among individuals."

In academic psychology, a heavy emphasis on biological evolution continued side by side with behaviorism. For example, in Murchison's 1935 *Handbook of Social Psychology* almost half of the pages were devoted to evolutionary problems ranging from bacteria to human life. Less than 5 per cent of the contents of the *Sourcebook* (edited eight years earlier by Kimball Young, whose affiliations had been in sociology) concerned such topics. In contrast to the Murchison *Handbook*, with its chapters on age, sex, maladjustment, and childhood, Young's volume contained sections on personality and social behavior, including selections on self, two chapters on prejudice, two chapters on social groups and their standards, and sections entitled "Leadership and Prestige" and "Collective Behavior," with chapters on public opinion and propaganda. The closest overlap between these two volumes was the topic of attitudes. In comparing the two volumes today, one cannot help noting that the topic headings in Young's 1927 volume sound more contemporary and reflect concern with actualities of social behavior not apparent in most of the 1935 Murchison *Handbook*. In fact, Robert French (1956) noted in his review of the more recent Lindzey-edited *Handbook of Social Psychology* that about three-quarters of the papers in the 1935 volume were devoted to "topics of scant concern" today. Social psychologists trained in academic psychology manifested less concern than did their sociological colleagues with social actualities or applied problems until the thirties (Cantril, 1934).

Some present converging trends in social psychology will be noted later in this chapter, but it should be noted here that their background is more complex than that of the two approaches sketched above. Besides the more traditional interactionist and behavioristic viewpoints, new trends arose in behaviorism itself, including attempts to digest Freudian conceptions (Dollard *et al.*, 1939). In general, the influence of Freudian theories became more evident in sociology (Burgess, 1939–40), in psychology, and in cultural anthropology (Hallowell, 1954). Psychologists became aware that anthropological findings in exotic cultures had relevance for their work, some of them embracing cultural relativism without full awareness of the implications of such a position for social psychology (cf. Murphy, 1949). Gestalt psychology made itself known in this country and influenced a number of social psychologists during the 1930's. There was much more to complicate this background, but this is perhaps sufficient to indicate the widened horizons and rapid pace of social psychology in the 1930's, as it hustled off in several directions.

With World War II, social psychology was "in demand" by government and military agencies. Studies on propaganda and morale, leadership selection, and "national character" were needed. Social psychologists were put to work side by side with colleagues who had considered themselves experimental psychologists or sociologists or anthropologists or political scientists. Cartwright wrote: "Practical problems of social engineering sprang up overnight which required solution before lunch" (1945, p. 67).

Regardless of how one evaluates the results (e.g., Katz, 1951), there can be little doubt that the research opportunities and facilities supplied during and since World War II by government and military, industrial, and private agencies have given more impetus to social psychology than could any professional efforts, no matter how dedicated. Literature on social-psychological investigations was classified by the *Psychological Abstracts* under "Social Psychology" for the first time in 1947 (after two decades as "Social Functions of the Individual" and one decade of "General Social Processes: Including Aesthetics"), but it has overflowed into almost every topical classification.

The sudden demand, broadened opportunities, and heightened interest in academic circles and outside brought social psychologists closer to the social actualities against which they must eventually test their theories. But a rash of hastily conceived investigations on topics of current interest inevitably tended to obscure any solid advance upon central problems in research and theory. In the interest of keeping the research grants coming and the research reputation of one's university or school rising, a problem suggested by one's next of academic kin was frequently investigated, with little attempt to relate the findings to earlier studies or to related topics.

Here the picture is deliberately drawn black and white to point up the glaring discrepancies and contradictions which anyone who surveys current literature is bound to find. Any pride in the achievements of social psychology over the past three decades must be tempered with awareness that considerable research is not channeled into coherent theory. Conceptual tools are still controversial. Research and theorizing flourish in certain specialized areas without recognition of their relevance to more general problems.

In progressing toward greater maturity as a scientific discipline, one necessary task is unification of conceptual tools. For example, the term *perception* is currently augmented by *social perception, sociometric perception, subception, perceptual defense, perceptual offense,* as well as W. I. Thomas' "definition of the situation," which is preferred by some in academic sociology. This is only one example of a problem area with overlapping and duplicating conceptual tools. The empirical referents of a number of historically important concepts might profitably be reexamined with the view of determining which of the present excessive number are more useful in handling relevant data, including the accumulating experimental results.

SOME PERSISTENT PROBLEMS OF INTERDISCIPLINARY INTEREST

Thus far, a definition of social psychology and its appropriate relations to cognate social disciplines have been suggested and the development of social psychology discussed. The necessity of interdisciplinary give and take became apparent in this discussion. These major points can be articulated through two illustrative problem areas which have persistently concerned all these disciplines, both in the past and at the present time. The problem areas concern small groups and individual-society relationship, including culture and personality.

SMALL GROUPS

Today the study of small groups is one of the most active research areas; it is "in vogue" in every sense. The mounting volume of publications in periodicals and books is an index of this trend. Leadership, supervision, and productivity in industrial plants, solidarity and morale, "group cohesion," problem solving, communication and decision-making processes are among the aspects being busily investigated. Considerably more space is now devoted to small-group research in collaborative volumes in social psychology (e.g., Lindzey, 1954; Maccoby *et al.*, 1958; Swanson *et al.*, 1952). Recently several books appeared dealing explicitly with small groups (Bass, 1960; Bonner, 1959; Cartwright and Zander, 1953; Hare *et al.*, 1955; Olmstead, 1959; Stogdill, 1959; Thibaut and Kelley, 1959). Surveys have been devoted wholly or largely to small-group studies (e.g., Allport, 1942; Cottrell and Gallagher, 1941; Faris, 1953; Kelley and Thibaut, 1954; Riecken and Homans, 1954; Roseborough, 1953). In 1954, Stodtbeck and Hare compiled a bibliography of small-group studies listing 1,407 publications.

The sources contributing to the increased activities related to small groups are diverse. A glance at the products reveals diversity of research and practical interests, confusion in the multiplicity of concepts and procedures used, and yet unmistakable leads for eventual unification of problems and concepts.

One source with healthy impact on current research stems from sociological studies such as those of Thrasher (1927), Anderson (1923), Clifford Shaw (1930, 1931), Hiller (1928), Zorbaugh (1929), and Whyte (1943). Most of these studies were carried out in the 1920's at the University of Chicago, primarily inspired by the searching mind of Robert E. Park.

Another important influence on small-group research stems from the concern of business and industrial agencies with efficiency in supervision and production. The results of this concern are well indicated by the work that has been done by Elton Mayo and his associates since the late 1920s (Mayo, 1933; Roethlisberger and Dickson, 1939), and by centers established later at Yale, Chicago, Cornell, and other universities. The movement is sometimes referred to as the "human-relations approach" in industry. As Arensberg pointed out, the development of the human-relations approach received added impetus in the 1930's from the practical concerns created by "labor unrest" (Arensberg, 1951). A few years after World War II, a book appeared under the title *Human Relations in Modern Business: A Guide for Action Sponsored by American Business Leaders* (Johnson *et al.*, 1949). It reflected the active interest of business circles in this research movement and its approach.

Another factor contributing to the study of group processes has certainly been the considerable interest of military organizations both in the United States and other countries in discovering quick and efficient techniques for selecting unit leaders (Ansbacher, 1951; Jenkins, 1947; O.S.S. Assessment Staff, 1948).

There were other important sources stimulating interest in small-group research. W. E. Newstetter and his associates utilized experimental manipulation and measurement techniques in summer camps (Newstetter *et al.*, 1938), and their group studies had considerable influence in arousing interest in "group work" in the social work profession.

In academic psychology, F. H. Allport (1924) followed German predecessors with an extensive series of studies which inspired other investigations. However, the works of Moreno (1953) and Kurt Lewin and collaborators (Lewin, 1939; Lewin, Lippitt, and White, 1939) probably had more direct effect in academic psychology in arousing interest in small-group research. Moreno's sociometric technique, which appeared in the United States in the mid-thirties, provided tangible representation of friendship choices among interacting individuals. A few years later, the demonstration by Kurt Lewin and his associates that various group atmospheres affect behavior differentially was highly effective in gaining acceptance among psychologists for the importance of group properties and encouraging their investigation.

The impact of these investigations in psychology may be difficult to comprehend without appreciation of their audience. The notion of emergent qualities in social-interaction situations, which Durkheim and other social scientists had emphasized and indicated empirically for years, fell upon deaf ears as long as most psychologists were preoccupied with models based on "mental chemistry" or "conditioned reflex." The emergence of social norms in social interaction had to be demonstrated in the laboratory before it was incorporated into the general repertory of psychology (cf. Newcomb, 1954). The experimental findings on groups appeared to be "old hat" to a good many sociologists, although increasing numbers became impressed by the methodological advantages of experimental investigation (Sherif, 1936).

Certain findings, however, were common in all of the foregoing movements in small-group research, and these findings provide the needed criteria for a sound definition of "group." Without some clear criteria, we are caught between rival definitions and descriptions, each claiming acceptance on the basis of particular views and research operations of its proponents. Stated broadly, it was repeatedly confirmed that stability and change of an individual's behavior in so many significant aspects of his living is inextricably related to his group ties. These ties are defined in terms of his group belongingness, his particular status and role relations within groups, and the group values or norms which he internalizes as his own.

In view of this general finding, it is not surprising that those studying supervision and productivity in factories soon found that serious headway required investigation of the organization (structure) and the set of norms that the workers considered their own (Roethlisberger and Dickson, 1939). Investigators of industrial relations found that incentive systems in a plant are effective for the rank and file within the acceptable bounds of rate setting established in their formally or informally organized groups. To the groups in question, rate setting is a protective measure defining the rate of work and production under given labor-management relations, financial arrangements, and technological conditions. As Whyte demonstrated in his recent book *Money and Motivation* (1955), one is always confronted with the fact that incentives and machines exert their influence within the framework of groups with more or less definite organizations and values.

Several investigators of attitude change on social issues have independently reached a similar conclusion concerning the significance of the individual's place in a group with definite values (Hovland *et al.*, 1953; Lewin *et al.*, 1945; Newcomb, 1943). And as studies of leadership progressed, investigators started to face the fact that apart from the structural (organizational) and normative properties of groups, the study of leadership runs into a dead end of total situational or task relativism (cf., Carter, 1953; Gibb, 1954).

When the study of groups starts with fragmentary factors and techniques, fragmentary data are obtained. Building a conception of groups from operations carried out on that basis is likely to end in defining aspects of more or less specific interaction episodes. The essential properties of groups, which have made their study so significant for social psychology, are necessarily obscured.

Investigations of groups actually functioning for more than a transitory interaction episode have demonstrated that a group structure (organization) which defines differentiated role and status relations of individual members and a set of norms (standards, values) are among their minimum properties (e.g., Hiller, 1947; Landesco, 1929; Shaw, 1930; Thrasher, 1927; Whyte, 1943). It can be said that the "groupness" of a group is proportional to the prevalence of such distinctive properties. Of course, there are other attributes of a group which should be studied exhaustively. But open-ended enumeration of dimensions and subsequent attempts at compounding them have not so far produced conceptions that are useful in handling social behavior in natural settings. There are limiting factors in every system, and they affect the main character of the system. If they are defined, then analysis of other properties and their interrelationships may proceed more effectively.

A survey of sociological studies of small groups, especially those in urban areas, provides inexhaustible leads for experimental testing. Briefly, such findings suggest the following account of group formation and its effects on individuals involved: individuals who experience motives, aspirations, deprivations, or frustrations as common tend to interact with one another with a high frequency. If the common motives are not directed toward goals whose attainment by one individual precludes attainment by the others, interaction tends to persist over a period of time. In the course of their interaction, statuses and roles are differentiated. Over a period of time, these relationships tend to stabilize in varying degrees (depending upon the individuals involved, extrinsic factors, and the relative effectiveness of group activities). The stabilization of status and role relations constitutes the group organization or structure. As group structure forms, norms are standardized, at least in matters with relevance to the common motives and aspirations which brought individuals together or which developed in the course of their interaction. In these matters, at least, the activities of the individual member are regulated internally by his membership in the structure, his particular status and role, and the group's norms.

Unless the group in question is totally isolated, it is bound to come into functional contact with other groups, small and large. Here the close examination of sociological findings on relations between groups (e.g., Berry, 1951; Goldstein, 1948; MacCrone, 1937) reveals that the particular pattern of intergroup relations established by a group in dealing with others is reflected in that group's norms for behavior. Accordingly, the individual member perceives members of an out-group in a friendly or hostile fashion, depending upon the norms toward the out-group established in his group (Sherif and Sherif, 1953).

Sociological studies of groups are replete with more specific findings which provide leads for experimental investigation. For example, the observation that the group members judge the performance of a low-ranking member with a consistent error of underestimation (Whyte, 1943) was the basis of experimental work dealing with judgmental variations as a function of the status of the individual performing the task (Harvey, 1953; Sherif, White, and Harvey, 1955). Similarly, observed instances of exaggeration of in-group achievements and depreciation of out-group performance suggested propositions for experimental testing concerning the effects of group membership and intergroup conflict upon judgment by members of the groups involved (Harvey, 1956; Sherif et al., 1954).

Unfortunately, there has been intellectual discontinuity in small-group studies, as Shils pointed out so emphatically (1948, pp. 26, 42). In practice, many psychologists in recent years have ignored the intellectual heritage, rich in data suggestive of significant problems and hypotheses, with direct bearing on man's relations in actual groups. Neglect of these group data, accumulated throughout many years in diverse localities, can hardly be justified on the grounds that social psychologists are interested in individuals and not in groups as such. These facts, primarily on the sociological level, give the social psychologist necessary information concerning the individual's relative place in the scheme of relationships that really count for him.

Of course, the social psychologist cannot stop at this point. He must proceed from this "microsociological level," borrowing a phrase from Newcomb (1954), to detailed analysis of the individual, his life history, the exact stimulus conditions confronting him, and his attitudes and motives operative at the time. At this psychological level of analysis, sheer improvisation from sociological data has not been notably helpful. On this score Strodtbeck and Hare's remarks concerning the neglect of experimental knowledge in social psychology are well taken (1954, p. 109). The investigator who goes to the considerable trouble of surveying available sociological data and then proceeds to more detailed analysis of individuals on the psychological level finds that the two levels of analysis are not contradictory. In fact, as we have seen, findings at one level serve as checks for the validity of findings on the other. For example, in The Jack Roller, Stanley's autobiography and the detailed life history and psychiatric reports contain detailed substantiation of the general trends of sociological data concerning the formation of groups and regulation of members' behavior within them (Shaw, 1930).

The methodological advantage of studying the individual's particular role and status in his group(s) prior to detailed analysis of his behavior can be illustrated briefly through the recent controversy over generality or specificity of leadership from situation to situation. The results of various leadership studies have been rather inconclusive. Some results, notably those of "leaderless-group" studies, favor the conclusion that leadership behavior is specific to given interaction and task situations. Other results point to continuity and consistency in leadership over a period of time. It seems likely that the results will be coherent if they are evaluated in terms of the relative stabilization of status and role reciprocities among the participating individuals at the time their behavior is assessed. Is the behavior in question being studied in a group with given structure and integration or is the behavior occurring in a new interaction situation among previously unrelated individuals?

Present evidence indicates that when there are no established reciprocities among individuals, leadership behavior is more closely related to the relative proficiency of individuals in the task at hand, thus rather specific to given situations (Carter, 1953; Gibb, 1954). On the other hand, if the individuals are members of a closely knit group, the relative weight of single tasks and situations in determining leader-follower behaviors is considerably reduced (e.g., Merei, 1949; Sherif and Sherif, 1953; Toki, 1935; Whyte, 1943). In this case leadership is more likely to be general from one situation to the next. The emphasis on organizational settings of leadership by Ohio State investigators and others (Pelz, 1951; Scott, 1953; Stogdill, 1950) is a significant advance in study of these problems.

Reference Groups. Discussion of some problems of interdisciplinary approach in small-group research requires consideration of the problems which brought the concept of reference groups to the foreground. The concept is widely used today by both psychologists and sociologists (Hartley and Hartley, 1952; Hilgard, 1953; Lindesmith and Strauss, 1949, 1956; Merton and Kitt, 1950; Newcomb, 1950; Sherif, 1948; Shibutani, 1955; Turner, 1956).

In modern societies, small groups are not self-contained closed systems. The individual member of a group has perceptual and/or conceptual access to a number of groups. The directions and goals of these various groups may be compatible or incompatible with one another. For this reason, no amount of exclusive concentration on face-to-face interaction processes within a single group furnishes a complete guide for studying behavior of an individual member.

Reference groups, that is, the groups to which an individual relates himself or aspires to relate himself as a part psychologically, may or may not be the groups in which he is actually seen or is registered as a member. An individual's reference groups may include membership groups or nonmembership groups. The social bases of the individual's standards of judgment, gratification, and attainment can be assessed only through ascertaining his reference groups. For this reason, the reexamination of a variety of attitudes of American soldiers studied during World War II (Stouffer *et al.*, 1949) in terms of the reference-group concept by Merton and Kitt (1950) marks a conceptual advance in attitude studies.

Analysis of the individual's reference groups is a significant step in understanding the influence of groups to which he does not actually belong in shaping his tastes, attitudes, and aspirations. Particularly in a vertically mobile multigroup society, many individuals set their goals in terms of more powerful and highly placed groups to which they privately aspire (e.g., Frazier, 1955; Johnson, 1941; Veblen, 1899).

Once the significance of the individual's psychological relatedness to various groups is ascertained, it will be easier to explain his compliance to group pressures, either with or without inner acceptance. This persistent problem was treated extensively by Piaget (1932), who utilized the concepts "autonomy" (i.e., regulation of one's behavior through rules cherished as one's own) and "heteronomy" (i.e., regulation of behavior through rules attributed to sources of authority). The problem was raised more recently by Festinger (1953a) in terms of "compliant behavior" with or without private acceptance.

Analysis of the individual's reference groups is, therefore, helpful in understanding the consistency of his behavior from day to day. It is equally valuable in analysis of inconsistent or contradictory behavior exhibited by the same individual in two different settings. For example, the individual member of a group with a nondiscrimination policy may reveal no prejudice while participating in deliberations of that group, but later may participate in a riot as an identified member of a neighborhood group, as observed during the Detroit race riots of 1943.

The concept of reference groups is a relational one. Analysis in terms of reference groups obviously requires collaboration at both sociological and psychological levels. Significantly, the term's first use by Hyman (1942) was directly tied to laboratory findings on the effects of reference points in judgment; its subsequent modification was based on sociological findings of the anchoring effect of in-group standards (Sherif, 1948), and after a period of some confusion (cf. Kelley, 1952), this usage is prevalent today both in sociology (Lindesmith and Strauss, 1949, 1956; Shibutani, 1955; Turner, 1956) and psychology (Hartley and Hartley, 1952; Hilgard, 1953).

INDIVIDUAL-SOCIETY RELATIONSHIP

The general problem of individual-society relationship towers over other common problems encountered by psychologists and social scientists. Persistent issues were inherited from philosophers, theologians, and political theorists of the past. The problem has been discussed under the labels "individual and the group," "culture and personality," "individual and society," and other paired polarities.

Until recently, major theories of individual-society relationship posited a picture of "original human nature" largely in the image of the prevailing temper and ideology of the times. The particular conception of "human nature" set the lines of the theory. At one extreme, human nature was depicted as an unfolding of biologically determined impulses and instincts. At the other, human nature was considered an infinitely plastic raw material molded in the image of a reified culture. Conflict was primarily between interested parties who were committed to unverified premises. No real progress was possible.

In recent years various scholars have attempted to reconcile the rival theories. For example, Homans (1950, pp. 316–333) grouped the historically significant theories under the headings "The Social Contract Theory" (Hobbes, Rousseau), "The Social Mold Theory" (Durkheim), and "Culture and Personality." He offered a reconciliation of these dichotomous approaches. These traditional theories place almost exclusive responsibility on either individual or the group for prevailing social life and man's fortunes or misfortunes within it. Homan's reconciliation recognizes that each of the various one-sided theories can account for phenomena in certain periods of time, but that a complete account of individual-society relationship requires bringing all of these time periods into the picture.

The picture of human nature which is emerging considers the human being as he functions at a given time in a particular society as a biosocial product (e.g., Asch, 1952; Ausubel, 1952; Mead, 1934; Murphy, 1947). The individual's consistent modes of behavior in personal and group relations and his persistent strivings toward values and goals are shaped interdependently by both his biological endowment and sociocultural influences. In this view, a conception of original human nature as an entity apart from the interaction of an individual in his social setting has proven to be untenable.

Some notion of original human nature was necessary as long as man's lasting and recurrent strivings were attributed primarily to biological endowment, as they were in McDougall's list of instincts (1923) or Freud's classification of "sexual instincts" and "death instinct" (Freud, 1927, pp. 54ff., 67). In such a doctrine, social organization, culture, and the entire scheme of human relations become matters of applied psychology. There is hardly place for emergence of social structure and other items of culture, or a human personality which is not reducible to the vicissitudes of instinctual impulses.

Concept of Ego (Self). When the individual's persistent motivational patterns manifested in characteristic modes of behavior are conceived as products of interrelated biosocial influences, preoccupation with an original human nature becomes unnecessary. If what is termed "personality structure" is revealed in anything, it is in the individual's characteristic modes of behavior. The focus of study in this area becomes, therefore, the problem of consistency in goal-directed behavior over a time span.

The regulative pattern lending characteristic *consistency* to the individual's goal-directed behaviors and to his performance of tasks in interaction with other individuals has been conceptualized in terms of the formation and functioning of the individual's ego or self. The concept of ego or self current in social psychology has nothing to do with the mystic halo surrounding the term historically. It has nothing to do with "homuncular entities" warring for domination of man's behavior (Ausubel, 1952). It is not akin to the notion of an "executive agent" that intrudes in ongoing psychological activity. Rather, it refers to a psychological formation that is an outcome of man's interaction with his surroundings. The biosocial formation termed "ego" or "self" consists of a system of relatedness to one's surroundings. In this system of relatedness, reciprocal expectations and ties with other people are crucial components.

Many psychologists and sociologists since William James' treatment of "social self" (1890) have contributed to a concept of ego or self as a developmental formation relating the individual to his surroundings (Sherif and Cantril, 1947, pp. 156–199). It is no accident that the authors who have offered theories of ego or self have been particularly interested in psychology-sociology relationships.

J. M. Baldwin described the development of self in terms of a "dialectic" process reflected in his dictum that "ego and alter are . . . born together" (Baldwin, 1895; cf. Baldwin, 1911). The sociologist C. H. Cooley presented an interactionist account of self as early as 1902 in his *Human Nature and the Social Order* (1902). Cooley unmistakably related development of self to the formation of "primary group" ties by the growing individual (Karpf, 1932, p. 300).

Probably the most thoroughly interactionist of the early twentieth-century social philosophers was George Herbert Mead (1934). Mead's "act" was not an isolated behavior unit, but referred to the complete pattern of interaction. In his words:

The social act is not explained by building it up out of stimulus plus response; it must be taken as a dynamic whole—as something going on—no part of which can be considered or understood by itself—a complex organic process implied by each individual stimulus and response involved in it (p. 7).

His theory of self dealt with an individual immersed in social "transactions." As an outcome of these transactions according to Strauss (1956) in his *The Social Psychology of George Herbert Mead*—

. . . the child learns not only to assume multiple positions vis-à-vis himself but to organize these positions into a system. Childhood games, Mead suggests are among the situations in which the child acquires the ability to do this. This generalized system of attitudes is termed "the generalized other." Mead's most distinctive characterization of self is in terms of the "generalized other" (p. xiv).

In the writings of Baldwin, Cooley, Mead, and some of their contemporaries, we find insightful attempts at viewing social behavior in terms of an ongoing interaction process in which a biosocial self or ego emerges. By and large, however, these brilliant insights were not conceptualized in a way permitting ready translation into a research program. The views of Lindesmith and Strauss were strongly influenced by Mead (e.g., Lindesmith and Strauss, 1949, 1956; Strauss, 1956), but Strauss comments: "There have been attempts to draw out of Mead's work very specific implications for empirical testing, but this has not proved very effective, at least as yet" (1956, p. xiv).

The conception of ego or self that is currently developing is based squarely on converging findings from a variety of research. The main outlines of this conception are derived from child development studies, experiments on ego-involvements, and anthropological findings.

Accumulating studies of child development (e.g., Ausubel, 1952; Gesell and Ilg, 1943; Piaget, 1932; Sherif and Cantril, 1947; Shinn, 1899; Wallon, 1933) contain ample evidence that an individual's ego or self is not innately given. Rather, their findings reveal the formation by the individual of relatedness to particular aspects of his life. This formation is not an immutable entity completely and finally structured by the age of six or the age of ten. Studies of adolescence (Ausubel, 1954; Horrocks, 1951; Jones, 1943; Kuhlen, 1951) show that noteworthy changes in the system of personal relatedness may occur during this transition period. Such changes may be intensified in sociocultural settings which are undergoing social change at an accelerated tempo (e.g., Davis, 1940; Lang, 1946). Changes may also occur in later life if the individual is confronted with serious problems which arouse conflict with present expectations and values in professional or other significant aspects of living. Old age in many societies is a transition period conducive to alterations in various components of the individual's ego formation.

Study of changes in the ego formation with changing social roles at given periods of life is helpful in achieving a formulation of ego or self which is generally applicable. This study implies an understanding of both the sequence and kind of developmental stages through which individuals pass in a society. It follows that cross-cultural comparisons are invaluable checks against an ethnocentric picture of self. The social psychologist finds relevant data in anthropological field work (e.g., Radcliffe-Brown, 1922; Radin, 1937; Rivers, 1924; Van Gennep, 1909).

In recent years, laboratory studies have demonstrated significant effects of ego-involvement in various psychological activities. The findings suggest the utility of the concept of ego in handling the consistency of characteristic modes of behavior and strivings. Are the behavior and strivings of the individual relatively consistent from situation to situation? There is evidence indicating consistency over a time span and, on the other hand, there is evidence of specificity of behavior to given situations. Certainly more experimentation and research are needed for any conclusive generalization. However, available experimental findings concerning the setting of goals (e.g., Holt, 1945; Lewin *et al.*, 1944), confidence (Klein, 1941), and specificity or generality of personal characteristics indicate that the person's behavior is consistent if the situation is ego-involving for him and is more variable if he is not ego-involved in the issue or situation at hand. Such experimental evidence led G. W. Allport, one of the outstanding "trait" psychologists of the thirties who favored the "generality" of personality traits (1937), to conclude that a trait may be general or specific depending on the degree of ego-involvement of the person in that respect (1943, pp. 472–474).

The conclusion reached here acquires added significance from relevant findings in child psychology. The growing child does not follow goals consistently until he becomes capable of setting up standards for his own behavior—an aspect of ego formation requiring conceptual development and mastery of language (Gesell and Ilg, 1943; Goodenough, 1945). Similar development is necessary for the appearance of consistent patterns of competitive behavior (Greenberg, 1932; Hirota, 1953; Leuba, 1933) and consistently cooperative behavior (Berne, 1930; Parten, 1933). During this same period, in a sociocultural setting where social distance is maintained toward certain out-groups, the child begins to exhibit prejudice in the consistent fashion prescribed in social definition (e.g., Clark and Clark, 1947; Goodman, 1952). The appearance of such consistent modes of behavior implies an internal patterning of motives which is here termed "ego" or "self."

There are, of course, inconsistencies in behavior in situations where the individual is ego-involved. In the brief discussion of reference groups, an example was given of personal inconsistency when the individual related himself to different reference groups with contradictory norms. Thoroughgoing study of behavioral inconsistencies needs to consider conflicting components of the individual's personal relatedness as they are situationally aroused over a period of time. However, it should also be noted that severe deprivations or frustrations usually produce striking inconsistencies of behavior in terms of the individual's "accustomed" self (e.g., Sherif and Sherif, 1956, pp. 433–443).

The conception of ego or self derived from the above findings can be summarized. *Ego* or *self* is a developmental formation in the psychological makeup of the individual, consisting of *interrelated attitudes* which are acquired in relation to his own body, to his own abilities, to objects, persons, family groups, social norms, and institutions and which define and regulate his relatedness to them in a number of concrete situations.

This conception takes into account cultural variations in ego formation inferred from observations in societies where individual behavior is predominantly competitive or primarily cooperative or primarily power-oriented or submissive, as the case may be. By relating ego formation to the individual's specific reference groups during his development, differences in modal behavior which are characteristic in the multiple and opposing groups of differentiated societies are amenable to psychological investigation. Changes, even transformations, in motivational patterns and behavior occurring in adolescence, in professional or marital life, in old age, and in critical situations can be analyzed without contradicting basic assumptions.

Conceiving of the individual's ego formation as a constellation of interrelated parts (attitudes) permits investigation of ego problems in specific dimensions. Unit parts (attitudes) of the ego formation are not fragmentary elements, but are interrelated. Being interrelated, the various parts may be conducive to an integrated pattern of motivation and hence behavior. Likewise, being interrelated, incompatible attitudes formed by the same individual become an important source of personal conflicts, as exemplified by the plight of many a professional woman who is torn between attitudes toward husband and home and attitudes toward her career.

Because the term "attitude" has been used in different senses historically and has at times been devoid of motivational character, additional words are necessary about the unit parts, which may be called "ego-attitudes." As used here, "attitude" denotes an internal variable, namely, a state of readiness which is learned and which involves a subject-object relationship. Characteristically, the individual in this subject-object relationship takes a positive or negative stand conducive to goal-directed behavior in relation to persons, groups, institutions, values, and other *classes* of objects. As such, attitudes do refer to acquired or sociogenic motives. As W. I. Thomas showed in the factually rich context of *The Polish Peasant in Europe and America* (Thomas and Znaniecki, 1918), a social attitude is always formed in relation to social stimuli, among which social values or norms constitute an important class.

In their recent book *Opinions and Personality*, Smith, Bruner, and White (1956) defined attitude in a similar way: "We define an attitude as a predisposition to experience a class of objects in certain ways, with characteristic affect; to be motivated by this class of objects in characteristic ways; and to act with respect to these objects in a characteristic fashion" (p. 33).

To psychologists of varying descriptions (e.g., Hilgard, 1953; Murphy, 1947; Snygg and Combs, 1949), it is becoming evident that a psychology of human motivation requires some such concept as ego or self. Amidst current neologisms positing dynamics of all sorts, it may sound a little pedestrian to make attitudes component parts of a concept such as ego or self. However, the individual's social attitudes, as components of his ego, do have motivational character. They affect his selectivity and goal-directedness even when other more "dependable" (Klineberg, 1954) or "biogenic" motives are aroused. For a human adult, sexual activity is not only a means of releasing sexual tensions, but it involves a social relationship in which his attitudes concerning personal qualities of the sex object and socioeconomic class may be of crucial importance (Ford and Beach, 1951). Likewise, eating, dressing, choice of dwelling are not only instances of tension reduction, but occasions for proving one's worth and distinction, as revealed in the choice of an eating place, the importance of the label in one's garment, the location of one's residence on this or the other side of the tracks (Veblen, 1899). The attitudes implied operate on a conceptual level and are not governed simply by homeostatic states of the organism.

If ego or self functions as a regulating agent from situation to situation, if relevant ego-attitudes normally regulate the functioning of other motives, shall we posit instinctive propensities at its basis? As noted earlier in this section, longitudinal studies of child development offer little justification for an instinctivist position. Without positing an instinctive basis, the motivational character of ego-attitudes can be studied through analysis of the effects of disrupting their subject-object relationships. Even in adulthood, our sense of personal stability continues to be dependent upon the perceived stability of the subject-object relationships implied in important ego-attitudes. Disruption of these relationships and out-of-the-ordinary events are conducive to feelings of uncertainty, insecurity, and anxiety. Experimental evidence has shown that even temporary disruption of physical anchorages for bodily orientation produces feelings of uncertainty, resulting in highly variable behavior (Sherif and Harvey, 1952). These crucial points, which indicate the feasibility of analyzing the motivational bases of ego-involvement without positing innate propensities, cannot be elaborated here (Sherif and Sherif, 1956, pp. 600–606). But a caution can be sounded against repeating the retreat of McDougall when he posited innate propensities for dominance, submission (self-abasement), etc., alongside a developmental picture of the "self-regarding sentiment" which remains to this day one of the most penetrating accounts of ego formation available (McDougall, 1923).

"*Culture and Personality*" *Approach to the Problem.* Among the most prominent interdisciplinary activities exploring individual-society relationships during the last two decades have been those labeled "culture and personality" and "national character" studies. The former have usually focused on smaller, less-developed societies, while investigations of similar problems in modern nations are termed studies of "national character." For purposes of the present discussion, distinction between the two movements is unnecessary.

Contemporary enthusiasm for studying culture and personality received its greatest impetus in the 1930's from the linguist-anthropologist Edward Sapir (1949, pp. 357–364, 507–597). In calling for study of "tangible problems of behavior rather than selected problems set by recognized disciplines" (1949, p. 513), Sapir hoped for the development of a genuinely "social" psychology which would leave the sociocultural investigator "free to study the rationale of group forms, group functions, group changes and group interrelationships from a formal or cultural point of view" (p. 364). The sociologist W. I. Thomas, whose interest in individual-society relationship was further stimulated by Sapir (Kluckhohn and Murray, 1948, p. xiii), contributed research orientation and conceptualizations in this area (Volkart, 1951). His influence was particularly apparent in the treatment of attitude-value relationships by Linton (1945), who also found Mead's concept of role useful in his development of "status personality" (cf. Becker, 1954, p. 150).

Gaining prominence and significantly deflecting the above influences, psychoanalytic orientation became predominant in "culture and personality" literature (Hollowell, 1954, pp. 202–209; Smith, 1954, pp. 37, 56). Comparatively few anthropologists find strictly Freudian interpretations of culture (Freud, 1938) palatable, and few would agree with the recommendation that psychoanalysis is necessary preparation for understanding problems of culture and personality (e.g., Roheim, 1949, pp. 587–588). However, the psychoanalytic influence on their studies persists. Its most widespread effect, even on nonpsychoanalytic writers, has been severe limitation of the problems chosen for study, the kind of variables investigated, and, consequently, the range of discussion and debate.

Typical research problems have concerned influences during very early childhood, particularly the effects of adult methods and manner of child rearing (e.g., Fromm, 1949; Kardiner, 1945; Lindesmith and Strauss, 1950; Whiting and Child, 1953). Literally all sorts of social attitudes and their relative salience for individuals in a given society have been attributed to hypothesized effects of adult treatment in early childhood. Yet serious questions remain concerning the influence of child rearing methods in personal development and the relationships between early childhood experiences and adult functioning (Lindesmith and Strauss, 1950; Orlansky, 1949; Sewell, 1952).

When research focus shifts to actual study of "modal personality" (e.g., Inkeles and Levinson, 1954; Linton, 1945), conceived as statistical expression of characteristics common to individuals in a group, the resulting evidence of group regularities may be proper data for sociocultural analysis. The modal personality thus attained will be a sociological construct even though it carries the "personality" label. In mutual accommodation to fundamentally conflicting assumptions, sociocultural investigators and psychoanalysts have sometimes arrived at formulations strikingly similar to the venerable dichotomy between individual and society. Thus in some of the literature, the "basic personality," "modal personality," or "social character" structure appears side by side with the "authentic individual," "the real self," or "deeper layers" of personality (Fromm, 1949; Kardiner, 1945; Linton, 1945). The latter is presumably immune to societal influences (cf. Lindesmith and Strauss, 1950, pp. 590f.).

If studies of culture and personality or national character are to be viewed as more than exciting literary adventures, sooner or later investigators will have to respect major methodological criticisms in their actual practice. Such criticisms have pertained to adequateness of sample within a society, reproducibility of procedures, and taking "responsibility" for stated hypotheses (e.g., Farber, 1955; Inkeles and Levinson, 1954; Klineberg, 1949; Kluckhohn, 1949). In particular, the existence of multiple groups in modern complex societies, and even in preliterate societies, requires specification of the group membership of individuals studied and of the range of group values within a society. Investigations oriented toward problems of multiple-group membership may very well lead to revision of concepts designating uniform or common characteristics for an entire society. Methodological improvements alone, however, do not guarantee more catholic selection of problems. Nor will technical refinements provide an escape from the theoretical confusion inherent in trying to reconcile "individualistic" or "reductionist" schemes of psychology with the fundamental premises of sociocultural study (Hallowell, 1954, pp. 95f., 207f.).

If as suggested in previous sections, a crucial problem of individual-society relationship concerns the consistency of the individual's characteristic motivational patterns, the concept of ego or self discussed here can aid in making research inroads in this area more rapid. While not identical with the totality of psychological organization usually designated as "personality," the concept deals with personal organization in terms amenable to the dimensional analysis necessary in actual research and in studying the interrelationships among evaluative dimensions. A concept of self was profitably employed by Gillin and Raimy (1940) in a research study and has been discussed in terms of culture and personality studies by Hallowell (1954).

It is suggested here that conceiving ego or self as a constellation of interrelated attitudes linked with identifiable reference groups will be particularly useful in studying psychological problems associated with culture change or acculturation (Broom et al., 1953; Herskovits, 1949; Thurnwald, 1932). Though not formulated in these terms, the Gillin and Raimy study consisted of eliciting responses to identify the individual's reference groups in order to explicate his self-conception. In a recent design for studying reactions to culture change (Spindler and Goldschmidt, 1952), the hypotheses concerned the relative incidence of "symptoms of personality disorganization" for individuals in "transitional categories" and those still closely related to traditional groups in a society. Further specification of conflicts in reference-group ties in terms of a particular individual's relevant ego-attitudes may be useful in delineating relationships between culture change and personality disorganization.

It should be noted that the currently developing concept of ego or self includes attitudes assigned, in orthodox psychoanalytic terminology, to a "superego." The inclusion of these attitudes, which incorporate values from authority figures as part of the ego constellation, is in harmony with anthropological findings that the relative frequency and social referents of feelings of guilt and shame following violations of social values vary from culture to culture, as do other ego-involved experiences (e.g., Ausubel, 1955; Klineberg, 1949).

SOME CONVERGING TRENDS IN SOCIAL PSYCHOLOGY

A backward glance at this discussion of social psychology and the social sciences will bring the remainder of the chapter into better perspective. As noted, social psychology as a scientific discipline is still in a formative stage. It cannot be asserted that even its subject matter is clearly delineated, as a glance at its textbooks readily indicates. The first task of this chapter, therefore, was an attempt to attain a workable definition of social psychology in order to talk about its relationships with cognate social disciplines. The main terms of the definition were derived from developments in psychology and social science, specified in their appropriate contexts. Social psychology was defined as the scientific study of the experience and behavior of the individual in relation to social-stimulus situations.

One of the main terms in the definition, namely, "social-stimulus situations," was the basis for articulation of social psychology–social science relationships. The give and take between the individual and the social-stimulus situations confronting him is on a meaningful, patterned level. Varieties of social-stimulus situations (including human groups and their culture, material and nonmaterial) are subject matters of sociology, cultural anthropology, and other social sciences. Analysis of social-stimulus situations as patterned events in space and time requires that the social psychologist borrow from the work of the social scientists. On the other hand, the study of experience and behavior necessarily takes the individual as its unit of analysis. Here, in turn, the social scientist is dependent on the psychologist. Illustrative problem areas where such a conception of distinctive yet complementary levels of analysis has or could prove fruitful were discussed briefly.

Despite continuing confusion and controversy over important concepts and preferred research orientations, there are convergences in social psychology today which can best be referred to as over-all trends.

On the whole, these trends are sufficiently general to transcend differences in preferred concepts and research topics. It should be noted, however, that they do not receive the same emphasis from all social psychologists. The emphasis of a given social psychologist may be on one or another of these trends, occasionally to the neglect of others. But it seems likely that every social psychologist has some concern and some part in all these trends and that social psychologists and social scientists have influenced one another.

Social psychologists of various persuasions seem to be concerned with the following trends:

1. A growing emphasis on studying social behavior within a framework of interacting influences, rather than concentrating exclusively on either internal factors (motives, effects of past experiences, organismic states, etc.) or external factors (e.g., groups, culture) as supreme determinants.

2. Positive efforts through cross-cultural and intergroup comparisons to achieve the perspective necessary to guard against ethnocentrism in drawing generalizations.

3. Increased utilization of scientific methods and techniques.

STUDYING BEHAVIOR AS A PRODUCT OF INTERRELATED EXTERNAL AND INTERNAL INFLUENCES

Not too many years ago, controversies between exponents of an individualistic approach and exponents of a group or culture-bound approach seemed endless. But a healthy conception emerged. It is that social behavior is not accountable solely on the basis of influences coming from the individual or solely on the basis of influences from groups and their culture. Rather, behavior becomes accountable when studied within the framework of interrelated external (e.g., social) and internal factors operative at a given time. In recent textbooks on social psychology, this conception of the joint determination of behavior is expressed in one form or another, with varying emphasis and with varying degrees of success in its application to the topics covered. The trend is reflected in textbooks by Krech and Crutchfield (1948), Newcomb (1950), Hartley and Hartley (1952), Asch (1952), and Klineberg (1954), to cite a few psychologists; it is reflected in the books of Faris (1952), Lindesmith and Strauss (1949, 1956) and Kimball Young (1956), to cite a few sociologists.

In bringing this trend to the foreground, Gestalt psychologists contributed substantially (e.g., Brown, 1936; Köhler, 1929; Lewin, 1935a). George Herbert Mead's conceptualization of the human "act," with emphasis on "outer" and "inner" aspects, was certainly influential, especially through his teaching (1934). Bartlett's investigations of memory were conceived in terms of such joint determination and were striking evidence of the utility of this approach to some American investigators (1932). Despite differences in terminology, the basic assumption of all psychologists who have contributed to the flourishing experimental investigation of "social perception" (e.g., Bruner and Goodman, 1947; Carter and Schooler, 1949; Luchins, 1944; Luchins, 1945; Proshansky and Murphy, 1942; Schafer and Murphy, 1943; Sherif, 1936) and "social judgment" (e.g., Chapman and Volkmann, 1939; Harvey, 1953) is that experience and behavior are jointly determined by external and internal factors. Such experimentation could not make headway without the assumption that reduced structure of the stimulus field permits maximal effect of internal influences (e.g., attitudes) in psychological structuring. I trust that these examples are sufficient to indicate the scope and interdisciplinary nature of this general trend. It has been variously stated, for example, in the writings of Cottrell (1942), Kluckhohn and Murray (1948, p. xi), and Murphy (1947).

The current need of research and theoretical development is a straightforward formulation of the frame of reference, consisting of functional relations among the interrelated external (stimulus) and internal factors that participate in shaping behavior. A diagram may be the simplest way to present the functional relationships of the frame of reference of an observed behavior. It is a representation of the main terms and the sequence of relationships. Interrelationships cannot be represented so simply. This diagram is a conceptual representation of a mode of analysis; it is not a picture of anything.

I will first note the sequence of relationships and then briefly characterize the main terms, basing my discussion on material presented in greater detail elsewhere (Sherif and Sherif, 1953, Chap. 6; Sherif and Sherif, 1956, Chaps. 2 and 3). Here generalizations are stated in categorical form. By necessity, they are given without qualifications and supporting evidence. We have found the scheme most useful in developing a program to study social interaction and individual functioning in an interrelated way (Sherif, 1954).

Note the direction of arrows in the diagram. Observed behavior, verbal or nonverbal, is not directly determined by external or internal influences. Observed behavior follows central psychological structuring, or patterning, of internal and external factors. Phenomenally, psychological structuring is revealed in perceiving, judging, remembering, imagining, and the like. In various situations, the relative weights of external and internal factors in psychological structuring differ, as will be mentioned presently.

Relations among external and internal factors constitute the frame of reference of a behavior or act, which can be adequately understood only within the frame of reference of which it is a part. Thus, conceived, an item of behavior (verbal or nonverbal) is a unit of psychological analysis. This has been the working conception in research practice for a good many psychologists for some time. Such a conception makes distinctions between fragmentary and unrelated reactions and an *act* (considered as situationally related and goal-directed) both unnecessary and confusing (e.g., Parsons and Shils, 1951, Chap. 1). Such a label as "act" might have been needed by George H. Mead to refer

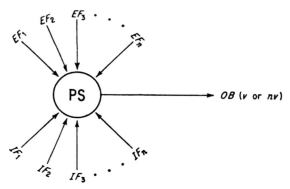

FIGURE 1. Diagrammatic representation of the frame of reference of an observed behavior at a given time. *OB* (*v* or *nv*): Observed behavior (verbal or nonverbal). *EF*: External factors (objects, persons, groups, cultural products, etc., in the external stimulus situation). *IF*: Internal factors (attitudes, emotions, states of the organism, linguistic concepts, effects of past experience, etc.). *PS*: Psychological (perceptual) structuring.

to the nonfragmentary and interrelated nature of human behavior during the decades when psychologists were dealing with behavior in terms of atomistic S-R bonds or sensations and images as elements of mental life.

Since an observed behavior follows central psychological structuring or patterning, experience and behavior constitute a unity (Murphy, 1947). Differences obtained between an expressed attitude on an issue and actual behavior in a relevant situation do not require a divorce of attitude (internal factor) from overt behavior. Rather, such contradictions imply a changed constellation of factors in the structuring of experience from the time when the individual was asked to respond to a direct question and the time when he confronted a relevant problem situation. Almost always different external factors are involved and internal factors other than the attitude in question are aroused.

"External factors" refer to stimulating situations outside the individual at a given time—objects, events, groups and their cultural products, including tools and other technological items. "Internal factors" refer to bodily states (fatigue, drowsiness, thirst), emotions, effects of past experience (including, as an important class, concepts derived from the language), attitudes, interests, and other social motives formed at the time. Internal factors are not observed directly. They are necessarily inferred from behavior (verbal or nonverbal) in relation to given stimulating conditions.

Psychological structuring is determined jointly by external and internal factors contributing in varying degrees in given conditions. In 1929, Köhler stressed the "bipolar character" of psychological structuring in these words: "Apart from drowsiness and similar states of low vitality, the organization of the total field will almost always have just that bipolar character, the self being directed to something else or from it" (p. 323).

In the joint determination of psychological patterning, we find a sound basis for *psychological selectivity*. The facts of psychological selectivity make it difficult to conceive of perception or judgment as simply cognitive affairs. In the "open" stimulus field encountered by the individual from day to day, in contrast to the "constricted" stimulus field presented in a laboratory experiment, what stands out for the individual as figure and what is relegated to the background are determined to a significant extent by motivational factors. Laboratory experiments for many decades have shown that only a limited number of stimulus items can be attended to, perceived, judged, or remembered at a given time. Which items are singled out of an open stimulus field is determined not merely by the compelling properties of the stimulus, but to a great extent by the motivational or attitudinal relevance of the stimulus to the individual. In this area, the social psychologist's findings on effects of attitudes or ego-involvement and the social scientist's findings on the patterned properties of social-stimulus situations can supplement one another.

The primary psychological tendency is toward structuring experience, and structuring ordinarily precedes the analysis of parts. (This is the reason why, during the period when analysis of elements was considered the main objective of psychology, graduate students had to be trained rigorously as observers before they could single out elements to report.) Internal structuring or patterning is not an additive affair. Objects and events in the external field are perceived or judged in terms of the relations of their parts rather than as discrete items. Likewise, internal factors contribute as related parts, rather than as isolated sovereign "movers" of behavior. External factors and internal factors contributing to psychological structuring become interrelated. Any item (external or internal) functioning in the system of relations, which constitutes the frame of reference at a given time, is affected by other factors. Herein lies the psychological basis of the differential or "emergent" effects of social situations as compared with individual situations.

Stimulus situations which are themselves highly structured, clear cut, or unequivocal set limits for alternatives in psychological structuring. Compelling stimulus structure in a given dimension permits comparatively little variation in the way people perceive or judge that dimension. Consensus of opinion concerning highly structured dimensions of a stimulus situation is reached very rapidly (Tresselt and Volkmann, 1942). The implications of this point are apparent in connection with the effects of material culture. Attempts to influence the individual toward an alternative which is contradicted by properties of stimulus situations are increasingly unsuccessful as the discriminated aspect becomes more clear cut; even individuals who are influenced are likely to see the situation as bizarre (Asch, 1956).

On the other hand, in stimulus situations lacking objective structure in one or several dimensions, alternatives for psychological structuring are increased. An application of this general principle for social psychology is that in social situations with ambiguous or equivocal aspects, the individual is more easily influenced by suggestions from others in perceiving or judging those aspects. This finding provides the sociologist with a psychological basis for some of his own recurring observations. The sociologist has observed that times of social instability and crises are fertile grounds for the rise and standardization of new slogans, new norms, and new forms of social organization (Blumer, 1946; Durkheim, 1915). The norm-formation experiments, which utilized the autokinetic effect as a situation lacking objective structure in a given dimension, were based both on the above psychological principle and on the observations by sociologists concerning such new standardizations (Sherif, 1936).

Experiments systematically varying external stimulus structure and covarying internal factors will clarify some problems of individual-society relationship. Promising starts have been made in this direction, as exemplified by the works of Coffin (1941), Luchins (1944, 1945), and J. D. Thrasher (1954). To summarize just one experiment, Thrasher covaried external stimulus in a given dimension and the nature of interpersonal relationships (friendship and nonfriendship between subjects). His results show that when the external stimulus field is relatively more structured, external stimulus factors weigh more heavily in determining judgment of the stimulus; but as the stimulus dimension being judged becomes less structured, the influence of internal factors (attitudes toward a friend) is relatively greater.

While denying the sovereign power of any set of factors for every instance of psychological structuring, the conception of joint determination outlined here implies that various factors in the frame of reference have differing *relative weights* at a given time. Such relative weights are not absolute, of course, being affected by interrelationships among various operative factors. Nevertheless, studies of social influence and motive arousal in situations of varying objective structure, such as those mentioned above, suggest a regularity or lawfulness of the conditions in which external factors or internal factors carry greater relative weights. Doubtless, systematic variation of factors affecting psychological selectivity will clarify further regularities.

In any specific research, it is necessary to recognize that certain factors function as *limiting* influences. Such limiting factors are decisive in determining salient characteristics of psychological patterning and hence behavior. They are referred to as "anchorages" or "anchoring agents." The currently developing concept of reference groups stemmed from a study of judgments of status (Hyman, 1942) which extended psychophysical experiments on reference scales and anchorages by using different groups as the standard for judgment. A reference group is conceived as a major anchorage for the individual in his social ties (Sherif and Sherif, 1956). With a shift in reference groups, significant changes occur in the individual's evaluation of various aspects of social life (e.g., Lewin and Grabbe, 1945; Merton and Kitt, 1950; Newcomb, 1943). Systematic investigation of the relative weights of factors under varying conditions is the most difficult but essential task of future research.

CHECKS AGAINST EFFECTS OF ETHNOCENTRISM

Perception and judgment of objects, persons, and events of the social world are influenced by the individual's internal standards or attitudes formed through contact with the social norms of his reference groups. As a result, there is a tendency to see things from the viewpoint of one's own group and to evaluate them in terms of its major premises. This tendency, referred to as "ethnocentrism" since Sumner's days, is not peculiar to members of any particular culture. Scientists are not immune to errors and distortions stemming from their ethnocentrisms. Scientists whose subject matter concerns human individuals, groups, and their products are necessarily in greater jeopardy than others from this source.

Anthropological studies like those of Malinowski, Boas, and Margaret Mead were profoundly influential in making social psychologists aware of the pitfalls of universalizing research findings obtained within their own sociocultural settings. Research on measurement of abilities and traits was also important in this respect. In the decades preceding the 1930's, research findings ranking various human groupings in terms of "superiority" and "inferiority" of intelligence were presented. The comparative and longitudinal research by Klineberg (1935a, 1935b) and others demonstrated convincingly that these rankings were altered when the findings were related to sociocultural conditions.

Subsequently, prominent investigators of psychological measurement have become aware that their tests are standardized on the basis of performance by individuals in specific societies and usually within a rather narrow segment of the population. The tasks chosen are those significant in the particular cultural group (e.g., Goodenough and Harris, 1950). Following their extensive survey of "individual and group differences in behavior," Anastasi and Foley (1949) concluded:

> Since all types of behavior are influenced by the subject's stimulational background, it follows that psychological data obtained within any one cultural group cannot be generalized to cover all human behavior. Many statements offered under the heading of general psychology are not general at all, but are based upon human behavior as it develops within a single culture (p. 838).

Anastasi (1953) has suggested that "culture-free" tests of abilities and traits are not feasible and that this can be demonstrated through contrasting results obtained when a trait or performance is selected in terms of its importance to a particular group. For example, a Draw-a-horse test standardized on performance by American Indian children worked to the decided disadvantage of white American children. Evidence indicates that similar differences result from evaluation of "personality" tests based on norms of different socioeconomic classes (Auld, 1952) or different cultural groups (Klineberg, 1949). It has been suggested that awareness of such sociocultural variations implies revision, possibly radical revision, in many concepts used in the study of abilities and personality. A concrete example is furnished by findings on intelligence testing in Peru where mental age and consequently intelligence quotient for school children are "in an inverse relationship with their Chronological Age" (Blumenfeld, 1956, p. 38).

Effects of ethnocentrism on drawing conclusions from social-psychological research can be illustrated briefly in the area of group research. During the decades 1910–1930, various scholars reported experimental results which on the whole seemed to indicate a tendency toward mediocrity of performance in groups. More recently it has been shown repeatedly that interaction in groups may result in improved performance and changed attitudes of individual members in socially desirable directions. Thus it cannot be concluded that leveling of performance toward the group mean is an inevitable consequence of group interaction. The results of performance in any particular group are dependent both on the nature of the task and on the properties of the group in question (cf. Kelley and Thibaut, 1954). Similarly, studies of the "group-decision" method for changing attitudes and behavior developed by Lewin and his associates (Lewin, 1952) suggest limitations in drawing general conclusions concerning its superiority over other techniques. Briefly, group-decision studies in the American setting reported more frequent attitude change and persistence of change when individuals participated actively in making a decision with an informal "resource person" than when given a lecture presenting information in favor of the advocated change. However, both for Hindu and German individuals, the group-decision technique proved relatively ineffective (Murphy, 1953; pp. 114–115; Weiss, 1956, pp. 66–67).

The fact that such checks have been made on these and other topics is evidence of the growing awareness among social psychologists that definite procedures are necessary to guard against ethnocentric conclusions. Since the social psychologist, like any human being, is psychologically related to certain groups—a national group, a socio-economic class, a school of thought, or a laboratory atmosphere—checks on the effects of his ethnocentrisms are becoming standard procedure in evaluating his conclusions. The checks generally recognized as helpful in minimizing ethnocentric generalizations and actually employed for this purpose include (1) cross-cultural comparisons, (2) comparisons among groups within differentiated societies, and (3) historical com-parisons within the same culture.

All such checks imply clear specification of the social-stimulus conditions under which findings are obtained. This is one reason why social-stimulus situations have been discussed rather extensively in this chapter and why their specification as external factors was stressed as an initial step, prior to investigation of their contribution in psychological structuring. As Daniel Katz has suggested, the "phenomenological bias" in much contemporary social psychology is sometimes responsible for serious neglect of important properties of social-stimulus conditions (Katz, 1951, 1955).

Cross-cultural, intergroup, and historical comparisons as checks against ethnocentrism do not imply an unbridled cultural or historical relativism. Cultural relativism notes observed cultural variations in behavior but carries the further unwarranted assumption that principles governing behavior have to be derived separately on the basis of each culture. Such a view amounts to assuming total determination of be-havior by social organization and culture (cf. Hartung, 1954). On the contrary, social psychology is proceeding more and more on the assump-tion that basic principles of psychological functioning are the same for all individuals, and that variations in behavior in different cultures are governed by the same principles. *In fact, cross-cultural and historical comparisons are necessary in order that general laws and principles can be attained in social psychology.*

The adolescent period represents a rather well-documented example to clarify the above point. Early investigators of adolescence in the United States, such as G. Stanley Hall, presented adolescence as a universal period of storm and stress. More recently, anthropological field work reported societies in which adolescence was a *relatively* smooth transition from childhood to adulthood. As a result, the view that adolescence was not a distinctive period of development except under highly restrictive and delaying sociocultural conditions prevailed. Careful inspection of comparative findings revealed, however, that even when relatively smooth, this transitional period was distinguished by interrelated internal changes (notably physiological) and changes in socially prescribed roles and statuses, both of which precipitate a process of re-formation of the individual's ego or self-constellation. The content, manner, and extent of change in ego-attitudes do vary from culture to culture. But recognition of basic uniformities permits active investigation of processes underlying reorganization during this period (Ausubel, 1954, pp. xiii; Bernard, 1942).

INCREASED USE OF SCIENTIFIC METHODS AND TECHNIQUES

Social psychology today is characterized by its active research orientation. Its textbooks, written by authors both from psychology and sociology departments, attempt to utilize research data whenever available, in contrast to the more speculative content of much influential literature of earlier periods. Efforts to devise more refined methods and techniques for obtaining data and for measuring and analyzing data have been a characteristic activity in the field in recent years. Particularly during the last decade, publications surveying problems and methods of research designs, of techniques employed, of actual conduct of research and treatment of data are distinctive evidence of this trend in social psychology (e.g., Jahoda et al., 1951; Katz, 1953; Lindzey, 1954).

It would be unfortunate to leave the impression that in social psychology scientific method is conceived in terms of research design and measurement techniques, independent of theory and concepts. It has been noted that development of integrative theory with direct bearing on actual research data is not proceeding as rapidly as refinement of techniques (e.g., Bruner, 1950). However, as Crutchfield (1954) and Robert L. French (1956) noted in their annual reviews in 1954 and 1956, respectively, the construction of theoretical models on a small scale is increasingly prevalent. Some of these efforts have attempted to propose mathematical definitions and postulates. As research and measurement techniques become more precise, the construction of mathematical models is likely to increase. At this stage of development in social psychology, J. R. P. French's statement of the frequent dilemma encountered in such attempts is pertinent. As he noted, "the very precision which gives power to the theory also tends to oversimplify it. For reasons of mathematical convenience one tends to make simple assumptions which so restrict the theory that it seems unrealistic compared to the complexity observed in social behavior" (1956, p. 181).

One notable feature of the trend toward refined procedures, techniques, and modes of analysis is its marked interdisciplinary character. Social psychology has borrowed techniques freely from research developments in fellow disciplines (e.g., content analysis, participant observation, analysis of interaction process, and several other "field" methods). Social psychologists have mingled freely with sociologists, political scientists, and investigators in applied areas in developing more refined survey methods, interviewing of various kinds, a variety of questionnaires, rating scales, attitude scales, and tests. They have been sensitive to techniques developed in child psychology (e.g., observation methods), experimental psychology, and clinical psychology (e.g., "projective" techniques), and prone to adapt them for use in their own research problems.

Because many of its investigators were nurtured in psychological laboratories, experimentation in social psychology has been a prominent activity, even more so since Murphy, Murphy, and Newcomb's *Experimental Social Psychology* in 1937. The advantages and prestige of laboratory experimentation have continued to attract social psychologists, whatever their academic origins, and to attract sociologists, notably those interested in small groups. While the range of topics investigated in the laboratory has greatly expanded, a growing number of investigators display healthy caution against unqualified reliance solely on the laboratory experiment. It has been noted that some "crucial variables and relationships cannot be reproduced under laboratory conditions" (Jahoda *et al.*, 1951, p. 337) and that in establishing necessary controls and manipulating conditions in the laboratory artifice may be the end product (e.g., Festinger, 1953b). As a result, serious discussions of the roles of the laboratory and the field in social-psychological research have been under way (e.g., Riecken, 1954). The problem of discussion has centered largely around when and how each method should be used to speed continued development of valid general principles.

The value of field research for laboratory experimentation is recognized both as a source of new hypotheses and as a check on the validity of conclusions (cf. Festinger, 1953, p. 141). Field work can, as in Newcomb's Bennington study (1943), provide crucial evidence of hypothesized relationships between social-stimulus conditions and psychological variables or, as in the analysis of survey data by Lazarsfeld and his associates (1955), it can indicate relationships obscured in the multifaceted nature of social life. Again, the participant observer can bring from his intensive and longitudinal study of social groupings a rounded "natural history," such as Whyte's *Street Corner Society* (1943). Here in the field of actual life are the variables and the relationships we must ultimately deal with. But how are we to bring them into the laboratory without mutilating their essential properties? And how are we to specify and refine our understanding of them without greater control than the field ordinarily permits?

There is, of course, no single solution, and explorations will continue. In the meantime, several steps seem to be proceeding simultaneously. On the one hand, design of laboratory experiments becomes more ingenious, and care in guarding against the possibilities of artifice is increasingly evident (e.g., Crutchfield, 1954; Festinger, 1955). On the other hand, efforts to improve the standards and techniques used in the field continue; the extensive use and improvement of sociometric techniques is only one example. In addition, at least since the Western Electric studies, there has been applied research or action research introducing changed conditions in the field (French, 1953). Such investigations, as well as detailed studies of "natural" change, like *The Invasion from Mars* (Cantril, 1940), are indispensable in keeping theory in close touch with real life and in suggesting hypotheses for further research. Yet applied research has some built-in handicaps. The investigator seldom has sufficient control to manipulate variables to the extent possible in the laboratory. He is sometimes under considerable pressure from the sponsors to restrict his research to problems which appear practical to them and which may or may not be practical in long-range terms (cf. Katz, 1951; Stouffer, 1950).

There is another possibility—that field and laboratory may be integrated in single research designs by establishing thoroughgoing control over a lifelike situation and by manipulating conditions to produce the social conditions found in the field, at least in their most essential aspects (Sherif, 1954). Such an approach cannot supplant field investigations, but it can bring the laboratory and its methods of control and techniques into the field when the problems of study are amenable to investigation in manageable social units.

An example of the above approach is our series of experiments on group formation and intergroup relations started in 1948 (Sherif *et al.*, 1961; Sherif and Sherif, 1953; Sherif *et al.*, 1955; Sherif and Sherif, 1956, Chaps. 6 and 9). One of the main theoretical objectives of these studies was demonstration of the feasibility of experimentation on intergroup relations. Initially, extensive surveys were made of empirical findings on friendship and hostility, and cooperation and competition between groups and their individual members. These surveys led to the generalization that a prerequisite for the experimental study of intergroup relations is the formation of delineated groups. Before it can be said that there are relations between groups, there have to be identifiable group organizations or structures.

Therefore, the design of the experiments was in successive stages to be carried out over a period of time. The first stage was devoted to the experimental formation of groups among previously unacquainted individuals. To control subject selection and ensure that backgrounds of subjects be homogeneous in crucial respects and to control conditions of interaction during the experiments, the location of facilities, and the timing of events, summer camps for boys in isolated sites were established as the experimental settings.

The group-formation hypothesis predicted that when individuals interact in a series of problem situations embodying goals that require coordination of activities for their attainment, a group would form, consisting of an organization of differentiated status positions and a set of norms peculiar to the group (Sherif and Sherif, 1953). Example of such a problem situation: Preparing ingredients available in bulk form, cooking them, and serving a meal when everyone was hungry.

Clearly, specific criteria had to be used for determining when groups were formed. In line with the discussion of small groups earlier in this chapter, the criteria included in the hypothesis for this purpose were (1) the rise of an identifiable status structure or organization, as measured by the relative frequency of *effective initiative* displayed by each member, and (2) the rise of an identifiable set of rules or norms, as measured by frequency and regularity of their observance and the spontaneous application of correctives by fellow members for behavior deviating beyond the latitude of acceptable behavior defined by the rules or norms.

When the criteria were satisfied by the formation of two groups, the second stage of the experiments was devoted to study of relations between groups thus formed. The hypotheses concerned the conditions of interaction between groups which would be conducive to hostility between them and to its reduction. Therefore, the two groups came into functional contact in a series of situations which involved competition and in which the attainment of goals by one group implied the deprivation or frustration of the other group. Example: A tournament of team games with prizes to the victorious group. As a result of successive win-or-lose encounters of this sort, readily identifiable unfavorable attitudes and consistently hostile actions developed between the groups. Operationally, unfavorable attitudes were measured by the frequency and stabilization of negative stereotypes of the out-group and its members, the "social distance" maintained between the groups, and manifest attempts toward hostile encounters.

In the last experiments (Sherif *et al.*, 1961), the final stage was devoted to conditions proposed as conducive to reduction of intergroup conflict. First, a series of situations was introduced involving physical *contiguity* in pleasant activities which each individual in the separate groups actively wanted. Examples: A sumptuous meal or an entertainment to which the two groups were invited to enjoy the same hall. These occasions for contact, which required no coordination of efforts to attain the desired activity, were utilized by each group for further recrimination and fights with the other.

In the second period of conditions for the reduction of intergroup hostility, a series of goals which were compelling and highly desired by both groups was introduced in apparently natural situations. The goal was attainable only through the joint efforts of the two groups. Examples: A threatened water shortage owing to dysfunction of the supply system; preparations for a much-desired outing which required greater efforts and resources than either group could provide separately. Such goals were termed "superordinate goals."

A series of situations embodying superordinate goals over a period of time did bring about a reduction of intergroup hostility and an increase in friendly relations between the groups, as measured by the reduction of unfavorable stereotypes and an increase in favorable conceptions of the other group and its members, as well as actions toward collaborating with the other group observed in situations prepared to test such reactions.

The advantages gained by integrating field and laboratory approaches when feasible are these:

1. By painstaking efforts, the naturalness of real life situations in the eyes of individual participants can be attained. In the group experiments mentioned above, the subjects perceived the experimental situation as a summer camp and did not suspect that from the beginning the conditions and activities in which they interacted were being controlled and manipulated. They were not aware that their behavior was constantly observed and rated. Every effort was made to make measurement techniques a natural part of the situation by presenting them in the form of activities appropriate in the situation.

2. Because experimental control extends to choice of subjects in accordance with specified criteria and to location of the experiment and activities engaged in, the precision of laboratory manipulation of variables need not be sacrificed. Since intergroup relations were focal in these studies, subjects were chosen to constitute homogeneous samples in order that differences in background (e.g., socioeconomic, religious, ethnic, educational) and personal characteristics (e.g., intelligence, modes of social "adjustment") would be minimized as prior sources of antagonism or friendship among them. Experimental locations were isolated and completely under the investigators' control. The proximity of subjects to one another and their activities could be varied according to predetermined plans. Thus, rather clear-cut evidence was obtained to test hypotheses based on sociological observations of the conditions of group formation and of specified intergroup relations (cf. Doby *et al.*, 1954, pp. 113–115). By introducing over a period of time activities and goals which required interdependent efforts by a number of individuals, social groups essentially similar to those of real life were produced among individuals who were not previously acquainted. These experimental conditions were sufficient for group formation, even when individuals had not initially expressed natural liking (in the form of sociometric choices) for other members.

In order to rule out possible explanation of group formation in terms of variables other than the experimental conditions, the stage of group formation in the first experiment in 1949 (Sherif and Sherif, 1953) was preceded by a period of freedom in the choice of associates in various activities. As a result, friendship clusters of two or three individuals began to form. In dividing subjects for the stage of group formation, these friendship clusters were deliberately split by assigning best friends to different groups. Thus, at the beginning of the period of group formation, only a third of the friendship choices were for individuals in the same group, while two-thirds were directed toward individuals in the other group. Following conditions introduced as conducive to group formation, the friendship choices were reversed and restricted almost exclusively to fellow members of one's own group (Sherif and Sherif, 1953, p. 268).

When conditions of initial contact between groups were planned so that one group could achieve the goal only by preventing the other group from doing so, group conflict resulted, as predicted. In the more recent experiment, the group conflict thus engendered was experimentally reduced through the introduction of a *series* of superordinate goals which were compelling and highly desired by members of both groups, but attainable only through the joint efforts of the two groups working together (Sherif *et al.*, 1961).

3. Because subject backgrounds and experimental conditions and their alteration are controlled, it becomes possible to specify crucial stimulus variables in the formation of social attitudes and to assess the psychological effects of these attitudes as a function of developing group membership through precise laboratory techniques suitably adapted to the phenomenally natural situations of the subjects. The group experiments utilized primarily judgmental reactions in relation to performance of laboratory-type tasks which could be introduced at critical choice points in the experimental design without unnecessarily cluttering the natural flow of interaction (Sherif and Sherif, 1956, Chaps. 6 and 9). Such techniques yield data in quantitative form.

In the highly complex setting of the field, in the laboratory-in-the-field, or even in some aspect of the field created in the laboratory, it is recognized that the selectivity of the investigator may influence the kind of data obtained and thus the kind of conclusions drawn. The most effective safeguard at present is the use of a combination of methods whose results can be checked one against another (cf. Katz, 1953; Lazarsfeld, 1944; Sherif, 1954). Thus in the group experiments referred to above, results obtained by participant observers were checked against independent ratings of other observers, sociometric techniques, stereotype ratings by the subjects, and several techniques adapted from the laboratory. The use of a combination of methods, continual cross-checking of laboratory and field findings, and feasible measures to integrate field and laboratory approaches may be among the steps toward ensuring the validity of generalizations based on social-psychological research.

FOUR

THE "INSTITUTIONAL" VS. "BEHAVIORAL" CONTROVERSY IN SOCIAL SCIENCE, WITH SPECIAL REFERENCE TO POLITICAL SCIENCE

With Bertram Koslin, Princeton University

As social psychologists, we are concerned with formulating research strategies for the study of attitudes and behavior in man's social relations. Problems of particular research interest include attitude-behavior relationships on political, economic, and other social issues. They include individual-group relationships, leader-follower relationships, and group-with-group relationships in various sociocultural settings. An integral and indispensable aspect of our research task is the specification of the stimulus conditions relative to which individuals' attitudes and behaviors are formed and function.

The task of specifying stimulus conditions in social psychology is no simple undertaking. Unlike the maze run by the rat, the pursuit rotor traced by the human hand, or a set of nonsense syllables to be memorized, stimulus situations in social psychology consist of complex and patterned events involving political, religious, economic, and other social objects, conditions, and relationships surrounding the individual. In specifying stimulating conditions, we are confronted with the occupational characteristics, educational level, political affiliations, ethnic affiliations, income levels, and power arrangements prevailing among the individuals we are studying and among other people in their psychological ken as well. In social psychology, constriction of the research perspective to the arrangements of the immediate location in which attitudinal responses are obtained, or in which interaction categories and spoken words of the respondents are recorded, amounts to neglect of some of the crucial independent variables operative in the situation, whether

The authors are grateful to Carolyn W. Sherif for her help in writing this paper.

Unpublished technical paper. Norman: University of Oklahoma, Institute of Group Relations, 1960. (Mimeographed.)

or not these variables are immediately apparent within the confines of the specific situation at that moment.

Concern with adequate specification of the stimulus characteristics of the setting in which reactions of individuals are studied, in order to test specified hypotheses, has necessarily led us to take cognizance of the contributions of the sociologist, the anthropologist, and the political scientist to detailed and appropriate specification of the properties of these social objects and relationships that constitute the setting. Cognizance of the sociologist's, anthropologist's, and political scientist's formulations and findings is necessary because the psychologist's descriptive improvisations of social organizations and institutions have fallen pitifully short of the mark, giving caricatured accounts of the properties of the sociocultural and political setting.

The recent, healthy trend for psychologists to borrow relevant findings from various of the social sciences has been reciprocated by the interest of the sociologist, the anthropologist, and the political scientist in formulations and research in psychology. This is as it should be. In the past, improvisations by the social scientist regarding the "nature of human nature," psychological dispositions, and "psychological laws" have not fared better than attempts by psychologists to improvise the nature of political, economic, and other social institutions.

DICHOTOMOUS APPROACHES AS STUMBLING BLOCKS
IN INTERDISCIPLINARY EFFORTS

In recent years, the willingness of psychology, on the one hand, and various social science disciplines, on the other, to exchange contributions has given rise to various undertakings, in the form of conferences, research, and publications, which may be referred to as *interdisciplinary* efforts. But as yet it can scarcely be said that the potential benefits of interdisciplinary efforts have been effectively realized. On the whole, interdisciplinary efforts in joint conferences and volumes have consisted largely of juxtaposing contributions by representatives of the various disciplines. It seems to us that one of the obstacles to effective interdisciplinary efforts is that conceptual approaches in the various disciplines are still formulated in terms of irreconcilable dichotomies—dichotomies that are part of our intellectual heritage and that may not be conducive to integrated formulations of human problems—that take account both of reacting individuals and sociocultural settings.

The dichotomous efforts to which we refer are epitomized by different labels in psychology, anthropology, sociology, and political science. In each case, however, the dichotomy is usually conceived as irreconcilable. In psychology, for example, the dichotomy is encountered in the study of leader-follower relations, of "voting behavior," of prejudice, and of "personality." Here the approaches are labeled the "individual" or "personality-oriented" approach as opposed to the "group" or "culture-bound" approach.

In cultural anthropology, the dichotomous approach is manifested in the stand taken by some younger anthropologists for the investigation of culture through "behavioral" study of a few selected individuals or "informants" using biographical techniques and psychological tests, as contrasted with attempts at theorizing on the basis of general outlines of kinship, value systems, and other characteristic cultural forms and trends (for example, Sherif, 1959).

We are all acquainted with a growing trend among sociologists who rally to the banner of "behavioral sciences" to concentrate on specific items of behavior by individuals in circumscribed social situations—such as hospitals, mental wards, conference rooms, and voting booths—without much concern over study of these situations relative to other aspects of the social systems of which they are parts. On the other side of the dichotomy are those who regard broad generalizations about social systems as the aim of sociology and who pay little attention to the validation of theory. In its more extreme instances, the view is manifested in grandiose theorizing of the armchair variety.

Since we are concerned as social psychologists with the study of political attitudes and behavior as they relate to a sociopolitical setting with its power arrangements, we naturally turn to the work of political scientists for accounts of the political system. But here, as well as in cultural anthropology and sociology, we are confronted with a dichotomous approach, reminiscent of those in other disciplines but now labeled "Institutional" vs. "Behavioral" approaches to the study of political phenomena.

The two approaches, which have crystallized since World War II, are succinctly summarized by Avery Leiserson (1958):

The oldest tradition in political science (as distinct from postulating and elaborating ideal forms of society and government) emerges in what may legitimately be called *institutional analysis,* i.e., the study of the historical, legal and structural development of political institutions, their modes of operation, and their differential effects in terms of general types of organizational behavior. Around the beginning of the present century there arose a new emphasis, associated with new developments in anthropology, psychology, and sociology, upon explicit observation and measurement of the perceptions and attitudes in the population at large toward politics. . . . In recent years, this . . . social-psychological, methods-oriented approach to politics in terms of people has acquired the label and status of behavioral analysis . . . (p. 369).

Let us consider some obvious implications of an "institutional" vs. "behavioral" dichotomy in approaching the study of sociopolitical life. If a "behavioral" approach is concerned primarily with the utilization and development of techniques for gathering data other than those traditionally employed, surely there would be little hew and cry about it. Only those with a lifetime commitment to an armchair base for grandiose political philosophy could have serious objection these days to more empirical data relevant to their problems of study or to additional techniques for securing them.

Evidently there is more to the problem faced by political scientists caught in an "institutional" vs. "behavioral" dichotomy than that. Everywhere, in the literature we have examined, the "behavioral" approach is characterized by sympathizers and critics alike as "concerned with individual behavior or with action in small, face-to-face groups and . . . a wide range of action not specifically relevant to any particular institutional context" (Truman, 1955, p. 209). So conceived, "behavioral analysis" is identified with analysis of items of individual behavior, whether these items are responses to a survey questionnaire, categories of response in interaction situations or in specified communication networks, or alternate strategies adopted by an individual faced with the necessity of reaching a decision.

This "behavioral" approach leads, say such critics as De Grazia, to disintegration of the problems with which political science is properly concerned into *"only* those bits of things that can be asked easily, *only* those partial things that can readily be seen, or *only* those incomplete aspects of things that can be manipulated numerically" (De Grazia, 1951, pp. 98–99). To use V. O. Key's phrase, the danger foreseen is that "substantive myopia be a consequence of methodological sophistication" (1956, p. 31).

The "methodological sophistication" attributed to enthusiasts of political behavior in contrast to those upholding an institutionalist approach seems to consist largely of adaptations of formal models originally formulated by mathematicians, of techniques borrowed from the psychological laboratory, and of survey research. The enthusiasm for "rigorous tools, focussing for the most part on individual behavior and attitude," Garceau (1951) commented, may tend toward the neglect of historical evidence and cross-cultural comparison.

If the "behavioral approach" as contrasted with the "institutional approach" in political science is indeed characterized by emphasis on measurement of response items from single individuals to the neglect of the organizational and institutional forms, the value systems, and the technological settings in which they occur, if laboratory or survey techniques have acquired such prestige that cross-cultural and historical comparisons may be neglected, then some questions raised in the history of social psychology may be relevant to issues currently discussed in political science.

"BEHAVIORAL SCIENCE" AND THE STUDY OF SOCIAL BEHAVIOR

We speak as social psychologists and thus as working members of a fairly young and developing discipline, itself racked with schisms. Psychology as a scientific discipline is properly concerned with the analysis of the experience and behavior of individuals. In this respect, social psychology cannot be divorced from psychology in general. It is a truism that a science of psychology is possible only through relating experience and behavior to the preceding and contemporary stimulating conditions in which the individual functions. Properly speaking, social psychology is distinguished from psychology only by its focal concern with individual experience and behavior relative to *social* stimulus conditions. Thus, as indicated at the outset, a crucial and necessary part of social-psychological investigation is specification of relevant social stimulus conditions and their properties.

What is meant by *social* stimulus conditions? Some psychologists would restrict the term to other individuals and interpersonal relations among them or to groups of individuals and relations among them. However, there seem to be no clear-cut criteria, except those dictated by disciplinary allegiances, for eliminating social organizations and institutions, values, and man-made objects from the "social" category, whether these are religious, economic, national, technological, or political arrangements, institutions, values, or objects.

If we may grant for the time being that the most significant stimulus conditions faced by an individual are "social" in this broad sense, how should these social stimuli be conceived? In older psychological traditions, the "stimulus" was conceived as a discrete item in the environment, perhaps a patch of light, a tone, or a touch of given intensity. Through several generations of experimental work, it became evident that the psychological significance of a particular stimulus item is dependent upon its relationship to other items immediately surrounding it as well as to factors coming from within the individual at the time, such as relevant past experiences, interests, and motives (see Sherif and Sherif, 1956, Chapters 1 and 2).

The implication for social psychology, perhaps of some interest to social scientists concerned with interdisciplinary efforts, is that a conception of "stimulus situation" that has functional value must consider specific objects, persons, and situations in their contextual and patterned relationships. In addition, it has been shown in the psychological laboratory that the individual's experience of the meaning of social stimuli is *immediate,* in the sense that reaction is to patterned regularities prior to any opportunity for differentiation and analysis of specific "elementary" dimensions and cues.

Here is the reason that, even on a psychological basis, the social psychologist must be concerned with the patterned properties of social objects, forms, and events. And this necessity brings him to the social sciences whose problems have properly and traditionally been concerned with the regularities of patterned actions, events, and objects in social life, and with the development, stabilization, and change of such regularities.

Because the task of specifying the properties of social stimulus conditions and settings logically leads the social psychologist to the work of his colleagues in anthropology, sociology, and political science, trends in those disciplines toward exclusive focus on the analysis of individual behavior seem regrettable, insofar as these trends detract from the investigation of the patterning and properties of human groups, institutions, their material achievements, language systems, and value systems. Carried to an extreme, such trends would result in the absorption of the social sciences by an all-embracing discipline studying individual behavior—which, of course, would be some kind of psychology.

Any partisan loyalties we may harbor as psychologists strengthen rather than dim our concern with psychological imperialisms in the social sciences. From the point of view of social psychology, the reduction of social stimulus agents to items of individual behavior, or even regularities in items of individual behavior, amounts to omitting essential properties of factors which are crucial independent variables in social-psychological research.

Of course, one can maintain that apart from individual human beings and their behaviors, there could be no institutions, no power arrangements, no group organizations, no value systems, no language, and no means of communication, transportation, or production. But once such products of human interaction come into existence, the behavior of individuals exposed to them cannot be adequately understood apart from them. Herein lies the futility of data summarizing individual social behavior apart from its context.

Certainly, man makes existing social forms and institutions; with equal certainty, social forms and institutions recast man as they develop and change. These products of human interaction can be and are studied in a meaningful way without reference to single individuals or their behavior if we are working on the level of the social sciences.

At this juncture the observations reported by Malinowski in 1922 on the Kula exchange system in the Trobriand Islands are instructive. The Kula exchange system is one of the institutions of tribal life that is interwoven, as Malinowski points out, with the religion, language, politics, and social organization of the Trobrianders. In order to understand the Kula exchange system it is necessary to relate it as a *part process* to the entire sociocultural setting of the Trobriands. This exchange institution is extensive, complicated, and yet well ordered. The islanders exchange, extend credit, "contract," and work at various specialized pursuits, and yet no single individual knows the outline of the Kula exchange system as a whole. Each knows his own motives, the purposes of individual actions, and the rules that apply to them. But when questioned about Kula, they responded with subjective impressions, with a few details concerning their direct experiences, but not with a coherent definition of the system. Not even a partial coherent account could be obtained. "For the integral picture does not exist in his mind; he is in it, and cannot see the whole from the outside" (Malinowski, 1922, p. 83).

Without knowing something about the Kula exchange system and how it fits into the entire sociocultural setting, without knowing something about its history, a "behavioral" scientist concentrating on items of individual behavior and experience would be apt to produce a good number of contradictory artifacts. He might report that the Trobrianders carry out an exchange system with two kinds of shells fabricated into necklaces and bracelets, but that it is meaningless since the majority of them cannot be worn for ornamentation. He might conclude that Kula is some sort of religious ritual, especially since no individual ever owns the ornaments but always has them on loan. Another "behavioral" investigator, perhaps struck by the similarity of these ornaments and the crown jewels (as was Malinowski), might reinterpret the findings. Still another "behavioral" scientist might discover by questioning informants that chiefs exchange with many; low status individuals with but a few. He might very well conclude that Kula is a feudal-like system for paying homage to others according to class. Yet another "behavioral" scientist may conclude that Kula is a true economic system: goods manufactured only in certain villages are transported hundreds of miles in exchange for other goods; the exchange of trinkets simply signifies business partners.

In the case of Trobriand Islanders, the additive sum of individual opinion and behavior does not give the adequate outlines of the Kula, an institution of far-reaching significance in the life of the islanders. In a similar vein, V. O. Key (1959) has questioned whether in the study of voting the sum of individual choices equals the collective end-product, the people's choice.

Whenever individuals, groups, and other units of analysis are investigated as parts of a superordinate or larger functioning system, a distinction drawn by Avery Leiserson (1958) has genuine significance: "the division of the population into political parties and groups . . . comprises the . . . definition of *political opinion,* as distinguished from the distribution of individual opinions without regard to organization that is called public opinion" (pp. 66–67). The attitudes of individuals functioning in terms of the groups to which they relate (reference groups) cannot be properly assessed or understood apart from their organizational context. In terms of political action the consequences are obvious: the more individuals are related to groups, the more these groups have an impact in politics. There is considerable difference between a distribution of opinions of unrelated individuals on some issue (for example, 10 per cent strongly pro, 15 per cent pro, 50 per cent undecided, 15 per cent con, 10 per cent strongly con) and two opposing organizations comprised of individuals with the same distribution of opinions.

ANALYTICAL LEVELS AND THE TIME DIMENSION

It is obvious in the foregoing discussion that the social sciences and social psychology are frequently approaching related problems, even the same problems, at two different levels of analysis, each employing appropriate units of analysis. Various problems of social systems, institutions, and sociocultural products are studied by anthropologists, sociologists, and political scientists. The units of analysis in social science need not be the behavior of individuals; more appropriately they may pertain to social groups, large organizations, political institutions, productive and distributive relationships, technological products and relations, religious institutions, music and art forms, language systems, and so on.

Whether working as a psychologist or as a "behavioral scientist" in one of the social sciences, the investigator seriously concerned with the human individual as his unit of analysis has to face the fact that individual behavior is not self-generating. Even the motives, desires, and aspirations that move men to create and change their social environment are inadequately studied apart from the properties of the social situations faced at a given time and those faced in the past. These properties are characteristically patterned arrangements among men and objects. We take it that such properties have something to do with the focus of "institutional analysis." If so, we wonder at the currency given to an irreconcilable dichotomy between "behavioral" and "institutional" approaches.

On the contrary, a conception of social disciplines working at a level of analysis with units appropriate to that level and of psychologists working at a level of analysis handling individual experience and behavior with appropriate units provides a method for cross-disciplinary checking of results. If a generalization concerning a particular problem reached at one level of analysis is valid, it is not contradicted by valid generalizations reached at another level and is in fact strengthened and refined by it. For example, the psychologist's findings that individuals behave differentially when participating in groups strengthens the sociological finding that collective interaction has properties peculiar to the group. In return, specification of group properties through sociological research and analysis permits the psychologist to identify variables producing differential behavior by the individual member. Thus the dichotomy between "behavioral" and "institutional" approaches is a false dichotomy engendered by our intellectual heritage and by the limitations of our disciplines at a given time in their history.

Likewise, the categorical assignment of longitudinal, historical methods to "institutional" analysis and of cross-sectional study at one point in time to "behavioral" analysis may describe what individuals are doing under the two rubrics, but it is neither inevitable nor desirable from the viewpoint of studying social behavior. On the contrary, the investigation of human social behavior must necessarily include longitudinal methods.

We propose to illustrate the main points made above with a brief discussion of the small group and a summary of some research by the senior author. That much-maligned and over-glamorized social unit, the group, has come to mean all things to all people. But, regardless of who is interested in the topic, a group is a *social* unit and its properties are properly defined at the social science level of analysis. Accordingly, before starting research on the small group, a survey of social science literature was made to extract the essential properties of a group (Sherif and Cantril, 1947; Sherif, 1948). A group was defined on the basis of these properties extracted from findings on actual groups in social life.

Briefly, the minimum properties of a group are that it consists of a number of individuals who, at a given time, stand in more or less definite status and role relationships to one another (*organization, leader-follower* relations) and who share a set of *values* or *norms*. This manner of defining a group is not an "operational" method, but the definition is operational in the sense that the existence of a group can be determined by definite criteria which square with repeatedly verified empirical findings and through specific research operations (Sherif and Sherif, 1953, 1956).

As thus defined, a group is necessarily *longitudinal*: status relationships and values (norms) develop only through a time period. An arbitrary collection of individuals brought together around a table to discuss something or passing notes in specified communication networks is not necessarily a group. Such transitory collections of individuals are merely "togetherness" situations.

By defining status relations in terms of relative standing in *effective initiative* demonstrated by individual members, the structure of the group becomes identical with its power arrangements. Here we follow the political scientist Meriam (1944), who observed that power was intrinsic in some form to every human organization.

The implication of this mode of defining "group" is clear: If, as a social psychologist, one is interested in studying the effects of groups on individual behavior or if, as a social scientist, one wishes to compare differing organizational forms, one first has to have groups formed *over a period of time*.

In experiments conducted by the senior author under natural field conditions that also permitted experimental control, groups were formed among unacquainted individuals over a *time period* by presenting a series of problem situations with genuine motivational appeal to these individuals, which required pulling together for their solutions (Sherif and Sherif, 1953; Sherif *et al.*, 1954). Sequentially, the attitudes and behavior of individual members of groups were studied as two groups, thus formed, came into contact. Since the research problem concerned intergroup attitudes and behavior, the first contacts between groups were in a *series* of situations over a *time period* in which the achievement and success of one group necessarily meant failure and defeat for the other. Of course, intense conflict developed between the groups and their members. Finally, facing the two hostile groups with a series of situations in which each group faced a threat or a much-desired goal that could be handled only by the efforts and resources of both groups pulling together, the conflict between them changed to friendly interchange. The attitudes and behavior of individual members were accordingly changed to friendly conceptions and acts toward the other group.

These experiments are very briefly summarized here, not for any direct relevance to political problems studied by political scientists, but to make a methodological point that may interest those concerned with the "behavioral"-vs-"institutional" dichotomy. The study of individual social behavior cannot be validly carried out in the abstract. The stimulus conditions facing the individual (here a "group" and then patterns of intergroup relations which cannot be extrapolated from intragroup relations) have to be specified in terms of their meaningful, patterned properties as they are studied at the level of social science analysis.

And, finally, the longitudinal sequence and patterning of events have to be brought into the analysis if the behavior of particular individuals at a particular time is to be understood. If an investigator had measured the attitudes and behavior of the individuals in the group experiments mentioned above during the height of intergroup conflict, without knowledge of the preceding series of events and the patterning of relations between the groups, he could only have concluded that he had stumbled upon a bunch of most disagreeable, perhaps frustrated and aggressive individuals.

Further, the behavior within the groups themselves could not be analyzed apart from the trends in intergroup relations, once the groups came into contact. The impact of conflicting intergroup relations changed the power structures within the groups, resulting in one group in a change of leadership, of course with attendant striking alterations of behavior by those involved.

If the research person interested in behavior of individuals relative to political issues and in institutional settings starts his research with definitions of the issues and of the settings and their power arrangements that square with the findings from the study of political institutions, then his research on individual behavior will supplement and will strengthen findings at an institutional level of analysis. The enticing end-result would not be a "behavioral"-vs-"institutional" dichotomy, but a rounded, integrated picture of the problem under study which included both institutional analysis and analysis of individual behavior within the appropriate setting.

In such integrated efforts on the part of colleagues in different disciplines, there is room for "behavioral" and "institutional" analysis, but no room for a "behavioral"-vs.-"institutional" dichotomy. For interdisciplinary integration must be both behavioral *and* institutional:

"Behavioral" in the sense that items of behavior are studied in their *time sequence* relative to the *patterned properties* of the social stimulus conditions.

"Institutional" in the sense that the patterned properties and relationships of social organizations and institutions are studied on their own level without reducing them to so many items of individual behavior *or their sums*.

PROBLEM OF VALIDITY AND THE CHOICE OF TECHNIQUES

In the 1930s sociologists and social psychologists participated in a trend toward measurement of attitudes and opinions on almost every conceivable topic. In the late Thirties and especially the Forties, survey research became an engrossing preoccupation for many. Meanwhile, successes in the psychological laboratory in studying certain social phenomena brought its methods to the attention of social scientists for the first time in a serious way.

Overwhelmed perhaps by the popularity and sophisticated nomenclature associated with those techniques, some social scientists have come to identify "science" with one or another of them. To some, the best data come from a laboratory. To others, survey research, the panel techniques, and the stratified sample offer the greatest promise.

In his own research efforts, the senior author has come to the conclusion that no one of these techniques is ever sufficient in itself for full study even of a problem of individual social behavior. In the study of complex social phenomena, the opportunities of investigator bias, overgeneralization, and neglecting crucial variables are so great that the only possible solution is the persistent use of a combination of all relevant techniques for data collection. Chief among these are historical and cross-cultural comparison and measurement of attitudes and behavior cross-sectionally by a variety of techniques (interview, attitude "scales," indirect techniques), content analysis, and, *finally*, experimental methods.

The experimental methods, as Gardner Murphy *et al.* (1937) commented with such wisdom over twenty years ago, are not and cannot be the starting point in investigation of a problem area in social life. They become appropriate only *late* in the sequence of research, after the main problems are sharpened, the main variables detected and defined in terms suitable both to the phenomena under study and to manipulation and measurement in the laboratory. As thus conceived, the laboratory method does indeed become a "crowning touch" in research.

But neither the experiment nor the survey nor historical research nor cross-cultural comparison is identical with scientific method in the human sciences. The use of a particular method does not make a science, as even the most cursory reading of the history of scientific thought will show.

V. O. Key commented that the blind application of particular techniques of study used with some success in other disciplines may well focus research on a narrow range of problems for which the techniques are particularly suited. The "imaginative contrivance" of new techniques suited to a "wider range of substantive problems," which Key (1956) called for, is surely part of the scientific development of any discipline. Rather than problems being formulated to suit available techniques or to meet the assumption of some statistical model, research tools should be forged to investigate social problems. Validity, as De Grazia (1951) emphasized, should take precedence over precision, and therefore research techniques that destroy, distort, or mutilate a problem under investigation are clearly inappropriate. Once these essentials are taken care of, it will be relatively easy to find the appropriate operational techniques and appropriate statistical modes of analysis that do justice to the properties of the problem at hand.

EFFORTS AT "BRIDGING THE GAP" BETWEEN "INSTITUTIONAL" AND "BEHAVIORAL" ANALYSES

Controversy between the adherents of a "behavioral" versus an "institutional" approach seems to have led to some healthy developments in social science and especially in political science, so far as we social psychologists are concerned.

For one thing, artificial boundary distinctions between disciplines are being weakened. Generalizations in political science are being tested against those of other social sciences; the findings of politics are being compared with those obtained in sociology, anthropology, economics, and psychology. There seems to be a programmatic effort in political science to implement in research Merriam's observation: "Obviously there is governance everywhere—government in heaven; government in hell; government and law among the outlaws; government in prison" (1944, p. 1).

This trend in political and other social sciences has led to increasing recognition that the findings of sister disciplines are important in understanding political, economic, religious, ethnic, occupational, interpersonal, and other aspects of man's social life (Apter, 1957). One sees evidence of a feeling that the knitting together of "institutional" and "behavioral" analysis is desirable.

Avery Leiserson (1953), for example, wrote:

The fact that we still find it necessary to differentiate between (a) patterns of political behavior common to both governmental and nongovernmental political situations, and (b) the specialized institutions and processes peculiar to government, is not conclusive evidence that common concepts of sufficient generality will not be found to integrate the data of interpersonal and institutional behavior into an inclusive, logically consistent body of theoretical propositions (p. 567).

Some social scientists have acknowledged that the integration of different *levels of analysis* is a necessity. If it is true, as Mills (1953) stated, for example, that "rigorous proof only exists on the molecular level," such integration will ultimately be necessary both in order to utilize rigorous methods as more than play things and to provide a firm factual base for broader theoretical attempts.

The adoption of an interdisciplinary, question-oriented mode of research has generated some confidence that the gaps which polarize "institutional" and "behavioral" analysis will be bridged in time by filling them up with appropriate research. The so-called "middle level" research is sometimes seen as the means of establishing connective tissue between "institutional" and "behavioral" analyses. "Middle level" research, it is thought, will bridge the vast gap between the poles of the individual, on one side, and government, on the other—a gap created by the old but persistent individual-vs-state dichotomy, as Garceau (1951) pointed out. Rather than viewing the process of government in terms of a direct relationship between individual and government, he suggested that by taking account of "multiple, parallel, collaborating and competing patterns of interaction linking citizen and active participants in key positions of decision-making" (Garceau, 1951, p. 71), progress will be made toward relating observable behavior to institutional patterns.

Question-oriented programs of research have served the function of heightening awareness of problems which arise when the techniques and concepts used in sister disciplines are applied in the study of political phenomena. On the whole, political scientists seem to be resisting naive buying of "behavioral" techniques and blind fact-gathering for its own sake (De Grazia, 1951; Garceau, 1951; Key, 1956; Leiserson, 1953). By emphasizing the scope, time dimension, and fluidity of politics reality checks on the concepts and methods in other social sciences have been applied. As a result it is already unfashionable in political science to argue for the kind of full-blown *reductionism* in research political scientists have encountered in other fields (Eckstein, 1956). On the contrary, the adherents of "behavioral research" in political science argue that there should be no neglect of institutional factors, no neglect of the time dimension, and no limiting of the scope of political processes in order to gather data here and now with available techniques (Eldersveld *et al.*, 1952).

One attempt to relate "institutional" and "behavioral" analyses in political science is incorporated in the work on decision-making. In this instance, a model of thinking and its associated "theory of games" has been borrowed and adapted for use in political science. Simon (1957), on the one hand, recognized that the assumptions of the formal model of decision-making concerning rational thinking are too restrictive and posed a model of decision-making which is less restrictive for "administrative man" (p. xxvii). On the other hand, Snyder and his associates (1954) employed a more common sense concept of decision-making as an analytic device for asking fruitful and significant questions in the study of international relations and politics in general.

Undoubtedly, the common-sense meaning of the term "decision-making" has facilitated its introduction into political science. But the implications of the current model and its assumptions have not been fully examined. The fundamental assumption made by some economists since the days of Bentham, and by some psychologists, has been that thinking is a process with a set of its own requirements or "laws." Requirements of what is involved in rational thought are defined in the form of a model, and most of the meager empirical research has been motivated to demonstrate the utility of the model (Edwards, 1954). Lying behind the economists' attempts to formulate a model of rational thinking is the effort to relate institutional patterns of economic systems to the behavior of individuals. In the process, institutional factors have been reduced to those few psychological factors logically required for the decisions of a rational man. More recently, the model for rational decision-making by individuals has been extrapolated in the field of international economics to the action of nation-states in the world market.

Snyder follows a similar procedure in his recent noteworthy contributions. Decision-making is placed in an organizational or situational context at the outset. "This means treating the decision-maker as an 'actor in a situation.' In turn, this means we make a basic choice to take as our prime analytical objective the recreation of the 'social world' of the decision-makers as *they* view it" (Snyder, 1958, p. 17). The conceptual analysis is, therefore, frankly psychologically concerned with perceptions, discriminations, goals, "standards of acceptability," and other psychological factors of decision-makers. The units of analysis are individuals, and the study of institutions, organizations, states, and relations between them is explicitly translated—that is, reduced—to study of individual actions: "*State action is the action taken by those acting in the name of the state.* Hence, the state is its decision-makers. State X as *actor* is translated into its decision-makers as actors" (Snyder *et al.,* 1954, pp. 36–37). Thus "institutional" and "behavioral" analyses are joined by reducing the institutional to the psychological as inferred from the actions of the "policy-forming man."

Certain implications of the mode of analysis represented in Snyder's work are pertinent to the discussion presented earlier in this paper. The problem is not whether organizational factors are brought into the picture, but *how* and *when* they are brought into the analysis.

The reduction of the sociocultural and political to the psychological leaves us with no better account for the emergence of new social and individual products than the "great man approach" or the individualistic personality theories such as psychoanalysis of which Snyder (1958) is so justifiably critical (p. 35). In a way, however, he does not make a clean break from the position of the reductionists. In formulating a psychology for decision-making in political situations, part processes are isolated from the total sociocultural context of which they are a systemic part. Yet it is by no means necessary that social changes ultimately affecting the basic assumptions and procedures in the state as defined have their loci in the part process studied.

As noted earlier, one of the clear lessons in the development of social psychology is that it is not possible to extrapolate uncritically from the behavior of individuals to behavior in togetherness situations, nor from group to intergroup relations. Even two individuals exert a differential effect on one another when they are brought together for the first time to decide on something. And the end product, whatever they decide, is not simply the average of the decisions of two individuals taken separately. Considerable evidence has mounted showing that thinking, perceiving, judging, indeed all cognitive processes are differentially affected if the individuals involved are functioning in interaction situations—all the way from mere togetherness situations, through interaction within their in-groups to interaction between two or more groups when their interests coincide or clash in various degrees (namely, intergroup interaction).

Therefore, these situations constitute one set of independent variables determining decision processes. They are *not* equivalent with the perceptions, "definitions of the situation," and decisions of so many individuals. Situations are also patterned through sociopolitical-socioeconomic systems of which they are parts and which are independent of the experiences of particular individuals.

In a like manner, if we want to know something about the attitudes and motives an individual brings to a situation, we (including the participant) infer them from experience and behavior in various situations. These situations are external to the single individual (probably every individual in China has an equal chance at birth of becoming Chinese). Therefore, no matter how far back in the individual's life history one wishes to proceed, patterned sociocultural factors constitute one set of independent variables. In an adequate social psychology the relationship of each of these stimulus conditions to one another must be taken into account. It would seem reasonable that the same considerations would affect the study of individuals who are decision-makers in the name of a state.

A particularly commendable and detailed effort to span the gap between the "institutional"-vs.-"behavioral" analysis was recently undertaken by Avery Leiserson (1958). Leiserson utilized a broadly conceived interaction approach for analyzing political processes in which "competent analysis of political organization includes not only the impact of structure and leadership upon behavior, but the consequences of attitudes, expectations, and demands (the social psychology of the groups composing its members and environment) upon structure, leadership, and functional performance of the political institution as a whole" (p. 371).

Since there seems to be a trend in political science toward harnessing data obtained by institutional and behavioral analyses, a few comments on methods of achieving an integration may be in order. Perhaps because of the neatness and apparent precision of "behavioral" data, there is a tendency to use them as criteria for sorting out significant "institutional" generalizations from insignificant ones. A theory of political parties thus achieved, however, becomes ultimately dependent upon "behavioral" data gathered mainly in the last two decades. Thus today's state of affairs as reflected in behavioral data becomes the prototype of political organization-participation everywhere and at all times past, present, and future. Historical perspective is sacrificed.

Another method in an attempt to reshuffle "institutional" and "behavioral" findings so that they fit an interaction framework is simply to *add* "behavioral" analysis to bolster "institutional" generalizations and *add* institutional generalizations to explain otherwise unconnected "miniscular" findings. In such additive analyses, factors related to different units of analysis are juxtaposed: Molecular findings are stretched to explain "institutional" observations and institutional generalizations are brought in *ad hoc* to explain "behavioral" findings (Mills, 1953, p. 272).

Such methods lead to a simple pooling of more or less discretely defined variables which are important aspects of a given topic. For example, the voting process is affected by institutions, ideologies, personality differences, identifications, cyclical fluctuations, electoral systems, regional variations, a host of variables psychologically important in non-voting, social structure, race or nationality, and so forth (see Leiserson, 1958). Integration of behavioral and institutional findings, on the other hand, requires that various factors be given appropriate weights in their relationship to one another as they determine the outcome.

By and large, political scientists seem to be interested in those aspects of individual behavior that are conceived as "significantly political: his voting behavior, his consumption habits of media of mass communication, his opinions on great issues, his direct participation in organized partisan groups, and . . . his apparent apathy and confusion in these respects" (Garceau, 1951, p. 70) as a means of shedding some light on the validity of institutional generalizations.

Adequate research planning in political behavior must take into account: (a) the problem of transforming descriptive accounts of policy-making institutions and processes into propositions about behavior in political situations, (b) the relating of these propositions to concepts and research techniques in other disciplines relevant to the area of political behavior delimited for investigation (Leiserson, 1953, p. 577).

This effort at making a tandem of "behavioral" and "institutional" approaches is not unlike the "ideal" research strategy of C. Wright Mills (1953): Institutional generalizations can be verified by molecular data if observations are garnered so that they are logically related, or constitute an "agreed upon" test of the generalizations in issue. For Mills, behavioral as well as institutional findings can be related to one another, each on their own level.

This procedure, which seems acceptable to political scientists, involves the constructing of "behavioral" indexes (logically related to institutional generalizations), which are incorporated into a polling schedule or some other technique. Following this procedure has led, however, to some contradictory findings. For example, V. O. Key and Frank Munger (1959) have criticized research motivated by a "behavioral" orientation which demonstrated that the "nonpolitical" group induces conformity to its political standards because it threatened "to take the politics out of the study of electoral behavior" (p. 281). Subsequently, with the "foremost motive . . . to choose variables which were political in quality," a research unit was conducted with the major finding: that attitudes toward the parties, the personal attributes of the candidates, and the issues of foreign and domestic policy have a profound influence on voting choice" (Campbell and Stokes, 1959, p. 363, 368).

Simple logical translation of institutional generalizations into "behavioral" indexes or "the formulation of hypotheses . . . [by] reduction of a functional proposition describing correlations [assumptions or postulates] to categories or attributes of people" (Leiserson, 1953, p. 579) runs the risk of restricting the findings to what the investigator is set to prove. This kind of approach may be *too* directed and lead, in the last analysis, to pre-determined results.

Such a research strategy in political science, anthropology, and sociology is apt to yield findings in these fields that are more or less contradictory and unrelated.

In the study of voting behavior, for example, much research has been conducted without due cognizance of the relationship of groups to the sociopolitical setting of which they are a part. In a like manner, studies designed to investigate political attitudes in the abstract—that is, without relating them to prevailing social patterns of group, intergroup relations, social movements, and international relations—have contributed findings that are difficult or impossible to organize into a coherent whole. On the basis of the available research findings, a whole series of questions could be asked: Have factors related to the personality of candidates, for example, always had the same weight in determining the vote? Could the international conflict in which the United States is presently engaged have something to do with the repeated finding that today the major parties in the United States are less divergent ideologically?

The methodological implication is that the first step in research on a particular aspect or particular part-process of social life is to conceive it within the framework of the sociocultural, economic, and political setting in which it operates. Otherwise "behavioral" research produces so many unrelated and disjointed "facts."

METHODOLOGICAL IMPLICATIONS

The foregoing discussion has implications for methodological approaches and research strategies in interdisciplinary efforts at achieving integrated accounts of problems interesting all the human disciplines. Foremost is the danger involved in simple extrapolation of findings obtained at one level of analysis to another.

One cannot extrapolate from findings on the effects of motivational urges of the individual (his hunger, his sexual desires, his desire for recognition and prestige) to explain the properties of group situations, as if the group situation were a void, as if the interaction process and the reciprocities that arise within it were but a play of shadows. So, too, it is impossible to extrapolate findings from group situations to handle the alignments, the conflicts, the bargaining of group with group. No group today exists in isolation. Its very formation and functioning may reflect its relatedness to other groups, organizations, and larger social units of which it is a part.

The extrapolation of the properties of interaction in groups to the explanation of relations between groups is a methodological error, implying that the *area of interaction between these groups* consisted of a vacuum or can be equated with the cozy atmosphere of a conference room. The character of intergroup relations is determined not only by the character of relations and norms that prevail *within* the groups but also by the process of interaction *between* groups—by a give-and-take process that may be full of tension or in a state of flow. Similarly, the fluid patterns of interaction in the early phase of a social movement are not predictable from the properties of groups that may be involved. Collective interaction has a focal point, but reciprocities among individuals are not yet stabilized (Sherif and Sherif, 1953).

If we are interested in what determines the vote of a single individual, if we are interested in determining why he makes a particular decision, why he has a given attitude, then his membership in and psychological relatedness to groups, to collectivities of various kinds, to ongoing social movements, to the nation-state must be taken into account. In short, his vote, his opinion, his decision must be studied relative to his reference groups and their properties.

A great number of laboratory experiments on judgment have shown that various factors interact in a relational way in determining the end product—the estimate, the goal set, the decisions. It is not permissible to predict the outcome without independent knowledge about these factors and their relationships. Similarly, the "psychological world" of the individual becomes understandable and predictable when we have knowledge of his place and function in the organizational scheme of the "social world" (which is external to him) gained independently of his behavior in a particular situation. Without such specification of the social stimulus situation faced at present and *over a period in the past,* the relative weight of a particular factor in forming his opinion, behavior, or decision at a particular time is indeterminate. Thus, at a particular time, an individual's involvement with a national or international issue may be the more weighty factor in determining his vote. Intergroup conflict, which usually has a long history, may emerge as the major factor in the individual's political behavior. Individuals in increasing numbers may become involved in social movements to establish welfare states, abolish the gold standard, or free the slaves. Unless these, together with other possible modes of relatedness are investigated, the measurement of behavior in any kind of situation with any kind of technique may tell us more about the technique than about variables producing the behavior. For example, if the influence of family membership in voting is under investigation, the relationship of families to the larger sociopolitical setting has to be considered if we want to formulate, in the last analysis, a coherent picture of voting behavior. Only by relating behavior to properties and trends of the socio-political-economic-cultural setting will we be able to integrate behavioral and institutional generalizations.

Generalizations by political scientists, anthropologists, and sociologists concerning the sociocultural setting should support and strengthen findings on the psychological level. Psychological generalizations should square with generalizations reached through studying social systems independently of the behavior of particular individuals. Without adequate knowledge of the social stimulus conditions confronting man, the study of experience and behavior is apt to become esoteric. Without an adequate social psychology, the social sciences are forced to forego interpretation of behavioral data or to invent their own psychologies for specific purposes.

FIVE

ANALYSIS OF THE SOCIAL SITUATION

Now I shall pursue this discussion by asking a question fundamental to the entire problem of the individual-group relationship, a question whose answer necessarily determines the conception of that relationship: "What constitutes the social situation for the individual, represented in his interpersonal and group relations?"

One of the most thriving activities in social psychology today is what passes under the name of "small group research." The more I study this thriving activity and the resulting host of publications, the more convinced I become that they are doomed to be a collection of disjointed and incoherent artifacts so long as they are not related to a framework of fundamental orientations concerning significant and persistent problems. An analysis of what constitutes a social situation is certainly among these fundamental orientations. Because of the absence of a unifying orientation, established generalizations in social psychology today are only a tiny fraction of the total output of publications from the universities and the military and industrial establishments, whereas there are hundreds of studies published that are labeled as studies of two-person, three-person, or n-person groups, studies of decision-making, and studies of coalition formation.

These are, of course, perfectly legitimate topics of study. But can they be studied adequately without first raising the question, "What is the social situation?" For example, is it just that the number of individuals varies—and so we have dyads, or triads, or quartets? Experiments have shown that the number of people is an important factor, but it is not the only significant factor. More important for the behavioral outcome may be such considerations as the prevailing relationships among the individuals as friends, or as enemies, or as collaborators for mutual benefit in a temporary crisis situation. The degree of ego-involvement that individuals have in the problem or task at hand can also be more important than the number of individuals participating.

From G. J. DiRenzo (Ed.), *Concepts, Theory and Explanation in the Behavioral Sciences*, Chapter 3, pp. 47–72. © Copyright 1966 by Random House, Inc. Pages 56–62 reprinted by permission.

To take another illustration: is a social situation characterized by the task or problem at hand, for example, as it is introduced by an experimenter in the laboratory? Can the experimenter even adequately describe the task or problem as an isolated factor? Here the evidence is contradictory and even conflicting, as one might expect. The task or problem introduced is always a task or problem for individuals with particular experiences, particular involvements, and particular skills.

In the study of any social situation—whether the problem is the effects of the number of individuals, whether the problem is the setting or the task, or whether it is the decision-making process—the factors under study have to be taken as parts of the social situation at hand. The need for considering different aspects of a social situation as part-processes within their appropriate framework is a problem of cardinal significance and not only in social psychology. It is also of cardinal importance in the study of all psychological problems, including those traditionally considered most basic and most elemental, such as psychophysics. The point was illustrated well by Harry Helson (1964) in his address in Philadelphia in 1963 upon receiving the APA Distinguished Scientific Contribution Award:

Let me begin by recalling an episode in the early 1930's when I gave a demonstration before the Optical Society of America of the inadequacy of the CIE (Commission Internationale de l'Eclairage) method of color specification. In this demonstration, although the stimulus *qua* stimulus did not change with change in surrounding, its color could be made anything we pleased by appropriate choice of the luminance and hue of the background color. In the discussion that followed, the late Selig Hecht, perhaps the leading worker in visual science at that time, arose and said: "Why do you complicate the problems of color vision by introducing background effects, Why can't you wait until we have solved the simpler problems before we go on to the more complicated ones?"

Helson continued his address with a list of subsequent discoveries in color vision that were possible only because he did *not* wait for the solution of so-called "basic" problems, but continued investigating the problems that he had formulated as basic—the problems of background and illumination in color vision. This work led him to develop a "frame of reference psycho-physics" with a fruitful line of experiments.

Helson's point is of great relevance to our present discussion. Let us pose the question: If there is a necessity, as demonstrated by Helson and his co-workers, for studying visual perception of a single patch of color within the context of its background, how much more compelling is the same principle in studying social behavior. How much more important it becomes to consider the social situation for a two-person or *n*-person group beyond the sheer presence of the two persons or the *n*-persons.

What is the background and the stimulus context for individual behavior in a social situation? Obviously the most concrete aspect is the presence of other individuals in face-to-face relations, and for some social psychologists, as we have said, their domain of study consists only of the study of person-to-person relations in face-to-face interaction. Of course these are important.

However, persons cannot be studied in *isolation*. At no time are persons in a socio-cultural vacuum, even in their moments of greatest intimacy. They have peculiar customs of inhabiting certain places and having certain histories. If we restrict our concept of the social situation to consist only of other persons here and now, we commit a fundamental error. There is a long tradition in experimental psychology that we specify the independent variables or experimental conditions. We take it for granted that an experiment on vision or audition will specify the light and sound frequencies presented, their intensity, and whether the experimental set-up permitted other light and sound frequencies to enter. We would severely criticize an experiment on learning as a function of drive and reward that did not specify how many hours the organisms were deprived and the quantity and kind of reward to be found in the goal box, as well as the dimensions of the paths leading to the goal object.

Applying the same standards, how can we possibly say that we, as social psychologists, are interested only in "personality" variables and that this is all we shall consider? We may temper this statement by saying that "sociologists" or "anthropologists" will study the rest of it, and that we are sophisticated enough to know that there are "variations." This amounts to saying: "I know that the behavior I am studying is affected by influences that are not apparent to my naked eye nor detected by my instruments and which I, as a researcher, am not controlling. But I am only interested in what *I* see and detect here and now." Unfortunately, much of the theory and research on social interaction among different combinations of individuals is about as near-sighted as this statement suggests. It is usually justified as being a study of "basic" features of personality or "pure" interaction process.

Unfortunately, however, personality is not an isolated phenomenon; "interaction" is not "pure process" devoid of *content*, devoid of *context* and background. Person-to-person interaction must be placed in a context and background, in turn. Interpersonal relations, among friends, or lovers, or enemies, do not take place in a vacuum. They take place in a restaurant, a bedroom, or an office, or a church, or a convention hall, or on a city street; or they take place in a psychological laboratory. In recent years, our attention has been called to the fact that the subject's appraisal of a situation and the setting can affect the outcome even of a psychologcal experiment. In any culture and in any specific situation, every social situation forms a pattern or context for individual behavior. What is being done to specify this context in contemporary psychology?

One of the noteworthy developments is the simple awareness of the variety of factors that may affect social behavior. Saul Sells has emphasized the point by his attempt to list the stimulus factors that may contribute to behavior variance under general headings; he has tried, in other words, to indicate the possibility of a taxonomy of the stimulus situation. His published volume of papers on this topic, *The Stimulus Determinants of Behavior,* provided, in my opinion, a sorely needed contribution to our field. But the sheer bulk of his listings is sufficient to show us that a "taxonomy" in the form of a syllabus is not a solution to the problem, valuable as it may be as a methodological device. At latest count, there were *over* 250 factors in his list. I do not think that his purpose in compiling it was to suggest that we should permute these 250-odd factors in *factorial* research designs.

Therefore, instead of a syllabus, I venture to repeat a simple classification of *sets* of factors that, as *sets,* enter into any social situation, even though particular sub-sets and their members may be present or absent in different cultures, and even though the *range* of the sets may differ in different cultures (which, in fact, it does). Here are the sets of factors in brief form.

(1) The set of factors pertaining to *individuals who participate* in the social situation. These include:

(a) The characteristics of the individuals, such as the number of persons, their ages, their sex, their educational, occupational, economic, and social attainments.

(b) The composition of the total participants in the social situation in terms of their similarities and differences in age, sex, homogeneity as to religion, class, and so on.

(c) Relations among the participating individuals. Are they strangers, friends, rivals, and in what combinations? To what extent are their relations stable or subject to change? This is a crucial sub-set of factors. To dramatize it, we may note that it makes a big difference whether a distribution of opinions—say, 40 per cent pro, 50 per cent con, and 10 per cent undecided—represents a collection of unrelated individuals or the membership of two well-organized groups and potential adherents.

(2) The set of factors pertaining to the *task, problem,* or *activity* at hand. Man's activities are, after all, of some importance to the study of his behavior. Is his task new or familiar, simple or complex, habitual or calling for creative efforts? Is it structured or unstructured in some degree in the structured-unstructured gradation?

(3) The set of factors pertaining to the *setting and the circum-*

stances surrounding it. These include the place, the material culture of that place, the objects and tools available, the facilities, the presence or absence of other people not involved in the task or problem at hand, and notably they must include the cultural and value orientations of the setting. There are, after all, appropriate settings for work, for problem-solving, for religious conversions, and for romance. These cannot be defined apart from a background of cultural values and status and role relationships.

(4) The set of factors pertaining to *each individual participant's particular relation to the above three sets of factors*. These include, among other things, his proficiency in the task or problem at hand, the degree of his enduring involvement in the problem, his attitudes toward other participants, his feelings of ease or discomfort in the situation, and so on.

One way of attempting to deal with these four sets of factors would be to vary the components of each set. If you are prepared to undertake this venture, you also should be aware that the relative *weights* or contribution of each to the behavioral outcome may vary in the following ways:

(1) The relative weights of different sets of factors may vary in different cultures. In fact, in different cultures the number of different factors and the range of different factors do vary.

(2) Within any given culture—including within the microculture of the psychological laboratory—the weights of different factors may vary. Thus, the task may be very important if the individuals are strangers and unfamiliar with the task; on the other hand, it may be a minor detail if they are comfortable companions and if the task is within the range of their experience.

(3) Finally, the relative weights, or significance, of the individuals participating, of the task or problem, and of the setting in which events take place vary according to the *temporal sequence* of events. This is a problem that we, as social psychologists, have left to the developmental area. But it is equally crucial in terms of the development of interpersonal, intergroup, and intercultural relationships. What may be crucial today—the old patterns of interaction and the old conceptions of tasks—may be "old hat" tomorrow. The problems of getting acquainted among strangers, for example, may give way to the efforts of interested parties and rivals to gain the day. Unlike "pure interaction" or "pure psychological process," the patterning of social life, and thus the patterning of the social stimulus situations for its participants, do not stay put with fixed and immutable weights.

I have, quite deliberately, concentrated so far on the various sets of factors and their variable weightings in social situations, because the overwhelming tendency among psychologists has been to over-simplify the context in which the individual-group relationship takes place. The traditional and sharp dichotomy between individual versus group appears hopelessly naive when we engage in the effort of analyzing the context of the social situation.

However, I should not like to leave the impression that the variability of the social situation means that no regularities are exhibited, nor the impression that prediction of behavior is therefore impossible. On the contrary, the social sciences have already, even in their infancy, demonstrated that certain variables are persistently weighty ones and that knowledge about these variables has striking predictive value for the student of individual behavior.

PART II

EXPERIMENTAL MODELS
FOR SOCIAL INTERACTION

S I X

SOME SOCIAL FACTORS IN PERCEPTION:
THE ORIENTATION

I. PROBLEM

That individuals may react differently to the same stimulus situations has become a truism in psychology. There are cases in which such internal factors as drive, attitude, affect, or emotional upset play the dominating part in determining the experiences and subsequent behavior. The concern of this study in social psychology is to note some social factors participating in the production of such differential response on the part of individuals.

Social psychology has studied individual differences in *response* to a social environment, but it has never recognized that each one of us *perceives* this environment in terms of his own personal habits of perceiving; and that cultural groups may differ from one another in behavior, because of fundamental differences in their ways of perceiving social situations. In the following paragraphs some cases reported by cultural anthropologists, revealing such differential group effects, will be reviewed. The psychological problem which they raise is the starting point for the experiments reported in this paper.

II. A REVIEW OF SOME OBSERVATIONS
OF CULTURAL ANTHROPOLOGISTS

Whatever society we take, no matter how primitive or developed, simple or complicated, we find standards, norms, conventions, customs, and values regulating to a great extent the conduct and shaping the mentalities, likes and dislikes of its members along economic, aesthetic, social, moral, political and other lines.

The individual acquires a certain set of norms from childhood on, no matter whether he wishes to do so or not, and *whether he is conscious*

From "A Study of Some Social Factors in Perception," *Archives of Psychology*, 1935, No. 187.

of the fact or not. Sapir (1928) has given a subtle analysis of this point in a recent symposium. These norms determine to a considerable extent the individual's ideas of good or bad, right or wrong, beautiful or ugly, and likewise his perceptual tendencies; *e.g., which aspects of a field of stimulation he will accentuate and which he will ignore.* For instance (to use the illustration cited by Sapir), a foreigner looking at the activities of a "primitive" group will often single out certain aspects that will be passed unnoticed by the natives as unimportant, or he will fail to notice certain parts that will be in the foreground from the point of view of the natives.

The norms may vary from society to society and from time to time. These variations may be comparatively slight within a given range, as is the case with societies belonging to the same culture (*e.g.,* Western culture), or they may be astoundingly great, as is the case with societies belonging to different cultures. The variation in norms and in perceiving, thinking, and reacting, may be so great that the norms appear stupid, and contrary to all notions of *"common sense,"* to a person whose thinking and behavior are regulated by norms of a different culture.

Some concrete cases showing wide differences from the norms of Western culture will show the point clearly. In order to emphasize the fact that these wide variations in norms are not restricted to the generally accepted variations in taste, fashion, social etiquette, standards, and manners of living, highly complicated aesthetic forms, and other affective phenomena alone, but that they are observed in cases relating to more psychological categories, the illustrations are chosen from the fields of space and time perception and experience of sense-quality.

We may start with a case of time reckoning. Radcliffe-Brown (1922, p. 311) reports:

> In the jungles of the Andamans it is possible to recognize a distinct succession of odours during a considerable part of the year as one after another the commoner trees and lianas come into flower. . . . The Andamanese have therefore adopted an original method of marking the different periods of the year by means of the odoriferous flowers that are in bloom at different times. *Their calendar is a calendar of scents.* (Emphasis ours.)

Here we see odors serving as *reference points* for time reckoning in place of the astronomical events so widely used. As Radcliffe-Brown explains, the odors play an important role, connected with magic, in the life of the Andamans. Therefore they are very sensitive to odors.

Different objects or events may be chosen to serve as reference points for time reckoning. Leona Cope (1919) gives some interesting cases:

> The Indian seems vaguely aware of the discrepancy between his lunar reckoning and solar year. Many tribes have no way of correcting their year count. In the calendars which have only twelve months, the Indians may unconsciously lengthen a month when it does not tally with the event for which

it is named, or they may insert another period. That the discrepancy was felt is shown by frequent references in the literature of the Indians to discussion and quarrels about which month it is or ought to be at a given time. The arguments apparently continue in such cases until, *through a comparison with the natural phenomena, matters are set right* (p. 137). (Emphasis ours.)

In another case sticks, standing for astronomical events, serve to supply reference points. "Often when the Indians agreed on a meeting at a particular time, they arranged bundles of sticks, from which they destroyed one for each day or night as it passed. When the last stick was gone they knew the appointed time had come. This method seems to have been common in the Southeast Woodlands and the Southwest." (Cope, 1919, p. 124).

A very striking case of variation in the experiencing of similarity has been observed by Malinowski. From his study of the Trobriands, Malinowski (1927) reports that the idea of resemblance between parents and offspring, or between children of the same parents, is controlled by strict social norms, which controvert evidence and our expectations in two respects.

First, resemblance to the father is considered "natural, right and proper. . . . Such similarity is always assumed and affirmed to exist." But it is a great offense to hint that a child resembles its mother or any of its maternal kinfolk. "It is a phrase of serious bad language to say 'Thy face is thy sister's,' which is the worst combination of kinship similarity."

Second, it is a dogma, with almost the strength of a taboo, that even brothers do not resemble one another, although each is said to be exactly like the father. Malinowski relates an incident illustrative of this. When he commented on the striking likeness of two brothers, "there came such a hush over all the assembly, while the brother present withdrew abruptly and the company was half-embarrassed, half-offended at this breach of custom." In another case, five sons of a chief were said to be exactly like the father. When Malinowski "pointed out that this similarity to the father implied similarity among each other, such a heresy was indignantly repudiated." (1927, pp. 87–92).

Here we see the influence of a taboo removing a perceptual relationship that might have been experienced otherwise, and a positive norm emphasizing a similarity which might not otherwise have been noticed.

The observations of the anthropological field workers *indicate that there is no strict finality* about the psychological color pyramid. *Cultural norms may determine at least slightly different color pyramids for different groups of people,* showing once more that there is no such thing as a generalized "normal *adult* human psychology." A quotation from Boas (1911) and some cases from other field observers will make the point clear.

For instance, it has been observed that colors are classified according to their similarities in quite distinct groups, without any accompanying differences in the ability to differentiate shades of color. What we call green or blue are often combined under some such term as "gall-like color," or yellow and green are combined into one concept, which may be "young-leaves color." The importance of the fact that in thought and speech these color-names convey the impression of quite different groups of sensations can hardly be over-rated (p. 199).

To give a concrete case, Margaret Mead reports of groups whom she studied, "Their color classifications are so different that they saw yellow, olive-green, blue-green, gray and lavender as variations of one color" (1933, p. 638). Likewise Wallis reports: "Not infrequently the savage *ignores* distinctions observed by us or cross-sections our distinctions. This frequently happens in color designations. The Ashantis have distinct names for the colors black, red, and white. The term *black* is also used for *any dark color,* such as blue, purple, brown, etc., while the term red does duty for pink, orange and yellow" (1926, p. 421).

From customs, traditions, and values which standardize our social attitudes one could furnish innumerable striking cases. But we shall restrict ourselves to a single example.

Sombre colors and depressed feelings are closely connected in our minds, although not in those of peoples of foreign culture. Noise seems inappropriate in a place of sadness, although among primitive people the loud wail of the mourner is a natural expression of grief" (Mead, 1933, p. 228).

In such a group it would show lack of understanding and be almost abnormal if one kept quiet and did not participate in the wailing. The famous Japanese smile at situations where the Westerner would show distress is pertinent in this connection. Therefore, there may be a great deal of truth in the statement of Benedict (1934) that "the definition of abnormality is to a great extent culturally determined," which follows as a corollary of the cultural determination of norms.

As any person who has observed two different cultures will agree, we could multiply these examples indefinitely. These are not weird and exceptional cases. They are articulate examples of differences in outlook due to variations in cultural norms. Neither are they anecdotes from the fond observations of curiosity seekers. To an individual who is brought up in accordance with a particular sort of norm about time, color resemblance, or family resemblance, these experiences are as "natural" as Arabic numerals are to us.[1] On the other hand, many norms or reference

---

[1] There is a profitable discussion of the development of number concepts in C. H. Judd's *Psychology of Social Institutions* (1926), which is appropriate in this connection for the fact that man did not find the numbers we use today, but developed them in the course of long history.

points observed in Western culture may look strange to a person who has not been brought up in it.

These variations in norms raise the problem whether the minds of primitive peoples operate in the same or in a different way from those brought up in Western culture. Some authorities like Levy-Bruhl think the primitive mind is in the "pre-logical" stage. This concept is futile, for when we examine the facts closely, the nucleus of all perceiving and thinking lies in established norms or reference points. What seemed pre-logical or illogical at first sight, ceases to be so. The whole problem is reduced to the relativity of established norms.

Reference points may change in the same individual. Some recent studies on attitudes (Allport, 1932) have verified the common observation that a person in this culture may give altogether opposite judgments about the same question. The same person says that he *is* opposed to playing cards and that he is *not* opposed to playing cards. If we take this rigidly and do not notice the connections in which they are given, these judgments appear illogical. But when we note the connections in which they are given, we see beyond the apparent contradiction. *As a member* of a certain church he is opposed to playing cards, but *as an individual* he has no objection, indicating two different reference points. In the same way, even the case Malinowski cites, which may look so absurd at first glance, may reduce itself to the existence of two sets of frames of reference. In both cases the culture provides the major premises. In one case it is the established tradition which dictates that a man resembles his father, and hence this sort of relationship is sought for and even assumed.

To secure objectivity in studying these social psychological matters, the social psychologist or sociologist has to acquire a certain "distance" from the norms which are implanted in him as a member of a group; otherwise his judgments will not be anything more than a collection of normative verdicts.

Now we are prepared to raise our problem in a more specific form. Since the variations in customs, attitudes, fashions, and standards can be summarized partly in terms of the relativity of social norms or frames of reference, the problem becomes essentially: *What is the psychological basis of these norms* or frames of reference, and how do they work? The specific task of this study becomes a psychological study of frames of reference. It is not the writer's aim to reach a short-cut generalization concerning the extremely difficult problem of the psychological basis of social norms. The task he sets for himself is to survey the results of some major psychological experiments having a bearing on the concept of reference points and to demonstrate experimentally the way in which the conclusions derived from these studies may be profitably extended to the formulation of problems in social psychology. Therefore, the work claims only to be an approach, which may be one of the steps toward a psychological explanation of the functioning of social norms.

If social psychology is to be psychological, it has to base itself on the results of experimental psychology and thus connect itself with the main bulk of psychology. Unfortunately this has not been the case with social psychology for the most part. It may be sufficient for the cultural anthropologist and sociologist to show the variations in individuals due to differences in culture and let it go at that. But it is just *at this point* that the main task of the social psychologist begins. It is his task to study the genetic development of these social and cultural effects in the individual, the perceptual problem of how the individual responds to the stimulus situations which involve social factors, and the learning problem as to how they become organized in him.

Already some real progress has been made towards a sound social psychology in the work of Piaget (1928, 1932). Tracing the transition from the predominantly autistic stage to the "logical" stage by following the language development of the child in a natural setting, he has shown us the *development of "communicable," logical thinking*, which becomes a problem of social psychology. For, as Piaget points out, what is considered *socially* logical, chiefly consists of sticking consistently to a *point of view* throughout, and these *points of view* are the socially accepted norms, which become also norms for the child through cooperation with others and through imposition on the child of definite responsibilities after he passes a certain age. In the "Moral Judgment of the Child" (1932) Piaget shows how the child, who does not at first draw a line between himself and his environment, whose behavior follows chiefly the "pleasure principle," and who at the start does not see that there are *rules of the game*, comes to realize that there are rules of the game if he wants to play with others, and that he stands in *certain relationships* to others, implying definite responsibilities. Such contributions make the development of logical thinking and the development of moral judgment into genuine psychological problems.

III. A REVIEW OF SOME EXPERIMENTAL FACTS IN PSYCHOLOGY

If one reviews experimental results from many different laboratories over a long period of time with the concept of reference point, or frame of reference, in mind, one cannot help noticing a convergence of findings. A brief review of these results is the special task of this section.

Before presenting these, it will be a useful introduction to mention another line of experiment, the work of Külpe and his followers on abstraction. We refer to the experiments in Külpe's laboratory beginning in 1900, on the influence of *Aufgabe* (task or instruction) on perception of stimuli presented. In these experiments he tachistoscopically presented to his subjects different stimuli, such as printed syllables. about which different aspects or "dimensions" could be reported; *e.g.*, the *number* of letters involved, the *locations* of the colors, or the *total pattern* composed by them. Külpe (1904) found that more items were noted and more correct judgments were made by the subject about that aspect of the stimuli which was called for in the *Aufgabe*. In other words, individuals notice more fully and more in detail the aspects of the stimulus-field that they set themselves to see or that they are set to see by instructions. Subsequently Yokoyama (Boring, 1924) and Chapman (1932) verified Külpe's results. All these experiments indicate that "the efficiency of report for all tasks is lower under an indefinite *Aufgabe* than under a definite instruction."

The set or attitude plays an important part in the field of perceptual organization, picking up certain parts in the field of stimulation as reference points. This is especially true in cases where the field of stimulation is not well structured. This is well illustrated in the following passage from Köhler (1930):

> There are cases in which all attempts to destroy, in actual analysis, a given form in favor of a certain other form are in vain. But distribute the furniture of a room in an irregular manner through this room; you will have rather solid and stable units, the single objects, but no equally stable and firm *groups* will be formed spontaneously with those objects as members. You observe that one group formation is easily displaced by another, depending upon slight changes of conditions, probably in yourself. It is evident that, under such circumstances, the *influence of changes in the subjective attitude* towards the field will be much higher than in the case of the solid units or stable groups. Even forces of no peculiar intensity will now be strong enough to produce new groups in a field which—with the exception of the objects in it—does not resist very much because its interior tendencies of group formation are too weak (p. 155). (Second emphasis ours.)

Such cases are of practical value in social psychology. When we observe with historical perspective, we notice that different people living in the same geographical area, facing the same nature, at different periods, may have, as we have seen, different sorts of time and space classifications, because different parts of nature were "standardized" as their frames of reference.

In the following paragraphs a brief historical review of the concept of reference points (or frames of reference) in experimental psychology will be given. The relationship implied in reference points is at the basis of the experiments reported in this study. "Reference point" is not a hypothetical concept. We find it involved in the comparatively simple forms of perception such as localization of a point on the skin and in visual perception of the localization of a short line. We find it involved in judgment, in psychophysics proper, in affectivity, and in personality, as some recent studies show. Let us review them briefly.

Henri studied localization on the skin over a period of years, 1892–

1897. He carried on his experiment at the Sorbonne first in 1892–1894, under the direction of Binet, and continued his experiments at Leipzig in 1894. Among his subjects were Külpe, Judd, Meumann, and Kiesow. He concluded that there are certain definite places that *form a frame of localization*. Spots are localized nearer these points of reference. The errors of localization take place accordingly. In Henri's (1895) own words, "*presque toujours l'erreur de localisation est commise dans la direction des points de repère que le suject a employés pour localiser le contact*" (p. 177). (Emphasis in the original.)

Henri carried the work further. In his dissertation at Göttingen (1897), he reports that when the subject uses one reference point (*point de repère* or *Anhaltspunkt*) within a cutaneous area, there appears a *constancy* in the direction of errors. With the shift of *Anhaltspunkte* there appears a corresponding shift in the direction of the errors of localization. This work is so basic in localization that it seems necessary to quote Henri at some length in connection with his description of the *variations in the error of localization with the shifts of reference points* (Anhaltspunkte).

Wenn man die Lokalisationsfehler betrachtet, so fällt sofort eine Konstanz in der Richtung der Fehler auf; in der grossen Mehrzahl der Fälle ist der Punkt zu nahe an irgend einer hervorragenden Stelle (Leiste, Knöchel, Rand, Gelenk, etc.) angegeben, und wenn die Versuchsperson für einen Punkt immer dieselben *Anhaltspunkte* braucht, so entsteht eine Konstanz in der Richtung der Fehler. Es giebt aber Punkte, für die es keine konstante Richtung der Fehler giebt, diese sind Punkte, welche die Versuchsperson in Bezug auf verschiedene *Anhaltspunkte* lokalisiert. Wenn z. B. der Punkt in der Mitte des Handrückens liegt, so schätzt die Versuchsperson manchmal die Entfernung zum Handgelenke, manchmal aber zu den Metacarpalköpfen oder zu den Sehnen der Finger, daher wird der Punkt in manchen Fällen zu nahe zum Handgelenke, in anderen Fällen zu nahe an die Finger verlegt. Im allgemeinen wird die Richtung des begangenen Fehlers durch die Unterschätzung der Distanz des Punktes von gewissen *Anhaltspunkte* bestimmt (pp. 37–38).

In subjective preferences we find the establishment of a *standard or reference point,* which is *peculiar to each individual.* Wells (1928) found this in an experiment in which he asked his subjects to arrange a series of pictures in order according to their preferences. Wells sums up the point thus: "If A and B arranged 10 pieces of music in order of preference, the *orders would center about each individual's own standard;* but if A, B, C, D, etc., arranged ten graduated weights the orders would theoretically all center about a common standard, the *objective order* of heaviness" (p. 172). (Emphasis ours.)

Hollingworth (1910) found the *establishment of a median value* in the comparison of sizes. "In the experiment on sensible discrimination we *become adapted to the median value* of the series, *tend to expect it, to assimilate* all other values toward it, and to greater or less degree to substitute it for them" (p. 468). (Emphasis ours.)

Gestalt psychologists furnish an infinite number of instances of *Verankerung* (frame of reference) by their insistence on the *member-character* of a part within an organized structure. Wertheimer (1925) in 1912 demonstrated that a line is experienced as horizontal or vertical in reference to the position of other things in the field of stimulation. Thus if the observer's visual field were objectively slanted by means of a mirror, a similarly slanted objective line tended to appear vertical, indicating that the position of an object is not perceived in respect to that object alone, but *by its relation* to the whole organized field.

Koffka made a special issue of the notions of "member-character" and "Verankerungspunkte" (anchorage points), and the importance of the ground for the figure. He summarized the facts and the argument on this point by saying, "all this means that a definite *single position exists only within a fixed spatial level. If the conditions for the formation of such a level are absent, localization is no longer possible;* for just as the level grows unstable, so does the single point within it" (1922, p. 570). (Emphasis ours.)

In discussing the ground (in relation to *figure*) he states,

. . . the ground has a very important function of its own; it serves as a general level (niveau) upon which the figure appears. Now figure and ground form a structure, consequently the former cannot be independent of the latter. On the contrary, the quality of the figure must be largely determined by the general level upon which it appears. This is a universal fact, observed in such products of culture as fashion and style. The same dress which is not only smart, but nice to look at, almost a thing of beauty, may become intolerable after the mode has passed (p. 566).

The ground is especially important in social psychology. Studies on social facilitation would gain much more sense if the subtle relationship between figure and ground were taken into consideration. For example, when two people are talking in a public place, their conversation and behavior are tinged by the properties of the whole "atmosphere."

In a recent article Lewin (1935b) shows the strength of the tendency to be "anchored" to a frame of reference ("ground"), of which the most important part is the social group to which one belongs. He also shows how every action one performs has some specific "background" and is determined by that background.

Beebe-Center (1932), who has done comprehensive work on affectivity, reports the relativity of affective judgments with a striking case. The observers were to judge pairs of stimuli. They were instructed to state in the case of each pair not only which stimulus was the more pleasant, but whether each was pleasant, indifferent or unpleasant. One observer reported that both stimuli were indifferent, yet one was more pleasant than the other. A sheer case of "illogic"—the same thing, indifferent and pleasant at the same time! The experimenter investigated the case further. He found that the observer had visualized a scale in his mind. The upper part represented pleasantness, the middle *part* (*not* the middle *point*) indifference, and the lower part unpleasantness. He placed the two stimuli in the middle within the indifference range, so reported "indifferent." Yet within the indifference range, one stimulus was above; *i.e.*, nearer to the pleasantness range, and accordingly he reported it as pleasanter. So the "illogic" turns out to be a perfectly natural case of *member-character. In relation to the whole scale,* both are indifferent; *in relation to each other,* one is more pleasant. Therefore, it is perfectly good logic, if the frames of reference are taken into consideration. This relational effect is not restricted to a few individual cases of affectivity alone. It applies to a whole array of facts that come under hedonic contrast.

The notion of the level of reference is becoming effectively utilized in the field of personality. Hoppe's (1930) work using the concepts of aspiration level (Anspruchsniveau) and ego level, and Frank's (1935) more quantitative work on the basis of these concepts are already steps in this direction.

From the point of view of its bearing on our own experiments, the general conclusion reached on the basis of the recent work on "absolute judgment" or single stimuli in psychophysics is important. This method goes back to Fechner, and to Woodworth and Thorndike's (1900) joint work. Wever and Zener (1926) revived it recently, and subsequent work has been carried on by Fernberger (1931), Bressler (1933), Pratt (1933), and others. These investigations show that in psychophysical judgments *the use of a standard stimulus is not a necessary condition to permit the observer to give a judgment about any stimulus in the series. After a few rounds of presentation, the observers establish a scale. The position of a stimulus is judged against the background of that scale.* Again we see a basic field of work in which frame of reference is involved.

In closing this review a case reported by Wever and Zener (1926) is pertinent. Using the method of "absolute judgment" or single stimuli, they gave an observer a "light" series of weights (84, 88, 92, 96 and 100 grams); after this series became an "established" scale for the observer, they suddenly introduced a "heavy" series (92, 96, 100, 104 and 108 grams). "The effect of the first series on the judgments of the second was quite evident for 20 or 25 presentations; *i.e.*, for four or five rounds judgments of the "heavy" *predominated* for all the stimuli; from this point on, however, the *judgments showed a redistribution* conforming to the second stimulus series." In other words, when for a stimulus (*e.g.*, 96 grams) the *"light series"* (*84–100 grams*) *is the frame of reference, the stimulus is experienced as heavy, but when the same stimulus is related to a heavy series, it is experienced as light.*

From this review one may conclude that a frame of reference is involved not only in perception or localization, but also in other psychological phenomena. Perhaps it may be involved in all psychological phenomena. If facts support this view, as there is reason to believe as the problem now stands, the psychologist will find in this tendency to experience things in a *relational* way, a sound foundation on which to build his social psychology.

After surveying several observations from the anthropological field workers, we had come to the conclusion that the diversity of patterns in different cultures may be expressed partly as differences in norms, or frames of reference. In the review that we have just made we have found the frame of reference a very important concept, the implications of which ran through many experimental findings. The relativity of norms in the social field on the one hand, and the implications of the frame of reference in psychological phenomena on the other hand, form the background for our experiments. They are useful for us at least in furnishing hypotheses for experimental test.

SEVEN

FORMATION OF SOCIAL NORMS:
THE EXPERIMENTAL PARADIGM

PROBLEM OF NORM FORMATION

Now, coming to concrete life situations, we find norms wherever we find an organized society, primitive or complicated. . . . We shall consider customs, traditions, standards, rules, values, fashions and all other criteria of conduct which are standardized as a consequence of the interaction of individuals as specific cases of "social norms." . . . These norms serve as focal points in the experience of the individual, and subsequently as guides for his actions. This need not always be a conscious function; many times it is effective without our awareness of it. We see the evidence of its effectiveness by its results, that is, in the behavior of the individual. The daily routine of everyday life is regulated to a large extent by the social norms in each society. As long as life with its many aspects is well settled and runs more or less smoothly from day to day, very few doubt the validity of the existing norms; very few challenge their authority. And the few who challenge them are considered to be doubting Thomases, eccentrics, trouble makers, or lunatics, and are reacted against with varying degrees of scorn or violence.

But when social life becomes difficult and there are stresses and tensions in the lives of many people in the community, the equilibrium of life ceases to be stable, and the air is pregnant with possibilities. . . . Under these delicate conditions the strength of the norms incorporated in the individual becomes uncertain and liable to break down. Such a delicate, unstable situation is the fertile soil for the rise of doubts concerning the existing norms, and a challenge to their authority. The doubt and the challenge which no one would listen to before, now become effective. These are times of transition from one state to another, from one norm or set of norms to another. The transition is not simply from the orderliness of one set of norms to chaos, but from one set of norms to a new set of norms, perhaps through a stage of uncertainty, confusion, and at times even violence. . . .

As a result of the strain and stress, of the confusion and uncertainty and feeling of insecurity, there may be action and reaction, apparent stability followed by fresh instability. The outcome is the final emergence or establishment of a stable set of norms having the status of standards. . . .

The study of the process of emergence or standardization of norms in actual life situations is an extremely complicated task. There are so many variables involved that cannot be directly observed. It may, therefore, pay us in the long run to start first with the study of the psychology of norm formation in a general way in a well-controlled laboratory situation. Yet what we shall undertake is really the study of the general psychological process involved in the formation of any norm, and not simply the explanation of the psychology of one particular norm. The test for such an approach lies in the applicability of the principle reached to the description and explanation of norms found in actual social life. Whether or not this is just one more psychological abstraction or laboratory artifact, which does not have anything to do with the true psychology of the formation of norms that are effective in everyday life, can be decided after it has met facts in the fresh and wholesome air of actualities. . . .

HYPOTHESIS TO BE TESTED

We have seen that if a reference point is lacking in the external field of stimulation, it is established internally as the temporal sequence of presentation of stimuli goes on. Accordingly we raise the problem: What will an individual do when he is placed in an objectively unstable situation in which all basis of comparison, as far as the external field of stimulation is concerned, is absent? In other words, what will he do when the external frame of reference is eliminated, insofar as the aspect in which we are interested is concerned? Will he give a hodgepodge of erratic judgments? Or will he establish a point of reference of his own? *Consistent* results in this situation may be taken as the index of a subjectively evolved frame of reference.

We must first study the tendency of the individual. We must begin with the individual in order to do away with the dualism between "individual psychology" and "social psychology." In this way we can find the differences between individual responses in the individual situation and in the group situation.

Coming to the social level we can push our problem further. What will a group of people do in the same unstable situation? Will the different individuals in the group give a hodgepodge of judgments? Or will they establish a collective frame of reference? If so, of what sort? If every person establishes a norm, will it be his own norm and different from the norms of others in the group? Or will there be established a common norm peculiar to the particular group situation and depending upon the presence of these individuals together and their influence upon one another? If they in time come to perceive the uncertain and unstable situation which they face in common in such a way as to give it some sort of order, perceiving it as order by a frame of reference developed among them in the course of the experiment, and if this frame of reference is peculiar to the group, then we may say that we have at least the prototype of the psychological process involved in the formation of a norm in a group.

THE AUTOKINETIC EFFECT: ITS POSSIBILITIES FOR OUR PROBLEM

With these considerations clearly in mind, our first task has been to find objectively unstable situations that would permit themselves to be structured in several ways, depending on the character of the subjectively established reference points. From among other possible experimental situations that could be used to test our hypothesis, we chose to use the situation that is suitable to produce autokinetic effects, as meeting the requirements demanded by our hypothesis.

The conditions that produce the autokinetic effect afford an excellent experimental situation to test our hypothesis. We can easily get the autokinetic effect. In complete darkness, such as is found in a closed room that is not illuminated, or on a cloudy night in the open when there are no other lights visible, a single small light seems to move, and it may appear to move erratically in all directions. If you present the point of light repeatedly to a person, he may see the light appearing at different places in the room each time, especially if he does not know the distance between himself and the light. The experimental production of the autokinetic effect is very easy and works without any exception, provided, of course, that the person does not use special devices to destroy the effect. For in a completely dark room a single point of light *cannot* be localized definitely, because there is nothing in reference to which you can locate it. The person looking at the light knows perfectly well that the light is not moving. These are facts which are not subject to controversy; any one can easily test them for himself. In this situation not only does the stimulating light appear erratic and irregular to the subject, but at times the person himself feels insecure about his spatial bearing. This comes out in an especially striking way if he is seated in a chair without a back and is unfamiliar with the position of the experimental room in the building. Under these conditions some subjects report that they are not only confused about the location of the light; they are even confused about the stability of their own position.

The autokinetic effect is not a new artificial phenomenon invented by the psychologists. It is older than experimental psychology. Since it sometimes appears in the observation of the heavenly bodies, the astronomers had already noticed it and offered theories to explain it.

We have studied the influence of such social factors as *suggestion* and the *group situation* on the extent and direction of the experimental movement. The study of the extent of the experienced movements permits a quantitative study for the approach to the formation of norms. We shall therefore report on the extent of movement.

PROCEDURE

We have studied the extent of the movement experienced in two situations: (1) when alone, except for the experimenter (in order to get the reaction of the individual unaffected by other experimentally introduced social factors, and thus to gain a basic notion about the perceptual process under the circumstances); and (2) when the individual is in a group situation (in order to discover modifications brought about by membership in the group).

The subject was introduced into the group situation in two ways: (1) He was brought into a group situation after being experimented upon when alone. This was done to find out the influence of the group situation after he had an opportunity to react to the situation first in accordance with his own tendencies and had ordered it subjectively in his own way. (2) He was first introduced to the situation in the group, having no previous familiarity with the situation at all, and afterwards experimented upon individually. This was done to find out whether the perceptual order or norm that might be established in the group situation would continue to determine his reaction to the same situation when he faced it alone. This last point is crucial for our problem. The others lead up to it and clarify its implications.

The subjects, apparatus, and procedures used will be only briefly outlined here. They are reported in full elsewhere (Sherif, 1935). The experiments were carried on in dark rooms in the Columbia University psychological laboratory. The subjects were graduate and undergraduate male students at Columbia University and New York University. They were not majoring in psychology. They did not know anything about the physical stimulus setup, or the purpose of the experiment. There were nineteen subjects in the individual experiments; forty subjects took part in the group experiments.

INDIVIDUAL EXPERIMENTS

The stimulus light was a tiny point of light seen through a small hole in a metal box. The light was exposed to the subject by the opening of a small shutter controlled by the experimenter. The distance between the subject and the light was five meters. The observer was seated at a table on which was a telegraph key. The following instructions were given in written form: "When the room is completely dark, I shall give you the signal *Ready*, and then show you a point of light. After a short time the light will start to move. As soon as you see it move, press the key. A few seconds later the light will disappear. Then tell me the distance it moved. Try to make your estimates as accurate as possible."

These instructions summarize the general procedure of the experiment. A short time after the light was exposed following the *Ready* signal, the subject pressed the key; this produced a faint but audible ticking in the timing apparatus indicating that the subject had perceived the (autokinetic) movement. The exposure time, after the subject pressed the key to indicate that he had begun to experience the movement, was two seconds in all cases. The light was physically stationary during the entire time and was not moved at all during any of the experiments.

After the light had disappeared, the subject reported orally the distance through which it had moved as he experienced it. The experimenter recorded each judgment as soon as it was spoken by the subject, writing each one on a separate sheet of a small paper pad. One hundred judgments were obtained from each subject. The subjects reported their estimates in inches (or fractions of inches).

The quantitative results are reported elsewhere. Here we shall present only the conclusions reached on the basis of these quantitative results, and give some important introspections that clarify these conclusions further.

The results unequivocally indicate that when individuals perceive movements which lack any other standard of comparison, *they subjectively establish a range of extent and a point (a standard or norm) within that range which is peculiar to the individual,* that may differ from the range and point (standard or norm) established by other individuals. In other words, when individuals repeatedly perceive movement which offers no objective basis for gauging the extent of movement, there develops within them, in the course of a succession of presentations, a standard (norm or reference point). This subjectively established standard or norm serves as a reference point with which each successive experienced movement is compared and judged to be short, long, or medium—within the range peculiar to the subject.

To express the point more generally, we conclude that in the absence of an objective range or scale of stimuli and an externally given reference point or standard, each individual builds up a range of his own and an internal (subjective) reference point within that range, and each successive judgment is given within that range and in relation to that reference point. The range and reference point established by each individual are peculiar to himself when he is experimented upon alone.

In the second series of the individual experiments, it was found that once a *range*, and a point of reference within that range, is established by an individual, there is a tendency to preserve these in the experiments on subsequent days. A second and third series of 100 judgments each show a median score for a given subject which is very similar to that found in the first series, but with a reduced variability.

The written introspective reports obtained from every observer at the end of the experiment further corroborate these conclusions based

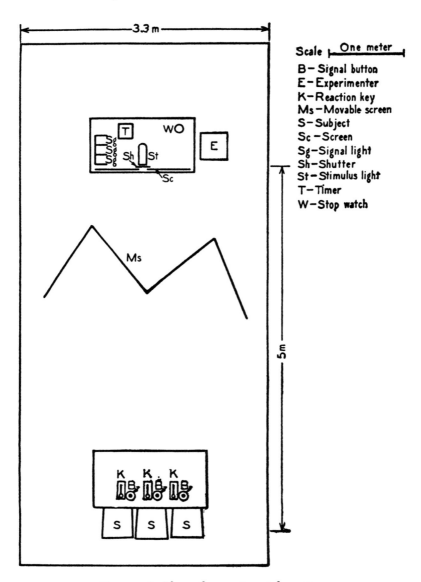

Figure 1. Plan of experimental room.

upon the quantitative results. Introspections of the following sort, which are typical, show that the subjects first found it hard to estimate distance because of the lack of externally given reference points or standards:

"Darkness left no guide for distance."

"It was difficult to estimate the distance the light moved, because of the lack of visible neighboring objects."

"There was no fixed point from which to judge distance."

Introspections of the following sort indicate that the subjects developed standards of their own in the absence of objective ones:

"Compared with previous distance."

"Used first estimate as standard."

This reveals once more the general psychological tendency to experience things in relation to some frame of reference. What we did in the group experiments was to carry this finding of experimental psychology into social psychology and note how it operates when the individual is in a group situation.

GROUP EXPERIMENTS

On the basis of the results given, the problem which we must study in the group situation becomes self-evident. The individual experiences the external field of stimulation in relation to a frame of reference. When a frame of reference is given in the objective situation, this will usually determine in an important way the structural relationships of the experience; in such cases all other parts will be organized as determined or modified by it. But at times such an objective frame of reference is lacking—the field of stimulation is unstable, vague, and not well structured. In this case the individual perceives the situation as shaped by his own internally evolved frame of reference. The questions that arise for the experiment in the group situation, then, are the following:

How will an individual who is found in the group situation perceive the stimulus field? Will there evolve in him again a range and a standard (norm) within that range that will be peculiar to him, as was the case when individuals were experimented on alone? Or will group influences prevent him from establishing any well-defined range and reference point within that range, and thus spoil his capacity to perceive the uncertain situation in any sort of order? Or will the individuals in the group act together to establish a range, and a reference point within that range, which are peculiar to the group? If such a range and reference point are established, what will be the influence of such a group product on the individual member when he subsequently faces the same stimulus situation alone?

The questions outlined above represent more or less pure cases. There are, of course, other possibilities that lie between these pure cases.

With these questions, we face directly the psychological basis of social norms. We must admit that we have reduced the process to a very simple form. But the first fundamental psychological problem is the way an individual perceives a stimulus situation. The behavior follows upon this perception rather than upon the bald physical presence of the stimulus. There is no simple and direct correlation between the stimulus and the subsequent behavior, especially on the level of behavior with which we are dealing. A simple perceptual situation is the first requirement for experimental analysis of the problem.

We purposely chose a stimulus situation in which the external factors are unstable enough, within limits, to allow the internal factors to furnish the dominating role in establishing the main characteristics of organization. This enables us to say that any consistent product in the experience of the individual members of the group, differing from their experience as isolated individuals, is a function of their interaction in the group.

We do not face stimulus situations involving other people, or even the world of nature around us, in an indifferent way; we are charged with certain modes of readiness, certain established norms, which enter to modify our reactions. This important consideration shaped the planning of the group experiments. We studied the differences between the reactions (a) when the individuals first faced our stimulus situation in the group, and (b) when they faced the group situation after first establishing their individual ranges and norms in the individual situation. Accordingly, twenty of the subjects began with the individual situation and were then put into groups in subsequent experimental sessions; the other twenty started with group sessions and ended with individual sessions.

This rotation technique enabled us to draw conclusions regarding the following important questions: How much does the individual carry over from his individually established way of reacting to a later situation when facing the same stimulus in the group? How much will he be influenced by his membership in the group after once his range and norm have been established individually when alone? How will he experience the situation when alone, after a common range and norm have been established peculiar to the group of which he is a member? In short, will the common product developed in the group serve as a determining factor when he subsequently faces the same situation *alone?*

The experimental setting was in general the same as in previous experiments. Of course, additional techniques were necessary to handle two or more members of a group at the same time. One major addition was the use of signal lights. As the subjects were new to the experimenter, he could not tell from the voice alone who was giving a judgment. So as each subject gave his judgment aloud, he pressed a push button connected with a dim signal light of a particular color by which the experimenter might know who the speaker was.

There were eight groups of two subjects each and eight groups of three subjects each. Four groups in each of the two categories started with the individual situation (one whole session for each individual), and then functioned as groups. Four groups in each category started in group situations for the first three sessions on three different days (all subjects of each group being present), and were then broken up and studied in the individual situation.

In order to make the relation of individual members to one another as natural as possible, within the limits of the experimental setting, the subjects were left free as to the order in which they would give their judgments. In fact, they were told at the start to give their judgments in random order as they pleased. Whether the judgments of the person who utters his first have more influence than the others becomes a study in leadership, which is a further interesting problem. Perhaps such studies will give us an insight into the effect of polarization on the production of norms in a group situation. But from the examination of our results, we can say that the reporting of the judgments has a gradual cumulative effect; aside from whatever influence the first judgment may have on the second or third at a given moment, the judgments of the third individual at a given presentation are not without effect on the subsequent judgments of the first subject in the round of presentations following. Thus the production of an established group influence is largely a temporal affair and not the outcome of this or that single presentation. We shall refer to this point again later.

Besides the quantitative judgments obtained during the experiments, the subjects were asked at the end of each experimental session to write down their introspections. Questions were asked which aimed at finding whether they became conscious of the range and norm they were establishing subjectively. These questions were: "Between what maximum and minimum did the distances vary?" "What was the most frequent distance that the light moved?"

Certain facts stand out clearly from our results. We may summarize these facts in a few paragraphs.

When an individual faces this stimulus situation, which is unstable and not structured in itself, he establishes a range and norm (a reference point) within that range. The range and norm that are developed in each individual are peculiar to that individual. They may vary from the ranges and norms developed in other individuals in different degrees, revealing consistent and stable individual differences. The causes of these individual differences are difficult problems in themselves, the understanding of which may prove to be basic to a satisfactory understanding of our problem. But for the time being it may be worth while to work on our main theme.

When the individual, in whom a range and a norm within that range are first developed in the individual situation, is put into a group situation, together with other individuals who also come into the situation with their own ranges and norms established in their own individual sessions, the ranges and norms tend to converge. But the convergence is not so close as when they first work in the group situation, having less opportunity to set up stable individual norms. (See left-hand graphs, Figures 2 and 3.)

When individuals face the same unstable, unstructured situation as members of a group for the first time, a range and a norm (standard) within that range are established which are peculiar to the group. If, for the group, there is a rise or fall in the norms established in successive sessions, it is a group effect; the norms of the individual members rise and fall toward a common norm in each session. To this the objection may be raised that one subject may lead, and be uninfluenced by other members of the group; the group norm is simply the leader's norm. To this the only possible empirical reply is that in our experiments the leaders were constantly observed to be influenced by their followers—if not at the moment, then later in the series and in subsequent series. Even if the objection has occasional force, the statement regarding group norms is in general true. Even if the group norm gravitates toward a dominating person, the leader represents a polarization in the situation, having a definite relationship toward others which he cannot change at will. If the leader changes his norm after the group norm is *settled* he may *cease thereupon to be followed,* as occurred several times strikingly in our experiments. In general, such cases of complete polarization are, however, exceptional. (See right-hand graphs, Figures 2 and 3.)

The fact that the norm thus established is peculiar to the group suggests that there is a factual psychological basis in the contentions of social psychologists and sociologists who maintain that new and supra-individual qualities arise in the group situations. This is in harmony with the facts developed elsewhere in the psychology of perception.

When a member of a group faces the same situation subsequently *alone,* after once the range and norm of his group have been established, he perceives the situation in terms of the range and norm that he brings from the group situation. This psychological fact is important in that it gives a psychological approach to the understanding of the "social products" that weigh so heavily in the problem of the stimulus situation.

DISCUSSION OF RESULTS

The experiments, then, constitute a study of the formation of a norm in a simple laboratory situation. They show in a simple way the basic psychological process involved in the establishment of social norms. They are an extension into the social field of a general psychological phenomenon that is found in perception and in many other psychological fields, namely, that our experience is organized around or modified by

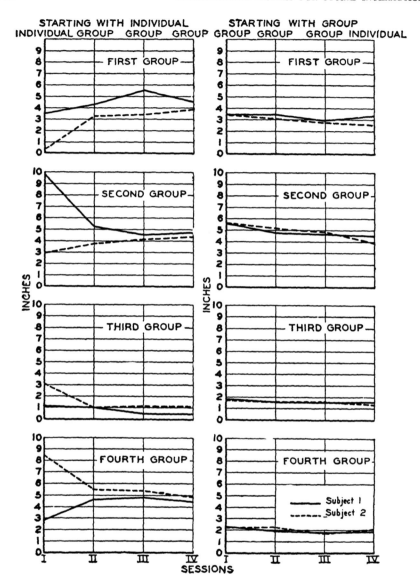

FIGURE 2. Medians in groups of two subjects.

frames of reference participating as factors in any given stimulus situation.

In our experimental situation, within certain limits, there is no "right" or "wrong" judgment. One subject demonstrated this spontaneously during the experiment, in spite of the fact that he was not supposed to talk: "If you tell me once how much I am mistaken, all my judgments will be better." Not being sure about the correctness of his judgments,

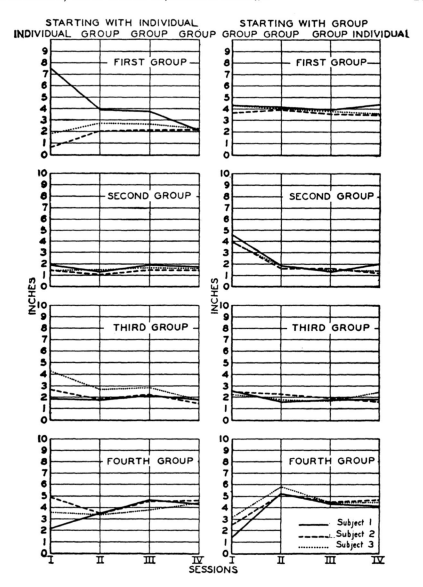

FIGURE 3. Medians in groups of three subjects.

the subject feels *uneasy*. This we know from the introspective reports. In the individual situation, the individual structures the unstructured situation by furnishing his own peculiar range and reference point. In the group situation the members of the group tend to structure the situation by converging toward a common norm in their judgments. If in the beginning of the experimental situation they start with divergent judgments, in the course of the experiment they come together, the divergent one feeling uncertain and even insecure in the deviating position of his judgments. This convergence is not brought about instantly by the direct influence of one or two judgments of the other members of the group. It exhibits a temporal pattern. The following introspection of a member of one of the groups, written in answer to the question, "Were you influenced by the judgments of the other persons during the experiments?" illustrates our point clearly. This subject wrote, "Yes, but not on the same observation. My judgment in each case was already made, and I did not change to whatever the other person said. But on subsequent observations my judgments were adjusted to their judgments. After a number of observations, the previous agreement or lack of it influenced me in adjusting my own perspective."

Despite the above case, every individual need not be aware of the fact that he is being influenced in the group situation, or that he and the other members are converging toward a common norm. In fact, the majority of the subjects reported not only that their minds were made up as to the judgment they were going to give before the others spoke, but that they were not influenced by the others in the group. This fact is in harmony with many observations in the psychology of perception; we know that the general setting in which a stimulus is found influences its properties, and that unless we take a critical and analytic attitude toward the situation we need not be aware that its properties are largely determined by its surroundings. This is the general principle underlying the psychology of "illusions."

It must be said that in our experimental setting the subjects are not moved by a common interest or drive such as is found in a group that faces a common danger, such as starvation or the cruel authority of a tyrant. In these vital situations there is a certain gap that has to be filled. Until this gap is properly filled, the instability of the situation continues. If the norms and slogans that arise under the stress of a tense and uncertain situation that requires a solution do not meet the situation adequately, the instability is not removed, and new norms and new slogans are likely to arise until the tension is removed. For example, in a hungry mass of people searching for food, a leader or a small party may standardize certain norms or slogans as guides to an outlook upon the situation and as guides to action. If these norms do not lead to the satisfaction of hunger, other leaders or interested parties may spring up and standardize other norms or slogans. This (dialectic) dynamic process moves on and on until the appropriate norms or slogans are reached that meet the situation best.

EIGHT

DIFFERENTIAL INFLUENCE:
PROCESS UNDERLYING SOCIAL ATTITUDE

From the foregoing experiments we conclude that when an individual perceives autokinetic movement which lacks an objective standard of comparison, and is asked during repeated stimulation to report in terms of the extent of movement, he subjectively establishes a range of extent and a point (a standard or norm) within that range which is peculiar to himself, differing from the range and the point (standard or norm) established by other individuals. When individuals face the same unstable, unstructured situation as members of a group *for the first time*, a range and a norm (standard) within that range are established which are peculiar to the group. When a member of the group faces the same situation subsequently *alone*, after once the range and norm of his group have been established, he perceives the situation in terms of the range and norm that he brings from the group situation. The ranges and norms established are not prescribed arbitrarily by the experimenter or by any other agent. They are formed in the course of the experimental period and may vary from individual to individual, or from group to group, within certain limits.

Our concern being the study of social influence, we may go further and put the question: can we experimentally make the subject adopt a prescribed range and norm directed by specific social influences?

Different kinds of social influences may be experimentally utilized to define certain prescribed ranges and norms. Among many possible ones we took the following: (*a*) The influence of group situations on the individual as a member of the group. We have already mentioned the main conclusion of this previous work. (*b*) The influence of the direct suggestion of the experimenter in raising or lowering the reported extents of movement. (*c*) The influence of a fellow member with prestige (cooperating with the experimenter) on another ("naive") member of the

From "An experimental approach to the study of attitudes," *Sociometry* (1937), 1: 90–98. Used with permission of J. L. Moreno and Beacon House.

group. (*d*) The influence of one naive member on the judgment of another. In this last case there is no prestige effect, because the subjects have not met each other prior to the experiment.

We shall say only a few words about the experiments under (*b*). If the subject is distributing his judgments, say, about three inches, without any socially introduced influence, the remark of the experimenter, "You are underestimating the distances" tends to raise the point round which the judgments are distributed to about five or six inches.

The following experiment under (*c*) shows how the autokinetic phenomenon can be utilized as a sensitive index of the prestige effect of one person on another. Here we report verbatim the account of an experiment with prestige:

"Miss X and I (Assistant in Psychology, Columbia University) were subjects for Dr. Sherif. I was well acquainted with the experiment, but Miss X knew nothing whatsoever about it. Since she was a close friend of mine, and I carried some prestige with her, Dr. Sherif suggested that it would be interesting to see if we could predetermine her judgments. It was agreed beforehand that I was to give no judgments until she had set her own standard. After a few stimulations it was quite clear that her judgments were going to vary around five inches. At the next appropriate stimulation, I made a judgment of twelve inches. Miss X's next judgment was eight inches. I varied my judgments around 'twelve inches and she did the same. Then I changed my judgment to three inches, suggesting to Dr. Sherif that he had changed it. She gradually came down to my standard, but not without some apparent resistance. When it was clear that she had accepted this new standard, Dr. Sherif suggested that I make no more judgments lest I might influence hers. He then informed her on a subsequent stimulation that she was underestimating the distance which the point moved. Immediately her judgments were made larger and she established a new standard. However, she was a little uneasy with it all, and before the experiment had progressed much farther, whispered to me, 'Get me out of here.'

"When we were again in my office, I told her that the point had not moved at all during the experiment. She seemed quite disturbed about it, and was very much embarrassed to know that we had been deceiving her. Noting her perturbation, I turned the conversation to other matters. However, several times during our conversation she came back to the subject, saying, 'I don't like that man' (referring to Dr. Sherif) and similar statements indicating her displeasure with the experience. It was not until some weeks later when she was again in my office that I discovered the full extent of her aversion. I asked her to serve as a subject for me in an experiment and immediately she exclaimed, 'Not down in *that* room,' pointing to Dr. Sherif's experimental room."

The experiment which will be given presently deals with the influence of a fellow member in the adoption of a prescribed norm. There were seven groups in this experiment, each group consisting of two members. In every group one subject cooperated with the experimenter, i.e., deliberately distributed his judgments within the range and around the norm assigned to him by the experimenter beforehand. The other subject was unaware of this predetermination. The degree of this "naive" subject's conformity to the norm and range of the cooperating subject may be taken as the index of the social influence. In all the groups the subject who was cooperating with the experimenter was the same person. This was done in order to keep the influencing member constant in all groups.

The range and norm prescribed for every group were different. For the first group, the prescribed range was 1–3 inches, 2 inches being the prescribed norm. For the second group, the prescribed range was 2–4, and 3 inches the norm, and so on to the seventh group for which the range and norm were 7–9 and 8, respectively. It will be observed that the prescribed range was rather narrow; consequently in the course of the experimental period the cooperating subject gave no judgments which deviated from the norm by more than one inch in either direction.

TABLE 1

Data from Group 1 Experimentally Obtained from "Naive" S

Prescribed	Session I (in group)	Session II (alone)
Range 1–3 inches	1–5 inches	1–4 inches
Norm 2 inches	3.36 inches	2.62 inches
No. of the 50 judgments falling within the prescribed range	41	47

In the first experimental session, both subjects (the cooperating and the "naive") took part. After each exposure of the point of light for two seconds, the subjects spoke their judgments aloud one at a time and the experimenter recorded these on separate sheets of different colored pads. In order not to stress the factor of primacy, the cooperating subject was instructed to let the other subject utter his judgment first, at least half the time. The social influence in our previous experiments with the autokinetic effect was found to be not so much a function of this and that separate judgments as of the temporal sequence of judgments. Fifty judgments were taken from each subject.

In the second session only the naive subject was present, so that we might see how much of the prescribed range and norm he carried from the first group session. In this individual session also, fifty judgments were taken. As the norm formation in the autokinetic effect is a fragile and, in a sense, artificial formation, such an arbitrary prescription may break down easily beyond a certain number of judgments. Our whole

point is that the autokinetic effect can be utilized to show a general psychological tendency and not to reveal the concrete properties of norm-
formation in actual life situations.

In the presentation of results we give the prescribed range and
norm, and the number of judgments of the "naive" subject falling within
the prescribed range, and his norms (as represented by the median of
the distribution of his judgments) in the first (group) and second (individual) sessions. The means and medians of the distributions of the
judgments given by the cooperating subject in the group sessions are
not exactly identical with the prescribed norms, though the modes and
ranges are the same. We did not think it necessary for him to memorize
a perfectly normal distribution. Our aim is chiefly to show a fundamental psychological tendency related·to norm-formation.

At the end of the second (individual) session the subject was asked
to answer in writing four questions related to the problem. The answers
to two of the questions further verify our former results. We shall therefore confine ourselves to the introspections given to the other two questions which are important for our present concern. These questions were:
(1) What was the distance that the light most frequently moved? (this
was formulated to find out whether the subjects became conscious of
the norm formed in the course of the experiment); (2) Were you influenced by the judgments of the other person who was present during
the first session? (this question was formulated in order to find out
whether the subjects were conscious of the fact that they were being
influenced by the cooperating subject).

The introspections of the subject in Group 1 are important for
any theory of suggestion and norm formation:

1. "Most frequent distance was 2 inches. Seemed to be more consistently 2 inches second day than on first day.

2. "Yes, they were despite my efforts to be impartial. Probably
many of my judgments were inordinately large because of small distances
given by other subject. I think this was an attempt at avoiding suggestion and in so doing going to the other extreme. I do not think I was
influenced by first day's judgments on the second day. I tried to be impartial in my judgments the first day. I felt resentment toward the other
subject the first day because of the successive equal judgments by him.
I tried to be objective toward this feeling: that is to banish the thought.
But I feel that this resentment caused my judgments to differ from his
by a greater amount than they would have if the judgments had been
kept separate; that is if I had not heard his judgments. The second day
I felt more independence in my judgments and I believe that these
judgments were therefore more accurate."

From these results we may conclude that the subjects may be influenced to perceive an indefinite stimulus field in terms of an experi-

mentally introduced norm. The degree of the influence may be different in different subjects, ranging from a large to a negligible amount. Even in the latter case, an influence on the norm (not in the range) is evident.

The introspections reveal that the subjects become conscious of the norm which develops in the course of the experiment. However, they need not be conscious of the fact that they are being influenced toward that norm by the other member of the group. In connection with this point, it is interesting to note that in some cases, the *conformity* to the prescribed range and norm when the *influencing* person is no longer present (Session II) is closer than the *conformity* produced by his actual presence.

It seems to us that the psychological process embodied in these facts may be basic to the daily phenomena of suggestion, especially to the role of suggestion in the formation of attitudes. It is not a rare occurrence in everyday life to react negatively or hesitatingly to suggestion on some topic raised by an acquaintance while in his presence, but to respond positively after leaving him (perhaps there is a disinclination to accept suggestions readily unless there is some strong prestige or pressing demand; to appear easily yielding is not so pleasant for an "ego").

Attitudes whatever else they may be, imply *characteristic modes of readiness in reacting* to definite objects, situations and persons. Our experiment has demonstrated in a simple way how a *characteristic* kind of readiness may be experimentally obtained in relation to an indefinite stimulus field. Perhaps this may constitute a step in the direction of the truly psychological investigation of attitudes.

NINE

THE PSYCHOLOGY OF SLOGANS

This paper aims to handle the psychology of slogans by the application of some major facts that come out persistently in the laboratory investigation of social influence—work which, in turn, is founded on such basic psychological phenomena as judgment and perception. As a new approach to the psychology of slogans it points to the possibility of achieving the all-important feat of welding together everyday actualities and usages with a conceptual scheme developed in laboratory research. This treatment, therefore, cannot be more than an outline.

We shall consider a slogan to be a phrase, a short sentence, a headline, a dictum, which, intentionally or unintentionally, amounts to an appeal to the person who is exposed to it to buy some article, to revive or strengthen an already well-established stereotype, to accept a new idea, or to undertake some action. As will be seen from examples to be given, slogans imply a value judgment.

From this characterization of a slogan it is evident that we do not find any basic difference between business and political slogans. Psychologically the basic dynamics involved in business slogans and political slogans is the same. The reasons for our contention will become clear as our main psychological points are developed. This must not be taken, however, as a denial of the specific properties of business slogans and the appetites and desires to which they appeal, or of political slogans and the situations from which they arise or utilize.

In noticing the importance of slogans in everyday life, social and even applied psychologists are lagging behind practical men who rise and fall by their deeds and words, unlike investigators in academic posts who may change their schemes once every few years without much consequence either to themselves or to their fellow men. Unless we deal with actualities our psychological scheme is but a high-sounding emptiness.

In the business world the importance of a good slogan or trade

From *Journal of Abnormal and Social Psychology* (1937), 32: 450–461. Reprinted with the permission of the American Psychological Association.

name is a recognized fact. A well-known advertiser's journal, *Printer's Ink,* has published thousands of slogans used in business in America. At least a few of them have an effect that lingers on.

Keep that School Girl Complexion
(Palmolive Soap)
Reach for a Lucky instead of a Sweet
(Lucky Strike Cigarettes)
The Nation's Host from Coast to Coast
(Childs Restaurants)
Berth of a Nation
(Greenport Metallic Bed Co.)
Built to Wear Without Repair
(H. Mueller Mfg. Co.)
Not an Accessory, But a Necessity
(Brown Spring Osler Co.)
Baking Aid that Nature Made
(Falk American Potato Flour)
Let Taylor Do Your Tailoring
(J. L. Taylor & Co.)
Money Saver—Butter Flavor
(Ohio Butterine Co.)
Time to re-tire
(Fiske Tires)

It is not within the scope of our paper to examine any one of these slogans separately. In passing we shall only point out that slogans are not magic ways of selling merchandise without offering anything substantial in return. The important and obvious thing for us to bear in mind is that business men, who would not throw out money for nothing, spend large sums in finding and advertising their slogans.

Even academic institutions, which already had their colors, insignia and mottoes, have started learning from business men. For example, a western university announced the following slogan in connection with its 1936 summer school:

Summer School where Summer's Cool

Practical politicians and other popular and religious leaders have already used slogans to arouse people to high patriotic, religious ardor. Since many people do not stop to investigate platforms, politicians try to catch them by slogans. Some of the following examples from American presidential elections summarize real issues; others are more or less catch phrases.

A Public Office is a Public Trust   (1884)

This slogan summarized the desire of the people to get rid of the corruption prevalent at the time. Here we cannot go into the history of every slogan.

Tippecanoe and Tyler Too	(1840)
Sound Money	(1896)
A Full Dinner Pail	(1896)
You Cannot Crucify Mankind upon a Cross of Gold	(1896)
Back to Normalcy	(1920)
Let's be done with Wiggle and Wobble	(1920)
G. O. P. = "Gas, Oil, & Petroleum"	(1924)
Keep Cool with Coolidge	(1924)
Coolidge or Chaos	(1924)
Two Chickens in Every Pot and a Car in Every Garage	(1928)
Bread, Bonus, & Beer	(1932)
In Hoover We Trusted; Now We're Busted	(1932)
Vote for Landon and Land a Job	(1936)

As will be readily noticed, at least a few of these slogans do not fit into the times. Slogans are especially effective at critical periods. This, precisely, is the point that we shall elaborate. It is especially in critical times that practical politicians utilize slogans most effectively in order to push people in the direction they wish them to go. A few examples from the critical periods of the war and post-war illustrate this point.

In America during the tense days of the World War, "He Kept Us Out of War" was an effective slogan in favor of Wilson's re-election. After America entered the War on the side of the Allies, the intense situation demanded its appropriate slogans, among which two good examples are: "A War to End War" and "Make the World Safe for Democracy." The suffragettes of America were quick to give their version of the famous slogans:

"He Kept Us Out of Suffrage" and
"Democracy Should Begin at Home"

In the confusion associated with misery and insecurity the Nazi propagandists, side by side with their insistence on slogans extolling Aryan blood purity, Nordic superiority and romantic Kultur, utilized socialistic slogans that fitted the temper of the German masses at the time.

Deutschland Erwache
Freiheit und Brot
Gemeinnutz vor Eigennutz
Brechung der Zinsknechtschaft

Some of the slogans used by the Nazis might very well be used by their socialist opponents. But the question as to whether their socialistic slogans are in harmony with the Aryan blood purity and Nordic superiority doctrines is not our problem here.

The "Share the Wealth" slogan of Huey Long is a similar slogan which caught the imagination of at least a portion of the petit-bourgeois population of America as the way out of their difficulties.

Likewise as part of the program to incorporate everything in Fascism, the Italian Fascists crystallized the chaotic and staggering situation in Italy for the time being. A few slogans may summarize this particular fascist solution (Zurcher, 1936):

> All within the State, Nothing outside the State,
>   Nothing against the State
> A Book and a Rifle Make a Perfect Fascist
> A Plow Makes the Furrow but the Sword Will Defend It

Nowadays the newspaper headlines in heavy print also serve somewhat as slogans in that they call attention in dramatic shortcuts to that aspect of the news which falls in harmony with the interests and prejudices of the power or powers that control the paper. The diametrically opposite headlines that conservative and radical papers extract from the same columns of news during the present Spanish Civil War are striking cases in point. As usual, Hearst papers utilize the occasion in a sensational way to stir up the readers in favor of fascism.

After this brief glance at the actualities in business, politics, and journalism, we may look for the psychological basis of the use and effectiveness of slogans. There are very few psychological studies on slogans. One interesting study is Lumley's *Slogans as a Means of Social Control* (1921). He calls attention to the dangers that are brought about by the abuse of slogans. His way of summarizing the effectiveness of slogans reads: "You cannot argue with disease germs. You cannot argue with slogans." Lumley does not offer any conceptual scheme in terms of which one can approach the psychology of slogans. His account is empirical. Approaching the subject with the common sense of everyday life, he says: "The features which make slogans so effective are too numerous even to mention, let alone to delineate, in this paper." Nevertheless, he cites fourteen features: (a) Rhythm; (b) Alliteration; (c) Alliteration and antithesis; (d) Ringing repetition of sounds; (f) Brevity; (g) Appeal to curiosity is not infrequent; (h) Punning; (i) Sentiment of patriotism; (j) The propagandists do not hesitate to enter, all unbidden, the inner sanctuary of one's private life; (k) Certain slogans appear to be meaty, the unavoidable conclusions of profound thought; (l) Authoritative note of slogans; (m) Many slogans are strictly class-appeals; (n) The apparent obviousness of meaning is an effective feature; (o) Obscurity of origin, combined with euphoniousness, timeliness, and other features, adds greatly to the strength of the slogan.

Certainly many of these items say something about the characteristics of slogans. In fact all of them may be true as separate items. But it will be readily seen that this enumeration of their features is not based on any consistent psychological principle. Some of the items characterize the external structure of the slogans, some the meaning, and a few the propagandist himself. Remembering the above items as useful discrete characterizations of the slogans, we have to go further into their psychology.

Some conclusions obtained in the laboratory investigation of basic psychological phenomena and also some recent results of experimental social psychology will shed light on our problem.

Experimentation with stimulus situations has shown that the stimulus field is organized into a definite pattern and that certain aspects stand out, the rest forming the background. If the stimulus field is itself patterned, the experienced pattern is determined by the conditions of the external pattern. If the stimulus field is not itself patterned, we tend to perceive it in some sort of pattern. Subjective rhythm read into the regular clicks of the clocks, or puffs of the locomotive, or the patterned perception of puzzle pictures, or of ambiguous Rorschach figures are examples of the point. Especially in cases where patterning is externally lacking do we tend to experience the situation by reading our own conscious or unconscious inclinations or interpretations into it. To perceive and experience things in some sort of pattern or order seems to be a basic and general psychological tendency.

Patterning is organized around some salient features or outstanding points of reference which are themselves part of the stimulating agents that form a functional unit at a given time. This fact has revealed itself in almost all fields of investigation—sensory phenomena, judgment, perception, memory, affectivity, experience of success or failure, etc.

With the shifts of the reference points there may result a reorganization of the whole pattern or structure. This is especially true in cases in which the stimulus field lacks intrinsic patterning. Some established attitude, some pressing desire, past acquaintance, or some other sort of preparedness may work in favor of singling this or that feature out of other possible ones.

This tendency to experience an indefinite, unpatterned, unstructured stimulus situation in some form of order has been shown in some recent experimental studies in social psychology. When a group of individuals face an unstable stimulus situation and are asked to report on some indefinite aspect of it, they tend to experience it in terms of a common range and a common reference point within that range, both of which are built up in the course of the group activity. Once the common reference point is established for the group, the individual member persists in adopting the common reference point even when he faces the same stimulus *alone* on subsequent occasions. [See Selections 7 and 8.]

It seems to us that the essential characteristics of the circumstances contributing to the rise and catching quality of the slogans are psychologically similar in essentials in spite of the fact that the experiments referred to above lack the concrete vitality and motivating direction of the actual situations. This is especially true of political slogans. The similarity lies in the fact that new slogans *also* arise or become effective when the situation people face is unstable, indefinite and demands a short epitomizing expression.

The case of business slogans is fundamentally similar. In business also, the persons who are interested in rendering their slogans effective have to launch their slogans on people who are more or less indefinite as to the articles or conveniences offered to them. It is difficult to know beforehand which slogans will catch and thus focus attention on this or that article. Usually the effective slogan is the one that appeals to a particular appetite, need, or other demand with a short-cut, simple expression whose features—such as rhythm, alliteration, punning—make its recurrence or repetition easy.

But none of these features is enough in itself to make a slogan effective. Otherwise it would be comparatively easy to sit down and construct a slogan. In actual practice, some of the best known slogans that make the most effective appeal—because they and not others are the best short-cut expressions of the situation on hand—have entirely accidental origin. A business man, Charles Pelham, vice-president of Fuller and Smith & Co., Inc., has recently made one point clear with the histories of some well-known business slogans, such as "The Nation's Host from Coast to Coast." From the delightful cases he collected the author reaches the conclusion that "if there is any conclusion to be drawn from these stories, it certainly is not that there is an approved way of going about formulating a slogan. Hard work may produce it and may not; a chance remark, a lucky eavesdropping, years of thought, or a moment's inspiration. To base a theory of the technique of inspiration on such material would plainly be stuff and/or nonsense."

What the business man noticed about slogans is also seen by the political observer who does not follow events merely from the irresponsible objectivity of his academic chair. What the business man characterized as the "casual and accidental," a political observer characterized as the "spontaneity" in the inception of the slogans. In our opinion "spontaneity" is preferable because "casual and accidental" smack of indeterminism. A slogan may have been formulated unintentionally or by some business or political propagandist. It catches the public imagination almost spontaneously when it fits in as a short-cut expression summarizing a directed and unsatisfied wish and carrying with it affective qualities of some established stereotypes if they exist.

In other words, slogans catch almost spontaneously when (and not before, because only a few might notice them) they stand out as short-cut characterizations of the direction and temper of the time and situation.

The difficulty in formulating an effective slogan that will catch like wildfire may be attributed to the fact that very few people can

hit on a happy combination that expresses the *temper* of the time best.
If this is not hit upon, mere structural qualities such as simplicity and
rhythm will not help much. It is because of this that the deliberate
propagandist or leader is not always the person who originates slogans.
They may originate from below. Before the famous slogans of the World
War became effective in America, a political observer shrewdly expressed this fact. In 1917, in an editorial in *The Nation* (June 21, p. 728)
the writer called attention to the characteristic of spontaneity with
which slogans catch, and concluded: "We do not know whence the
American slogan for the present war will come. It may come from the
White House or from the vaudeville stage or from the common life.
But it will be set in motion without forethought, it will make its way
at first without public notice, and before we are aware we shall have
it." This observation is in essential harmony with the conclusion reached
by the business man.

The psychological properties of slogans come into high relief when
we take into account the rise and effectiveness of slogans in times of
panic, critical situations, or revolutionary moments. Ordinarily the
routine of daily life is regulated by more or less well-established norms—
i.e., customs, traditions, modes, various kinds of well-implanted social
values. Some of them become ossified stereotypes, and the flow of social
life and human relationships as regulated by these norms and stereotypes
is almost taken for granted.

But in critical times when the existing norms or stereotypes are
no longer sufficient to regulate the new conditions, the situation upset
by the rise of new and heretofore unaccounted factors and relationships
has to be reformulated. The new situation produces its own appropriate
norms. For any group co-activity that lasts for any length of time results
in a set of norms that defines the desired ends and taboos of the group.
And slogans, especially at the time of crises and tension, become short-
cut battle cries of the situation which may be used or abused as magic
focal catchwords for intense action and feeling. Thus slogans may serve
as crystallizing points in the confusion of a crisis which tends to develop
into a new regulation of a new order.

The extent of upset may vary—it may affect and reformulate one
aspect of group life, or it may affect the whole structure of society. Especially in cases where the whole structure of society is affected, we see
masses moving intensely and summarizing their movement with certain
sharp slogans. At such times people are not in the mood to read or hear
long political speeches or platforms. Slogans and headlines that fit into
the temper of the movement are the things that count.

Let us take, for example, two important revolutions from history,
the French and the American Revolutions. One of the most important
slogans in the world's history is the "Liberty, Fraternity, and Equality"
of the French Revolution. This revolution started at a time of tyranny

and oppression, when the French masses lived under destitute conditions while the privileged minority took pride in being useless in the world of luxury and fantasy of their class. There was no longer any connection between economic and social realities and the superstructure of norms and etiquette. The French Revolution "arose from the ever increasing divorce between reality and law, between institutions and men's way of living, between the letter and the spirit (Mathiez, 1929, p. 1). When a superstructure of norms is separated too much from the basic realities, sooner or later that superstructure suffers. The objective realities force themselves through the destruction of the degenerating and parasitic superstructure to a new order. When life was becoming unbearable the old traditions and superstitions began to lose their grip on the French masses. Therefore, religious life, an important part of the superstructure, "no longer had any attractions" (p. 13), and "the innovators now won the day" (p. 3).

When again and again the good life promised by virtues of loyalty to values and institutions is not fulfilled, people wake up and challenge them. If the unfortunate conditions of living are intensified by new crises, things move faster and come to the point of explosion. This is what happened during the years just preceding the French Revolution. A few concrete items will give a clearer picture:

> At Abbeville there were 12,000 workmen unemployed, at Lyons, 20,000 and the numbers at other places were in proportion. At the beginning of the winter, which was a very hard one, it was necessary in the large cities to organize workshops supported by charity, especially as the price of bread was constantly rising. The harvest of 1788 had been much below normal. The shortage of forage had been so great that the farmers had been forced to sacrifice part of their cattle and to leave some of their lands uncultivated, or else sow it without previous manuring. The markets were short of supplies. Not only was bread very dear, but there was a risk that it would run short. . . . The wretched people cast covetous glances upon the well-filled barns in which their lay and ecclesiastical lords stored up the proceeds of their tithes and their rents in kind (Mathiez, 1929, p. 34).

The effect of this situation in individual experience is well expressed in the words that Taine puts into a peasant's mouth:

> I am miserable because they take too much from me. They take too much from me because they do not take enough from the privileged classes. Not only do the privileged classes make me pay in their stead but they levy upon me ecclesiastical and feudal dues. When from an income of a hundred francs, I have given fifty-three and more to the tax collector, I still have to give fourteen to my seignor and fourteen more for my tithe and out of the eighteen or nineteen francs I have left, I have yet to satisfy the excise-officer and the salt-tax-farmer. Poor wretch that I am, alone I pay for two governments—the one obsolete, local, which is today remote, useless, inconvenient, humiliating, and makes itseelf felt through its restraints, its injustices, its taxes;

the other new, centralized, ubiquitous, which alone takes charge of every service, has enormous needs and pounces upon my weak shoulders with all its enormous weight (Gottschalk, 1929, p. 39).

This is the time when the individual, and many others like himself, is open to new possibilities. In fact, people feel the need to hold on to something new; the whole of life has to be reformulated. Therefore,

the rising was directed not only against those who were speculating in foodstuffs, against the old system of taxation, against internal tolls, and against feudalism, but against all those who exploit the populace and live upon its substance. It was closely connected with the political agitation. At Nantes the crowd besieged the Hotel de Ville with cries of "Vive la Liberté" (p. 35).

In this atmosphere of unrest, confusion, and ferment, the slogan "Liberty, Equality, and Fraternity" emerged as a magic torchlight which crystallized the aspiration of the masses in a short-cut way.

Now let us turn to the American Revolution and look at the conditions from which some of its well-known slogans emerged.

Long before the outbreak of the American Revolution and especially during the ten years preceding it, commercial legislation in the colonies was in a state of anarchy. The chronic confusion that accompanied the shifting conditions under which "American business and agricultural enterprise was growing, swelling, and beating against the frontiers of English imperial control," was augmented by a business depression following the war of 1763, and Grenville's program for relieving English taxpayers with American taxes.

In the swift reaction that followed, inflated prices collapsed, business languished, workmen in the towns were thrown out of employment, farmers and planters, burdened by falling prices found the difficulties of securing specie steadily growing.

By the new imperial program, the evils of the depression were aggravated (Beard and Beard, 1930, p. 201, 211).

"No Taxation Without Representation" was the slogan that rallied the colonists up and down the seaboard in overt protest: a boycott of English goods, riots in the large cities, tarring and feathering of tax collectors, the destruction of imported goods and royal officials' property.

Once the revolution broke out, new slogans arose. Resolving the crisis with rebellion and independence came so swiftly that many colonists who were firmly for "No Taxation Without Representation" did not accept this method. A number of slogans evolved to sanction the course that had been taken; for example, "Resistance to Tyranny is Obedience to God."

More serious than the doubts of those who hesitated to defy authority was the want of unity among the thirteen colonies, a lack leading to uncertainty on the battle field and disorganization in civil life. Even the indefatigable cheer-leader for the revolution, Thomas Paine, said:

When I look back on the gloomy days of last winter and see America suspended by a thread, I feel a triumph of joy at the recollection of her delivery and a reverence for the characters which snatched her from destruction.

There was no administrative machinery ready-made to coördinate activities. "Exactly the opposite was true; they had to creat everything national out of a void—a government, a treasury, an army, even a bookkeeping system, and agencies for buying supplies" (Beard and Beard, 1930, p. 135).

To make matters worse, the revolutionaries themselves within each state were divided into opposing factions that nullified each other's work and sometimes came to blows. The merchants and property owners were intent upon overthrowing the feudal mercantilism of England, while the mechanics, small farmers and laborers were anxious to utilize the upheaval to abolish the remnants of feudalism within the indigenous social structure.

Unity of action against the external foe could alone meet the situation, and slogans to that effect were effective and widely circulated: "United We Stand, Divided We Fall"; and "If We Don't Hang Together, We'll All Hang Separately."

Anybody who reads John Reed's *Ten Days That Shook the World* and goes through the misery and starvation depicted there, can easily understand why such slogans as "All Power to the Soviets" and "Peace, Bread and Land" became signals that stood out in the midst of destruction and wretchedness as symbols of a new life.

We have tried to give a psychological characterization of the rise and effectiveness of slogans. Our chief point is that slogans are short-cut expressions arising in confused and critical situations. This does not mean that these short-cuts necessarily express the true and objective solution of the problems they are facing. We have not even implied this. At critical times, such as ours, demagogues may arise and catch the temper of the times, uttering slogans which may move millions of people temporarily. The analysis of actual forces and the evaluation of the correctness of the solutions offered lie outside the limits of our discussion. But it may be safe to say that the more correctly and the more objectively a set of slogans expresses the underlying forces in a critical situation, the more vital and lasting they will prove to be. Slogans of liberty and equality at times of tyranny and oppression, and of peace and bread at times of insecurity and war, scarcity and starvation, will keep on moving the masses as magic torches, since they express a deprivation and tension that shakes the very depths of human life.

TEN

CONFORMITY-DEVIATION, NORMS, AND GROUP RELATIONS

With Carolyn W. Sherif, Pennsylvania State University

There are certain questions that should be raised at the outset in dealing with the problem of conformity and deviation. I shall start by raising them. Then some laboratory studies of the normative process which underlies conforming or deviating behavior will be summarized, and limitations of the confines of the traditional laboratory in handling basic problems of conformity and independence will be discussed. This will lead us to the necessity of research on normative process within the framework of the properties of groups. It will be concluded that research and experimentation thus formulated will yield a basis for realistic evaluation of the norm system of a group from the point of view of social stability and social change.

PROBLEM OF CONFORMITY AND DEVIATION

An item of behavior, taken in and by itself, cannot be labeled either conformity or deviation. There is no such thing as conforming or deviating behavior in the abstract. The terms "conformity" and "deviation" make sense when at least the following questions are raised:

1. Conformity to *what?* Deviation or departure from *what?* Always, conformity is conformity to *something.* Deviation is departure from something, whether the referent of that "something" is made explicit or not.

What is that "something"? The referents may be the prevailing, the usual, or expected ways of doing things in the individual's surroundings. This is the *normative* basis of the problem. The referents may be the individual's particular place or position in the scheme of interpersonal or group relationships. This is the *organizational* basis of the problem. Does the individual accept and behave in terms of the place and position expected of him and his kind in the scheme of things?

2. What is the relative importance of the behavior area in which conformity or deviation occurs? For example, is it a matter of whether a father takes care of his family as he should, or is it a question of whether he keeps up with the baseball scores in the World Series as his friends do?

3. Is the normative basis of the behavior in question shared and upheld by other groups to which the individual is related in some capacity? Or do his multiple groups put contradictory or even conflicting demands and expectations on the individual for his behavior in given dimensions? This of course relates to the problem of integration or conflict of social values in the psychological world of the individual.

4. The fourth question concerns whether conformity and deviation occur primarily through coercion or threat of subsequent coercion and force, or whether the behavior in question is prompted by the individual's inner convictions and personally cherished values.

5. What are the *alternatives* available for the individual in the stimulus situation with respect to the area of behavior in question? Are there many, few, or none? Are they clearly defined or difficult to distinguish? In other words, what situational factors enter into the picture, both as to the physical setting and the other people involved?

When studied in the context of these questions, conforming or nonconforming behavior can be taken as an index of the degree of stability or the extent of change in the human relationships of a given setting and specifies whether stability or change occurs primarily as a consequence of coercion or primarily through the voluntary inter-action of individuals. Thus viewed, conforming behavior and noncon-forming behavior can serve as a basis of evaluating the trends in human relationships: how a group is doing and in what directions it is headed.

These are among the basic problems for any human group. They are all the more vital in this modern shrinking world. Whether we like it or not, peoples and groupings are being brought into closer functional relationships. Scarcely a group is left which is contained within itself as a closed system. What a particular group is doing and where it is headed have wide impacts on other peoples. The implication of this enlarging interdependence of peoples is rather obvious, namely a norma-tive system which transcends restrictive, monopolistic loyalties and conformities still surviving from relatively more closed group patterns of previous periods.

RESULTS OF NEGLECT OF ISSUES

Apart from the questions just raised, that is, questions of the refer-ents of conforming behavior, of the relative importance of the area of behavior, of the integrated or conflicting character of the normative bases of the behavior in question, of how conformity is brought about, conforming and nonconforming behavior cannot be studied as a scientific problem. Neglect of one or the other issues raised here has resulted in a spate of literature in recent years by social psychologists, social scientists, and essayists, which at its best is healthy social critique and at its worst boils down to a romantic protest and a cry for heroes.

We even read discussions of whether man is by nature a conformist, a submissive prey of social winds and tides, or whether by nature he is a seeker of truth, hence required by his own nature to be independent. Such formulations are reminiscent of the old controversies over human nature by instinct theorists of whether man is altruistic or selfish, cooperative or competitive, acquisitive or sharing. Now the argument seems to be transferred to the cognitive sphere.

By implication, those who would define "human nature" as basically conformist or as basically independent praise one kind of behavior and damn the other. Yet by formulating the problem in this dichotomous form in the abstract, conforming behavior or deviating behavior cannot be evaluated in a consistent fashion.

Taking a stand as an apologist of conformity can amount to the praise of blind subservience. On the other hand, singing the praise of nonconformity apart from evaluation of the norm or value to which it is related may lead to an absurd dilemma. Let's just cite a few cases of nonconforming behavior, such as driving down the middle of the road, monopolizing a conversation, deliberate plagiarism, or stealing. Of course, those who see virtue in nonconformity in its own right would protest these crass examples. For praise of nonconformity is made of righteous nonconformity. This is exactly the point. Nonconformity or conformity cannot be evaluated in its own right apart from its referent, namely the normative basis of the behavior in question.

NORMATIVE PROCESS IN THE LABORATORY

I shall first consider the formation of the normative process as studied in the psychological laboratory, with special reference to variations in results owing to the kind of controlled stimulus setup presented to the subjects.

The study of norm formation in the laboratory has been undertaken through producing a characteristic mode of behavior relative to the aspect of the stimulus situation experimentally introduced. This production embodies the bare essential of norm-regulated behavior.

MODES OF BEHAVIOR AND STIMULUS PROPERTIES

If the stimulus arrangement provided by the experimenter is objectively well graded or has compelling anchorages, the ensuing uniformity of behavior relative to it is determined by these salient features of the stimulus conditions. As a result of repeated encounters with them, characteristic modes of behavior come into close fit with the stimulus properties.

Tresselt and Volkmann (1942) clearly demonstrated the principle in their study dealing with the production of uniform opinion by non-social stimulation. These authors formulated the principle in question as follows:

Each person in a group says what he does not only because he has been persuaded by argument, induced by reward, compelled by pressure, guided by past experience, or influenced by the voiced opinions of other people; he says it also because he faces a restricted range of social or nonsocial stimulation, and this range has determined his scale of judgment (p. 243).

When stimuli are presented serially over a period of time, the range representing categories of behavioral uniformity to particular items is appropriate evidence for inferring the formation of a *psychophysical scale*.

The study of stimulus relationships affecting the formation and functioning of psychophysical scales cannot occupy our attention further at this time. It has been carried to a rather sophisticated level in recent years through the efforts of such contributors as Graham (1952), Helson (1959), Johnson (1955), Stevens (1957), Volkmann (1951), and others.

For the present discussion it is sufficient to emphasize that the normative process can be determined primarily by the range and salient anchorages of the stimuli to which individuals are exposed repeatedly. I strongly suspect that the principles to which we have alluded underlie the similarity in characteristic modes of outlook in technological matters by various human groupings scattered over wide geographic regions, but exposed to similar technology (Sherif, 1948; Sherif and Sherif, 1956). If so, the rapid shift in psychophysical scales following the introduction of new stimulus values may be pertinent to understanding the relatively faster assimilation of new technological items as compared with new social concepts. This refers, of course, to the well-known empirical facts formulated by sociologists and anthropologists as the "cultural lag."

Of course, weights, lines, and sounds do not have an exclusive copyright on compelling stimulus characteristics. Stimuli with social relevance, including verbal statements, may have such compelling properties as well. In his study on stimulus conditions as factors in social change, Cohen (1957) at the University of Oklahoma studied changes in norms as a function of alteration in the range of social stimulation faced by the subjects. By scaling statements of undesirable behavior of the kind used earlier by McGarvey (1943), Cohen selected moderately undesirable acts, such as "fishing without a license." Subject pairs were to come to an agreement in rating how desirable or undesirable these acts were. Exposed to the restricted range of items, control and experimental pairs rated them similarly (see Figure 1). In the second

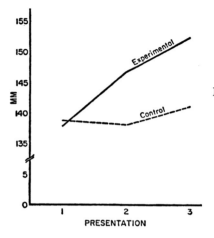

FIGURE 1. Mean ratings of moderately undesirable behavior items. (Drawing based on data from Cohen, 1957.)

experimental presentation, very undesirable behaviors, such as "kidnapping a baby for ransom," were included. As Figure 1 shows, the somewhat undesirable behaviors were agreed to be more desirable, thus showing the well-known contrast effect owing to the dastardly acts introduced in the second presentation. The differences between the experimental and control subjects were maintained in the third session when individuals rated the behaviors alone, indicating a normative process primarily determined by the exposure of interacting individuals to specified ranges of stimulus items. It is in this sense that conformity is related to the formation of psychophysical scales.

LABORATORY STUDIES

Now let's turn to laboratory studies on the formation of *psychosocial scales:* scales of characteristic modes of behavior whose formation may be influenced by the relationships among interacting individuals. Features of man's relationships with man become most salient as determinants of his conformities precisely when the stimulus situation they face together is highly fluid and provides various alternatives.

This observation has been made time and again by social scientists. I was first impressed with it upon reading Durkheim's accounts of the formation of *representations collectives* in out-of-ordinary interaction situations and the accounts of Chicago sociologists—notably Clifford Shaw, Thrasher, and Zorbaugh—of small group functioning in interstitial areas of large cities. Even in the midst of "social disorganization," in the sociological sense of that term, an orderliness prevails in the social life of these small groups. How does the normative process take shape under such conditions? How do new standards of conduct arise in out-of-ordinary situations, times of crisis and the breakdown of established conformities?

RESEARCH ON NORM FORMATION

These were among the questions that led to the laboratory norm-formation experiments which utilize the autokinetic setup as a fluid stimulus in the dimension in question amenable to various alternative modes of behavior (Sherif, 1935, 1936). The problem was conceivéd in terms of stabilization of behavior over a period of time, and not as a question of whether an individual is susceptible to suggestion in this or that particular round of judgment. Contrary to Durkheim's view, even when the individual is alone and not interacting with others, his psychological functioning becomes organized and exhibits emergent properties. This was the finding of the individual sessions. As some of you know, after the individual faces such a situation repeatedly, his behavior stabilizes within a characteristic range and around a modal point with reduced variability.

When individuals face the autokinetic setup together, over a period of time a convergence of the individual behaviors occurs, resulting in similarities not initially present. But the norm that emerges during interaction is not an average of the individual norms. Nor is it necessarily identical with the initial behavior of one or the other individual, although a large prestige or status differential may almost produce this result. To specify the normative outcome further, the relationships of individuals in a particular interaction process have to be delineated. However, once formed, the convergent behavior is not dependent upon the *immediate presence* of other individuals. In subsequent sessions when the individual was alone, behavior was still regulated by the normative process.

It was suggested that when the individual changes his verbal reports in the presence of another person making somewhat different judgments, he is not really *seeing* the stimulus any differently, but is simply changing his behavior in order to avoid disapproval and appear agreeable. Certainly this does happen in some situations. A recent experiment by W. R. Hood and the writer (1957) was designed to investigate whether or not behavior in the highly unstructured autokinetic situation represented such public compliance. Procedures were planned to eliminate suspicion that the experiment had anything to do with social influence and to remove the immediate presence of another person or the sound of his voice at the time judgment was rendered. The subject simply overheard another person making twenty judgments while waiting his turn to make estimates by himself. One sample overheard judgments ranging from 1 to 5 inches and another sample overheard reports ranging from 6 to 10 inches. Figure 2 summarizes judgments made when the subjects were alone, by showing the proportions of judgments 5 inches or less and 6 inches or more under these two conditions. Later, when asked what extent of movement they had usually seen, the subjects' estimates did not differ significantly from their own median judgments

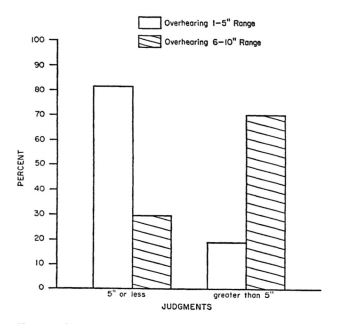

FIGURE 2. Proportions of judgments 5″ or less and greater than 5″ for two conditions. (From Hood and Sherif, 1957.)

in the situation. We may conclude, I believe, that in this situation, individuals "call them as they see them" and they see them as influenced by judgments previously overheard. There is no evidence of a discrepancy between judgment and verbal report.

JUDGMENTS AND LIMITS

Can we say, then, that in highly fluid situations, the relationships among individuals determine behavior altogether, and that the "sky is the limit" as far as the extent of social influence that can be achieved? We cannot. For even in this highly unstructured situation, the size of the room, as the individual can determine it—from finding his way about, from echo and the like (Sherif and Harvey, 1952)—the subject-to-light distance, exposure time, intensity of the light, and other stimulus arrangements set rather definite limits upon the extent of movement perceived. If another person's judgments exceed these limits too far, they are unlikely to exert any determining role at all.

Whittaker (1958) showed this at the University of Oklahoma by having planted subjects make judgments which exceeded the individual's largest estimate made previously when he was alone. For different samples, the "plant" made judgments ranging upward from magnitudes 1 inch larger, twice, eight, or twelve times larger than the maximum

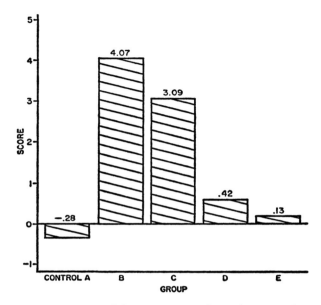

FIGURE 3. Mean difference scores for judgments alone
and with "plant." (From Whittaker, 1958.)

estimate the individual had given when alone. Figure 3 summarizes
the results in terms of the average difference between means of the
individual and together sessions. It may be seen that the partner's judgments had a significant effect when they exceeded the previous maximum
estimate by 1 inch and upward, that the effect decreased when his
judgments were twice as great, and that no significant effect was found
when the partner's judgments were eight or twelve times as large. These
latter changes do not differ significantly from those for the control group,
which simply judged alone a second time. Analysis in terms of frequency of judgments exceeding the individual's initial range when
alone leads to the same conclusion. We conclude "the sky is *not* the
limit" in the effectiveness of attempted influence even in a highly unstructured situation.

Furthermore, once a psychosocial scale has been established, the
experimenter cannot play around indefinitely, introducing new social
anchorages in order to change it. This is in some contrast to laboratory
findings on psychophysical scales, which reveal strikingly quick adaptations to changes in the stimulus values presented. The successive introduction of conflicting social anchorages produces breakdowns of a
psychosocial scale, as Norman Walter's experiment at the University
of Oklahoma (1955) shows. Walter was interested in what would happen
to an established psychosocial scale for judging autokinetic movement

when conflicting reports from equally good sources were presented successively. A few days after the individual established a characteristic range and mode of behavior alone, he was informed casually of the performance of students at a university with high prestige in his eyes. The figure given was actually either the 90th or 10th percentile of his own previous estimates. The result was a significant shift toward the figure introduced, with greatly reduced variability, even a greater reduction than for control subjects whose variability decreased regularly during four sessions on different days without procedural changes. At a third session three or four days later, a second "data report" opposite in direction to the first was given experimental subjects, this one from another institution of about equal prestige in his eyes. The typical result was a shift in behavior back to the region of the initial norm established when alone, but with increased variability. Finally at a fourth session, the experimenter discredited both reports by saying the results were suspected of error. The result was further marked increase in variability such that a breakdown in the normative process ensued.

ANCHORAGE POINTS AND BEHAVIOR

The effect of systematically reducing the number of anchorages available in the stimulus arrangement is to increase the probability that characteristic behaviors developing as individuals face the situation repeatedly will be significantly influenced by relationships among the individuals. This generalization is supported by the findings of various studies, and James Thrasher (1954) tested it in a single design. His stimulus setups represented three gradations of stimulus structure. Judgments were obtained from individuals alone, then in pairs composed either of good friends or initially neutral persons. In the situation with the most stable anchorages available in the stimulus setup, neither friends nor neutral individuals affected each other's behavior significantly. But in the least structured situation, the relationship among the individuals as friends or as initially neutral decidedly affected the normative process. The intermediate situation produced results intermediate between these two.

LIMITATIONS OF LABORATORY CONFINES
FOR VALID RESEARCH STRATEGY

The general conclusion to be drawn is that the choice of the stimulus setup in the laboratory determines to a great extent how effective social factors introduced by the experimenter will be. If the structural properties of the stimulus arrangements allow no alternatives, social factors introduced will play relatively little part in patterning characteristic behavior. If the stimulus conditions provide alternatives in his sizing up of them, the likelihood of compliance to social influences introduced by the experimenter will increase. There are a good many combinations and gradations in between the stimulus situations representing these two extremes. If space permitted, we could draw upon experiments by Asch (1952), Coffin (1941), Luchins (1944), Mausner (1953, 1954), and others to accentuate this conclusion.

Frequently, the manipulator in public relations, the demagogue in public affairs enjoys a cynical glee at the compliance and malleability of people owing to the muddied atmosphere which the manipulator and demogogue themselves have helped manufacture. It is a laudable antidote against such cynical views of human affairs to set up experiments in the laboratory with clear-cut stimulus arrangements and to present results showing that people are independent in their appraisals of the situation, that they do not blindly succumb to false social influences. However, the demagogue himself seldom works with a situation as clear-cut as, say, matching a pencil to a yardstick, when he attempts manipulations. He fishes in muddied waters, unless he feels that brute force is on his side.

COUNTERACTING MANIPULATION

Perhaps the more effective way of counteracting such situations may be a concentration on analysis of conditions which render people susceptible to manipulative influences. Here one problem is *what* is presented at all, in the first place. All the information, all the news fit to be presented in speech and mass communication media on vital matters which lie far beyond the individual's perceptual range come to him through the *selectivity* of people in control of the mass media. Especially in the contemporary scene, when man is faced with the problem of taking sides, making decisions, and expressing opinions on issues that relate to the use of atomic energy, foreign aid in distant lands, or the merits or demerits of a balanced budget, he gets most of his information through the mass media or from other persons who got it from the mass media. The problem of *selectivity* in *what* is presented is at least as important as that of the presence or absence of alternatives once a situation requiring a decision is encountered. Furthermore, we suspect that in problems such as those just mentioned, man's ethnic, religious, and political ties may be weighty factors in determining which side is taken and which decision is made. If so, it is a bit unrealistic to study conformity and nonconformity in an arbitrary situation within the confines of the traditional laboratory and to declare the generalizations reached on this basis as the verdict of psychological science.

The study of the relative contribution of selected stimulus factors, in which almost infinitely fine gradations of structure are possible, and of selected social factors which are also numerous, is an interesting psychological problem. A good many psychologists could devote their whole lifetimes to it. But no amount of concentration on all the variations between a sharply defined stimulus setup at one extreme and a highly fluid setup at the other, and no amount of technical refinement within the traditional laboratory setting will settle for us the important question of what are *typical* conditions conducive to the production of various modes of compliance and independence to social influences.

It is not yielding or being independent to discrete and transitory social influence that brought about concern over problems of conformity and independence in human affairs on the contemporary scene. That is why my brief report of experiments dwelt mainly upon studies of the normative process producing a characteristic attitude and mode of behavior to its referents over a span of time. Studies of yielding and independence in relation to one-episode social influence are reminiscent of Allport's early studies of "social decrements," "social increments," and "social subvaluents" through what is referred to as the study of "pure social effect." Such studies have only limited bearing on problems of conformity and deviation in which the individual's self-esteem, status, and work in relation to other persons significant in his scheme of things are at stake.

INTERACTION CONDITIONS

The settings in which compliance and noncompliance become important problems cannot be determined within the confines of the traditional laboratory setting. Here we have to extend our research perspectives and put validity checks upon ourselves to catch the essential properties of actual situations conducive to various modes of compliance or independence. In order to achieve this perspective, intimate familiarity must be achieved first with interaction settings in which an integral aspect is that of compliance or independence in behavior. And the proper focus for developing valid research strategies is upon the formation and functioning of actual groups in both their ingroup and intergroup interactions.

CONFORMITY AND NONCONFORMITY IN GROUP RELATIONS

This brings us to the central part of my presentation. The representative, the typical problems of conformity and nonconformity can be more effectively singled out through due recognition of man's behavior relative to significant other persons. Significant other persons stand in specifiable relationships to the individual—friendly or unfriendly, pulling together or pulling apart. Conforming or nonconforming behavior makes very little sense when it is not analyzed within a framework of these relationships. An observation will illustrate the point. In 1958, a group of liberal students at a southwestern university were interested in persuading restaurants and soda fountains in the area to cater to Negro students. The representative response of the shopkeepers was that they were willing to do so but each individual was concerned about what the other shopkeepers in the area would do. Our image of ourselves, our appraisals of our own practices, are not self-generating. They are not independent of our relatedness to people significant in our eyes, whether these significant people are seen as friend or foe. This point will be specified further in connection with the properties of groups and ingroup and outgroup demarcations.

It may not be too far off the mark to maintain that man's relation to significant others is, on the whole, in terms of his membership in various groups, such as family, club, fraternity, occupational outfit, religious or political outfit of some sort. If the problem of conformity and independence is formulated within a framework of the individual's group setting we are confronted head on with relationships in which the problem is an ever-present, integral aspect of interaction situations day in and day out, and not an incidental side issue. If the problem is formulated within the concreteness of group relations, as these relations unfold in the actualities of social life, then conformity or nonconformity acquires a functional significance which is mutilated when either is considered apart from these relations, as by those who advocate a doctrine of an irreconcilable individual–group dichotomy. The social philosophy which puts issues in dichotomous either-or form, that is either *for* the individual or *for* the group, starts with the categorical assumption of individual and group as irreconcilable entities or antithetical polarities, as though demands and interests of one are necessarily in conflict with the interests of the other for all occasions. Within the framework of man's ties with other men in lasting relationships, the conflicting or harmonious character of interests is itself a problem of study. With the vantage point thus gained, the external stimulus, whether it be sharply defined or fluid and uncertain, can be studied as it becomes relevant to relationships among individuals facing definable problem situations.

MEMBER'S EXPERIENCE OF CONFORMITY AND INDEPENDENCE, AND PROPERTIES OF GROUPS

A rounded analysis of the important problem of the individual's experience when he complies and when he is independent in specific instances of his group relations should start with specification of the essential properties of the group itself and the individual member's psychological relationship to these properties.

The concept "group" means all things to all people. Various concepts are offered in the academic market place today in the name of operational definitions. Not infrequently, the model and technique are derived from more established sciences without due concern for their appropriateness as tools for valid study of human group problems. Unless the appropriateness of the proposed techniques and models is examined relative to the essential properties of actual groups, they are doomed to inefficacy in yielding valid results which can be generalized to handle the individual's behavior in his actual group setting.

EARLY STUDIES

Prompted by this serious methodological concern with formulation of valid problems, we undertook an extensive survey of sociological field studies dealing with properties of small groups. We turned to this literature for the simple reason that sociologists have priority in their concern with the properties of actual small groups and have collected considerable empirical data on the topic (Faris, 1953). These surveys were a first step in our ongoing research program on formation and functioning of groups in both their ingroup and intergroup relations, in which the problem of conformity and deviation is an integral part. They are presented in various publications (Sherif, 1948, Chaps. 5 and 6; Sherif and Cantril, 1947, Chap. 10; Sherif and Sherif, 1953, Chap. 8; 1956, Chaps. 5, 6, and 7).

These early surveys deliberately centered on informally or spontaneously formed small groups in order to start with group formations which are the creation of voluntary and free interaction among the individual members, and not the product of an organizational blueprint with rules and bylaws handed down by a governing body with outside authority. From this survey, several generalizations about the properties of small groups were extracted. Here we touch only on the minimum essentials.

It is extracted that any small group functions as a delineated social unit. The members have a rather clear notion who is in, who is out, and also the marginal ones who did not quite make it at the time.

It is extracted that the individuals who achieve accepted membership in groups can be ordered at a given time along a status hierarchy from the leader down to the position at the bottom. This property of status differentiation need not be brought about through a formal vote or through formal codification on paper. The relative status position that a given individual member occupies is operationally inferred from the relative frequency of *effective initiative* that he achieves in starting and carrying out activities and projects in which the membership as a whole participates. This result is confirmed by sociometric choices of the group members along dimensions of effective initiative as well as popularity. The status differentiation of the members constitutes the *organization* of the group and embodies the *power* aspects of relations within the group.

The psychological counterpart of the emergence of group structure or organization is revealed through reciprocal performance expectations of members, not through dictates of an outside authority, but on the basis of their experiences of the relative contributions of each member in previous efforts towards solution of common problems.

PROPERTIES OF "GROUPNESS"

Another essential property of groups, extracted from a survey of empirical field studies, is a set of values or *norms* shared by group members. It can be said that the "groupness" of the group as a more or less lasting social unit may be best defined in terms of these essential properties, viz., organization or structure and a set of values or norms (*cf.* Homans, 1950). More transitory social situations which lack these properties may be referred to as mere aggregates or togetherness situations.

The set of values or norms of a group (variously referred to as its code, standards, or rules) has probably a more direct bearing on the problem of conformity and deviation. There would be no persistent problem of conformity or deviation if there were no norms to conform to or deviate from: a question raised at the start of this discussion. As long as there are values or norms shared, upheld, and cherished by group members, compliance to and deviation from them are ever-present concerns.

In the literature, there is confusion in regard to the concept "group norm." As long as a norm is property of the group, upheld by members as "theirs," a norm is an expected and even ideal mode of behavior for them and does not refer necessarily to the statistical average of the behavior of members (Freedman *et al.*, 1952).

The *social attitude* of the individual, determining characteristic and persistent modes of behavior to relevant stimuli, be they other persons, groups, activities, institutions, or symbols, is derived from those expected, or even ideal modes of behavior referred to as a group norm. A norm is a group property and, as such, is a sociological designation. The individual's social attitude is the consequence of internalization of the norm by the individual. Social attitudes define the individual's relatedness to stimuli in question—to other persons, groups, symbols, etc.—and his stance for or against them. As such, social attitudes may be referred to as his ego-attitudes or, if you like, self-attitudes. The individual's experience of self-identity, his feelings of stability (security), his strivings toward expected and ideal goals consist in large part of ego-attitudes derived from his membership character in given groups during his life history.

This being the case, norms are not rules or standards of behavior devoid of motivational and emotional warmth. Social attitudes formed relative to group norms define a substantial part of the individual's goal-directed behavior, which is the earmark of any motivational state.

The motivational-emotional character of norm-regulated behavior is not a mystery if we consider the rise and stabilization of norms in spontaneously formed groups. Small groups arising on an informal basis in actual life are outcomes of interaction among individuals with motives perceived as common, be they common deprivations and frustrations—such as those experienced by youngsters in slum areas—or desires for social distinction and exclusiveness with appropriate facilities and prestige symbols—such as those characteristic of clubs mushrooming in residential extensions of large cities like Los Angeles, Houston, and Chicago. As anyone familiar with the history of labor organizations in this country knows, it was the common urge for mutual protection and improvement of working and wage conditions which prompted the banding together of laborers in the latter half of the 19th century, at first secretly and then in public forms which foreshadowed the modern labor unions. The norms cherished as almost sacred and upheld most tenaciously in word and deed by labor organizations to this very day are those related to the motivational issues that brought the early workers together—collective bargaining, the right to strike, seniority rights, the closed shop, minimum wage, and so on. The motivational bases of such norms are readily seen when one of the members deviates from the hardwon standards. Not just a few administrators, but the rank and file have coined labels and developed corrective measures for deviations they consider as selling out their interests. A similar analysis of motivational bases in the rise and functioning of norms can be applied to management and business organizations.

In short, norms arise and are stabilized relative to motivationally important relationships and activities. Serious issues of conformity and nonconformity arise relative to norms pertaining to matters of consequence to the group, its existence, its perpetuation, its solidarity and its effective functioning toward central interests and goals. Therefore, it is somewhat unrealistic to dwell upon cases of conformity or nonconformity in matters considered peripheral to the scheme of things by the group in question, such as the hobbies engaged in by members privately. This question of the relative importance of the behavior area was one of those which opened this presentation. In this connection, it is essential that the investigator recognize that the importance of a norm in the scheme of a particular group may or may not correspond to the importance and seriousness of the issue in question in determining the course of human relations in a larger sense. For example, in this country until recently, many organizations, including labor, considered political matters as the politician's realm.

LATITUDE OF ACCEPTABLE BEHAVIOR DEFINED BY NORM

Now we turn to discussion of a concept which will provide us with a baseline for classifying given behavior as conforming or deviating and for evaluating unique personal variations of individuals in this respect. Norm-regulated behavior cannot be represented as a single point. The expected or ideal behavior within the bounds of a given norm is represented by a range of behaviors, which we have referred to as a "range of tolerable behavior" and "latitude of acceptance," and shall here term "latitude of acceptable behavior" (Hovland, Harvey, and Sherif, 1957; Sherif and Sherif, 1953, pp. 198, 207*f*; 1956, pp. 171, 533).

As long as behavior falls within bounds defined by this range, it will not call for correctives applied to cases of deviation (Jackson, 1960). Behavior outside the limits is viewed as objectionable by other members and will arouse spontaneous correctives from the membership, even without deliberate formal action. In our present ongoing research on naturally formed groups in settings differentiated as to social rank in several southwestern cities, we find that an important difference between groups distinguished as to their solidarity is the extent to which the membership actively participates in correctives for deviating behavior (Sherif, 1959; Sherif and Sherif, 1960). Solidarity is measured by members' behaviors when the leader is present and absent, by their secrecy and exclusiveness relative to outsiders, by relative coordination of role performance in the face of mildly threatening situations. The group with greater solidarity by these measures is also the group whose members react to a man when a member deviates from an important norm.

Of course, the usual routines of social life run within the bounds of acceptable behavior. Like the oxygen in the air which is noticed only when the concentration falls, the reality of norms and their limits are seen most strikingly when correctives and constraints are aroused by deviation, as Durkheim so aptly noted.

NORMS, LATITUDE, AND BEHAVIOR

The latitude of acceptable behavior varies in magnitude according to the importance of the norm for the group. The more consequential the issue at hand, the more constricted the latitude of acceptable behavior. Conversely, the more peripheral the issue, the greater the variability encompassed by the latitude of acceptable behavior. In matters bearing closely on the existence and perpetuation of the group, the latitude of acceptable behavior is constricted, unless the group is in a state of disorganization. And, at times when the well-being of the group becomes an acute problem, it is constricted still further. In our experiments on group formation and intergroup relations in 1949 and 1954, groups met in intense competition for a single goal over a period of several days. At the height of the group conflict growing out of this competition even a slightly kind word about the out-group was seen as almost treasonable; whereas, a little earlier, similar acts were acceptable in the spirit of good sportsmanship (Sherif and Sherif, 1953; Sherif et al., 1954). It is not hard to find parallels of this constriction of the latitude of acceptable behavior in the political scene of recent years.

Along the lines of previous studies in relation to the closed-shop issue in 1948 by Hovland, Volkart, and Sherif and the prohibition issue in Oklahoma by Hovland, Harvey, and Sherif (1957), our study during the 1956 election campaign (Sherif and Hovland, 1961) verified the constricted latitude of acceptance in matters vital to the existence of a group. In this experiment, the task was to indicate acceptance and rejection of nine statements ranging from extremely pro-Republican (labeled A) to extremely pro-Democratic (labeled I) on the issue of the election of presidential and vice-presidential candidates of the two parties. The finding pertinent to our present discussion was that identi- fied members who were actively campaigning at the time for their respective parties, viz., members of Young Republican and Young Dem- ocratic organizations in several universities in the Southwest, included fewer stands in their latitudes of acceptance and rejected an extended range of stands as compared with individuals not identified organiza- tionally with either party, who had more extended latitudes of accep- tance around the stand they endorsed (see Figure 4).

BEHAVIORAL LATITUDE AND POSITION IN THE GROUP

The latitude of acceptable behavior on a given issue varies also with the position the individual occupies in the group. I strongly suspect that position in the group and importance of the norm interact in rather complex fashion to define the limits of the latitude of acceptable behavior for a particular individual relative to a particular norm. But it should be mentioned that the leader, as a member of a group, is not immune to correctives. If his nonconformity pertains to a matter of sufficient im- portance, the end result may be his decline in the power hierarchy.

The concept of latitude of acceptable behavior is explicit recog- nition of the fact that no two individuals in the same group uphold the norms to the same degree, nor are cases of nonconformity involving different individuals ever identical. There are individual variations in both conformity and nonconformity owing to unique personal character- istics of the individuals in question. These individual variations are psychological facts which should be included in an adequate con- ceptualization. Perhaps some of the difficulty encountered in doing so stems from the tendency in psychology to categorize individual variations as though they referred to events in an altogether different universe of discourse than social behavior. If unique individual varia- tions are ordered relative to a baseline defined by the latitude of acceptable behavior and the range of rejected behavior on the issue in question, we may achieve a reference scale more meaningful than

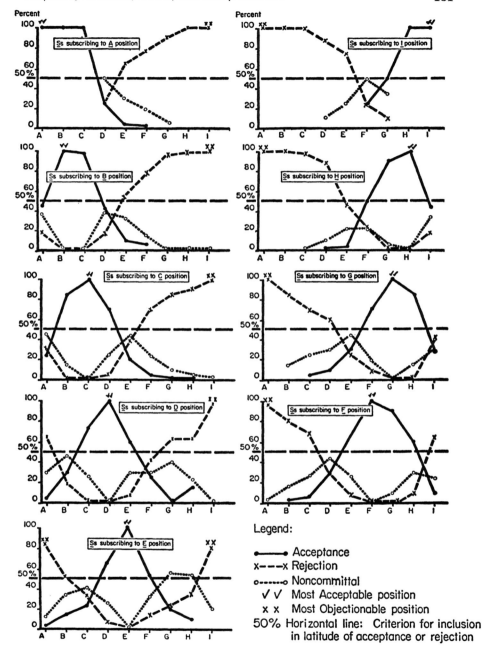

FIGURE 4. Latitudes of acceptance and rejection for stands on a political issue by individuals upholding different position: A (extreme pro-Republican)) to I (extreme pro-Democrat).

hypothetically constructed scales dictated by worn-out typologies and computational convenience (Hood and Sherif, 1955).

CONFORMITY-DEVIATION AND CHANGE IN INTERGROUP RELATIONS

As concluded in the last section, a norm emerges in relation to significant aspects of the existence and activities of the group. The prevailing pattern of relations of a given group with others is certainly a significant concern for its members. In the course of friendly or hostile, cooperative or competitive traffic between groups, norms emerge which regulate the intergroup attitudes and behavior of the members of the ingroup toward the outgroup and its members. If the character of this traffic is positive, if the goals of the respective groups do not conflict, if interests of groups do not clash, the norms regulating attitude and behavior are friendly and favorable. If the groups are striving towards goals whose attainment implies gain for one group while signifying loss and defeat for the other, the intergroup norms are unfavorable and hostile. In line with the specific character of the norms, qualities or stereotypes are attributed to the outgroup, being positive or negative depending on the character of the intergroup relations. This process underlies the close or remote "social distance" at which another group and its members are kept.

GROUPS AND NEGATIVE STEREOTYPES

In our 1949 and 1954, experiments on group relations mentioned earlier, groups in conflict developed unmistakable negative stereotypes and each group viewed the other through the widening gap of social distance which appeared irreconcilable to the members of both groups. In the 1954 experiment, these negative stereotypes were changed and the social distance between the groups reduced to the point of mutual acceptance. A brief background is necessary to explicate the conditions bringing about this positive change.

In these experiments, groups formed as social units when individuals who were initially unacquainted were brought together in activities with compelling goals whose attainment required joint and coordinated action on the part of all individuals. As a consequence of interaction in such conditions over a period of time, groups emerged with organizations and with norms, as is characteristic of groups in actual life. When two groups had thus developed independently as social units, they were brought together for the first time in the second stage of the experiment, in a series of reciprocally competitive activities, in which the victory of one meant the defeat of the other, with attendant reward and glory for the victor and disappointment and frustration for the vanquished group. In the course of these encounters, the initial sportsmanship toward the adversary went into a sharp decline and was supplanted by derogatory invectives and open expressions of hostility.

In time, unfavorable adjectives, such as "stinkers," "cheats," "sneaks," became stabilized in word and deed as the picture of the adversary. As intergroup conflict increased, cooperation and solidarity *within* each group reigned supreme.

At this point, members of each group were disinterested in any *information* about their adversary which might have changed their views of them; they were adamant in their insistence that they did not even want to be in the same situation as the other group. Therefore, the ground was not favorable for *negotiations between the leaders.* When brought into physical proximity in activities enjoyable to each group separately, the *social interaction situations* were utilized for furthering the mutual derogation.

None of the measures just mentioned could have been effective in changing the reciprocal hostility to intergroup cooperation or in changing the highly unfavorable stereotypes to a congenial picture of the outgroup. Of course, the threat of a common enemy is usually conducive to burying the hatchet for the time being, but this measure, which had been effective in 1949, was discarded because of its temporary nature and because it simply widened the sphere of group conflict.

THE OUTGROUP AND ATTITUDE CHANGE

The experimental procedure that proved to be effective in changing attitudes and behavior toward the outgroup was the same in conception as that which had resulted in the individuals banding together in group organizations in the first place: viz., the introduction of problem situations and goals which individuals could not ignore but whose solution and attainment required that all of them pull together. When the problem situation involves two or more groups, the goals conducive to opening interchange between their respective members and laying the ground for mutual efforts could only be those with *urgency* for members of all the groups involved, but which cannot be attained by the resources and efforts of the groups separately. The coordination of all efforts in the same direction must be required to reach the goal, which may be avoiding a common disaster or may be ends mutually beneficial and satisfying to all. Such goals are *superordinate* to each of the groups in question. Through the introduction of, not one, but a *series* of superordinate goals, social distance between the groups in the experiment was reduced and stereotypes changed from largely unfavorable to generally favorable pictures of the outgroup. Figure 5 shows the combined ratings of the outgroup on several traits made by members of the respective groups first at the height of intergroup conflict, and later, following the series of superordinate goals.

The process of change involved shifts in conforming behavior and changes in what constituted nonconformity. The friendly interchange and mutual cooperation between members of the different groups which characterized their relationships following the series of superordinate goals were viewed by members of each group as conforming to the developing group trend. They were not considered deviation, as they certainly would have been during the earlier period of intergroup hostility when a friendly gesture would have been regarded as "indecent."

CONFORMITY-DEVIATION AND SOCIAL CHANGE IN THE LARGER SETTING

Conformity and deviation have been discussed in this paper in terms of normative process in small groups spontaneously organized by individuals with motives and problems seen as common, whether these motives relate to common conditions of the natural settings or to experimentally created problem situations. In such groups, whatever the organizational form and the character of the norms may be, they are not handed down by an outside authority. They are outcomes of the interaction process among the individual members, of course, as influenced by their previous group memberships and the setting in which they function. Each individual attains a position in the group through his relative contribution and efforts, and his position is not fixed once and for all. Each had some hand in shaping the norms of the group and can have a hand in changing them through further interaction.

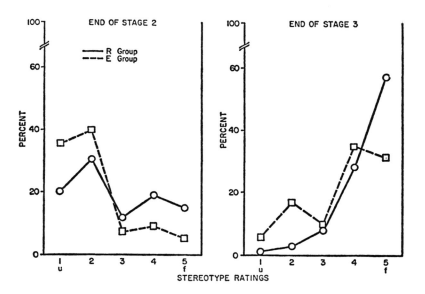

FIGURE 5. Ratings of the outgroup during intergroup conflict (left) and reduction of conflict (right). (From Sherif et al., 1954.)

Such is not the case in traditional groups and formally organized groups in the larger cultural setting. We cannot adequately touch upon the questions raised at the beginning of this paper without at least mentioning conformity and deviation as they occur in such organizational frameworks.

LARGER SETTINGS

Many organizations in the larger setting are handed down through the generations and some are deliberately organized with blueprints, rules, and regulations put down on paper by personages or governing bodies in power. As a result many individual members have had nothing to do with shaping the organizational patterns and normative system. Not infrequently, the norms and organizational forms, which might have been appropriate under conditions at the time of their appearance, prevail now more through the heavy hand of tradition or through active efforts of those interested in their perpetuation.

The larger setting is further confounded by multiple groups in which individuals may have overlapping memberships, and by sizable power differentials between various groups in the scheme of things. In the highly differentiated modern scene, the individual may be faced with contradictory, even conflicting modes of compliance from his multiple groups. He may also experience in a personal way the power differential between his own groups and others in the setting.

Problems suggested by formal organizations and multiple groups have been investigated especially by sociologists—Durkheim, the Lynds, Merton, and Williams, to mention only a few. Here I can only cite a few of the pyschological questions these topics impose upon us without marshalling factual evidence.

We may note, first of all, that when normative systems are upheld by the heavy hand of tradition and coercion, with little voluntary acceptance by the bulk of the individuals involved, informal groups usually arise within the formal outfit, as has been observed in industrial and military organizations. In such cases, the individual's compliance with inner acceptance is to norms of the informal groups to which he actively contributes. It may be suggested as a hunch to be tested that the greater the appeal of informal groups within formal organizations, the greater the secrecy observed in maintaining the existence of informal groups, the greater is the likelihood that the norms and rules of the formal organization have lost their effectiveness in regulating the behavior of the individuals involved.

The formal organization is one of the settings, so prevalent in modern differentiated societies, in which an individual's membership group (in this case, the formal organization) may not be his reference group, that is the group to which he relates himself psychologically or aspires to belong. Other common instances of discrepancies between the individual's membership groups and his reference groups owe their existence to the anchoring effects of the more powerful groups for individuals situated at lower levels in a setting which sanctions upward mobility.

CONFLICT AND THE INDIVIDUAL IN THE GROUP

The individual living his existence in membership groups with set modes of conformity while simultaneously relating himself psychologically to other groups or aspiring to belong to other groups is bound to experience frustration and personal conflict, at least at times. Many a man, dissatisfied and frustrated in his association with a given group, in which whatever compliance he observes is through coercion or fear of coercion, strives to break away from it and its norms. However, the efforts toward the break are not the end point in this picture. Usually the break, when it is made, is from one constellation of human relationships toward another. Thus, resistance and tendencies to deviation from the norms of one group are supplanted by active searching for new anchorages which the individual can accept as his own.

Perhaps this picture may have some relevance for issues of change. It suggests that active nonconformity to the norms of a membership group which require coercion for their observance, which arouse frustration in man and conflict between men rather than understanding and cooperation, is but one part of the picture. The completed picture is not a state of normlessness, but a search for normative bases which are not conflicting, not frustrating, not self-degrading to the individual.

The elevation of nonconformity alone to the level of a slogan has its roots in an untenable dichotomy between individual and group, in a preconceived inevitability of clash between the two. Such a stand cannot account for changes in human relationships or their normative bases.

If normlessness is not the end result of social change, then the human sciences face a more vital and difficult task than merely demonstrating the blinding and degrading effects of certain norms. The task requires some valid criteria for singling out prevailing norms which produce these effects and for deliberate choice of values and organizational forms conducive to behavior which is enriching and "self-actualizing" for individuals in their social relationships.

SUMMARY AND CONCLUSIONS

In all phases of his daily living—social, political, economic, religious—man is confronted today with pressures and exhortations to regulate his behavior within advocated molds and directions.

Concerned with the plight of those of their fellow men who have fallen prey in blind conformity to such pressures and exhortations, psychologists and social scientists have advanced various antidotes. One attempt in this direction is the cult which almost elevates nonconformity in its own right to a pedestal of virtue. Such attempts are laudable from the point of view of intent. But their realistic adequacy as effective measures is a different matter.

Even the most ardent proponent of nonconformity would not praise stealing simply because it is a nonconforming deed. Indeed, conformity is condemned because of concern over widespread degradation of moral and artistic values, of repressive restrictions on human expression and the rights of man, of arbitrary limitations to human dignity and potentialities. In short, the plea for nonconformity is made in the name of values or norms which were themselves formulated through a long and arduous stretch of human history. But as long as the analysis and the plea center on conformity or nonconformity in the abstract, there is no adequate basis for evaluating conforming or nonconforming behavior. And the exhortation to individual man to assert his independence of a mountain of social pressures may not be an adequate way to move the mountain.

An item of behavior, whether in social, political, religious, or economic spheres, cannot be characterized by itself as either conforming or deviating. It is always conformity or deviation relative to some premise, canon, standard, or value—in short, to some norm. Therefore, the primary question to be raised becomes: "Conformity or nonconformity in relation to what practice, what value, what moral standard, or what norm?"

Social values, moral standards, or norms are products of interaction among human beings over a period of time in matters of consequence to their mutual and individual concerns. Thus, issues of conformity and nonconformity which make the problem so urgent for study are not one-episode affairs involving momentary, transitory social influence on inconsequential matters. For these reasons, the traditional laboratory setting is far from adequate for studying significant problems of conformity and deviation.

On the whole, the traditional laboratory experiment takes the individual from a context of relationships with other people involving matters of mutual importance to expose him briefly to a momentary situation arranged by the experimenter. There is sufficient evidence to conclude that the experimenter's success in demonstrating susceptibility to conform in the laboratory is inversely related to the degree of structure, the number and clarity of alternatives available in the stimulus situation the experimenter has arranged for the subjects. Thus in a highly unstructured situation with various alternatives, the subject may conform almost invariably to definitions introduced by the experimenter. To conclude, therefore, that he is basically a conformist would be quite in error. Likewise, demonstration of righteous protests by individuals exposed to easily discriminable stimuli and a fantastically false consensus by others is scarcely evidence for man's basic independence.

The attribution of either blind subservience to the group or independence to the basic nature of man rests on an untenable dichotomy between individual and group. An adequate approach must begin with a clear statement of the place of norm-regulated behavior in psychological functioning. Even a single individual faced with a perceptual situation for which he has little in the way of established guide posts for evaluation, comes *in time* to a stabilized mode of behavior, as experiments have shown. At the basis of this tendency toward stabilization lies man's capacity to regulate his behavior through conceptual categories.

Normative regulation of behavior is also conceptual regulation, and without it, human morality of any kind would be inconceivable. It is precisely the normative regulation of behavior that permits human action to transcend demands of the immediate social surroundings, as well as to conform to them, to delay momentary impulses, and to resist the promptings of transitory emotional states. Normative regulation, properly conceived, is not alien to man's nature, but one of its distinctive features. In specific situations, the process may lead either to conformity or nonconformity.

Those canons, values, or norms relative to which conformity or nonconformity become important problems are integral aspects of man's relations with other men. These relations involve lasting expectations, reciprocities, and responsibilities, and their patterns constitute the individual's group relations. Thus the realistic, the significant setting for study and analysis of conforming behavior is the setting of human groups, large and small.

Some kind of norm system is one of the essential features of any human group, be it a club or church, a sect or professional group, or even a group whose major tenets involve nonconformity to prevailing societal norms.

When man enters into repeated interaction with others, directed toward similar concerns and goals, he takes part in a process of norm formation and stabilization. Once a normative system is stabilized, the individual member who took part in its creation regulates his behavior within the bounds it defines as acceptable, even without external pressures and sanctions. Both our research and considerable empirical findings demonstrate that the bounds defined by group norms are perceived by the single member as his own *latitude of acceptable behavior*. Behavior outside of this range is evaluated as objectionable. Henceforth, social control is achieved in part through the autonomous regulation of behavior by individual members. And when it relies exclusively on external pressure and coercion, changes in the normative structure may be anticipated.

Therefore, the question of concern to those who are disturbed with the plight of men caught in pressures toward certain molds of conformity should not be evaluation of conformity or nonconformity in the abstract. The first question must be conformity to what norm? Answers to this question entail not only the external referent of the behavior, but the context of group relationships in which it occurs and the voluntary or coercive nature of its regulation. Then analysis of the appropriateness or inappropriateness of the norm in question for the situation and in terms of other criteria may begin with an adequate basis. If on this basis, norms are found inappropriate, a related task becomes discovering the processes leading to perpetuation of dysfunctional norms, including notably, interested parties engaged in active efforts to that end.

A closely related task is assessing the demands placed upon the individual by conflicting norms—for example, norms of altruism preached on Sunday and norms for the hard facts of business and professional practice. The existence of mutually conflicting values or norms characteristic of highly differentiated Western societies today, as various social scientists have pointed out, is responsible in no small part for psychological conflict with attendant wear and tear and restlessness so widely reflected in contemporary novels and social science literature.

If, as it would seem, the interdependencies of human development and human groups are becoming increasingly closer and wider in scope, then the analysis demands a flood of light upon the consequences of maintaining obsolete, constrictive norms perpetuated through ethnocentrisms and activities of particularly interested groups. The appropriate changes in norms are, of course, part of the problem of social change. If the social scientist or psychologist backs away from this problem, he is backing away from the course of intellectual history. For good or evil, human relationships and their norms have changed and they will change. The challenge of understanding the process and the directions it takes must be met if we are seriously concerned with man's creative development and larger self-fulfillment. The two are not independent.

ELEVEN

A STUDY IN EGO FUNCTIONING:
ELIMINATION OF STABLE ANCHORAGES
IN INDIVIDUAL AND GROUP RELATIONS
With O. J. Harvey, University of Colorado

This study attempts to investigate the effects of various conditions of situational uncertainty on ego functioning through simple judgmental reactions. By situational uncertainty we mean situation surrounding the individual which lacks stable spatial and other anchorages, consequently, making it impossible or hard for the individual to determine his bearings in relation to objects and individuals in the situation.

This is not a study of judgmental processes *per se*. The fundamental conceptual approach of studying attitudes, ego-attitudes, and other internal factors through "cognitive" processes such as judging, perceiving, remembering, etc., is becoming the main approach in the experimental study of these central topics of psychology.[1] The present study is an application of this general approach to the problem of anxiety or insecurity.

A number of experimental findings and observations of man's reactions under varying degrees of instability, confusion, and chaos in

From *Sociometry* (1952), 15: 272–305. Reprinted with permission of J. L. Moreno and Beacon House.

The study reported here was made possible by financial aid under a contract between the Office of Naval Research and the Research Institute of the University of Oklahoma. The authors are grateful to ONR, to Dean Laurence H. Synder, director of organized research at the University of Oklahoma, and to Dr. L. E. Swearingen, director of the Research Institute at the time of the main experiment. All experimental work reported here was carried out by O. J. Harvey. Preliminary work was done by D. Swander. Norman Walter participated in pre-testing trials of the main experiment. Charles Shedd made a survey of literature on anxiety which was useful in the writing stage. We are grateful to Professor Caspar Goffman, formerly of Oklahoma, now professor of mathematics at Wayne State University, for advice and work in the treatment of results.

[1] This approach is well represented in Bartlett (1932), Blake and Ramsey (1951), Bruner and Krech (1949–50), Coffin (1941), Harvey and Sherif (1951), Sherif (1935, 1936, 1948), and Sherif and Cantril (1947).

life situations offer promising leads for testing recent theoretical formulations in ego psychology experimentally. The present study is regarded as a preliminary attempt in this direction. Since the experiment is developed from leads implicit in these experimental findings and concrete observations of life, implications of the experimental part acquire significance *only* against this background.

At this early stage of the development of ego psychology, which encompasses problems of identifications with individuals and groups, problems of anxiety, security-insecurity, etc., it will be very immature to plunge into the abstractions of laboratory situations without a constant effort to relate relevant laboratory situations and life situations. Such a constant effort will be more than rewarding because by so doing we avoid the danger of finding mere artifacts, good only on paper, and can obtain valid findings which can be translated into the world of reality in life situations.

SOME RELEVANT EXPERIMENTAL FINDINGS

The reactions of individuals to stimulus situations with relatively little objective structure are largely determined by variations in social and internal (motivational, attitudinal) factors. For this reason the autokinetic situation is admirably suited for studying such variables experimentally. In the middle thirties, Sherif (1935) showed the effects of certain social factors in judgments of extent of apparent movement and characteristic variations from subject to subject in distribution of judgments. The subject in the autokinetic situation finds himself in a room completely dark except for the periodic appearance of a tiny pinpoint of light. Since he has no way of knowing whether or not his judgments are correct, the subject feels uneasy (Sherif, 1936, p. 107). Seated in the dark room, uncertain of whether or not he is reacting appropriately,

at times he feels insecure about his spatial bearing . . . some subjects report that they are not only confused about the location of the point of light; they are even confused about the stability of their own position (Sherif, 1936, p. 92).

When the individual's judgments of movement differ considerably from those of a prestigeful partner, he may, as in Sherif's study of attitude formation (1937), become disturbed and uneasy, especially if no common norm is achieved or maintained. Murphy (1945) has suggested that under these circumstances "the insecurity of the untrained observer, the need to see as a trained observer did, was the chief dynamic factor involved . . ." (p. 4).

In short, insecurity or anxiety of varying degrees is situationally aroused in the autokinetic experiment. In this unstable, uncertain situation, establishment of or convergence toward a common norm is accompanied by a reduction of these insecurity feelings (Sherif, 1936,

p. 110). As Kelman says, in his study of experimentally induced success and failure, "the establishment and use of a standard give the individual a basis for his judgments and therefore reduce his anxiety" (1950, p. 279).

As Sherif's experiments showed, the individual facing the situation alone establishes a more or less characteristic range and norm for his judgments; and individual variations in reaction to the judgments of others in a group situation are striking. In extending the work on individual characteristics, Bovard (1948) found that changes in scatter and means between individual sessions and sessions with a prestigeful partner on the same day were highly correlated with the degree to which the social norm was carried over in an individual session four weeks later.

In the clinical area, pronounced individual differences have been found among various patients in mental hospitals by Voth (1947). Patients in anxiety states were among those perceiving "more pronounced" movement. Following metrazol shock treatments, patients frequently show "very distinct reduction in movement" p. 800).

Klein and Schlesinger (1951) found significant quantitative and qualitative differences in reactions to apparent movement of forms among groups previously selected as "form-labile" and "form-bound" on the basis of criteria from Rorschach scores and protocols.

F. Schumer (1949) showed that individuals who were found to be "movement oriented" on the basis of a Rorschach index revealed significantly less convergence toward a group norm in the autokinetic situation than "non-movement oriented" individuals.

In Kelman's study of "suggestibility" in the autokinetic situation (1950), differential insecurity was produced experimentally by telling one group of subjects that most of their judgments in an individual session were correct, and another group that most of their judgments were incorrect. Individuals in the "success" group were subsequently less susceptible to the judgments of a "planted" subject than individuals in the "failure" group.

IMPLICATIONS OF OBSERVATIONS FROM LIFE SITUATIONS
FOR OUR PROBLEM

Experimental study must ring true to the characteristics of situations and behavior in the run of things in men's lives. For our problem we are specifically concerned with life situations of little structure, that is, situations with few stable anchorages. An example is the battlefield in modern mechanized war. In his description of the modern battlefield, Marshall (1947) wrote, "The harshest thing about the field is that it is *empty*. No people stir about. There are little or no signs of action. Over all there is a great quiet which seems more ominous than the occasional tempest of fire" (p. 44). This is in contrast to the recruit's expectations after being trained in the presence of great numbers of men and massive mechanical power all around him. But "he finds himself suddenly almost alone in his hour of greatest danger, and he can feel the danger, but there is nothing out there, nothing to contend against" (p. 45). "There is nothing to be seen. The fire comes out of nowhere. But that is all that he knows for certain" (p. 47). As the men scatter under fire, they may even be out of sight of one another. And, as Vilfroy's account of the early days of the war in France (1940) puts it, he feels utterly alone, "forward and isolated" (Vilfroy, 1942, p. 105).

Another example is the situation of soldiers on board ship, bound for an invasion. The present situation is clear-cut enough, but the future is unknown. It was Ernie Pyle's insightful observation that

I don't believe one of us was afraid of the physical part of dying. That isn't the way it is. The emotion is rather one of *almost desperate reluctance to give up the future*. I suppose that's splitting hairs and that it really all comes *under the heading of fear. Yet somehow there is a difference.* . . . When we huddled around together on the dark decks, it was these little hopes and ambitions that made up the sum total of our worry at leaving, rather than visualization of physical agony to come (Pyle, 1943, p. 4. Italics ours).

As Stouffer *et al.* (1949) indicated, the result of such situations is anxiety and insecurity for the individual. In behavioral terms, one fruit of such unstructured situations of stress is a decrease, at least temporarily, in behavior governed by group standards for action or by possible realistic requirements of the situation, and an increase in behavior aroused by the individual's anxieties. Marshall (1947) observed that as men spread apart under fire, they move "individually to whatever cover is nearest or affords the best protection." Some may use their equipment, timidly at first. Others do nothing, either because lacking instructions they don't know what to do or because "they are wholly unnerved and can neither think nor move in sensible relation to the situation" (p. 48). When the men cannot see one another under enemy fire, "all organizational unity vanishes temporarily. What has been a force becomes a scattering of individuals" (p. 129).

Those who have spent considerable time in prisoner-of-war camps report that the uncertainty of present and future life led frequently to increased individual fantasy and increasingly difficult relations with fellow prisoners.[2]

At a simpler level, Pyle (1943) contrasted the behavior of infantry men, who were most exposed to continuing chaos and uncertainty even as to where and when they would sleep or eat, and sailors, who

[2] E.g., Vaughan (1947) describing a civilian concentration camp in the Philippines, pp. 133–134.

at least had a ship to call home. The sailors were "more like themselves. They didn't cuss as much or as foully as soldiers. They didn't bust loose as riotously when they hit town" (p. 3).

The individual, in a situation having few or no anchorages to guide him, caught in the throes of anxiety, tries to establish some level of stability. He seeks to find some standard and is susceptible to accepting a standard from another source. Take, for example, the pilots preparing to take off from a ship before daybreak. On a completely dark deck, they must find their ships. "Old hands get used to memorizing the *relative positions* of all the planes the afternoon before the next morning, which helps" (Wordell and Seiler, 1943, p. 26). It is a common enough observation that some conclusion to awaiting an indefinite future, even finally entering combat, may bring intense relief and stabilization, in spite of objective dangers in the certainty (Simpon, 1943, p. 4).

Marshall (1947) investigated the problem of why enemy fire against an advancing infantry line invariably caused a delay of from 45 to 60 minutes. His observations (of eleven infantry companies and one reconnaissance troop) led him to conclude that the line did not proceed until *effective communication* was restored. This might be simply one bold individual standing up and shouting "Follow me! We're going on!" (p. 130). If withdrawal becomes necessary, but is not coupled with some brief explanation (e.g., "Get the hell out of here and follow me to that tree line on the far side of the creek"), panic is likely to result.

In such stress situations, where the individual perceives only confusion, he may long for something or someone to provide standards of conduct. Thus soldiers caught in a hasty withdrawal of British forces after the breakthrough by Rommel's army in Libya, completely surrounded by confusion "bewilderment and fear and ignorance" *wanted* to receive orders (Moorehead, 1942, pp. 69–71). Here is the statement of a veteran wounded in the North Africa campaign:

One time we begged our lieutenants to give orders. They were afraid to act because they didn't have the rank. We took a beating while they were waiting for orders—how did they know the commander hadn't been knocked off? (Stouffer *et al.*, 1949, p. 117).

In the absence of other anchors or standards for anticipating the future, men put their faith in the wisdom and experience of the captain of their vessel or the pilot of their plane (e.g., Pyle, 1943, p. 4; Rehm, 1945, p. 7). In such situations, the individual becomes increasingly dependent upon his own group for feelings of security (e.g., Stouffer *et al.*, 1949, p. 144; Marshall, 1947, pp. 129–130).

In short, the effect of extreme stress, uncertainty, lack of stable anchorages may be to increase suggestibility—in the sense of increasing the likelihood of accepting a standard for behavior from a source other than the individual's own. When shared with others, this increasing desire for some stable anchorages leads to the rise and spread of *rumors,* as the study and reports of rumor have amply shown (e.g., Allport and Postman, 1947; Caplow, 1947; Lucas, 1944, p. 66; Robinson, 1944, p. 64; Pyle, 1943, pp. 9–10; Chunn, 1946, pp. 107–109; Holman, 1942, pp. 93–94; Booker, 1946, p. 196; Vaughan, 1947, pp. 133–134).

Rumor may, of course, be based on some specific event or action which is not defined for those watching. Marshall (1947) who investigated the sources of panic which occurred in battle during World War II concluded that *in every case "the common denominator" was that "somebody failed to tell other men what he was doing"* (p. 146). Thus, in one case, a sergeant wounded during battle dashed back to a first aid station without telling his squad why. They took after him, and the rumor spread through the whole line, "The order is to withdraw."

The acceptance of an inappropriate or erroneous standard in a situation of intense stress and uncertainty often leads to panic. Turning to examples more familiar to social psychologists, it is no coincidence, as Cantril (1947) pointed out, that the panic following Orson Welles' "Invasion from Mars" followed the tense, jittery days of the war crisis of September, 1938, while this country was still in a period of depression. Similarly, the "phantom anesthetist of Mattoon," Illinois (Johnson, 1945), made his appearance during the war and predominantly among *women* of lower economic and occupational groups, many of whom (among those who responded) indicated trouble with "nerves."

THE THEORETICAL BASIS OF THE STUDY

The concepts of anxiety, insecurity, inadequacy, aloneness, etc., which all express personally felt, painful experiences of being out-of-tune, uneasy with oneself, have become at present central topics in the writings of authors seriously concerned with the plight of man living under the strains of the modern world. Such concepts are central in the analysis of modern man presented by Fromm, Horney, Murphy, Harry Stack Sullivan and others.

The present investigation is undertaken as an experimental approach to the study of some phases of ego problems. As recently stated by Mullahy in a symposium devoted to the topic of anxiety to which various authors contributed, there is no agreement as to what is meant by anxiety (Mullahy, 1950). For example, "some include fear under anxiety, others do not. This is no mere matter of terminology. Until we decide precisely what we are talking about, we can have little agreement on what causes anxiety, and what function or functions anxiety serves . . ." (p. 44).

If there is no differentiating criterion between fear and anxiety, between fear and insecurity, or between fear and experience of aloneness, then in the interests of parsimony we should list them all under fear and not unnecessarily multiply terms in such a complicated area. We have, therefore, to justify anxiety, insecurity and similar concepts with some differentiating criterion. Traditionally some authors defined fear in terms of stimuli which are definite and identifiable, and anxiety in terms of indefiniteness of stimulus situations. If such were the case, the most convenient way to deal with the problem might be to speak of fears caused by definite stimulus situations and fears caused by indefinite stimulus situations.

It seems to us that the differentiating psychological criterion between fear on the one hand and such states referred to as anxiety, insecurity, etc., on the other hand, is furnished by those who study these problems in the developmental sequence of the individual.

Developmentally the appearance of fear in the human infant is prior to the appearance of anxiety. In order for anxiety to appear there has to be a certain degree of ego development. To this effect Harry Stack Sullivan (1947) writes:

Along with learning of language, the child is experiencing many restraints on the freedom which it had enjoyed up till now. Restraints have to be used in teaching of some of the personal habits that the culture requires everyone should show, and from these restraints there comes the evolution of the self system—an extremely important part of the personality—with a brand-new tool, a tool so important that I must give you its technical name, which unhappily coincides with a word of common speech which may mean to you anything. I refer to *anxiety*.

With the appearance of the self system or the self dynamism, the child picks up a new piece of equipment which we technically call anxiety. Of the very unpleasant experiences which the infant can have we may say that there are generically two, pain and fear. Now comes the third (pp. 273–274).

Likewise, the state of *insecurity,* in a strict sense, does not appear until a certain degree of ego development in the form of formation of certain interpersonal ties has taken place. To this effect another insightful student of ego development and functioning (Ausubel) states: "Security needs, of course, cannot arise until some notion of self is formed and until the infant is mature enough perceptually to appreciate his executive dependence" (1952, p. 333).

It seems to us that the above line of developmental observations gives us leads to make clear-cut differentiations as to the nature of anxiety, insecurity and the like. *In such states there is always ego reference,* whether it be conscious or not. The study of anxiety or insecurity, will lack its main component if the concept of ego is not brought into the picture and made central in the handling of these problems. Hence our understanding of anxiety, insecurity will increase hand in hand with increase of our understanding of ego development and functioning.

A host of empirical observations leads us to define ego as a developmental formation or "Sub-system" in the psychological make-up of the individual consisting of functionally interrelated attitudes which are acquired in relation to his own body, members of his family, social groups, objects, values and institutions which define and regulate his relatedness and hence behavior in so many concrete situations.

Ego consists of ego-attitudes formed in the life history of the individual defining, regulating his relatedness to situations, objects, individuals, groups, etc. His personal stability, personal security then, consists of the stability and continuity of these relations defined and regulated by these developmentally acquired and functionally interrelated ego-attitudes. When the stability of these relations defined by ego-attitudes is disrupted, when the ties between the individual and other persons and groups defined by his ego-attitudes are impaired, when values implied in these ego-attitudes are threatened, or when activities of the individuals towards goals determined by his ego-attitudes are thwarted with subsequent experience of failure, the consequence is ego-tension, the degree and consequnce of which will vary from case to case. We use ego-tension as a generic term to refer to painful, unpleasant experiences such as anxiety, insecurity, personal inadequacy, aloneness, shame, etc., none of which can be accounted for without bringing the ego-system into the picture. When ego-tension is caused by failures or potential failures crushing or threatening our sense of adequacy, our sense of self-esteem, or by actual or potential blockage of the individual's ego-involved goals, the appropriate term for *ego-tension* in such cases may be *anxiety*. When the ego tension is the outcome of the disruption of the stability of our bearings or ties (ties of belongingness) in relation to our physical or social surroundings, when it is the consequence of blows suffered in the course of status strivings, the more appropriate term may be *insecurity*. When the ego-tension is due to physical or psychological isolation from individuals or groups we are identified with or aspire to be identified with, the appropriate term for this psychological state may be *aloneness*. When ego-tension is aroused by being caught in a situation in which our action or predicament is negatively at variance from the level of ego values, the resulting product may be referred to as *shame*. In cases in which the variance or deviation of experience and behavior is related to the few most central, fundamental ego values the resulting ego-tension may be appropriately termed the experience of *guilt*.

We should also mention ego-tensions due to *conflict*. These cases of ego-tensions are due to our being caught in a situation which demands contradictory roles in relation to that situation. These kind of ego-tensions, which are so frequently encountered in "casually patterned" societies with contradictory values existing side by side, have been treated extensively in the writings of sociologists, psychologists and novelists who are seriously concerned with the plight of modern man. One good illustration of the point is the case of the professional woman who cherishes the notion that her accomplishment is on a par with the top-notch males in her area but who cannot participate in a convention to share the honors with her male colleagues because of the demands of her husband (the demands of the husband reinforced by the prescriptions of social norms concerning the female role in society). Another example of the point is the case of the minority group member who constantly tries to be treated in harmony with the values embodied in the constitution of the country, but who is constantly frustrated because of these claims. Or, take the case of the minority group member whose identification is split between the country of which he is formally a member and another group physically far away, thus trying to have his cake and eat it at the same time.

We have to limit this discussion of ego-tensions to the lines of the particular problem of the present experimental study. The particular ego-tension in question is insecurity. It should be said, at this point, however, that there are cases of ego-tensions in which it is difficult to decide whether anxiety or insecurity would be a more appropriate label. For example, in the case of the present study the conditions are such that both the bearings of the person in relation to his surroundings and his sense of adequacy in the given task are involved.

Anxiety in its milder or neurotic form expresses a state of ego-tension which is the by-product of experienced threats or uncertainties, real or imagined (for present or future) which are felt as directed at our personal goals, personal values, hopes of success in relation to these goals and values which constitute the core of personality. Or when, under critical circumstances, the stability of our physical and social bearings are disrupted with the subsequent experience of not being anywhere definitely, of being torn from social ties of belongingness, or when nothing but a future of uncertainty or blockages is experienced as our lot, the by-product is the experience of insecurity. The individual tossing in such a state of anxiety or insecurity flounders all over in his craze to establish for himself some stable anchorages. The fluctuations of his experience and behavior are greatly increased. In our opinion great fluctuations or variability in experience and behavior occur *first,* even in cases of persons who may *eventually* turn into themselves to build internally paranoid anchorages which are completely out of line with the facts of reality surrounding them.

The consequences of the ego-tensions, anxiety or insecurity are a state of restlessness, floundering all over to find some stable anchorages, heightened fluctuations of behavior. If these states of anxiety or insecurity are widespread among the individuals of a group, the result is an increased degree of suggestibility, the increased credulity for events that are bizarre and unexpected, a greater degree of susceptibility to the spread of wild rumors, the greater likelihood of panics. In the experimental findings presented previously, we gave evidence of the greater variability of reactions and greater suggestibility under conditions of uncertainty and failure. We gave various illustrations of some consequences of conditions of uncertainty and confusion.

In line with the illustrations already presented, the following passage from *The American Soldier: Combat and Its Aftermath* sums up clearly what we have tried to state regarding the effects of conditions of confusion, uncertainty which lack stable anchorages:

> In combat, the individual soldier was rarely sure of what had just happened, what was going on at the moment, or what was likely to occur next. He was subject to continual distraction by violent stimuli, and lived always under the tension of expecting the unexpected. This kind of unceasing confusion—the lack of firm constants to which behavior could be oriented—exposed the individual to insidious anxieties. All people need some stability in their environment; it has been repeatedly shown that *personality integration and the development of regularized patterns of behavior are strongly conditioned upon the existence of stable referents for activity. One of the prime functions of any sort of social organizations is to provide the individual with a dependable set of expectations.* Unless one knows, at least within broad limits, what behavior to expect from others, the very concept of adjustment becomes meaningless. So it is that the uncertainties and confusions of combat were themselves identifiable sources of stress. The frictions of battle, the mistiness of knowledge that goes under the name of "the fog of war," could be minimized by good provisions for transportation and communication, and by good discipline and administrative organization; but *uncertainty* always remained (Stouffer *et al.*, 1949, pp. 83–84, italics ours).

PROBLEM

The problem is the experimental production of a state of anxiety or insecurity through elimination of stable anchorages in the situation. If this first part of our problem is demonstrated, then our next task will be to reduce ego-tension (anxiety, insecurity) thus produced through the introduction of a few salient stable anchorages.

From a methodological point of view if we can exactly specify the course of elimination of stable anchorages and if the criterion of the appearance of anxiety or insecurity can be expressed in a clear-cut way in terms of the spread of judgments rather than in descriptive phrases, we shall be on firmer ground in the study of the complicated matters of ego-tensions.

The statement of the problem as a production of a state of anxiety or insecurity through elimination of stable anchorages in the situation is too general a statement for an experimental study. It has to be specified to lead us concretely to the particular study and the appropriate procedures to be used. In psychological and especially psychiatric literature, the general case is neurotic anxiety or neurotic insecurity when these problems are dealt with. Besides these extreme cases, there are cases of anxiety or insecurity which are experienced for the duration of a temporary threat or potential threat to our ego values and goals, which are experienced for the duration of a temporary state of loss of our physical or social bearings under confusing and uncertain conditions. Ausubel, a keen student of ego problems, included a section on situational anxiety in his recent book on *Ego Development and the Personality Disorders* (1952). He shows that when an individual faces a situation that constitutes a challenge to his sense of adequacy, the result is the experience of anxiety which may last for the duration of the situation at hand. In our experimental procedure, we aimed to produce a state of situational anxiety or insecurity through eliminating spatial anchorages as much as possible for the subjects in a task that requires spatial orientation. (This is especially true in the case of condition C, see pp. 205f.) The psychological basis underlying this assumption is the following: One of the earliest phases of ego development in infancy is the delineation of bodily self from surrounding objects. Henceforth, the bodily self is a main anchorage in making spatial localizations as pointed out by W. Stern years ago. But this main anchorage (viz., the delineated bodily self) is not independent of the stability or instability of other anchorages in the surroundings. As the surrounding space relations become more unstructured or surrounding space anchorages are eliminated, the stability of the spatial bearings of the bodily self become increasingly difficult. So much so that some of the S's in our situation with least structure spatially lost their orientation. They reported walking towards West while they were actually moving South, or even a few reported moving West while they actually were moving East. The discovery on their part that their actual direction was at variance with their experience of direction in such a seemingly simple task of finding their seats in complete darkness was conducive at least to a mild degree of situational anxiety.

The importance and implications of this general tendency for ambiguity and unstructuredness to lead to some degree of insecurity or anxiety for ego psychology has been emphasized previously:

Even in cases of relatively simple events, ambiguity or unstructuredness delays the judgment time and renders judgmental activity rather tense and difficult. This is not a pleasant experience even on its simplest level. The ego is no exception to the general principle. Once it is formed with all its diverse ties in relation to goal objects, persons, and groups which stand in different degrees of affective relationship to it, the ego has to be anchored safely in many capacities. When these ties are disrupted, we experience insecurity and loss of personal identity. In fact, the feeling of personal security consists mainly of the stability of these ties which originally constitute the formation of the ego (Sherif, 1948, p. 273).

The above line of psychological bases of our problem recently received a clear confirmation from a clinical psychologist. To this effect Abt (and Bellak, 1950) states:

Clinical experience with a number of the projective methods has established my conviction that when any psychological task is ill defined, and when in addition the stimulus field is either quite ambiguous or new in the experience of the subject, the testee tends to react with anxiety, which may be either minimum or strong [pp. 56–57]. . . . I suspect, on the basis of certain experimental findings arising both from the laboratory and from social psychology, that as the stimulus field becomes progressively more and more unstructured—a process that forces the individual to rely increasingly upon internal or subjective factors in perception—there is a tendency for his anxiety level to increase markedly [pp. 53–54].

HYPOTHESES

On the basis of the experimental findings presented, empirical observations reported, and the theoretical leads developed, it seems plausible to advance the following hypotheses to be tested:

The more unstructured and uncertain (with fewer definite anchorages) is the stimulus situation which the individual faces—

(a) The wider is his range or scale of judgments, thus revealing greater variability in judgments of the individual.

(b) The greater is the magnitude of the norm around which the individual scatters his judgments.

(c) The more accentuated are the differences between the judgments of individuals, this tendency being considerably reduced in group situations.

(d) The greater is the degree of convergence of judgments between individuals in group situations.

SUBJECTS

Altogether, 85 subjects took part in the present experiment.[3] Each of the final experimental groups for the three experimental conditions consisted of twenty subjects (half male, half female). Each of these sixty subjects participated in two sessions, one individual and one group session under the appropriate condition.

The remaining 25 subjects were used in pre-testing the experimental conditions which were finally adopted in this study. Of this number,

---

[3] These 85 subjects include only those used in the pre-test and experimental session of the main experiment reported here, the procedures of which were formulated for pre-testing after extensive preliminary work. This preliminary work. which was an exploratory attempt to find appropriate procedures, was carried out by D. Swander. The present report does not include any subjects or results from this preliminary work, which was presented as an experimental term paper in a graduate course at the University of Oklahoma, May, 1951.

nine were utilized in pre-tests of Conditions A and B, and sixteen were pre-tested under Condition C.

All subjects were college students who were not familiar with the autokinetic phenomenon. Subjects were paired on the basis of a criterion of homogeneity. In all cases, males were paired with males, and females with females. Subjects were placed together who did not differ markedly in age, college classification, or ethnic background. To exclude the effects of prior relationships among the subjects, subjects paired in the group sessions were not acquainted with one another. Subjects were assigned to one of the three experimental conditions on a random basis.

APPARATUS

The general disposition of the apparatus, which consists mainly of a small pin point of light exposed through a circular hole one millimeter in diameter, and a subject identification system, is essentially the same as that used by Sherif in earlier work. Two major improvements were made on the apparatus: The exposure time of three seconds (constant for all conditions) and signal to the experimenter (five seconds before the appearance of the autokinetic light) were altogether automatically controlled instead of being manually operated.[4] The source of the autokinetic light was a small radio dial bulb burning at approximately normal brilliance on 6–8 volts.

The appearance of the autokinetic light, the exposure time and signal to the experimenter were controlled by relay circuits which were set in operation by the contact of electrically sensitized copper bosses mounted on Paklite disks with stationary spring loaded plungers. The three Paklite disks on which the bosses were mounted at appropriate locations to regulate automatically the timing of the autokinetic light, exposure time and signal to the experimenter, were driven by a Telechron synchronous motor at one revolution per minute.

PROCEDURE

All subjects participated first in an experimental session *alone,* and then (after an interval of from two to seven days) they were placed in a *group* session in pairs of two. The explanation given all subjects for being paired was that it should make the task easier as well as taking less time.

In both the individual and group sessions of the three conditions, each subject gave fifty judgments at a distance of 21 feet from the autokinetic light. If the subject, or subjects, failed to report movement

---

[4] The apparatus was designed and constructed by Ralph Fearnow, formerly of the Physics shop of the University of Oklahoma.

of the light within 30 seconds after it appeared, the estimate was re-corded as zero and the experimenter pressed a control key causing the light to disappear. There was a time interval of 1 minute between the disappearance of the light and its reappearance for a new judgment. The exposure time for all subjects was 3 seconds, i.e., there was a 3-second interval between the time the subject pressed his key indicating perceived movement and the disappearance of the light. All judgments, pertinent remarks and other behavior of the subjects were recorded by the experimenter.

After the second, or group, session, each subject filled out a ques-tionnaire which contained items concerning his opinion on the positive or negative effect of another person's presence and estimates upon his own judgments, and his feeling of certainty accompanying the judg-ments. All subjects were then paid for both sessions at the rate of 65 cents an hour.

Conditions A, B, C: Since the purpose of the study was to examine the effects on judging an ambiguous stimulus of three degrees of experi-mentally induced uncertainty, the three conditions were made to rep-resent gradations or degrees of difficulty in the form of fewer anchorages in the situation. Physical anchorages were eliminated as described below. *The role of the experimenter was defined differently for the three con-ditions,* since preliminary exploratory work indicated that the experi-menter, through friendly conversation and directions, was providing (social and spatial) anchorages in an uncontrolled way.

The three conditions ranged from A, the relatively easy and simple, through B, of intermediate difficulty, to C, the most uncertain and difficult.

CONDITION A

This condition was intended to produce the least uncertainty among the subjects. To effect this, the experimental situation was made rela-tively simple and the role assumed by the experimenter was one of informality and friendliness. The experimental room for this condition (15 by 28 feet) was much smaller than for the other conditions (81 by 54 feet). Subjects had a brief glimpse of the interior, the seat, table and of the space relations in the room. Thus the subject in Condition A had some opportunity to orient himself in relation to definite anchorages, such as walls, chair, table, etc.

Individual Session. The attempt was made to establish rapport by spending several minutes with each subject in informal and friendly conversation before the experimental session. The subject was assured the task was simple and easy, that there was no doubt that he would do well. In short, *in Condition A the experimenter was as friendly and encouraging as possible.* After ascertaining if the subject "was about ready to try your luck at judging distance," he was instructed: "Now I will take you to a dark room where I will show you your chair. Your only task will be to judge how far a point of light moves."

The subject was then taken to the experimental room. As he entered he was, by a brief flash of light, shown his seat and table on which there was a switchbox connected to the autokinetic apparatus. He could dimly see the walls of the room. As soon as he reached his chair, the door was closed, leaving the room in total darkness. The curtain, which prevented the subject's seeing the end of the room containing the apparatus, was then withdrawn and the experimenter went to the apparatus in a confident manner.

Approximately 5 minutes elapsed before the subject began his judgments in order that the degree of dark adaptation would approximate that of subjects in the other conditions (especially Condition C) in which a longer period was required for the subject to find his seat. During these few minutes, the experimenter continued to carry on informal and friendly conversation with the subject.

Then the subject was instructed:

You will be shown repeatedly a point of light like this. [The light was shown.] It shall always appear in this same place. Several seconds before the light is to appear I shall say "Ready," then the light will appear. After a short while, the light will begin to move. As soon as you see it move, press the button. Remember, do *not* press the button when you first see the light, but press it as soon as you see the light begin to move. After you have pressed the button, release it. Presently the light will disappear. After the light has disappeared, tell me the total distance the point of light moved, trying to make your estimates as accurate as possible.

We are not interested in the direction of the movement, but only in your estimate of the total distance the point of light moved.

Is there anything that is not clear?

Subjects were instructed to give only the total distance and not the direction so that in the group session they would not be reporting movement in different directions, which would have aroused strong suspicions among them.

After two practice trials, each subject gave fifty judgments. Throughout the experimental session, the experimenter remained friendly and responsive to the subject.

Group Session. The procedure here differed from the individual session only to the extent necessary for adaptations to a group situation. The experimenter tried to perpetuate any rapport established in the first session, as well as attempting to contribute to a positive interaction between the subjects. After several minutes of conversation among the subjects and experimenter, the subjects were taken to the experimental room. The only difference in the instructions was that the subjects were instructed that after they had pressed their keys and the light had disappeared, they were to:

Give your estimates of the distance the light moved, one of you at a time. As you give your estimate, press the key in front of you again and release it immediately. [This permitted the subject to be identified by signal on the apparatus before the experimenter.] It does not matter which of you gives your estimate first; but in order that you will not be influenced by the other person's estimate, let the same person not give his (her) estimate first every time.

CONDITION B

This condition was between A and C in difficulty. *The greatest difference between Conditions A and B was in the size of the experimental room.* This room, 81 by 54 feet, was formerly a theater on a Navy base. It was located in a larger, vacated building in which there was no activity except the experimentation. On the way to the experimental room, it was necessary to traverse a dimly lighted corridor. *The experimenter sought to establish rapport with the subject in the same way as described for Condition A,* but this was undoubtedly made more difficult because of the less pleasant setting in the abandoned recreation hall.

Individual Sessions. Before going to the experimental room, the subject was instructed: "I will take you into a dark room where I will lead you to your chair. Your only task will be to judge how far a point of light moves."

Unlike Condition A, the subject never saw the space relations inside the experimental hall. The experimenter entered the darkened room ahead of the subject, and taking his hand, led him to his chair, which was 10 feet from the door. To reassure the subject, the experimenter acted very confidently in the dark, especially in leading him to his chair. After about 5 minutes of dark adaptation, the same procedure was followed as for the individual session in Condition A.

Under Condition B, the subject had little idea of his relationship to the room. The fact that the room was so large produced such acoustical conditions that the subjects had a difficult time estimating their distance from the experimenter (an important index employed by many in their attempts to find some means to aid them in the accuracy of their judgments).

Group Session. The procedure for this situation was practically identical to that described for Condition A, group session, the exception being that the subjects held hands and were led to their seats by the experimenter. The instructions were the same as for the group session, Condition A.

CONDITION C

This was intended to be the situation in which spatial anchorages were eliminated as much as possible, hence the most difficult. *The experimenter made no attempt to establish rapport with the subjects, being matter of fact instead of warm and cordial, and engaging in only the necessary minimum of conversation throughout the sessions. More significant than the changed air of the experimenter was the increased difficulty in the experimental conditions.* The experimental room was the same one used for Condition B, but several factors were introduced which made it much more difficult (See Figure 1).

At a distance of 12 feet from the entrance, stairs were placed containing 4 steps in the front and 3 steps down in the back. The area of the room was marked off with ropes so that the only way the subject could reach his chair was by passing over the stairs (unless he crawled through the ropes, which none did). The ropes were introduced after preliminary work showed that the subjects in search of their chairs usually ended up at the right or left wall. They tended to stick by the wall despite instructions from the experimenter on how to find their goal. Therefore, in order to eliminate vertical anchorages as much as possible, rope barriers at hip level were used. It should be pointed out, however, that when subjects lost their way and came to the ropes, the ropes did not provide any definite anchorage as to their exact location.

After finding the stairs and passing over them, it was necessary for the subject to turn exactly 45 degrees to his left and proceed straight for 39 feet before reaching his goal (chair). There was nothing between the stairs and the chair but space.

Certain landmarks in simple relation to the subject's chair were set up in order that the experimenter could direct him to his seat when he became completely lost (see Figure 1).

Individual Session. Before going to the dark room the subject was instructed:

You are to enter a dark room. [The subject had been shown the entrance he was to use previously.] After you have gone through the door, you are to pull it tight behind you and pull the curtains closed, too. [The curtains were used to insure against light leakage.] Then place your back to the door which you have just entered and walk straight ahead. You will come to some stairs. When you have passed over the stairs, stop and turn left 45 degrees, and walk straight in the direction you are then facing. You will come to your chair and a table in front of it. After you find your chair, sit down and face directly forward.

Is there anything that is not clear?

The subject was then left in an office, several doors from the experimental room, while the experimenter made his way to his chair in the experimental room. He then called the subject, who could not tell from where in the experimental room the sound had come. As soon as the subject had closed the door of the experimental room, the experimenter started recording by stop clock the time it took for him to reach his chair, as well as all pertinent remarks of the subject. The experimenter maintained complete silence despite frequent attempts of the subjects to establish contact by asking for direction and aid. The experimenter's

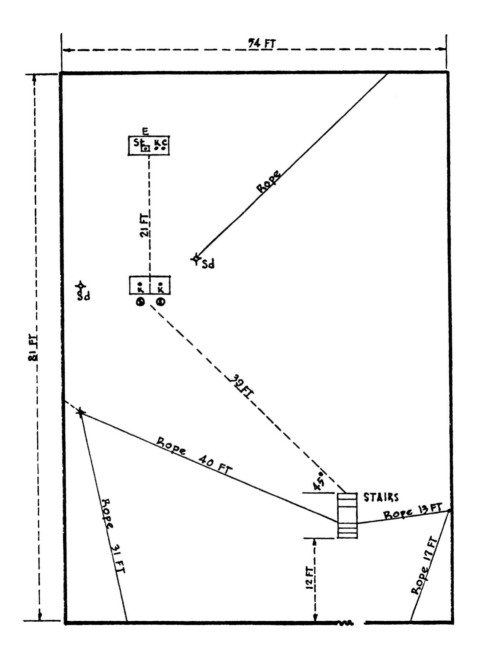

FIGURE 1. Disposition of the experimental setup for condition C.

silence was broken only after the subject had wandered for 3 minutes without finding his chair, had expressed the fact that he was lost and had given up, or had reached his chair. When the subject became lost the experimenter directed him to his chair by explaining the relationship of certain landmarks to the subject's table.

After the subject had reached his chair, either through his own ability or by directional aid, he was instructed:

> There is a table in front of you. On this table there is a box with a button on it. You will be shown a point of light like this. [Light was shown.] It will always appear in this place. Several seconds before it is to appear I shall tap like this. [Experimenter tapped the table with a pencil.]

The tapping was substituted for saying "ready" to reduce further the contact between experimenter and subject.

The rest of the procedure was the same as that for the individual sessions in Conditions A and B.

Group Sessions. Here the subjects sought their seats in pairs. Before entering the dark room, the same instructions as for the individual session of Condition C were given. After the subjects had reached their chairs, the same procedure as for the other group sessions was followed except that instead of saying "ready" before the appearance of the light, the experimenter tapped his pencil.

RESULTS

In line with the statement of the problem and the hypotheses advanced, the treatment of the data is made in terms of comparison of ranges and norms of judgment under Condition A, B and C in individual and group situations. Attention should be called to the fact that the crucial comparisons are between data obtained under Condition A (relatively easy condition) and Condition C (the condition of greatest uncertainty).

The formulation of our problem and hypotheses derived from experimental and empirical findings indicated that the more uncertain, the more chaotic the situation the individual faces, the greater the likelihood of individuals floundering around. In view of this, the gross measure of statistical range acquires special importance. Figure 2 shows striking differences in the scope within which individuals distribute their judgments under Conditions A, B and C. Under Condition C, in which all anchorages were eliminated as much as possible, this scope becomes startlingly large when compared with that of the more usual autokinetic situation (Condition A), which though vague and indefinite affords a few anchorages for the individual.

METHOD OF ANALYSIS

Since the frequency distributions under our various conditions are not normally distributed, it was decided that non-parametric tests (i.e., tests which do not depend upon the form of the frequency distribution) be used wherever feasible. It was found that this could be done in comparing the judgment ranges and medians of individuals under the various conditions. The non-parametric test used is the so-called sign test. Our use of this test is in modified form. The test as used by us, with the modifications explained, is as follows:

Suppose a random variable has a certain probability distribution, and two samples A and B of the same size N are taken at random and are both ordered according to size from the smallest to the largest:

$$\text{A:} \quad X_1 \leqq X_2 \leqq \ldots \leqq X_N$$
$$\text{B:} \quad Y_1 \leqq Y_2 \leqq \ldots \leqq Y_N$$

Consider the set of differences:

$$\text{D:} \quad X_1\text{-}Y_1, X_2\text{-}Y_2, \ldots, X_N\text{-}Y_N$$

The expected values of the number of positive entries and the number of negative entries in D are the same. The sign test given in Dixon and Massey (1951) Table 10, may accordingly be used. Our modification, a minor one, is in noting that an arbitrary prescribed method of pairing the observations from the two samples may be used, without impairing the validity of the sign test. The method of pairing used here is obtained by ordering the sample values from the smallest to the largest.

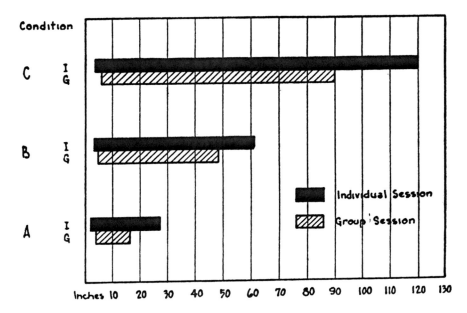

FIGURE 2. Spread of individual judgment ranges under conditions A, B, and C in individual and group situations.

Regarding the comparison of variation of judgment ranges and medians between individuals under the various conditions, the standard F test was used. This was done with reluctance, since there seems to be no non-parametric test available at the present time for comparing measures of spread. In crucial comparisons, from the point of view of hypotheses, the F ratios are so large that, at least in these cases, the deviation from normality is not likely to affect the conclusions.

Comparison of judgment ranges for individuals under Conditions A, B, C. Table 1 gives ranges in judgments for twenty individuals in

TABLE 1

Judgment Ranges Under Various Conditions in Individual and Group Situations

	CONDITION A		CONDITION B		CONDITION C	
	Ind.	*Group*	*Ind.*	*Group*	*Ind.*	*Group*
1.	2	4	3.5	4.5	3.5	6
2.	2.75	5	4.5	4.5	14	8
3.	4	5	5	6	14.5	8
4.	4.5	5	6	6.5	21	11
5.	5	5	6	7	21	12
6.	5	6	7	8	21	14
7.	5.5	6	8.5	9	23	22
8.	7.5	7	14	11	23	22
9.	8.5	8	15	12	24	22
10.	9	8	18	12	29	22
11.	10	8	22	18	31	23.5
12.	11	8	24	24	37	24
13.	12	8	35	24	44	24
14.	12	8	45	24	54	24
15.	13	10	47	25	58	30
16.	14	10	48	35	60	32
17.	15	12	58	42	70	32
18.	17	12	58	42	71	35
19.	17	16	60	48	120	60
20.	27	16	61	48	120	90

The ranges in individual situations (Session I) and group situations (Session II) under Conditions A, B, C. The ranges under alone and group sessions are arranged in ascending order and the rows do not represent the ranges obtained from the same subject in individual and group sessions. Range in inches.

alone situation and group situation under each of Conditions A, B and C. These will be labeled A_I, A_G, B_I, B_G, C_I and C_G. The test outlined above is applied to comparisons between A_I and B_I, A_I and C_I, B_I and C_I, A_G and B_G, A_G and C_G, and B_G and C_G, and also between A_I and A_G, B_I and B_G and C_I and C_G. The results are shown in Table 2.

From the results presented in Tables 1 and 2, it may be inferred that:

1. The greater the uncertainty and stress, the more individuals fluctuate in their judgments.

TABLE 2

Sign Test Comparing Judgment Ranges of Individuals under Conditions A, B and C in Individual and Group Situations

	Between	Number Positive[°°]	Number Negative	r[°]	
	A_I and B_I	20	0	0	P < .01
	A_I and C_I	20	0	0	P < .01
BETWEEN	B_I and C_I	19	1	1	P < .01
CONDITIONS	A_G and B_G	19	1	1	P < .01
	A_G and C_G	20	0	0	P < .01
	B_G and C_G	14	3	3	P < .05
BETWEEN INDIVIDUAL	A_I and A_G	13	6	6	P = .17
AND GROUP	B_I and B_G	12	6	6	P = .20
SESSIONS	C_I and C_G	19	1	1	P < .01

[°] $r = 3$ is .01 probability level for $N = 20$, (Table 10, Dixon and Massey, 1951).

[°°] The number positive is the number of pairs in Table 1 for which the difference between the range for the individual under the second listed condition and that for the individual under the first listed condition is positive; e.g., the number of pairs for which the score under B_I exceeds that under A_I in Table 1 is the score under number positive for "A_I and B_I" in Table 2.

2. The results for the comparison of C_I and C_G indicate that the fluctuation of judgment is significantly reduced in the situation of greatest stress, Condition C, by group interaction, while this is not true in the comparison of group and individual sessions under Conditions A and B.

Comparison of variation of judgment ranges between individuals under Conditions A, B, C. It is also of interest, regarding Table 1, to see whether there is more variation between individuals in situation C than, say, in situation A. Table 3 gives the results of F tests applied to the data of Table 1.

The results of Table 3 permit the following inferences:

1. These results indicate considerably more variation of judgment ranges between individuals under Condition B than under Condition A and even more strikingly greater variation under Condition C than under Condition A in both alone and group situations.

2. They also indicate more variation of judgment ranges under Condition C than under Condition B; and more variation in alone situation than in group situation, under each of Conditions A, B and C, but not nearly in the same degree as, say, between Condition A and Condition B.

TABLE 3

Comparison of Variation of Judgment Ranges Between Individuals under Conditions A, B and C in Individual and Group Situations

(For 19 × 19 degrees of freedom .05 and .01 probability levels of F are 2.2 and 3.0 respectively (Snedecor, 1950)

	Between	F Value	
	A_I and B_I	12.6	P < .005
	A_I and C_I	28.4	P < .005
BETWEEN	B_I and C_I	2.3	P < .05
CONDITIONS	A_G and B_G	18.7	P < .005
	A_G and C_G	30.9	P < .005
	B_G and C_G	1.7	P > .05
BETWEEN INDIVIDUAL	A_I and A_G	3.1	P < .01
AND GROUP	B_I and B_G	2.1	P > .05
SESSIONS	C_I and C_G	2.8	P < .03

Comparison of medians of judgments under Conditions A, B, C in alone and group situations. The medians of judgments of individuals under Conditions A, B and C in alone and group situations are presented in Table 4.

The results of the sign test comparing medians of judgments of individuals under Conditions A, B and C in alone and group situations are presented in Table 5.

From the results presented in Table 5, the following inferences can be drawn:

1. The results indicate that individuals have significantly higher medians under condition of maximum uncertainty (Condition C) as compared with conditions of less uncertainty (Conditions A and B). The greater the uncertainty and stress the greater the median value of judgments.

2. Under the condition of greatest stress (Condition C) the medians of judgments are significantly reduced by group interaction; while this reduction is not nearly as high under Conditions A or B.

The results of F tests comparing fluctuation of judgment medians between individuals under our various Conditions A, B, and C in individual and group situations are presented in Table 6.

The following inferences can be drawn from the results in Table 6:

1. The results indicate greater variation of medians of judgments

between individuals under Condition B than under Condition A, and more variation under Condition C than under Condition A to an even greater degree, in both alone and group situations. Thus, the greater the degree of uncertainty and stress the greater the fluctuation of judgments between individuals.

2. They also indicate significantly more variation between the medians of judgments of individuals in alone situation than in group situation under Condition C. The same effect is observed under Conditions A and B but not to the same degree as under Condition C.

During the group sessions, the judgments of the subject pairs con-

TABLE 4

Medians of Judgments under Conditions A, B, C, in Individual and Group Situations

	CONDITION A		CONDITION B		CONDITION C	
	Ind.	*Group*	*Ind.*	*Group*	*Ind.*	*Group*
1.	1.20	1.90	1.70	2.31	2.87	3.73
2.	1.56	2.29	2.78	2.58	5.78	4.40
3.	2.23	2.45	2.81	2.91	6.80	5.00
4.	2.50	2.52	2.91	4.31	7.75	5.00
5.	3.00	2.89	4.11	4.42	8.33	5.33
6.	3.17	3.50	4.15	4.85	8.35	5.48
7.	3.24	3.86	4.80	5.33	9.50	6.25
8.	3.50	4.31	6.00	5.53	10.50	7.00
9.	4.66	4.56	6.44	5.90	12.69	7.12
10.	4.69	5.00	8.40	6.56	12.73	8.27
11.	5.00	5.08	9.67	7.92	12.75	8.86
12.	5.50	5.12	9.82	7.92	17.29	8.92
13.	5.91	5.17	11.61	9.82	17.61	10.36
14.	7.60	5.50	11.67	10.00	20.75	11.64
15.	8.36	6.12	14.00	10.80	22.00	11.67
16.	8.43	6.26	16.75	11.00	27.45	12.50
17.	10.91	6.56	17.80	15.75	36.65	12.61
18.	11.00	10.86	33.18	18.67	48.00	12.92
19.	16.28	11.00	33.94	18.78	52.00	24.00
20.	17.34	12.18	43.00	20.67	72.00	25.39
Median of Group	4.85	5.04	9.04	7.24	12.74	8.56

The medians in individual situations (Session I) and group situations (Session II) under Conditions A, B and C. The medians under alone and group sessions are arranged in ascending order and the rows do *not* represent the medians obtained from the same subject in individual and group sessions.

Confidence limits of the median for Condition A (individual) at 95% confidence, as computed by the median limits test (Dixon and Massey 1951, p. 254; Table 25, p. 360) lie between 3.17–8.36, and for Condition C (individual) between 8.35–22.00. This indicates almost no overlapping in the confidence limits of the medians for the individual sessions of Conditions A and C. Confidence limits of other medians are intermediary between these extremes with various degrees of overlapping in the expected direction.

Median in inches.

TABLE 5

Sign Test Comparing Judgment Medians of Individuals
under Conditions A, B and C in Individual and Group Situations

	Between	Number Positive	Number Negative	r	
	A_I and B_I	20	0	0	P < .01
	A_I and C_I	20	0	0	P < .01
BETWEEN	B_I and C_I	20	0	0	P < .01
CONDITIONS	A_G and B_G	20	0	0	P < .01
	A_G and C_G	20	0	0	P < .01
	B_G and C_G	18	2	2	P < .01
BETWEEN INDIVIDUAL	A_I and A_G	11	9	9	P > .25
AND GROUP	B_I and B_G	14	6	6	P > .10
SESSIONS	C_I and C_G	19	1	1	P < .01

verged toward one another in varying degrees under each of the three
experimental conditions (A, B, C). The medians of blocks of ten judgments were plotted serially for each subject in individual and group
sessions. These curves revealed convergence throughout the course of
the group sessions. It should be noted, however, that convergence did
not always result in a lowering of the individual's norm (median) as
would be expected if a general "leveling effect" were operant as the
chief factor. The individual medians were raised or lowered in the
group interaction depending upon the relation between subjects established in the group session.

As the results in Tables 2, 5 and 6 indicate, variability and medians
of judgment of individuals were reduced in the group situation under
all experimental conditions, the differences between individual and
group situations being most significant for Condition C. (However, this
tendency is not clear in Table 3.) Since the direction of these shifts was
toward the partner's norm, these results indicate convergence of judgment in the group situation, especially under Condition C.

Further suggestive indication of this greater convergence under
conditions of greatest uncertainty is revealed in the percent shift in

$$\text{medians from the individual to the group session} \frac{(\text{Mdn.}_I - \text{Mdn.}_G)}{\text{Mdn.}_I}.$$

(This method of computation is open to obvious and serious criticism,
since it assumes that the proportion has some psychological validity
regardless of the absolute values of differences and initial medians.)

The mean of these percent shifts for Condition A was 41.8% and that of Condition C was 53.4%. In Condition A, twelve subjects had less than 35% shift; in Condition C, five subjects had less than 35% shift. For the reasons mentioned above, these findings are considered merely suggestive. Another interesting trend in the results of Condition C was for the greatest percent shift in medians to be found among the subjects with the largest initial median and Q (individual session) of the pair. With one exception, this was the case for every pair under Condition C.

TABLE 6

Comparison of Variation of Judgment Medians between Individuals under Conditions A, B, and C in Individual and Group Situations

	Between	F Values	
	A_I and B_I	5.5	P < .005
	A_I and C_I	14.6	P < .005
BETWEEN	B_I and C_I	2.7	P < .05
CONDITIONS	A_G and B_G	3.3	P < .01
	A_G and C_G	3.4	P < .01
	B_G and C_G	1.0	P < .05
BETWEEN INDIVIDUAL	A_I and A_G	2.1	P > .05
AND GROUP	B_I and B_G	3.3	P < .01
SESSIONS	C_I and C_G	8.6	P < .005

Observations of the experiment and the reactions of subjects on the questionnaire indicated certain complications in the group situation under Condition C which are relevant to any conclusions drawn from the above results and which will be discussed below.

Other data of particular significance. In the study of a complex problem such as ours (viz., ego problems), it is not sufficient to present only statistical analysis of results, no matter how impressive our confidence levels. We have to look for supporting evidence as well. In our opinion, some of the behavior of the subjects and their own perceptions as to what happened during the course of the experiment are at least equally revealing. Responses to the questionnaire items, spontaneous remarks of the subjects and their behavior confirm and sharpen the statistical analysis revealing significant differences, especially between Conditions A and C.

One questionnaire item concerned the subject's difficulty in making judgments. Under Condition A (relatively easy), fourteen or 70% of the subjects indicated that "estimates were easy" or "no major difficulty in any estimates." In contrast, 90% of subjects in Condition C (with fewest anchorages) reported difficulty in half, the majority, or most of their estimates, only two subjects indicating that their "estimates were easy."

Content analysis of answers to an open general question asking for the subject's reaction to the individual session revealed increasing uncertainty and confusion from Condition A to Condition C. In Condition A, five (25%) subjects indicated uncertainty as contrasted to nine (45%) in Condition B and thirteen (65%) in Condition C. Typical comments of subjects in each condition reveal qualitative differences even in this experienced uncertainty, among those who spontaneously included it in their responses:

Condition A: "I felt ill at ease, but curious."
Condition B: "Bewildered. I don't ever remember even being in such complete darkness. And it was a little nerve wracking."
"Very unsure and a little afraid, not of anything in particular, just of a strange and totally unexplained situation."
Condition C: "Felt helpless and ill at ease—was very puzzled."
"Completely confused. Lost as heck."

Further spontaneous remarks of the subjects substantiated this supposition that uncertainty and instability were not only experienced more frequently under Condition B and especially C, but that such uncertainty was more intense in the latter conditions. For example, one subject in Condition B remarked: "The first time when I was there by myself, it sometimes seemed as if the room was moving with me. Sometimes it seemed like my chair was turning over to one side. When I would move my feet away from a spot and replace them, it seemed like the floor was laying at an angle."

In Condition C, the most difficult and uncertain condition, there were frequent attempts by the subjects to anchor themselves to some physical point in the vast space of seeming emptiness. It was the usual practice, when finding a line, to hold on to it and follow it back and forth several times. Some found an object and then would radiate out from this, going a counted number of steps in one direction, retracing these steps to the object and going a certain number of steps in another direction or an increased number of steps in the same direction. There seemed to be a tendency to hang on to an object once discovered. One female subject typifies the more extreme behavior of those who reluctantly gave up their physical anchorages to continue in their search for the chair. This girl, after having difficulty in finding and crossing the steps, wandered back and forth several times following a line and then exclaimed: *"I can't tell which way is forward."* Finally she bumped back into the stairs and just gave up. After she stood still and completely quit for three minutes, the experimenter, with much difficulty, directed her to her seat.

Subjects under Condition C in the alone situation often asked the experimenter for directions and aid to their goal. In this condition, as well as in Condition B, subjects frequently asked their distance from the experimenter in an effort to have some yardstick for judging their location and that of the light.

In the *group situation,* subjects often remembered from the first (individual) session some physical anchorage in the room and its relation to the chair. Such subjects tried to make their way to these remembered points and to get their bearings from there, with varying degrees of success. As a result of this and the presence of another person, about half of the subjects in Conditions A and B stated in response to an open question that they felt more at ease in the group situation than the individual. Seven subjects in Condition C volunteered that they felt more at ease in the group situation. There is some evidence that some subjects in the group situation under Condition C felt new uneasiness and some resentment. While 65% of subjects in Condition A preferred to make their judgments in the group situation, only 35% of those in Condition C preferred the group situation. Another 35% preferred to judge alone as compared with 20% preferring the individual session under Condition A. (The remaining subjects were "indifferent." The above percentages for Condition B are 45% and 30% respectively.)

Similarly 45% of subjects in Condition C felt that their partner's estimates were a hindrance in making their own estimates, as compared to 10% in Condition A and 30% in Condition B. One subject in Condition C, for example, remarked: "I'm afraid I wasn't accurate on that [group session]. I didn't feel as alone but I wondered if she [her partner] were criticizing my estimates." Another wrote that he preferred to be alone because "presence of another hinders me in being sure of estimates."

Such representative data indicate rather clearly that some subjects in Condition C were made to feel insecure when their rather unstable norms from the individual session were assailed or disagreed with by another person. Because of wide individual differences between medians and ranges in the individual sessions of Condition C and the relatively small number of subjects, subjects of several pairs initially had widely differing norms when they entered the group situation. As indicated on page 214, subjects under Condition C actually tended to converge toward the judgments of their partners to a relatively greater degree than did those in Condition A. However, the above data indicate that some subjects in this condition of greatest uncertainty (C) gave ground begrudgingly, but did so nevertheless because of the greater insecurity of their grounds.

While there is no doubt that in some conditions of extreme uncertainty, actual clashes may occur traceable to widely differing standards of individuals, we do not believe this would be the case if the relationship between the individuals were one of mutual dependence, rather than one of annoyance or resentment. The present experimental set-up was not sufficiently conducive to the establishment of mutual dependence between subject pairs. For this reason, our hypothesis (d) predicting greater convergence in the group situation under conditions of greater insecurity and uncertainty has probably not been adequately tested in spite of favorable statistical results (only the results of Table 3 are not clear in indicating this tendency). As a first step in doing so, we would want, in a condition of great uncertainty, to establish a relationship of mutual dependence between subjects prior to their judgments. In short, this hypothesis should hold true when individuals in a condition of great uncertainty find another person or group as their main anchorage in the situation. In lieu of establishing such a relationship, a person of considerable prestige as partner would be an interesting possibility. A negative test of this general hypothesis would be to create between two individuals a relationship of mutual distrust and suspicion or resentment prior to the judgment.

SUMMARY AND CONCLUSIONS

This study is presented as an experimental contribution to an aspect of the psychology of ego functioning. Specifically, it attempts to investigate the effects of situational uncertainty on ego functioning. The basic assumption is that the ego of the individual, which implies his characteristic relatedness to his surroundings as reflected in his characteristic reactions, is built up in relation to physical and social anchorages from childhood on. The stability of his ego, hence the consistency of his reactions, is dependent upon the stability of these physical and social anchorages. As the physical and social anchorages become more unstable, more uncertain, the individual's personal bearings become more unstable, more uncertain. This condition of instability, of uncertainty is thus at the basis of the experience of insecurity. Psychological states of anxiety or insecurity always involve ego reference. Insecurity is that state of ego tension produced by actual or perceived shattering of physical or social anchorages, or actual or perceived uncertainty of one's physical or social grounds in the present or in the future.

The psychological consequences of the actual or experienced loss of physical and social bearings are at least *initially* increased fluctuations, variations in reactions, floundering around in search of something to hold on to, strivings to re-establish some level of stability through available anchorages.

The specific problem of the study was to produce situational insecurity by elimination of spatial anchorages, thus affecting the stability of some of the developmentally earliest ego relationships, viz., spatial anchoring of the self. Variability of behavior was tapped through simple judgmental reactions, with the assumption that even the most complicated motivational states are reflected in such reactions.

In line with the leads derived from our previous work, the autokinetic situation was utilized. On the basis of preliminary trials, three conditions representing three degrees of uncertainty were chosen. In the main experiment, sixty subjects took part. All were normal university students who were not previously acquainted with the autokinetic situation or with one another. Under all conditions, each subject took part in an individual session, and later a group session. There were ten subject groups under each experimental condition.

In line with our hypotheses, it was found that:

(a) The more uncertain the situation, the greater the range within which judgmental reactions are scattered.

(b) The more uncertain the situation, the greater the magnitude of the norm or standard around which judgments are distributed.

(c) The more uncertain the situation, the larger the differences between the ranges and norms of judgment of different individuals.

(d) The more uncertain the situation, the greater the tendency, on the whole, toward convergence in group situations.

The tendency under (d) is stated with qualifications due to the nature of specific procedures in the present study and the perceived relationship between the subjects.

This approach to the complicated ego problems, which are considered more and more as central in understanding human personality under various conditions of life, has the advantage of tying together (a) findings and theoretical formulations concerning ego formation and functioning, (b) empirical observations concerning the effects of actual conditions of uncertainty and stress on human experience and behavior, and (c) the study of motivational and attitudinal factors through the paradigm of relatively simple judgmental and perceptual reactions developed during the past two decades.

PART III

THE SELF
AND REFERENCE GROUPS

TWELVE

THE SELF AND REFERENCE GROUPS: MEETING GROUND OF INDIVIDUAL AND GROUP APPROACHES

The problem area of this monograph concerns man's perception and conception of himself as an individual living in a physical and social world. The considerations which have led social philosophers, psychologists and social scientists again and again to a concept of self-ego may be broadly summarized as follows: first, characteristic "consistency" of the person's behavior from one situation to another; and, second, the experienced and observed "continuity" of this consistency over a time span.

The pictures of human motivation based on the studies dealing with the effects and relative importance of various single motives (hunger, sex, sleep, security) provide bits of items that sorely need the integrating component that runs through them all. For example, human sexual activity (within certain limits) is not only a problem of bodily homeostasis, it is at the same time a problem of establishing secure and reliable personal ties or a problem of personal conquest. Likewise, beyond the level of bodily subsistence, activities engaged in to satisfy hunger involve, at the same time, problems related to congenial companionship, distinction, and status.

In all these activities engaged in under the goal-directed promptings of this or that particular motive, there is the involvement of the person with characteristic claim or self-picture of the individual that provides the unique consistency of the individual from situation to situation. The insistence on this involvement of the self-picture of the individual in so many diverse activities and situations is an insightful

Carolyn Sherif effectively participated in the collection of data for this paper and in writing it.

From F. N. Furness, Ed., *Fundamentals of Psychology: The Psychology of Self.* Annals of the New York Academy of Sciences (1962), pp. 797–813. Reprinted with permission of the New York Academy of Sciences.

anticipation on the part of "personalistic" psychologists such as Wilhelm Stern and Mary Calkins.

However the great task now is to go beyond these insights hitherto advanced only with occasional observations and incomplete case histories. The objective of the present paper is to move toward some aspects of these "next steps" by operationally demonstrating some relevant dimensions of this psychological consistency-inconsistency problem in the area of individual-group relationship.

An attempt will be made to establish, on the basis of research findings, that the concept of reference groups, as will be defined and discussed in relation to the self concept, provide the necessary meeting ground of individual and group approaches in handling the consistency or inconsistency of the individual in his human relations.

DEFINITION OF THE PROBLEM AREA

When an individual forms a "self-image" as a successful student, a popular social mixer, a doctor, a soldier, a fashion model, a good family man, a writer or an artist, his behavior toward a wide variety of persons and objects acquires consistency as evidence seems to indicate. Then, the stand or role he takes relative to so many particular items in his environment ceases to be so many isolated, discrete, and unrelated items. These images of himself require long range adjustments in his experience and behavior over a time span (cf. Murphy, 1947, p. 715).

The terms "self" and "ego" have almost as many meanings as there are writers who have used them. For this reason I shall start by characterizing self or ego as the concept will be discussed in this paper. I say "*the* concept" because I shall use "self" and "ego" interchangeably. In fact, I should prefer to use neither, because of their confused and even muddied histories. However, I have not come up with anything better than "X," which unfortunately implies an unknown quantity. The physicists have used almost all of the Greek letters, and even nonsense names have their connotations.

When I speak of "self or ego," I refer to a developmental formation —a "subsystem"—within the psychological make-up of the individual, borrowing the term "subsystem" from Koffka. This developmental subsystem consists of interrelated attitudes formed by the individual in relation to his own body and its attributes, his capacities and skills, to objects, other persons, family, groups, social values and institutions. These attitudes which may be properly designated as ego attitudes define and regulate the individual's relatedness to such objects in concrete situations. They are inferred from characteristic and consistent modes of behavior of the person, whether manifested in words, expressions or deeds.

A few words about this characterization. It *does* take the mystery and the drama away from the concept of self. The concept of attitude cannot compete in appeal value or glamor with "the inner self," the "real self," or even "super-ego." However, I am a social psychologist interested in research, specifiable and communicable research strategies and operations on problems of the self. If anyone wants a phenomenological or philosophical definition of self to be explored intuitively, that is perfectly all right for him. Intuitions and research, however, are not the same. Investigation and experimentation require definitions conducive to analysis in terms of specified dimensions and their interrelationships.

If we examine empirical studies, we invariably find that self or ego problems are always studied in terms of a person's positive or negative stands, images or fixations he forms relative to persons, objects, groups, values, events in past or present, in terms of his attractions and aversions, his strivings and goals for the future. The evidence is always the individual's words, his expressions, postures and actions, whether these are obtained on the psychiatrist's couch or in a laboratory.

There is another empirical justification for conceiving of self or ego in terms of a constellation of attitudes. The self is not a unitary structure, even though component parts are functionally interrelated. This assertion is in agreement with literature on the self from William James (1890), Cooley (1902) and McDougall (1908) right down to contemporary accounts by Gardner Murphy (1947), Snygg and Combs (1949) and others. The constituent parts of the self are interrelated. However interrelationship need not mean integration or a unitary structure all of one piece. In fact, *because* of the interrelated character of attitudes composing the self, there may be conflicts between the component parts. A modern professional woman who finds herself in a situation that in one breath taps her identity as a professional person, an attractive woman, and a mother can give us examples of such conflicts.

SELF AS A DEVELOPMENTAL FORMATION

As defined here, the self is a developmental formation: a product of biosocial development and learning in interaction with other people. The constellation that defines an individual's conception of himself, his attributes and qualities relative to his psychological world is not innate, as has been demonstrated time and again.

About fifteen years ago, we surveyed the developmental literature from a wide variety of sources and found remarkable convergence on this point (Sherif and Cantril, 1947). Empirical observations from as early as those of Tiedemann in 1787 (Murchison and Langer, 1927), Darwin (1877), Preyer (1890), James Mark Baldwin (1895), Millicent Shinn (1899) and Cooley (1908) to the more recent work of Piaget (1926, 1928, 1932), Wallon (1933), Gesell and his associates (1934) and Goodenough (1945) are in compelling agreement, even though points of emphasis and temporal sequence of appearance of component parts are still matters of controversy. There are not many generalizations in psychology with such widespread support from such diverse sources. We had better pay some respect to its implications.

The behavior of a young infant is consistent only for the duration of a bodily state, such as hunger, sleep or discomfort, or for the immediate duration of a stimulus. In fact, consistent differentiation of his own body from surrounding objects requires a complex of different experiences.

The timing and objects of psychological relatedness vary for different children and in different social settings. Everywhere, however—everywhere—the appearance of consistencies in perceptions of self and of others is contingent upon interaction with other individuals and upon the attainment of communicable language. It is primarily the conceptual attainments that harness the highly affective and motivational ties of self with the environment into stabilized attitudes in more or less durable forms.

There are profound implications in a conclusion reached by James Mark Baldwin in 1896, a conclusion based on his observations of his own children that directly influenced later work by Cooley and by Piaget. In Baldwin's words: "The *ego* and the *alter* are born together. . . . Both . . . are thus essentially social" (1895, p. 338). Here lies the basic inadequacy of those individualistic approaches to the self that posit the unfolding of deep-seated impulses and complexes as the basis of the individual's social behavior, divorcing the self from the "alter," which was an essential aspect of the very process of self-identification. This time honored conception amounts to positing an immutable and self-generated self or ego as Essence that is static and contained within itself. As David Ausubel concluded in his scholarly survey of ego development in his book, *Ego Development and Personality Disorders,* "There is no predetermined course or sequence of events which reflects the unfolding of a detailed blueprint designed by inner impulses" (1952, p. 44).

Without pretense at an adequate account of the formation of self even within the bounds of a single culture, we may summarize briefly broad trends of development, following Gardner Murphy's illuminating account (1947). The earliest manifestations of self-awareness, he proposed, are part of a perceptual stage consisting chiefly of demarcation of bodily self from surrounding objects, which is followed by the acquisition of immediate roles and *traits* or qualities associated with them. Thus, when the child has distinguished "me" from "you" in a concrete sense, his developing linguistic capacities permit the concept of self as a *boy* or a *girl,* then as a *good* boy or a *pretty little* girl. The traits associated with these roles are then elaborated to include various ways of appearing and acting and dressing appropriate to a boy or a girl. Developmentally, the last stage involves relating oneself to significant groups and classes of persons. This stage requires a clear distinction between "we" and "they" and involves traits, qualities and stereotypes attributed to "us" and to "them."

The level of conceptual development required for distinctions between "we" and "they" to become consistent is revealed in fascinating detail in studies of group and racial awareness such as those by Ruth and Eugene Hartley and their co-workers (for example, R. Horowitz, 1939; Hartley *et al.*, 1948) and by Mamie and Kenneth Clark (1940, 1947). Interestingly enough, among children studied in the United States, the gradual clarification of concepts of "I," "we" and "they" occurs during the preschool years and is accompanied by the appearance of consistency in a variety of other social behaviors, such as consistent competition with others, consistent cooperative play, consistency in sympathetic responses to another's distress and sociability (for example. Greenberg, 1932; Leuba, 1933; Hirota, 1951; Berne, 1930; L. B. Murphy, 1937; Parten, 1932, 1933).

The setting of consistent standards or goals for one's future performance relative to others is one of the later developments in ego formation, appearing around the age of five to six among children studied by Gesell and Ilg (1943) and Goodenough (1945).

These broad trends in formation of self or ego emphasize a conclusion: The ego of the individual is not self-generated. Despite its highly affective and motivational and emotional character, emergence of self is conditional upon processes of development and learning in interaction and communication with other individuals in specific physical and social settings.

Indeed, no man is an island. His very self owes its chief characteristics to processes of give-and-take with other individuals and to physical and conceptual encounters with the world he lives in. Among the significant features of that world are the human groups in which he moves from childhood on: family; play groups; school; friendship clusters; neighborhood, church, occupational, professional and work groups; and political organizations.

The remainder of this paper will discuss the self as related to groups, their status and role structures, and their values or norms, especially in terms of reference group ties.

MULTIPLE GROUPS AND CONCEPTUAL LEVEL OF FUNCTIONING

If conceptions of self and of alter are "born together," an individualistic approach to study of the self is doomed to be one-sided. No matter what the repercussions and vicissitudes of particular life experiences, accounting of the individual's self development requires specific reference to both subject (that is, the person himself) and object (that is, other person or persons) in these experiences. Even the most individual-centered of all modern writers, including Freud, have considered ego in relation to at least one human group: the family.

The antithesis of an individualistic approach—cultural or group determinism—is likewise one-sided and, hence, it runs into difficulties equally severe. It is simple enough to point to individuals with modes of behavior, striving and goals differing from those of other members of the groups in which they actually move. In fact, most individuals do not appropriate to themselves all of the values or standards of the groups in which they live or have lived.

The problem of the reciprocal relationships between the individual's self and groups or culture owes its complexity primarily to two sets of facts. One set of facts has already been mentioned, namely the individual's capacity to function conceptually and to relate himself in consistent fashion to persons, groups, events and goals not immediately present in his environment and over extensive time periods. The vehicle of extending one's self in space and time consists of concepts provided by language.

The second set of facts are properly sociological, namely the existence of modern man in highly differentiated societies composed of overlapping and at times conflicting human groupings or organizations, small and large. Individuals find themselves in multiple groups and come to relate themselves to various of these organizations, not just to one or two (E. Hartley, 1951).

These two sets of facts produce the frequent phenomenon of man conforming, passively enduring or rebelling in an immediate social setting while relating himself to other settings and goals. The most obvious example is the self identification of the great bulk of people in the United States with a "middle class," although the very concept of middle class implies that some people must be "not middle" but lower class (Centers, 1952). Interestingly enough, the tendency toward "middle class" identification is even greater among adolescents and, for adolescents, greater for girls (Centers, 1950).

The failure of either monopolistically "individualistic" or "group-centered" approaches to handle such problems is dispelled by a concept explicitly relating the self to the world of real social groups. Social groups can be and are studied objectively by sociologists without necessarily requiring reference to the self conceptions of the particular individuals. Research on self, however, must refer both to actual social groups and the individual's own relatedness and perceptions of them. The integrating concept to interrelate the two may be the concept of "reference groups."

The concept of reference group is a psychological one, defined from the point of view of the individual's relatedness. In the way of definition, reference groups are those social units to which the individual relates himself or *aspires* to relate himself psychologically. These groups may be the actual groups in which he moves from day to day. However, they may be groups with which he is not actually associated. He may even have no direct contact with them. His conception of them may not correspond closely with their nature, manifest values and goals as studied objectively on a sociological level.

Because of these very real possibilities, the investigator interested in self or ego ties is forced to consider the individual's relatedness both with membership groups—groups in which the individual actually moves —and other reference groups, with which he may or may not be in actual intercourse. When an individual finds his belongingness, his sense of identity as a person with some place in life within his membership groups, these membership groups are at the same time his reference groups. His self may be properly studied as a member of these groups.

In this changing world, however, not infrequently we find a discrepancy between the individual's membership groups and his reference groups. Of course, the very fact of existing in a group setting, within an organization with its values and goals and pressures toward conformity, is significant. Psychologically, however, there are profound differences between inwardly cherished values and goals of a group and conformity merely for the sake of surviving in a setting while inwardly relating oneself to other values. The latter state is being experienced today by a good many individuals who oppose segregation but face ostracism in their neighborhoods, loss of jobs, even violence, if they do not conform to local customs.

EVIDENCE OF SELF-REFERENCE GROUP TIES

Suppose we simply ask a person to answer the question, "Who am I?" This was done by Bugental and Zelen (1950) and by Kuhn and McPartland (1954). Their findings seem to indicate that about three fourths of the people asked this question start with a personal pronoun or, more often, their names—those "handles" of identity, as McDougall called them. The great majority of responses then locate the individual in a social context, giving sex, occupation, social and family status, nationality and religion. (Members of minority groups rather consistently include their ethnic or religious affiliation. Women, more than men, refer to their roles in the family. Characteristically, people seem to exhaust all of the labels placing them in a social context before getting to descriptive or idiosyncratic responses. In fact, it is evidently the disturbed individual who skips this process of locating the self in its social context and replies, as did a woman in a therapy situation reported by S. S. Sargent: "Oh, I'm just a fat old thing.")

These descriptions by which individuals typically define themselves —these statements, "I am a doctor," "I am a Baptist," "I am a Republican," "I am Italian"—are not discrete items. As Centers found in his studies of class identifications, if people relate themselves psychologically to the same groups, their attitudes tend to be similar although, objectively, they move in different circles (1952, p. 308).

References group ties are manifold, but not discrete. A change in reference groups involves a shift of an entire constellation of attitudes. Such changes were reported by Newcomb (1948) in the well-known study of attitude change by girls from largely conservative backgrounds as they became active participants in the liberal atmosphere at Bennington College, Bennington, Vermont, of the New Deal 1930s. Mere presence at the college was not sufficient for this shift, for some girls never accepted Bennington as their reference group.

In a beautifully conceived experiment in the natural conditions of a college campus, Siegel and Siegel (1957) showed the differential effects of membership and reference groups on that cluster of attitudes defined by the California E-F scale, which I prefer, with Ruth Hartley (1957), to conceive as a measure of "acceptance of the cultural *status quo*" in so many respects. The students in this experiment all voted by secret ballot that they wanted to live in the most prestigeful dormitory units. Scores on the E-F scale were higher for girls in those units. The girls who failed in their desire to live in this select atmosphere, but who subsequently chose to remain in the less distinguished company where they had been placed, showed the greatest change of attitudes. That is, the greatest attitude change was for those who adopted the group in which they found themselves as their reference group.

Finally, as evidence of the manifold effects of reference group ties of the self, let us consider briefly the shifts in importance of the individual's different reference groups as he progresses from childhood through adolescence. During adolescence, the values and goals of parents become less important, at least for a time. When parental values conflict with the standards of the peer group, it is the peer group that wins more often than not, as Rosen (1955), among others, has shown.

(This can be illustrated with a personal and somewhat frivolous example. Recently, in honor of the centennial of the Civil War, the school in Oklahoma attended by our 14-year-old daughter [an eighth grader] held a costume party. Afterward she described this colorful event, for which a "Mason-Dixon Line" had been drawn down the center of the room. When asked whether she sat with the "South" or the "North," she replied, "The South, of course." Her mother said, "What do you mean, 'of course'? I've never heard you express sympathy with the Southern cause, and your great-grandfather was in the Union army." The reply was, "Oh, mother, don't be silly. Only the seventh graders sat on the North, and all my friends were on the South.")

The adolescent's heart lies where his friends are, to an extent that, in specific situations, *their* judgments, even *their abilities* are considered superior, on the whole, to parents'. In a doctoral thesis at the University of Oklahoma, William Prado (1958) measured this shift in relative importance of family and age-mate reference groups from childhood to adolescence. He deliberately chose boys who valued their fathers highly and interacted with them easily and warmly. Each boy watched his father and a close friend perform an eye-hand coordination task in which the outcome could only be guessed, because the situation was set up so that they could not ascertain exactly the actual performance. In the experiment the boys guessed the scores their father and friend had made. The task offered no particular advantage to either father or friend, nor was it directly related to attitudes toward father and friend. Yet children 8 to 11 years old estimated their fathers' performance higher than the performance of their friends, while the adolescents (14–17 years old) estimated their friends' performance significantly higher than their fathers'.

When reference groups shift in importance, a host of attitudes and expectations do concomitantly change.

Thus far I have tried to illustrate specifically the value of the reference group concept as a meeting ground for individual and group or cultural approaches to problems of the self. The data collected by both approaches become pertinent to the study of self since the reference group concept relates the individual's self in so many aspects or dimensions to the sociocultural context in which it forms and functions.

The possibilities of this conceptual tool have been explored in recent years for handling personal problems encountered by *marginal persons*: that is, persons caught betwixt and between membership and other reference groups and unable to anchor the self securely in either (e.g., Sherif and Sherif, 1953, pp. 172ff.; 1956, pp. 635ff.). Such marginal positions are frequently encountered among members of minority groups rising in the social structure, but they are also prevalent in the intermediate links of many large organizations, such as the foreman in industry and the noncommissioned officer in military organizations.

While the analysis of personal disturbance is not my forte, I have been sufficiently interested in the links between self stability and environmental stability to experiment, with O. J. Harvey (1952), on the effects of uncertainty generated by situations depriving the individual of stable and dependable physical guides. If loss of stable physical landmarks in the environment can, as this experiment showed, result in extreme variability of judgment and expressed feelings of personal disorientation and floundering, I am impressed with the possibilities of systematic study of reference group ties, their stability or lack of stability, among disturbed individuals.

(In this connection, Louis McQuitty's comparison of responses to items on personality inventories by normal community populations and by hospitalized mental patients is instructive. One of McQuitty's outstanding findings [1950] was that "the successive answers to personality inventories by disintegrated personalities are those characteristic of diverse categories of people" [p. 468], indicating the idiosyncratic and yet floundering nature of the origin of their responses.)

REFERENCE GROUPS AS ANCHORS FOR THE SELF

As an integrative concept, the concept of reference groups has been widely used in recent years by psychologists and sociologists alike, at times in different senses. It faces the danger of becoming a magic term to be invoked descriptively to explain anything and everything under the sun. For this reason it will pay us to examine briefly the research background from which the concept stems. Elsewhere we have reviewed the background and history of the concept in some detail (Sherif and Sherif, 1953, 1956).

When individuals face a situation in which they have an established level of achievement but are also made aware of the achievement of other groups whom they regard as superior or inferior, the position of their own group relative to the group in question serves as the main anchor—or standard, if you like—in setting goals for their own performance. Chapman and Volkmann demonstrated this in an experiment which has served as a model for numerous others during the last two decades. The conception of this experiment is based on prior work on judgment, as indicated by the general principle that served as the starting point of Chapman and Volkmann's pioneering study. In Chapman and Volkmann's words, setting personal goals "may be regarded as a special case of the effect upon a judgment of the frame of reference within which it is executed" (p. 225).

What Chapman and Volkmann actually showed was that college students raised and lowered their estimates of their own anticipated performance when given the alleged performance of groups they considered "inferior" or "superior" to their own in that respect. They were not told in the instructions of the experiment to consider their own relation to these groups. They *spontaneously* used the level of their own groups as an anchor or standard, relative to the perceived achievement of the groups in question. Hyman, in 1942, used the same conception to show that an individual's concepts of his own status are tied to the relative standing of groups in relation to which judgments are given.

Let us make this notion of the individual's reference groups as anchors for his judgments, perceptions, and behavior more concrete. The phenomenon of "rate setting" in industrial establishments using the piece-rate system of payment is well known (Roethlisberger and Dickson, 1939). Briefly, if the work output designated as standard is 100 per cent, and a bonus can be gained for work exceeding it, it is found that workers characteristically perform within a narrow range of 100 per cent.

The system is obviously designed to encourage production. However, even though the workers are perfectly capable of exceeding 100 per cent, only a few consistently break the limits thus set to gain the bonus. Such persons are called "rate busters" by the others, a derogatory term summarizing a host of informal pressures and even sanctions put upon these workers to slow down. W. F. Whyte, in his *Money and Motivation* (1955), estimates that "rate busters" constitute only about 10 per cent of the workers in a factory using this monetary incentive device.

M. Dalton studied the backgrounds, the in-plant and out-plant activities of rate busters and other workers, and came up with the fascinating finding that rate busters characteristically came from "farms or . . . urban lower-middle-class families—both types . . . being strongholds of the belief in economic individualism" (Whyte, 1955, p. 42), while other workers were typically from urban, working class backgrounds. The rate buster is either a "lonewolf" in the factory and outside of it or a person with strong upward mobility who "cuts himself off from others on the same level and seeks association with those of superior status" (p. 42). Thus the rate buster's past membership groups and present reference groups are different from those of the other workers studied.

These findings have a great deal to tell us about motivations and goals. Obviously a worker takes home more pay if he exceeds 100 per cent. However, only a small fraction actually do so, even though excess production is perfectly feasible for most of them. The reason is that the norms of the informal group of workers regulate the individual's behavior. In other words, he gives up more pay to take home to his family in order to keep his friendships and self-respect in the eyes of people that really count in his evaluation, namely, his reference group. In short, reference-group norms are the main anchors by which he sets his own personal level of achievement. He typically reacts with a sense of outraged righteousness toward those who consistently exceed the norm.

We are reminded here of the studies by Hinckley and Rethlingschafer (1951) and by Marks (1943) showing that one's own height or one's own skin color serve as anchors in judging the height or skin color of others. This "autistic" tendency operates within limits set by objective perception of heights and skin colors near the extreme ends of the continuum. Similarly, the clear realities of group life set limits within which individuals establish levels for their own achievement and goals for the future.

SELF-RADIUS AND GOALS RELATED TO DIFFERENT REFERENCE GROUPS

Three years ago we started a program of research involving the study of self-reference group ties, conceiving of reference groups as anchors for the self system whose effects could be studied through the individual's perceptions of his environment, through his evaluations, and through the goals he sets for personal attainment. The remainder of this paper will summarize results of this research particularly pertinent to the central theme presented thus far.

The findings I shall summarize were obtained as part of a research program studying intensively the behavior of members of naturally or spontaneously formed groups functioning in differentiated sociocultural settings. This program that I am directing has been supported by the Hogg Foundation for Mental Health of the University of Texas, Austin; the Society for the Investigation of Human Ecology, New York; and the Rockefeller Foundation, New York. Data concerning American Indian groups were obtained with support from the Office of Naval Research, Washington, D.C. All of the findings reported here were obtained by Carolyn Sherif, Research Associate at the Institute of Group Relations at the University of Oklahoma.

The research strategy of this program starts with selection of specific sociocultural settings that can be differentiated and ranked in terms of ecological and sociocultural measures. The settings themselves are studied further through survey techniques in order that their physical features and populations may be fully delineated for the purpose of studying small groups within them. Small groups are selected for intensive study within each setting—first on a sociological level focusing on their organization and values or norms and, finally, concentrating on the patterned behaviors of their individual members for a period of five to six months. Our aim is to integrate these various data into a single design with the objective of intensive analysis of the behavior of members in specified groups. Since we have reported the plan and early results of this program elsewhere (M. Sherif, 1959; M. Sherif and C. Sherif, 1960; M. Sherif, 1960; C. Sherif, 1960), I shall proceed directly to the aspect of the research most directly relevant to this paper.

The research is social-psychological. Therefore, unlike a sociological or anthropological investigation in which one can quite properly study the settings and groups without necessarily getting concerned over the self-conceptions of individuals within them, we were faced with some missing links. The underlying rationale was that if the physical and social arrangements in an area, including the behaviors of its residents, vary over a period of time within definable ranges, then these arrangements would affect the pursuit of one's interests in that setting and play a part in creating a picture of one's personal plight or fortune, as the case may be. Furthermore, the range of possibilities, of alternatives, and of conceivable goals in the setting should contribute to setting limits of the individual's perceived self radius in different dimensions.

This line of reasoning led to questions that were to be answered by concrete research findings: *Do* individuals living in areas differentiated in terms of sociocultural and ecological measures perceive themselves and others differently? Are their conceptions of achievement and their personal goals different in educational, occupational, material and financial matters, and in interpersonal and intergroup relations? The answers to these questions were sought through responses to Self Radius and Goals Schedules administered to high school students in the areas of study. The data to be reported are based on responses of 1,220 individuals from "high-," "middle-" and "low-" rank areas in San Antonio, Texas, with its Spanish-speaking population particularly in the low-rank area; from similarly ranked areas in Oklahoma City; from a small university community; from an all-Negro school in Oklahoma City; from a school whose students are American Indians born and raised in Oklahoma; and from a school in Oklahoma whose students are 85 per cent Navaho, from the reservation of New Mexico and Arizona.

First, in what respects are the conceptions of individuals living in such diverse settings in the United States today similar? The over-riding commonality in the findings is in conceptions and goals related to material possessions and attainments. (Consider their perceptions of the neighborhood in which they live and their expressed desires of where they want to live. Those living in high-rank areas in San Antonio or Oklahoma City want to stay there. Sixty-five per cent of those in low-rank areas want to move and, specifically, to move into sections of the city most desirable from a material point of view. Thus there is an inverse relationship between social rank of neighborhood and frequency of the desire to move to another part of town.)

For example, the desires for an automobile and for specific makes and models of automobiles are similar in all areas studied, although, of course, actual possession of cars differs tremendously. The proportion of individuals aspiring to own a Cadillac or Oldsmobile does not differ significantly in the areas studied (in fact the only difference found was that the Navaho Indians frequently aspire to a pick-up truck rather than to a passenger car).

While individuals in all of these areas value and want similar material possessions, they differ significantly in their conceptions of the associated achievements necessary to attain them. We tried to establish in so many respects what was conceived as a minimum—that is, a bottom level in the individual's eyes—and a maximum representing high achievement for him, and, in addition, his own personal goal for himself within these bounds. This range represents the radius of achievement the individual sees as acceptable for him, and his own goal can be located within that radius.

For example, in the high-, middle-, and low-rank areas in Oklahoma City we asked how many years of school are (1) required for a person to be considered "educated"; (2) are necessary for a person "who wants to do the things I want to do"; and (3) the amount of education "I want myself." For more than 80 per cent of those in the high-rank area, these figures were identical, namely, a university education. In the low-rank area, the great majority regarded a high school education as all that was necessary, and more than one half also indicated that this defined an "educated" person and was what they themselves desired to achieve.

As might be expected, the populations also differ with respect to their conceptions and goals in occupations. For example, as compared with the white university town population, the conceptions of the prestige of various occupations by Negro and Navaho subjects differ. Navaho subjects tend to perceive the prestige of low-prestige occupations as higher than white subjects. Negro subjects tended to perceive an occupation as having either very high or very low prestige. (These trends are not simply characteristic response tendencies by these groups for the scale used to secure their judgments. The same rating scales were used for judgments of other dimensions but these trends were not obtained for other dimensions.)

The level of occupational goals varies with the rank of the area. Furthermore, when individuals in low-rank areas are asked what kind of work they *expect* to get rather than what they *want* to achieve, a significant proportion shifts to work still lower on the occupational ladder (McNemar test of change). It is as though this question reminded them of a few hard realities that they had forgotten. Even without this reminder, however, the ceiling for their goals is lower than that in more favored settings.

The very conceptions of the financial achievements necessary to attain the telephone, television set, clothing and automobiles that all desire differ in the different settings. These include concepts of how much spending money one needs, the minimum and maximum expenditures necessary to buy acceptable clothing and the concepts of how much income is necessary just barely to get along, on the one hand, and to be "really well off," on the other. For example, in the high-rank area of San Antonio, the median income per week considered just barely enough to live on was about $60 a week, and the median "to be really well off" was about $318 a week. Within this range, personal goals for income were set comfortably at a median of $230. In the low-rank, Spanish-speaking area, the minimum figure was about $35 a week, the maximum was about $83, and the personal goal was about the same; the subjects were putting their personal goals at the very top of their range of desirable income. Confidence limits computed for these medians show no overlap between these population estimates whatsoever. Relative to their conceptions of what is desirable, the Spanish-speaking youth are actually setting their goals higher than those in the high-rank areas. In other words, persons in the low-rank area are aiming at the very top of their more limited conception of what is desirable, while those in the high-rank area are aiming at a goal well below the top of their more extended range of what is desirable.

Even these financial matters, which often seem trivial and unpsychological to psychologists, are affected by the cultural values of one's reference groups. By and large, the trends in our data on financial conceptions follow the relative economic ranks of the areas. However, there was one notable difference. Conceptions of the cost of a gift for a dear friend or relative clearly reflecting reciprocal interpersonal expectations reveal the gift-giving tradition of American Indian life, particularly for the relatively least acculturated group in our samples, the Navaho. Conceptions of the least and the most that should be spent for a gift are highly standardized between $2.50 and $10 for all other groups. However, the Navahos conceived this range between about $6 and $18. Furthermore, the cost of a present "that I would be proud to give" is typically located at about $5 for other groups, but the Navaho's pride in a gift is associated with the maximum he could manage, as shown by the median of about $17.

ILLUSTRATIVE FINDINGS

As illustrative of other data, I now propose to present briefly some findings concerning the number and nature of the groups that individuals from these different backgrounds consider most like themselves—most acceptable to them personally—and those considered least like themselves. On the average the white respondents identified themselves only with white native-born and English, considering themselves least close to Russians and African Negroes. It should be added that there was a strong tendency in all groups to use only the acceptable segment of the rating scale, a tendency undoubtedly reflecting the normative trend toward tolerance in the United States today, since ratings of other items on the same kind of scale did not cluster in the acceptable segment in this way.

Negro subjects regarded a total of eight groups as like themselves, including white native-born, English, Mexican, American Indian, Italian, Spanish-speaking, African Negro and, of course, American Negro (groups perceived as least close to themselves were German, Jew and Russian).

The Oklahoma and Navaho Indians grouped white native-born with their own American Indian group, and both rated Russians and African Negroes as most distant. In addition, however, Navahos accepted at the same level as themselves the English, Mexican, and Spanish-speaking groups, while the Oklahoma Indians accepted the American Negro. Unlike other groups, Navaho subjects rated as most distant from themselves those groups with which they have had little or no contact but are traditionally held in high regard by white, native-born populations, such as Norwegian, Belgian and other north-European peoples.

(It is at least of passing interest that about 10 per cent in each of these populations failed to differentiate among the groups at all, that is, simply rated them all alike as acceptable to them.)

In short, the radius of one's self, the level of achievement seen as necessary, as desirable, and as a goal for one's self are tied to the conditions, to the arrangements, to the values or norms of one's reference group. Strivings and desires function within the bounds set by the reference scales prevailing in one's reference groups. To place individuals with different reference scales on the same continuum and to evaluate

their goals and achievements by common standards is to obscure fundamental problems of motivation that make the study of the self a central
problem area, at least in social psychology.

The potential value of dimensional analysis of the various related
aspects of the individual's self ties is shown, I believe, by a recent experimental study by Carolyn Sherif (1961). Using data already obtained
from the Self-Radius Goals Schedules, she first made estimates of the
range of acceptability—that is, the latitude of acceptance—encompassed
by prevailing norms in Navaho and white high school populations in
several dimensions. Next she obtained independent estimates of the
relative personal involvement in these dimensions by a paired-compari-
son technique.

The experiment itself consisted of obtaining evaluative judgments
from individuals in these two settings with differing latitudes of acceptance, using the "own categories" technique that allows the subject
freedom to use any number of categories he chooses and to label them
himself (Sherif and Hovland, 1953).

Each individual evaluated four series of items that varied in personal significance to him, ranging from a neutral series of items (numerals) to a highly involving series (names of ethnic groups). One half
of the individuals from each group was given items that were largely
within the latitude of acceptance prevailing in his group. The other half
evaluated items that covered the gamut from acceptable to highly objectionable items.

The findings in this experiment supported the hypotheses and can
be summarized briefly as follows:

(1) Indian and white subjects did not differ significantly in the way
they categorized a neutral series (numbers). However, the number of
categories used by the two groups in evaluating the ego-involving materials did not differ ($F = 4.98$, $p < .05$, 1 and 68 df). For both groups,
the more ego-involving materials were evaluated with fewer categories
than the less ego-involving materials ($F = 17.02$, $p < .001$, 3 and 204
df). In other words, the more personally involving the material, the
greater the tendency for individuals to evaluate specific items as either
within the norms of their reference group, and hence acceptable to them
personally, or as *outside* of the norms of their reference group, hence
objectionable to them personally. This tendency was greater for the
Indian subjects.

(2) The experiment showed that the individual discriminates more
keenly within the prevailing latitude of acceptance when he is not faced
with deviant items. When faced with a large number of objectionable
things, he is prone to regard anything *within* the norm as more acceptable than he does when faced simply with variations within the norm.

(3) General principles governing "assimilation" and "contrast"

effects in judgment are also applicable to personal evaluations when the individual's latitude of acceptance is conceived as the anchor or standard for judgment. (The background and recent research on assimilation-contrast effects in psychophysical and social judgment is reviewed in the forthcoming book *Social Judgment* by Sherif and Hovland.)

In other words, the individual with a narrow latitude of acceptance relative to the series being evaluated not only rejects items deviating from the norms, but piles them up to a significant extent in the extremely objectionable category in line with the previous findings in this regard. The individual with a broad latitude of acceptance relative to the series tends to assimilate slightly deviant items toward his most acceptable category. It seems to us that such findings have significance in understanding more precisely the circumstances in which an individual will feel threatened, insulted or otherwise violated personally in the face of words or actions deviating from the norms of his reference group.

By specifying the range of acceptability defined by reference-group norms, the relative personal significance of the various norms or values to individuals, and then studying individuals' evaluations within this framework, the experiment demonstrates how data traditionally associated, on the one hand, with a cultural approach and, on the other, with a psychological approach can be integrated. Even variations in personal consistency were amenable to analysis within this framework, as evidenced by a low but significant intraclass correlation among the number of categories used by the same individuals for different materials ($.388$, $F = 4.53$, $p < .001$, 68 and 204 df).

SUMMARY

In this paper I have attempted to point to the inadequacy inherent in either a primarily group-centered or a primarily individual-centered approach to problems of the individual's personal relatedness to his environment. On the other hand, data concerning the individual's socio-cultural setting and data concerning his self conception can be integrated theoretically and in actual research practice through the reference group concept. As ancillary to the concept of self or ego as a constellation of inter-related attitudes, the reference-group concept directs attention to the subject-object relationships implicit in any motivational system. The object may be immediately present in the environment, or the self may be tied to it on a conceptual level; that is, the object may be beyond the confines of the person's immediate perceptual reach in space and time. Through continued analysis of the individual's relatedness to his reference groups in various specific dimensions and study of the kinds of interrelationships among these dimensions, we may be in a better position to assess the individual's unique personal consistencies, as well as inconsistencies, over a period of time.

THIRTEEN

THE PROBLEM OF INCONSISTENCY
IN INTERGROUP RELATIONS

The problem of consistency and inconsistency in intergroup relations is not a separate issue. Emphasis of this point is necessary if we are to achieve an adequate handling of the problem in research and in practice. As in many other areas, research efforts in this area are doomed to failure so long as the problem is taken as an isolated topic of investigation. Nor will such an approach be of substantial help to men seriously concerned with doing something about this vital matter in human relationships. In fact, practitioners and men of good will in education are rightly becoming suspicious of the value of the prescriptions "handed down" to them by the research people. Too often, such prescriptions fall pitifully short of the scope and diversity of the concrete experiences faced in the field of realities—realities which are not infrequently grim.

In this paper, I shall not try my hand at writing a rounded social psychological account of consistency-inconsistency in intergroup relations. An adequate social psychology of this serious issue can come only after we learn more about the underlying phenomena which have been more familiar topics of study for the social psychologist. Certainly the problems of attitude, attitude change, group membership, and ego functioning are among them. The aim of this paper is to relate briefly the topic at hand to these more familiar basic problems and to call attention to a few implications derived on this basis.

The issue of consistency-inconsistency in intergroup relations is another current issue which can be handled only as part and parcel of persistent major problems to which it is organically related (Sherif, 1948b). To start with the obvious fact, such inconsistencies in intergroup relations cannot be considered apart from the reality of the *institution* of social distance (prejudice)—the standardized scale of social distances at which one group is placed in relation to other groups. Many—by no

From *Journal of Social Issues* (1949), 5 (3): 32–37. Reprinted with the permission of the Society for the Psychological Study of Social Issues.

means all—campers in an interracial camp, caught *temporarily* in the atmosphere of the camp situation, may reduce the social distances at which the groups of fellow campers are placed, thus revealing reduction in prejudice. But when these same campers return to their own customary group setting, they may and do (as evidence indicates) return to their roles as good members of their own group. The out-groups which were treated perhaps with fairness or even cordiality in the camp situation are put back on the social distance scale in the positions standardized in the in-group.

It is evident, then, that in order to have any understanding of the inconsistency of behavior in such situations, we must first have a clear picture of the institution of social distance. The necessity of keeping in mind the prevailing social distance scale becomes evident when one examines the extensive, but all too frequently one-sided studies and practical efforts aimed at reducing or eliminating prejudices. On the whole, such methods as contact (even contact in group situations), information, instruction, resort to mass media of communication and other propaganda devices have been disappointingly unrewarding. In some cases, such well-meant efforts have produced bitter fruit—different kinds of "boomerang" effects. In our opinion, these disappointing results are due to the one-sidedness of the approaches used. The factors which investigators overlooked proved to be more potent than those with which they happened to be preoccupied.

In the case of consistency-inconsistency in intergroup relations as well, it may be rewarding to postpone for a time concentration on the topic itself and to look *first* at the implications of the social psychological phenomena that underlie prejudice.

An undue emphasis on individual childhood frustrations and other frustrations, on an authoritarian atmosphere of the family and of other agencies of child training, on aggressive tendencies thus engendered in the development of individuals leads to some variety of "displacement" theory of prejudice. All these are genuine problems to be taken up in later stages of the analysis. However, exclusive preoccupation with such part-problems is doing gross injustice to the broad scope of the topic. At this date, it should have been accepted as a well established fact that prejudice is a standardized social institution for the country like any other social institution. Its existence is quite independent of the particular life histories of the individuals in terms of their degree of contact with groups in question, information about them, etc. This fact has come out time and again in studies such as those of Bogardus, F. H. Allport, Meltzer, Zeligs and Hendrickson, Hartley, Murphy and Likert, and others. As good members of their group, the relatively better adjusted majority of the in-group shares the institution of social distance. Response to the individuals belonging to various out-groups is regulated by the position of those groups on the social distance scale. The concentration on individual frustration, aggressions and other individual factors can shed light on a limited area—the area of the degree of intensity with which the particular individual reveals his prejudice.

An adequate account of prejudice as a social institution goes well beyond the scope of competence of the psychologist. With all the social, economic, political, religious factors coming into the picture, this task lies largely in the domain of the social scientist. Therefore, the psychologist has to learn from the social scientists in this area before he can do justice to the topic.

It is the psychologist's job to study how the individual acquires the attitude of prejudice in the process of his becoming or being a member— and a good member—of his family, school, church, club, union, business organization, and social class. This is a specific case of the acquisition and functioning of an individual's attitudes in relation to any social institution or norm. As was convincingly established by Horowitz (1936) over a decade ago, prejudice is derived from membership in a community and not primarily by contact with the individuals of the group against whom prejudice is directed.

Since the attitude of prejudice is an attitude which in our eyes defines our standing in relation to the members of other groups, since it is a factor in appraising the worth of other people in relation to us, it is an ego-attitude. This fact is borne out by the findings of the Hartleys and the Clarks that the ego must reach some certain degree of development before a consistent pattern of prejudice is established in the individual. In other words, the development of prejudice and ego development go hand in hand. *The individual's attitudes of prejudice are consistent parts of his ego constellation.* The theoretical elaboration of the above statements and factual evidence on which they are based is presented elsewhere (Sherif and Cantril, 1947; Sherif, 1948).

Reactions of the individual in intergroup relations are ego-involved reactions. The behavior of the individual in relation to the members of any out-group is not determined in a major way by the specific properties of the stimuli at hand (including the persons in question), but is altered, distorted, accentuated, minimized, etc., largely as determined by the interiorized values on the social distance scale. The perceptual selectivity and distortions so frequently observed in intergroup relations are the outcome of ego-involvements.

But the ego-attitudes concerning various groups are not the only constituent of the ego. Other ego-attitudes function as part of the ego at a given time—ego-attitudes related to membership in the family, in church, school, club, clique, gang, sex, business, union, etc. There are also more specific ego-attitudes defining the individual's specific *role* or relative position in such groups. These various ego-attitudes, which may be activated singly or in some combination by the properties of the specific situation at hand, may or may not be compatible. If they are *incom-*

patible, the individual will be reacting one way in one situation and the opposite way (contradictory way, if you will) in another situation, as determined by the requirements of his different roles in the two different situations. For example, take the painful dilemma in which the modern professional woman is frequently caught. As a woman (in the feminine role), she is supposed to and she wants to react in a certain way. As a lady, she wants to observe certain niceties. As an engineer, doctor, or research worker (in the professional role), she has to and wants to live up to the expectations of her professional colleagues. In the privacy of her home with her husband or child, she may behave in a consistent way in her feminine role without contradicting herself. In sorority reunions or at purely social meetings, she may consistently behave like a lady. In her office or in a professional meeting, she may be her professional self more or less consistently. But it is a common occurrence in highly complicated modern societies to have this person caught in a situation which puts contradictory demands on her as a woman, as a lady, and as a professional person. Caught in such a situation, she will probably contradict either her womanly self, or ladylike self, or professional self, depending on the relative strengths of her various selves and the significance of the situation to her. This is especially true if she is a person of more than ordinary intensity.

Let us apply this kind of analysis to the contradictory behavior of the Detroit union members cited by Dr. Jahoda. These union members, who were taught and practiced non-segregation in their union activities, "actively participated in the race riots in 1943." If these union members had been *nothing but* the good and staunch union members that they were, they would not have participated in the race riot or in any act of discrimination. But they were also members of a neighborhood group, a church, ethnic group, and—as they are reminded in so many ways, directly or indirectly—of a "race" which they have learned stands at definite distances in relation to other "races" and groups. When this self (as member of an ethnic or racial group) was aroused, they acted this time as staunch members of their "racial" group. They followed the dictates of being "regular guys" in this situation no matter how contradictory such dictates were to other roles. In fact, they probably acted with a feeling of righteous indignation against those whom they considered to be the offenders.

Another illustration of such contradictory ego-attitudes is the case of young factory girls who, after "discussing the goals of life came to a unanimous decision that 'being happy' was the most desirable goal." During this discussion, the girls were shown two pictures—one of a smiling working class girl, the other a serious looking wealthy girl. From the smiling appearance, the girls characterized the working class girl as happy, while the serious look indicated to them that the wealthy girl was not happy. Yet, their aspired identification was with the leisure class girl. The contradictory reaction of these girls was due to the fact that they were, of course unwittingly, using different and contradictory premises. When discussing the goals of life in a general way, they naturally chose happiness as the goal of life. Almost anyone, living under any social system, would choose happiness as the goal of life. But when faced with the *concrete* alternative of identifying themselves either with the serious looking wealthy girl or the smiling working girl, their persistent and intense yearnings were activated. In the culture in which they live, through movies, schools, novels, radio, society columns in the papers, face-to-face and indirect media of influence their aspirations in the matter of identification are well ingrained. Thus their *aspired* self has strongly become the wealthy girl. She is the embodiment of the finishing school girl, the debutante, the movie star, so omnipresent in every conceivable means of mass communication as the significant, successful, desirable person.

These illustrations are sufficient to clarify the main point. What is designated as the ego (self) of the individual really consists of a host of attitudes learned in relation to persons, things, institutions, groups, norms with which he has been in contact. Especially in highly complicated modern societies of the West today, it is not a *unitary* ego which is involved in various situations. In one situation, one ego-attitude is involved; in a different situation, another ego-attitude or set of attitudes is activated as determined largely by the demands of the particular situation. As we have seen, various ego-attitudes of the same individual need not be compatible. When ego-attitudes are incompatible, the resulting reactions are usually contradictory to each other. (Therefore, the indiscriminate use of such terms as "ego-structure," as though the ego of the average modern man were a unitary, integrated whole, simply perpetuates a conventional psychological fallacy.) Herein lies, in our opinion, the psychological basis of most inconsistencies of individuals' reactions, especially in intergroup relations. As a good member of a union which has taken a definite anti-discrimination policy, the individual does not dare to and will not indulge in acts of discrimination, much less race rioting. But, like many of his fellow union members, he is other things at the same time. He is also a member of an ethnic group. In fact, he felt himself a member of an ethnic group (with all its auxiliary memberships) before he came to know himself as a union member. It is no wonder that in a conflicting situation, he reacts in a way contradictory to his union loyalties.

Anyone who keeps a clear picture of ego development in mind will find some well meaning attempts to better group relations rather naive. A boy goes to an interracial camp. It is unrealistic to assume that the camp situation is more than a small transitory segment of his life. He is primarily a member of a family, an ethnic group, a play group—

these are the groups which contribute heavily in the composition of his ego. A boy who behaved nicely in such a camp situation can hardly be expected to behave in the same way in his school, street or family situation when he knows that he will be laughed at, punished, or ostracized for such behavior.

The modern version of attitude change studies by "restructuring perception" is, of course, based on one important conclusion—that group situations can be created in which learned ways of perceiving and categorizing can be altered. But it is scarcely realistic to assume that perceptions "restructured" in a new group situation or attitudes altered in a liberal situation will become the lasting perceptual reactions or attitudes of the individual. The individual does not stay in such especially created situations for long. The objective situation in which he is customarily situated is the angle from which he sees and reacts to the world. To claim greater validity for situations in which perceptions are restructured than for the more or less permanent objective situations is a dangerous subjective tendency in psychology. Rather the results of such studies provide clear proof that perceptual lines or categories drawn in group situations are not immutable and can be changed. This is one thing. The problem of the durability of such changes and of making them last is the great problem challenging us all.

The inconsistent behavior in intergroup relations is not due only to external "cross pressures." However, such "cross pressures" certainly do play a part in some cases. For example, a white boy may want to play with Negro boys because he heard or read something that this was the right thing to do. In some cases, he will not even try to put the idea into practice out of fear of correctives from his playmates, family, and other grownups.

But in many cases, the *external* "cross pressures" need not be the cause of inconsistent behavior in intergroup relations. Our idea of what we are, what other groups are, what is desirable for a person to be, what is a desirable position to occupy, who are desirable persons to associate with, who are the persons who should be put at a distance, are derived in their major outlines from our reference groups. However, in time they seem to be our very own. The individual is simply not aware of their derivation. As Hartley indicated, white children, especially older ones, are often unable to say how they acquired their prejudices. The impact of external pressures is not even needed to regulate behavior under these circumstances.

In summary, the issue of consistency and inconsistency in intergroup relations is not a separate issue. Any adequate approach to the problem both in research and in practice, requires that it be taken as part and parcel of persistent major problems to which it is related. We have to keep in mind the picture of the institution of social distance and the implications of the psychology of ego development and functioning. An adequate account cannot be achieved by psychologists alone; it requires the close collaboration of social scientists in various areas. We have to make revisions on our hasty generalizations concerning attitude change derived mainly from studies done in artificial, transitory situations. With these considerations in mind at every step of the way, research on the issue of consistency and inconsistency in intergroup relations can be conducted in proper perspective.

THE ADOLESCENT IN HIS GROUP IN ITS SETTING
A. Theoretical Approach and Methodology Required
With Carolyn W. Sherif

This chapter and [the next] report a research program on natural groups of adolescents which was initiated in 1958 and is still in progress. The research program focuses on the attitudes, goals, and behavior of individual members in the context of their group and their particular socio-cultural setting. It attempts to study interpersonal relations, attitudes, behaviors and misbehaviors when these occur, in numerous interaction episodes over months. The groups under study are groups of the members' own creation or their own choosing, that is, their *reference groups.*

This chapter summarizes the theoretical guidelines and the empirical basis for a multifaceted research program requiring a combination of psychological and sociological procedures. The intimate relationship between theory and research methods will be articulated through discussion of the choice of data-gathering techniques and the timing of their introduction in the study of natural groups. We have reached the conviction painfully that free or arbitrary choice of methods is not possible in the study of actual groups which possess the essential properties defining "groupness." The nature of the groups sets definite limits on the range of methods that are appropriate.

. . . Our book, *Reference Groups: Exploration into Conformity and Deviation of Adolescents* (Sherif and Sherif, 1964) presents more details of the research program, its findings up to 1962, and the leads derived from them that are applicable to current problems of adolescent misbehaviors and the wastage of talents and energies in socially harmful channels.

From M. Sherif and Carolyn W. Sherif (Eds.). *Problems of Youth: Transition to Adulthood in a Changing World.* Chicago: Aldine Publishing Company, 1965.

This chapter is based on the senior author's invited address to Division 9, American Psychological Association, Los Angeles, September 6, 1964. Since 1961, the Research has been supported by grants from the National Science Foundation.

NECESSITY FOR MULTIFACETED RESEARCH DESIGN

The individuals studied in the research program are adolescents. As outlined in the Introduction, the dilemmas of this period, in a culture itself undergoing rapid social change, produce a broad and intense motivational base for group formations in all walks of life. The adolescent period is a paradigm for studying the individual-group-society relationship in its clearest manifestation. As such, the issues of theory and research into youthful behavior are essentially the same as those in the study of human social behavior at any period of life.

We start with a premise based on a host of empirical findings. The premise is that adequate study of the behavior of individual group members must include specification of the group properties and the part played by the individual.

Obviously, however, groups do not rise and function in a vacuum. Even though they are units with distinctive patterns of their own, groups are not closed systems defining their own universe. The claims of a group and the goals it pursues are related to the settings in which the group functions. That part of the setting which raises issues and problems about goals and collective efforts to attain them is the sociocultural setting.

Even though our interest is the individual behavior of group members, the components and events comprising the sociocultural setting cannot be reduced to psychological terms. They are *out there* relative to an individual. They are not reducible to "psychological constructs," as cogently noted by Roger Barker (1963). The sociocultural setting and its various aspects can be and are studied in their own right, by sociology, anthropology, and other social sciences, quite apart from the psychological study of particular individuals immersed in them.

Of course, there can be no denial that a person's psychological world is the world he actually experiences. But this experiential fact should not be stretched into a denial of an equally unmistakable fact: sociocultural products are *out there* as stimulus conditions for the individual, affecting his behavior and his success or failure in attaining his goals. This is the case even though he may not be aware of their impact. We cannot derive an adequate conception of the sociocultural setting merely from the psychological worlds of individuals in it without falling into a fruitless circle of reductionism.

Therefore, we must conclude that adequate study of individual behavior must include the specification of both the individual's groups and the sociocultural setting in which they form and function. The difficult research task is hitting upon concepts of analysis and procedures appropriate to each domain, namely, the individual, the group, and the sociocultural setting. Necessarily, the research task is *interdisciplinary*, to use a very fashionable term which is often misapplied. In a multifaceted research program which includes the study of individual-group-setting within the same design, the appalling gap between laboratory research and field research may narrow in a relatively short time.

If it is to achieve its purpose, such research must also interrelate its several facets without falling into a bias favoring either an individual group, or cultural approach. Proper operational procedures and the interrelationship of the various aspects will contribute to resolving a number of theoretical or doctrinal conflicts (as represented by the "institutional" vs. "behavioral" controversies in social science [cf. Sherif and Koslin, 1960], and the schisms between proponents of research on small groups and large organizations). In the present conception, individual behavior is seen in the context of groups and larger organizations. Small groups, in turn, are not viewed as units in their own right, but as parts of a larger social system. Our research program is an attempt in this direction.

THE RESEARCH DESIGN IN THREE FACETS

Mindful of the range of influences on the formation and functioning of human groups and the behavior of members, we designed our research to include operations appropriate for the behavior of individuals, for their groups, and for the sociocultural setting. In specifying the gross characteristics of the setting, as well as the prevailing patterns of values or norms within it, we relied heavily on methods, procedures, and findings of social scientists. After all, social scientists have developed tools and collected a wealth of data on the regularities of the sociocultural setting and the properties of groups. It is wasteful for social psychologists to start from scratch or to improvise tools without discovering those available in other academic disciplines.

The research program has three main facets, which may be summarized as follows:

1. Since the focus of the program is social-psychological, the concentration of procedures and data is on selected small groups of adolescents and their members. Clusters of teen-age boys (13-18 years old) are selected on the basis of their frequent and recurrent association in specified locations. Each group is studied intensively for periods from six months to a year. A combination of techniques is used in collecting data, including observation, behavior ratings by regular observers and independent raters, informal sociometric techniques, situational tests, and case history materials. The distinctive research strategy is that the boys are not aware that they are research subjects or that they are being observed for research purposes.

Behavior in the groups has included both socially acceptable activities, and deeds socially unacceptable to an extent that they would be

labeled "delinquent" if detected by adult authorities. The basis for selecting groups is their regular and recurrent association, not whether they
behave properly or misbehave, or have been labeled socially acceptable or
delinquent. For purposes of comparison, groups are selected from settings
of low, middle and high socioeconomic rank and from urban neighborhoods with different ethnic populations.

2. A second facet of the research is specification of the characteristics of the particular sociocultural settings where the small groups function. Such characteristics were conceived as stimulus conditions, relative
to the attitude and behavior of the individuals studied. Therefore, we
could not be content with a blanket, over-all characterization of the setting or with improvised descriptions of it. We relied especially on the
Shevky-Bell social area analysis (Shevky and Bell, 1955; Bell, 1958)
which yields concise indicators of what is meant by low, middle and high
social ranks, and their gradations.

3. For social-psychological analysis, specification of only major characteristics of the setting is not sufficient. Certain aspects of the sociocultural setting have greater salience than others, particularly for individuals
in the adolescent period. A large research literature shows that, during
the adolescent period, individuals are particularly attuned to others in
their own age set. Accordingly, special emphasis is given in the research program to collecting data on the bounds of acceptability and
on the goals prevailing among representative samples of teen-age youth
in each sociocultural setting. These data indicate what youth in different
areas regard as "socially desirable" and undesirable, and where they set
their sights for achievement in various respects. Thus, cultural values can
be compared between areas to ascertain which are common to them all
and in what ways they differ. In turn, the concepts and goals prevailing
among youth in a given area can serve as a baseline for assessing the
relative typicality or deviance of individual members of a group being
studied within that area.

INTERDEPENDENCE OF THEORY AND RESEARCH

We sought research methods from the social sciences as well as
psychology, and we relied on the empirical findings in both as the basis
for concepts and theory. Concepts and theory enter into research from
the very beginning, when the investigator formulates the problem of
study. They influence what kind of data he gathers and what data he
disregards. They affect the selection of data-gathering techniques, the
manner in which the data are used, the analysis, and the interpretation of
findings. Consequently, it is fitting to examine the theoretical and methodological problems of interdisciplinary research, which the adequate study
of youthful behavior must be.

In social science and psychology, there are grand theories of the individual-group-society relationship. The present approach, however, did not derive from a grand theory, though that might have greater esthetic appeal. Few, if any, of the grand theories are formulated to encompass the gamut of influences shaping behavior and to guide research operations at three different levels of analysis (individual, group, cultural).

Nor does the present approach stem from theoretical models borrowed (or smuggled) from more established and prestigeful sciences. Formal models of the relationships among the multifaceted data are the *goal*, so that, ultimately, we can express events and their relationship in five pages instead of five hundred. Because of the current fad, even craze, for models in psychology and social science, we shall be explicit about the limitations placed on data gathering by premature adoption or formulation of a formal theoretical model.

The indiscriminate use of models based on analogy with other sciences has proceeded with a singular lack of concern for the crucial question of the isomorphism between the models, and the events and actualities of which they are supposed to be models. Such concern should be the basis for accepting or rejecting a model. If it is not, the model restricts the range of data collected, conveniently pruning branches of unwanted facts to the point of focusing on tiny and barren twigs of trivia.

The common pitfall in borrowed models was emphasized recently in a presidential address to the Division of Engineering Psychology of the American Psychological Association, a rather unexpected source. Chapanis (1961) observed that attempts are seldom made to validate borrowed models and that those who work with them typically end up being "intrigued with essentially trivial problems."

Model building by making analogies with a more established science is not a monopoly of our time. There was the "mental chemistry" model of Wundt and Titchener, which now lies at dead end. There was the organic analogy of Herbert Spencer, which fared no better. Some mechanical and hydraulic analogies still flourish, but a similar fate for them is inevitable. As Emile Durkheim (1915) and others put it, social life and human value systems are not on a continuum with physical and biological events. They have properties of their own, not to be found through analogy with physical sciences.

The issue at hand, however, is not model building as such, but the proper basis for building them. The first step toward adequate models of social behavior and its social setting starts with formulating the proper questions and defining problems. In order to take this first step, a period of concentration on the actualities of our topics is essential. These actualities must be explored at the level of the complexity which is characteristic of problems of individual-group and sociocultural relationships.

To gain the effective tools for the logical and mathematical formalization so essential for precise model building, we have to define our problems and their properties more clearly. Unfortunately, at this erratic stage in the study of human affairs, even the basic problems at stake have not been formulated in stable form.

This is a plea for a disciplined phenomenology as an *initial step* in formulating problems. This is only an initial step, but one which serves generously as we venture on into research and theoretical interpretation.

As an illustration, consider the study of the formation of social norms in the laboratory through utilization of the autokinetic phenomenon (Sherif, 1935, 1936). This experiment is frequently cited as an example of the precision to be gained from laboratory models (cf. Cartwright and Zander, 1960). Yet it did not originate in the techniques and procedures of the psychological laboratory—it started with a lesson learned empirically in the actualities of social life: that social norms or standards arise when conditions in the lives of men are fluid, uncertain, or in crisis. From this lesson, it was then a matter of devising an appropriate laboratory condition to represent this fluidity and uncertainty; the autokinetic setup was one of several such conditions suitable for the problem. The same concern with observed actualities was the basis for the conception of our experiments on intergroup relations, which have been presented elsewhere (Sherif and Sherif, 1953; Sherif *et al.*, 1961). We are proceeding from such an empirical basis in studies of attitude and attitude change (Sherif, Sherif, and Nebergall, 1965).

The present undertaking on adolescents in their groups presents the investigator with much more challenging and difficult tasks than does experimentation. In the open field of actual life, event follows event, and none can be controlled and manipulated as the investigator chooses.

What guidelines do social science and psychology give us for raising crucial problems and formulating hypotheses? Necessarily, we can give only brief and essential examples of empirical findings that are established with sufficient stability to serve as a basis for research.

EMPIRICAL BASIS FROM SOCIAL SCIENCE AND PSYCHOLOGY

From the empirical findings of sociologists, especially from the Chicago school of the twenties and thirties, we learned of the universality of group formations whenever individuals interact with similar motivational promptings. These motivations may be deprivations, frustrations, or desires for earthly goods and political power. This generalization, based on empirical facts, provided the basis for hypotheses both for our experimental studies of group formation and intergroup relations, and for the present research.

As noted earlier, we also learned, primarily from findings by adolescent psychologists, of the motivational dilemmas common to this period. At the same time, we noted in anthropological reports that these dilemmas varied in their severity because of cultural arrangements (cf.

Sherif and Cantril, 1947). These reports also confirmed the generality and significance of group formation during adolescence.

From studies of both small and large organizations, we learned that human groups have properties more complex than merely an un-differentiated state of interdependence among individuals (cf. Homans, 1950; Blau and Scott, 1962). In actual groups, we learned, the inter-dependencies can be specified in terms of a differentiated and hierarchical pattern of positions, with decided implications as to what each individual can or cannot do in effectively initiating activities for others in the pattern without being challenged by them.

We learned from the studies of sociologists and anthropologists that every group possesses a set of regulations and standards—that is, a set of social norms—defining a latitude of acceptable behavior, includ-ing the ideal, as well as a range of unacceptable attitudes and actions which will bring forth scorn and sanction from others in the group.

Likewise, we have relied on guidelines from empirical findings in psychology. The findings from psychology have been particularly useful in developing behavioral indicators for the individual-group relationship; the hierarchical arrangements within groups, bounded by the end-posi-tions of "leader" and "man at the bottom"; and the way members of an in-group evaluate each other and out-groups. We found invaluable leads in the accumulating empirical facts in the psychology of perception (especially on perceptual selectivity), the psychology of judgment and motivation, and child psychology. We were concerned with including the sociocultural setting explicity partly because of the unmistakably established findings on background and context effects in the psychology of perception and judgment. Because of their far-reaching implications, these findings will be summarized.

Even the simplest judgment is a comparison process, not immune to the effects of its context or background. As Helson demonstrated, the color judgment of the same patch of material "could be made anything we pleased by appropriate choice of the luminance and hue of the background color" (Helson, 1964, p. 26). Context and background effect are considerations even in a relatively simple judgment of a patch of color or a weight of so many grams. How much more crucial they should be in considering an individual's judgment, perception, and other re-actions in his social relations!

Social relations constitute the context of individual attitude and behavior. Background and context intrude even into the carefully con-trived confines of an experimental interview or testing situation. There is much more to a contrived laboratory or testing situation than what catches the eye or what the experimenter's instruments can record. The context is not merely the experimenter's stimulus material and special in-structions. The experimenter himself, the way he is appraised by the subject, the surroundings, the presence or absence of other individuals and the subject's appraisal of them—all these intrude into the shaping of performance.

No wonder, then, that a whole movement on the "social psychology of the psychological experiment" is developing to articulate the hitherto unaccounted-for or neglected ingredients that go into the making of any situation. The trend is well represented in the experiments of Orne (1962) and Rosenthal (1961). Only a few of the recent contributions to this strengthened sensitivity to context and background can be cited here.

That the characteristics of the administrator make a difference on intelligence tests is forcefully brought to our attention once again in recent surveys by Pettigrew (1964) and Martin Deutsch (1964). Even more closely related to our own research is the report by Pearl in Chapter 5 of [Problems of Youth], where he compares interviews with delinquents made by graduate students with those made by other delinquents. "When graduate students conducted the tape-recorded interviews, they confirmed the usual conclusion that lower-class youth were inarticulate. But when lower-class interviewers canvassed the same persons, responses were entirely different. The subjects were animated and highly verbal."

Stevenson and Allen (1964) reported recently that the response rate in a motor task differs according to whether the experimenter is male or female; and Pishkin (1964) showed that errors in concept identification by schizophrenics were significantly affected by whether the experimenter was present or absent. Finally, we note the finding that the context of interpersonal relations in a hospital ward has produced not only behavioral variations, but also significant metabolic alterations (Schottstaedt, Pinsky, Mackler, and Wolf, 1958).

In brief, the context and background of human behavior produce significant variations, whether or not the investigator includes them in his study design. If we would understand the sources of behavioral variation, there seems to be no question about including the sociocultural and group contexts of behavior. Sober consideration of the research findings on context and background effects led to our inclusion of the sociocultural setting and group properties in the design, and to the methods chosen or developed for the study of behavior in groups.

CONCEPTS GOVERNING THE CHOICE OF RESEARCH METHODS

Since our research program focuses on the intensive study of natural groups of adolescents, the major hypotheses and data-gathering techniques for their assessment pertain to the behaviors and attitudes of individuals in such groups. The prerequisite to an adequate study of individual behavior in a group context is a definition of the properties of actual groups and their interaction processes.

Our definition of the properties of groups is based on extensive surveys of empirical findings on group formation and functioning in different social spheres, as documented in our own earlier publications (1948, 1953, 1956).

The term "natural group" is used in these chapters to designate the origins of the groups, and carries no evaluative implication. Particularly in the case of adolescent groups, it is convenient to distinguish groups formed through the informal interaction of members from those instituted by adults, a board of officers, or a council.

We are referring to groups in a technical sense, specifying the properties that distinguish a group from casual collective encounters, from temporary "discussion groups," and from experimental groups collected on an *ad hoc* basis. A formally instituted body may or may not become a "group" in the precise sense to be defined here.

In the first place, a group is a human formation formed over a given time span through interaction of individuals. It is a *social unit*. Its bounds define who is "in" and who is "not in." The criteria for membership and other properties of the group may or may not be codified explicitly as verbal rules.

The essential condition for the formation of a human group is interaction over a period of time among individuals with similar concerns, similar motives, similar frustrations, or, generally, a *common dilemma* which is not effectively dealt with through established social channels and arrangements. In other words, people in the same boat of misery or unfulfilled desires love company. They tend to interact with one another.

Repeated interaction in a variety of tasks by individuals with some common striving leads to differentiation of functions in activities, along with the coordination of effort. The differentiated functions are stabilized in time as *roles with differing status*. This differentiation of roles and statuses *over a time span* is the pattern of the human group.

Over a time span this patterned give-and-take interaction of individuals produces a *set of rules or norms* for the regulation of attitude and behavior within the bounds of the group and toward outsiders. The rules or norms that are salient in the eyes of members are those that pertain to the existence and continuation of the group and to spheres of activity related to the common motivational concerns which initially brought them together.

In summary, the minimum and essential properties of a group consist of (1) a pattern or organization of member roles, differentiated as to status or power as well as to other functions; and (2) a set of values or norms regulating behavior, at least in spheres of activity frequently engaged in by the group.

The "groupness" of a group is, therefore, a matter of degree. It is proportional to the extent that the status and role pattern is stabilized, and to the extent that member behavior is effectively regulated by a set of norms pertaining to their recurrent activities.

Now let us consider some implications that these properties of groups have in developing research procedures which will yield valid and reliable data on interpersonal relationships within the group and on the attitudes of individual members.

First, the unit character of a group implies a context for behavior which is, in some degree, "private." The "privacy" of in-group interactions develops from the motivational basis which brings the members together and the prolonged give-and-take among them.

Groups do not form and function for the benefit of an investigator. On the contrary, their very nature militates against his intrusion. The gross intrusion of an outsider into significant ongoing events will affect the usual context for behavior of members. This is particularly true if the outsider is identified as a *researcher*, an *investigator*, or anyone intent upon manipulating their behavior. We determined, then, to avoid making members aware that they were being observed and studied. This decision meant that our data had to be obtained in numerous interaction episodes at times and in places not under the observer's control. Observers were instructed to avoid, as much as possible, any interruption of the free flow of interpersonal give-and-take among members.

The definition of the group in terms of differentiation of status and role relationships and a set of norms did not specify that the individual members could or would report on leader-follower relations or on their conformity to group norms. In fact, we have records in our research of numerous expressions of the following sort: "We have no leader." "We have no boss." "We are all equal." Despite such reports, it was possible to rank these same individuals as first, second, third, down to lowest, in terms of their *effective initiative* in activities of the group. Effective initiative is an operational index of *power* in any organization.

In brief, the properties of groups led to inferences about the procedures necessary to study them adequately—namely, that the primary source of data was to be observation of interaction episodes over a period of time, without the awareness of members, and without undue cluttering of the flow of interaction by research techniques. These decisions, in turn, required adjustments to a common problem in field observations, the problem of checking reliability of observations.

In [the next chapter] the operational procedures, including the criteria for assessing group properties, are summarized in more detail. Here it is sufficient to note that the selective bias of a *single observer* was minimized by using a *combination of methods* for data collection. The use of a combination of data-gathering techniques permits findings by one method to be checked against those yielded by another. This is the best insurance against observer bias. The methods included adaptations of techniques ordinarily considered distinctive to the controlled laboratory situation, for example, rating methods and situational tests.

HYPOTHESES BASED ON EMPIRICALLY DERIVED CONCEPTS

From the properties of groups and their formation, several hypotheses about member attitudes and behavior were deduced. The major hypotheses of our research program and a string of auxiliary predictions are spelled out in *Reference Groups* (Sherif and Sherif, 1964).

Here we have deliberately selected hypotheses of major import for youthful behavior. The research program has collected pertinent data both in the study of natural groups, as summarized in the next chapter, and in laboratory experiments based on the same conceptualization, reported in this chapter.

Here, then, are general predictions deduced from the empirically derived concept of group:

1. To the extent that a group organization (role and status relations) is stabilized, the norms or standards for behavior in activities focal in interaction become *binding* for individual participants.

("Binding" means here, psychologically binding, such that conformity to the norm occurs because the person considers the norm in question as *his personal* guideline, not as one imposed on him. One index of the extent to which a group norm is binding for the individual is his behavior in compliance to its bounds when he is out of the reach of other members, and there is no threat of sanctions for deviation.)

2. The *salience* of various groups for the individual is a function of the extent to which its activities bear on motivational concerns he shares with the membership.

("Salience" refers here to the relative importance of the group as reflected in his behavior, especially in his choices or preferential judgments.)

3. Conformity to an established norm by new participants in the interaction pattern will be a function of the extent to which the conditions giving rise to the norm continue. Conversely, deviation from an established norm is a function of its "arbitrariness" relative to current motivations and circumstances faced by members.

("Arbitrariness" may be defined operationally in terms of the difference between the established norm and a norm stabilized in the current situation by individuals who have had no contact with the established norm.)

4. The extent to which an individual's behavior in group activities is predictable is a function of his position in the status organization and the degree of the group's stability.

(The last section of this chapter will spell out the curvilinear relationship between status and predictability of behavior.)

STABILITY OF STANDARDS FORMED IN GROUP VS.
MERE TOGETHERNESS SITUATIONS

An operational distinction can be made between mere *compliance* to the demands, pressures or suggestions of other individuals in an immediate situation, and the concept of *conformity* to the group.

Conformity, properly speaking, refers to behavior within the bounds of standards (norms) stabilized in prior interaction situations. The extent to which group norms are psychologically binding for the individual member may be tested by observing his behavior when he is *not* in contact with other members. It was predicted that the extent to which standards are psychologically binding would vary with the degree of stability in the interpersonal (role) relation among the individuals who participated in their formation.

In a laboratory experiment undertaken with the support of our research program, N. P. Pollis investigated this hypothesis by comparing conformity to standards which had been formed in interpersonal relationships of varying stability. He tested the hypothesis by first establishing standards for behavior (judgment), and then putting the individual in a transitory "togetherness" situation where the others confronted him with conflicting judgments. The question, then, was to what extent would the individual comply with the immediate social influences of others, or conform to his previously established standard in a novel situation.

The experiment was preceded by sociometric study of the sophomore class of a college, conducted under different auspices than the experiment so that the subjects would establish no connection between the two. On the basis of this study, subjects were selected from the intermediate range of general social standing on the campus. Certain well-defined cliques (groups) were discovered. It was also possible to specify which individuals were not personally acquainted.

In the first session of the experiment, each of the 144 subjects participated either (a) alone, (b) together with someone he did not know personally, or (c) together with a fellow group member. These three conditions defined variations in the stability of interpersonal relationships.

The task was to judge the frequencies of auditory pulses produced by an Eico audio-generator. A series of pulses was presented, consisting of random arrangements of four different pulse rates. Each pulse rate lasted 3 seconds and was followed by a 6-second rest period.

The task was sufficiently subject to error that Pollis found it feasible to train subjects to three different ranges of judgment by identifying the slowest and fastest rates differently in his instructions. Thus, he established three different judgment ranges, each among one-third of the subjects: low, middle or high. The purpose of this variation was to provide a pool of subjects with differing established ranges for a second session.

In the second session, each subject served with two others, none of whom were fellow group members. In the first session, one had stabilized his judgment range alone, one together with another student with whom he was interacting for the first time, and one with a fellow group member. Each of these three had formed a different range for judgment in session 1 (low, middle, high). The possible effect of the source in speaking judgments within these ranges was controlled by systematically counterbalancing the range established in session 1 and the social situation in which the individual had formed it. In other words, in session 2, the group member in one triplet started giving the high range; in another, the middle range, in another, the low range.

Two measures were used to test the hypothesis. First, the percentage of each individual's judgments in session 2 that fell *within* his range for session 1 was used as the measure of his *conformity* to the standard formed in session 1. Second, the percentage of judgments by other subjects in session 2 that fell within his range of judgments was a measure of their *compliance* with him in the immediate togetherness situation.

Figure 1 presents the findings on *conformity* to initial standards formed in session 1. If the hypothesis is correct that standards are psychologically binding to the extent that interpersonal relations among those who form them are stable, conformity would be greatest for individuals who formed standards in the *group* situation. It would be next greatest for standards formed in mere togetherness situations in session 1, and least for individuals who stabilized their own standards alone. The cumulative percentages in the figure show that the hypothesis is supported. Measures computed trial by trial revealed that these significant differences were not merely a result of initial trials.

Figure 2 gives findings on the relative *influence* in session 2 of subjects who had formed their standards alone, together, or in a group. It shows the average percentage of the judgments made by the two other subjects which fell within the individual's range. In other words, these percentages indicate the relative influence exerted by the subject on others present in the session. It may be seen that those who formed their scales in a group situation both conformed to them more (Figure 1) and exerted the most influence on others, that is, complied least in session 2. Individuals who had formed standards alone were least influential and most compliant in session 2.

This experiment by Pollis verifies in more precise form a recurrent observation in our study of natural groups. Being a member of a group with shared standards for behavior renders the individual *less* compliant to outsiders in a transitory situation. To the extent that he is part of patterned interpersonal relationships, the standards formed in that pattern are psychologically binding for him. Through *conformity* to group standards, he is less easily swayed by momentary influences and pressures in a different direction.

The implication that *conformity* to group standards produces greater

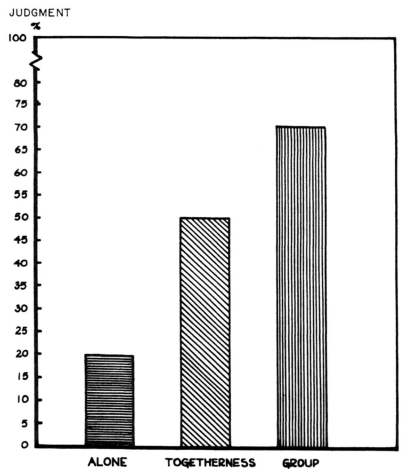

FIGURE 1. Adherence to norms initially formed in situations with varying stability of interpersonal relationships

independence by the individual in outside encounters is paradoxical only when the terms are defined without considering his social background and the context of the immediate interaction situation. The definition of the properties of a group implies definite consequences for individuals belonging over a period of time.

SALIENCE OF DIFFERENT REFERENCE GROUPS

The research program on groups of the adolescent's own choosing has yielded abundant evidence of the salience of these reference groups

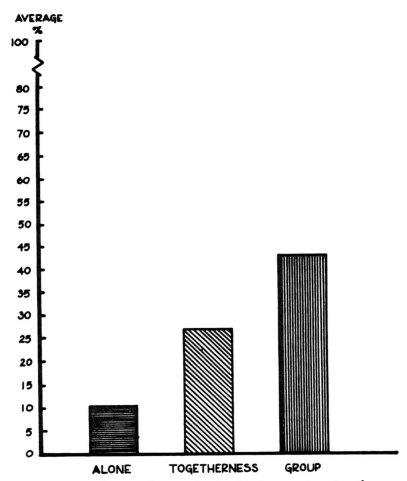

F<small>IGURE</small> 2. Relative influence of others' judgments in a togetherness situation by persons whose norm was formed initially in situations of varying stability

for the members. In making choices between their activities and standards and those of family, church or school, they frequently neglected the latter. As noted in the Introduction, a shift in the salience of age-mate and family reference groups is a general phenomenon of the adolescent period in this society. An experiment by Prado demonstrates behavioral consequences of this shift by a comparison of children's and adolescent's judgments on the competence of their fathers and their best friends.

Prado selected 25 boys eight to eleven years old and 25 boys fourteen to seventeen years old, who consistently selected their father as the most valued and trusted parent. This stringent criterion for selection minimized the possibility that adolescent boys were simply rebelling against unusually authoritarian fathers. Similarly, Prado obtained the boys' sociometric preferences in order to single out their best age-mate friend.

Bringing each subject to the laboratory with his father and his best friend, he had the father and the friend perform a simple eye-hand coordination task (throwing a dart at a target), so arranged that the outcome was indeterminate. Each subject judged, in turn, the performance of his father or friend with scores from 0 to 24.

If appraisal of performance indicates the salience of reference groups, it is reasonable to predict that children would estimate their fathers' performance higher than that of their friends; while adolescents would estimate their fathers' performance *lower* than they estimated that of friends.

The results showed significant differences. Of the children, 20 of the 25 did estimate their fathers' performance as superior to that of age-mate friends (mean difference = + 3.5 points). Conversely, 19 of the 25 adolescents appraised their fathers' performance as *lower* than that of their friends (mean difference = − 2.6).

Although the exact outcome was indeterminate, some real differences in the skills of the fathers and friends could have affected the boys' judgments. But actually, 17 of the 25 fathers of adolescents performed as well or better than their sons' pals, and only 13 of the 25 fathers of children equalled or outstripped their child's friend. In a reanalysis of Prado's data, we have found that, ignoring the *direction* of error, there are not significant differences in the children's and adolescents' accuracy in judging. In both age groups, average error in the fathers' performance was approximately 4.5 points, and the average error for friends somewhat less (3.5 points).

Considering the errors as overestimations and underestimations of performance, we can compare the difference between errors for fathers and errors for friends as an index of the extent to which the father is favored over the friend or vice versa, taking into account differences in performance. If the difference is *positive*, the father was favored over the friend. If the difference is negative, the friend's performance was favored over the father's, despite differences in skill.

Figure 3 presents the findings. On the average, children overestimate their father's performance, even with differences in performance controlled (Mean difference = + 2.35). Adolescents underestimate their fathers, with performance level again adjusted (Mean difference = − 3.64). (A test of the significance of these differences between errors for fathers' and friends' performances yielded t = 3.72, p < .001.)

A subsidiary finding in Prado's research supports the hypothesis

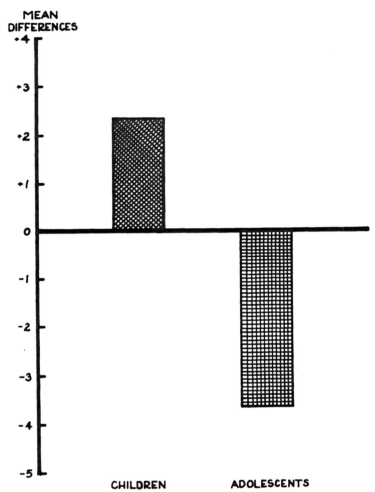

FIGURE 3. Overestimation by children and underestimation by adolescents of parent's performance as compared with best friend's

that the shifting salience of reference groups in adolescence is related to the motivational concerns the members share. He found that adolescents engaged in a significantly greater number of activities with friends than did younger boys, even though the two age groups did not differ in their consistency in choosing the friends in question. Since both children and adolescents in this study actually preferred their father as a parent, the logical inference is that the adolescent's activities and free time are focused more on common concerns with age-mates than are a younger child's.   .

CONFORMITY TO NORMS AS A FUNCTION OF
THEIR ARBITRARINESS

If group norms become psychologically binding for individual members, without threat of disapproval, why do an individual's patterns of conformity change? Why do the values or norms of one group persist even when membership changes over successive generations, while those of another group disappear as the last member leaves?

Relative to youth problems, we suggested in the last section that adherence to group norms varies with the salience of the group. This salience shifts from childhood to adolescence, primarily because the dilemmas of adolescence in modern societies are shared with age-mates more than with one's family.

It is equally true that when adolescents gain mature roles, or are thrust into them by circumstances, the salience of age-mate reference groups diminishes. Adults say there is nothing like a job or marriage to "settle down" the wild, rebellious, or "silly" behavior of their offspring and his crowd. His motivational concerns no longer intersect so extensively with those of his age-mates.

But what of the transmission of group norms and customs over time? The transmission of a group, carrying the same identity and similar norms, to a new membership is a distinctive feature of human societies. It is observed in informal social life as well. In the next chapter, we summarize the intensive study in our research of three generations of boys living in the same neighborhood, each of whom belonged to the same group as a teenager.

When a group has established norms for behavior, and new members come as older ones depart, what conditions lead to the maintenance of the group norms in substantially similar form, and which ones are conducive to their alteration?

Our hypothesis predicts that one important variable affecting the transmission of norms and the extent of conformity to them by new members is the degree of their arbitrariness relative to current conditions facing the group. When a norm is transmitted by older members to a new generation of members, its "arbitrariness" can be defined relative to the conditions in which the new generation functions. The norm developing in those conditions *without* an enculturation process by older members can be termed *least arbitrary*.

If the arbitrariness of norms is an important variable in conformity-deviation, it will help explain the continuity of groups of boys who grow up in the same neighborhood, relative to the changes occurring in the neighborhood and the city of which it is a part.

For these reasons, a laboratory experiment was initiated (as part of our research program) to examine how differing degrees of arbitrariness affected the conformity of succeeding "generations" in the laboratory. Data were collected by Mark K. McNeil with assistance from Michael Lauderdale, both assistants in the program at the time. The autokinetic phenomenon was chosen as the situation to be appraised by the subjects.

As in the earlier studies of norm formation by Sherif (1935, 1936), a norm for behavior in this situation was defined as a common range of judgment around a modal point, stabilized over time by two or more individuals. Individual conformity is defined as a judgment falling within this norm; deviation, a judgment outside the norm.

In this situation, the degree of arbitrariness of a norm could be defined operationally as the extent to which a prescribed and transmitted norm differed from the range and mode of judgments stabilized under the same laboratory arrangements *without* the introduction of a norm transmitted by "planted" subjects.

The general sequence of procedures followed those used in a study by Jacobs and Campbell (1961), who, through instructions to "planted" subjects, introduced an arbitrary norm of 15.5 inches with a range of one inch. They followed the progress of the norm through successive generations by replacing one of three planted subjects with a naive subject after each block of judgments, and then replacing an experienced subject with a new naive subject at the start of each succeeding block.

Since degree of arbitrariness was our main interest, three degrees were standardized in our laboratory: (I) not arbitrary; (II) an arbitrary norm chosen not to overlap the range of Condition I and with a higher mode (a range of 9-15 inches around a mode of 12 inches); (III) more arbitrary norm not overlapping Condition II and a still higher mode (15-21 inch range and 18 inches mode).

In Condition I (not arbitrary), four naive subjects gave 30 judgments each of the extent of autokinetic movement; then each in turn was replaced by a new naive subject in the succeeding "generations," and so on, through eight generations of 30 judgments each. In Conditions II and III, a preliminary "enculturation" phase consisted of three generations, with the prescribed norm being given by three, then two, then a single planted subject, who in turn was replaced by a naive subject. Eight generations of naive subjects followed, the transmitted norm being traced over these.

The subjects were high school students (ages 16-19). A total of 66 naive subjects participated in two replications of each condition.

The major hypothesis was that degree of conformity over successive generations would decrease (and deviation increase) as a function of the degree of arbitrariness of the transmitted norm. In order to test this hypothesis, it was also necessary to demonstrate the following: (a) a norm formed in Condition I would be transmitted with only minor variations as personnel changed, and (b) the enculturation procedures in Conditions II and III did produce conformity to the prescribed norm by naive subjects.

The findings can be summarized briefly as follows:

1. The norm formed by subjects in the first generation in Condition I (not arbitrary) was within an interquartile range of 4-8 inches, with a median and mean of 6 inches. The means and medians of seven successive generations were around 4 inches with an interquartile range from 3 to 6 inches. In short, after the second generation, the norm in Condition I was transmitted with only minor variations.

2. The enculturation by planted subjects in the more arbitrary conditions did result in conformity by naive subjects. In Condition II, 100 per cent of their judgments fell within the prescribed range, and 90 per cent of the judgments conformed in Condition III (most arbitrary), as shown in Figure 4. Similarly, the median judgments of naive subjects in Condition II were very close to the prescribed median of 12 inches (11.7 inches); and the median for Condition III during enculturation was 16.5-17.5 inches.

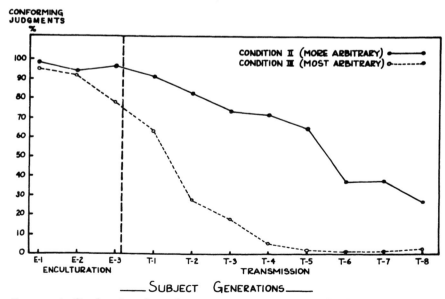

FIGURE 4. Conformity through successive generations of laboratory subjects as a function of the arbitrariness of norms

3. The prescribed norm in Condition II was transmitted to the first generation, consisting entirely of naive subjects, 100 per cent of their judgments conforming to the transmitted norm. In the most arbitrary condition (III), there was some deviation from the prescribed norm by the first generation of entirely naive subjects, but 63 per cent of their judgments conformed to the transmitted norm.

Figure 4 gives the percentages of judgments by naive subjects which fell within the prescribed norm for Conditions II and III through three enculturation and eight transmission generations. Conformity to the prescribed norm was significantly greater at every generation in the less arbitrary condition (II). The rate of increase in deviation was clearly more rapid in Condition III (most arbitrary).

Figure 5 presents the median judgments of naive subjects, generation by generation. The greatest shift away from the transmitted norm and toward the "natural" norm of Condition I was in the most arbitrary condition, with half of the downward trend occurring by the third trans-

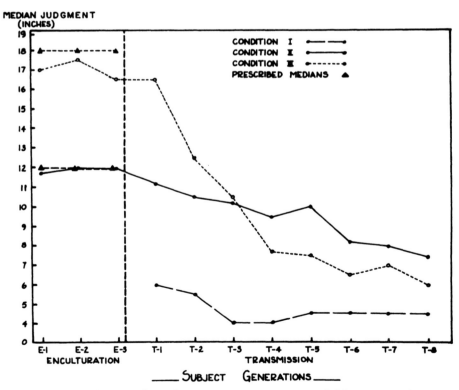

FIGURE 5. Conformity through successive generations of laboratory subjects compared to prescribed medians and "natural" norm

mission generation. The change was more gradual in Condition II (less arbitrary), with the median judgments less toward the "natural" norm even in the last generation of subjects.

The general theoretical inference from this experiment is that conforming behavior by individuals occurs in a context of social interaction which is inevitably related to the conditions, problems and tasks which confront them. The norms stabilized are products of both the interaction process and the conditions in which it occurs. With successive generations of membership, conformity to established norms for behavior is an inverse function of the arbitrariness of the norms. However, deviation by individuals results in new, less arbitrary norms which, in turn, are transmitted to new members. [The next chapter] presents an example of this process in three generations of boys belonging to a neighborhood group in a large city.

GENERALITY OF GROUPS AND THEIR PSYCHOLOGICAL CONSEQUENCES

In the research program on adolescent reference groups, we were impressed once again with the generality of group formations in all walks of life during this age period. Whether the groups are labeled cliques, friendship circles, chums, crowds, or gangs seems to depend much more on the social rank of the neighborhood than on their essential properties.

All have differentiated patterns regulating their interpersonal relations. All have rules, customs, fads—in short, norms—regulating behavior in their activities. These are the minimum essentials of a group.

These groups of adolescents were formed, or joined, on the members' own initiative, through interactions among individuals sharing the dilemmas of status and motivation common during adolescence in this society. The status differentiation which developed was not imposed on them; the norms were not considered arbitrary impositions on the members.

The individual had a hand in creating the properties of the group, or had selected it. The group was his—a context where he could have personal ties with others, could amount to something in ways not available elsewhere, could accomplish things as a person. It contained others whose acceptance he wanted, whose yardsticks were his personal gauges for success and failure, whose approval brought inner warmth and whose disapproval left him miserable.

Psychologically, therefore, the basis of group solidarity, of conformity to group norms without threat of sanctions, of the binding nature of group rules even when they conflict with those of parents and officials, lies in the personal involvement of members. The self-image of the individual consists, in large part, of his ties with his reference group and the yardsticks it provides. The continuity of his ego identity from day to day depends to a large extent on the stability of his ties with members and on their consistency in appraising him according to the patterned relationships and norms shared in common. They are among the stable anchorages in his world. The disruption of their stability affects him as surely as the sudden lack of stable guideposts in his physical surroundings (cf. Sherif and Harvey, 1952).

Groups of the individual's own choosing are not the monopoly of adolescents. They are formed whenever people see themselves in the same boat, whether this be a neighborhood, a large organization (such as the military, industrial plant, or prison), or in a crisis situation. It is true, as Zorbaugh (1929) reported some years ago, that the slum has its gangs and the Gold Coast has its clubs. These are all human groups with consequences—good or evil—for the attitude and behavior of individuals composing them.

IMPLICATIONS FOR VALID STUDY OF BEHAVIOR IN GROUPS

Groups are not formed to be studied by outsiders. They are not formed for the benefit of a reformer. They are not formed to tolerate criticism, advice, or unfavorable evaluations by outsiders. They are formed by individuals with similar concerns. They have designs and ends of their own. They have properties of their own, which are reflected in the attitude and behavior of members toward each other and toward outsiders.

Therefore, if we would study individuals who belong to groups, the cardinal research strategy must be a design that places the behavior of members *within* their groups, and places the groups, in turn, within their sociocultural setting. The selection of methods, procedures and research models is not a matter of convenience or the arbitrary preference of the investigator. If they are to yield valid data, the methods and procedures must accommodate the properties of groups as they actually form and function.

In terms of the properties of groups, as spelled out in this chapter, certain methods are appropriate and certain are inappropriate. Furthermore, the appropriateness or inappropriateness of methods depends on the *time* at which they are used. The properties of groups require a procedural *sequence* of steps.

The issue is not merely whether or not data can be collected, for some kind of data can almost always be obtained. The issue at hand is the *validity* of the obtainable data. This issue is bound to be confronted more and more seriously as social scientists and psychologists are called upon to contribute to baffling human problems ranging all the way from delinquency and school dropouts to segregation, prejudice, and other threatening problems of intergroup relations.

The basic criterion for securing valid data on groups and their members is that procedures and techniques be *timed* so that members will not view the event as an unwarranted intrusion or imposition by an outsider. This is the reason why, from the beginning, a special effort was made in our research not to arouse the group's awareness that an observer was studying them and rating their behavior.

To the extent that a group is at odds with established routines and channels for behavior, they not only have designs of their own, but also *secrets* about these designs. Whether or not their behavior is socially acceptable to adults, most adolescent groups do have plans which they consider *private*, especially from grownups, who seldom "understand" them. (See, for example, the Introduction to [*Problems of Youth*]).

To the extent that group members consider their affairs "private," they erect walls of resistance to any outsider. The appropriate timing and sequence of research procedures are, therefore, contingent upon steps to bring down first these walls of resistance and then the walls of secrecy.

In short, the timing and sequence of research procedures must be planned in terms of the degree of *rapport* established with group members, particularly those of higher status who are most obligated to protect the group's privacy. Results from the more usual research procedures—interviews with direct questions, questionnaires, sociometric choices, laboratory procedures requiring the cooperation of subjects—are less than worthless if introduced before rapport is firmly established. They are misleading. Very early in our research, this realization was forced upon us by an incident involving the untimely use of sociometric techniques.

The observer had had considerable give-and-take with the group for several months. In securing sociometric choices, he talked individually to each boy, inquiring whom he liked to "hang around with" most. The answers seemed free and courteous, but revealed the futility of such a procedure when rapport is no deeper than surface courtesy. The boys were all telling the observer that their best pals were boys about ten or twelve years old, most of them younger brothers.

The cycle of procedures for study of groups, as developed in our research, and problems of developing and assessing rapport, are discussed in the next chapter.

PREDICTABILITY OF BEHAVIOR STUDIED IN ITS APPROPRIATE CONTEXT

A serious pitfall in research is the tendency to select a particular mode of behavior, often because it is socially unacceptable, and then to "explain" it through postmortem analysis without specifying the background and context of the events in question. In experimentation, this tendency leads to laboratory models with little bearing on the actualities of the field. In the field, it leads to failures in predicting behavior and, practically, to views impeding the development of preventive measures.

In studying youthful behavior, we have been equally interested in those attitudes and actions which are socially acceptable and those which are not. There cannot be one social psychology for acceptable behaviors and another, entirely different, social psychology for unacceptable ones. In both cases, general psychological principles must be sought which take into account the background and context of behavior.

PREDICTION AND THE SOCIAL CONTEXT OF YOUTHFUL BEHAVIOR

A research design to accommodate all the influences shaping behavior and to secure valid, reliable indicators of behavior as it actually occurs is essential in developing a base for making predictions. We have secured data on planning, decision-making, and actions that members considered secret and would not have exposed to any adult with authority. Frequently, the events had consequential outcomes for the individuals.

A case in point was our prediction of two school dropouts some weeks before they occurred. The prediction was based on extensive evidence that the two boys were highly committed members in a group in which the high status positions were held by boys who had left school. The two continued in school under pressures from parents and teachers. They were not failing. But in their group, derogation of school as a place for "sissies" was common. They had no close personal ties with schoolmates. Being in school deprived them of time when other members were doing "interesting" things. First one, then the other boy stopped attending school, a few months short of graduation.

The study of behavior in its group context has been severely hampered by a moralistic view which condemns group influence as a sign of individual weakness or even pathology. This view is blind to the fact that group influence on individual behavior may be for good as well as for evil.

In our research, we encountered numerous instances of an official tendency by community authorities (school, recreation leaders, parents) to minimize even the existence of groups within the area of their work. Apparently the tendency is nationwide in scope, as indicated in a report for the Committee on the Judiciary of the U.S. Senate in the following words:

We further encountered difficulties when confronted in many communities with the attitude that the mere existence of any gang or gang problem constituted a failure of responsibility of the agencies, so that the type of reports made by these agencies were less than complete. In several cities we found, based on our own investigations, discussions, and contacts made with gangs, gang workers, police on the beat, teachers and citizens, a wide discrepancy between their off-the-record statements and the official reporting regarding the existence of gangs, their antisocial behavior, and the degree of problem they created. (U.S. Senate Report, 1961, p. 12)

Yet, ignoring the group context of behavior will continue to lead, as it has in the past, to failures of prediction in research and to continued "surprises" at a community level. For example, the following type of news item is not unusual:

The uncovering by police (Sunday) of a ruthless, pistol packing gang of 20 or more youthful LeDroit Park Ramblers (in Washington, D.C.), who are suspected of engineering over 80 "hustles" in 6 months has left area youth workers shocked. . . . Playground officials, the Recreation Department's roving leaders, the Junior Police and Citizens Corps, the LeDroit Park Civic Association, and the Youth Aid Division of the police department had all been unaware even that a group of youth using the name of "Ramblers" existed. (U.S. Senate Report, 1961, p. 12)

The deeds and misdeeds of youth cannot be predicted solely on the basis of class membership, nor solely on the basis of family relations, nor through any theory advocating a single sovereign cause. It should be sobering for both theorists and practitioners to read a recent report ascribed to the Pennsylvania Chiefs of Police Association (in the same Senate report) which concludes that "the broken home and unemployed and socially handicapped youth can no longer be solely blamed for juvenile crime." Several examples are cited of serious violations by youth from comfortable neighborhoods.

An equally strong case could be made that theories advocating oversimplified etiology cannot account for socially acceptable behavior. The etiology of behavior, whether acceptable or not, must include the context of membership in natural groups, in whose formation and functioning many influences participate. These influences stem from the individual and his background, from the sociocultural setting in which he develops, and from the prevailing images of success and achievement set by people who count in his eyes, whether these people are immediately present or are reflected from the mass media. All of these contribute to the natural reference groups of age-mates in which youth moves and to their directions, which may be for good or for evil.

PREDICTION AND GENERAL PRINCIPLES OF BEHAVIOR

The greatest promise for a theory to enable prediction lies in identifying general principles that are equally valid in the laboratory and in the rich context of the field. The experiments summarized earlier in this chapter are examples of research utilizing general principles of judgment with relevance for behavior in social actualities. Thus, Pollis' study showed that the tendency toward compliance with others' judgments is modified by the individual's background, specifically by whether his standards were formed in a group or in a less stable interpersonal context. Prado used the general finding of systematic variations in judgments of performance to index shifts in the salience of reference groups from childhood to adolescence. As a final example from this research program, we will mention continuity of a basic principle of judgment discovered in the interaction patterns of adolescent groups in the field.

The interpersonal relations among contemporaries are patterned affairs. To some extent, an individual regulates his behavior relative to others, and to that extent his behavior becomes predictable in a variety of situations. In comparing the ratings made by observers with the sociometric choices made by members of the relative power (effective initiative) in a group, we have found that predictability of behavior is related to the individual's position in the group structure. But the relationship is not a linear function of relative power; it is curvilinear. As [the next chapter] will show in more detail, consistency and confidence in ratings are invariably greater regarding the leader and other high status persons, followed by ratings of those with lowest status. Variability in rating is greatest in the intermediate ranks.

Thus, we see in the patterning of group interpersonal relations a phenomenon which has been extensively studied in the psychophysical laboratory—namely, *end-anchoring.* The extreme representatives of a set of stimuli are singled out most readily and used as standards for assessing the others. In natural groups, the leader position is typically the most potent anchor; the lower positions are rated with less variability than intermediate levels.

The extent to which end-anchoring of the group structure occurs, the stability of the structure, and the number of status categories (or levels) from top to bottom vary considerably in natural groups, as they do in larger organizations. The variations, in turn, are affected in a crucial way by the relation of the small group to its setting. Thus, the stability of the leader position, which is the upper anchor, as well as the extent of differentiation in the pattern, are strikingly dependent on *what* the members engage in and on what their dealings are with others in the setting— both other groups and adult authorities. The changes in the status patterns which we have observed as they happened resulted from external changes in the settings—changes in the opportunities faced by the members or exposure of their most private activities by adult authorities.

But, whatever the variations, differentiations according to the effectiveness of initiative and patterns of deference among members was the rule in these natural groups. This phenomenon is the invariant consequence of prolonged interaction among individuals facing common problems. Which individual will occupy what status position, and which individual will succeed in changing his position, rests on unique personal characteristics of individual members—their contribution relative to the demands of group activities in which certain personal characteristics matter. These are fascinating problems of individual differences to be explored in the research program as it continues.

CONCLUSIONS

The properties of natural reference groups do limit the range of procedures and the sequence of their application in collecting valid data. Much more effort and patience are required than in laboratory research. But within the approach outlined here, precise and reliable measurement is within the grasp of field research. Laboratory methods of assessment can frequently be adapted for this purpose. And with greater specification of the variables, findings in the field become the proper basis for laboratory research.

When small groups and their members are studied relative to their sociocultural settings, and the setting studied relative to the groups within it, the dichotomy between small group research and research on large organizations will disappear. The "psychological" and the "sociological" study of social behavior will supplement one another, instead of being monopolistic preferences of their respective disciplines.

The contributions of particular individuals, for good or for evil, can be studied to any desired degree of elaboration within their appropriate behavior settings. The appropriate behavior settings are patterned affairs, consisting of the individual's reference groups and the sociocultural setting of which these reference groups are parts. Personal skills and qualities are not contributed in the abstract. Unique individuality shows in the ways an individual interacts with others in activities and situations important in their concerted undertakings. These interactions provide the context for his own attitude and behavior.

On the basis of the theoretical and methodological background presented here, the research on adolescents in their groups in their settings is summarized in the next chapter. It is our conviction that the approach outlined is equally viable for the study of behavior at other age periods, taking into account the changes in the setting and their salience throughout development.

FOURTEEN

THE ADOLESCENT IN HIS GROUP IN ITS SETTING
B. Research Procedures and Findings
With Carolyn W. Sherif

In this chapter, we will outline the procedures and research tools developed for intensive study of natural groups on the basis of the theoretical guidelines presented in [the preceding chapter]. Findings from our research on youth in various settings within urban areas of the southwestern United States are incorporated throughout the chapter.

The procedures and tools in this research program are not entirely distinctive—if there is innovation, it lies in procedures for studying behavior in natural groups of adolescents without arousing awareness of research intent. Nor do we propose that all the findings on adolescent youth are unique to our research. As indicated in the last chapter, we have freely utilized previous research from psychologists and social scientists as bases for hypotheses, concepts, and research procedures. We would be surprised if our findings bore no relation to those previously reported on American youth.

On the contrary, our purpose is to demonstrate the importance of incorporating the many influences on youthful behavior into single research designs. The neglect of some facets has led in the past to emphasis on one particular point to the neglect of others in theories of adolescent behaviors and misbehaviors. We have had ample opportunity to see the fruitlessness of one-facet theories, whether they focus exclusively on early childhood development, intrapsychic conflicts, sexual development, social class or local subculture.

A theory capable of accounting for the behavior of individuals interacting with others in definite habitats—that is, social-psychological theory —must be based on an integration of findings about all the significant influences affecting behavior. These include the motivational dilemma of the adolescent in his society; the person he is at the time, including his skills and his desires to be part of some scheme of human endeavor; the influences from other people who *count* in his eyes; the properties of his relationships with those people; the values and facilities of his sociocultural setting; and the setting's place in the larger social scene.

From M. Sherif and Carolyn W. Sherif (Eds.), *Problems of Youth: Transition to Adulthood in a Changing World.* Chicago: Aldine Publishing Company, 1965.

If a theory is to be adequate, its development must proceed hand in hand with the development of operational tools for research incorporating all the significant variables. Without such tools, no theory can link its concepts together and deal with empirical relationships, no matter how elegant it may sound. And without a theory to integrate the significant variables affecting adolescent behavior, practical measures for preventing the wastage of youthful potentialities can only proceed on a hit-or-miss basis.

RESEARCH PERSPECTIVE ON ADOLESCENT BEHAVIOR

Let us sum up the general features of the adolescent period, since the influences that an adequate research design must study follow from these features.

First, the adolescent is a human male or female with at least a decade of life behind him. His body and its functioning are beginning to change toward that of an adult human. As they do, he is expected to alter his behavior toward others and toward his current and future responsibilities. Although ordinarily he wants to do so, these behavioral alterations can be achieved in a consistent way only if he changes his picture of himself relative to others. Thus they demand changes in self or ego-attitudes in various respects.

Second, in modern societies, the motivational problems that come with physical changes and the necessity of changing one's self-image are further compounded by ambiguities in adult definitions of the transition period. The general characteristics of the period as defined, or left undefined, produce strong motivational problems and dilemmas which are, indeed, common to all youth in some degree.

Third, adolescent behavior under the grip of these motivational problems and dilemmas is not entirely unique to the adolescent period. Similarities may be observed among any individuals presented with a motivational problem. A frequent response, when individuals perceive that others share their problem, is to come together in regular association. Since age-mate association is both permitted and encouraged in modern societies, youth do gravitate toward one another, associating more frequently and more intensely than in earlier childhood. The domain of other adolescents becomes a reference set of greater salience than that of adults or younger children (as demonstrated experimentally in [the preceding chapter]).

Fourth, regular associations among individuals of any age with common problems acquire distinctive properties. These include some patterning or organization of interpersonal dealings, and some agreement as to what objects and behaviors are acceptable and which are not, what is to be prized and sought, and what is "ideal." These two properties—patterned interpersonal relations and shared yardsticks for evaluation—are the minimums defining a human group. Thus, group formations proliferate during adolescence.

Fifth, what the individual adolescent desires, what he sees as the ideal, what he does in concert with age-mates, the character of their group and its products, are not *direct outcomes* of the motivational problems which bring him to his fellow group members or which he discovers he shares with them. Here, we must consider both the immediate sociocultural setting and its facilities, and the values of the larger society of which they are parts.

During adolescence, the character of the general culture and the immediate circumstances of living take on new and added significance. The radius of self-concern is expanding beyond its more limited scope of childhood and extending further into the future. Even in the immediate present, the adolescent is more tuned to sociocultural influences and his society's adult success images. He is more mobile than a child.

The point may be illustrated briefly: In our research, we found that boys and girls in the southwest come to feel, by the age of seventeen or eighteen, that it is their inalienable right to have a car. A car is seen as a *necessity*. Particular kinds, models, and colors desired are specified to the last detail. There can be no doubt of the motivational press behind these desires, nor of their relevance to other common motivational problems (including notably those related to prestige, contacts with and conquests of the opposite sex). However, it is impossible to understand this phenomenon apart from an understanding of the "car culture" in American life, with its mass salesmanship and broad impact on social life.

The general "car culture," combined with physical characteristics and facilities of southwestern cities, has made possession of a car the ideal in all kinds of neighborhoods, rich and poor. Having or not having a car, as well as the kind of car it is, affects one's status and prestige with those of both sexes. The desire for a car is certainly a "psychological need" as experienced by the individual. But this need and the resulting development of a subculture with stylized patterns of driving around, of joy rides or outright theft, would be bizarre phenomena if a researcher should attempt to study them apart from the widespread importance of a car in American life, and the differential availability of cars in different settings. The "need" for a car, as well as "needs" for thrills, or for defiance, or for "acting out," are meaningless apart from the character of the sociocultural settings in which they have been nourished and shown in action.

ESSENTIAL FACETS IN RESEARCH DESIGNS ON ADOLESCENT BEHAVIOR

If, as in our research, we wish to study adolescents as individuals, we must incorporate into the design at least the major sets of influences that affect their attitudes and behavior. This is equally true whether our problem concerns adolescent accomplishments in socially desirable directions, or their undesirable modes of activity, such as drug usage or car theft. Within the general problem of adolescence as defined in a society, we have seen that the sociocultural setting and its values are major influences, particularly those values prevailing among the reference set of teenagers. Finally, the design would be incomplete without including study of the individual's reference group of age-mates, and his relationship to them and to other groups in his ken (family, school, church groups, etc.).

As outlined early in the last chapter, the design of research included three main facets to accommodate these major influences. The next sections describe the operational steps in the three facets, with emphasis on the intensive study of behavior in natural groups of youth. Finally, findings in the three facets are summarized to indicate their interdependence.

SOCIOCULTURAL SETTINGS OF BEHAVIOR

To be sure, there must be a division of labor in the sciences of man. Study of sociocultural settings is a sociological or anthropological task. If the task has not been done as specifically as necessary for research on particular adolescents, then the investigator must "act like a sociologist" for the time. He can get help from social scientists, borrow their tools, or secure a collaborator, but he cannot ignore the task as being irrelevant to his own interests. Nor can he evade the task by assigning a blanket label to the setting, such as "lower class," "middle class," or "ethnic subculture." This evasion would be analogous, for example, to an experimenter in color vision saying: "I am studying color vision in an illuminated laboratory. But I do not know how much or what kind of illumination it is, because I am not a physicist or electrician. Information of that kind isn't my job."

Like the physical surroundings, the social habitat has regularities in structure, time sequence, and recurrence of events. For example, the range and standards of living in a neighborhood where adolescents live and meet indicate a patterned set of circumstances. These circumstances are pertinent to what youth do, how they spend their time, where they spend it, and even what they consider suitable activities during leisure hours. Boys in favored neighborhoods of high socioeconomic rank own cars, have comfortable homes, and ample spending money. They will think of leisure related to their cars, their visits and parties in each others' homes, and outlays of money for dates and professional entertainment. They are extremely mobile. In fact, the entire city is "their oyster," which makes their study unusually difficult. The contrast in mobility and attitudes is striking in an urban neighborhood where cars are not available, homes poor and crowded, and money lacking.

In our research, residential areas where the youth live are studied through first-hand exploration, mapping of facilities, available municipal statistics, and (in neighborhoods with Spanish-speaking residents) block surveys to check the extent of acculturation among residents. Looking for ways of indicating features of the setting, we found that Shevky and Bell had developed a social area analysis based on census tract statistics. A limited number of census measures, combined appropriately, serve to indicate relative ranks of areas in significant respects. These indicators seem to account for the major sources of variance in a host of discrete statistics on urban areas. Each is associated, therefore, with correlated information not included in the analysis.

Bell's chapter in [*Problems of Youth*] obviates the need of presenting the three indicators in social area analysis in detail. They are, however, (1) socioeconomic rank (2) degree of urbanization and family conditions, and (3) ethnic status of the population and their concentration in an area. In addition to being reproducible and communicable, these indicators have the advantage of showing gradations in a coordinate system based on standardized scores. For example, it is possible to specify that one area of low socioeconomic rank is not as "low" as another. Or, a low rank area is not as urbanized as one of middle rank in the same city; that is, there are fewer apartments in the low rank area, more children, and fewer mothers who work. Clearly, the ecological conditions are quite different in the two neighborhoods, apart from socioeconomic level. Life in this low rank area, with its shabby two- and three-room houses, is likewise different from that in a comparably poor tenement neighborhood of a large eastern city.

Specifying ethnic status of the residents is equally important, though not always sufficient for our purposes. In some areas, with a sizable proportion of Mexican-born citizens, we have conducted block surveys to assess the relative acculturation, on the basis of length of residence and style of living. Indications of relative acculturation to U.S. life were, for instance, the type of pictures on the walls and the cultivation of yards, ranging from the flower-pot culture of the Mexican to the green lawn of the "Anglo." The advantage of such specification of the setting can be illustrated, and may be similarly illuminating in other sociocultural comparisons, for example, between neighborhoods of Negroes raised in urban settings and those peopled by recent migrants from rural areas.

In this instance, we found that a group of adolescent boys in a "Latin" neighborhood had very little interest in organized sports, unlike most of their counterparts in other areas. When we found that their neighborhood was among the least acculturated to American life, they appeared as fairly representative of their immediate setting, although otherwise these boys' lack of interest in sports would have seemed extremely atypical. This information also clarified the frequent observation that whenever one of these boys spoke English to his fellows, he was chastised to remember he was "Mexican." (Their Spanish, however, would not have been altogether understandable in Mexico.)

Later in the chapter, the dangers of blanket conclusions about youth in a given socioeconomic level or subculture will be mentioned. We warn against generalizing about youth in any given stratum without sufficient evidence and against viewing any stratum as an isolated phenomenon. We stress both the importance of a comparative approach to youth from different backgrounds and the relationships among different strata in a society. After all, socioeconomic strata are characterized as "low," "middle," or "high" in rank according to social criteria as well as economic needs for physical well-being. The ill fate or good fortune of a particular stratum is, therefore, conditional in part upon the larger social system.

ADOLESCENT VALUES AND GOALS WITHIN THE INDIVIDUAL'S SETTING

For a particular adolescent, the values and goals of other youth in his ken are salient aspects of his environment. Whether his personal radius for achievement and his potentialities are in line with theirs or not, he knows full well that his actions are gauged relative to their standards, which are revealed to him time and again in episodes of action, appraisal, approval, disapproval, notice and notoriety, or, worst of all, ignominity and personal oblivion.

For such reasons, one facet of the research program assessed conceptions of propriety, of achievement, and of success in the various sociocultural settings. A paper-and-pencil form presented as an opinion survey was administered to representative samples of secondary school students in the study areas. To date, three versions of this form have been used with many identical items in each. Throughout, the aim has been to devise items on significant aspects of adolescent life in forms which will yield a *range* of conceptions, from the acceptable minimum to the personal ideal. The content areas include conceptions of leisure time and activities, work and future occupations, school and academic goals, financial and material necessities and goals, parental regulation and controls, proper modes of behavior, desirable associates, and personal success and aspiration. The data are analyzed both in terms of the bounds of acceptability and achievement prevailing in a neighborhood and of the distribution of individual responses within these bounds.

In other words, the data in this facet are sociocultural data on the adolescents themselves. In view of the school context in which the forms are administered, the data are most accurately interpreted as indicating what youth regard as "socially desirable," in Allen Edwards' use of that term (1957). However, in a school setting, young people do not always respond readily in terms of personal experiences or specific social relationships. The records contain overheard statements such as, "Boy! Did I feed them a line." In non-school situations in which the same forms have been administered, observers who have established more rapport with boys than most other adults have encountered resentment to some items, particularly those pertaining to areas where adults are usually excluded. Recent administration of the forms in detention and reformatory settings also indicates evidence of attempts at dissimulation, but the data here differ from those obtained in school settings from youth with comparable socioeconomic backgrounds.

The different pattern of responses in different sociocultural settings, and some evidence of dissimulation, support our interpretation that these data express youths' conceptions of what it is socially desirable for them to report. But even these conceptions of "lines" to give adults vary in several important ways, and are interesting data in themselves, revealing socioeconomic and cultural differences.

Since one's self-radius for achievement is, in part, a function of what one conceives as socially desirable, the differences between the bounds prevailing in different sociocultural settings have important psychological implications. Even if not followed, the prevailing bounds in a social setting are significant as stimulating (external) conditions for the individual youth. Their salience can be illustrated briefly.

In a lower middle class area suburban to a large city, one small group of boys studied in our research for nine months had all dropped out of school. Although some of them had been prevented from re-entry by school authorities, the majority had been subjected to persuasive and coercive efforts by their parents to continue in school. One parent had even given a bribe—a new car—as the reward for school attendance, to no avail. By their actions and in conversations, these boys deprecated school attendance. They were, however, fully aware that among their agemates outside their group, high school graduation was the minimum standard for achievement. Their awareness was revealed in repeated instances of withdrawal from the "school crowd" as "snobs," in their unanimous agreement about the impossibility of returning to the local high school, and by statements by all but one member that they intended to finish school in a neighboring town or "in the army" eventually, thereby reaching a par socially and occupationally with their contemporaries.

The data on prevailing self-radius and goals of youth in different urban areas are used in four ways:

First, to detect values and goals upheld by common consent of youth in different areas.

Second, to detect differences between the areas in these respects.

Third, to assess the homogeneity or heterogeneity of standards prevaling among adolescents *within* an area.

Fourth, to form a basis of comparison for assessing the typicality or deviance of the attitudes and goals expressed by members of small groups studied in an area.

INTENSIVE STUDY OF SMALL GROUPS WITHIN EACH SETTING

Within each neighborhood of low, middle or high socioeconomic rank, the attitudes and behaviors of boys in informal groups of their own choosing are studied intensively over periods of time ranging from six months to a year. This focal facet of the research is carried out in the field —in the natural habitat of boys themselves.

In this aspect, we had to face seriously the problems of research method arising from the context effects discussed at some length in [the preceding chapter]. The very nature of research by people into the current behavior of other persons raises issues which are by no means so obvious in the other sciences. One of these is how to establish research contact with the phenomena under study without fundamentally changing them.

Admittedly, astronomers had the problem of research contact with the heavenly bodies. The technological means for observation (telescopes, electronics, satellites) have not yet substantially affected the movements of heavenly bodies nor their nature.

In the study of human behavior, however, there is growing evidence that technological devices and instruments may be inimical to approaching the phenomena of interest. Their usefulness begins *after* the investigator has solved the problem of getting close enough to human beings to study them without letting them know they are under observation.

Therefore, the intensive study of behavior in natural groups proceeded from the premise that the timing and selection of research procedures should be such that they would have little effect on the group and its members. This is the reason for all of the efforts to keep group members from being aware that they were being observed for research purposes.

In the varied and changing field of social actualities, a single observer will inevitably choose facts selectively. It was our second premise that selectivity could best be minimized if the observer focused on one aspect of the interaction process at a time, and a variety of independent data-gathering techniques were introduced at choice points. In appropriate sequence, the observer's reports and ratings of behavior were checked against ratings from an independent observer, from sociometric interviews with group members, from interviews with adults who knew them, and from public records pertinent to their past activities. The use of a combination of techniques in a variety of situations over time is the best way to insure validity of findings, which cannot be guaranteed by sophistication in test design, or in planting recording devices, or in later analysis.

To date, the study of 24 groups of boys (ages 13-18 years) has been completed through the cycle of steps envisaged. The difficulties, and in some cases failures, in completing the study cycle would make a fascinating chapter in themselves on the rigors of social research. These difficulties range all the way from practical problems of carrying out procedures in a particular setting, to some observers' lack of persistence and interfering preconceptions on the nature of research. Many of the latter preconceptions, formed in other training, must be revised in an attempt, such as ours, to fit research procedures to the actualities of the field, rather than vice versa. The real challenge of social research is to secure precise and manageable data that faithfully reflect the actual properties of events.

THE OBSERVER BEING OBSERVED

When an observer begins to hang around in the vicinity of a group, there is always a period when the members observe and scrutinize *him*. The observer being observed by his subjects is one instance of a general phenomenon of person perception: first impressions are invariably accompanied by efforts to *place* the person and his presence in our area in some social categories.

For this reason, the prime criterion for placing an observer is his "fit" with the predominant socioeconomic and cultural background of the residents. In appearance, speech, and manner, he must blend into the scene. Even then, the recurring presence of a strange face in familiar surroundings calls forth questions about why he is there and what he intends to do.

In our research, the observer is instructed to develop first a reasonable pretext for his presence that circumstances cannot contradict even before he makes contact with a cluster of boys. Preferably, the pretext is one which will bring the boys to the observer because of their own interest in his activities or possessions (for example, his athletic equipment, or his car).

The age difference between observer and observed is another factor to be reckoned at this stage. Our observers are ordinarily in their early twenties, slightly older than the group members they observe. This has proven necessary for two reasons: First, the observer must be trained and mature enough to follow procedures in step-by-step fashion. Second, an adolescent observing adolescents is in the constant danger of becoming *part* of their group, competing for status, and seeing the interaction process from his particular role in the structure.

Fortunately, we discovered that adolescent boys in most communities do have contacts with slightly older males and are, in fact, somewhat attracted by the possibility of contact with a person representing what they may become. The age factor, therefore, has not been insurmountable when the observer succeeded in establishing his presence as a sympathetic, possibly helpful young adult—somewhat like an older brother.

Still, for weeks or several months, the observer is observed. He is asked pointblank who he is, his connections, why he is around, and what he is doing. Over the course of time, the boys check up on his replies before they start opening up to him. The observer is still denied the luxury of direct questions to the boys. The procedures he employs are planned in step-by-step fashion to gain data while strengthening rapport.

The initial and most difficult period in the intensive field study of natural groups is making contact with the members and overcoming their wall of resistance and secrecy about their more private activities. It challenges the patience and skill of the observer. Depending on these as well as on the group, the study has sometimes not progressed beyond the period of the observer being observed. We suspect that in most such cases, the rigid walls of resistance and secrecy indicate tightly knit groups with stable organizations and binding commitments in activities of an illegal or antisocial nature.

DEVELOPING AND GAUGING RAPPORT

Once contact with group members has been made, the real cycle of procedures in the study of natural groups begins. However, the particular methods used, and their sequence and timing, are planned to coordinate with the development of rapport between observer and group members.

In the early period, no techniques are introduced that require probing questions or other assaults on the privacy of group activities. The observer simply reports on what he sees and rates member behavior after leaving the group. No other techniques are used until the observer is tolerated by members in activities and in discussion of matters considered exclusive and private.

Gauging the degree of rapport is too critical to be merely a matter of intuition. We utilize a combination of indicators in deciding on the timing of the procedures in the study cycle. Indicators of degree of rapport include these signs: the observer's success in finding the various places the group congregates when not in plain public view; the members' tolerance of his presence in these more private places; the degree of intimacy of activities the members discuss freely in his presence; the extent to which members welcome him into activities which they would hide from other adults.

Valid data on group properties and member attitudes can be obtained only if rapport is developed. For this reason, ratings by independent observers, sociometric choices, interviews and other procedures that assume cooperation with the researcher (without dissimulation or fabrication) are kept for near the end of the study cycle. Collection of case history materials is the final step in the cycle. Data obtained from all of these procedures can then be cross-checked against the mass of documentation of member attitude and action which has been collected during interaction episodes.

Developing rapport and adjusting procedures to the changing degree of rapport are continuing processes. Recently one of the observers (Mr. Lauderdale) attempted to conduct individual interviews with items from the Self-Radius and Goals schedules; this followed seven months of observation, during which he had been permitted to learn some of the more intimate secrets of the group including drinking, sexual activities, and incidents involving the police. The individuals responded freely enough about money, jobs, leisure activities, and the like. But he reported responses ranging "from apparent indifference and withdrawal to outright hostility" when he queried them about school experiences and about their special friends. "Remarks ranged from simply 'I don't know' to explanations that 'I don't like to answer questions because someone might try to get something on me,' or 'You're sure full of questions, aren't you? I don't like snoopy questions from my friends or anyone else.' "

Another observer (Eduardo Villarreal), who returned to a group he had studied about three years earlier in order to check on present membership, reported that new members were withdrawn and suspicious even though the older members introduced him as an old "camerado." The newer boys relaxed only after questioning him themselves to find out exactly what he was up to.

THE STUDY CYCLE

The complete study cycle is accomplished through ten successive sets of instructions to observers, followed as rapport warrants going on to the next step. The instructions are revised regularly on the basis of new research experiences, but they are substantially the same as those presented as the appendix of our book (Sherif and Sherif, 1964). Here, the steps will be summarized briefly along with definitions of the principal measures to be used by observers.

First, a group is singled out for observation on the basis of observed frequency of association among a specifiable cluster of boys between 13-18 years in specific locations (recreation center, pool hall, drive-in, vacant lot, etc.).

Second, after establishing rapport to the point that he is tolerated by the boys in locations and activities other than those of their initial encounter, an observer directs his attention to the status or power relations among the individuals. The prime criterion for status or power in the group is defined by the concept of effective initiative, or the extent to which suggestions made by the various individuals are actually followed at that time or later. Allied observations pertinent to ratings of status or power include concrete examples of deference, effective dominance, or submission.

Although the pattern of power relations, as defined above, is not the only dimension differentiating the attitudes and behaviors of members in a group, it is the most useful dimension for predictive purposes. If one knows which boy has most frequently suggested alternatives that the others actually translate into common decisions and actions, he has found the operational *leader* of the group. If he can rank other individuals in the same respect, he has a powerful predictive device for what may transpire among them. The observers in our research have been able to do this, and the fact that the resulting pictures of group structure are invariably hierarchical reflects something about the nature of social power. Unlike some other attributes, individual power is necessarily limited by the nature of interaction. If members adopt the suggestion of one member, those made by others are bound to be neglected for the time.

Of course, other dimensions contribute to the differentiation of individual roles in a group: popularity, special skills in activities valued by members, and special resources, such as money, a car, or a home for entertaining. However, any one of these dimensions, so frequently taken by responsible adults as *the* criterion for adolescent standing, is imperfectly correlated with status (power) in their actual interactions. (Cf. Sherif and Sherif, 1964, Chapter 7.)

Third, the observer focuses on the prevailing customs, procedures and norms of the group. He looks for collective products of their interaction—procedures typically followed in frequent activities, common jokes and sayings, signs of dress or decoration, names for "us" and "not us," and expressions or deeds denoting what is considered acceptable, unacceptable, desirable, or unsuitable enough to demand reprimand or punishment. These normative properties are assessed in three ways:

1. Observation of distinctive similarities in expressed attitude and behavior among members that differ from those in other circles or groups.

2. Members' reactions to the usually acceptable range of behavior, including rewards and approval for praiseworthy actions and various forms of punishment or disapproval, indicating deviation.

3. A new member's conformity over time with established procedures, modes of attitude and action.

Next, the observer's ratings and reports are checked through independent techniques, including ratings of a significant group activity by an independent observer, sociometric ratings obtained from the members individually in informal interviews, and situational tests devised especially to create forced choices between association with the group and other activities.

Finally, through interviews with the boys, parents, teachers and other adults, as well as any available records in school or community, a "natural history" of the group and the backgrounds of particular members are reconstructed. The observer also maps the spread of the dwellings of the members, which indicates the effort they make to associate, especially when they do not have transportation available. It is noteworthy, perhaps, that only one of the groups studied thus far has been clustered within the same block. Even "neighborhood" groups are scattered over considerable areas, which shows something about the mobility of urban life for adolescents, but also reveals a selective process in the formation and membership criteria in these groups.

MEMBER BEHAVIOR PREDICTABLE IN TERMS OF GROUP PROPERTIES

Through these procedures, we have specified the essential properties of adolescent groups and their changes over time. These group properties, and the individual's place in the group, provide a powerful basis for predicting adolescent behavior, whether desirable or not. The extent to which behavior is regulated by group membership is related to a person's standing in the group. The degree to which group norms are binding for an individual is related to the stability of his relationships with other members (as demonstrated experimentally in the last chapter).

Being part of recurrent interactions among contemporaries means, for the individual, that he will to an extent regulate his behavior relative to others. Hence, the stabilized patterns of interaction in a group and the individual's location in the pattern affect his treatment of others, their treatments of him, and how closely he adheres to group norms.

LINKING FIELD OBSERVATIONS WITH PRINCIPLES
DERIVED IN THE LABORATORY

In our earlier studies of group formation and intergroup relations in summer camps (Sherif and Sherif, 1953; Sherif *et al.*, 1961), we observed certain regularities in the formation of group structure. Invariably, the first signs of structure were the stabilization of the top and bottom levels of status or power. An observer watching the groups in a variety of activities could consistently rate the persons highest and lowest in effective initiative long before he could differentiate intermediate positions. The boys themselves also agreed more consistently in choosing who was most and least effective in initiating their activities and getting things done.

It is striking, therefore, that the end-anchoring perceived by group members (indicated by their sociometric choices) is similar to the judgments of status by an observer. On the basis of the ratings made by observers of 24 groups, we have constructed a theoretical diagram showing the end-anchoring of an observer's judgments over several blocks of observation periods. Actual data necessarily deviate in detail from the theoretical curves, depending on the number of individuals in a group, changes in membership, or shifts in activities which affect the group structure. Nevertheless, the phenomenon in question was found for each of the groups studied.

Figure 1 represents the average variations in observer's ratings of effective initiative of group members over a substantial block (10) of observation periods, each an hour or longer. Each point on the graph represents the average changes, from one observation period to the next in a given block of observations, in his ratings for members in different segments of different status (base line). In other words, the base line represents the average rating for members during a block of observations;

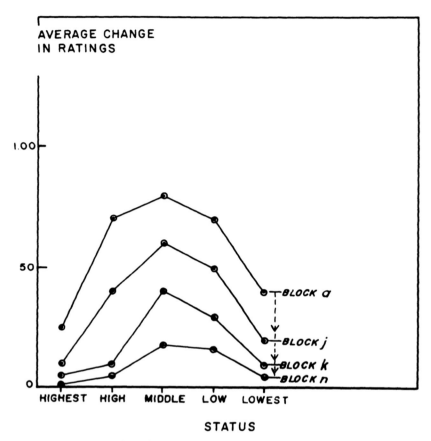

FIGURE 1. End-anchoring in observers' judgments of status in natural
groups over time

the ordinate indicates average shifts from one period to the next. For
example, if the observer changed his ratings on an average of one status
rank for each of ten periods, a point would be located on the ordinate at
.9. Or, if he changed his rating by five ranks twice throughout the block,
the average change would be 1.00. Such large shifts usually reflect a
process of change in the status structure.

Each curve in the figure represents a different block of observations,
lasting around a month, from Block a, during the early weeks of observation, to Block n, when the observer has been with a group several months.
End-anchoring is revealed in the observer's greater consistency in rating
persons in the highest (leader) and lowest (bottom) positions than in the
intermediate ranks. The slightly lower variations for high status ranks

just below the leader and for low ranks just above the bottom represent empirical findings. The intermediate ranks are typically most subject to change.

In our data, the introduction of a new member increases the variation in ratings for other persons near the status level where he first enters the group. If he is a friend of a low status member, variability increases in the low status ranks. If, on the other hand, he immediately shows some highly prized skill or possession, his presence increases variability in ratings of high status ranks. Changes in group structure for other reasons (for example, significant changes in activities, or departure of a member) are similarly reflected in sharp increases in variability of the observer's ratings.

Figure 2 represents the observers' average ratings of *confidence* in how they ranked status from time a (bottom) to time n (top), when they had become closely familiar with a group. Since the confidence ratings

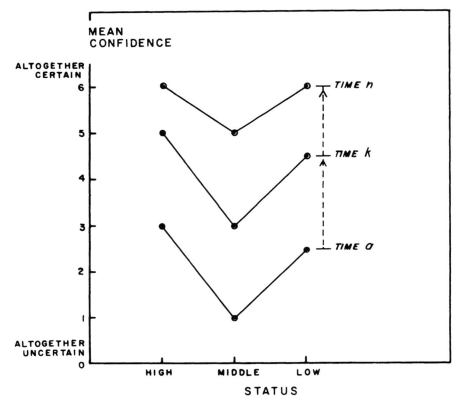

FIGURE 2. End-anchoring revealed in confidence of observers in judgments of status in natural groups

were introduced more recently, this theoretical figure is based on the ratings of fewer groups. Each time he ranks members according to effective initiative, supporting each rating with concrete observations of behavior, the observer indicates how confident he is of each rating, from "altogether uncertain" (0) through "wavering between certainty and uncertainty" (3) to "altogether certain" (6). Figure 2 shows that early in observation (time a) observers are generally uncertain of their ratings, and that their confidence increases over time (to time n). The end-anchoring effect also shows here, in the consistently higher confidence for the high and lowest positions.

Is the end-anchoring effect in group structure solely a perception of the observer, or does it reflect also a reality of group life? Independent raters have agreed closely with the observer when given sufficient opportunity to observe the group, and group members themselves agree more closely in sociometric choices at the highest and lowest levels. End-anchoring seems to be a general phenomenon in perceiving interaction patterns in a group. Furthermore, the ratings by observers can be reconstructed by a content analysis of the concrete events in which members show varying degrees of effective initiative.

We have been asked if the more dominant anchoring position of the leader indicates that groups possibly form through clustering around one individual. On the basis of our research evidence, we feel that this explanation is not sufficient. In only two or three groups have we been able to ascertain that the boys came together initially around a given individual whose initiative was accepted from the beginning. These were all fairly unstable groups. But in the majority of cases, we have found that the leader position has evolved during day-to-day interaction, rather than being the cause for interaction. Our observations include cases of leadership changes, reflected in temporarily increased variability of the observer's ratings of the high status levels, and then followed by renewed end-anchoring on the new leader.

In short, the predictability of individual behavior regarding effective initiative in interactions with others is related to status in the group, in a curvilinear fashion. The curvilinear end-anchoring effect is strikingly similar to that reported in the psychological laboratory for judgments of any series with well-defined end stimuli (for example, series of weights, lines, or sound intensities).

This finding has both practical significance for the prediction of adolescent behavior in natural groups, and theoretical significance in the study of human behavior. We see here the operation of a well-established principle of psychophysical judgment, namely that variations in judgment are smallest for well-defined extremes in a series and greatest for intermediate values. Our conceptualization underscores the operation of this general principle in field observation. The differences between judgments of series of objects and judgments of individuals interacting as members of a social unit indicate that the operation of the general principle should be analyzed discerningly.

In both the psychophysical laboratory and the field ratings of status, the extreme items (objects or persons) serve as anchors, as revealed by reduced variability in judgments. However, lower variability in judging the top position than the bottom is a peculiarity of the human organization, not found in judgments of physical series. One might conclude from this that the general principle is not, after all, general. But another conclusion is that any general principle of human behavior must take account of the context and the particular properties of the stimulus situation. This is our conclusion.

The top rank position in a human group is a more important anchor than the lowest position because of the properties of human organization. These properties are not present in a series of weights, lines, or sound intensities. So the general principle is valid in both psychophysical and psychosocial judgments if the special characteristics of the stimulus situation are taken into account: in this case, the fairly equal importance of end items for ordering a series of physical stimuli, and the inequality of the leader and lowest positions in a human group for ordering those intermediate in position. This demonstrates one way of bridging the appalling gaps still prevailing between field studies and the more precise laboratory approach to the study of human behavior.

LATITUDES OF ACCEPTANCE AND REJECTION
DEFINING INDIVIDUAL CONFORMITY

The individual's position in his group structure provides still another basis for prediction—the extent to which his behavior will fall within a range of variation defined as acceptable by other group members. This latitude of acceptance varies with the significance or importance of the activity for the group. Its limits are defined operationally by behavior indicating common disapproval, threats, or actual punishments.

In every group we have observed, the latitude for acceptable variation in individual behavior has been smallest for matters affecting the maintenance of the group and its solidarity in the face of outside threat (from other groups of age-mates, parents, school authorities, police, etc.). This narrowing of the limits on behavior in the face of outside threat has long been noted in "gangs," especially those involved in illegal activities. It is equally true for groups in activities which are not defined as socially deviant.

For example, one group observed in our research made a great point of "good sportsmanship" in encounters with other groups of age-mates. Nothing called forth disapproval, scolding, or threat of isolation so quickly as unnecessary roughness in a game with other boys or being a "poor loser," despite the fact that the same behavior was accepted when these boys played among themselves. In several groups, the common desire to do things together conflicted with parental requests to do homework. The member who dared tell his parents that they were not actually studying together, but playing records, was treated as a child at least and in some cases as a traitor. Similarly, in a high rank area, the reputation of members as "smooth" but proper young men was zealously guarded for the benefit of the attractive "nice" girls and their mothers. Members who found a younger or less cautious girl willing to engage in sexual contacts were severely chastised if they made it a public matter, outside of their private circle.

In the groups we observed who engaged in definitely illegal activities, the boy who welched out through fear or who "squealed" was treated either to a "good beating" or to ostracism. In these cases, the maintenance of the group as a unit, unsullied by adult or police surveillance, made the norm of privacy in group activities essential. "Getting caught" at an illegal act (carrying a weapon or stealing, in these cases) was a reason for group censure, since it endangered other members. Two group leaders who were caught were both chastised severely by others for being foolhardy and taking risky actions.

Figure 3 shows the relationship found between the range of individual variations permitted and the relative importance of the activity for the group. The latitude of acceptance (ordinate) is narrowest in matters of greatest importance for maintaining the group and its standing as a unit. The latitude is broadest for those matters of least importance, particularly those involving activities strictly within group confines.

The relationship depicted in Figure 3 is further complicated, however, by the relative status of members in the group. Figure 4 shows two curves of the relationship between the latitude of acceptance (ordinate) and the relative status of group members (base line). In matters of minor importance to the group (top curve), the latitude of acceptance is greater for high status members, especially the leader, and smaller for low status members. In other words, especially within the group, the leader and his high status cohorts typically have considerable leeway in regulating behavior relative to others; it is the low man on the totem pole who is continually being nagged, laughed at, or barred from play.

On the other hand, in important matters (lower curve) the leader is expected to be exemplary; even slight deviations on his part arouse questioning, criticism, or scolding from other members. For example, in several groups where money is scarce, it was observed that the leader consistently pitched in with all of his funds or with more than the others, and that this was expected of him. If he indicated that he planned to spend it in other ways, he ran the risk of being called stingy. Similarly, the high status

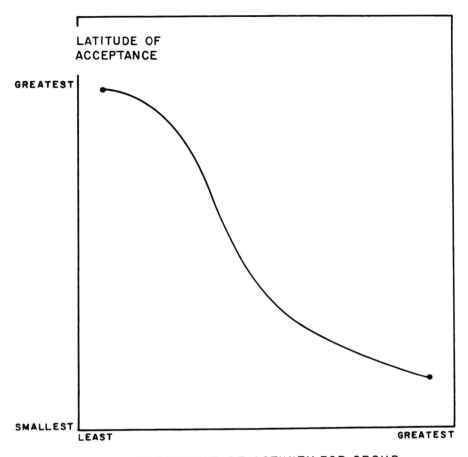

FIGURE 3. Range of individual variations acceptable in natural groups as a
function of importance of activity

member with a car was expected to have it available for group activities,
and conflicting plans on his part brought forth cries of "he thinks he's too
good for us." In the same activities, however, a low status member could
beg off without anyone expecting any more of him. He was saving money
for shoes, or his sister needed the car. "What do you expect of *him,*
anyway?"

To sum up: In observations of natural groups of adolescents, we
have found a relationship between the person's status and the expectations
others have for his behavior in various respects, as well as his expressed

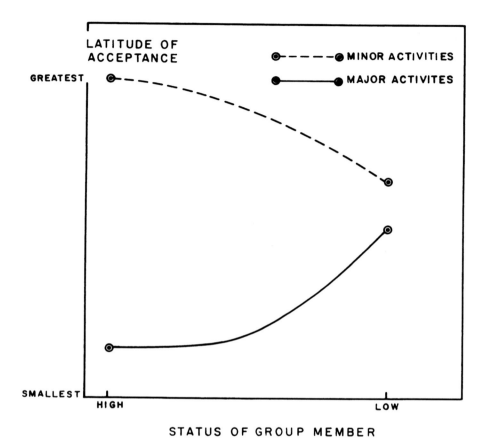

FIGURE 4. Conformity in natural groups as a function of member status and importance of activity

attitude and actions. These relationships hold promise as a base for predicting adolescent behavior. Relative effectiveness of an individual in initiating activities for other members is most predictable at the top of the status structure (most effective) and at the bottom (least effective). Adherence to group norms (expressed as the range of variation in individual behavior which does not call forth sanctions from others) is most strict for all members in matters of importance to the group. However, the acceptable latitude varies with the person's status. The more significant the activity for the identity and continued maintenance of the group as a unit, the narrower the latitude of acceptance for all members, the latitude for the leader being smallest. The more incidental the activity, the broader the range of individual variations without arousal of sanctions, the latitude for the leader being greatest.

INTERDEPENDENCE OF SOCIOCULTURAL SETTING AND
GROUP PROCESS IN ADOLESCENT ATTITUDE AND BEHAVIOR

The larger social scene, the neighborhood with its prevailing values and facilities, and the informal social relationships with age-mates do not act independently in influencing adolescent attitude and behavior. The rest of the chapter summarizes generalizations from our findings, with illustrations, that show the interdependence of these influences. No one of these, considered by itself, is more important than another *in every case.* Our main generalization is that it is impossible to determine the more significant source unless all are included in the analysis.

Many of our generalizations have concerned differences between different settings. Therefore, we begin on a contrasting note: there are unmistakable similarities between youth in widely different settings in the United States.

SIMILARITIES IN ATTITUDE AND BEHAVIOR IN DIFFERENT AREAS

Contrary to some popular theories about youth of different classes, we found that certain values and ambitions unmistakably marked the adolescent in the United States. Though differing in appearance, following different fashions in dress, sometimes speaking different languages, youth in all areas cherished an image of individual success as an adult, as it is spelled out through the magic symbols purveyed by television, advertising, movies, magazines, and popular books. This was true of members of groups studied intensively. The ingredients of the image were desired by nearly a hundred per cent of every sample of high school students studied: cars, comfortable homes, attractive clothing, appliances, telephones, radios, TV sets, money for entertainment, including movies. Regardless of what they have or what is available, youth in settings of low, middle and high rank want the "good things of life," as defined in mass salesmanship so characteristic of this country today.

Another finding common to youth in all areas was their orientation toward age-mates as the reference set. This was strikingly apparent in observations in every setting. The school samples, for example, asked why "school is fun"—three-fourths of the replies pertain specifically to the opportunities that school gave to interact with age-mates.

It should also come as no surprise to find, as we have, a common and intense interest in the opposite sex at this period. Observations of the small groups of boys are peppered with references to girls. In the surveys of school students, the interest is more hidden because of the tendency to give "socially desirable" answers (a problem mentioned earlier). However, it was readily revealed in the great majority of youth by their answers to the question, "What do you and your friends talk about?" (After starting to write, then erasing, the word "sex," one boy substituted "girls."

He was overheard to say "I don't want those people to think I'm a sex fiend.")

Another similarity was the ability to distinguish what adult authorities consider "right" and "wrong." Given a list of forty-five actions, youngsters in very different settings rated their acceptability-unacceptability in much the same way. These were teen-agers attending school, not dropouts. Therefore, it was gratifying to read a recent report of similar findings by Short and his co-workers (1963), who compared nondelinquent and officially delinquent youth on a written questionnaire. Of course, some youth in both samples may have violated the precepts in question, but it seems that violation because of ignorance of what society deems acceptable, or of what deviation is considered serious, is more rare than some theories of lower class youth or of psychopathology would lead us to believe.

In the small groups studied intensively in different neighborhoods, the finding most common to all was the boys' insistent desire to do things on "our own," without adult programming or supervision. Since these expressions and this active search for "freedom" are manifested in every area, the ecology and rank of each neighborhood become very important in determining whether the "freedom" is found in a friend's house, in one's car, behind a pool room, or in the streets.

DIFFERENCES BETWEEN YOUTH IN DIFFERENT SETTINGS

Youth living in areas differentiated by socioeconomic level and cultural composition are well aware of these differences. As reported earlier (Sherif and Sherif, 1964), we have found that those living in low rank areas freely express their desire to move to a high rank area, while those in high rank areas express contentment with their present circumstances and derogate the schools and type of persons found in lower class settings.

Differences between neighborhoods are apparent to the naked eye, of course. What is not so apparent is the effect that the differences in facilities have on a youth's actual mobility, his access to adult programs designed to improve his social mobility, and his ease in entering any situation peopled by those whose appearance and manner identify them as residents of an area differing substantially in rank.

Like other investigators, we found that youth in different neighborhoods set levels for personal goals according to the socioeconomic level of the neighborhood. However, we also found that the differences in goals are accompanied by differing conceptions of achievement. Figure 5, for example, presents recent data from one city, collected in areas which are upper middle, lower middle, and low according to the Shevky-Bell index of socioeconomic rank. The low rank area is largely Spanish-speaking; the lower middle is mixed (Spanish-speaking with some Negroes); the upper middle area is mixed ("Anglos" with some Spanish-speaking persons).

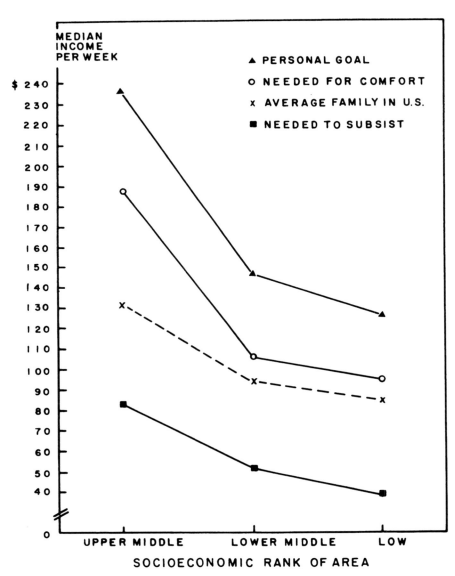

FIGURE 5. Conceptions of subsistence, "average income," comfort, and personal goals for future income as a function of socioeconomic rank of neighborhood

The triangles in the figure represent the median values of personal goals for estimated income (per week) when one is adult and married. The personal goals vary, on the average, with the socioeconomic level of the area.

The figure also shows the median estimates obtained from the youth of the amount needed per week for subsistence (bottom bars), for comfort (circles), and the estimated income of the "average American family" (X). As the figure shows, youth in all three areas are "ambitious" according to their own conceptions of achievement, that is, according to their conceptions of enough to be "really well off" (circles). However, the upper middle rank conception of comfort is higher than the goals set, on the average, in the other areas.

These, and similar data on success in school and occupation, seem to belie the notion that middle or upper class youth are necessarily more ambitious or achievement-oriented than those in lower ranks. Those from areas of lower rank are ambitious relative to their own ideas of achievement, and even more ambitious relative to their own parents' achievements (cf. Sherif and Sherif, 1964).

The data on samples of youth in school do not represent completely the values and goals of all youth in an area, because varying proportions have withdrawn or are barred from public school. A further finding on school youth in the various areas will help us in analyzing the social situation of those who withdraw from school.

HOMOGENEITY—DIVERSITY OF VALUES IN SETTINGS OF
DIFFERENT SOCIOECONOMIC RANK

In analyzing data obtained from youth in schools in the areas where our small groups were found, we were not entirely prepared to find that the least diversity of individual values and goals was found consistently in schools serving areas of higher socioeconomic rank. This discovery of so many like-minded students is a comment on the residential arrangements in large cities and on the cultural situation of youth in high rank areas. In these high rank areas, students had the least individual variation in personal goals, or conception of success in education and use of leisure time.

In both middle and low rank areas, greater heterogeneity was found in the values and goals of the student body, with actual cleavages into distinct social strata being characteristic of the middle rank schools (so classified on the basis of modal parental occupation and education). Even in schools serving areas of low rank, only in matters which are strictly financial (income, spending money, and the like) did the like-mindedness equal that of students in high rank areas.

Figure 6 represents the personal goals for education in three schools, in terms of years of schooling desired. The ordinate represents

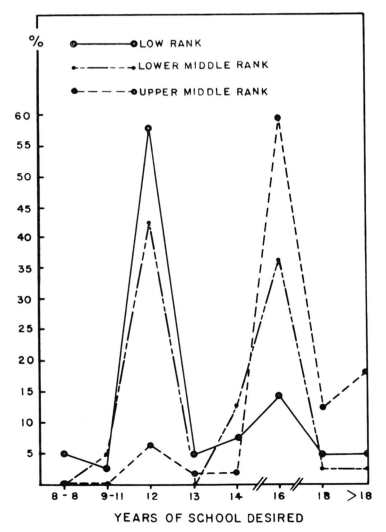

FIGURE 6. Personal goals for education in neighborhoods of
different socioeconomic rank

percentage of the samples, and the curves give the distribution of goals
in a school of low rank, lower middle rank, and upper middle rank in a
city where free transfer is permitted. (These are the same three schools
whose financial goals are represented in Figure 5.)

This figure represents one example of the greater diversity in values
found in the lower rank areas. Ninety per cent of those in the high rank

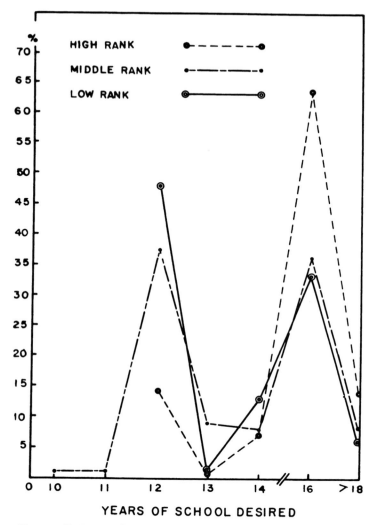

FIGURE 7. Personal goals for education in low, middle and
high socioeconomic rank in city with higher median
educational level

school (dash line) desire to complete college (16 years) or more advanced degrees (18 or more years). Greater diversity is evident in the
low rank area (solid line), although the mode is for high school diploma.
The distribution of responses in the lower middle rank area is strikingly
bimodal (broken line).

Figure 7 presents comparable data from a different city in which transfers are seldom granted, and the median educational level is substantially higher. The middle rank school (broken line) serves a large and diverse section of the city; but the low rank school is located in the oldest portion of the city, where most residential areas are of low socioeconomic rank, with a substantial Indian-Mexican-Negro minority. The distributions for both low and middle rank areas are clearly bimodal, while that for the upper rank area (dash line) again represents greatest homogeneity.

These findings have led us to suspect that some theorists on lower class life may have overlooked the actual diversity within lower class settings, perhaps because of their preoccupation with specific social problems. We suggest that generalizations about the characteristics and values of a class or ethnic grouping must specify carefully what values are involved, and how widely they are shared, before referring to distinct "subcultures" in different settings.

Specification of the homogeneity or diversity of the sociocultural setting proves helpful in understanding the nature of adolescent groups in that setting.

DIVERSITY OF THE SETTING AND CHARACTERISTICS
OF GROUPS WITHIN IT

Let us start with a picture of what went on in the groups studied intensively in our research. What people do and talk about when they get together regularly of their own accord can tell us a great deal about them. The boys in our groups engaged in a great range and variety of activities. As noted previously, these invariably included girls, cars, and sports, in all but the least acculturated neighborhoods. During a considerable portion of the observation time, nothing seemed to happen: youth spend a lot of time hanging around, driving around if they can, while rehashing the past, planning an evening or a future scheme. The apparent aimlessness of much of the activity conceals active evaluations of things past and planning of things important to them. The discussions and plans revealed the boys' overwhelming desire to know themselves and each other as (near) adults, and to do things they wanted, on their own, without programming or intervention by adults.

Frequently, doing things on their own as adults involved activities deemed improper for the age level, even immoral or illegal. This was true in middle and high rank neighborhoods as well as low rank, even though most of the groups and their members were not labeled as "delinquent" by police.

All of the boys were concerned about their "manliness" (though this meant somewhat different things in different settings), with clothing fads, and with other cultural trends available in the larger setting. Each boy translated these trends meaningfully for himself in relation to the others in his group. For example, the discussion and consumption of alcohol were so frequent that it seemed that drinking must be considered a sign of adult-ness for a young male—at least, the ability to talk about drinking.

We have not yet found a group which specialized in one sort of forbidden activity. On the contrary, groups emphasizing drinking not only tolerated non-drinkers but had many other activities. There were groups which engaged in theft (usually in twos or threes), and others which tolerated such activities by only two or three members. Observations of drug usage were remarkably similar to those involving alcohol. Although not all members participated, it was invariably a social affair.

The observations in these respects are difficult to reconcile with the sociological classification of groups into *types* on the basis of their activities. Particularly obscure, in terms of our observational material, is the classification of drug usage or alcohol as "retreatist." If one may infer any centralized purpose, our data imply that these activities are, on the contrary, ordinarily social—a means to enhance attraction and prestige (even though they may be carried to the point where the individual becomes "withdrawn" into unconsciousness or hallucinatory behavior, as in paint solvent or glue sniffing).

Activities labeled delinquent if detected by adult authorities were not distinctive to groups in any setting, nor the exclusive specialization of any one group. Nevertheless, frequent "delinquent" activities had decided consequences for the character of the group. Roughly proportional to the frequency of forbidden activities (not necessarily illegal ones), the groups became highly *secretive*. The frequency of activities involving such violations of adult dictums was, in turn, a function of the amount of time spent together; the wall of secrecy shielding members was the most impenetrable for groups which associated most frequently.

The total amount of time spent together, the secrecy of the group, and the absorption of individuals in their group activities to the exclusion of others were related to the homogeneity or diversity of the settings. By far the most homogeneous of the settings studied in our research were the least acculturated, low rank areas populated by persons of Mexican origin, and another low rank area populated by poor whites at considerable distance from the city center and from schools.

The one group of Negro boys studied in the Southwest were in a much more diverse setting, by virtue of proximity and contact with school youth and recreational agencies, which reflected the hope from the nationwide movement for equal opportunities. For example, Negro youth in school set their goals for education on a par with those of school students in the highest rank areas of their city, although not half of their parents had finished high school. Of course, these findings depend on circumstances in the cities in question, and cannot be generalized to other regions.

Whether labeled delinquent or not, the groups in the most homogeneous settings of low rank were also the most solid and stable. The boys' perception of great differences between themselves and anyone outside "my neighborhood," inadequate and crowded homes, difficulties in achieving in school, real deprivations of physical needs—all of these circumstances combine to make the adolescent group the central place for each boy as an individual, where he can find pleasure and entertainment and, in some cases, necessities not provided elsewhere. These boys were the least mobile. Leaving the area involved considerable planning and effort, and often subjected them to the suspicious eyes of police.

Given these circumstances, the ecology of the immediate neighborhood and its facilities become weighty matters. Interference in using the facilities is eliminated only when the group defines a territory which is its own, which it is known to claim, and, hence, which represents the group's investment in prestige. When the boys went outside the territory, or when others came in, there were occasions of gang fighting, complete with weapons. Such incidents were recalled later with excitement and pride by members. They looked for accounts of them in the papers.

To assess this love of violence and bravado, it is essential to bear in mind that it was not directed to fellow group members, even though adolescent boys are not habitually gentle with one another. Nor was violence directed to members of those other groups with whom relations were friendly. The violence occurred in conflict with individuals defined by the boys as enemies, a capsule formula used to justify the actions of one's group in conflict, whether the opponent be another informal group, a club, the police, or a nation.

We cannot share the cynical view that violence is a prime value for adolescent boys, and that their efforts to avoid it are superficial. The difficulties of avoiding violence between conflicting groups are well known in adult life today. There is little reason to expect small groups of adolescents to succeed better, even when they genuinely desire not to get into trouble.

In fact, there were repeated observations that groups involved in conflict had made efforts to avoid it. Avoiding trouble was frequently discussed; precautions against it were quite as observable as the violent actions, though less dramatic. They "cased" a place for the presence and location of antagonists before entering. They avoided going into places where trouble might start. Joel Garza, one of the observers, recorded a half-hour episode during the intermission of a drive-in-movie, to which he had driven a group by no means noted for shrinking from conflict. A rival group was spotted between their car and the rest room; with considerable self-control, the members laid a strategy to use the facilities without encountering the rivals.

Much attention has been devoted to the pleasure, or even "thrills," which adolescent youth say they derive from violent encounters with an enemy, from a forbidden joy-ride, or theft with one's fellows. We suspect from our observational data that these "thrills" have something to do with the effect of interaction among individuals who feel they "belong" together, who are open with one another, and who derive satisfaction from concerted efforts not available to them in the formal arrangements of living. Such exhilaration and "thrills" have also been reported by members of groups engaging in concerted activities toward desirable ends. In such a group situation, it is thrilling to win a ballgame, to elect a member to the student council, or to hold a party.

GREATER VARIETY OF GROUP CHARACTERISTICS IN DIVERSE SETTINGS

Most of the groups studied intensively in our research came from more diverse settings, which were characterized not only by greater variations in values but more opportunities for mobility and choice. In such settings, we find groups composed of individuals with differing backgrounds and aspirations; groups whose activities place them in opposition to the predominant values in their setting; and groups of boys directed outside of their immediate settings by the pull of opportunities seen elsewhere.

Using the prevailing values of the immediate neighborhood as a yardstick, we find that one group of boys in a lower rank neighborhood is quite atypical in several respects. Because of success in grade school athletics, these boys were imbued with the goal of "making" the high school team. Unlike the local "toughs" on their streets, they not only continued into high school, but chose a school far across the city because it had the best teams. Dubbed "Escuelantes" (school boys) by others in their neighborhood, they have not performed well academically and have not made the school team. Most of their leisure time is spent together, warming up, practicing, talking about sports and glorifying the heroes of their school teams. It would be gratifying to report that the aspirations of this group reflected their parents' efforts, but their personal histories offer no such reflection. Three of the boys are illegitimate sons of servicemen, and none of the families provides the "solid, middle class" concept of achievement.

After being with this group for several months, the observer concluded that their chances of making the school teams were slim, for they were smaller than most varsity athletes. He reported that the intensity of their concentration on the school team and their own skills was so great that, at times, it seemed (in his eyes) to be almost fantasy. But the group process has kept the boys in school, and he predicts they will complete it.

By contrast, another group, composed of lower middle class boys in a predominantly middle rank area, had all dropped out or been expelled from school. In terms of their future hopes for jobs and income, the members proved to be quite typical of school students in their community, with their goals in these respects clustering around the median.

But their own initial encounters and continuing activities have focused on the pursuit of pleasure in cars, pool halls, and with girls. This kind of group activity required considerable outlays of spending money (over ten dollars a week), more money than 99 per cent of the students in their former school feel is needed. Together, these boys have their "fun" and secure spending money to support it by sporadic odd jobs. Meanwhile, the joint pursuit of such fun has resulted in several members being sent to "training schools" by the authorities. None of these boys is "mentally handicapped" in terms of standardized tests, and the parents of some have exerted strong but unsuccessful pressures on their sons to return to school and keep away from "the boys."

Still another group, which met regularly at a public center in a low rank area, was primarily recreational. In many respects, the members were diverse in their attitudes and aspirations. For example, two boys dropped out of school in 10th and 11th grade, two intended to graduate, one planned to go to further training, and one wanted to finish college. Although this was not a very solid group, its pull on members is so strong that the parents of the boy with college ambitions moved out of the neighborhood, where they had lived many years, in an attempt to break the association.

These examples are sufficient to indicate the variety of adolescent groups to be found in areas providing some diversity and, especially, some mobility to members. The immediate neighborhood, the family, the school, the images of success in society are not clearly "to blame" for the directions taken by any of these groups, yet they are all involved. To some extent the directions taken hinge upon the selective process of interaction among adolescents who, for the time, find some significant psychological identity within the group circle. The directional power of such groups must be included in the picture in order to understand why the Escuelantes are so directed outside their neighborhood, why the dropouts have resisted persuasive and corrective efforts to bring them into line, and why a recreational group seems threatening to the parents of a boy who wants to go to college.

Ordinarily, most of these groups last only a few years, until members leave the area, get jobs, go to school or military services, or marry. Their transitory nature makes their little "organizations" and their little "cultures" no less real, nor does it lessen their impact on individual members as long as they last.

THREE GENERATIONS OF A YOUTHFUL NATURAL GROUP

The reality of the little "cultures" of adolescent groups may be seen more clearly if one could see what happened when at least some of the members "stayed put," did not leave the neighborhood, or did not enter into formal social relationships fundamentally different from those of adolescence. Such an opportunity arose in the research project in a neighborhood of low socioeconomic rank with a population of Mexican origin. The transmission of a group identity and its culture (norms) through three generations of adolescents was traced.

Early in the research project, a group of adolescent boys called "Los Apaches,"[1] was observed for several months by Eduardo Villarreal. Subsequently, he has carried through the observation cycle on an "older generation" of former members, ranging in age from 23 to 36 years, still living in the same area. Then he returned to find the current membership of Los Apaches, which had changed in the interim. Thus, it is possible to compare the norms and status relationships in three generations of members during a period when the neighborhood itself was essentially the same, but life in the city underwent considerable alteration (roughly, since the postwar period).

When first observed, Los Apaches consisted of twelve boys, with other occasional hangers-on. (See Sherif and Sherif, 1964.) Most of its members were known to police and detention home officials for stealing, carrying weapons, and engaging in fights with a rival group—the Lakesiders. Currently, nearly three years later, those who were members at that time have apparently escaped serious convictions. Some of them have jobs, are thinking of getting married, and are not active as Los Apaches members.

The observer could find very little change in the customs or norms of Los Apaches during this time. A "lieutenant" took over the leadership position when the old leader got a job and a steady girl whom he is thinking of marrying. Several new members have been added, some at high status levels. The rivalry with the Lakesiders continues, and seems to be even more important in group discussions. Occasionally, the members steal (always in twos or threes); a member of the older generation remarked, "These boys have more money than we used to get." Beer, solvent-sniffing, and marijuana are included at group get-togethers; there is always as much beer as money and ingenuity permit.

The young adults (now the older generation) meet regularly at favorite beer joints, a member's house, or night spots. They all quit school in the elementary grades, and all have unskilled jobs, with the exception of an auto mechanic and a shoe repairman. With very few exceptions, the observer reports, they seek sexual relations frequently while they are out together, even though most of them are married.

The members of the older generation belonged to Los Apaches at different times, when each was in his teens. Although the name *Los Apaches* was adopted when one of the younger adults was a member, all the men refer to the age-mate group by this name. They all still refer to to the Lakeside as the rival group, even though few of them now en-

---

[1] Like other identifications in published reports of this research, this name is fictitious.

counter adults who were Lakesiders when they were Los Apaches. Those who did belong to the group at the same time reveal closer attachments than those who did not, as revealed by patterns and frequency of visits, lending money, or borrowing a car. A former leader (El Apache) is among the highest in status in this older generation group.

By observations over a considerable period of time, and at an arranged picnic for older and younger generations, it was ascertained that the older generation of young adults has very little contact with the recent or present membership of Los Apaches, except in the parental home of one member of each of the three generations. One other possible exception is that the present generation has, on occasion, sought help or a car from the older generation during conflict with the Lakesiders, which the older generation refused. The former leader (second generation, now almost twenty) and other older adolescents make moves to be accepted by the older generation. But the present membership (13 to 18 years old) preserves a respectful distance from their elders, in line with cultural expectations.

Older generation adults say that the present generation is not as tough as they were and does not get into as much trouble, chiefly because they have more money from parents and can borrow cars. But, they say, Los Apaches and Lakeside will "always" be rivals, and the younger members agree. All ages hold an implacable dislike for "perros" (police), but the older generation says the police are also less tough now than they used to be.

These are some changes in the group as seen through the eyes of former members. The observer reports other differences traceable to the changing times: The younger generation places a much higher value on education, although none has gone further than the ninth grade. The younger generation uses slang identical to that of the older generation (Spanish), but speaks English more frequently. Unlike the adults, who strongly prefer Mexican popular music, the younger generation both prefers and sings the current popular songs in English.

In short, as a miniature culture, Los Apaches has endured with minor changes, but has reflected the impact of broader culture change. The impact of the group may still be seen on the young adults who no longer see themselves as members, but in fact continue to interact in a group with a broader age range.

IMPORTANCE OF ADOLESCENT REFERENCE GROUPS
TO INDIVIDUAL MEMBERS

The groups studied in this research, formed by individuals of their own choice, are important to their individual members. Our evidence shows many instances of individual preference for group activities and values over those of family, church, school, girl friends, and even reasonable considerations of personal safety.

It is also undeniably true that the informal groups of age-mates were of greater import for boys whose past history and present circumstances offered few other sources for a stable definition of self in relation to other human beings. These were not just boys from broken homes, for some had stable homes and were devoted to their parents. They were not only the poverty-stricken youth, for some had more than the necessities of life. They were not just school failures, for some were progressing in school. They were not all members of subordinated cultural minorities. When the entire set of such unfavorable circumstances prevailed in extreme degrees for some boys, they produced the strongest attachment to an adolescent group. However, these circumstances did not guarantee that a boy would belong or would be attached to his group.

Attachment to a group meant that the individual also had to be accepted by the others, live up to them, and prove himself a reliable and worthy member. Many boys who had unfortunate social circumstances in home, school, and community did not belong to a group because they could not achieve this necessary acceptance. Some had been expelled from groups.

The boy who was accepted, could live up, could prove himself reliable over a time, was usually among the more able, the more sociable, the more responsible to his fellows. Such personal attributes were necessary to gain status in any of the groups, regardless of other prerequisites for particular groups (for example, smoothness, or toughness, or daring). Having a secure place, especially a high place, among one's fellow-members further enhanced the importance of the association for the individual.

Thus, we have an apparent contradiction: Those to whom the group became most important as individuals, those most devoted to its tenets and outlook (whether socially desirable or undesirable) are likely to be individuals who display, *within* their groups, certain qualities usually prized by society. These qualities include loyalty, responsibility, and consistency in dealing with one's fellows. These very qualities may contribute to the individual's performance of antisocial actions directed toward outsiders or the larger community.

This generalization in no way condones those activities and norms of a group which are socially undesirable. If these are malicious, undesirable, or destructive, they should be denounced. But generalization does imply that adolescent attitudes and behaviors which are traceable to interaction in their reference groups cannot be defined within the traditional lexicon of psychopathology, or by new labels for the same pigeonholes.

CONCLUSIONS

In reporting on the research program, it has been our aim to emphasize the multifaceted nature of influences shaping social attitude and behavior of individuals, for good or for evil. We have focused on participation in reference groups of age-mates because of a conviction that many aspects of the immediate and larger sociocultural setting are filtered to the individual adolescent through this highly salient medium.

The findings have shown that adolescent reference groups are patterned affairs, with power relations and "cultures" (norms) of their own. Attitude and behavior of particular individuals vary in terms of their places in these informal social schemes. The larger social scene, the immediate setting, and the age-mate group are interdependent influences in the life of particular adolescents. Especially when the immediate setting offers diverse alternatives, the interaction patterns and goals of the groups may become decisive in choosing among these alternatives.

For the single individual, participation in a reference group of age-mates may be beneficial for his future, or it may have disastrous consequences. In either case, an adequate theory of his attitude and behavior cannot rest with assigning labels of social approval or disapproval, mental "health" or "illness," to the individual. It is necessary to develop an adequate theory of individual behavior in close alignment with empirical findings on personal background, on associations with other humans who count in his eyes, and on the sociocultural setting. The social conditions in which he acts do not merely offer opportunities or hindrances to his strivings as a human individual; they also offer success pictures which affect *what* he will strive toward.

PART IV

CONCEPTS, ATTITUDES, AND EGO-INVOLVEMENT

FIFTEEN

SOME SOCIAL-PSYCHOLOGICAL ASPECTS
OF CONCEPTUAL FUNCTIONING

In this early stage of social psychology—for that matter of psychology in general—I believe our most fruitful efforts are in the formulating of clear, significant problems. Adequate conceptualizations and technical refinements will follow if pertinent problems are raised at the outset. During this discussion, I shall attempt to raise some problems which seem significant for a social-psychological accounting of conceptual functioning.

It is necessary to add, however, that the concepts I shall be concerned with are not merely those used by an elite group of research scientists. In a psychological sense, we cannot differentiate such concepts from those used in everyday life. I shall speak of concepts as those which the individual shares with his group, small or large, and which are standardized for that group and, hence, are used as communicable symbols. In this sense, it is unthinkable to speak of concepts which are not crystallized in words or symbols.

The major approach (but not the only approach) to the study of symbolic processes by psychologists has been the studies of "concept formation." Concept formation is defined by one experimenter in the area (Smoke, 1946) as "the process whereby an organism develops a symbolic response—usually, but not necessarily linguistic—which is made to the members of one class of stimulus patterns, or to an aspect of such a class, but not to other stimuli" (p. 97). Such reaction to members of a group or class of stimuli as equivalent or similar has been observed

Carolyn W. Sherif has collaborated with me both in the selection of material and in the writing of this paper. Work on this paper, including the collection of material and the preliminary study of naming was done in 1947–48 while I was a Rockefeller Foundation Research Fellow at Yale University. I am grateful to Professor Carl I. Hovland, Chairman of Psychology at Yale, and to the Rockefeller Foundation for making this study possible.

From *The Nature of Concepts, Their Inter-relation and Role in Social Structure*. Proceedings of the Stillwater (Oklahoma) Conference sponsored by the Foundation for Integrated Education, 1950.

313

in simple form on the sub-human level (Morgan, 1943). For example, members of sub-human species have responded to triangularity *per se*, regardless of size or position.

With human subjects, the procedure in most concept formation studies involves repeated exposure to a series of stimuli which may be grouped according to certain physical characteristics into one class but not into another. A nonsense syllable given by the experimenter is to be associated with the "correct" members of the class. Usually no rewards are given other than those that might accompany a good performance in the task.

There have been fruitful attempts along this traditional line of study. For example, Heidbreder (1945) has demonstrated in a series of experiments that concepts of concrete objects are attained with greater ease than concepts of more abstract relationships.

The classical concept formation studies on the whole have emphasized a logical inductive process at the expense of motivational and functional variables operating in most life situations. However, a more serious inadequacy of this line of approach is the neglect of one of the most characteristic features of concepts on the human level—namely, their *shared* character. In human society, concepts *are standardized;* they become common property of the group. Concepts are accumulated in human groupings and passed to coming generations. In the terminology of Charles Morris (1946), concepts of a language are *comsigns,* i.e., standards common to members of a group.

Although concept formation, in the sense of a reaction to a group or class of stimuli as though they were equivalent, may be quite properly studied on the sub-human level, the formation and standardization of *comsigns* or language signs are peculiar to the human level (Yerkes, 1943; Schneirla, 1948). The human organism is the only one in the animal kingdom capable of developing and mastering a systematic code of language signs. This capacity is basic to the qualitative variations distinguishing the behavior of man from other primates (Schneirla, 1948), and, in fact, one may say, to the appearance of human culture. Physiologically, this capacity appears to be associated with the increased extent and complexity of the cerebral cortex in man (Schneirla, 1948). When the factors leading to such qualitative differences between the symbolic reactions of sub-human and human organisms are ignored, we are eventually caught in a sort of reverse anthropomorphism—a "zoomorphism" in which the heterogenous linguistic activities of man are interpreted in terms of the symbolic responses of the rat or chimpanzee in the laboratory.

Valid comparisons can perhaps be made between the generalizations of the young child beginning to talk and those of sub-human animals. The child's acquisition of his "first words" is a slow process, marked by trial and error. However, the period of laborious trial and error learning of words is comparatively brief and is followed by an almost dramatic surge in vocabulary development so characteristic that some investigators have called this period the "naming stage." In her recent survey, McCarthy (1946) found the literature on vocabulary development in general agreement that "vocabulary appears to increase rather slowly at first, then, quite rapidly throughout the preschool period."

Estimates of children's vocabularies give striking evidence of this spurt in language acquisition. In M. E. Smith's study (1926) of children from the ages of eight months to six years, the vocabulary increased *five-fold* between the *eighteenth and twenty-first months*. (These data may be plotted as in Figure 1.)

In short, at some time around the second year of life, vocabulary development is sharply accelerated. This rapid increase in the acquisition of words seems to involve a generalization of greater scope than any hitherto achieved—a generalization cutting across the sensory mo-

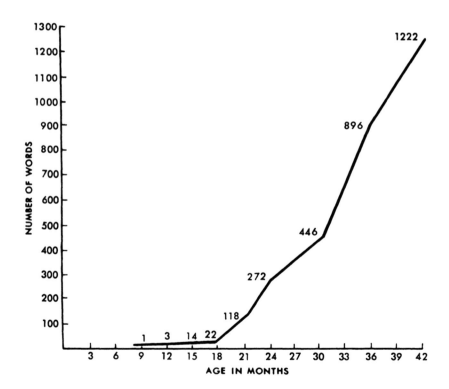

FIGURE 1. Vocabulary increase from 8 months to 42 months. (Adapted from M. E. Smith, [1926], Table 8, p. 54).

Note the sharp increase in size of vocabulary beginning at about 18 months of age.

dalities which adults can express in some such phrase as "everything has a name."

The functional significance of the child's early words will be mentioned in another context. Here it is sufficient to note that this generalization—that "things have names"—is closely related to the use and acceptance of the instrumental function of words. Speech activity becomes an effective means of satisfying the child's needs and bringing other persons into his activity for aid, comfort and play. In this period, a new and solely human striving appears—namely, a *striving to learn the names of things*. It may be indicated at first by the child's own primitive sounds and gestures, such as "eh-eh-eh." Later, we see the familiar picture of the two-year-old pointing again and again to objects and repeating insistently, "What's dis?" Linguistic responses acquired by this short-cut method come to supplement and, in time, to replace other forms of response. In fact, it is during this period that the symbolic activities of sub-human animals and those of human children come to a parting of the ways. At the beginning of the nine-months period in which the Kellogs raised their own son and an infant chimpanzee together, the chimpanzee surpassed the boy in many respects, including response to human words. But in spite of the fact that the boy was somewhat retarded linguistically in terms of established vocabulary norms, he was easily surpassing the ape around the age of two (Kellog and Kellog, 1933).

The symbolic behavior of sub-human animals is characteristically bound to more or less discrete and immediate perceptual situations. Pre-human gestures, vocalizations, and response to human words are not removed from the motivational and emotional situations in which they occur (Schneirla, 1948). While the symbolic behavior of the young human is similarly tied to concrete perceptual situations and routines, normal children advance to a level of *conceptually* symbolic functioning. It is within the bounds of known physiological facts and harmonious with behavioral observations to assume that the achievement of a conceptually symbolic level of functioning is closely related to the maturation of the human central nervous system. The validity of this relationship is indicated especially by the breakdown of conceptual functions with pathological degeneration of cortical tissue in disease (such as paresis), brain tumor, or injury (Schneirla, 1948).

When the human child attains that generalization embodied in the notion that "things have names," which is revealed by a marked acceleration in vocabulary development around the age of two, he has taken the first major step away from the perceptually symbolic level— in which behavior is bound to immediate objects and situations—toward a *conceptually* symbolic level of behavior. This conceptually symbolic level of behavior is distinctly a human attainment which is basic to the understanding of the psychological development of the human individual.

EFFECTS OF CONCEPTS ON HUMAN BEHAVIOR

Perhaps the most important and certainly one of the most distinctive effects of concepts in human behavior is their categorizing effect in relation to those objects, situations or relations to which they refer. When objects or persons, situations, etc., are subsumed under a common name, perception of and response to the various stimuli tends to be similar as determined by the meaning, i.e., by the *generalization,* crystallized in the name. The name functions as a category to which stimuli either belong or do not belong. Response to stimuli in the same category tends to be similar. For example, in one study (Miller and Dollard, 1941), young children were taught to call two very different stimulus objects by the same name. It was found that "other responses (such as reaching for the object) are more likely to generalize from one to the other than when the two objects have been given different names."

This categorizing effect of concepts has long been noted by various authors in several fields. In a more philosophical vein, we find this fact stressed by such writers as Ernst Cassirer (1946) and De Laguna (1927). Ethnologists have gathered extensive evidence substantiating this point and some, notably Edward Sapir (1949), have emphasized it in their writings. More recently, Kluckhohn and Kelly (1945) generalized as follows concerning such comparative findings:

A language is not merely an instrument of communication and for rousing the emotions. Every language is also a device for categorizing experience. The continuum of experience can be sliced very differently. We tend all too easily to assume that the distinctions which Indo-European languages (or our own particular language) force us to make are given by the world of nature. As a matter of fact, comparative linguistics shows very plainly that any speech demands unconscious conceptual selection on the part of the speaker. No human organism can respond to all the kaleidoscopic stimuli which impinge upon it from the external world. What we notice, what we talk about, what we feel as important is in some part a function of our linguistic patterns. Because these linguistic habits tend to remain as unquestioned background phenomena, each people tends to take its fundamental categories, its unstated basic premises for granted. It is assumed that others will think the same way, for "it's only human nature." When others face the same body of data, but come to different conclusions, it is seldom thought that they might be proceeding from different premises. Rather it is inferred that they are "stupid" or "illogical" or "obstinate" (pp. 100–101).

Research has yielded considerable evidence of the categorizing effect of concepts in various psychological functions. In perceiving and remembering, it has been found that the introduction of a concept affects subsequent response in terms of the name or symbol. For example, studies by Bartlett (1932), Gibson (1939), and by Carmichael, Hogan and Walter (1932) have shown that if a form or object is given a familiar name, either by subject or experimenter, its reproduction is altered in the direction of the name. After surveying the relevant literature, McGranahan (1936) concluded that:

The effect of language on perception appears to be to make features of the objective world that are represented by language forms stand out in greater articulation, to give greater individuality to the object or event represented, to cause similarities to be seen in things similarly represented, and in general to influence perception in the direction of the speech-forms (p. 202).

It is well established that all perceptions, judgments, etc., take place within a frame of reference. The more salient factors, either internal or external, serve as anchorages or reference points in terms of which reaction is made. By their nature, language concepts provide organized and crystallized anchorages which determine response in a major way. Because of its categorizing effect, it is probably language more than any other *single* factor which lends to the perceptions of human adults their highly organized character.

In learning situations of human adults and children who have gained some instrumental mastery of language, symbolic factors usually enter at the outset because of their involvement in the perceptual process. In a good many experiments on human learning, linguistic factors are, therefore, uncontrolled. The investigator often presumes that only those factors which he introduces into the situation are operating. When experimentally introduced into the situation, linguistic factors alter the usual course of the learning process observed on the sub-human level. Trial and error behavior is considerably reduced or even eliminated. For example, when human subjects are instructed of the sequence of stimuli in a conditioning experiment (e.g., a *green light* followed by *shock*), the number of trials exerts no consistent effect on the strength of the conditioned response. Learning may occur in one trial. *Similarly,* the learned response may be extinguished in one trial by new verbal cues (Cook and Harris, 1937).

Resistance to conditioning may increase with the entrance of symbolic factors. Genetically, the speed of conditioning has been found to decrease around the ages of three to five years when the child achieves instrumental mastery of his verbal processes (Razran, 1935).

Other experiments have demonstrated that conceptual factors substantially increase the speed and efficiency of discrimination (Hilgard *et al.*, 1937), maze learning (Warden, 1924), learning of motor skills (Goodenough and Brian, 1929), and problem solving (Long and Welch, 1941, 1942; Welch and Long, 1943).

In an ingenious experiment, Pyles (1932) found that the learning of three-dimensional objects by children ages two to seven years was directly influenced by whether or not the objects were *named.* The greatest difficulty was encountered in learning unnamed objects. Next in order of difficulty came objects assigned nonsense names by the experimenter. The greatest ease in learning was found for objects named as familiar animals.

In summary, after a child has achieved the generalization that "everything has a name," the learning process can be short-circuited. The trial-and-error encounters with stimuli characteristic of learning by sub-human animals and human infants give way to a predominantly deductive process in which responses to whole groups of objects and persons are learned by the acquisition of a name or concept. It is this *telescoping* of the learning process which makes possible the inculcation of so many social concepts in the form of short-cut dictums. The child's concepts of objects, persons, and relationships in the social world are frequently attained more by the dictums of adults than by contact with the actual stimulus situations. For example, young children, even though they have had no contact with Hindus or Turks, acquire concepts of Hindus and Turks with appropriate accompanying attitudes. The mere fact that a particular person or object is placed in one category rather than another has unmistakable psychological consequences. But, in the case of most social stimuli, the consequences are more far-reaching, because their conceptual categorization establishes the social world as the child comes to see it.

It is this acquisition of concepts which makes possible the formation of attitudes toward the many objects, persons, and situations in the child's world. Through the formation of such attitudes, the child is eventually enabled to relate himself *psychologically* to his environment. In early infancy the child does not clearly distinguish between his own body and its desires and the external world. This distinction cannot be made accurately *until crystallized in the concepts of "me," "mine," and "I."* A host of distinctions must be made—for example, the ability to locate events accurately in the past, present, or future—an achievement which occurs very gradually. Further conceptualization of persons and objects with the accompanying formation of appropriate attitudes leads to the formation of a personal identity having definite psychological relationships with other persons and groups. These attitudes are, then, *ego attitudes,* largely formed in relation to standardized concepts or norms (Sherif and Cantril, 1947). They determine the personal identity of the individual as he experiences it, and they constitute his ego or self. Until such conceptual distinctions are made, the child cannot begin to set up future standards or goals for his own behavior. According to Gesell and Ilg (1943), the setting of goals for the future does not begin until around the age of seventy-two months, that is, after a considerable degree of development of conceptual functioning.

This ego development—the acquisition of concepts pertaining to objects, persons and relationships in the social world and the formation of attitudes psychologically relating the individual to these stimuli—

constitutes the main core of human socialization. The work of ethnologists convincingly shows that the individual becomes altruistic, individualistic, competitive, favorably inclined toward *this* group of people, antagonistic toward *that* group, as determined by the norms or concepts existing in the society of which he is a member.

This idea is best expressed in the imposing work of Gardner Murphy on *Personality,* which is the most comprehensive synthesis of what little we know on personality to date (1947). The self is not an innate entity which is present at birth. Its development is a naturalistic process as the child comes into contact with his environment. The main lines of the development of self are presented by Gardner Murphy in three stages. At its earliest stage, the development of self may be characterized as primarily *perceptual*—this is when one's own body is clearly delineated from surrounding objects; when attitudes and identifications develop in relation only to persons who are immediately present within his perceptual range, and who are instrumental in satisfying his needs. Then, as his ability to comprehend qualities develops, the self begins to acquire qualities or traits. Later, as his conceptual functioning develops, his self becomes more and more a *classificatory* system. This classificatory system implies drawing family lines, lines of social membership, church membership, ethnic group membership, etc., with all the appropriate attitudes that go with each one of them.

From the consideration of the vastly significant effects of concepts in human psychological development, it does not follow, as some might conclude, that every reaction, social response, or psychological process is determined solely or even chiefly by verbal factors. Every reaction is jointly shaped by internal or internalized factors and by external stimulating conditions operating at the time in their functional relationship. As we shall see in more detail in a moment, it is obvious that the conceptual classifications in a society and the generalizations made by children are not based primarily on logical processes or objective common properties of stimuli. In the great proportion of instances, motivational and affective factors enter to determine the stimuli subsumed under a concept and, hence, to determine its *meaning*. On the other hand, it is factually erroneous to consider the process one of mere *subjective* categorization. This is the frequent implication of uncritical attempts to demonstrate the relativity of concepts in different societies. Objective stimuli almost always enter into the drawing of conceptual distinctions. Further, when the discrepancy between behavior and objective reality becomes too great, there are forces *from* society (in the case of the child) or *within* society tending to bring the two into closer correspondence.

In this connection, we must note that concepts themselves are at the outset *by-products* of interaction of individuals in human groups, in their efforts to satisfy their needs and to deal with their environment.

It seems that the vocabulary of a group or society, hence its classifications of things, reflects the practical activities of the group in dealing with life processes (Malinowski, 1930). It can be expected that in *relatively* isolated small human societies, the range of vocabulary will be proportional to the range of objects, persons, situations, etc., which have functional significance in their on-going vital activities. Of course, in relation to complex societies, this point would have to be altered substantially, especially because of the acquisition of words from other societies, and other complicating factors in the complex culture.

It has frequently been observed that the concepts in primitive societies differ widely from those made in the languages of more developed societies. As Hocart rightly pointed out (1912), such differences are *not* indicative of the inferior generalizing power of the primitive mind or some other peculiarity of primitive mentality. Rather such differential classifications stem from differences in the vital activities carried on by the groups in specific environments; they are standardized to deal with such differences. It is not possible in this paper to do more than suggest examples of such differential classifications. (I am grateful especially to Dr. Clelland Ford of Yale University for suggesting much of the body of literature we have studied in this connection.)

As an example, the Masai of East Africa are a nomadic group whose chief occupation is cattle raising. The Masai have as many as seventeen terms for cattle—separate words for a cow with one calf or two calves, a sterile cow, etc. (Merker, 1904). The chief crop of the Ifugao of the Phillipines is rice, and it is called by twenty different names during various stages of planting, growth, harvesting, etc. (Barton, 1930). In the Solomon Islands, one of the staples is nuts. Two nuts so alike in appearance as to seem identical except in size are given different names. These names indicate important distinctions, for the nuts—so vital in the economy—have different seasons, are gathered differently, are cracked and preserved differently. In fact, in terms of the activities related to them, the two nuts are similar only after they are roasted or made into pudding. And then, they are called by the same name (Hocart, 1912).

While gardening and animal-raising groups may have many names for those plants or animals vital in their economic life, they may have only very vague concepts of objects not important to them. Malinowski (1930) noted that a plant or bird with no value to the group for the larder or clothing was dismissed with some phrase such as "Oh, that is just 'bush,'" or "merely a flying animal." On the other hand, in those groups in which hunting or gathering are the chief means of livelihood, especially against great odds as among the Arunta of Australia or the Siriono of Bolivia, names have been standardized for almost all the neighboring flora and fauna (Spencer and Gillen, 1927; Holmberg, 1946).

In our study of five Turkish villages with differential degrees of isolation from modern industrial life, we found a general relationship between the mode of life and the concepts relating to such fundamental functions as timing and estimating distances. Concepts of time and distance in the most isolated villages were vague and inaccurate. The greater the functional contact with modern industrial life, the more precise and accurate the concepts of time and distance became (Sherif, 1948).

Of course, it is not necessary to go outside of one's own society to find examples of concepts arising in the course of group activities. Concepts of obvious functional value to the users form in gangs of youngsters and adolescents in large cities, as reported by Thrasher (1927). In prisons, at least a portion of the argot originates in the prison situation and reveals concepts related to the more prominent aspects of the depriving prison life (Clemmer, 1940). In the British Armed Services, 230 neologisms—entirely new words—were reported to be standardized during the early years of the recent war (Hunt and Pringle, 1943). The sources, forms, and phonemic properties of such new words are, of course, complicated problems which lie beyond the ken of the psychologist. They are rather subjects for the students of language.

Now I shall take a brief glance at the functional significance of children's vocabulary development. In the activities of the human individual, as well as in group interaction, symbolic responses are *by-products,* first. As Lewis has clearly pointed out (1936), language activity is at first merely an accompaniment to other forms of response in the child's efforts to satisfy his needs, secure aid, comfort, etc. Only gradually does speech *replace* other responses. The child's earliest sounds are primarily an expression of his needs and affective state and are directed only secondarily toward objects or persons (Lewis, 1936; McCarthy, 1946). As the child discovers that his sounds have consequences on the course of his activities and begins to use them instrumentally, objective reference becomes more prominent. Still, the words of young children may be used in such an extensive fashion that they are practically unintelligible to an adult. Children's words take on approximate dictionary meanings very gradually, and only then with considerable correction and pressure from adults and with the child's emerging desire to conform to adult usages. This fact is well illustrated by the definitions acceptable at various age levels on the Stanford-Binet test of intelligence. At the lowest age levels, acceptable definitions are simply in terms of the object's *use.* Thus, an orange may be defined as "we eat it for breakfast." The series of studies conducted by Piaget (1928) on children's language development revealed and traced these developments in fascinating detail. This intimate link between motivation and concepts does not suddenly break with the attainment of conventional usages. Psychologically, concepts are all connotative in some degree. The denotative and connotative character of concepts cannot be separated from a psychological point of view. This is entirely harmonious with what is known of other psychological functions. For example, perceptions are not merely cognitive affairs. They are always jointly determined by internal affective and motivational factors and by external factors. Of course, the relative contribution of affective and cognitive factors varies in different instances.

In some cases, children standardize names or labels peculiarly their own for objects which have functional value in their activities. For example, Watt (1944) reports that a sixteen-month-old child standardized the label "yo-yo" for objects which he could carry by handles. Another group of portable objects—those without handles—was called "go-go."

Such unique standardizations by young children have also been observed in the case of children in groups. Jespersen (1923) reports that twin boys five and a half years old, who were frequently left to shift for themselves, developed a whole set of words. When left alone, they "conversed pretty freely and in completely unintelligible gibberish." As a matter of fact, unique standardization of words by twins is common enough to be noted in standard texts on "speech defects" (Berry and Eisenson, 1945; Van Riper, 1947). I am grateful to Professor John W. Keys of the Department of Speech at the University of Oklahoma for calling this fact to my attention and also for reporting his own observations of the peculiar words of twins. In one family, the twins developed several special words. One word, "tedaden," was used in the children's communications to mean "climb upon." Another word, "ding-a-ding," was used to mean "trade" or "you give me what you have and I'll give you what I have."

Of course, such childhood standardizations ordinarily pass into oblivion, partly through adult pressure and in part because the motivations and events so crystallized by the children are more or less specific to situations in which they have participated and are not shared to any degree by others.

With such facts as these in mind, we could expect that names or labels are likely to be produced when an individual or a group of individuals attempts to deal with unnamed objects, situations, or relationships having motivational value to them. Such a tendency was found in a study we made of young children. Specifically, pre-school children were placed individually and in small groups in a situation in which the only means of securing a much-desired toy was by a verbal response. Since the children were all from the lower economic levels (most of them came from a school in a poorer section of New Haven), it was possible to present toys which were highly prized and which were also unnamed by the children. Adult pressure favoring one kind of verbal response in preference to another was at a minimum. Yet, after the children faced this situation individually several times, all but two children out of twenty-two standardized a label for at least one of the toys. In the group situation, labels were standardized by all of the groups and were shared by every individual member. No doubt the standardization of names in the group situations was achieved so readily because they were advantageous in coordinating the play activities of the group.

So far, I have touched briefly upon several topics related to the social psychology of conceptual functioning—namely, the greatly accelerated development of vocabulary around the age of two in the *human* infant, the structuring and categorizing effects of concepts or language symbols on perceptions, learning, motives, ego development, etc. Also, I pointed briefly to the functional significance of concepts or symbols in relation to the vital motives of the individual and the group. These topics raise fundamental problems in any serious psychological theorizing, particularly in the field of social psychology. We could, therefore, continue this paper from now on along one of several equally significant alternatives.

In view of the particular interest of this conference in integrated education, I propose to devote the rest of this paper to an alternative which has serious practical, and hence educational, consequences in human relations as well.

This educational issue which is rather widely discussed by ethnologists, sociologists, psychologists, as well as by semanticists in recent years, is related to the well-known fact of the structuring and categorizing effect of concepts or symbols. It is mainly through the vehicle of language (concepts or symbols) of his group that the individual acquires the culture and techniques of his particular civilization, whatever this particular civilization may be; that his perceptions, learning, and attitudes are structured and categorized, subject, of course, to variations due to individual differences. Alongside of these achievements made possible by language, we must also note that it is through the vehicle of language, through concepts and symbols, that he acquires the established traditional prejudices, stereotypes, superstitions, erroneous generalizations concerning nature around him and people within and without the range of his perception. Through the existing concepts of the group, which he acquires through the years of childhood and adolescence in the process of socialization, his mind is already made up for him about things, about the nature of human relations, about goodness or badness of people, about the superiority of inferiority of *this* or *that* group. Through the established concepts in daily usage in his group, his attitudes about things and people are already made for him, in many cases, even before his actual contacts with the referents of these concepts. Even after he has a chance to come into contact with the situations and people in question, his perceptions, his evaluations in the face of actual contacts are colored by his already existing attitudes mainly derived through the concepts of his group. For these vital concepts of everyday life concerning relations between man and woman, between professions, between groups and classes of people, are not mere cognitive affairs, scientifically attained on solidly established facts and their functional relations. These concepts embody demarcation lines and heavily loaded positive and negative attributes or characteristics. It is for this reason that attempts to bring about positive changes in attitudes by bringing together individuals belonging to antagonistic groups have been, on the whole, singularly unrewarding. In view of the indications of the accumulating evidence in the psychology of perception and attitudes today, it would be surprising if the attempts to bring about significant shifts in attitudes on the basis of actual contacts *alone* were effective. For we do not see with our eyes alone, and hear with our ears alone, but we see and hear, at the same time, with our attitudes, of which the major ones are *verbally* acquired. And, I suspect, the scientists, even research scientists, do not constitute an exception to this rule, especially when they are outside of their own lines of specialization.

I have time to illustrate the idea presented in the preceding paragraph only with one example. It deals with the concepts related to the psychological nature of the two sexes, male and female, prevalent in the Middletown intensively studied by Professor Robert Lynd of Columbia University. In Lynd's words,

[But] this culture says not only that men and women do different things; they are different kinds of people. Men are stronger, bolder, less pure, less refined, more logical, more reasonable, more given to seeing things in the large, but at home needing coddling and reassurance, "like little boys." Women are more delicate, stronger in sympathy, understanding and insight, less mechanically adept, more immersed in petty detail and in personalities, and given to "getting emotional over things" (Lynd and Lynd, 1937, p. 176f).

Naturally, these conceptions of the psychological nature of man and woman come in as important factors in determining the reciprocal attitudes and roles of the growing boy and girl.

Some of the most serious instances of the stereotyping effects of the standardized concepts are in the field of intergroup relations. Consider such concepts as Gentile, Jew, American, Turk, White, Negro, Christian, Mohammedan, and for that matter, labor, capital, strike, production, etc. Any individual classified under any of these terms, or even the very mention of these words, immediately arouses positive or negative qualities in the eyes of the person facing him, as determined by the particular characterization of these terms in his respective group.

In view of the stereotyping and even blinding effects of such concepts prevalent in everyday life situations for millions of people, the educational or practical *problem* is self-evident. This huge educational problem cannot be even adequately approached until we attain scientifically valid concepts and generalizations in major areas of human relations and unify them into an integrated account of human relations.

After achieving this integrated account of human relations in terms of the special conditions of one nation alone, the *first* educational task, it seems to me, is to make them prevail, not only in the citadels of advanced learning, in colleges and universities, but through all stages of education, in the nursery, at home, in play, in the club and professional organizations, etc.

In the light of even meager evidence concerning the effects of attitudes and ego-involvements, one can say with some assurance that the introduction of courses in scientific method or courses in the analysis of concepts in colleges will not safeguard against the stereotyping effects of the concepts coming down from the past.

In this connection it is relevant to question what per cent of young people *do* change their concepts acquired in their home and communities on the basis of courses in biology, psychology, and sociology taken in their school years.

It is relevant to question how many students change their distance or prejudice scale acquired in the community with which they identify themselves, after learning in their anthropology courses the loose popular usage of the concept of "race." How many of them modify, on the basis of comparative data of an ethnology course, the conception of "human nature" they picked up in the image of their particular culture? The weight of evidence as presented by the studies of F. H. Allport, Eugene Hartley, and others indicates that there is little difference between college and non-college populations in these matters.

By the time students come to high school, not to mention college and university, their ideas concerning human relations, both on the inter-personal and intergroup level, are already formed, as prescribed by the existing concepts of their group. Their conceptions of their roles as man and woman, their conceptions of what are proper and improper personal relations, how distant or close given groups should be held in relation to themselves, are already formed as prescribed by the definitions of their group in these matters. We may question again the effectiveness of the scientific concepts and generalizations concerning these very matters taught in psychology or sociology courses. I suspect with good reason that such scientific concepts and generalizations superimposed in the formal school courses (which are taken in many cases simply to add so many points toward graduation) have only limited effects. Whereas, the attitudes and identifications taken in more naturally, almost like the act of breathing, from the widely prevalent concepts of their group concerning these very matters are the ones, on the whole, which have greater psychological weight and, hence, are likely the ones to be carried into real life situations in school and thereafter. For the attitudes derived from the widely prevalent concepts of our group are not viewed as so many bits of information; they *do* become a part of ourselves; they constitute the more or less stable anchorages of our personal identity. It is not surprising, therefore, that when confronted with concepts widely at variance with the established attitudes concerning human relations, the students feel uneasy, even insecure, about things. Most of them carry over the prevalent attitudes acquired from their communities when they settle down as citizens in their respective communities. I must add, however, that there are a few who try to readjust their outlooks in terms of the scientific concepts taught in their courses and acquired in the intellectual atmosphere of the school. But these few are the ones who become *personally involved* in the subject matter of the new concepts.

As an antidote to the stereotyping effects of concepts, it is suggested that the abstract nature of general concepts be stressed, and reactions be based on actually observable events and cases. It is stressed by semanticists especially that there is no such entity as the generalized cow or tree. What actually exists are Cow 1, Cow 2, etc. Likewise, there is not such an entity as the Negro, which is a concept that comes rather high on the abstraction ladder; but actually there are Negro 1, Negro 2, etc., each representing individual differences—intelligent ones, dumb ones, good ones and bad ones, as is the case in any other group. This process analysis is carried further and further. For example, to stress the fact that even a single individual is not a fixed entity throughout the course of his life history, it is suggested that we think and react to Mr. X not as Mr. X in a cut-and-dried way, but instead as Mr. X 1949 and Mr. X 1950, etc.

The efforts of semanticists in this direction are certainly laudable. But it does not really give us a realistic antidote against the stereotyping effect of concepts which lead us to various erroneous and harmful types of behavior.

The semantic antidote exemplified above overlooks a basic psychological tendency of human beings. This basic psychological tendency of the individual is to think and react in relation to objects, situations, and people in terms of generalized standards or concepts—in short, in terms of their established frames of reference. This is true both in relation to situations which are designated as merely cognitive as well as situations loaded with value properties. This basic psychological tendency of reacting in terms of already existing generalized standards or concepts is responsible for the relative consistency of the individual personality under varying conditions from day to day. On the other hand, it is responsible also for the stereotyping, narrowing-down effects when concepts not founded on fact come into play. We would be in a continuous state of suspense—a state which is painful—if we were to postpone judgment, evaluation, etc., until all the relevant data were made available from day to day in so many varied situations. The exceptional research worker, who at times has to stay in suspense until the necessary data are in before he can formulate a statement, knows

too well with what great efforts this suspense is achieved and at what
price in nervous strain. It is too much to expect this achievement from
millions of citizens who are rightly less troubled with suspending
judgment until all the relevant facts are available. Life would be
miserable, indeed, if people were to spend their time and energy on
Cow 1, Cow 2, etc. Even highly trained research scientists usually do
not practice this when they are not in the field of their special training.
They usually react as other citizens in their community. It would be
very instructive from this point of view to collect pronouncements of
physical scientists of various nations during the last twenty years, for
example, concerning the nature and goals of human relations, and to
find what per cent of these pronouncements reflect scientifically valid
concepts and what per cent are concepts reflecting their particular
identifications with particular groups.

The basic psychological tendency to perceive, to evaluate and
react always in terms of certain generalized standards, anchorages,
or symbols can be illustrated by various experiments in the fields of
judgment, perception, attitudes, etc. Especially in cases of stimulus
situations which are vague or unstructured and lack sufficient objective
cues, the subjects do not announce that they do not have the necessary
objective data to arrive at judgments, to structure perceptions, to formulate conclusions; on the contrary, they *do* form judgments, they do
structure perceptions and draw conclusions, usually on the basis of
anchorages or standards they themselves provide internally. For example, experiments utilizing the autokinetic situation have given us
significant leads along these lines. Here, I can take time to cite only
one concrete example, deliberately from the field of human relations.
Dr. Eugene Hartley, in one of his studies of prejudice (1945), inserted
names on non-existent groups to the list of actual groups to be rated by
his subjects along a social distance scale. The subjects were students
of some Eastern universities, one of them being one of the oldest and
best-known institutions in America. The subjects did not stop in rating
when they came to the names of non-existent groups. They did not say,
"we never heard of these groups and therefore we cannot rate them."
They went ahead and rated them, and their ratings were, on the whole,
on the general level of their prejudice toward other groups. In other
words, they carried over their generalized level of prejudice to non-
existent groups. Thus, these university students, including those from
the famous university, who are among the better trained youngsters
in scientific methods, took definite stands concerning even mere names
to which they were exposed for the first time. It seems to me that the
results of this study, which serves as a paradigm of several studies,
stands in bold relief as a warning against the unreality of such attempts
exemplified in the Cow 1, Cow 2, instead of a generalized Cow approach.

It seems to me that the conclusion to be drawn from all these considerations is evident. Concepts enter into psychological functioning of the individual as categorizing and structuring factors. Because of their weight as categorizing and structuring factors, concepts which are not scientifically validated have a stereotyping and blinding effect on the experience and behavior of individuals. At least a great majority of the concepts in everyday use by millions of people today are concepts which are not scientifically valid. The effective antidote is *not* to superimpose on them in the course of education the meager facts in the sciences of human relations as they exist today. In view of the general categorizing tendency of concepts at the human level of psychological functioning, the approach that suggests as an antidote taking every single case on its own merits or demerits is unrealistic. If concepts are in use as standardized and shared property of the group, they cannot help being effective. Therefore, the only effective way of getting rid of concepts which lead us into blind alleys is to replace them with scientifically valid ones, all the way through. The field of human relations is still in a primitive stage. Therefore, it is in this huge vital field that the attainment of scientifically valid concepts is most urgent. It may be that, if an integrated scheme of valid concepts is attained in the field of human relations, the existing dichotomy between science and ethics, between theory and practice, between heart and reason, will evaporate into thin air, and future generations will not be bothered with major problems of concepts vs. values in their educational policies.

SIXTEEN

SOME NEEDED CONCEPTS IN THE STUDY
OF ATTITUDES: LATITUDES OF ACCEPTANCE,
REJECTION, AND NONCOMMITMENT

Perhaps more effort and words have been poured into the study of social attitudes than into any other single problem area in social psychology. Under the labels of *attitude* and *attitude change* or one of the mushrooming neologisms, research on social attitudes continues to increase. This is as it should be.

From childhood on, the individual encounters objects, persons, and groups with insistent labels of approval, disapproval, or other value shadings attached to them by people important in his eyes. Of course, the process is seldom a one-way street. In the interaction process between him and others, the individual's desires as they are formed at the time, his strivings to belong and to prove himself play their part.

Whether his social attitudes are formed through interaction with other individuals or are primarily shaped by dictums, pronouncements, or exhortations of others, the state and particular brand of an individual's socialization can be expressed in terms of the attitudes which he has formed relative to stimuli within his psychological world. Stimuli relevant to his attitudes are selectively perceived and reacted to in a characteristic way. In no small measure, his appraisals, and hence his reactions to these stimuli are in terms of his attitudes towards them. Appropriate attitudes are involved when he is interacting in small groups, when he is exposed to communication from newspapers or television, and when he is deciding on a course of action. The importance attached to the study of attitudes is understandable.

What is not entirely understandable is the nebulous state of conceptions in this central problem area. No wonder that research results have frequently been difficult to evaluate. Until recent years, no greater

From J. Peatman and E. L. Hartley, Eds., *Festschrift for Gardner Murphy.* Copyright © 1960 by Harper and Brothers. Used by permission of Harper and Row, Publishers.

confusion prevailed than in research attempting to change social attitudes through communication. Reported results were inconclusive and even contradictory. Significant changes toward the position presented in communication were reported, but so was "no change"; and still other studies resulted in change in the opposite direction (Murphy, Murphy, and Newcomb, 1937; Williams, 1947; Hovland, 1951, 1954).

Much confusion may be avoided in research if the properties of social attitudes which have made their study essential in any scheme of social psychology are kept in clear focus. Attitude change studies gain coherence and predictions become possible when the properties of the individual's attitude are analyzed in relation to the properties of the stimulus material to which he was exposed.

Within the limits of available space, concepts found useful in recent research on social attitudes will be discussed, a study analyzing *latitudes of acceptance and rejection* on a political issue will be summarized, and the implications of this mode of analysis for attitude change studies will be indicated.

PROPERTIES OF SOCIAL ATTITUDES

Social attitudes are learned relative to a stimulus or stimulus class, such as social objects, other persons, groups, or institutions. Thus they always imply a subject-object relationship (Thomas and Znaniecki, 1918). The positive or negative values which the individual attaches to things, persons, or groups are usually outcomes of interaction between him and others, in which process his desires to be accepted, to belong, to prove himself, to amount to something play a crucial part. Thus a major source of the content of social attitudes is the values or norms of the individual's reference groups.

What does it mean for the individual to have an attitude towards a group, a church, a country, a political or economic issue? The attitude defines his positive or negative relatedness to its referent. Once a stimulus class is charged with value, the individual sees things related to it in a *characteristic* way, in a *selective* way, and he reacts accordingly. It is from the characteristic and selective mode of behavior in given conditions that an attitude is inferred (Campbell, 1950).

Events in line with his attitude are desired and satisfying. Events out of line or contrary to it produce dismay, annoyance, and disappointment. Thus a social attitude has the essential earmarks of a motive. There is good reason for using "sociogenic motives," "acquired drives," and "social attitudes" as equivalent terms.

The relationship defined by an attitude is not usually expressed in neutral terms, but in emotionally charged terms. A Baptist, for example, does not express his attitude toward his church by saying: "I formed a positive opinion of this particular church, and therefore I prefer it."

He says: "I *am* a Baptist." A disrespectful remark from an outsider hurts and, if possible, a corrective reaction is meted to the offender.

Much of what is included in one's sense of self-identity and self-esteem consists of subject-object relationships implied in the social attitudes formed during one's particular life history. If not transformed under specifiable conditions, social attitudes are lasting and not transitory affairs. Confusion in definitions of social attitudes can be reduced by including their motivational and (more or less) lasting properties therein. Transitory or motivationally neutral opinions and sets produced for the performance of laboratory tasks can be designated by concepts other than "attitude."

CATEGORIZATION OF ITEMS RELEVANT TO AN ATTITUDE

What is the consequence of having a positive attitude towards one's own group? That group is placed high in acceptance and other groups are ranked in descending order, usually in terms of definitions of those groups prevailing in one's own reference group. Similarly, upholding a stand on a controversial issue amounts to categorizing other stands on the issue, say, along the acceptable-objectionable dimension, in terms of their relative distance from the one the individual upholds.

The behavior from which attitudes are inferred always involves a judgmental process. In 1934, Gardner Murphy made me keenly aware of this general fact by calling my attention to an observation by Wells (1908). Wells noted that the ordering of a series of weights was in terms of the objective gradations of the series, whereas the ordering of pieces of music was in terms of the preference standard of the individual.

Even when order remains constant, the groupings of items into categories may vary as a function of attitude. In a recent study by Carolyn Sherif (1958), subjects sorted 100 cards into as many or as few categories as they saw fit. For one group of subjects, a number from 1 to 100 appeared on each card. For the experimental group, the same numbers appeared preceded by a dollar sign, and the instructions were to consider each card as a price tag on a garment. In the first case, the cards were categorized in terms of convenient groupings of the decimal system. In the second case, categorizations clearly reflected the income and prestige levels of the subjects, and the resulting differences in what was considered "cheap," "reasonable," "dear," etc.

When the individual has a definite attitude relevant to stimulus material, he brings established categories to the task of dealing with it. His own stand delineates the bounds of his tolerance or acceptance, and is customarily a major anchor in his judgments. This set of categories constitutes his *reference scale* for the placement of items in that universe of discourse. In our research we have frequently encountered spontaneous protests from a subject that the scale he was instructed to use did not extend far enough, or that it was too extensive for him to make proper ratings. Closer examination of such cases revealed lack of fit between the categories imposed by instructions and the reference scale the individual had formed in regard to the issue at hand.

Categorization of items relevant to attitudes is equivalent to evaluation, and evaluation presumes the placement of items into categories. The judgmental and motivational processes producing the behavioral outcome are inextricably intermingled.

SOURCE OF THE INDIVIDUAL'S REFERENCE SCALE
AND A BASELINE FOR RESEARCH

In the psychophysical experiment, the subject judges a stimulus as to weight, intensity, or extent relative to a standard stimulus of specified value, or to the repeated presentation of a series of graduated stimulus values. The keenness of his judgment, the effect of the series, and anchoring effects are gauged against known stimulus values.

In social life, the individual is ever passing judgments on a social issue in terms of the reference scale he has formed in his previous encounters with that issue. The reference scales used by different individuals vary in range and in the widths of the segments each finds acceptable and objectionable. Here the scale of categories prevailing in the individual's reference groups, ranging from the limits of acceptable categories to the limits of unacceptable categories on the given issue, is a useful counterpart of the objective series values against which judgments are gauged in psychophysical research. The categories prevailing in a group provide a *psychosocial* scale against which the differing ranges of individual reference scales, the different stands upheld by different individuals (including the deviates or nonconformists) can be assessed.

The limits of possible positions on an issue are the bounds of conceptual categories available in the social setting. For example, one would have difficulty if he asked the Siriono of Bolivia to group more than three items into categories because their number system consists of 1, 2, 3, and then "much" or "many." Likewise, in a social setting where wines are not differentiated and labeled by different names, it would be foolhardy to ask subjects to rank wines as to, say, their appropriateness for different occasions. In a setting where there are no different shadings on a political issue, the available categories would accommodate only similarity to the prevailing stand and "different."

The use of forced choice between two stimuli at a time (paired comparisons) and establishing a rank order on this basis are, of course, always procedurally feasible. But the results of this method reflect the discrimination ability of the person rather than the cutting points which characteristically define the direction, tolerance limits, and rejections of the attitude in question. The primary and crucial cutting points in attitude research are the limits of categories defined as acceptable and as unacceptable. From the point of view of attitudinal categorization, say, on racial discrimination, the fundamental step is to ascertain that being discriminated against in housing, in work, or in school are all placed in an undesirable category by those subjected to them. Ordering within the acceptable and unacceptable categories is a technical step that should follow. But if investigation starts with forced choices, the main boundary conditions are obscured, and the cutting points arrived at in the analysis may be sheerly arbitrary. Beebe-Center (1932) made a similar comment on the limitations of forced choice in discussing judgments of pleasantness and unpleasantness.

In sum, the prevailing psychosocial scales categorizing positions represented in a sociocultural setting and prevailing in an individual's reference groups can be used as a baseline in research. Against this baseline, the relative positions of particular individuals, the widths of their tolerance range, the degree of their conformity or nonconformity can be advantageously computed.

CHARACTERISTIC DISTRIBUTION OF JUDGMENTS AND NUMBER OF CATEGORIES AS AN INDEX OF AN ATTITUDE

By focusing upon the judgmental processes involved when the individual reacts to stimuli relevant to an attitude, certain predictions were possible (Hovland and Sherif, 1952; Sherif and Hovland, 1953). The predictions were based (1) on the demonstrated effects of affectively charged internal anchors on the placement of items in a series (e.g., Volkmann, 1936; Hunt and Volkmann, 1937); and (2) on the demonstrated liability of ambiguous stimuli to displacement as a function of motivational factors (e.g., Chapman and Volkmann, 1939; Proshansky and Murphy, 1942; Marks, 1943). These predictions were as follows:

1. Individuals with strong attitudes (i.e., ego-involved) on an issue will tend to bunch together a disproportionately large number of items in extreme categories at the expense of intermediate categories.

2. Individuals with moderate positions and little ego-involvement with an issue will distribute their judgments more evenly throughout the categories.

3. The items which are liable to displacement towards extreme categories will be middle-of-the-road (neutral) items and not those sharply defining a position.

4. Individuals upholding strong stands will concentrate more judgments at the extreme segment of the scale *opposite* to their own stand on the issue. In other words, highly ego-involved individuals upholding stands near the extremes will be "choosy" in accepting items, thus lumping a much greater number of judgments into the segment of the

scale which is objectionable from their standpoint. This well-known tendency is expressed by partisans of public issues in the form: "Those who are not definitely for us are against us," and may be conceptualized as a *raised threshold of acceptance* and *lowered threshold of rejection*.

5. When individuals are given freedom of choice as to the number of categories they will use in placing items on an ego-involving issue:

a. Persons with strong attitudes will use relatively fewer categories and will concentrate their judgments at the two extremes of their "own scale," the greater frequency being at the extreme *opposite* to their own stand.

b. Persons with moderate positions will use a more extended scale consisting of a relatively larger number of categories than that used by those upholding an extreme position, and will distribute their judgments more evenly throughout the scale.

These predictions were tested in research on judgments of the favorableness or unfavorableness of statements to the social position of Negroes. Of the 300 subjects (college students), about one-third were Negro students. The statements sorted were 114, ranging from those clearly favorable to the social position of Negroes through definitely anti-Negro expressions originally used by Hinckley (1932). The sortings were made under two procedures:

1. *Imposed categories* procedure: Ss were instructed to sort the statements into 11 categories.

2. *"Own categories"* procedure: Ss were to choose as few or as many categories as they saw fit, with category one being defined as "most unfavorable."

In the first session, part of the subjects judged under the imposed category condition and the others under the "own categories" procedure. In the second session about two weeks later, the sorting conditions for the two groups were reversed.

The results support the predictions stated above. The checks introduced make explanation of the results in terms of carelessness in sorting extremely unlikely. Subjects were not told at the first session that a second session would occur. Yet those subjects who concentrated their judgments at the extreme segments of the scale under the imposed category condition were the ones who used only three or four categories under the "own categories" procedure. The same pattern of frequency appeared under the "own categories" condition in more accentuated form, with a disproportionately large number piled in the extreme category opposite to the subject's own stand on the issue.

It is suggested that the "own categories" procedure for judgment in which a sufficient number of middle-of-the-road or ambiguous items are presented may be used as a quantitative "projective" technique in assessing attitudes on controversial issues. The subject is instructed to sort the items in terms of their "pro" and "con" nature. The number of categories used and the degree of concentration of judgments in extreme categories reveal the strength of the attitude. The characteristic distribution of judgments reveals the position that the subject upholds, the neutral items being displaced predominantly toward the extreme opposite to his own stand on the issue. Perhaps the "own categories" procedure may be useful in assessing the rigidity or flexibility of the person in given matters.

LATITUDE OF ACCEPTANCE AND LATITUDE OF REJECTION

We have seen that a person strongly committed to a stand on an issue becomes highly selective in admitting statements to categories acceptable to him. His threshold of acceptance is raised, and his threshold for rejection is lowered. Thus he tends to lump together a disproportionately large number of items into objectionable categories. This tendency has been observed frequently. For example, Johnson (1955) reported that persons holding extreme stands towards war gave negative judgments more frequently and with greater confidence than did individuals with more moderate positions.

For the study of reaction to communication and attitude change, the consequence of raised and lowered thresholds can be measured in terms of latitudes of acceptance and rejection for items on an issue. The customary use of a single score or average to represent the individual's attitude on an issue obscures these significant relationships. Individuals upholding the same modal point on an issue do differ concerning their personal involvement and the other positions on the issue which they will also accept or tolerate. They do differ in regard to the limits of their tolerance, beyond which all other positions on the issue are flatly rejected as objectionable, even as obnoxious.

The *latitude of acceptance* may be defined as consisting of those positions on an issue that the individual finds most acceptable, plus other positions also acceptable to him. The *latitude of rejection* consists of those positions on the same issue that he finds most objectionable, plus other objectionable positions on the issue.

Our first attempt towards assessing latitudes of acceptance and rejection, carried out in 1948–1949 by the writer, C. Hovland, and E. Volkart as a pilot study, utilized the "closed shop" issue. The second was carried out in 1952–1954, and utilized the prohibition issue in Oklahoma (Hovland, Harvey, and Sherif, 1957). The unpublished research to be summarized here was carried out in Oklahoma as part of a collaborative research project with Hovland, and utilized the issue of the 1956 presidential election.[1]

[1] The collaboration of Dr. Henry Pronko, University of Wichita; Dr. Robert Scofield, State University of Oklahoma; Dr. Jack Douglas, W. R. Hood, R. Killian, W. LeFurgy, George Rucker, and L. La Fave, all of the University of Oklahoma at the time, is gratefully acknowledged.

On the basis of the previous studies, the hypotheses were:

1. The latitude of rejection of individuals committed to an extreme stand on an ego-involving issue is greater than the latitude of rejection of individuals with a moderate position on the same issue.
2. The latitude of rejection of individuals committed to an extreme stand on an ego-involving issue will be relatively greater than their latitude of acceptance.

The study was carried out in two sessions of which the first was devoted to procedures designed to ascertain the attitudes of the subjects in terms of their latitudes of acceptance and rejection. Here we can only mention in passing the results of the second session in which communication was presented and reactions to it obtained.

The issue of the presidential and vice-presidential candidates in the 1956 election was suitable for testing the hypotheses because adequate numbers of subjects upholding differing stands were readily available and because the issue held nation-wide interest at the time.

For the purpose of securing latitudes of acceptance and rejection on the election issue, nine statements were prepared after extensive pretesting. The statements ranged from an extremely pro-Republican position through a middle-of-the-road position to an extremely pro-Democratic position. For purposes of analysis, the nine positions were designated by the letters A through I. Statements A, E, and I are reproduced below:

A. The election of the Republican presidential and vice-presidential candidates in November is absolutely essential from all angles in the country's best interests.

E. From the point of view of the country's interests, it is hard to decide whether it is preferable to vote for presidential and vice-presidential candidates of the Republican Party or the Democratic Party in November.

I. The election of the Democratic presidential and vice-presidential candidates in November is absolutely essential from all angles in the country's best interests.

The complete set of nine statements (A to I) was mimeographed on each of four sheets of paper. On the first sheet, subjects indicated the statement "most acceptable" to them; on the second, they indicated other statements also acceptable to them. The positions checked on these two sheets provided the data on their latitudes of acceptance. On the third sheet, subjects checked the statement "most objectionable" to them, and on the last sheet they checked other objectionable statements. The checkings on these last two pages yielded data on their latitudes of rejection. Subjects were not forced to check any statements in regard to which they chose to remain *noncommital,* and such results were classified accordingly.

The statements were designed to prevent a "ceiling effect." In fact, our results reveal a reluctance to endorse extreme end items (statements A and I), even by subjects selecting a position next to the extreme as the one most acceptable and actively committed to one of the major parties as campaign workers.

Results are based on data from 406 subjects from college populations in three universities in the Southwest. The median age was slightly over 21 years, and 78 per cent of the subjects were 25 years or under. A special point was made to obtain members of the Young Republicans and the League of Young Democrats who were engaged in campaign activities at the time (the month preceding the election). In addition, some small groups in university dormitories with known stands on the issue were obtained. The responses of these subjects served to check the validity of the results.

In part of the analysis, subjects were classified according to the position they chose as "most acceptable." Then the frequencies with which these subjects accepted, rejected, or remained noncommittal on each of the remaining eight positions were determined. From this analysis, nine graphs were constructed, each representing the frequencies of responses by subjects with a different stand on the election issue.

On each graph, the various positions on the issue are shown on the abscissa, ranging from A (the extreme pro-Republican position) to I (the extreme pro-Democratic position). The ordinate represents the percentage of subjects upholding a given position who accepted, rejected, or remained noncommittal to the other eight positions on the issue. The first graph, for example, represents the acceptances, rejections, and noncommittal responses of subjects checking the most pro-Republican position (position A) as "most acceptable." The adjacent graph represents the responses of subjects checking the most pro-Democratic position (position I) as "most acceptable." The solid line represents the percentage of subjects accepting given positions. A double check mark is located above the "most acceptable" position, which is, of course, 100 per cent in each figure. The long-dash line represents the percentages of subjects rejecting given positions, and the short-dash line indicates the percentages of noncommittal responses. The most objectionable position for subjects is represented by XX. For example, the most objectionable position for subjects at position A is the I position.

A definite criterion was necessary in order to make generalizations about latitudes of acceptance and rejection of individuals who find different positions as "most acceptable." The criterion used was the placement of a given statement within the "acceptable," "rejected," or "noncommittal" category, as the case might be, by 50 per cent or more of the subjects. In each figure a heavy dash line represents this 50 per cent cutting point. When a percentage of acceptance or rejection is above the 50 per cent line, we included that position in the latitude of acceptance or the latitude of rejection of that subject group.

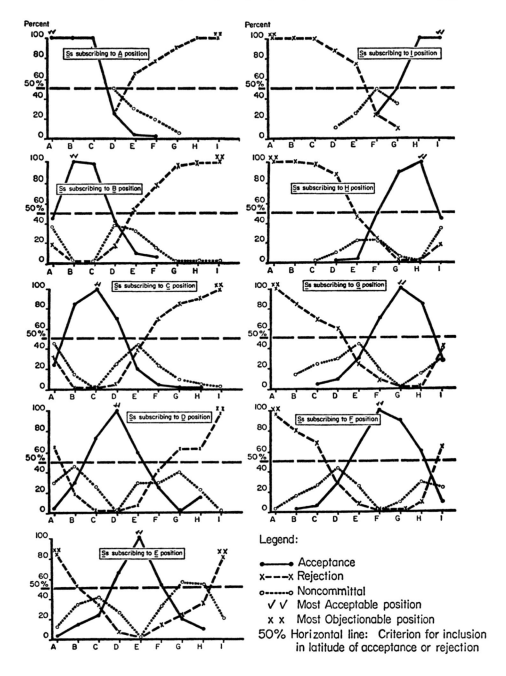

Latitudes of acceptance and rejection for individuals upholding given positions on a controversial issue.

Note that the distributions for subjects holding pro-Republican positions (graphs on the left for positions *A–C* in particular) are the reverse of those for subjects holding pro-Democratic positions (graphs on the right for positions *I–G*). The figures are presented side by side for easy comparison, and it may be seen that one of each pair appears to be almost a *mirror image* of the other. The figure for subjects at the middle position (*E*) is at the bottom. These subjects include equal numbers of positions in the latitude of acceptance and latitude of rejection. The distributions for rejection and the noncommittal classification are bimodal.

The results shown by these graphs quite clearly support our hypotheses, namely, that the latitude of rejection of individuals upholding extreme stands is greater than the latitude of rejection of individuals upholding moderate positions, and that, for individuals with extreme stands, the latitude of rejection is greater than the latitude of acceptance.

We were also interested in determining whether our hypotheses would be supported by analysis of the relative sizes of the latitudes of acceptance and rejection for each individual. Therefore we divided the subjects into three classifications on the basis of their own positions on the issue: extreme pro-Republicans (checking positions *A*, *B*, or *C* as most acceptable); extreme pro-Democrats (at positions *G*, *H*, or *I*); and moderates (at *D*, *E*, or *F*). In each of these classifications we determined the number of individuals whose latitude of acceptance was greater than their latitude of rejection, the number whose latitude of acceptance was smaller than their latitude of rejection, and the number whose latitudes of acceptance and rejection were equal in size. All of the differences in the resulting 3×3 table were in the predicted directions.

The overwhelming majority of subjects upholding extreme positions had latitudes of acceptance which were smaller than their latitudes of rejection, while this pronounced trend was not evident in the case of moderate subjects. Chi square analysis yielded a value of 26.34, which is significant at less than .001 level for 4 degrees of freedom. Separate analysis indicated significant differences between extreme pro-Republican subjects and moderate subjects, and between extreme pro-Democratic and moderate subjects. Differences between extreme pro-Republican and extreme pro-Democratic subjects were slight and not significant, as was predicted.

SOME IMPLICATIONS FOR REACTIONS TO COMMUNICATION AND ATTITUDE CHANGE

One implication of our research is that reaction to communication presenting a given position on an issue will not depend solely upon the relation between the position the individual chooses as his "own stand"

and the position advocated in communication. His judgment of the communication is affected also by the distance of the position advocated from the limits of his latitude of acceptance. We found, for example, that a communication presenting a stand somewhere near the middle-of-the-road is judged differently by moderate subjects with broad latitudes of acceptance than by subjects with extreme views and narrow latitudes of acceptance (Hovland, Harvey, and Sherif, 1957).

The individual whose latitude of acceptance extends to a position close to that presented in communication or propaganda is likely to *assimilate* the position presented in communication, i.e., to regard it as closer to his own stand on the issue than it actually is. As a result he is more likely to be influenced by the content of communication.

The individual with a narrow latitude of acceptance whose limit is farther from the position presented in communication reacts quite differently. In this case, the result is akin to the *contrast* phenomena in judgment and perception. The individual judges the communication as more divergent from his own stand on the issue than it actually is. He is irritated by the communication. He may even become more uncompromising in his stand than he was initially. We suspect that the relationships and judgment processes involved are pertinent to an explanation of the well-known boomerang effects in propaganda.

From a theoretical point of view, the results demonstrate the relevance of assimilation and contrast effects found in laboratory studies of judgment and perception to the study of effects of communication advocating a point of view on a controversial social issue.

SEVENTEEN

THE SOCIAL JUDGMENT-INVOLVEMENT APPROACH
TO ATTITUDE AND ATTITUDE CHANGE

With Carolyn W. Sherif

This paper concentrates on the rationale and empirical basis of the social judgment-involvement approach to attitude and attitude change. At the point where our approach makes unequivocal predictions about attitude change without preparing loopholes for retreat, we shall evaluate its position relative to the cognitive dissonance approach. The factual support and procedural details may be found in sufficient detail in Sherif and Hovland (1961) and Sherif, Sherif, and Nebergall (1965).

The social judgment-involvement approach is not based on a preconceived formal model, although a valid model is the desired ultimate goal. It does not attempt to contrive procedures that fit data into interval or ratio scales with a zero point, as represented in the measurement of temperature. A two-inch segment is part of a total length of ten inches. But in the analysis and measurement of a social attitude, a lesser position on the same side of the issue is not necessarily included in the range of positions acceptable to a person committed to an extreme position. For example, the position of "desegregation at a reasonable pace" will be jeered by the person who stands for "desegregation *now*," and he will place it in the detestable category of "tokenism."

The social judgment-involvement approach is modest in its point of departure. As its point of departure, the social judgment-involvement approach adheres to an unbiased and disciplined *phenomenology*, in the sense that it assesses the extent of acceptance and rejection on significant social issues without imposing fixed measurement indicators that represent the individual's stand on an issue as a single point (for example, as a mean or a single composite score). In this regard the present approach continues in the tradition of social perception or social judgment. It attempts to learn from actualities—namely, the actualities of individuals who uphold a position when they place relevant items into

Paper presented at the American Psychological Association, Chicago, September 3, 1965.

categories that are acceptable or objectionable to them or, for reasons of their own, prefer not to place them in either acceptable or objectionable categories.

The satisfaction of hearing a communication whose message falls within one's range of acceptance and the tension aroused by being exposed to a discrepant communication are not accounted for through analogy with a physical model. As Emile Durkheim stated so forcefully decades ago, events of social life are not merely carryovers of physical events and cannot be extrapolated on a continuum of physical events. The formulation of the present approach relies heavily on established findings regarding the judgment process and on findings about the characteristic consistency of behavior revealed in experimental studies of ego-involvement in perceiving, judging, and learning. Every attitudinal reaction implies an evaluative comparison or choice among alternatives, which is a judgment process. Whenever these alternatives are personally significant, the self-concept is involved in the process.

Therefore, as an important basis of our approach to attitude and attitude change, we relied heavily on principles developed by experimentalists working in judgment area. In *Social Judgment* with Carl Hovland, we looked into the implications of various psychophysical methods for the study of attitudes. In this area we found very useful guidelines in the work on affective judgment by Beebe-Center (1932), in the work of experimentalists like John Volkmann (1936, 1951), W. A. Hunt (1941), and Harry Helson (1964) studying the effects on judgment of external and internal anchors that are near or remote relative to the object of judgment.

The social judgment-involvement approach welcomes the charge of being crude and primitive at this early stage of the game. It welcomes this charge as long as it succeeds in specifying the degree of discrepancy between a communication and the person's own position, in making unequivocal predictions about the direction of attitude change toward or away from a communication, and in predicting susceptibility or resistance to change even before an attempt is made to change the person's attitude. The approach offers operational indicators for degree of ego-involvement in terms of the relative sizes of the person's latitudes of rejection and noncommitment, as will be specified later.

The present approach starts with the following crucial questions: *What is it* that is to be changed when a person is exposed to a communication or some other attempt at attitude change? *What is it* that is resistant to change? Is it his guesses about the number of beans in a jar, or leaves on a tree, or grains of sand in a square yard of beach? Or is it his views on his family, how he as a person stacks up in relation to his contemporaries, or the worth of his religion, his politics, his profession, his country, or his way of life? It is one thing to change from one brand of chewing gum or tooth brush to another brand of chewing gum or tooth brush. It is quite another thing to change the person's stand toward persons, objects, groups, beliefs, and institutions that he accepts or rejects as related to himself with all the commitments, identifications, and emotional reverberations associated with them.

A definition of attitude is necessary to develop adequate operational tools for assessing attitude and attitude change and for measuring the degree of discrepancy between an attitude and communication intended to change it, beyond the vague statement that the communication is "similar" or "discrepant." The definition developed in our approach is based on a great body of evidence, and it leads to methods for specifying the structure of an individual's attitude.

Definitions of attitude (that is, *what* is to be changed) have all had certain essential features in common. Almost invariably, representative definitions of attitude specify in one way or another that attitudes are acquired, or learned, and that attitudes are inferred from the *characteristic, consistent,* and *selective* modes of behavior of the same individual over a time span. These criteria for attitude have been stated since the writings of W. I. Thomas, the sociologist; through those of the psychologists Murphy, Murphy, and Newcomb; G. W. Allport; Donald Campbell; and the series of volumes from the Yale Communication Program by Carl I. Hovland and his associates.

Underlying the characteristic, consistent, and selective modes of behavior is a comparison process, and every comparison implies a judgment process. In selecting one alternative over others, the individual both discriminates among the alternatives and reveals his preference somewhat as follows: This one is acceptable or desirable or "the one for me." In avoiding certain alternatives, he compares and evaluates them: This is objectionable or disgusting or "these people are definitely not my kind." He reveals a set of categories for evaluating the available items within the stimulus domain in question.

Accordingly, the present approach developed the following definition of attitude, that is, *what* it is that changes or resists change: *Operationally, an attitude may be defined as the individual's set of categories for evaluating a stimulus domain, which he has established as he learns about that domain in interaction with other persons.* The data from which attitudes are inferred, therefore, are his consistent and characteristic categorizations, over a time span, of relevant objects, persons, or communications into acceptable and objectionable categories. Change is inferred from the alteration of the individual's acceptance-rejection pattern. Therefore a close understanding of this acceptance-rejection pattern and the analysis of measurable changes in the acceptance-rejection pattern have been our main task in the present approach.

Proceeding from the definition of attitude, let us specify three concepts for purposes of assessing the structure of an attitude.

1. *Latitude of acceptance.* If a person voluntarily states his view on a topic, he usually gives the position most acceptable to him. The latitude of acceptance is simply this most acceptable position plus other positions the individual also finds acceptable.

2. *Latitude of rejection.* The position most objectionable to the individual, the thing he most detests in a particular domain, plus other items or positions also objectionable to him define the latitude of rejection.

3. *Latitude of noncommitment.* While accepting some and rejecting others, the individual may prefer to remain noncommittal in regard to certain positions. Ordinarily, these are the "don't know," "neutral," "undecided," "no opinion," or "no comment" responses in public opinion surveys. In all of our research in this area, the individual has been required only to indicate the most acceptable and objectionable positions, being free to accept or reject other positions but not forced to do so. The positions he does *not* evaluate as either acceptable or objectionable constitute his *latitude of noncommitment.* As we shall see, some of the most useful predictive indicators discovered in our research pertain to the latitude of noncommitment, that is, the positions on which he prefers to remain noncommittal.

Now let us see some advantages of specifying the structure of the person's attitude in terms of latitudes of acceptance, rejection, and noncommitment. First, individuals finding the same position as most acceptable do differ in their tolerance for other positions and in the range of their rejections. Second, the latitudes of acceptance, rejection, and noncommitment differ systematically for persons upholding different positions according to their degree of involvement in the issue at hand.

We shall draw some conclusions based on studies of two different national elections in two different parts of the country, in which attitudes were assessed twice about a week apart for over 1,500 persons. In addition, these conclusions are verified by subsequent studies on several other issues, including the labor-management issue by Alvar Elbing (now of Dartmouth College), the farm policy issue by James Whittaker (now of North Dakota State University), the prohibition issue, desegregation issue by L. La Fave (now of Indiana State University), and the re-apportionment issue by John Reich (of the University of Colorado).

Figure 1 is a summary of the relative sizes of latitudes of acceptance, rejection, and noncommitment on the 1960 election issue. It shows the mean number of positions in the latitude of acceptance, rejection, and noncommitment for persons taking each of nine positions as *most acceptable to them* (their own positions). The person's own position is given on the baseline from A, the most extreme Republican, to I, the most extreme Democratic position. The ordinate represents the aver-

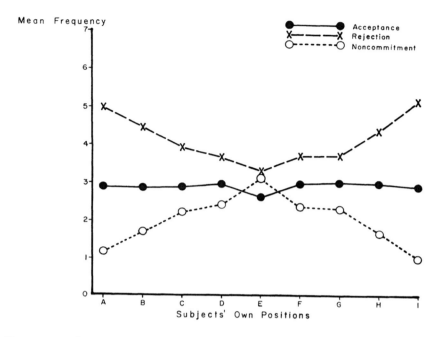

FIGURE 1. Election issue—1960, Pacific Coast. Sizes of latitudes of acceptance, rejection, and noncommitment.

age or mean number of positions. Solid dots indicate the mean number for acceptances, X's the mean number of rejections, and the white circles represent the mean number of noncommitment. Note that the means for the latitude of acceptance form almost a straight line near three, regardless of a person's own position. The dip at E (the nonpartisan position) reflects the heterogeneity of these persons. About 17 per cent found *only* the E position acceptable, and a substantial proportion were "leaners" accepting only one other position on either the Republican or Democratic side. Relationships between the size of the latitude of rejection and the person's own stand, and between noncommitment and the person's own position are both significant.

Specific conclusions can be drawn from the data:

1. The means for the latitude of acceptance form almost a straight line near three positions—with a noteworthy dip for E position (that is, for nonaligned subjects).

2. The latitude of rejection increases in size as a curvilinear function of the extremity of the person's commitment.

3. The latitude of noncommitment is also curvilinearly related to extremity of commitment, but inversely so, approaching zero for sub-

jects with greatest commitment. In fact, it is zero for an appreciable number of highly committed subjects.

Several studies using different issues have reported much higher levels of noncommitment than those found in the studies of national elections just before they occurred, and also a much greater frequency of attitude change. Therefore, the frequency of noncommitment by the person on different issues can serve as a predictive indicator of his relative ego-involvement in them. We have successfully used the relative size of the latitude of rejection as an indicator of high and low involvement for placements of communication by different individuals on the same issue.

The rationale for using the size of the latitude of rejection as well as the size of latitude of noncommitment as more discriminating indicators for ego-involvement is worth noting, for it leads to another facet of the research program. We knew that the more extreme stands were taken on the election by active proponents of the respective parties, for the most part. *There is considerable evidence from other research showing a general relationship between extremity of position and degree of involvement in an issue* (Cantril, 1946). However, some persons in our research chose a moderate and even a nonpartisan position as most acceptable but rejected five or six positions out of the total nine. They gave other evidence of considerable involvement in the election. Fortunately, we had additional evidence that frequent rejection is associated with high involvement on an issue. The latter data provided the basis for predictions about reactions to communication. These were experiments on the individual's *own categories.*

THE INDIVIDUAL'S OWN CATEGORIES

Predictions about placement of communication and attitude change were based on a principle of judgment established in the psychophysical laboratory and verified in studies of social judgment. Very briefly, judgment of particular objects shifts systematically, depending upon the standard or anchor used for comparison. A standard very different from the objects judged shifts judgment *away* from it—this is a *contrast* effect. A standard or anchor resembling one of the things to be judged shifts judgment *toward* the standard—this is an *assimilation* effect.

The person with an attitude comes to a situation designed to change his attitude with his own categories for evaluation. The present approach predicts that his own stand (as represented by his latitude of acceptance) will serve as the major standard for comparison to the extent that he is involved in the objects being judged. His placement of particular communications will vary systematically with their discrepancy from his stand. With small discrepancies, the communication will be categorized nearer the person's stand, that is, *assimilated toward it*. As the difference between attitude and communication increases, the communication will be contrasted with the person's stand, that is, seen as increasingly more different from his position than others see it.

As applied to social judgment, the principle may be illustrated by the early studies of Sherif and Hovland in the early 1950 s. In these experiments, the subject's task was completely objective. He was to categorize a series of statements according to how favorable or unfavorable they were to the status of Negroes. Note that he was *not* asked to check his acceptances or rejections on the issue. In one condition, with *imposed* categories, he was to use eleven categories, as prescribed in the Thurstone method for equal-appearing intervals. In the other, he was left free to use any number of categories in any way he chose, in order to differentiate the statements as to how favorable or unfavorable they were to Negroes. In short, the Own Categories method was used.

The findings in this and subsequent studies using the method of the individual's own categories have substantiated the following generalizations:

1. If a person has an attitude toward a stimulus domain, he comes to the task of judging relevant communication (statements) with a set of categories that are at the same time evaluative, affective, or motivational in nature, as well as cognitive. They are his own categories.

2. If he is highly involved in the topic at hand, the task of categorizing communications becomes an evaluative task for him, even though he is instructed to judge them according to objective, non-evaluative criteria.

3. To the extent that he is ego-involved, wittingly or unwittingly, he will use his own position as a standard or anchor for placing the statements. His placements will reveal a *raised threshold for acceptance* and a *lowered threshold for rejection*. Thus, his latitude of rejection is disproportionately greater than his latitude of acceptance. The disproportion is revealed in his categorizations by a greater reluctance to place statements in categories he accepts and a tendency to lump all of those he rejects into one broad segment.

4. The highly involved person tends to use fewer categories than a less committed person.

These effects occur when a highly involved person categorizes statements *relevant* to his attitude, we repeat, even when he is not instructed to express or check in terms of his attitude. Therefore, the Own Categories procedure is proposed as an indirect or disguised method for attitude and personality assessment. Proportional to his involvement in the material, the individual will (1) use fewer categories and (2) distribute items into them quite unequally, with a relatively small mode at his most acceptable position and a larger mode in the segment most objectionable to him.

PLACEMENT OF COMMUNICATIONS AS BASIC
TO PROBLEMS OF ATTITUDE CHANGE

The basic information for predicting a person's reaction to a communication (or some other medium for changing his attitude) is his placement or categorization of its position relative to his own. Ample evidence is accumulated to show that a communication is judged to be factual, unbiased, fair, and pleasing in proportion to its proximity to the person's latitude of acceptance or nearby in his latitude of noncommitment. Conversely, reactions to communication as propagandistic, false, and biased increase as the difference increases between the individual's own stand and the position advocated.

Of greater theoretical interest are the factors affecting the individual's placement of a communication as resembling or diverging from his stand in some degree. One major variable is the degree of the person's *involvement* on the topic. If it is unfamiliar or a matter of complete unconcern, there is no issue of psychological tension aroused by a communication discrepant from the person's position. Here, we have a situation for attitude formation or learning, but not attitude change. Psychologically the situation in which an individual already has some kind of established attitude is quite different.

If he is involved in his stand, the person uses his own position as an anchor for assessing the position advocated in the communication. If it is near his latitude of acceptance or within his latitude of noncommitment, he is likely to assimilate the advocated position toward his stand, seeing the message as more similar to his views than it is. Furthermore, he regards it as factual and fair. But the range within which this assimilation occurs varies *inversely* with the degree of his ego-involvement. The higher the involvement, the narrower the range of assimilation. Beyond this range, similarity between one's own stand and the communication decreases in his eyes, proportional to the discrepancy between the person's own stand and the position advocated. Likewise, the assessment of the message as fair, factual and true decreases.

In studying placements of communication on the 1960 election campaign, we divided persons upholding each of the nine positions as most acceptable, according to the size of their latitudes of rejection, using it as an indicator of degree of ego-involvement. The less ego-involved persons, with small latitudes of rejection, assimilated communications toward their own position over a wider range of discrepancies. Highly involved persons, who had the same latitude of acceptance but greater latitudes of rejection, exaggerated the divergence of the same message—that is, contrasted it to their own stand.

Obviously, the properties of the communication itself affect its placement. Clear-cut statements of extreme positions are not subject to assimilation-contrast effects to any appreciable degree. The less extreme, and especially the moderate statements are the ones subject to systematic displacement, even though they are somewhat *pro* or *anti*. A great deal needs to be done to specify what makes communications subject to displacement. We know that ambiguity of position is part of the picture. When situations are fluid, rumors are quickly accepted. In case of doubt, the person uses his own standard for assessing such situations.

ATTITUDE CHANGE

Now we are in a position to assess some advantages accruing from the approach for measurement of attitude and attitude change and to compare some of its predictions.

1. The present approach provides concepts and operational tools for assessing *when* a communication will be seen as so discrepant by the person that it does arouse tension, instability, dissonance, disequilibrium, incongruity, or imbalance. From at least the time of William James, in one form or another, the phenomenon of tension and irritation has been noted in response to a situation violating values the person holds near and dear. *This is nothing new.* The challenge in this respect is to specify the degree of discrepancy that arouses these feelings of tension. Certainly it is not adequate to deal with discrepancies only in terms of the "logical obverse" or the number of "elements" dissonant in logical terms.

2. Unlike predictions "generated" from cognitive dissonance theory, the present approach predicts *less* susceptibility to change when the issue is very important to the person, that is, when he is more ego-involved. *Susceptibility to change can be predicted by the present approach from the size of the latitude of noncommitment as well as the size of the latitude of rejection.* There is considerable evidence now that moderately committed persons with larger latitudes of noncommitment shift their attitudes in experiments approximately twice as frequently as highly committed persons. Highly committed persons displace discrepant communications away from their own stand; and if they change at all, it is most frequently away from the communication or by retrenchment in their own stand.

3. The predictions from the present approach about attitude change as a function of discrepancy between communication and the person's attitude are different from those of cognitive dissonance formulation. Dissonance theory has been interpreted to mean that greater changes *may* occur with greater discrepancies. Therefore, we must soberly repeat that our approach predicts a curvilinear relationship, as clearly specified in *Social Judgment* (Sherif and Hovland, 1961). Specifically, increasing attitude change is predicted with increasingly discrepant communications *within the range of assimilation*, but decreasing change

is predicted thereafter, proportional to the discrepancy as the communication falls deeper within the latitude of rejection. We predict without qualification that a highly committed person exposed to an extremely discrepant communication of brief duration will *never* react to it by changing his attitude toward the communication. He will feel irritated, derogate the communicator, speak to his friends about it, but he will never resort to the alternative of changing toward communication in order to reduce his irritation, tension or dissonance.

The apparent contradiction in results reported by various researchers about attitude change and the discrepancy problem is no contradiction when the conditions of the various experiments are specified. When thus specified, the results fall into a pattern. Predictions from cognitive dissonance theory and the present approach are similar only within certain definite conditions, that the social judgment-involvement approach specifies. These conditions are those affecting the assimilation range, hence the segment of positions conducive to increasing attitude change. The conditions which increase the assimilation range are as follows:

1. Low ego-involvement, or no attitude at all at the outset.
2. Ambiguous communications or highly ambiguous, unstructured situations to be judged.
3. Highly valued sources in terms of the person's reference groups.

Most studies showing greater change with more remote communications have used a limited range of discrepant communications. Even with low involvement, ambiguous communications, or highly valued sources, the present approach predicts that a communication sufficiently discrepant will reduce attitude change. Studies showing a curvilinear relationship have for the most part used issues in which some involvement could be demonstrated and the positions advocated have extended to extreme discrepancies.

Specification of the structure of a person's attitude in terms of latitudes of acceptance, rejection, and noncommitment permits both predictions about susceptibility to change before any change is attempted at all, and predictions of the direction and pattern of change. Blind predictions on the direction of change were made for attitudes assessed during the 1960 election campaign about a week apart. They were based on the pattern of acceptances and rejections in the first session. Accurate prediction was made for over 70 per cent of the subjects. This and a number of other possibilities opened by the approach await further exploration.

On our part, we are interested in utilizing the methodological advantages gained in this approach for further studies of individuals in their groups. An individual's attitudes are not acquired or changed in thin air, but with reference to his fellow men, for they are the ones with whom we have ties, claims for recognition and for amounting to something. Therefore, we see the next major step in the social judgment-involvement approach as the study of interaction in reference groups, of the kind exemplified in our previous experiments on the formation and change of attitudes within and between groups and our intensive studies of natural groups reported in our *Reference Groups* (1964). Eventually, accurate prediction of attitude change hinges upon the individual's relative involvement in several universes of discourse. This issue is closely related to his roles in various reference groups and to their values.

EIGHTEEN

THE OWN CATEGORIES PROCEDURE
IN ATTITUDE RESEARCH

With Carolyn W. Sherif

The Own Categories Procedure is a general method for the study of social attitudes that avoids certain limitations inherent in many available models for attitude measurement and provides more information about the individual's attitude than most other procedures. The procedure yields quantitative indicators of the individual's attitude and the degree of its importance to him, through the number of categories he uses and the pattern of his judgments in the categories.

We shall first describe the procedure and summarize very briefly the theoretical basis for its use in attitude research. Next, we shall describe research findings that indicate some major variables affecting the measures yielded by the procedure. Finally, we shall discuss briefly the utility of the procedure in attitude research.

This paper is a highly condensed version of one chapter and other portions of *Attitude and Attitude Change: The Social Judgment-Involvement Approach* (1965). Previous statements and research findings appeared in *Social Judgment* by Sherif and Hovland (1961).

DESCRIPTION OF PROCEDURE

The term "Own Categories" reflects the translation of the conception of attitude into operational procedures. Attitude is conceived as a set of *evaluative* categories which the individual has formed (or learned) during his interaction with persons and objects in his social world. When faced with persons, objects, or events relevant to his attitude, the individual uses these categories for classifying specific items as acceptable-unacceptable, good-bad, truthful-erroneous, or other appropriate evaluative terms. In this sense, they are his "own categories" for

Paper prepared for the Symposium on Attitude Measurement and Change, International Congress of Applied Psychology, Ljublyana, Yugoslavia, August 6, 1964. (Translated in *Bulletin du C.E.R.P.*, Paris, 1964, 13, 185–197.)

evaluation, as contrasted with the division of a stimulus domain under labels arbitrarily imposed by an authority figure, an experimenter, or a survey interviewer. They are his personal reference scale for appraising the stimulus domain in question.

To the extent that the object of the attitude is socially relevant, individuals belonging to the same group or culture will share rather similar attitudes; hence, each individual's own categories are not necessarily unique to him. The bounds of their acceptances will vary within a range defining the "proper," the "acceptable," and the "desirable" ways of viewing the stimulus domain and of behaving toward it in their group or society. This range of positions defined as acceptable, plus a range of positions defining what is unacceptable in a group or society, represents one social norm in their set of values or norms, which is an important aspect of its culture.

The Own Categories Procedure begins with the preparation of a set of items relevant to an attitude. These items may be objects, pictures, or verbal statements about some topic or issue. Their content may vary; however, the logic of the procedures need not change with the content. Major criteria in assembling the pool of items will be specified later. In research thus far, the number of items has varied from 25 to more than 100.

The individual's task is simple and natural in any culture where sorting objects is a familiar task. He is instructed to sort the pool of items into any number of piles, or categories, that seems to him necessary, so that items within each category seem to him to "belong together." The dimension or attribute which he is to judge is specified clearly. For some research purposes, he is told to categorize them in terms of their acceptability to him.

If, however, the aim is a "disguised" or "indirect" test of his attitudes, instructions are used that do not arouse his awareness that his stand is under the scrutiny of a stranger, or researcher. He is then told to place the items into categories as objectively as possible in terms of how "favorable" or "unfavorable" the items are toward the persons, events, issues or objects in question. For example, he may be told to categorize statements concerning Negro citizens of the United States in terms of their "favorableness" to the status of the Negro. One extreme category is specified in instructions; for example, "Put the statements most unfavorable to Negroes in the first pile." Otherwise, utmost caution is used to avoid hints as to the number of categories to be used, and the individual is free to distribute the items into categories in any way he chooses.

When his task is completed to his satisfaction, the individual is usually asked to order his categories. He may be asked to label or describe them, either in terms of the explicit criterion stated in instructions or in terms of their acceptability-unacceptability to him personally. These variations depend upon the research purpose and hypotheses.

THEORETICAL BASIS OF THE PROCEDURE

The present approach started with the search for reference scales that are psychologically and socially valid for the study of attitude and attitude change. In an unpublished study in 1948 (Sherif, Volkart, and Hovland), we found that the bounds of the positions accepted and rejected on a social issue vary, even for persons holding the same position as most acceptable. A series of studies on a variety of social issues over the last fifteen years has confirmed the early finding, namely that the ranges of the positions that an individual accepts, rejects, and toward which he remains noncommittal (when not required to evaluate every position) vary systematically according to his personal involvement in the issue (Sherif and Hovland, 1961; Sherif, Sherif, and Nebergall, 1965). There is a high probability that the individual who endorses an extreme position will rank that issue high in importance, within his scheme of personal priorities. But those adopting a moderate position with equal ardor display patterns of acceptance-rejection-noncommitment similar to their more extreme counterparts.

Specifically, we found that individuals highly involved in some stand on a social issue reject many more positions than they accept and readily evaluate almost every position as acceptable *or* objectionable. (Their *latitudes of rejection* are approximately twice the size of their *latitudes of acceptance*, and noncommitment approaches zero.) Proportional to his lack of involvement, the number of positions the individual accepts and rejects become approximately equal and his latitude of noncommitment increases. This means that highly involved persons have a much broader latitude of rejection than persons less concerned and that they remain noncommittal toward fewer positions, even when not required to evaluate all of them.

What psychological principles underlie these differences in the size of the individual's latitudes for acceptance, rejection, and noncommitment? We had no factual basis for positing a typology of individuals as to the range of their tolerance or for unmeasurable "psychodynamic mechanisms" that would account for the different patterns. We still have no such evidence. We sought a theoretical basis for the phenomena sufficiently broad to encompass the considerable factual evidence that a particular individual may tolerate differences on issues of little concern to him—to the point of self-contradiction—while seeing a matter of high personal concern in terms of "black and white." There is also evidence that the ranges for toleration and condemnation vary from one human group to another.

We found such a basis in the psychology of judgment, studied for decades in psychological laboratories in various countries. Our account of the principles essential to the present approach is necessarily brief and sketchy (see Sherif and Sherif, 1956; Sherif and Hovland, 1961; Sherif, Sherif, and Nebergall, 1965). Whether the object of judgment is a weight, the length of a line, a person's skin color, or a girl's beauty, judgment is rendered relative to the immediate stimulus context in which it appears and to preceding contexts.

For example, quite apart from one's attitude on the issue of the segregation of public schools according to skin color or national origin, a statement such as "We must keep the future interests of school children in mind" is appraised differently when preceded by other statements opposed to segregation, on the one hand, or favoring segregation, on the other.

But not all the stimuli present or just preceding a judgment have equal weight in affecting the outcome, even in the psychophysical laboratory where the stimuli are motivationally neutral. In the orthodox psychophysical methods, the standard stimulus presented with each new stimulus for comparison is more influential than others less frequently presented or not designated as a standard (Helson, 1959, p. 591). Such frequently presented stimuli, or those designated as standards, become anchors for the individual's judgments. Lacking an explicit standard, the individual typically uses the most extreme stimuli presented to him as anchors in sizing up the intermediate values; the end stimuli thus contribute more than others to his judgment of a particular member of the series (Parducci, 1963).

An anchor stimulus or a designated standard enhances the accuracy of judgment for items coinciding with it in value, but it produces systematic shifts or "displacements" in judgments of objects differing from it in varying degrees. An anchor differing slightly from the object of judgment results in displacement *toward* the anchor. This is an *assimilation effect*, well known in studies of perception and now established in judgment (see Sherif, Taub, and Hovland, 1958; Parducci and Marshall, 1962; Helson, 1964). With increasing discrepancies between the anchor and the object of judgment, assimilation ceases and displacement begins to occur in a direction away from the anchor; the difference between the anchor and the object is exaggerated. This is the well-known *contrast effect*. Assimilation and contrast in judgment are complementary phenomena governed by the relationships between anchor and object of judgment.

In 1950, a series of studies was initiated to clarify the differences and similarities between judgments of neutral and socially relevant items, ranging from experiments with lifted weights to studies of the scale values of attitudinal statements. On this basis, a conceptual approach was developed that does account for the distinctive patterning of latitudes of acceptance-rejection and that provides the theoretical basis of the Own Categories Procedure. The approach is based on the relationships governing assimilation-contrast effects, taking into account the following generalizations:

A. If a person has an attitude toward the stimulus domain, his judgments of specific objects in that domain are, to some extent, relative to the categories of his own reference scale, in addition to the context of immediate and preceding stimulation.

B. To the extent that the domain has high priority in his scheme of personal relatedness with his social world, his latitude of acceptance becomes an anchor or standard for his placement of other items in the domain. In other words, the range of positions acceptable to him becomes an anchor proportional to his personal involvement in upholding it.

C. To the extent that his own position becomes the most salient anchor in the situation, the individual's categorization of items is *evaluation* of the items. There is now a considerable body of research supporting this statement (Sherif, Sherif, and Nebergall, 1965). Even when instructed to heed only the stimulus attributes of the items and categorize them on an impersonal dimension, the highly involved individual performs the task in terms of his agreements-disagreements with the items, including his assessments of their truth and falsity. One may temporarily force him to follow instructions by insisting that he compare one item with another, as in the method of paired comparisons. He *can* discriminate among the items but, barring special arrangements requiring him to do so, he simply does not divorce the task of judging the items from his evaluations of them.

D. When his own stand is the anchor, other items will be displaced toward his acceptable category (*assimilation*) or away from it (*contrast*), proportional to their proximity or difference from his own stand. The additional, necessary condition for these systematic displacements is that the objects lack, in some degree, objective properties which are readily and uniformly perceived as defining membership in a particular category. For example, strongly worded statements of an extreme position on a social issue are not displaced systematically to any significant degree. They are readily identified as extreme positions in terms of the prevailing social realities. Systematic displacements are found, however, for less extreme and intermediate positions on the same issues.

With these four additions, the theoretical approach accounts for the phenomena which are used to study attitudes with the Own Categories Procedure.

RESEARCH USING THE OWN CATEGORIES PROCEDURE

Using this conceptualization, Sherif and Hovland (1953) predicted that individuals strongly involved in problems of the status of Negro citizens would (1) use fewer categories for judging statements on the issue than less involved individuals, and (2) place fewer statements in the category of items most acceptable to them than in the category most objectionable to them. The subjects were highly involved Negro students (who were the first admitted to a previously white university), active white participants in the desegregation movement, Negroes at a segregated university, a few consistently anti-Negro whites, and un-selected white students. They sorted 114 statements prepared by Hinck-ley as the preliminary pool for item selection for a Thurstone attitude scale. The pool contained pro-Negro and anti-Negro statements with a large number of intermediate items having high Q values (high vari-ability). The statements were sorted by the Own Categories Procedure, either two weeks before or two weeks after the same subjects judged them using eleven categories as prescribed in the Thurstone "equal-appearing intervals" method (Hovland and Sherif, 1952).

They found that highly involved persons, judging these statements in terms of their favorableness-unfavorableness to Negroes, produced bimodal distributions of the statements into categories: Intermediate categories were neglected, while a disproportionate number of items was placed in the extreme category farthest removed from the position the individual found acceptable. The bimodal distribution was greatly accentuated under the Own Categories Procedure because of the sig-nificant tendency for highly involved persons to use fewer categories. In fact, the most militant Negro subjects, on the average, used fewer than four categories, placing 65 of the 114 statements in a single cate-gory highly objectionable to them and 27 in a category acceptable to them. In comparison, unselected white students placed 43 statements in objectionable categories and 38 in categories they later indicated were acceptable.

Using a combined index of skewness of the judgment distribution and number of categories, Sherif and Hovland found that these two measures differentiated between their subject groups according to their personal involvement in the problem of the status of Negroes. Propor-tional to their involvement, their threshold for acceptance was raised; this was indicated by a smaller mode in the distribution of judgments in acceptable categories. Their threshold of rejection was lowered; this was indicated by the disproportionately high mode of the distribution of categories they later said were objectionable. These peaks in the dis-tribution reveal the individual's acceptable and objectionable categories, the objectionable category being wider.

LATITUDE OF ACCEPTANCE AS ANCHOR IN EVALUATION

Carolyn W. Sherif (1961) compared the evaluative and non-evalu-ative categories of American Indian and white high school students of comparable educational level. Since the ranges of acceptable items varied according to their cultural backgrounds in several respects, it was pos-sible to show contrasting evaluations of the same items by the Indian and white students according to their latitudes of acceptance, while demonstrating that their categorizations of neutral items did not differ.

Using the Own Categories Procedure, each individual sorted four sets of items. The Indian and white students categorized series of digits

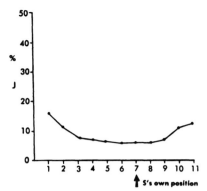

FIGURE 1. Distribution of percentages of judgments by moderate, less ego-involved subjects on the social position of Negroes, using imposed categories. Number of imposed categories = 11. (From Hovland and Sherif, 1952.)

Imposed categories from the category most unfavorable (1) to category most favorable (11), the arrow indicating the own position of subjects.

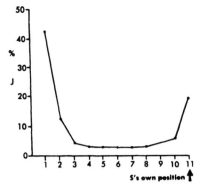

FIGURE 2. Distribution of percentages of judgments by highly ego-involved subjects on the social position of Negroes, using imposed categories. Number of imposed categories = 11.

Imposed categories for subjects whose own position was category 11 (most favorable to Negroes). Note the neglect of intermediate categories and the greatest mode at the extreme opposite to their own position.

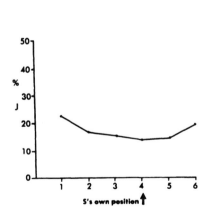

FIGURE 3. Distribution of percentages of judgments by less ego-involved subjects on the social position of Negroes with the Own Categories Procedure (adapted from Sherif and Hovland, 1953).

Subjects using 6 categories with Own Categories Procedure. The Own Categories range from most unfavorable (1) to most favorable to Negroes (6). Note that the distribution is fairly even as in Figure 1.

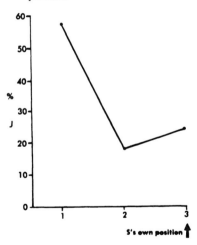

FIGURE 4. Distribution of percentages of judgments by highly ego-involved subjects on the social position of Negroes using the Own Categories Procedure (adapted from Sherif and Hovland, 1953).

Subjects using 3 categories in Own Categories Procedure. Note the accentuation of the bimodality in Figure 2 owing to the greatly reduced number of categories used by the subjects.

(numbers) in comparable fashion, attempting to fit the items into equal categories according to the decimal system. Their categories for *evaluating* the same digits when preceded by dollar signs differed significantly from these; differences between the Indians and whites were significant.

Having previously conducted a cultural survey, Sherif (1963) knew that the prevailing bounds for acceptable expenditures of money differed. For example, reflecting an elaborate tradition of gift-giving in their culture, Indians considered much larger sums of money necessary for an appropriate gift than whites did, but deemed much smaller sums acceptable for wearing apparel than whites did. When evaluating the series of numbers as dollar values, their latitude of acceptance was the main anchor, with the result that their evaluative categories were highly unequal when the range of prices exceeded acceptable bounds. To the extent that the price range was beyond acceptable bounds, the discrepant items were lumped together in one category as extremely objectionable.

This experiment showed that the "relativity of judgment" is not solely in terms of the immediate and preceding stimulus context of judgment but is also affected by the individual's own categories for what is acceptable and objectionable whenever *evaluations* are rendered. For this reason, the Own Categories Procedure is suitable for assessing similarities and differences in reference scales prevailing in different cultures even when the objects of evaluation are not extremely involving to the individuals.

SALIENCE OF ATTITUDINAL ANCHORS VARIES WITH DEGREE OF INVOLVEMENT

Carolyn W. Sherif's study also showed that the number of categories used varied systematically according to the individual's relative involvement with the four different sets of items. On the average, all subjects used more categories for the digits than they did for series of socially valued items. The three sets of socially valued items were ranked in personal importance by a paired comparisons procedure. The number of categories used in evaluating them differed, in turn, according to their rank in personal importance.

More categories were used for the monetary values than for descriptions of interpersonal behavior, and the fewest categories were used for assessing the desirability of interpersonal contact with members of different ethnic groups. An intraclass correlation of .38 for the number of categories used by the same individuals for the four different materials was significant, but sufficiently low to indicate that most of the variance was accountable to the differing personal relevance of the item content.

A recent experiment by Glixman (1965) with different subjects and stimulus materials supports this conclusion. He reported that individuals used fewer categories in appraising descriptive statements about themselves than in sorting familiar objects, even though a much larger number of the self-descriptions was presented. He also reported correlation coefficients for individual consistency in number of categories used for three item contents, which vary around 0.35 for his different subject samples.

It may be objected that significant differences in number of categories used by the same individuals in categorizing sets of items that differ in personal import are confounded by differences in the stimulus material itself—by the experimenter's incapacity to equate the range of the domains in question, and so on. The objection is appropriate. In this connection, a research thesis by John Reich (1963) directed by M. Sherif is pertinent.

Reich studied the own categories of mature women between the ages of 35 and 50, with median years of schooling exceeding four years of university study. The attitude in question concerned legislative reapportionment. As a result of the growth of urban areas, the number of representatives to the state legislature from different districts no longer represented the relative sizes of their populations. Reich secured active members of the League of Women Voters, which had dedicated its major efforts to remedying this situation, as individuals highly involved in the issue. The less involved subjects were women schoolteachers, who also favored reapportionment but were not particularly concerned with the issue, as indicated by lack of overt acts and expressions of opinion. The two samples were matched by age and education as closely as possible.

Persons who *opposed* reapportionment changed their stands during the study. A federal court ruling that the legislature *must* reapportion shifted the anti-reapportionment subjects to a pro-reapportionment position according to an out-moded formula which no one had supported up to that time. We mention this change to emphasize that the individual's own categories are inevitably tied, to some extent, to the reference scales prevailing in the social realities of his time and place. Similar shifts in the positions on psychosocial scales have been observed in the United States over the past century by groups favoring and opposing a federal income tax and, more recently, desegregation of public facilities.

From a pool of 120 statements on the issue of reapportionment, Reich chose 60 from pretests with 79 subjects. Fifteen were consistently judged as *pro,* fifteen consistently as *anti,* and thirty had been judged with high variability. In categorizing these sixty statements by the Own Categories Procedure, 74 per cent of the highly involved women used four or fewer categories, while only 26 per cent of the teachers used such a small number. The less involved teachers placed about the same number of statements in favorable and unfavorable categories, but the highly involved League members placed over half of the statements in unfavorable categories, which they found extremely objectionable.

The League members saw the issue in "black and white," and

mostly "black," despite the fact that they were equally well educated and highly conversant with the complexities of legislative reapportionment. Because of their superior information on the issue, they doubtless *could* have made finer discriminations than the teachers. The fact is, that given the opportunity to categorize the positions in their own way, they did *not* make fine discriminations.

THE CRUCIAL ROLE OF THE INTERMEDIATE ITEMS

An earlier study of La Fave and Sherif (1962) provided convincing evidence that the distinctively bimodal distributions of judgments obtained by the Own Categories Procedure occurred through systematic displacements of the intermediate items. Twenty-five items on the issue of desegregation of public facilities were selected through pretests in order to have five representatives in each of the following classes: Very Integrationist, Integrationist, Moderate, Segregationist, and Very Segregationist. Variability in placement of the items in the two extreme categories was low. Three samples judged the position of these 25 statements under the Own Categories instructions.

The highly involved, favorable subjects were 95 Negroes from a state Negro university in the southwest; the least involved were 144 unselected white undergraduate students in a desegregated university. In an effort to secure highly involved, anti-Negro subjects, 78 members of a college fraternity with strong ties to southern tradition were used. The fraternity members, however, were a heterogeneous lot, as noted in the next section.

Owing to the small number of items (25), variations in number of categories used were less than in other studies previously cited. However, 92 per cent of the Negro subjects used four or fewer categories, and fully 68 per cent used three or fewer. In comparison, 46 per cent of the unselected white students used five or more categories for the 25 items. Of the southern fraternity members, 77 per cent used four or fewer categories.

Over 87 per cent of Negroes placed more items in categories which they labeled as favoring segregation than in those favoring desegregation. Among southern fraternity members, the distribution was reversed by 59 per cent of the sample; that is, more judgments were made as favoring desegregation. Unselected white students distributed their judgments more evenly, 55 per cent of them placing equal numbers of items in favorable and unfavorable categories.

Tracing down the items responsible for the bimodal distributions of most Negro and a majority of southern fraternity members, La Fave and Sherif were able to show that they occurred through systematic displacements of thirteen statements which were intermediate to the extremes and had high Q values. The Negro subjects, using fewer categories, accumulated such statements in categories unfavorable to integration—a contrast effect relative to their own pro-integration stand. The southern fraternity members, a majority of whom opposed integration, accumulated such statements in categories favoring integration—again a contrast effect.

This research shows the importance of one of the major requirements in preparing a pool of items for the Own Categories Procedures: The array must include, between the extremes, a large number of items which are "intermediate" in position or are ambiguous in their position with respect to the extremes. Judgments of such items are characterized by great variability. They are, in short, items that are typically discarded in the construction of most conventional attitude tests as too variable.

Studies by Zimbardo (1960) and La Fave *et al.* (1963) show that the characteristics of such items that make them subject to systematic displacement according to the individual's attitude are not adequately described simply as "ambiguity" and that the inclusion of adjectives with positive or negative connotation reduces variability in placement. The items we have found most suitable are those representing positions on an issue which are not well-known, positions which are the object of wide disagreement (for example, "neutrality" on a "hot" intergroup or international issue), and statements whose meaning is "indeterminate." An example of the latter is borrowed from Zimbardo's study (1960) of university students majoring in science or in the humanities, namely: "Anyone who has known a scientist personally will know why science is where it is today."

The second major requirement for preparing a pool of items is that the range or variety should be large, including extreme positions on social issues or, in cross-cultural comparisons of reference scales, covering a range beyond usual experience and tradition. This requirement reflects the fact that the particular range of values presented for judgment does affect the placement of particular items.

For example, Carolyn Sherif (1961) found that Indian and white students used narrower categories, thus discriminated more keenly, when presented a range of items that were largely acceptable to them than when objectionable items were also included. This corresponds to the well-known tendency to see fine shades of difference when dealing with friends or allies, but to ignore many of these differences when one's friends are compared with enemies.

COMPARISON OF FINDINGS FOR AND AGAINST
THE OBJECT OF ATTITUDE

In the studies reviewed thus far, the use of few categories and the bimodal distributions of items in them have been shown most decisively for individuals who uphold stands intensely favorable toward the objects. The practical reason for this deserves comment. In selecting highly involved subjects, we have relied as much as possible on their known public actions and statements on the issue in question. Particularly in relation to the Negro issue, it has not been possible to obtain subjects who publicly state and act upon an anti-Negro position.

In an effort to remedy this lack, we have used not one but a combination of criteria for an *anti* position, including conventional paper-and-pencil tests of attitude toward the Negro, self-ratings, and observation of behavior. On the basis of these criteria, we found that only 41 of the 78 southern fraternity members could be classified as consistently anti-Negro.

The inconsistencies we have found were traceable to self-reports of attitude *or* paper-and-pencil tests. The explanation is not complex. There is a collegiate norm, which prevails among students in all but a few places, that makes an open stand against the Negro simply "not the thing to do." In their self-ratings and paper-and-pencil tests, aware that the researcher is interested in their attitudes, many individuals respond in terms of the *researcher's expectations,* rather than in terms of their views—which they subsequently belie through anti-Negro statements to friends and sympathizers. The "social desirability" (Edwards, 1957) of their responses is the salient consideration in the research situation. Avoidance of this problem is a major advantage of the Own Categories Procedure, since it may be presented as a completely "objective" task to the subject.

In view of the lack in other studies, the use of overtly *anti* subjects by Kathryn Vaughan (1961) is particularly significant. Vaughan conducted her study near the United States-Mexican border, where persons of Mexican origin compose a substantial portion of the population, and in another part of the same state about 600 miles north, where such persons are not common. In the vernacular, persons of Mexican origin or descent are called "Latins" (a more polite term than some others) and non-Latins are "Anglos."

Replicating the Sherif-Hovland study (1952, 1953), Vaughan compared the placements of statements about Latins, with eleven categories prescribed in instructions and with the Own Categories Procedure. She constructed a pool of 103 statements, selecting sixty which were composed of five sub-sets—two sub-sets consistently placed at the extremes, two with moderate variability but scale values on either a favorable or unfavorable side, and one sub-set with extremely high variability.

The results for the eleven instructed categories represent a striking mirror image of those found for Negro and pro-Negro whites in the Hovland-Sherif study (1952). Intermediate categories were neglected by intensely anti-Latins, their extreme category for pro-Latin statements was very broad, and a smaller mode in the distribution of judgments occurred at the extreme anti-Latin end, with which they agreed. Residents of the area with sparse Latin population, and little concern with it, distributed their judgments fairly evenly over the eleven categories.

The same trends were greatly accentuated using the Own Categories Procedure. Over 85 per cent of the anti-Latins used three or fewer categories, while almost 92 per cent of the uninvolved subjects used four or more categories. The range was two to five categories for involved anti-Latins and two to eleven for uninvolved subjects, but only 8 per cent of the latter used three categories or fewer.

Vaughan at no time requested any statement as to which categories were acceptable or objectionable to the subjects, but she reported that many of the highly anti-Latin persons had great difficulty in following instructions to categorize the statements objectively as favorable-unfavorable to Latins. They kept insisting that many of the statements were "not true," and they had all sorts of "facts" to prove it. This observation represents the considerable evidence that the individual's Own Categories for acceptance-rejection do serve as the reference scale for his placements, even when he is warned not to use them, providing the object of judgment is important to him.

CONCLUDING REMARKS

The Own Categories Procedure does not suffer from certain limitations of most available techniques for attitude measurement. Its logic does not derive from statistical or physical models for measurement, but from widely general principles of psychological functioning.

The task required of the individual does not presume a common culture or educational level, but is applicable with changed content to any cultural setting where objects are sorted.

It may be used in the study of attitudes without arousing the individual's awareness that *his attitude* is being explored for research purposes.

It yields quantitative measures both for the location of his acceptable and most objectionable categories and his degree of involvement in the matter. A restricted number of categories with the greatest mode in the judgment distribution at the objectionable segment and a secondary mode at the acceptable segment is typical of highly involved persons. To the extent that the individual is little involved in the matter at hand, his distribution of the items approaches more equal divisions into a greater number of categories. In this event, the acceptable and objectionable categories may be ascertained *after* he has sorted them, from the labels he uses for the various categories.

When appropriate for the research purposes, the individual may be asked directly to evaluate the objects in terms of his acceptances-rejections. By varying the stimulus material, it is possible to assess individuals' categories relative to those prevailing in their own and different cultural groups and to predict their reactions to cultural items deviating from their latitudes of acceptance. In fact, we believe that findings on the individual's own categories will have much greater predictive value than most conventional tests yielding a single position to represent the individual's attitude.

For example, in our study of reactions to communications on the 1960 presidential election we found that highly committed partisans of the major parties judged a communication mildly favoring their opponent as much more extreme than it was—contrasting it to their own position by displacing it *away* from their own position. Less involved persons adopting the *same* position as most acceptable assimilated the identical communication *toward* their own position. This finding is predictable when one knows that the less involved person has a more finely differentiated set of categories and that he is noncommittal toward those in the segment of positions presented by the speaker. The highly involved person, on the other hand, has very broad categories, including one or more for objectionable positions, and his latitude of rejection covers moderate positions.

In our opinion, the use of similar theory and procedures for the study of reactions to sociocultural change and innovation is one of the most exciting among several problems to be explored through the Own Categories Procedure.

PART V

EXPERIMENTAL AND
FIELD RESEARCH:
MAN IN IN-GROUP AND
INTERGROUP RELATIONS

NINETEEN

THE NECESSITY OF CONSIDERING CURRENT ISSUES AS PART AND PARCEL OF PERSISTENT MAJOR PROBLEMS

In psychology, the sharp demarcation between the "pure" and "applied," between academic austerity and concern with consequential events of everyday life seems to be losing its high-handed grip. The impact of recent momentous events and the demands of actual social life for academic people to deliver the goods have been so compelling that the scholar can no longer afford to move "in the domain of bare existence," as Titchener put it. Research psychologists in industrial, genetic, social and other fields of psychology, including those working in the traditional field of sensation, are earnestly engaged today in studies which have direct bearing on the practice of day-to-day affairs.

Evidence of this healthy trend is particularly prevalent in social psychology, perhaps because the most controversial and consequential problems of today's unsettled and critical world are *social*. The effects of technological, economic, political and military events are unmistakably reflected in the unstable and strife-ridden relationships of the small and large social units. Problems of war and peace, of autocracy and democracy, of the impact of atomic energy, problems of inter- and intra-group relationships, of prejudice, of the individual in social change, of attitudes concerning every conceivable topic obtained through a host of public opinion and academic organizations, are among the front-line topics of study for social psychologists today.

Yet, in spite of this flourishing concern over current social problems, it cannot be said that we are close to having a consistent social psychology which actually has weight in the formulation of *lasting* practical policy. Consequently, the studies, in general, stand as separate patches, each with its merits and demerits. On the whole, such studies become the talk of the town, with a varying radius of circulation and

From *International Journal of Opinion and Attitude Research*, 1948, 2: 63–68.

effect, only to be shelved in the library when the run of events brings
other issues to the spotlight. It may be that such undertakings would
have more than seasonal significance if they were conceived and executed in full view of the persistent major problems. For the specific
content of such problems may change, but the variables at work persist
in spite of variations in time and locality. If such studies are then related to the concepts which recur as central in our field, instead of
being stated only in terms peculiar to the scope of the issue at hand,
they would contribute to the accumulation of a unified body of social
psychology, thus in a larger way enhancing their own effectiveness in
social life. In short, the thesis of this paper is that the good will which
leads investigators to tackle the study of current social issues will in
the long run reach further if the issue at hand is first related to persistent problems and then formulated in terms of central concepts of
psychology. In this brief paper I can illustrate the point in a summary
way by considering only one topic from several possible good ones. I
happened to choose the topic of *prejudice*.

Undoubtedly due to its consequential effects in human relationships, a great deal of work has been done on the topic of prejudice
against various groups. It is safe to assume that there cannot be separate psychologies of prejudice in relation to this or that group, but that
they are specific cases of the general picture of prejudice. This general
picture of prejudice is, in turn, part and parcel of the psychology of
social attitudes and of identifications. It seems to me that the studies
and the practical measures proposed and tried out here and there to
stamp out prejudice will gain real weight as a field of research and
greater effectiveness in practice, if, *at every step,* they are related to
and appraised in the light of the persistent and basic findings in the
psychology of *attitudes,* the psychology of *ego development,* and of
groups.

What is this general picture of prejudice? In a few sentences, only
a general statement can be given, glossing over all the observed variations and necessary modifications. Any observer who has lived in different countries with traditionally established human relationships cannot
help but notice that each social group has its peculiar scale of prejudice
or social distance. Unfortunately, so far the quantitative work has been
done only in one country—namely, in America. Therefore, we can speak
more definitely about the American scene.

The investigations of Bogardus (1933), Guilford (1931), F. H.
Allport and Katz (1931), Hartley (1946), and others, carried out over
a period of years using different methods, indicate that there is a
rather well-established scale of social distance or prejudice for the
country, cutting across regional, ethnic and occupational differences
on the whole. Near the top of the scale come Americans, Canadians
and English. Then follow the French, Norwegians and other Northern

Europeans. Southern Europeans, such as Italians and Spanish, and then Jews follow in descending order. At the bottom of the hierarchy are placed Negroes, Hindus, Chinese and Turks. The exact standing of each group may change within narrow limits, but in general they fall within the same segment of the scale. One exception occurs in the social distance scales reported by members of the groups whose places are low on the established scale. They tend to place their own special group high, keeping the rest of the scale intact. This indicates that they are ego-involved first in their own groups and then as members of the country as a whole. It may be that by so doing the members of discriminated groups also are contributing their bit to the perpetuation of the existing scale of prejudice.

The values on the scale, which may be designated as *positive* at the top and *negative* at the bottom, are revealed as so many corresponding *attitudes* in terms of single individuals. As is the case with all attitudes, attitudes of social distance render individuals possessing them highly selective in their reactions (positively or negatively) in relation to the members of groups in question. When individuals come into contact with members of the various groups who do not fit into the expectations produced by their place on the scale, the tendency, on the whole, is to regard these members as exceptions or deviations while keeping the scale intact.

Evidence seems to indicate that attitudes of prejudice are not built up on the basis of contact with members of the groups in question, but are derived from the prevailing social distance scale in one's own group (e.g., Lasker, 1929; Hartley, 1948). That is, an individual's prejudices are acquired as he becomes a member of his group. In other words, the attitudes of prejudice, as well as other attitudes, are *learned*. An adequate psychology of learning will ultimately give us the basic principles underlying the attitude of prejudice as well as other attitudes. In the meantime, social psychologists have to stress the theoretical and practical implications of the following findings.

Genetically, prejudice is manifested in a *consistent* way only after the child has developed and learned to grasp the actual scheme of social distances and proximities in his surroundings. As the studies of the Hartleys and Clarks (1939, 1940) have shown, the behavior of very young children toward members of socially stigmatized groups is first kept in line by grownups. Increasingly with age comes an awareness of one's own group and other groups and their relative positions in the existing scheme of social relationships. It is no coincidence that this increasing awareness and increasingly *consistent* manifestation of a scale of prejudice occurs during the stage when the child is becoming able to participate actively in group activities—that is, when he can *psychologically* become a member of a group. At this stage too, his prejudiced reactions result not merely from the dictates of his grownups, but from the approvals and disapprovals, and the pressures of his play and school groups, and from *himself*. The social distance scale, acquired from his groups, becomes so much a part of himself—of his ego—that the individual usually becomes unaware of their derivations but considers them his own (Hartley). In this sense, the positive and negative values of the social distance scale of his group become *ego-distances* of the individual members. In short, the formation of attitudes of prejudice is one aspect of ego formation.

The above considerations, stated in a nutshell form, lead us to conclude that the attitude of prejudice is a product of *group membership*. It is produced in the individual member in the same way as his other attitudes—for example, his attitude toward a flag, family, school and work. In order to become a member of his group in good standing, he is bound to share the prejudices of the group as well as its positive values, if a scale of prejudice exists in his membership group. If he does not share these prejudices existing in the group, that is, does not observe certain discriminations and behave accordingly, he becomes a *deviant* or non-conformist. A great majority of the individuals in every group certainly strive to become members in good standing, especially at times of greater social stability. The findings of the representative studies (such as Hartley's [see Horowitz 1936, 1937] and Murphy and Likert's, 1938) that the effect of *contact* with the members of discriminated groups is negligible and that correlations between *information* and prejudice are rather insignificant are among the weighty substantiations of the above conclusion. The fact that there is positive correlation between being a non-conformist or "dissident" and freedom from prejudice in a social scene where the scale of social distance exists adds its weight in the same direction. The finding of Allport and Kramer (1946) and a 1947 survey in Berlin that the degree of religious observance and the degree of prejudice go together (*Herald Tribune*, 1947) become perfectly intelligible in the light of the indication of the above material.

At this point, the converging findings of psychologists and sociologists concerning the properties and products of group interaction, positive and negative "in-group" and "out-group" relationships become handy. The experience and behavior of the *identified* member reflects the properties and products of his membership group. Once the "in-group" and "out-group" delineation becomes an accentuated affair, the individual member reveals characteristic attitudes appropriate to the norms standardized for "in-group" and "out-group" relationships. If the relationship between the "in-group" and "out-group" is integrated and positive, the standardized attitude toward the "out-group" in question and the members thereof is favorable; if not integrated, it is unfavorable. The individual member, on the whole, simply has to conform to these standardized relationships in order to achieve and retain a status in his group, which is of greater importance to him than bits of information and bits of personal experience and occasional dictates of his good will. In the works of Thrasher, Zorbaugh, Clifford Shaw, Landesco, Whyte and others, one finds a mine of significant evidence to this effect. It becomes evident, then, that the core of the perpetuation or change of the existing scale of prejudice lies in the integration or lack of integration of the direction and interest of group relationships; and in terms of single individuals, in his conformity or non-conformity to the norms of his group. The most striking substantiation of this finding came out in Newcomb's comprehensive Bennington study, which is perhaps the most effective investigation of attitude change to date. To summarize the main findings of the study in a few words, the presence or absence of change of attitude and the degree thereof is a function of the degree of the individual's assimilation to the atmosphere of the new community.

On the basis of these findings, it may be said that current studies concerned with individual differences in the manifestation of prejudice may gain much if they place their subjects *first* as members of a social group and keep the implications of this group membership in mind at every step of their analysis. The degree of prejudice manifested by a single individual acquires specific significance only in relation to a scale of prejudice—which is a group product. From the practical point of view, the individual manifests acts of prejudice because of a social background of prejudice. Otherwise, he would be prevented from these acts or even punished or ostracized by his own group. People commit harmful acts under some stress or tension against persons for whom they have no prejudice. If we call every evil act prejudice, prejudice ceases to have any consistent meaning.

In conclusion, it seems that there is a disparity between the indications of the representative research material and the efforts of those who are concerned with the current problems of prejudice and who are trying to deal with them in terms of propagation of information and increased individual contact or in terms of transitory group situations which are ineffective in bringing about lasting changes in the attitudes of the individual. This disparity points to the necessity of pulling together the items of practical concern and the indications of converging lines of persistent problems. With a comprehensive approach thus achieved, the efforts of men of good will to eliminate prejudice may be rendered less wasteful in the long run.

TWENTY

INTEGRATING FIELD WORK AND LABORATORY
IN SMALL GROUP RESEARCH

The study of small groups has become one of the most flourishing areas of research, involving men in various social sciences and psychology. The influences responsible for the increased preoccupation with small groups spring both from developments within various academic disciplines and from agencies instituted for devising practical solutions for immediate application. Brief mention of influences contributing to the flourishing state of affairs in small group research will be helpful as orientation:

1. Theoretically and empirically, works of sociologists have historical priority in showing persistent concern with the topic of small groups (Faris, 1953). Since the early 1920's a definite research development in sociology related to small groups has been carried on, as represented by the works of men like Thrasher, Anderson, Clifford Shaw, Zorbaugh, Hiller, and Whyte. In the recurrent findings reported in this line of research, which was carried out over a period of a good many years, one cannot help finding crucial leads for a realistic approach to experimentation in this area.

2. Another group of the major instigators of the extraordinary volume of small group research stems from the practical concern of business and military agencies. A series of studies initiated by Elton Mayo and his associates at the Harvard Business School in the late 1920's has proliferated in various institutions, both academic and technological. Another impetus along this line came from the concern of military agencies for establishing effective techniques for the assessment of leaders.

3. Another major influence in the development of small group studies comes from psychological research. Regardless of the theoretical treatment, the results of psychological experiments almost always showed differential effects on behavior when individuals undertook an activity

From *American Sociological Review* (1954), 19: 759–771. Special Issue on Small Groups. Reprinted with permission of the American Sociological Association.

in relation to other individuals or even in their presence, as can be ascertained readily by a glance at Murphy, Murphy, and Newcomb's *Experimental Social Psychology*. F. H. Allport's experiments which started around 1915 are illustrative of this point. In the 1930's, it became increasingly evident that social behavior (cooperation-competition, ascendance-submission, etc.) could not be properly studied when the individual is considered in isolation. Psychological "trait" theories or personality typologies fell far short in explaining social relations. Therefore, when Moreno's work appeared in this country in the mid-thirties presenting his sociometric technique for the study of interpersonal choices and reciprocities among individuals (i.e., role relations), it quickly found wide application. A few years later Kurt Lewin and his associates demonstrated the weighty determination of individual behavior by the properties of group atmosphere. This line of experimentation was the basis of other subsequent studies coming from the proponents of the Group Dynamics school. Some other major influences coming from psychology will be mentioned later.

INTERDISCIPLINARY COOPERATION AND THE CONCEPT OF "LEVELS"

It becomes apparent even from a brief mention of the background that men from various disciplines contributed to make the study of small groups the going concern that it is today. As a consequence there is diversity of emphasis in formulating problems and hypotheses, and diversity in concepts used. This state of affairs has brought about considerable elbow-rubbing and interdisciplinary bickering among sociologists, psychologists, and anthropologists. In this process and through critical appraisal of each others' approaches, the interdisciplinary approach has become a necessity for achieving a rounded picture.

Faced with the task of dealing with both psychological and sociocultural factors in human relations problems, psychologists have too often yielded to the temptation of improvising their own "sociologies" in terms of their preferred concepts. Sociologists, on the other hand, have sometimes engaged in psychological improvisations. While sociological or psychological improvisation at times proves necessary on the frontiers of a discipline, it is difficult to justify on topics for which a substantial body of research exists in sociology or in psychology, as the case may be.

On the whole, interdisciplinary cooperation has usually turned out to mean rallying psychologists, sociologists, anthropologists, and other social scientists to toss their theories and concepts into the ring. But, mere juxtaposition of utterances made by psychologists, sociologists, etc., in the same room or between the covers of the same book does not bring interdisciplinary cooperation. Nor is interdisciplinary integration possible by laying down segments from each discipline along the same line—one yard from psychology, one yard from sociology, then a foot each from history and economics.

The outlines of an interdisciplinary approach appear more clearly with the realization that "psychological" and "sociological" signify different levels of analysis. Men studying human relations are approaching related, similar, or even the same problems at different levels of analysis, necessitating units and concepts appropriate for dealing with events on that level. If we are working on the psychological level, our unit of analysis is the *individual*; hence our treatment must be in terms of his psychological functioning—in concepts such as motives, judging, perceiving, learning, remembering, imagining, etc. If we are working on a sociological or cultural level our concepts are in terms of social organization, institutions, value systems, language, kinship systems, art forms, technology, etc.[1]

The concept of levels holds a fairly obvious but invaluable check on the validity of research findings. If it is valid, a generalization reached on a topic at one level of analysis is not contradicted and, in fact, gains support from valid generalizations reached at another level. For example, the psychologist's findings of differential behavior of an individual when participating in the activities of his group should be (and are) substantiated by findings on the sociological level, namely that collective action in a group has properties peculiar to the group. Checking and cross-checking findings obtained at one level against those obtained at another level on the same topic will make interdisciplinary cooperation the integrative meeting ground that it should be.

During the last century in the social sciences and more recently in psychology, the dependence of sub-units upon the setting or superordinate system of which they are parts has gained increased attention, especially in view of unrewarding attempts to account for the functioning system in an additive way. Understanding part processes is possible only through analysis of their relations within the functioning system, as well as by analysis of unique properties of the part process itself. Unless knowledge of the superordinate or larger functioning system is gained first, before tackling the part processes, there is the likelihood of unwarranted generalizations concerning the parts, and misinterpretation of the true functional significance of the processes observed.

In this connection, an illustration from Malinowski (1922) is instructive. Malinowski describes the complex exchange system of the Argonauts of the Western Pacific called the Kula. The Argonauts themselves

---

[1] "The human group is an organization of two or more individuals in a role structure adapted to the performance of a particular function. *As thus defined the group is the unit of sociological analysis*" (Freedman, Hawley, Landecker, and Miner, 1952, p. 143, emphasis added).

have no knowledge of the *total outline* of any of their social structure. . . . Not even the most intelligent native has any clear idea of the Kula as a big, organized social construction, still less of its sociological functions and implications. If you were to ask him what the Kula is, he would answer by giving a few details, most likely by giving his personal experiences and subjective views on the Kula. . . . Not even a partial coherent account could be obtained. For the integral picture does not exist in his mind; he is in it, and cannot see the whole from the outside.

This point can be illustrated in relation to small group studies. Since Lewin's experiments in the 1940's comparing lecture and group discussion methods in changing attitudes, various studies have shown that *in the American setting* skillfully conducted group discussion in which members participate is more effective than lecture presentation of the same material. On the basis of results obtained in the American setting, it would seem that the superiority of group discussion methods might be universal. That this is not the case is indicated by one of the studies in the Unesco project in India (Murphy, 1953). In an attempt to modify caste attitudes among college students in India using various methods, the greatest changes arose as a result of a lecture method using emotional appeals. The experimenter wrote: "Contrary to our original expectation and hypothesis, these young boys do not seem to be in a position to exploit fully the discussion technique, in bettering their social relationships. Does it indicate that our boys have got to be used to the democratic ways of discussion and at present prefer to be told what are the right attitudes rather than to be allowed to talk them out?" Within a social organization whose values clearly encourage dependence on authority and effectively discourage settling issues on a give-and-take basis in small sub-units, particular dependencies may become so much a part of the individual's ego system that group discussion techniques would be less effective than methods more in harmony with the social organization in which they take place.

Such comparative results illustrate the value of starting *first* with due consideration of the sociocultural setting with its organization and values before generalizations are made about small groups functioning as parts of that setting (cf. Whyte, 1951; Arensberg, 1951). For small groups are not closed systems, especially in highly complex and differentiated societies such as the United States.

Facts obtained concerning the group setting are in terms of concepts and units at the social or cultural level of analysis. They will not give the step-by-step analysis of the particular interaction process; they will not be adequate for the task of dealing with interpersonal relations or the behavior of particular individual members. At this point, psychological concepts are needed for a detailed analysis of reciprocal relations, for handling motives, perceptions, judgments, etc.

EXPERIMENTAL STEPS TOWARD INTEGRATION

The rest of the chapter will be devoted to a summary statement of the prior attempts on our part toward pulling together some relevant findings in sociology and in psychology in the study of small groups. In these attempts the guiding considerations have been the following:

1. To extract some minimum generalizations from the sociological findings on small groups on the one hand; on the other, to extract relevant principles from the work coming from the psychological laboratory.

2. To formulate problems and hypotheses relating to one another the indications of the two sets of relevant findings, that is, from sociological and psychological research.

3. To test hypotheses thus derived with methods and techniques which are appropriate for the particular problem—experimental, observational, sociometric, questionnaire, or combinations thereof, as the case may be.

Let us start with the term "small group" itself. The term "small group" is coming to mean all things to all people. If the concept of small groups is considered at the outset, research on small groups will gain a great deal in the way of selection of focal problems for investigation, and hence effective concentration of efforts.

"Small group" may mean simply small numbers of individuals. If this is the criterion, any small number of individuals in a *togetherness situation* would be considered a small group. But a conception of small groups in terms of numbers alone ignores the properties of actual small groups which have made their study such a going concern today.

One of the objectives of concentrating on small group research should be attainment of valid generalizations which can be applied, at least in their essentials, to any group and to the behavior of individual members. Accordingly, one of our first tasks was that of extracting some minimum essential features of actual small groups from sociological work. In this task there is a methodological advantage in concentrating on *informally organized groups*, rather than formally organized groups in which the leader or head and other positions with their respective responsibilities are appointed by a higher authority, such as a commanding officer or board. In informally organized groups, group products and the particular individuals who occupy the various positions are determined to a much greater extent by the actual interaction of individuals. If care is taken at the beginning to refer to the general setting in which small groups form and function, their products and structure can be traced through *longitudinal observation* of the interaction process.

On the basis of an extensive survey of sociological findings, the following minimum features in the rise and functioning of small groups were abstracted:

(1) There are one or more *motives* shared by individuals and conducive to their interacting with one another.

(2) *Differential effects* on individual behavior are produced by the interaction process, that is, each individual's experience and behavior is affected in varying ways and degrees by the interaction process in the group.[2]

(3) If interaction continues, a *group structure* consisting of hierarchical status and role relationships is stabilized, and is clearly delineated as an *in-group* from other group structures.

(4) A set of norms regulating relations and activities within the group and with non-members and out-groups is standardized.[3]

Interaction is not made a separate item in these minimum features because interaction is the *sine qua non* of any kind of social relationships, whether interpersonal or group. Since human interaction takes place largely on a symbolic level, *communication* is here considered part and parcel of the interaction process.

When group structure is analyzed in terms of hierarchical status positions, the topic of *power* necessarily becomes an integral dimension of the hierarchy. Power relations are brought in as an afterthought only if this essential feature of group hierarchy is *not* made part of the conception of group. Of course, power does in many cases stem from outside of the group, and in these cases the nature of established functional relations between groups in the larger structure has to be included in the picture.

Our fourth feature relates to the standardization of a set of norms. The term "social norm" is a sociological designation referring generically to all products of group interaction which regulate members' behavior in terms of the expected or even the ideal behavior. Therefore, norm does not denote average behavior.[4] The existence of norms, noted by sociologists, has been experimentally tested by psychologists in terms of convergence of judgments of different individuals (Sherif, 1936), and in terms of reactions to deviation (Schachter, 1952). A norm denotes not only expected behavior but a *range of acceptable behavior*, the limits of which define deviate acts. The extent of the range of acceptable behavior varies inversely with the significance or consequence of the norm for the identity, integrity, and major goals of the group.

With these minimum essential features of small informally organized groups in mind, a group is defined as a social unit which consists

---

[2] This feature, long noted by sociologists, has received repeated laboratory confirmation by psychologists, as mentioned earlier.

[3] It is not possible here to review sociological findings on which these features are based or to discuss them more fully. They have been elaborated in our *Psychology of Ego-involvements* (with H. Cantril, 1947), Chap. 10; *An Outline of Social Psychology* (1948); and *Groups in Harmony and Tension* (1953), Chap. 8.

[4] Cf. Hiller (1947); Freedman, Hawley, Landecker, and Miner (1952).

of a number of individuals who, at a given time, stand in more or less definite interdependent status and role relationships with one another, and which explicitly or implicitly possesses a set of norms or values regulating the behavior of the individual members, at least in matters of consequence to the group.

Common group attitudes or sentiments are not included in this definition because social attitudes are formed by individuals in relation to group norms as they become functioning parts in the group structure. At the psychological level, then, the individual becomes a group member to the extent that he internalizes the major norms of the group, carries on the responsibilities, meets expectations for the position he occupies. As pointed out by various authors, his very identity and self conception, his sense of security become closely tied to his status and role in the group through the formation of attitudes relating to his membership and position. These attitudes may be termed "ego-attitudes" which function as constituent parts of his ego system.

On the basis of findings at a sociological level, hypotheses concerning the formation of small in-groups and relations between them were derived and tested in our 1949 camp experiment (Sherif and Sherif, 1953). One of the major concerns of that study was the feasibility of experimental production of in-groups among individuals with no previous role and status relations through controlling the conditions of their interaction.

The hypotheses tested were:

(1) When individuals having no established relationships are brought together to interact in group activities with common goals, they produce a group structure with hierarchical statuses and roles within it.

(2) If two in-groups thus formed are brought into functional relationship under conditions of competition and group frustration, attitudes and appropriate hostile actions in relation to the out-group and its members will arise and will be standardized and shared in varying degrees by group members.

As sociologists will readily recognize, testing of these hypotheses is not so much concerned with the discovery of new facts as getting a clearer picture of the formative process under experimentally controlled conditions. It aims rather at singling out the factors involved in the rise of group structure, group code or norms, and in-group–out-group delineations which will make possible their intensive study with appropriate laboratory methods on the psychological level.

To test these hypotheses, 24 boys of about twelve years of age from similar lower middle-class, Protestant backgrounds were brought to an isolated camp site wholly available for the experiment. The early phase (Stage 1) of the study consisted of a variety of activities permitting contact between all the boys and observation of budding friendship groupings. After being divided into two groups of twelve boys each, in order to split the budding friendship groupings and at the same time constitute two similar units, the two groups lived, worked, and played separately (Stage 2). All activities introduced embodied a common goal (with appeal value to all), the attainment of which necessitated cooperative participation within the group.

At the end of this stage, there developed unmistakable group structures, each with a leader and hierarchical statuses within it, and also names and appropriate group norms, including *sanctions* for deviate behavior. Friendship preferences were shifted and reversed *away* from previously budding relationships *toward* in-group preferences. Thus our first hypothesis concerning in-group formation was substantiated.

In the final phase (Stage 3) of the 1949 experiment, the two experimentally formed in-groups were brought together in situations which were competitive and led to some mutual frustration, as a consequence of the behavior of the groups in relation to each other. The result of intergroup contact in these conditions was enhancement of in-group solidarity, democratic interaction within groups, and in-group friendship, on the one hand. On the other hand, out-group hostility, name calling, and even fights between the groups developed, indicating that in-group democracy need not lead to democratic relations with outsiders when intergroup relations are fraught with conditions conducive to tension. The resistance which developed to post-experimental efforts at breaking down the in-groups and encouraging friendly interaction indicates the unmistakable effect of group products on individual members. Thus the results substantiated the second hypothesis concerning determination of norms toward out-groups by the nature of relations between groups and demonstrated some effects of intergroup relations upon in-group functioning.

One of the main methodological considerations of this experiment was that subjects were kept unaware of the fact that they were participating in an experiment on group relations. The view that subjects cease to be mindful that their words and deeds are being recorded is not in harmony with what we have learned about the structuring of experience. The presence of a personage ever observing, ever recording our words and deeds in a situation in which our status and role concerns are at stake cannot help coming in as an important factor in the total frame of reference. Therefore, in our work, the aim is to establish definite trends as they develop in natural, life-like situations and to introduce precision at choice points when this can be done without sacrificing the life-like character which gives greatest hope for validity of these trends.

The study just summarized illustrates the testing of hypotheses derived from sociological findings in experimentally designed situations. The next point relates to psychological findings, generalizations, and laboratory techniques relevant for the study of experience and behavior of individual group members. Here our task is to achieve a more refined analysis on a psychological level of individual behavior in the group setting through precise perceptual and judgmental indices. If such data obtained through precise judgmental and perceptual indices and other appropriate techniques are in line with findings concerning group relations on the sociological level, then we shall be moving toward integration of psychological and sociological approaches in the study of group relations.

Here only the bare essentials can be stated of the psychological principles from a major trend in experimental psychology which are utilized in designing the experiments to be reported.[5]

Judgments and perceptions are not merely intellectual and discrete psychological events. All judgments and perceptions take place within their appropriate frame of reference. They are jointly determined by functionally related internal and external factors operating at a given time. These interrelated factors—external and internal—constitute the frame of reference of the ensuing reaction. Observed behavior can be adequately understood and evaluated only when studied within its appropriate frame of reference or system of relations. The external factors are stimulus situations outside of the individual (objects, persons, groups, events, etc.). The internal factors are motives, attitudes emotions, general state of the organism, effects of past experience, etc. The limit between the two is the skin of the individual—the skin being on the side of the organism.

It is possible, therefore, to set up situations in which the appraisal or evaluation of a social situation will be reflected in the judgments and perceptions of the individual. In short, under appropriate and relevant conditions, the way the individual sizes up a situation in terms of the whole person he is at the time can be tapped through apparently simple perceptual and judgmental reactions.

An additional principle should be clearly stated because of certain conceptions in psychology which imply that perception is almost an altogether arbitrary, subjective affair. If external stimulus situations are well structured in definite objects, forms, persons, and groupings, perception will correspond closely to the stimulus structure on the whole. This is not to say that functionally related internal factors do not play a part in the perception of structured situations. The fact that some well-structured situations are singled out by the individual as "figure" rather than others indicates that they do. Such facts are referred to under the concept of *perceptual selectivity.*

---

[5] Fuller accounts of these principles from the works of psychologists and their background may be found in M. Sherif, *The Psychology of Social Norms* and *An Outline of Social Psychology*; Sherif and Sherif, *Groups in Harmony and Tension*, Chap. 6.

If, on the other hand, the external field is vague, unstructured, in short, allows for *alternatives*—to that extent the relative weight of internal factors (motives, attitudes) and social factors (suggestion, etc.) will increase. It is for this reason that the exhortations of the demagogue are relatively more effective in situations and circumstances of uncertainty. Since perceptions and judgments are jointly determined by external and internal factors, it is possible to vary the *relative · weights* of these factors in differing combinations, giving rise to corresponding judgmental and perceptual variations. This has been done in various experiments. In a study carried out as part of our research program at the University of Oklahoma, James Thrasher co-varied the stimulus situation in gradations of structure and the nature of interpersonal relations of subjects (strangers and friends) to determine the reciprocal effects of these variations on judgmental reactions. It was found that as the stimulus situation becomes more unstructured, the correspondence between stimulus values and judgment values decreases and the influence of social factors (established friendship ties in this case) increases (Thrasher, 1954).

Following the implications of the above, it is plausible to say that behavior revealing discriminations, perceptions, evaluations of individuals participating in the interaction process as group members will be determined

—not *only* by whatever motivational components and unique personality characteristics each member brings with him,

—not *only* by the properties of external stimulus conditions (social or otherwise),

—but as influenced, modified, and even transformed by these and by the special properties of the interaction process, in which a developing or established state of reciprocities plays no small part. Interaction processes are not voids.

The starting point in our program of research was the experimental production of group norms and their effects on perception and judgment (Sherif, 1936). This stems from our concern for experimental verification of one essential feature of any group—a set of norms (feature 4 of small groups above). Groups are not transitory affairs. Regulations of behavior in them is not determined by the immediate social atmosphere *alone*.

Especially suggestive in the formulation of the problem was F. Thrasher's observation on small groups that behavior of individual members is regulated in a binding way (both through inner attachment and, in cases of deviation, through correctives applied) by a code or set of norms. Equally provocative in this formulation was Emile Durkheim's *Elementary Forms of Religion*, in which a strong point was made of the rise of *representations collectives* in interaction situations and their effect in regulating the experience and outlook of the individual.

After thus delineating the problem, the next step was to devise an experimental situation which lacked objective anchorages or standards (i.e., was vague or unstructured) in order to maximize the effects of the social interaction process. When individuals face such an unstructured stimulus situation they show marked variations in reaction. However, such marked individual variations will not be found if the stimulus is a definite, structured object like a circle or a human hand. There will be agreement among individuals, on the whole, when they face a circle or a normal hand even if they are five thousand miles apart and members of different cultures. The fact of objective determination of perception and judgment and the ineffectiveness of social influences (suggestion, etc.) in relation to structured stimuli was clearly noted in the original report of this experiment in several contexts. In a larger publication, in order to stress cases of objective determination of psychological processes, a chapter was devoted to the effects of technology and its decisive weight in determining social norms and practices, with numerous illustrations from various parts of the world. Among them was our study conducted in the early 1940's of five Turkish villages with varying degrees of exposure to modern technology, specifically dealing with the compelling effects of such differential exposure on judgmental, perceptual, and other psychological processes.[6]

The experimental situation chosen for the study of norm formation was the autokinetic situation (the apparent movement of a point of light in a light-proof room lacking visible anchorages). The *dimension* chosen was the extent of movement. As this study is reported in detail in various places, I shall give only the bare essentials.

First it was established that the judgment of the extent of movement for given brief exposures varies markedly from individual to individual. Then individuals were brought to the situation to make their judgments together. If, during the course of their participation, their judgments converge within a certain range and toward some modal point, we can say they are converging to a common norm in their judgments of that particular situation. It is possible, however, that this convergence may be due to immediate social pressure to adjust to the judgments spoken aloud by the other participants in the situation. Therefore, going a step further, if it is shown that this common range and modal point are maintained by the individual in a subsequent session on a different day when he is alone, then we can say that the common range and modal point have become his own.

The results substantiated these hunches. When individuals face the same unstable, unstructured situation for the first time together with other participants, a range of judgment and a norm within it are established which are peculiar to that group. After the group range and

---

[6] See M. Sherif, Contact with modern technology in five Turkish villages, pp. 374–385 in Chap. 15, *An Outline of Social Psychology* (1948).

norm are established, an individual participant facing the same situation *alone* makes his judgments preponderantly in terms of the range and norm that he brings from the group situation. But convergence of judgments is not as marked as this when individuals first go through individual sessions and then participate in group sessions.

When the individual gives his judgments repeatedly in the alone situation, the judgments are distributed within a range and around a modal point peculiar to the individual. This finding has important theoretical implications. The underlying psychological principle, in individual and group situations, is the same, namely that there is a tendency to reach a standard in either case. Here we part company with Durkheim and other sociologists who maintained a dichotomy between individual and social psychology, restricting the appearance of emergent properties to group situations alone. In both cases, there are emergent properties. In the individual sessions they arise within the more limited frame of reference consisting of the unstructured stimulus situation and special psychological characteristics and states of the individual; whereas in togetherness situations the norm is the product of all of these within the particular interaction situation. The norm that emerges in group situations is not an average of individual norms. It is an emergent product which cannot be simply extrapolated from individual situations; the properties of the unique interaction process have to be brought into the picture. Therefore, the fact remains that group norms are the products of interaction process. In the last analysis, no interaction in groups, no standardized and shared norms.

In a subsequent unit, it was found that a characteristic mode of reaction in a given unstructured situation can be produced through the introduction of a prescribed range and norm (Sherif, 1937). When one subject is instructed to distribute his judgments within a prescribed range and around a modal point which vary for each naive subject, the preponderant number of judgments by the naive subjects come to fall within the prescribed range and around the modal point introduced for them, and this tendency continues in subsequent alone sessions. This tendency is accentuated if the cooperating subject has prestige in the eyes of the naive subject. These findings have been substantiated in a number of studies. For example, it has been shown that the tendency to maintain the prescribed range persists after several weeks (Bovard, 1948). In a recent experiment Rohrer, Baron, Hoffman, and Swander (1954) found that social norms established in the autokinetic situation revealed a rather high degree of stability even after a lapse of one year. This stability of an experimentally produced norm acquires particular significance in view of the facts in the study that (a) the subjects had first formed individual norms on the basis of actual movement *prior* to the establishment of divergent norms in a social situation and (b) the norms stabilized in the social situations were revealed after the lapse of one year in *alone* situations, i.e., without further social influence.

The actual presence of another person who makes judgments within a range prescribed by the experimenter is not essential. Norman Walter (1952) demonstrated that a prescribed norm can be produced through introduction of norms attributed to institutions with high prestige. A prescribed distribution of judgments given by tape recording is similarly effective (Blake and Brehm, 1954). A prescribed range can be established, without social influence, through prior experience in a more structured situation with light actually moving distances prescribed by the experimenter (Hoffman et al., 1953).

The advantages of a technique such as the autokinetic device for studying norm formation and other aspects of group relations are: (1) Compared with gross behavioral observations, it yields short-cut precise judgmental indices along definite dimensions reflecting an individual's own appraisal or sizing-up of the situation. (2) The judgmental or perceptual reaction is an *indirect* measure, that is, it is obtained in relation to performance and situations which do not appear to the subject as directly related to his group relations, his positive or negative attitudes. The feasibility of using judgmental variations in this study constituted the basis of its use in subsequent studies dealing with various aspects of group relations.

At this point, longitudinal research will bring more concreteness to the process of norm formation. As Piaget (1932) demonstrated in his studies of rules in children's groups, the formation of new rules or norms cannot take place until the child can perceive reciprocities among individuals. Until then he abides by rules because people important in his eyes or in authority say that he shall. But when the child is able to participate in activities grasping the reciprocities involved and required of the situation, then new rules arise in the course of interaction, and these rules become his autonomous rules to which he complies with inner acceptance. Although in contrast to some still prevalent psychological theories (e.g., Freud), these longitudinal findings are in line with observations on norm formation and internalization in adolescent cliques and other informally organized groups. These are among the considerations which led us to an intensive study of ego-involvements, and to experimental units tapping ego-involvements in interpersonal relations and among members occupying differing positions in the status hierarchy of a group.

These experimental units represent extensions of the approach summarized to the assessment of positive or negative interpersonal relations, status relations prevailing among the members of in-groups, positive or negative attitudes toward given out-groups and their members.

The first units along these lines dealt with interpersonal relations. It was postulated that since estimates of future performance are one special case of judgmental activity in which motivational factors are operative, the nature of relations between individuals (positive or negative) will be a factor in determining variations in the direction of these estimates. This inference was borne out first in a study showing that estimates of future performance are significantly affected by strong positive personal ties between subjects.[7] In a later unit, the assessment of personal relations through judgments of future performance was carried to include negative interpersonal relations as well as positive (Harvey and Sherif, 1951). In line with the hypothesis, it was found that individuals tended to over-estimate the performance of subjects with whom they had close positive ties and correspondingly to underestimate the future performance of those with whom they had an antagonistic relationship.

The study of status relations in small groups followed (Harvey, 1953). This study is related to feature 3 of the essential properties of groups discussed earlier in this chapter, namely, the rise and effects of a status structure. Observations by the sociologist, William F. Whyte, gave us valuable leads in formulating the specific problem of this study. During one period, a Street Corner clique that Whyte observed was engaged seriously in bowling. Performance in bowling became a sign of distinction in the group. At the initial stage, some low status members proved themselves on a par with high status members, including the leader. This ran counter to expectations built up in the group hierarchy. Hence, in time, level of performance was stabilized for each member in line with his relative status in the group. In the experiment, Harvey first ascertained the status positions of individual members in adolescent cliques. This was done through status ratings by adults in close contact with the subjects, through sociometric ratings from clique members, and through observations of some of the cliques by the experimenter during their natural interaction. Cliques chosen for the final experiment were those in which there was high correspondence between the status ratings obtained.

The overall finding was that the higher the status of a member, the greater his tendency and that of other group members to overestimate his future performance. The lower the status of a group member, the less is the tendency of other group members and of himself to overestimate his performance, even to the point that it is underestimated. If these results are valid, it should prove possible to predict leaders and followers in informal groups through judgmental variations exhibited in the way of over- and under-estimations of performance.

In the summer of 1953 our first attempt was made at a large-scale experiment starting with the experimental formation of in-groups themselves and embodying as an integral part of the design the assessment of psychological effects of various group products.[8] This assessment involved laboratory-type tasks to be used in conjunction with observational and sociometric data. The overall plan of this experiment was essentially like

---

[7] Study by C. W. Sherif summarized in M. Sherif, *An Outline of Social Psychology*, pp. 289–292.

[8] This experiment was carried out with a grant from the Rockefeller Foundation.

that of the 1949 study which was summarized earlier. However, it required carrying through a stage of in-group formation, to a stage of experimentally produced intergroup tension, and finally to integration of in-groups. The scope of this experiment embodying laboratory-type procedures at crucial points in each stage proved to be too great for a single attempt. During the period of intergroup relations, the study was terminated as an experiment owing to various difficulties and unfavorable conditions, including errors of judgment in the direction of the experiment.

The work completed covered the first two stages and will be summarized here very briefly. The plan and general hypotheses for these stages are similar, on the whole to those of the 1949 study summarized earlier.

Prior to the experiment, subjects were interviewed and given selected tests administered by a clinical psychologist. The results of these assessments are to be related to ratings made by the experimental staff along several behavioral dimensions during the experiment proper when in-group interaction had continued for some time.

At the end of the stage of group formation, two in-groups had formed as a consequence of the experimental conditions, although the rate of group formation and the degree of structure in the two groups were somewhat different.

Our hypothesis concerning experimental formation of in-groups substantiated in the 1949 study was supported. As a byproduct of in-group delineation we again found shifts and reversals of friendship choices *away* from the spontaneous choices made prior to the division of groups and *toward* other members of the in-group.

At the end of this phase of in-group formation, just before the first scheduled event in a tournament between the two groups, psychological assessment of group members within each status structure was made through judgments obtained in a laboratory-type situations. In line with methodological concerns mentioned earlier in the chapter, the experimental situation was introduced to each group by a member of the staff with the proposal that they might like to get a little practice for the softball game scheduled later that day. When this proposal was accepted, the experimenter took each group separately and at different times to a large recreation hall where he suggested turning the practice into a game, in which everyone took turns and made estimates of each others' performance. This was accepted as a good idea. Thus each boy took a turn at throwing a ball at a target 25 times and judgments of his performance were made by all members after each trial.

It should be noted that in previous studies, judgments of future performance were used as an index. The important methodological departure here was using as the unit of measurement the difference between actual performance and judgment of that performance *after* it was executed. In order to do so, the stimulus situation had to be made as unstructured as possible so that the developing status relations would be the *weighty factor* in determining the direction of judgmental variations.

In line with our hypothesis in this experimental unit, the results indicate that variations in judgment of performance on the task were significantly related to status ranks in both groups (Sherif, White, and Harvey, 1955). The performance of members of high status was over-estimated by other group members; the performance of members of low status tended to be underestimated. The extent of over- or under-estimation was positively related to the status rankings. Variations in judgment of performance on this task were not significantly correlated with skill, or actual scores, of members. This should *not* be interpreted to mean that skill can be discarded as a factor, or that it would not be highly related to judgmental variation in a more structured task. Of the two groups, skill seemed to be of *relatively* greater importance in the group which achieved less stability and solidarity. This is one of several indications that the relationship between judgmental variation and status rankings is closer in the group of greater solidarity and greater stability of structure. This finding of a relationship between degree of stability of the structure, on the one hand, and psychological response of members as revealed in their judgments, on the other, points to the necessity of systematic concern with the degree of group structure and solidarity as a variable in small group studies. In particular it should be brought systematically into the study of leadership and problems of conformity (Sherif, 1954).

We hope to gain greater understanding of the relationship between stability of group structure and psychological reactions as revealed by judgmental indices through a new study designed for this purpose. In this attempt the task will be held constant and the degree of established status relationships among subjects will be varied. At one extreme, subjects will be complete strangers; at the other extreme, subjects will be members of highly structured groups. The hypothesis to be tested is that judgments will be more a function of actual performance in the task in the case of strangers, and progressively more a function of existing status relations and less of skill with the increasing degrees of stability of group structure.

Following the experimental assessment of psychological effects of group structure in existing and in experimentally formed in-groups, the next step in our program of research was to extend the use of judgmental variation techniques to the level of intergroup relations among already existing groups. Such an experimental unit has recently been completed by O. J. Harvey (1954). Harvey investigated relations between existing informally organized groups and their effects on in-group functioning and on evaluations of the in-group and out-group. Organized cliques were chosen on the same basis as those in the study of status relations in existing informally organized groups already summarized. In the first experimental session, in-group members judged each other's performance on a task. In the second session, two cliques with either positive or negative relationships with each other were brought to the situation together. Here a similar procedure was followed, with in-group members judging performance both of other in-group members and performance of members of the functionally related out-group. In addition, subjects rated in-group and out-group members on ten adjectival descriptions presented on a graphic scale. These ratings were included to yield data relevant to our hypothesis concerning the nature of group stereotypes in the 1949 study and those of Avigdor's study (1952) on the rise of stereotypes among members of cooperating and rival groups.

Results obtained in this experiment bear out the hypotheses. Greater solidarity was evidenced in the in-group when negatively related outgroups were present, as revealed by an increasing relationship between judgmental variation and status ranks and by greater overestimation of performance by in-group members. In-group performance was judged significantly above that of out-group members when the groups were antagonistic, which was not the case when the groups present were positively related to each other. Finally, results clearly show a much higher frequency of favorable attributes for in-group members (e.g., "extremely considerate," "extremely cooperative") and a much higher frequency of unfavorable attributes given members of an antagonistic out-group (e.g., "extremely inconsiderate," "extremely uncooperative"). The difference between qualities attributed to in-group members and members of friendly out-groups is much smaller and not so clear-cut, as would be expected.

Thus, having demonstrated the feasibility of experimental study of norm formation, of status relations within groups, and of positive and negative attitudes between groups through laboratory-type techniques, on the one hand, and, on the other, experimental production of in-groups themselves in two previous studies, our next step is to carry through the large-scale experiment along the lines of our 1953 attempt which will pull together all of these various aspects into one design. Judgmental indices reflecting developing in-group and intergroup relations are to be obtained through laboratory-type techniques at choice points in a way that does not clutter the flow of interaction process. These judgmental indices can be checked against data obtained through more familiar observational, rating, and sociometric methods. If indications of the findings through judgmental processes are in line with the trends obtained by gross observational and other methods, then we can say the generalizations reached are valid. If this can be established, the laboratory-type experiment can be offered as a more precise and refined method of assessing the effects of interaction processes in group relations.

This approach, which considers the behavior of individuals as an outcome of interaction processes into which factors enter both from the individual himself with his unique characteristics and capacities and from properties of the situation, affords a naturalistic behavioral setting against which the claims of various personality tests can be evaluated.

The successive phases of this comprehensive experimental plan are:

1. Experimental production of in-groups themselves with a hierarchical structure and set of norms (intra-group relations). In line with our 1949 and 1953 studies, this is done, not through discussion methods, but through the introduction of goals which arise in the situations, which have common appeal value, and which necessitate facing a common problem, leading to discussion, planning and execution in a mutually cooperative way.

2. Bringing into functional relations the two experimentally formed groups in situations in which the groups find themselves in competition for given goals and in conditions which imply some frustration in relation to one another (intergroup tension).

3. Introduction of goals which cannot be easily ignored by members of the two antagonistic groups, but the attainment of which is beyond the resources and efforts of one group alone. In short, *superordinate goals* are introduced with the aim of studying the reduction of intergroup tension to derive realistic leads for the integration of hostile groups.

This experimental plan was carried out during the summer of 1954 at Robbers Cave in Oklahoma.

TWENTY-ONE

EXPERIMENTAL STUDY OF INTERGROUP RELATIONS

The main aim of this paper is to give a summary report of a preliminary experiment dealing with inter-group relations. It may be relevant at the outset to state briefly the approaches leading to the formulation of the study and hypotheses to be tested. Naturally the design and the points which will be particularly stressed follow the leads from these approaches.

The topic of inter-group relations is the most complex, the most baffling of all social psychological problems. This statement is, of course, a confession of ignorance. The study of group relations on the psychological side alone necessarily involves all major topics of psychology—motivation, judgment, perception, learning, attitudes, ego-involvements, effects of social situations etc. These major topics are each in themselves far from being settled matters; they are still controversial topics. Some psychologists seem to advocate that from a strictly scientific point of view it might be wise to postpone tackling the problem of group relations until the basic topics of psychology are more or less established beyond being merely so many points of view of different schools.

But in the present-day world of flux, tension, and conflict among human groupings, the concern over group relations has forced itself into the foreground. As a consequence, several universities and other organizations are rapidly making provision for the study of group relations. An ever-increasing number of social psychologists and men in related fields are moving to concentrate their work in this area. Taking note of the feeble and helpless state of academic discipline of social science today in comparison to the startling new developments in physical sciences, an increasing number of writers point out the urgency of making rapid strides in the study of human relations.

Although the need is urgent, real progress in the study of groups is still impeded by the well-worn grooves of certain historical approaches which were based on insufficient data and hence were one-sided. The alternative on the positive side is not the creation of a vast new terminology. We can more safely proceed by following the leads of a few well-grounded lines of facts, which seem to be converging.

One such well-grounded line is the fact that the individual reacts differentially as a member of group situations as compared with individual situations. His judgments, his perceptions, and his motives in group situations are determined not only by the individual characteristics that he brings into the situation, but also by the structural properties of the group situation and his particular place in it. By structural properties of group situations, I mean simply the reciprocal functional relationships that operate between different parts in a given situation at a given time. This basic fact has become almost a truism in social psychology on the basis of experiments carried out during the last two decades. The differential effects of even transitory group situations on various psychological processes such as "association" and affectivity, etc., were almost without exception discovered in the experiments of the previous decades. The varied findings of this earlier period concerning such differential effects acquire more integrated significance when viewed in terms of the structural effects mentioned above, rather than as merely added or subtracted "social increments" and "social decrements." In short, the differential effect of group situations is not an additive process.

Such differential reactions do not pop up suddenly in group situations alone. The judgment of a stimulus within or outside of a scale, within limits, is not determined only by its individual properties, but also by its relation to other parts of the scale which set the limits, that is, the main anchoring points. Likewise, properties of a perception are determined by the reciprocal effects of all internal and external factors that operate at the given time, the totality of which constitute the *frame of reference* of the reaction in question. If even the perception of simple lines and circles is determined not only by their own properties in isolation, but as structurally affected by the presence of other stimuli at the moment, it is a sterile effort to try to build up the account of reactions of the individual members in social situations on the basis of the discrete accounts of the individual and stimulus situation. This consideration becomes even more imperative when we realize that total situations are more complex and at times more compelling than the presence of lines or other stimuli in the proximity, or than some experimentally introduced anchorages.

The above line of evidence was included in this chapter after some hesitation. It is stated and demonstrated in any elementary textbook. Yet the implications of this basic fact for our problem and certain historically important modes of approach are crucial.

For example, in his "Group Psychology and Analysis of the Ego" (1922), Freud states:

From our point of view we need not attribute so much importance to the appearance of new characteristics. For us it would be enough to say that in a group the individual is brought under conditions which allow him to throw off the repressions of his unconscious instincts. The apparently new characteristic which he then displays are in fact the manifestations of this unconscious, in which all that is evil in the human mind is contained as a predisposition (pp. 9–10).

It seems to me that the whole indication of the findings of the experimental work of the last fifteen years or so is in the opposite direction— that is, in the direction of emphasizing the major importance of *the new characteristics* generated in group situations. In the current attempts to eliminate prejudice, hostility, and other harmful attitudes, and to build up new identifications, the positive effects of the group situations are being brought into the foreground as perhaps the most effective method.

To be sure, there are cases of group situations which produce effects conducive to aggressive, cruel, and impulsive actions on the part of an individual member (e.g., a lynching party). These cases represent one kind of the differential effects of group situations. On the other hand, there are other cases of the differential effects of group situations which are conducive to behavior of a high degree of cooperation, solidarity, and, at times, self-sacrifice hardly possible if the individual stopped to calculate in isolation the pros and cons of the consequences.

Another example of such one-sided emphasis in dealing with group relations is represented by the attempts to solve everything through *leadership* alone. Of course leadership is important and exerts greater influence in the orientation of the group, for good or for bad, than do other parts of the group. But this influence of leadership is limited within certain bounds. Leaders who go too far beyond these bounds are repudiated. The leadership position is also within the hierarchical scale of positions of the group. The attempts based on the assumption of unlimited powers of leadership in the solution of group problems do not, therefore, promise solutions of lasting value.

Of course, the most flagrant illustration of misleading and, in this case, thoroughly untenable approaches is any *racist doctrine* which attempts to explain the gaps and conflicts among human groupings on the basis of alleged inherent superiority or inferiority of the groups in question. To this audience I hardly need mention the fallacy of race doctrines. Such doctrines are nothing but self-righteous justifications of the beneficiary groups for the purpose of perpetuating existing inter-group relationships.

The adequate line of approach to the problem of group relations is, then, the study of the experience and behavior of individuals in intragroup and inter-group relations as affected by the group situation and group membership. Therefore, it becomes imperative to study the individual's inter-group behavior on the level of differential experience and behavior as affected by his actual participation in the group activity in progress or as affected by his membership in his group when he is reacting alone to other groups or their members. This does not preclude the study of his special personal motives, attitudes, intelligence, and other individual capacities. On the contrary, the very notion of differential experience and behavior is meaningless unless two kinds of data are related to each other: (1) data concerning individual motives, attitudes, characteristics, and capacities of the individual, (2) data concerning products generated in the group situation.

In concrete terms this means the necessity for studying group relations on the group level. It is almost stupid to make tautological statements like this, but, unfortunately, the tenacity of outworn approaches forces one to make such statements. The extrapolation from the individual motives, attitudes, characteristics, traits, and capacities *alone* in explaining group phenomena have led us up blind alleys. As psychologists, even of the social brand, neither can we be satisfied by merely noting the characteristic features and trend of the group as a whole; we must make our observations in terms of the reactions of single individual members and as intensively as possible. Therefore, at this early stage, we, as social psychologists, can deal only with intra- and inter-group relations of small groups, whose individual members can be singled out and observed in space and time. Since small groups do possess at least the minimum structural characteristics or features of groups of any size, the likelihood is that we can more effectively extend the generalizations obtained from them to the inter-group relations of larger social units than has been the case heretofore.

The *informally* or *spontaneously* structured small groups such as cliques and gangs are particularly suited for our purpose. The *formally* organized small groups, such as an army squad or staff members of a university department, have features which make them unsuitable for such studies. In the formally organized groups there are too many outside pulls and pushes which are themselves highly complex. For example, in a formally organized small group, such as a small army unit, the statuses of members are assigned from without, as are the major rules and regulations.

In informally or spontaneously structured small groups, whatever status a member acquires, and the upward or downward shifts from it, are determined by the interaction of individual members within the group, each member with ascertainable personal motives, characteristics, and capacities. Even the leader himself is not appointed from without, with instructions to behave in specific ways. He achieves a position of leadership in the process of group interaction through personal characteristics that enable him to move to the top in that particular group. In such spontaneously structured groups, whatever decisions, standards, or norms are upheld and followed are the ones that either generate in the process of group interaction or are adopted by the group as their own. It seems to me that the inter-group harmony and alliance, friction and conflict, among these informally structured groups embody some crucial prototype illustrations of the inter-group relations of larger social structures.

With such considerations in mind, since 1936 I have been trying to learn as much as possible about these informally organized in-group structures. The works of such investigators as Thrasher, Zorbaugh, Clifford Shaw, and William Whyte are highly illuminating in this respect. The accumulating data on clique formation and functioning coming both from psychologists and sociologists are organically related to the work of these investigators. A survey of data dealing with other kinds of informally structured small groups will further elucidate these converging lines of research.

The social psychologist cannot help finding in the above works, accumulating since the 1920's, results which fit the emerging trend of the last fifteen years or so in his own field. In the sociological works mentioned above, one finds concrete and recurring illustrations of the facts of differential experience and behavior, the rise of standardized group norms, the formulation of group decisions, the interdependence of the reactions of the individual members on functional reciprocal relationships within the group structure. This literature also offers ample evidence of the considerable determination of the behavior of individuals in inter-group relations on the basis of their group membership.

The survey of literature on informally structured small groups forces one to take note of certain features which are common to all such small groups. We take our lead to the study of inter-group relations from the implications derived from these features. (In this connection I am deliberately using the empirical and harmless word "feature" without putting any special conceptual significance into it. Each one of these features embody one or more basic topics of psychology, namely motivation, perception, judgment, learning, attitudes, ego-involvements, individual differences, etc.) The following *four* are certainly among the features that stand out in any of these informally structured groups. Here I can only cite them briefly. Elsewhere I have said a little more about each one of them (Sherif, 1948).

1. There are common *motivational* factors that bring the eventual group members into interaction and that determine the shorter or longer duration of this interaction. In the case of one group, the *dominant* motivational factor may be material deprivation, such as deprivation of food; in the second group the *dominant motivational* factor may be sex; in the third it may be *insecurity*; in the fourth it may be *recognition* and *social prestige*, etc. It is factually erroneous, therefore, to posit any one single motive (such as Eros or sex, hunger, or some alleged ego-drive)

as a sovereign instinct, drive, or need which holds groups together in every case.

The dominant motivational factor, whatever it may be, certainly is a weighty determinant of the direction of the particular activities of the group, the character of group products that will arise in time, and the determination of the special statuses and roles each member will occupy.

Once the statuses and group products become more or less stabilized for the group (as we shall see in features 3 and 4), the ways and means of satisfying even the dominant motive which was initially responsible in bringing the individuals together tend to be regulated in terms of the group structure.

2. Now a few words on the *second feature*, namely, the *differential effects of group interaction* on the experience and behavior of individual members. Not only motives, but all the psychological functions, feeling, perceiving, judging, thinking, and reasoning, etc., are modified in group situations. As we have said, the differential effects of group situations are not merely additive or subtractive affairs. Rather, they are *structural* changes which can be adequately understood in terms of their *membership-character* in relation to the total situation. This key concept of *membership-character*, so rightly stressed by Wertheimer, Köhler, Koffka, and Lewin, is indispensable for any understanding of group situations.

These structural changes, I must stress again, do not pop up only in group situations, as some leading sociologists like Durkheim and his influential school advocate. They are observed in the perception and behavior of the individual in any kind of situation in which new factors enter with a certain measurable degree of weight or compellingness.

3. Now I come to the *third feature*, and this embodies the promise of the starting point for a more adequate study of group relations. If the group interaction is not a transitory affair, but lasts for some time, a *more or less* stable group structure takes shape, with established, though by no means immutable, *statuses* and *roles* for individual members, from the leader on down. Groups are necessarily hierarchical affairs. The smooth functioning of group activities requires a hierarchical organization and more or less stabilized roles, which imply more or less stabilized relationships in terms of reciprocal expectations, etc.

With the stabilization of the group structure with relative statuses, which I repeat are not immutable and frozen, corresponding relative weights of *power* arise among the individual members. These *power* relationships are among the topics that are sorely neglected by the majority of social psychologists today. In view of the overstressed emphasis on getting the *leaders* of various groups into a conference room and settling all the points of conflict by discussions there, it should be pointed out that the status and power of the leaders, even though greater than that of others, are not unlimited. The leadership position, too, is a position within the hierarchical scale of the group. If the leader steps out *beyond certain bounds* in his group or in conference with the leaders of other groups, he also is subject to the correctives of the group (drop in his position, loss of prestige, repudiation, being dropped out altogether, and even severely punished).

From the point of view of inter-group relations, the most important consequence of group structuring is the delineation of *in-group* from *out-groups*. The development of in-group and "we-experience" is accompanied by the demarcation and setting of boundaries from out-groups. All these in-group delineations and the setting of boundaries from out-groups are reflected through self-justifying, self-glorifying, and self-righteous attitudes about the in-group and gradations of friendly or hostile attitudes concerning the out-groups thus marked off. The possibilities suggested by the fact of in-group and out-group delineation provide us with a sound basis for the formulation of hypotheses concerning inter-group relations.

4. The *fourth* feature of these groups is the rise of a set of standards, values, or *norms*. In groups in which no standardized norms exist, such norms arise in the course of group interaction. The major *ego-attitudes* of the individual member are formed as a result of his membership in the group and his other reference groups. As this point is expanded elsewhere, I shall not take time now to elaborate it.

The above features concerning intra- and inter-group relations unmistakably point the directions for an adequate program of a co-ordinated series of experiments in this vital area. Also, they warn us against drawing conclusions concerning inter-group relations on the basis of the properties of in-group relations only. To date, experimental studies of group relations have concentrated mainly on intra-group relations. Kurt Lewin and his associates have demonstrated the differential effects on individual members of different group situations created by three different types of leadership—namely, democratic, autocratic, and laissez-faire. Yet the democratic, autocratic, and laissez-faire character of *in-group relations* thus produced do not necessarily determine the character of *inter-group relations*. For example, in Lewin's experiment friction occurred between the democratic and laissez-faire groups and a "war" broke out. The democratic group did not stop to think of a democratic way to settle the affair: democratic procedure was something to be practiced within the group. The fight that developed was hardly a democratic method of solution. In short, in-group democracy does not necessarily imply democracy toward out-groups, even though we may preach it.

Therefore, it becomes imperative to consider the consequence of in-group formation in relation to other groups. This will give us more promising leads in handling inter-group problems such as group tension and group prejudice.

As we noted in citing the main features of in-groups, one of the products of group formation is a delineation of *"we"* and *"they"*—the *"we"* including the members of the in-group. The *"we"* thus delineated comes to embody a whole host of qualities and values to be upheld, defended, and cherished. Offenses from without or deviations from within are promptly reacted to with appropriate corrective, defensive, and, at times, offensive measures. A set of values, "traits," or stereotypes are attributed to all those groups and individuals who comprise the *"they"* group from the point of view of the *"we"* group. Such attributed traits may be favorable, unfavorable, or both, depending upon the nature of the relations between the groups in question. If the interests, directions, or goals of the inter-group relationship in question are integrated or harmonious, the *"they"* group is pictured in a positive or favorable light. However, if the activities and functional views of the two interacting groups clash, then the characteristics attributed to the out-group are negative and derogatory. If one group takes the position that another group is in its way, that for some reason the other group interferes with the goals or interests of the *"we"* group, or that it should be working in the interest of the *"we"* group, all sorts of stereotypes develop to justify this position. All race-superiority doctrines are deliberate or unconscious justifications for this kind of relationship.

This fact, in favor of which ample evidence can be piled up from the sociological studies of small groups as well as from race-relations studies, comes out also in experiments which are *not* primarily designed to study in-group and out-group delineation. For example, in the study of Sears, Hovland, and Miller (1940) of the effects of frustration caused primarily by sleep deprivation, it was observed that an in-group formation was in the making. Jokes and unflattering adjectives were bestowed not only against the experimenters in question, but against psychologists in general. Likewise, in the Minnesota starvation study during World War II, the men sharing semistarvation "built up a tremendous in-group feeling that tended to exclude both their non-starving friends and administrative and technical staff" (Guetzkow, 1946). In short, the world was delineated into "haves" and "have-nots," with appropriate attitudes.

A PRELIMINARY STUDY OF INTER-GROUP RELATIONS

The indications of the converging lines achieved by the experimental work of psychologists, and the rich sociological findings on small groups, show us the way to formulate more fruitful problems, hypotheses, and experimental designs concerning the vital topic of inter-group relations. The study reported in broad outline in this paper stems from the above considerations.

This study of group relations was conducted in a camp in Northern Connecticut during the summer of 1949 with the active and generous backing of Professor Carl I. Hovland, chairman of the Department of Psychology, Yale University.[1] It was carried out in the conviction that experimental study of the essential variables underlying group tension will contribute effectively to a more realistic approach to problems of inter-group tensions in actual life situations. The study represents an attempt to include within a single experimental design the study of in-group properties and of inter-group relations. The dominant idea in its conception was to create controlled situations which would make possible (1) the formation and functioning of in-groups, and (2) inter-group relations between these experimentally produced in-groups.

On the basis of lessons learned from the sociological and psychological study of the properties of small in-groups and functional relationships between in-groups, the following hypotheses were formulated:

1. When individuals having no established relationships are brought together in a group situation to interact in group activities with common goals, they produce a group structure with hierarchical positions and roles within it. The group structure tends in time to generate byproducts or *norms* peculiar to the group, such as common attitudes, positive in-group identifications, nicknames, catchwords, etc.

2. The second part of the hypothesis is related directly to inter-group relations. If two in-groups thus formed are brought into functional relationship, positive or negative out-group attitudes and appropriate friendly or hostile actions in relation to the out-group and its members will arise, depending upon the harmony or friction between the goals of the two groups. The testing of this hypothesis also involves in prototype form the process of the rise of group stereotypes.

The *third part of the hypothesis* is related to individual achievements and strivings for position within the in-groups as determined by more or less unique individual factors. Since this aspect of the study will be presented elsewhere, we need not deal with it in this broad presentation.

SUBJECTS

In order to test these hypotheses, it was necessary to eliminate, insofar as possible, group formation and positive or negative relations between groups on the basis of background factors such as ethnic differences and differences in class, religion, education, age, sex. etc. In short, the subjects had to be *homogeneous* in as many background and individual respects as possible.

Interviews were held with parents of prospective subjects in their homes and with the ministers of their church groups. Information sheets were filled in for each subject, including the relevant background ma-

[1] The study was financed by a grant to Yale University from the research division of the American Jewish Committee, N.Y. I am deeply grateful to the Committee and its director of the research division, Dr. Samuel Flowerman, for the grant.

terial as well as the subject's interests, play-group activities, school experiences, etc.

The possibility of grouping together on the basis of previous acquaintance was minimized by selecting subjects from different neighborhoods and towns of the New Haven area, such as West Haven and Hamden. There were thus no definitely established friendship bonds among the subjects.

Prior to the experiment, several tests were administered to the subjects by Professor Richard Wittenborn and Dr. Elmer Potter at the Yale Psychology Department. The tests were deliberately administered prior to the appearance of the subjects at the experimental situation. In order to prevent any suspicion on the part of the subjects that these tests would be related to observations of their behavior in the main experimental situation, the test administrators never appeared on the scene while the experiment was in progress. The tests given included an intelligence test, the Rosenzweig Picture-Frustration test, and selected pictures of the TAT.

In attempting to satisfy this criterion of *homogeneity* of subjects, we selected 24 boys of about twelve years of age, all coming from settled American families of the lower middle-class income group in the New Haven area. All of the boys were Protestants. In fact, nineteen came from the same denomination, and the other five from highly similar denominations. The educational opportunities and backgrounds of the boys were similar. The group had a mean I.Q. of 104.8. All the boys might be called more or less "normal"; none were "behavior problems."

With these factors equated as much as possible, the kind of groupings, statuses within groups, and attitudes which were to be produced between groups could not be attributed to such cultural and social background factors as ethnic, religious, or class differences, or to existing friendship bonds.

The possibility remained that the formation of a particular in-group might be determined chiefly by personal preferences or attractions among the boys, or by their common personal interests. It was necessary, therefore, to plan the experiment in such a way that the weight of personal preferences and interests and personality factors between the experimental groups could be neutralized.

DESIGN AND PROCEDURE

Stage I was planned as the period of spontaneous groupings on the basis of personal inclinations and interests. All activities were campwide with a maximum of freedom and "mixing up" of the boys in various games and camp duties. Thus, it became possible to ascertain budding friendship groups and, more or less, to equate the weight of personal factors in the two experimental groups of Stage II.

Stage II was designed as the *stage of in-group formation* of two experimental groups as similar in composition as possible. Each experimental group would participate separately in activities involving all of the members of the group. Activities were chosen on the basis of their motivational appeal and their involvement of the whole group. Different activities afforded varied situations in which all members of a group could find opportunity to participate and "shine." All rewards given in this stage were made on a group-unit basis, not to particular individuals.

Stage III was planned to study *inter-group relations* between the two experimental in-groups thus produced when brought into contact (a) in a series of competitive activities and situations, and (b) in mildly frustrating situations caused by one group to the other. The frustrating situations were arranged in such a way that the blame or responsibility for the frustration would be placed on the experimental groups and not on the adults in the situation.

The particular activities chosen in the three stages were selected from those for which the boys themselves expressed preference. They were timed in terms of the demands of the three stages of the study. Thus the activity and situations in which the boys participated had the motivational value of life situations and were not simply situations prescribed by adults. They will be described in more detail later.

The experiment was conducted at an isolated camp site near the Massachusetts state line and lasted for eighteen days. The nearest town was eight miles away, and there was no bus service in the neighborhood; consequently there were no distractions from neighborhood soda fountains, movies, townspepole, etc. Neither boys nor staff members were permitted to have any visitors during the course of the study.

The site consisted of about 125 acres of land, largely hills and timber, with a stream suitable for swimming and fishing running through it. There were two bunkhouses, a mess hall, kitchen, infirmary, administration building, latrines etc., and broad level areas for athletic events.

Before giving a more detailed description of the three stages of the experiment and the main results it is necessary to emphasize the techniques of observation and the role of adults in the camp. Of course, it is well known that individuals behave differently when they know they are being observed or studied, especially by psychologists. The consideration cannot be "allowed for" or explained away. Therefore, all those associated with the study were strongly urged to prevent the boys' suspecting that their behavior was being observed or that various periods of camp activities were planned. The parents and boys were simply told that new methods in camping were being tried out.

The bulk of observational data was obtained by two participant observers who were graduate students. They acted as counselors to the two experimental groups. Each participant observer had the assistance of a junior counselor who was under his direct control and was instructed to follow his lead. Since the junior counselors were experienced in camping activities, the participant observers were comparatively free to observe their groups and to stay with them throughout the camp period. However, the participant observers were instructed not to make notes in the boys' presence unless the situation clearly called for writing something, such as a cabin discussion in which "minutes" could be taken down. Otherwise, the participant observers withdrew or surreptitiously jotted down short notes which they expanded each evening after their boys were asleep.

The other staff members, including an official camp director, activities director, and nurse, were instructed to perform their duties in the camp in strict accordance with the planned activities and stages. The specific demands of the experiment for the next day were discussed in detail each night after the boys' bedtime and after the main observations for the day were obtained from the participant observers.

As far as the boys were concerned, therefore, the situation was as natural and attractive as the usual summer-camp situation. For this reason, and to satisfy the criterion of homogeneity among subjects and staff members, the author appeared on the premises as a caretaker with the name of "Mr. Mussee." This gave me freedom to be at crucial places at crucial times doing odd jobs without attracting the boys' attention. In addition, it was sometimes possible to make naive statements to the boys and ask naive questions about matters which every other staff member was expected to know as a matter of course. For example, I usually pretended not to know what group a particular boy belonged to, and I was sometimes able to elicit information that might not have been easily available otherwise.

According to the participant observers and other staff members, who were instructed to watch carefully for any sign to the contrary, this role of caretaker was never suspected. Some typical examples of the boys' reactions to Mr. Mussee will illustrate the role. For example, the rather patronizing attitude accorded a caretaker is seen in one boy's reaction when Mr. Mussee was following his group to a cook-out. The boy yelled: "Hey, Mr. Mussee, hurry up. We can't wait for you!"

On the last day, when the whole camp was breaking up and the premises were being cleaned, the caretaker was busy putting data in order and did not appear. Several boys, not seeing him at his job, complained, one of them remarking, "Where the hell is Mr. Mussee? This is his job."

In addition to observational data, charts of seating arrangements at meals, of bunk choices, of athletic teams chosen, of partners or buddies in various activities and situations were made for each day throughout the camp. A record was kept of all outgoing and incoming mail. Postcards were recorded.

One more point related to group technique is fundamental in understanding the results which will follow. This point concerns the counselors and other members of the staff. The counselors (i.e., participant observers) were in the camp primarily to observe. They and other staff members were *not* to be leaders in the usual sense at boys' camps. They were instructed, rather, to look after the safety of the boys, and to set things right if behavior went too far out of bounds. Neither the counselors nor the boy leaders were asked to exercise any particular kind of leadership technique, democratic or authoritarian. Nor was authority to be delegated or suggested to the boys by the staff members. The tendency to depart from the observance of these instructions on the part of any staff member was forcefully called to his attention so that it might be corrected. The boy leaders and their lieutenants emerged from the ranks of the two experimental groups in the course of group interaction, especially during the stage of in-group formation (i.e., Stage II).

As mentioned earlier, the daily camp program was made up of the activities for which the boys themselves expressed preference. If a hike was scheduled, the boys were left to their own devices in organizing it. Of course, they were given tents, canteens, food, equipment, etc., as they asked for them and were given any necessary help. The boys were not preached to or organized from above to discuss among themselves the manner in which they would execute their activities. It was their affair and their discussion and their action. On the whole, the demands of the situations, not adult leadership, led the groups to discuss their affairs collectively. For example, the participant observer at one time gave his group a whole watermelon, leaving the division strictly to them. On another occasion, four large chocolate bars were given to each group of twelve boys as a reward in their collective Treasure Hunts. The ways in which the watermelon and chocolate were distributed were up to the boys.

RESULTS

From this study, several types of data were obtained:

1. The main data related to group relations, that is, to in-group formation; the rise of group structure with relative positions and leader-follower relations; the development of in-group products, including in-group and out-group attitudes; and the development of inter-group tension, with rudimentary stereotypes and attitudes of prejudice.

2. Data were also collected concerning individual factors determining particular statuses and roles within the group. Groups are necessarily hierarchical, and it is such individual factors which largely determine the position which each member occupies. For example, when we classify our data, it will be possible to relate intelligence and certain measures from the TAT and Rosenzweig Picture-Frustration test to statuses attained and behavior in the actual group situations.

3. Finally, a special study was made of two boys in the camp, one in each experimental group, who were lowest in their groups in participation in group activities and inconsistent in their identifications. From

these data, we will develop some valuable hints for the study of *marginality* and *social isolates*.

Since the principal problem of the study concerns inter-group relations, our concern here will be only with those results most directly related to group relations. Within the limitations of this paper, we shall have to concentrate on the main trend in formation of in-group and inter-group relations without going into details other than those necessary to make this trend clear.

Stage I, which lasted three days, was the stage of "natural" groupings based on personal likes and dislikes and common interests. As mentioned before, the main purpose of Stage I was to rule out, or at least to minimize, the possibility of interpreting results of the experimentally induced in-group formations and inter-group relations of later stages on the basis of personal inclinations of the individual members for one another. Therefore, during Stage I, all of the 24 boys were put in one large bunkhouse.

It should be emphasized that the boys were free to select their own bunks, seats at meals, buddies for play activities, athletic teams, etc. All activities were camp-wide, i.e., potentially including all boys.

At this stage an informal poll of preferred activities was taken with the promise that activities would be scheduled which the boys liked best. The main results of this poll were as follows:

Softball and hiking—20 choices each
Football—14 choices
Swimming—13 choices
Soccer—12 choices
Fishing—9 choices
Ping-pong—7 choices
Horseshoes and volleyball—5 choices each
A number of other activities were given choices of 4 or less.

At the end of Stage I, popularity ratings (sociograms) were obtained during informal interviews held on the pretext of getting suggestions for favored activities and for improving the camp. As other such studies have found, the sociograms showed the boys clustering in budding friendship groups of two, three, or four boys. These sociograms served as the most important criterion in assigning the boys to the two experimental groups for the period of experimental in-group formation of Stage II. In addition, the two experimental groups were equated in other respects insofar as possible without violating the requirements of the sociogram results. Chief among these other characteristics were size, strength, ability in games, intelligence and personality ratings previously made on the basis of the tests by Professor Wittenborn and Dr. Potter.

The division of the subjects into the two experimental groups was deliberately done to split the budding friendship groups which had developed. For example, if two boys showed preference for one another, one was put in one group and the other boy in the second group. If more than one friendship choice was made, we attempted to put the boy in that group holding the *fewest* of his friendship choices. Therefore, at the start of Stage II—the stage of experimental in-group formation— the number of friendship choices given to members of the experimental in-group was fewer than the number of friendship choices given to members of the experimental out-group.

TABLE I
Total Choices of Friends, End of Stage I

	Choices Received by:	
Choices Made by:	*Eventual Red Devils*	*Eventual Bull Dogs*
Eventual Red Devils	35.1%	64.9%
Eventual Bull Dogs	65.0%	35.0%

One of these experimental groups came to be known as the Red Devils, the other as the Bull Dogs. Therefore, it will be helpful to refer to them by these names although at this point in the experiment the groups had existence only on paper. As Table I shows, of the total friendship choices made by boys who were to become Red Devils, only 35.1 per cent were choices of other boys assigned to their group. The remainder, almost two-thirds, of the friendship choices made by future Red Devils were directed to boys who were placed in the Bull Dog group, that is, the out-group.

Similarly, only 35 per cent of the total friendship preferences of boys who were to become Bull Dogs were for other future Bull Dogs. Sixty-five per cent of their friendship choices were for boys who were placed in the Red Devil group.

Stage II, which lasted five days, was the stage of experimental in-group formation. The subjects were divided into two groups as described. The groups lived in separate bunkhouses. As it happened the Red Devils, as they were to be known, voted to remain in the old bunkhouse, while the Bull Dogs voted to move to the new bunkhouse.

It had been anticipated that this split into two groups might not be taken easily by some of the boys. In fact, one boy cried for ten minutes at his separation from another camper with whom he had struck up a friendship in the preceding days at camp. For this reason, immediately after the bunkhouse change was made, cars took each group separately from the camp for a hike and cook-out. It will be recalled that hiking had shared first place on the boys' preferred activities, being chosen by twenty boys. The cook-out supplies were particularly sumptuous, including steak for broiling over an open fire.

During Stage II, the two experimental groups were separated as much as possible. They lived separately, ate at separate tables, served on K.P. on alternate days, and engaged separately in frequent hikes, overnight camping trips, etc. Swimming was scheduled separately for the two groups, and each very soon found their own special places some distance apart. One of these swimming places, the Bull Dogs', was secret from the other group.

Each group chose its own special hide-out in the woods in opposite directions from each other. When leaving their hide-out, one group devised an elaborate plan of departure in groups of two or three designed to camouflage the direction of their hide-out.

The activities of Stage II required that members of each group cooperate collectively in achieving their ends. In addition to hiking, overnight camping trips, and swimming, each group had a "Treasure Hunt" and engaged in group games such as fox and hounds, or bean toss, in which each member had to collect a certain number of beans to win a group reward. A small sum of money ($10.00) was given to each group to spend as they chose. Considerable group effort went to improving their cabins, stenciling insignia on T-shirts, making standards, etc. In addition, one of the groups sometimes chose to engage in craftwork, collecting wildlife, and the like. These varied activities afforded *ample opportunity for each boy to show his worth in some line of pursuit.*

One of the major findings of the study in line with the hypothesis was the formation of a well-defined in-group organization or structure. By in-group structure is meant simply the development of relative hierarchical positions within the group unit ranging from highest to lowest position. In addition to evidence from the sociograms, the hierarchical roles were manifested in terms of successful or unsuccessful initiation of group activities, the greater or lesser responsibility taken in their planning and execution, the degree of adherence to the line of activity taken by the group, the source and effectiveness of group sanctions, etc.

The accompanying sociograms reveal the hierarchical positions of boys within each experimental group in terms of *popularity* (see Figs. 1 and 2). They can be considered as a measure of *one* index of group structure. The important factor which such sociograms do not adequately reflect is *power relationships* within the group. For example, in the Red Devil group, L. is revealed as receiving one more friendship choice than S. However, S. acquired and maintained power over L. and other members high in status and, partly through these boys, over the Red Devil group (see below). In the Bull Dog group, the boy H. exerted greater direction over the group than the popularity rating alone indicates, by virtue of his ability and acknowledged leadership in athletic events, even though he yielded to the overall leadership of C., the Bull Dog leader.

In the Bull Dog group, a boy named C. rose to leadership by his greater contribution in the planning and execution of common activities

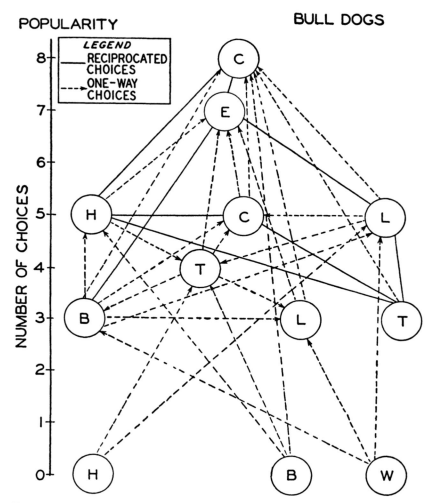

POPULARITY   BULL DOGS

FIGURE 1. End of stage II, in-group formation: Friendship preferences of Bull Dogs.

and by regulating and integrating the tasks and roles of the group members. At the outset, this boy successfully swung the vote to move to the new bunkhouse. His suggestions on improving the bunkhouse, for example, by putting the letter "B" on the door and by building a chinning bar, were, from the first, almost always adopted as good ones. He proved to be very effective in leading the group on their first hike. He was the boy who most frequently helped another in his group: for example, once by bandaging a blister, another time by fixing a belt. It was C. who

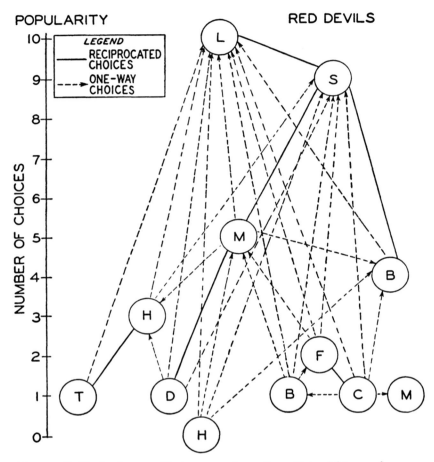

FIGURE 2. End of stage II, in-group formation: Friendship preferences of Red Devils.

mapped out the devious route designed to conceal their hide-out in the woods. He frequently praised other group members and instigated group praise. An instance of the latter occurred after the group had worked long and hard on a project to improve their secret swimming pool. C. said, "We did a good job, boys. We should be proud of ourselves." This was followed by cheers for the group effort and C.'s suggestion that they give the pool a name.

The Bull Dog group was, then, focalized around C.'s leadership. However, he did not lead in every situation. For example, he was not as good in athletic events or those requiring muscular skill as a boy named H. H. took over the lead in such situations with C.'s approval.

However, C. would occasionally overrule a decision of H.'s in such a situation, telling him, for example, not to put in a substitute player in a game; and H. would comply. A third popular boy, E., was delegated authority by C. in other tasks, such as camping or hiking.

In some contrast to the Bull Dog group, the boy who became recognized as leader of the Red Devils, S., won his position chiefly by virtue of his daring, athletic skill, and "toughness." He is noted as successfully leading the group in games and in daring expeditions. He was overtly recognized as "the captain" by other Red Devils. Yet S. tended to be "cliquish," confining his favors and most of his attention on the whole to a few other boys high in status, and preferring to be with them. He sometimes enforced his decisions by threats or actual physical encounters. On some later occasion, he even encouraged and participated in an attack on two members low in status in his own group. For this reason, S.'s leadership position was sometimes shaky. In fact, on the basis of popularity ratings at the end of Stage II, another boy, L., received one more choice from the group than did S. (see Fig. 2). As it happened, S. retained power over his lieutenants, including L., and these boys in turn had effective and consistent influence over the rest of the group. It was the consensus of the staff that L. could have taken over the leadership of the group if he had wished to. For some reason, he remained subordinate to S. personally and in the group. S. once announced to the group: "My first successor is L." Later, at a time when his leadership was very shaky, he referred to L. as "the co-captain." Actually L. at no time asserted leadership over S.

S.'s prestige in his group was revealed when he spoke of his coming birthday and the boys found that he would be only twelve years old. They all expressed surprise with such remarks as, "I thought you were at least fifteen!"

Within both groups, there was competition for status as exemplified by the struggle between L. and H. of the Bull Dogs. L. tried to compete with H. in athletic events. But all the boys recognized that his performance did not measure up to H.'s. As a result, L. openly resented H.'s higher status, making remarks such as "Why does H. get to do everything?" On one occasion, H. physically squelched L.'s strivings. In this conflict, C. (the leader) tried to placate L. In spite of L.'s dissatisfaction with his status, he became increasingly identified with the group. One day, some group members expressed a desire to have the horseshoe stakes moved closer to their cabin. L. and H. tried to pull them from their present location. As the others in the group came along, L. successfully tugged them out of the ground and fell to the ground exhausted. In response to their cheers, he replied, "It was me and H."

Along with the formation of a more or less definite group structure, with which we have dealt only sketchily here, each group developed strong in-group feelings of *loyalty* and *solidarity* within the group and of identification of varying degrees with its activities and products. This in-group identification is illustrated by the reaction of the in-groups to those members who continued to mingle with boys in the experimental out-groups several days after the division into two groups at the end of Stage I. For example, three members of the Red Devil group, all low in the status hierarchy, were branded as "traitors" and even threatened with beatings until they saw less of the boys with whom they had been friendly in Stage I and who became Bull Dogs. When one of the counselors returned from a necessary trip to the cabin of the other group, he was greeted with cries of "Traitor!"

Even the most retiring and ambivalent members were *at times* caught in the in-group. For example, one boy who was lowest in the Bull Dog group for participation, and was caught between loyalty to the group and waves of homesickness, was observed driving a long stick into a piece of red paper, saying, "That's what we'd do to the Red Devils."

An example of in-group identification is a boy's reference to his cabin as "home." He asked the boy leader if he had some equipment "at home." The leader asked, "Which home?" and the boy replied, "Our cabin, I mean."

Along with the group structure, products were standardized by the group, which in turn served to further solidify the in-groups. Obviously one example of such standardization was the names for the groups. The choice of these names was without doubt influenced by the larger setting—Bull Dogs, for example, being a symbol of Yale. Most of the boys were quickly given nicknames in their group: in the Bull Dog group, the boy named Emerson was dubbed "Radio," Luden was called "Coughdrop," and other nicknames clearly referred to the individual characteristics of the boys. H., the boy athletic leader, was admiringly called "Horrible H.," another lad was named "Screwball." Interestingly enough, the leader of this group, C., was the only boy in this group respectfully called by his own first name—Lee. The leader of the Red Devils was tagged to typify his toughness and attractive blond appearance as "Baby Face." Other nicknames in this group were "Bones" for a thin boy and "Lemonhead" for L., a boy with a rather long skull.

Each group came to prefer certain songs. In some of them they inserted their own group's name in a glorifying fashion and the names of the other group in a less complimentary way.

Both groups standardized methods of punishment. In the case of the Red Devils, as we have mentioned, sanctions were imposed by S., the leader, through threats or actual encounters. Wayward Bull Dogs, on the other hand, were kept in line with a system of sanctions suggested and always imposed by C., the leader. Although he once was observed verbally threatening a boy, C. relied on the method of sanctions rather consistently. A Bull Dog who got out of line had to remove a certain number of heavy stones, usually ten, from the Bull Dog Pond. This method started when the boys were improving their secret swimming place by damming it and removing rocks. They actually succeeded in raising the water level six inches.

One of the *crucial tests* of the study was whether or not these experimentally introduced in-group relationships would bring shifts or reversals in the friendship ties which began to form in Stage I on the basis of personal likes or affinities. At the end of Stage II, sociograms were obtained through informal talks with each boy. In obtaining these sociograms, it should be emphasized that the boys were free to mention those boys they liked to be with best *in the whole camp*, i.e., from the other group as well as their own.

The results indicating that such reversals were indeed found can be summarized as shown in the following table:

TABLE II

Total Choices of Friends, End of Stage II

| | *Choices Received by:* | |
Choices Made by:	Red Devils	Bull Dogs
Red Devils	95.0%	5.0%
Bull Dogs	12.3%	87.7%

For comparison purposes the reversals of friendship choices obtained at the end of Stage I, the stage of natural groupings, and at the end of Stage II, the stage of experimental in-group formation, are presented together in Table III. It becomes sharply evident from this comparison that the friendship preferences of these boys were at first predominantly for members of the experimental out-groups. During Stage II, shifts in friendship choices occurred which were definitely in the direction of the members of the developing in-groups.

TABLE III (Composite Table)

Total Choices of Friends at the End of Stage I and End of Stage II
(Note the Reversals)

| | | *Choices Received by:* | |
	Choices Made by:	*Eventual In-Grroup*	*Eventual Out-Group*
End of	Eventual Red Devils	35.1%	64.9%
Stage I	Eventual Bull Dogs	35.0%	65.0%
End of	Red Devils	95.0%	5.0%
Stage II	Bull Dogs	87.7%	12.3%

It is evident from these tables that after the stage of in-group formation was completed, the members of each experimental group predominantly preferred to associate with members of their own in-group.

Very briefly, we will summarize the results of Stage II. In line with the first part of our hypothesis, it was found that when the two experimentally produced groups were brought together in situations and activities calling for group cooperation toward common goals, an unmistakable in-group structure developed with hierarchical positions and roles within it. The structure was not static, changing with situations within certain limits. As the group formed, the members achieved positive in-group identifications and common attitudes toward the group. By-products or *norms* peculiar to the group were standardized—nicknames, catchwords, ways of doing things, sanctions, preferred songs, etc.

Before going on to the results of Stage III, the period of inter-group relations, it is necessary to emphasize one more finding of Stage II which is related to in-group formation and *specifically related to the cultural background of the subjects.* Along with the delineation of the "we" or in-group, the two experimental groups referred to the "they" or out-group frequently and in a clear-cut way, even though there was comparatively little functional contact between the groups.

More than this, these groups of boys immediately and spontaneously began to make *comparisons*, not just in terms of "what *we* have or do, and what *they* have or do," but in terms of "their lousy cabin," "our pond is better," and even "those low kind." They began to express a desire to each other and to the staff to compete with the other group in games, with considerable assurance that their own group would win. In fact, on the second day of Stage II which followed the rather strenuous hike and cook-out for each group separately on the first day, signs of competitive attitudes between the two groups were mounting. The groups devoted a good share of this second day to the more leisurely activity of improving their respective bunkhouses and surroundings with the help of their counselors. During this activity, comparisons between the efforts of the groups cropped up and boundaries were drawn around the bunkhouse areas. The boundary questions led to disputes between some members of the two groups and some raiding of each other's cabins. This raiding was carried on in a rather playful and adventurous spirit and had the effect of intensifying the developing in-group demarcations. Since the main aim of Stage II was to produce in-group formations through cooperative group interaction rather than through opposition or competition in relation to an out-group, possible contact between the two experimental groups was further reduced during the following days of Stage II by keeping their activities farther apart through overnight hiking, swimming separately, and cook-outs in their respective hide-outs.

This rather strong desire to compete and the spontaneous derogation of the other group in *specific* respects probably *stems from the cultural*

*background and specific socialization of these boys in a competitive so-
ciety.* However, these instances of competitive feelings and, in some
cases, of derogation, were *not* at this stage *standardized* in the sense that
they were consistent modes of response to the out-group and its members. They were confined chiefly to the urgent desire to participate in
the most attractive of all pastimes for American boys of this age—competition in sports. There was no consistent day-to-day tension or hostility
between the groups at this stage.

   In Stage III, the stage of inter-group relations which formally lasted
nearly five days, the two experimental groups—each with varying degrees
of in-group structure and strengthening friendships within the in-group
—were brought into functional relationship with each other in competitive
and mildly frustrating situations. The frustrating situations were planned
in such a way that *on the whole* they seemed to one group to have been
caused by the other.

   At the beginning of Stage III, a series of competitive games was
announced as though giving in to the boys' requests. The plan was for
each group to receive a certain number of points or credits for winning
athletic events during the coming days and for the excellence of performance in camp duties, such as cabin cleaning, K.P., etc. This point
system, which was explained and given to each group orally and on
typed sheets, was simple and clear. However, it allowed for some manipulation by the staff in the points given at cabin inspection, K.P., etc.
It was possible, therefore, to keep the number of points attained by each
group within a surmountable range until near the end of the contest,
thus keeping up the strivings of both groups to win. For example, victory
in athletic events brought about 15 points, whereas 1 to 10 points could
be given for K.P. duties. Since such duties were performed separately,
this manipulation did not arouse too much suspicion. The staff agreed
that both sides were evenly matched in sports in terms of the size and
skill of individual members.

   A poster with two thermometers was placed on the bulletin board
and the rising score of each group filled in. This poster became a center
of attention for the competing groups. The prize to the winning group,
which was displayed and much admired, was twelve four-bladed knives
—one knife for each member of the winning group.

   The effects of competitive games were not immediate. Observers all
noted considerable "good sportmanship" on the part of the two groups
at the start. For example, after the first contest, the winning group spontaneously gave a cheer for the losers; and the losers, though still scattered
around the field, responded as a group with a cheer for the winners.
However, as the contest series progressed, this cheer changed. It started
out as "2–4–6–8, who do we appreciate," followed by the name of the
other team. It changed to "2–4–6–8, who do we appreci*hate*."

Each day of Stage III began with a Tug of War between the two groups (see Fig. 3). In this contest, the group members organized themselves and exhorted each other in the intense common effort. As it happened, the Red Devils lost the first contest. Their reaction to the loss represents one of many *perceptual distortions occurring in the group situations.* (We mentioned previously the group's exaggeration of their leader's age by three years.) All Red Devils were convinced that the "ground was against us." They spent most of the morning discussing this and their strategy for the next Tug of War. The following day, this group was on the verge of winning the Tug of War when the Bull Dogs' leader began a series of shouts and encouragement to his boys. This apparently made possible a "second wind" in which the Bull Dogs regained their lost ground and finally defeated the Red Devils again. This time, the Red Devils rationalized their defeat by agreeing that the Bull Dogs "must have done something to the rope."

The series of games also included softball, soccer, and touch football. These contests tended to solidify further the in-group structure and loyalty. For example, one of the Bull Dogs became ill and was unable to participate in one of the games. He and other members of his group cried. The boy who was ill said that if the Bull Dogs won the series, he would not accept a knife because he had "let them down." But the other boys shouted down this sacrifice, gave him a cheer, and loudly proclaimed that he was "one of them."

In the Red Devil group, one of the members low in status, a boy named F., revealed increasing identification with the group during this period. When the Red Devils were trailing the Bull Dogs with two outs, and no one on the bases, F. came to bat and was tagged out with a ground ball. He sobbed for some time and went off by himself, saying to a counselor, "I lost the game for us." He was almost afraid to show his face in the Red Devil cabin; but his group never mentioned the

FIGURE 3.

incident and were, in fact, kind to him. This incident typifies the manner in which *group efforts and goals* became intensely *personal* ones for the individual members.

As mentioned earlier, inter-group rivalry and hostility increased rapidly during the days of the competitive contest. During one game when the boys were becoming overheated, a staff member cautioned a Red Devil not to drink too much water, because he might get sick. At this, a Bull Dog called out in a nasty tone, "Let him drink all he can. He's a Red Devil." Such expressions of hostility became increasingly frequent.

As the contest progressed, the Bull Dog group pulled out in the lead, probably because of their highly effective organization directed by C. and, in athletic events, led by H. The Red Devils responded to their increasingly apparent losing position by labeling the Bull Dogs as "dirty players." They were sure that they could win if the Bull Dogs were not "such cheaters." They said, "At least we play fair." By the contest's end, the words "dirty players" and "cheats" were almost synonymous with Bull Dogs as far as the Red Devils were concerned. Of course, the Bull Dogs denied such charges and even recognized the role of their more integrated group structure in their performance with such remarks as "We win because we have an organization."

The cumulative effect of the competitive games caused considerable group friction and, to the Red Devils, considerable frustration. The common expression of the winning Bull Dogs and the losing Red Devils in pictures taken immediately following the victory of the Bull Dogs in the athletic series conveys an objective glimpse of this fact.

The winning Bull Dogs were tremendously elated at their victory. The reward of knives was distributed by C.'s suggested method—each boy was blindfolded and chose a knife from a bucket. Thus, not even the high-status members had advantage in choosing preferred colors, etc.

The losing group, the Red Devils, was by this time weakened. In their case, the group failure was conducive to disintegration. S., the leader and athletic captain, was bitter and began blaming and ridiculing members of his own group. At the same time he retired more and more to the company of his lieutenants. This was resented by Red Devils lower in status. Until the Red Devil group experienced an attack from the Bull Dogs and even fought with them at a later time, there was considerable disorganization.

In addition to this competition in Stage III, there were also arranged situations in which it seemed that one group interfered with or frustrated the other. Several such incidents were planned by the staff, but they could not all be carried out because of the extreme effectiveness of the first ones. The examples given were carefully recorded and, with the background of the two crystallized but hostile in-groups, constitute a little experiment in themselves. Unfortunately, many fascinating details must be omitted in this presentation.

On the evening of the victory of the Bull Dogs over the Red Devils in the athletic series and camp competition, both groups were asked to attend a party in the mess hall. By careful timing and by indirectly interesting one group in something else momentarily, the participant observers were able to see to it that the Red Devils got to the mess hall a short time before the Bull Dogs. None of the subjects in either group suspected that this timing was deliberate.

The refreshments of ice cream, cake, etc. were on a table. Half of them had been battered, broken, or crushed; the other half remained whole and delectable. When the first group (the Red Devils) arrived, they were told to go ahead and take their share of the refreshments, leaving half of it for the Bull Dogs, who were late. As we know, the Red Devils were the defeated group and had expressed in no uncertain terms their frustration and envy of the Bull Dogs for winning the prize.

Faced with the refreshments, half fresh and appetizing and half broken and crushed, the Red Devils chose the good portion and carried it to their own table. At this point the Bull Dogs arrived. Upon seeing the sorry-looking refreshments left for them, and the feasting Red Devils, they immediately protested by sulking and by remarks of hostility against the Red Devils. The Red Devils were quick to justify their actions in terms of "first come, first served," which became the standardized justification for all Red Devil members.

The Bull Dogs discussed the possibility of throwing their beaten-up cake at the Red Devils, but decided against it on the grounds that, after all, it would taste good. They went to the far corner of the mess hall and proceeded to hurl insults and names at the Red Devils. The names were by now standardized, among them being "dirty bums," "rotten jerks," "pukes," and several more objectionable terms.

The Red Devils ate their refreshments in righteous indignation, referring to the Bull Dogs as "dirty players," "cheats," etc. The most vociferous Red Devils were four boys at the bottom status level in their group. The leaders remained more sullen and resentful of the "unjustified" attack. L., the leader's chief lieutenant, told the group to "ignore it."

When they finished, the Red Devils left the mess hall, but one of the stragglers caught sight of the Bull Dogs dumping their dirty plates and ice cream cartons on the Red Devil table. He became involved in a physical altercation which was stopped by the counselor when one Bull Dog pulled out his knife, opened the blade, and had to be restrained from brandishing it.

This event, which the Bull Dogs saw as the doings of the Red Devils, set off a series of raids and fights which soon had to be stopped by all means. The next morning, the Red Devils deliberately dirtied up their table at breakfast to make the clean-up work hard for the Bull Dogs, who were on K.P. that day. When the Bull Dogs saw the messy table, they decided to mess up the table further and leave it. C., their leader, was against this action, but the group went ahead and he joined in. They smeared the table with cocoa, sugar, syrup, etc., and left it. It was soon alive with bees and wasps. The group hung the walls with threatening and derogatory posters against the Red Devils.

The upshot of this was that at lunch that day the two groups lined up across the mess hall from each other and began to fight—shouting, throwing knives, cups, etc., and becoming so excited that intervention became necessary.

No one of either group knew who started the fight. Each was sure it was someone in the other group.

At this point, it was quickly decided by the staff to stop Stage III of the experiment immediately and to concentrate on breaking down the in-groups. The decision was to stop the intense inter-group conflict by any means necessary and then to initiate a camp program in which all boys would participate on a campwide basis. The experiment, from the point of view of controlling the situation, was over at this point. There was no systematic attempt at integration after Stage III. The instructions to all the staff members were to do away with the hostility as much as possible in order to send everyone home feeling good. In this period, a great deal of information and significant leads were gained for the future study of integration of hostile groups and elimination of hostility, which is certainly the pressing problem to be tackled.

In spite of the genuine efforts of the participant observers and junior counselors to stop the fighting, the acts and words of hostility continued. The Bull Dogs raided the Red Devil bunkhouse to regain a supply of green apples which they had stored as ammunition "just in case," and which the Red Devils had taken from them.

At the instigation of a counselor, the Bull Dogs decided to send H. on a "peace mission" to the furious Red Devils. H. was chosen because his athletic prowess was admired by all the camp and because during the athletic series he had remained on somewhat better terms with the Red Devil leader than had any other Bull Dog. However, the formerly temperate Red Devil leaders, S. and L., who had advised the group to "ignore" the Bull Dogs, turned down H.'s efforts. In spite of their counselor's argument, the Red Devils declined to settle with the Bull Dogs until they had had a chance to "get even." H.'s "peace mission" ended in inglorious failure: he was chased from the Red Devil bunkhouse in a hail of green apples.

The Red Devils were observed going on unauthorized expeditions to collect green apples and were later instructed that there was to be no more fighting. Pictures were taken of this secret expedition.

In spite of the fact that the Red Devils were dead-tired from the activities of the day, these youngsters succeeded in awakening and dressing at 2 A.M. with the intention of raiding the Bull Dogs. This attempted raid was an "upper-crust" affair, led by S. and his lieutenants. The raid was stopped by the participant observer and junior counselor, who were asleep in the cabin, when one of the would-be raiders kicked over a barrel of green apples which were to be used as ammunition. Since it was dark, no one could be sure who did this. The boys were in general agreement on a culprit who himself vigorously denied the charge, saying that S., the leader, made the noise. After going back to bed, the Red Devils were stopped from raiding again at 6 A.M. the same morning. Both groups were made to dump the ammunition they had hoarded.

The degree of hostility between the two groups can be clearly seen in the posters which were made by the boys and hung in the mess hall and in each others' cabins. These posters were made in every case by boys low in status in their respective groups. This, along with other evidence which has been touched upon, suggests that manifestations of inter-group hostility and rivalry of group members low in status may at times be more intense than the manifestations of members higher in status. It seems likely that the members low in status, having greater strivings for status within the group, may go to greater lengths in trying to gain recognition by showing their identification and loyalty to the in-group (Figs. 4 and 5 are examples of these posters).

In brief, the consequences of the inter-group relations in competitive situations and in frustrating situations which members of one group perceived as coming from the other group were: (1) to solidify the in-group belongingness and solidarity, to enhance in-group democracy, and to strengthen in-group friendships; (2) to generate and increase out-group hostility, to produce derogatory *name-calling* which came close to standardizing of negative stereotypes in relation to the out-group (i.e., *rudiments of prejudice*).

Thus, we see in a concrete way that in-group democracy and cooperation does not necessarily mean democracy and cooperation with the out-group and its member, if the directions and interest of the groups are in conflict.

In dealing with inter-group relations, the vital interest and directions of the groups in their day-to-day living have to be given their due weights. The attempts to bring people into contact in a group situation and to change their perceptions and attitudes without giving proper weight to the *vital interests* of group members is hardly more than playing with shadows. *The facts of structuring and re-structuring perceptions and attitudes are not arbitrary affairs.* They are organically related to the motives sanctioned and regulated by actual group memberships.

It is not possible here to deal at any length with other aftermaths of this experiment. After Stage III, the boys were brought together once

FIGURE 4.

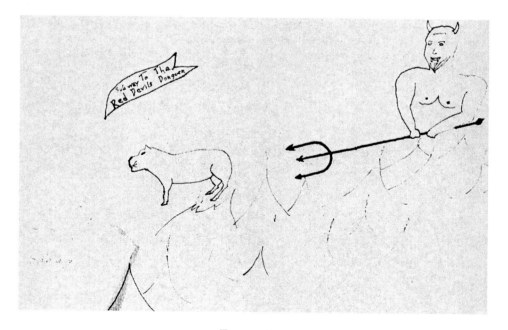

FIGURE 5.

more. Their tables were separated so that all boys would "mix up," and they were encouraged to do so by the counselors. With some persuasion, the groups attended birthday parties, camp fires, and other activities together. Individual competitions, track meets, a stunt night, etc. were held.

Probably the most effective event for the breaking up of the in-groups was a campwide softball game in which a team chosen by the boys from the entire camp competed with an outside group of boys from the neighboring town. In this, the boys participated *as campers*, not as in-group members. However, it should be recognized that any future experiment designed to study the process of integration between two such hostile in-groups should hardly be started by uniting the in-groups against still another in-group.

The postexperimental period did relieve a good deal of the generated tension, in that there were no more collective fights. However, the evidences of the in-group lines developed during the experimental period were observed on subsequent days. Seating arrangements, friendship preferences, etc. continued to follow group lines on the whole. On the last night of camp, the boys of the two experimental groups insisted that they wanted separate campfires because they wanted to be "by themselves" for the last time. In spite of their mixing, the old names and songs for the opposite group cropped up occasionally at these gatherings.

EXPERIMENTAL INDICATORS FOR MEASURING GROUP RELATIONS

Before closing this general report of our study, I would like to emphasize one theoretical and methodological point that has served as the guiding principle in the conception and execution of our investigation. This guiding principle, as has been pointed out earlier, has been that the reactions (perceptual, judgmental, etc.) of the individual take place within their appropriate reference frames. Following the implications of this principle, it is becoming more and more evident that perceptual, judgmental, motivational, and other reactions of the individual member in a group situation can be adequately understood only by placing him in the group setting of which he is a part. And this, in turn, implies that *the effects of group situations and participation as a group member will be reflected even in the relatively simple discriminations (judgments), perceptions, and other reactions of the individual.* This being the case, the effects of the group situation, and the changes brought about in attitudes toward the in-group and the out-group and their respective members, can be studied in terms of precise laboratory experiments, such as the currently accumulating judgment and perception studies. This will constitute a significant advance in method over observation of actual behavioral events alone. The actual behavioral events are more difficult to observe with precision and present baffling problems in their ordering along definite dimensions. If the psychological significance of the actual behavioral events can be epitomized and measured in terms of representative judgmental and perceptual situations, we shall be achieving a methodological gain close to the laboratory level.

In the observational data, we have concrete leads for reducing the gross behavioral trends to clear-cut perceptual and judgmental situations. For example, in competitive games, the members of the opposing teams were very keen in catching even the slightest errors or fouls committed or supposedly committed by their opponents. Such errors or alleged errors instantaneously brought forth shouts of protest from the group concerned, almost to a man. Correspondingly, any success exhibited by their in-group players brought forth almost unanimous cries of elation. In instances of dispute where errors or fouls were not so clear-cut, both groups invariably lined up against each other and the referees to prove that their opponents were in the wrong, citing all kinds of "observations" to substantiate their point. Following this lead, after in-group and out-group delineation is experimentally produced and tension is mounting between groups, members of opposing teams can be brought into controlled situations to study their perceptual selectivity and distortion. For example, a series of pictures can be designed in which the face of the player committing an error or achieving a success is not clear. These pictures can be shown to members of each of the groups for a suitably short time, and the groups' identifications obtained for the individuals in the pictures who are in error or are achieving success. In line with the findings concerning perceptual selectivity and shifts brought about by motivational factors, it can be predicted that picture identification will significantly follow group lines—the number of identified heroes being greater on the in-group side and the number of culprits being greater on the antagonistic out-group side.

Another good possibility is the use of the autokinetic situation, which can be employed in different ways to produce significant trends along group lines. For example, one such possibility is to get the scale of distribution and the norm of judgments first *individually* from the members of opposing groups. The members could then be paired, with one member of the pair from each of the opposing groups. Also, the individuals would be paired with other members of their in-group. It can be stated as a plausible hypothesis that the departure from the individual norms of the first individual session in the direction of a common norm in a subsequent group situation will be greater in the case of the in-group pairs than with the pairs composed of in-group and out-group members.

The above are two of several possible judgmental and perceptual situations which can be utilized to measure group effects. Such controlled study of the effects of experimentally produced group situations could be made in relation to other functions as well. Rote learning and selective forgetting could be studied easily by presentation of simple verbal stimuli, such as lists of adjectives. It would be interesting, for example, to compare the rate of learning and retention by in-group members of uncomplimentary adjectives when these adjectives are applied to their in-group and when applied to the out-group and its members.

Through such an approach, judgmental, perceptual, learning, motivational processes can be studied in a unified experimental design in a group setting *which is itself experimentally produced.*

This study was not carried out in a sadistic spirit to generate group tensions. It was carried out with the conviction that we must attain a clear understanding of the underlying factors producing friction and tensions among human groupings if we are to deal with them effectively. Otherwise, our efforts in the direction of their elimination will continue to be wasteful. The real advances in medical sciences have been achieved, I believe, by going at the outset to the causation of disease.

Our next step will be the study of integration in inter-group relations. We have already learned a few lessons from the present study which are in line with the more empirical data of men in the social sciences. These may serve as the basis for further hypotheses and experimentation.

TWENTY-TWO

APPROACH, HYPOTHESES, AND GENERAL DESIGN
OF INTERGROUP EXPERIMENTS

The focal concern of this study is intergroup relations. As an experiment in social psychology, it undertakes to trace over a time period the formation and functioning of negative and positive attitudes of members of one group toward another group and its members as a consequence of experimentally introduced situations. Therefore, the main hypotheses relate to attitudinal and behavioral trends predicted as a result of controlled alterations of the conditions in which experimentally formed in-groups interact.

The general trend of findings from the sociology of small in-groups and their intergroup relations and relevant findings from the work of experimental psychologists led us to the experimental study of the problem of intergroup relations in successive stages. In the present undertaking (Summer, 1954) it will be carried out in three successive stages. The main features of these three successive stages are the following:

Stage 1: Experimental production of in-groups with a hierarchical structure and set of norms (intra-group relations). In line with our 1949 and 1953 studies, this will be done, not through discussion methods or through lecture or exhortation by resource persons or experts, but through *the introduction of goals that rise as integral parts in the situations, that have common appeal value, and that necessitate facing a common problem, discussion, planning, and execution in a mutually cooperative way.*

Stage 2: Bringing the two experimentally formed groups into func-

Mimeographed and distributed to staff and a number of colleagues in various universities by the author as principal investigator prior to experiments and included in M. Sherif, O. J. Harvey, B. J. White, W. R. Hood, and Carolyn W. Sherif, *Intergroup Conflict and Cooperation: The Robbers Cave Experiment,* Norman: University of Oklahoma, Institute of Group Relations, 1961. (Multilithed.) It is reproduced here in substantially the original form including the use of *future tense* in referring to various steps and procedures of the design. The experiment was supported by a grant to the author from the Rockefeller Foundation in 1952.

tional relations in situations in which the groups find themselves in competition for given goals and in conditions which imply some frustration in relation to one another (*intergroup tension*).

Stage 3: Introduction of goals which cannot be easily ignored by members of the two antagonistic groups, but the attainment of which is beyond the resources and efforts of one group alone. Such goals will be referred to as *superordinate goals* throughout this report. Superordinate goals are to be introduced with the aim of studying the reduction of intergroup tension in order to derive realistic leads for the integration of hostile groups. Considerations which led to the selection of this approach rather than other possible alternatives (such as a common enemy, leadership technique or discussion techniques) are stated briefly in the discussion of Stage 3 in the last part of this report.

It should be emphasized at the outset that individuals brought into an experimental situation to function as small groups are already members of actual groups in their social settings and thus have internalized values or norms (that is, attitudes) which are necessarily brought to the situation. With this consideration in mind and in order to give greater weight to experimentally introduced factors in the situation, a special effort will be made in this study not to appeal to internalized values or to prestige symbols coming from the larger setting in the formation and change of positive or negative attitudes in relation to respective in-groups and out-groups.

BACKGROUND OF THE ABOVE SUMMARY

The rationale that underlies the above formulation of our approach to the study of intergroup relations stems from relevant findings in both sociology and psychology. They are stated more fully elsewhere.[1] Here only a summary statement of these lines of development will be given.

Empirical observations by social scientists and inferences made by psychologists without direct experimental verification present a rather confusing picture at the present time. Therefore it is necessary to state precisely the sense in which the concept "group" and the issue of relations between them (intergroup relations) are used here:

A group may be defined as a social unit (1) that consists of a number of individuals who, at a given time, stand in more or less definite interdependent status and role relationships to one another and (2) that

---

[1] Leads derived from the field work of sociologists concerning relations of small groups are summarized in M. Sherif and H. Cantril (1947), Chap. 10; M. Sherif (1948), Chaps. 5–7; Sherif and Sherif (1953), especially Chap. 8.

Psychological principles derived from the work of experimental psychologists and utilized in our previous work as well as the present undertaking are summarized in M. Sherif (1936), Chap. 3; Sherif (1948), especially Chaps. 4, 7, and 9; Sherif and Sherif (1953), especially Chap. 6.

explicitly or implicitly possesses a set of values or norms of its own regulating the behavior of individual members, at least in matters of consequence to the group.

In order that this definition not be unwieldy, common attitudes, common aspirations, and goals are omitted. Such shared attitudes, aspirations, and goals are related to and, in fact, are implicit in the concept of common values or norms of a group. From the point of view of the members within the group, these social units may be referred to as *in-groups*. Again from the point of view of a member within the group, those social units of which he is not a part psychologically or to which he does not relate himself may be referred to as *out-groups*. It follows that the term *intergroup relations* refers to the relations between two or more in-groups and their respective members. Whenever individuals belonging to one in-group interact, collectively or individually, with another group or its members in terms of their group identification, we have an instance of intergroup relations.

From a survey of empirical literature it can be stated that intergroup attitudes and behavior regulated by them are produced in the form of social distances and standardized stereotypes as a consequence of functional relations between in-groups. Once these intergroup attitudes and stereotypes are standardized they take their place in the cultural repertory of the group and in many cases, through the vehicle of language, outlast the very functional relations which were responsible for their rise.

These functional relations between groups and their consequences, rather than the study of the deviate individual, constitute the central problem of intergroup relations. Of course, this does not imply a denial of various unique influences in the life history of the individual member (such as personal frustrations, special hardships in the family or other situations). Such personal influences in the life history may have a great deal to do with the individual becoming a nonconformist or deviate in terms of the prevailing scales of attitudes of his group. But such unique or personal influences *do not determine the scale themselves*. Rather they come in an important way to determine the particular place the individual will occupy within these scales or, in the case of nonconformists or deviates, the acceptance of a position outside of the scale.

Considerations determining the approach, plan, and hypotheses: At present there are various and conflicting psychological approaches to the study of intergroup relations. It seems that no amount of argument on an abstract level will prove the advantage of one approach over another. Certain of the empirical considerations that led to the approach to be used in this study will be mentioned briefly in the pages that follow.

The consequential intergroup behavior of individuals (largely revealing friction and tension at the present time) is in terms of their membership in their respective groups. Intergroup behavior of an individual which deviates considerably from the prevailing trends is not a typical case. If the individual's intergroup behavior is too much out of line with the prevailing trend of his respective groups, it is brushed aside or dealt with as *deviate* by other members.

One approach to intergroup relations is through the study of *leadership*. Even though leadership undeniably contributes great weight in the shaping of intergroup relations, concentration of research on leadership alone leaves out functional ties to which leadership itself is organically related. Such an approach is in contradiction to the main trend in leadership studies today. These studies are increasingly pointing to the necessity of considering leadership in terms of the whole state of reciprocities within the group.

Another approach in intergroup problems concentrates efforts on *in-group relations*. Empirical data seem to indicate that the nature of intergroup relations need not be in line with the prevailing character of in-group relations. This approach, which concentrates on improving in-group relations in order to improve intergroup relations, ignores the demonstrated consequences attributable only to the particular character of the interaction process *between groups*. Solidarity within the group need not be transferred to solidarity between groups, and in fact may contribute to sharpened delineations between groups with all the attendant byproducts.

In short, the conception of the present study differs markedly from existing theories which posit one factor or a few factors as sole or primary determinants of the course of intergroup relations. (1) Inherent superiority of human groups; (2) national character ("war-like people," "peaceful people"); (3) deep-seated innate instincts of aggression or destruction; (4) frustrations suffered individually; (5) direct economic gain; and (6) the character of leadership—all are variously advanced as sole or primary determinants of intergroup relations. Each of these theories still has its strong supporters.

The present approach does not deny that some such factors may, singly or in combination, be operative as factors in determining the course of intergroup relations (excepting specifically the first and third listed above). "National character," frustrations suffered in common and experienced as a common issue, certain economic gains that become shared goals, or the particular character of the group's leadership may variously become the more weighty determinant of intergroup relations under a given set of circumstances.[2]

But conflicting evidence leads us to assert that the weighty factor determining intergroup relations will not be the same for all circumstances. For example, in settled times when in-groups are in a state of greater stability, national character as formed at the time and the existing scale of social distance (or prejudice) will regulate, on the whole, the

[2] The present approach is elaborated more fully in Sherif and Sherif (1953), 182–90, 296–307.

particular pattern of intergroup relations. But in times of greater flux or crises (due to the impact of technological, cultural, socioeconomic, and even military events) some other factor or factors take the upper hand.

One primary point of departure in our approach, then, is the principle that various factors are functionally interrelated. In this respect the present approach is opposed to theories which make this or that factor sovereign in its own right; it attempts rather to ascertain the relative weights of all the possible factors that may be operative at the same time.

The functional relatedness of various factors leads us to the cardinal psychological principle of our whole plan of study: In the study of (intra- and inter-) group relations the relative contribution of given external stimulus factors and internal factors pertaining to participating individuals (hunger, sex, status desire, complexes, etc.) have to be analyzed within the framework of the ongoing interaction process among the members in question.

The relative contribution of an external stimulus factor, or an attitude, a drive, or other internal factors, cannot be simply extrapolated from individual situations to interaction situations. Interaction processes are not voids. Whatever drives, motives, or attitudes the individual brings into the situation operate as deflected, modified, and, at times, transformed in the interaction process among the several individuals (who stand or come to stand in time in definite role relations toward one another).

The application of this cardinal principle to the study of group relations is derived from more basic findings in the field of judgment and perception. The judgment of a given weight is not determined solely by its absolute value but also, within limits, by its relative position in the scale of which it is a part and by the presence or absence of other functionally related anchoring stimuli with values within and without the scale. Likewise, placement of attitudinal items on a scale with categories specified by the experimenter or with categories chosen by the subject is determined not only by whatever intrinsic value these items may have when considered singly, but also by their relation to one another and their relation to the stand that the individual has taken on the issue.

Following the implications of this general psychological principle, it may be plausible to state that behavior revealing discriminations, perceptions, evaluations of individuals participating in the interaction process as group members will be determined *not* only by whatever motivational components and personality characteristics each member brings with him, *not* only by the properties of stimulus conditions specified in an unrelated way, but as influenced, modified, and even *transformed* interdependently by these and the special properties of the interaction process, in which a developing or established *state of reciprocities* (roles, statuses) plays no small part. The developing state of reciprocities between individual members can be measured in various differentiated dimensions (for example, status, popularity, initiative, etc.).

In short, one cannot directly extrapolate from the knowledge of stimulus conditions alone or motivational components of participating individuals alone, but one has to study behavior in the framework of the actual interaction process with its developing reciprocities.

Carrying this line of conceptualization to the area of intergroup relations, one should start with the recognition that *the area of interaction between groups* cannot be directly extrapolated from the nature of relations within groups or prevailing practices within them, even though a careful analysis of intragroup relations is an essential prerequisite in any approach to intergroup relations. Numerous instances of intergroup relations in which the pattern (positive or negative) is different from the pattern prevailing within the respective in-groups might be mentioned.

The interaction process between groups and its consequences have to be studied in their own right in addition to studying relations prevailing within the in-groups in question.

The conceptual orientation outlined above determined:

1. The formulation of specific hypotheses.
2. The design of the experiment through three successive stages.
3. The choice of criteria in selection of subjects and the choice of setting that will not permit the direct intrusion of influences other than those experimentally introduced.
4. The special considerations related to observational and experimental techniques to be used in the collection of data, and the specific roles staff members will occupy.

METHODOLOGICAL CONSIDERATIONS

The problem of intergroup relations has not been made the domain of experimentation. Literally, there are only a few studies specifically designed to experiment on intergroup relations. Therefore, the present study undertakes to define main functional relations involved in the problem and to point to some unmistakable trends on the basis of data obtained.

In experimental study of intergroup relations it is necessary that various conditions *between* groups be experimentally introduced and manipulated, the nature of these conditions being defined, and the consequences of their variation predicted.

Recent research in both psychology and sociology and indications of attempts by practitioners in this area are making it increasingly evident that theoretical and practical problems of group relations, including attitudes and change of attitudes regulating behavior of individuals within their respective groups (in-groups) and with out-groups, have to be studied in terms of the *interaction processes* within and between appropriate group settings.

The usual practice in attitude studies has been to study the effects of already existing attitudes, or to measure attitudes that are already formed. When carried out apart from particular group settings, the study of motives (drives), frustrations, past experience, etc., (which are certainly operative in the formation, functioning, and change of social attitudes pertaining to group relations) has given us items of information whose validity has not been proven in actual issues of group relations. The attempt in this study is to trace the formation, functioning, and change of attitudes towards one's own group, toward its various members, and towards out-groups and their members within the setting of group interaction processes, and as consequences thereof.

In-groups themselves and the attitudes of members towards one another and toward the in-group as a whole are to be experimentally produced. In other words, *group attitudes (both intra- and intergroup) will start from scratch and will be produced as a consequence of interaction processes in intra- and intergroup relations through the introduction of specified experimental conditions.* The methodological gain from the experimental production of attitudes whose effects or change are to be studied or measured needs no elaboration.

Considerations such as those briefly mentioned above determine the approach taken, the specific hypotheses formulated, and the design of the experiment in three successive stages in the present 1954 study. Likewise they determine the choice of particular methods and cautions to be pursued in the collection of data.

To approximate as much as possible the natural process of spontaneous group formation, of in-group and out-group delineation with its consequences so abundantly reported in the literature on small groups, *subjects will be kept unaware of the fact that this is an experiment on intergroup relations.*

Data concerning in-group formation (Stage 1) and intergroup functioning (in Stages 2 and 3) will be obtained through participant observers who are perceived as part and parcel of the situation by the subjects. All of the staff members directly in contact with the subjects will participate in the role of usual camp personnel, or some role not out-of-ordinary in a camp situation. Moreover, the participant observers should not be detected by the subjects while recording observations contrary to the natural functions of their announced roles. The argument that subjects cease to be mindful that their words and other behavior are being observed and recorded is not in harmony with what we have learned concerning the structuring of perception. The presence of a personage ever observing, ever recording our words and deeds in a situation in which our status and role concerns are at stake, cannot help coming in as an important anchorage in the framework of the interaction process in question. Candid recordings of conversation and moving pictures taken at choice points without the awareness of the subjects will be valuable in addition to other observational data.

All the goals in the in-group stage and in the negative and positive intergroup stages will be introduced through conditions inherent in immediate situations (such as eating, overnight camping, or some activity expressly desired by the subjects), and not in the form of abstract incentives distantly related to the immediate goals of ongoing activities and situations. For example, attainment of food will be introduced, not as a hypothetical problem or discussion situation, but through arranging conditions at a time when group members are getting hungry in a place where no other food is available so that members have to cooperate with one another to prepare available ingredients with facilities in the situation. (*After* subjects take the initiative along some plan, all necessary help and skill can be extended to carry out their plan more effectively.)

The technique of *problem solving*, that is, attainment of goals introduced in the manner described above, will not be through methods introduced by the experimenter, such as *discussion method* or *lecture method*. One of the guiding principles in the present study is that an actual problem situation faced by group members, as a common goal to be attained or a common deprivation to be taken care of, will necessarily lead to various suggestions, counter-suggestions, proposals and their weighing—in short, to discussion by group members.

When the group is faced with a situation involving common goals or deprivations, group activity will arise. This group activity may be in the form of suggestions from various members, leading to discussion, decisions, planning and execution. When group activity in relation to common goals is initiated, effective ways of dealing with the situation may involve group discussion, or analysis of the situation by a member who is conceded to know more about the topic than others, or (especially if the group is well-structured or the situation and available means sufficiently compelling) more direct action by higher status members or by the whole group may be taken. Those familiar with sociological findings on informally organized small groups, know well that such groups, facing plans to be executed or problems to be solved, do discuss, do plan, and do execute plans. In this interaction process involving an actual problem or goal situation perceived as common to the group, discussion of alternatives has its place, at times exhortations (lectures) and skills of particular members in verbal and nonverbal ways have their places. The various activities involved in the interaction process—namely, discussion, exhortation, planning, and execution—may be carried out in sequence, or in rapid succession, or the common decision may be implicit in the action itself, if the goal and means stand out clearly. The sequence followed and methods used will be determined in part by the nature of the problem, in part by the particular character of group structure (in which leadership, as part and parcel of the hierarchical structure of the group, plays no small part), in part by the particular set of values or norms prevailing in the group, and also by the character and norms of the general socio-cultural setting of which the group in question is a part.

Emphasis on studying the interaction process in a natural setting, while approximating experimental control and techniques, does not eliminate the possibility of checking the validity of observed trends by precise laboratory techniques at "choice" points. If there is any validity in the recent generalizations concerning perceptual and judgmental variations ("distortions") as a function of attitude or motive, relevant perceptual or judgmental tasks of the type used in the laboratory can very well be introduced at a few choice points. The stimulus materials used in these experimental units are of an indirect and unstructured type not involving direct questions about developing group attitudes. The procedures are perceived by the subjects as part of the camp activities, and not as experiments which clutter the flow of their interaction process.

In fact, on the methodological side, the plan of the study aims at two additional objectives:

1. The first involves the introduction of laboratory-type experimental procedures as supplements for obtaining data concerning the effects of group interaction with the aim of establishing short-cut methods for tapping behavioral trends to supplant laborious, gross behavior observations (see experimental units at the end of Stages 1, 2, and 3 later in this report).

2. The second is to secure personal data (for example, intelligence, personal characteristics) through available testing procedures which can be related to various dimensions of behavior manifested in the interaction process in various stages. This aspect is not to be carried out in the present 1954 study owing to lack of facilities. As this line of research develops it can be brought to the foreground as one of the important problems.

SUBJECTS

Subjects will be 24 twelve-year-old boys from established Protestant families of middle-class socioeconomic standing, who are normal (no "problem" cases), who have not experienced any unusual degrees of frustration in their homes or other situations, who are not school or social failures (no isolates), and who have a similar educational level.

A nominal fee of $25 or less will be charged. This nominal fee will give us the privilege of asking parents not to visit their boys during the experiment. Staff members will have no visitors.

THREE SUCCESSIVE STAGES AND THE HYPOTHESES

The hypotheses will be listed under their appropriate stages, since the account of these stages specifies in outline the conditions under which the particular hypothesis holds true.

Our general hypothesis in regard to intergroup relations (which is the main concern of the present study) is that intergroup attitudes and behavior are determined *primarily* by the nature of functional relations between groups in question (*and not primarily* by the pattern of relations and attitudes prevailing within groups themselves, *nor primarily* by the deviate or neurotic behavior of particular individual members who have suffered more than the usual degree of frustration in their personal life histories).

Both the 1949 and 1953 experiments started with a stage of spontaneous friendship choices.[3] This stage, to which the first days of the experiments were devoted, was introduced to rule out the possibility of attributing the experimental in-group formation to personal affinities that subjects develop for one another. This alternative explanation was ruled out on the basis of reversals of friendship choices away from interpersonal preferences and in the direction of the experimentally produced in-groups in our 1949 and 1953 experiments. The stage of interpersonal friendship choices, therefore, is eliminated from this 1954 undertaking, and the study is designed in three stages instead of the more complex four-stage design of the 1953 attempt.

In the two previous studies, the assignment of the subjects to two experimental groups was done towards the end of the first stage, that of spontaneous friendship choices. The basis for this division was not only the splitting of spontaneous friendship choices but also matching the groups as much as possible in terms of observed skills, athletic ability, and so forth, as well as in terms of data collected during the period of subject selection. Since dropping the period of spontaneous friendship choices eliminates the possibility of actual observation at the camp prior to assignment of subjects to two groups, we have to rely exclusively on the data from the observations at schools, teacher evaluations, school ratings, and data from interviews in actual home situations during the subject selection period. Utmost care will be exhibited by staff members to obtain two groups matched in as many dimensions as possible relevant to the activities that will be introduced, especially those to be utilized in the intergroup stages.

---

[3] A brief summary of our 1949 experiment was presented in Rohrer and Sherif (1951), Chap. 17. A fuller account of that experiment is given in Sherif and Sherif (1953), Chaps. 9 and 10. A short report of the completed part of the 1953 experiment is given in Sherif, White, and Harvey (1955).

STAGE 1: (5–6 DAYS) EXPERIMENTAL IN-GROUP FORMATION

The chief aim of Stage 1 is the production of in-groups through manipulation of conditions in which interaction takes place. This step is necessary in order that intergroup relations may be studied between in-groups, whose formation and functioning can be specified.

With the aim of specifying the formation and structure of the experimental in-groups, the two groups will be kept apart and their activities separated as much as possible, especially during the first days of this stage. Otherwise any functional contacts between the two groups would certainly have some consequence both for in-group formation and for the later stages of intergroup relations.

Conditions conducive to bringing about in-group formation (with hierarchical statuses and roles which will be clearcut at the upper and bottom ends of the hierarchy) will consist of a series of common and interdependent activities prompted by goals integral to the actual situations in which the subjects find themselves (for example, getting a meal when they are hungry or water when thirsty). The attainment of the goal will necessarily require cooperation and reciprocal relations. As a result, the initial discussion and the activities that follow will be real to the subjects, unlike discussion topics introduced or hinted by experimenters (or leaders) which are not immediately inherent in the situation. (Topics used in many discussion group studies are often conducive to individual "shining" in verbal skills or debating.)

The effects of the series of activities conducive to group formation will be studied in terms of:

1. Behavioral observations—verbal and non-verbal.

2. Ratings of *emerging* relationships by the participant observers (looking from outside).

3. Sociometric ratings in several relevant dimensions (looking from inside).

4. Experimental indices in terms of judgmental and perceptual variations reflecting the reciprocal role and status attitudes that emerge among group members toward each other. Before these indices are obtained, we can make predictions of the direction and degree of such variations.

As emphasized in the introductory theoretical and methodological considerations, the focal point is to maintain the natural flow of the interaction process within groups and, later, between groups under conditions which appear lifelike to the subjects. Any observational procedure, or laboratory-type experiment or repetition of sociometric tapping, which clutters the flow of interaction is antithetical to the main conception of this study. Therefore, only one judgmental experiment will be used during the stage of in-group formation. It is perfectly feasible to design an experiment primarily to study in-group formation and related problems and to devote the entire time to it. In that case, of course, it would be possible to introduce various experiments studying the progressive development of in-group structure and its effects on in-group members.

Hypothesis 1 (Stage 1)

A definite group structure consisting of differentiated status positions and reciprocal roles will be produced when a number of individuals (without previously established interpersonal relations) interact with one another under conditions which (a) situationally embody goals that have common appeal value to the individuals, and (b) require interdependent activities for their attainment.

The hypothesis above is formulated on the basis of empirical findings by sociologists like Frederick Thrasher, Clifford Shaw, and William Whyte. These and other authors stated generalizations in line with it. Our findings in this respect will serve as experimental verification. This hypothesis was supported by the results of both our 1949 and 1953 experiments cited previously.

The hypothesis will be considered to be verified if the individuals can be placed on a pyramidal hierarchy (the leader being at the apex) on the basis of observational data, status ratings of subjects in the respective groups by participant observers, and sociometric indices.

Observational data: The ratings of *emerging* status relations will be a part of the daily observational reports of the participant observers. Thus, the ratings will serve as a day-to-day index of the trend from mere togetherness situations (in which unstable, transitory differential effects are manifested) to various degrees of stabilization of established reciprocities which constitute the *group structure* at a given time. When three consecutive ratings (especially of positions at the top and bottom of the status hierarchy) by participant observers of their respective groups show a high degree of correspondence, we can say a definite in-group structure has formed. *At this point* the similar ratings independently made by junior counselors and other staff members who have had sufficient contact with the groups may be used as further checks. At that time, *sociometric ratings* and the judgmental experiment with the target board will be introduced (see below).

Observational data consisting of the frequencies of *suggestions* for activities made by various members and the proportion of acceptance and observance of these suggestions will be obtained. The latter measure might be termed the *initiative ratio.*

Other observational data along various dimensions will be desirable. Observers will make their ratings of group structure along these dimensions.

Frequency of suggestions (for engaging in this or that activity, etc.) addressed *to* various group members is one such dimension. It is a plausible hunch that the number of suggestions for group activities that are *received* by various members will be proportional to the status each achieves in the group. When members are placed according to the frequencies of suggestions addressed to them, we may be getting a placement of members pyramidal in shape very much like the one mentioned above. It is plausible to state this tendency in the form of an auxiliary hypothesis:

Hypothesis 1a (Stage 1)

If a definite group structure develops, it will be reflected in a consistent pattern in directions of communication. The specific pattern in direction of communication will be as follows: *The higher the status of a group member the greater the frequency of suggestions (for group activities) addressed to him.*

It seems feasible to represent the pattern in directions of communication visually in the form of a chart. We should think that through the course of a study such as this, variations in such charts would be obtained. The chart of directions of communication at a given time will correspond closely to the chart of initiative ratios and the pattern of judgmental variations in the way of overestimations and underestimations of performance. A suggestion for activities coming from any member may be kicked around among the group. Even if it is not initially addressed to the top position (leader), but to middle position members or lieutenants, it will be kicked around until a nod expressing approval or, at least, no disapproval from the top position member (leader) is perceived.

Sociometric data:[4] Sociometric data obtained from the subjects themselves along various dimensions (popularity, initiative, degree of service for the well being of the group, etc.) will be significant indices in terms of relations perceived by the group members themselves. The sociometric indices (looking from within) should give very much the same trend as those represented in the ratings, frequencies, and charts obtained through observational data mentioned above. We shall consider this hypothesis verified only in cases in which there is a high degree of correspondence between observational, sociometric, and experimental indices.

Experimental indices to be obtained through laboratory-type judgmental experiments introduced at this point: Recent findings which indicate the feasibility of measuring attitudes and other motivational components through perceptual and judgmental indices suggest that the reciprocities developing among members of a group as status and role

---

[4] It was thought that obtaining sociometric indices three times (once at the end of each three stages), asking the same or similar questions within a three-week period might appear repetitious (if not suspicious) to the subjects. Therefore, in line with our main concern not to clutter the natural flow of the interaction process, it was decided prior to the actual start of the experiment to restrict sociometric choices to the intergroup stages (2 and 3) and forego them at the end of the in-group stage.

relations will be reflected in the differential ways group members perceive and judge one another. One index of these differential judgments as a function of relative statuses or roles will be based on the tendency to expect higher or lower performance in activities engaged in by members occupying various status positions. (Differential expectations proportional to status positions occupied.) Relative over- and underestimates of performance in experimentally introduced tasks may be utilized to measure indirectly the status hierarchy of group members. If this proves to be the case, such experimental indices can be developed to check the validity of gross observational findings, and eventually to supplant them. Such an attempt will be made in this study with the following hypotheses:

If Hypothesis 1 holds, it can be predicted that:

Hypothesis 1b (Stage 1)
(1) The higher the status of a member in the group, the greater his tendency to overestimate his performance in an activity the group engages in.

(2) The higher the status of a member in the group, the greater the tendency of other group members to overestimate his performance.

(3) The lower the status of a member in the group, the less his tendency to overestimate his performance in an activity the group engages in.

(4) The lower the status of a member in the group, the less the tendency of other members to overestimate his performance, even to the point of underestimating it.

This psychological tendency was demonstrated in established informal cliques in an experiment at the University of Oklahoma carried out as one unit of a research project supported by the Office of Naval Research.[5] However, in that study indices used were estimates of future performance, whereas in the 1953 study mentioned above direct judgments of performance were used.[6] The experiment to be introduced here follows the procedures used in 1953 utilizing direct judgmental indices.

Hypothesis 2 (Stage 1)
When individuals interact under conditions stated in hypothesis 1, concomitant with the formation of group structure, norms will be standardized regulating their behavior in relations with one another and in practices and activities commonly engaged in.

This hypothesis is also based on empirical findings by sociologists and on studies of adolescent cliques, and will be experimentally verified in this study.

The group norms that are standardized will be expressed as atti-

---

[5] Harvey (1953).
[6] Sherif, White, and Harvey (1955).

tudes and conforming behavior of individual members. The production
of a set of standards or norms can be verified by observing the reaction of
group members to deviations from it. When there is a norm regulating the
interpersonal relations of in-group members in terms of their established
statuses and roles or regulating behavior in some practice or activity, it
can be predicted that behavior by a group member deviating from the
norm will arouse corrective reactions from other group members. (This
applies also to norms regulating behavior toward out-groups which will
become prominent in Stage 2.) The corrective measures or sanctions may
range from actual punishment meted out to the deviate through "silent
treatment," scorn, ridicule, criticism, expressions of disapproval, to
amusement, varying according to the importance of the norm violated,
the degree of deviation, and the status of the individual. Facts relating to
reactions to deviation are reported by sociologists and also in the experiment by Schachter and others.

STAGES OF INTERGROUP RELATIONS (2 AND 3)
As stated earlier in our definition, intergroup relations refer to interaction between two or more groups collectively or between their
respective members. In our study, intergroup relations refer to interaction
between the two experimentally produced groups (as formed in Stage 1)
and their respective members.

Stages 2 and 3 constitute the main stages of this experiment. All of
the previous work in Stage 1 (in-group formation) leads up to them.
Stage 2 is the tension or friction phase of intergroup relations. Stage 3
is the integration phase of intergroup relations.

STAGE 2: (4–6 DAYS) INTERGROUP RELATIONS: FRICTION PHASE
Relations between the experimentally produced groups start with
a friction phase because the major problem of intergroup relations today
is the reduction of existing frictions between various groups. For this
reason, the phase of friction is preceding the attempt to reduce tension
and to integrate groups into cooperative activities with common goals.

Friction between the two groups will be brought about through the
introduction of two sets of conditions:

1. During this stage the two groups will be brought into contact in
a series of *competitive* activities in the form of a tournament of events
which will yield cumulative scores with a reward for each member of the
winning team. However, these individual rewards can be obtained only
by being a member of the winning group and cannot be won individually.
In other words, in order to win the award individually the members of
each group are to contribute their individual bits to the winning of the
team.

2. Introduction of situations which will be perceived by one group
as *frustrating* and which will be perceived as caused by the other group,
and not by the camp administration. This was tried with positive results
in 1949. The situations will embody goals which can be attained by one

group and not by the other, in such a way that both groups will perceive the other as an obstacle in its way to attaining the goal.

In line with the methodological point that the subjects should not perceive this as an experiment on intergroup relations, conditions set up in Stage 2 and 3 conducive to group frustration and friction, or to integration as the case may be, must be designed in such a way that the subjects cannot assign the source of these conditions to the staff. They must be planned in such a way that it is not possible for group members to ascertain by checking verbally with the members of the other group that someone (the staff) has been manipulating conditions.

Our general hypothesis is that subjects who did not have appreciable contact with members of the opposite group during Stage 1 will develop negative attitudes verging on enmity towards the out-group which is perceived to be in their way for the attainment of goals shared in common within their group. Negative intergroup attitudes, such as prejudice, develop whenever any out-group is perceived as frustrating or as an obstacle. (In short, norms regulating behavior toward out-groups, like social distance norms, are standardized group products.) Negative attitudes toward out-groups will be generated situationally under these conditions and will tend to persist even though the individual members in question have not undergone any special degree of frustration in their life histories. Applying this general statement to the particular case of intergroup relations in this study, our specific hypotheses will be:

Hypothesis 1 (Stage 2)

In the course of competition and frustrating relations between two groups, unfavorable stereotypes will come into use in relation to the out-group and its members and will be standardized in time, placing the out-group at a certain social distance (proportional to the degree of negative relations between groups).

Evidence for the rise of stereotypes will be obtained by recording derogatory adjectives and phrases that are used to refer to the out-group. The specific competitive and frustrating situations and the activities and verbal utterances relating to out-groups will be noted. If possible, the frequency of references made to out-groups (positive or negative) and of activities undertaken relating to out-groups, both in intra- and inter-group situations, should be recorded. Such conditions, verbal utterances and activities in relation to the out-group constitute the steps on the basis of which stereotypes are built. In time all members of the out-group will be perceived in terms of the generalizations encompassed in the standardized stereotypes. This aspect of our study constitutes a contribution to the formation of norms of social distance (prejudice) which prevail in social groups. The tendency toward stereotype formation was noted in our 1949 study and verified in a more systematic way in R. Avigdor's doctoral thesis.[7]

---

[7] Avigdor (1951). For a brief summary, see Sherif and Sherif (1953), 290–95.

In addition to observational data, the rise of stereotypes will be tapped through two experimental units introduced at this stage:

1. Experimental indices reflecting the reciprocal intergroup evaluations in terms of stereotype ratings (testing Hypothesis 1, Stage 2). This is essentially the technique used by Avigdor.

2. Experimental indices revealing overestimation of performance of in-group members and underestimation of performance of out-group members. In this unit a bean-toss contest between the two groups will be introduced. The contest consists of rapid gathering of as many beans as possible by all members of each group within a brief time period. After the contest, beans presumably picked up by each member will be projected on a screen, identifying with each projection the individual who presumably collected them. Actually the same number of items will be projected each time in the same confined area, the items being spread in somewhat different arrangements. Estimates of the number of beans will reflect overestimation of the performance of in-group members and underestimation of the performance of out-group members. This tendency can be stated in the form of specific hypotheses:

Hypothesis 1a (Stage 2)
In-group members will tend to overestimate the number of items purportedly obtained by in-group members and underestimate the number of items attributed to out-group members.

Hypothesis 1b (Stage 2)
The degree of this tendency manifested will vary according to the status (low or high) of in-group and out-group members in question.

The feasibility of the two experimental units—namely, assessment of differential judgments of performance of members of in-groups and out-groups and differential rating of qualities in so many relevant dimensions —has already been clearly established in an experimental study carried out in our project.[8]

These data from assessment techniques as well as sociometric choices will be obtained again at the end of Stage 3, and will serve as an index of decrease of unfavorable attitudes toward out-groups in that stage.

Hypothesis 2 (Stage 2)
The course of relations between two groups which are in a state of competition and frustration will tend to produce an increase in in-group solidarity.

Increased group solidarity will be revealed in the expressions of

[8] O. J. Harvey, An Experimental Investigation of Negative and Positive Relationships between Small Informal Groups Through Judgmental Indices. Unpublished doctoral dissertation, University of Oklahoma, 1954; see Harvey (1956).

glorification of the in-group and of "feats" of members, especially those of high standing. Increased encouragement of efforts of in-group members in a way not manifested during the period when the in-group was not in contact with the out-group will be another indication. Additional behavioral data in support of this hypothesis will be derived from the experimental units described above.

Hypothesis 3 (Stage 2)

Functional relations between groups which are of consequence to the groups in question will tend to bring about changes in the pattern of relations within the in-groups involved.

This hypothesis should hold true for both positive and negative intergroup relations of consequence. (See also last paragraph of this report.) The changes in in-group relations can be measured in terms of popularity and status of in-group members in various respects. The degree of consequence of intergroup relations for the group in question can be measured by the frequency of references to the out-group and by the amount of planning and activity engaged in within the in-groups in relation to the out-groups.

One way of testing this hypothesis is through special attention to ratings of status relations within the groups by participant observers. These ratings should be continued throughout the intergroup phases with the expectation that some important changes in the functional relations between groups will produce consequential changes in the in-group structure as stabilized at the end of Stage 1. The participant observers' ratings will be checked with independent ratings by other observers in contact with the groups, thus contributing to the reliability of the data.

The hypothesis is predicted for both parties (winning and losing groups in our study). In the case of the group suffering defeat the impact of intergroup relations may be to the extent of *disorganization* of the in-group pattern, which will be marked by shifts in status positions occupied by various members.

Related to the above hypothesis is a subsidiary one concerning the functioning of low status members of the two contending groups. This has theoretical implications in view of present-day controversies. It can be stated as follows:

Hypothesis 4 (Stage 2)

Low status members will tend to exert greater efforts which will be revealed in more intense forms of overt aggression and verbal expressions against the out-group as a means of improving their status within the in-group.[9]

---

[9] This hypothesis does not imply that high status members will not initiate and actively participate in intergroup conflict. In line with one of the major tenets of *Groups in Harmony and Tension* (Sherif, 1953), intergroup behavior in conflict

An empirical test of this subsidiary hypothesis will be found in observation and comparison of the hostile and aggressive reactions of low status members toward the out-group when reacting in the presence of in-group members high in status and when reacting when high status members of their in-group are not in the immediate vicinity.

STAGE 3: (6–7 DAYS) INTERGROUP RELATIONS: INTEGRATION PHASE

This stage constitutes the crucial and novel aspect of this study. Deliberately the attempt to bring about cooperation between groups follows a stage of friction produced between them experimentally. This should be the attempt in studies aiming at reduction of group tensions. Production of harmony between groups which are not in a state of tension does not present much of a problem in terms of intergroup events today.

There are various possibilities or alternatives for the study of reducing intergroup tensions. One alternative could be called the "common enemy" approach. Empirical evidence and a tryout of this measure as an expedient manner of reducing post-experimental hostility in 1949 indicates that this measure can be effectively used. But it implies conflict between larger group units.

Another alternative would be to arrange a series of events in which achievement of individuals can be made supreme. But this would simply achieve disruption of the in-groups. In terms of actual happenings in intergroup events, the use of this measure in an experimental study would be unrealistic and would have few if any realistic implications for the reduction of intergroup tensions. As noted earlier, actual intergroup tensions take place either collectively between group units or between individual members of the in-groups reacting in terms of their group identifications.

A third alternative would be through leadership techniques. With appropriate manipulation this measure can be made effective. But in actual groups, intrusion of an outside person as a leader is not a welcome one. In actual groups, leaders, too, are part of the group structure, and they have to function within certain bounds in whatever initiative they take. For this reason, manipulation of conditions through leaders who are not part and parcel of the groups in question has little implication for the state of intergroup relations that actually exist.

Such considerations led to the choice of the alternative to be used in this study. The main feature of the alternative chosen is the introduction of *superordinate goals* which are integral to the situation and which cannot be ignored by the groups in question. The main criteria in the choice of procedures to be introduced in this integration stage will be

---

or cooperation consists mainly in participation in the intergroup trends of one's group. A line of activity in positive or negative intergroup relations will be ineffective unless high status members either take a lead or assent to the developing intergroup trend. If they stay in the way of an unmistakable trend in intergroup relations or deviate from it markedly, the consequence will be a sinking in the group hierarchy (see Hypothesis 3, Stage 2).

that goals of sufficient strength to the groups in question be superordinate, in the sense that the resources and energies of any single group will be inadequate for the attainment of the goal, thus creating a state of real and/or perceived interdependence. Situations will be planned and listed before the experiment in which such a state of interdependence inheres keeping a sufficient level of motivation that members of groups are directed toward the superordinate goals, and introducing a series of stimulus conditions which will make the facing of the superordinate goals and the modes of their attainment compelling.

The superordinate goals will not be introduced abruptly right after this stage starts. Initially some contact situations will be introduced. At these occasions the groups will have to be in close physical proximity under conditions in which expression of their hostility toward one another will not be very appropriate. Of course, mere get-togethers or contact will not materially help reduce the friction. The aim of this early period is to create the possibility of *communication* between members of the two respective groups. For example, the improvised birthday of an outsider (preferably a local personage not related to the subjects positively or negatively in an appreciable way) to which both parties are invited would be an example of such an occasion. The early phase of Stage 3 will thus consist of occasions that will give the two groups opportunity for *contact* or communication.

Hypothesis 1 (Stage 3)

It is predicted that the contact phase in itself will not produce marked decrease in the existing state of tension between groups.

The persistence of tension will be revealed in reactions showing resistance to cooperation with the out-group, in spite of contact, and persistence of negative stereotypes. If this prediction holds, it will eliminate the alternative hypothesis that contact in itself will bring about reduction of tensions.

After a series of contact situations, a series of superordinate goals will be introduced—goals which cannot help having appeal value to the members of both groups. The following are examples of superordinate goals inherent in a situation for members of both groups concerned, the attainment of which is dependent on collaboration on the part of both groups: (1) A project related to some improvement of the water tank on the hill and the pump near the reservoir, since the tank provides water for members of both groups. (2) Creating a situation of interdependence in a joint overnight camp in which members of both groups will need mutual aid for their meal and sleeping facilities. Probably the increased social suggestibility in new situations or situations of uncertainty may be utilized to enhance the effects of the conditions of interdependence. (3) Other examples already suggested by staff members are the possibilities of utilizing the swimming pool or the truck (which brings their provisions), for example, having the truck in a rut deep enough to require the combined efforts of both groups to free it.

Hypothesis 2 (Stage 3)

When groups in a state of friction are brought into contact under conditions embodying superordinate goals, the attainment of which is compelling but which cannot be achieved by the efforts of one group alone, they will tend to cooperate toward the common goal.

Hypothesis 2a (Stage 3)

Cooperation between groups necessitated by a series of such situations embodying superordinate goals will have a cumulative effect in the direction of reduction of existing tensions between groups.

Even though the groups are brought into situations which permit communication between them and then situations requiring their collaboration toward a common goal, the effects of friction produced in Stage 2 will tend to persist, along with the by-products of this friction. One of the indices important in the study of the changes in this stage, in addition to observational data giving a gross account, will be the decrease in expressions of resistance to collaboration with the out-group, which will be strong at first.

Observational data will be collected in the mess hall and other situations involving choices (of seating arrangements, etc.) to check the extent of intermingling among members of the two groups.

Another way of gaining evidence of reduced tension will be a decrease in the actual use of derogatory terms and expressions toward the out-group. After the series of superordinate goal situations has exerted a cumulative effect, the rating of relevant stereotypes will be repeated. The "bean-toss" experiment or a similar procedure will be applied here if it can be carried out without spoiling the flow of the interaction process.

Toward the end of Stage 3 sociometric choices will be obtained again. It is predicted that in comparison to those obtained at the end of Stage 2 there will be a marked increase in choices of out-group members.

As predicted in Hypothesis 3 (Stage 2), intergroup relations developing in interaction directed toward superordinate goals will also tend to bring about changes in in-group relations. As in the case of the friction phase (Stage 2), proportional to the demands for intergroup cooperation, there may be changes in in-group structure. A special note should be made here of those who are contributing more to intergroup cooperation, for example, lieutenants who exhibit strivings toward still higher positions in the in-group structure and those in marginal roles. Effective cooperation will be brought about when high status members or members on the move to higher status through activities in the area of intergroup relations take a hand in initiating in-group moves toward cooperation and in participating in intergroup communication related to superordinate goals.

TWENTY-THREE

SUPERORDINATE GOALS IN THE REDUCTION
OF INTERGROUP CONFLICT

In the past, measures to combat the problems of intergroup conflicts, proposed by social scientists as well as by such people as administrators, policy-makers, municipal officials, and educators, have included the following: introduction of legal sanctions; creation of opportunities for social and other contacts among members of conflicting groups; dissemination of correct information to break down false prejudices and unfavorable stereotypes; appeals to the moral ideals of fair play and brotherhood; and even the introduction of rigorous physical activity to produce catharsis by releasing pent-up frustrations and aggressive complexes in the unconscious. Other measures proposed include the encouragement of co-operative habits in one's own community, and bringing together in the cozy atmosphere of a meeting room the leaders of antagonistic groups.

Many of these measures may have some value in the reduction of intergroup conflicts, but, to date, very few generalizations have been established concerning the circumstances and kinds of intergroup conflict in which these measures are effective. Today measures are applied in a somewhat trial-and-error fashion. Finding measures that have wide validity in practice can come only through clarification of the nature of intergroup conflict and analysis of the factors conducive to harmony and conflict between groups under given conditions.

The task of defining and analyzing the nature of the problem was undertaken in a previous publication (Sherif and Sherif, 1953). One of our major statements was the effectiveness of superordinate goals for the reduction of intergroup conflict. "Superordinate goals" we defined as goals which are compelling and highly appealing to members of two or more groups in conflict but which cannot be attained by the resources and energies of the groups separately. In effect, they are goals attained only when groups pull together.

From *American Journal of Sociology* (1958), 63: 349–356. Reprinted with permission of the University of Chicago Press.

INTERGROUP RELATIONS AND THE BEHAVIOR OF GROUP MEMBERS

Not every friendly or unfriendly act toward another person is related to the group membership of the individuals involved. Accordingly, we must select those actions relevant to relations between groups.

Let us start by defining the main concepts involved. Obviously, we must begin with an adequate conception of the key term—"group." A group is a social unit (1) which consists of a number of individuals who, at a given time, stand in more or less definite interdependent status and role relationships with one another and (2) which explicitly or implicitly possesses a set of values or norms regulating the behavior of individual members, at least in matters of consequence to the group. Thus, shared attitudes, sentiments, aspirations, and goals are related to and implicit in the common values or norms of the group.

The term "intergroup relations" refers to the relations between two or more groups and their respective members. In the present context we are interested in the acts that occur when individuals belonging to one group interact, collectively or individually, with members of another in terms of their group identification. The appropriate frame of reference for studying such behavior includes the functional relations between the groups. Intergroup situations are not voids. Though not independent of relationships within the groups in question, *the characteristics of relations between groups cannot be deduced or extrapolated from the properties of in-group relations.*

Prevalent modes of behavior within a group, in the way of co-operativeness and solidarity or competitiveness and rivalry among members, need not be typical of actions involving members of an out-group. At times, hostility toward out-groups may be proportional to the degree of solidarity within the group. In this connection, results presented by the British statistician L. F. Richardson are instructive. His analysis of the number of wars conducted by the major nations of the world from 1850 to 1941 reveals that Great Britain heads the list with twenty wars— more than the Japanese (nine wars), the Germans (eight wars), or the United States (seven wars). We think that this significantly larger number of wars engaged in by a leading European democracy has more to do with the intergroup relations involved in perpetuating a far-flung empire than with dominant practices at home or with personal frustrations of individual Britishers who participated in these wars (Pear, 1950, p. 126).

In recent years relationships between groups have sometimes been explained through analysis of individuals who have endured unusual degrees of frustration or extensive authoritarian treatment in their life-histories. There is good reason to believe that some people growing up in unfortunate life-circumstances may become more intense in their prejudices and hostilities. But at best these cases explain the intensity of behavior in a given dimension (Hood and Sherif, 1955). In a conflict between two groups—a strike or a war—opinion within the groups is crystallized, slogans are formulated, and effective measures are organized by members recognized as the most responsible in their respective groups. The prejudice scale and the slogans are not usually imposed on the others by the deviate or neurotic members. Such individuals ordinarily exhibit their intense reactions within the reference scales of prejudice, hostility, or sacrifice established in their respective settings.

The behavior by members of any group toward another group is not primarily a problem of deviate behavior. If it were, intergroup behavior would not be the issue of vital consequence that it is today. The crux of the problem is the participation by group members in established practices and social-distance norms of their group and their response to new trends developing in relationships between their own group and other groups.

On the basis of his Unesco studies in India, Gardner Murphy concludes that to be a good Hindu or a good Moslem implies belief in all the nasty qualities and practices attributed by one's own group—Hindu or Moslem—to the other. Good members remain deaf and dumb to favorable information concerning the adversary. Social contacts and avenues of communication serve, on the whole, as vehicles for further conflicts not merely for neurotic individuals but for the bulk of the membership (Murphy, 1953).

In the process of interaction among members, an in-group is endowed with positive qualities which tend to be praiseworthy, self-justifying, and even self-glorifying. Individual members tend to develop these qualities through internalizing group norms and through example by high-status members, verbal dicta, and a set of correctives standardized to deal with cases of deviation. Hence, possession of these qualities, which reflect their particular brand of ethnocentrism, is not essentially a problem of deviation or personal frustration. It is a question of participation in in-group values and trends by good members, who constitute the majority of membership as long as group solidarity and morale are maintained.

To out-groups and their respective members are attributed positive or negative qualities, depending on the nature of functional relations between the groups in question. The character of functional relations between groups may result from actual harmony and interdependence or from actual incompatibility between the aspirations and directions of the groups. A number of field studies and experiments indicate that, if the functional relations between groups are positive, favorable attitudes are formed toward the out-group. If the functional relations between groups are negative, they give rise to hostile attitudes and unfavorable stereotypes in relation to the out-group. Of course, in large group units the picture of the out-group and relations with it depend very heavily on communication, particularly from the mass media.

Examples of these processes are recurrent in studies of small groups.

For example, when a gang "appropriates" certain blocks in a city, it is considered "indecent" and a violation of its "rights" for another group to carry on its feats in that area. Intrusion by another group is conducive to conflict, at times with grim consequences, as Thrasher (1927) showed over three decades ago.

When a workers' group declares a strike, existing group lines are drawn more sharply. Those who are not actually for the strike are regarded as against it. There is no creature more lowly than the man who works while the strike is on (Hiller, 1928). The same type of behavior is found in management groups under similar circumstances.

In time, the adjectives attributed to out-groups take their places in the repertory of group norms. The lasting, derogatory stereotypes attributed to groups low on the social-distance scale are particular cases of group norms pertaining to out-groups.

As studies by Bogardus show, the social-distance scale of a group, once established, continues over generations, despite changes of constituent individuals, who can hardly be said to have prejudices because of the same severe personal frustrations or authoritarian treatment (Bogardus, 1947).

Literature on the formation of prejudice by growing children shows that it is not even necessary for the individual to have actual unfavorable experiences with out-groups to form attitudes of prejudice toward them. In the very process of becoming an in-group member, the intergroup delineations and corresponding norms prevailing in the group are internalized by the individual (Horowitz, 1944).

A RESEARCH PROGRAM

A program of research has been under way since 1948 to test experimentally some hypotheses derived from the literature of intergroup relations. The first large-scale intergroup experiment was carried out in 1949, the second in 1953, and the third in 1954.[1] The conclusions reported here briefly are based on the 1949 and 1954 experiments and on a series of laboratory studies carried out as co-ordinate parts of the program (Sherif, 1954).

The methodology, techniques, and criteria for subject selection in the experiments must be summarized here very briefly. The experiments were carried out in successive stages: (1) groups were formed experimentally; (2) tension and conflict were produced between these groups by

[1] The experimental work in 1949 was jointly supported by the Yale Attitude Change Project and the American Jewish Committee. It is summarized in Sherif and Sherif (1953), Chaps. 9 and 10. Both the writing of that book and the experiments in 1953–54 were made possible by a grant from the Rockefeller Foundation. The 1953 research is summarized in Sherif, White, and Harvey (1955). The 1954 experiment is summarized in Sherif, Harvey, White, Hood, and Sherif (1954). For a summary of the three experiments, see Chaps. 6 and 9 in Sherif and Sherif (1956).

introducing conditions conducive to competitive and reciprocally frustrating relations between them; and (3) the attempt was made toward reduction of the intergroup conflict. This stage of reducing tension through introduction of superordinate goals was attempted in the 1954 study on the basis of lessons learned in the two previous studies.

At every stage the subjects interacted in activities which appeared natural to them at a specially arranged camp site completely under our experimental control. They were not aware of the fact that their behavior was under observation. No observation or recording was made in the subjects' presence in a way likely to arouse the suspicion that they were being observed. There is empirical and experimental evidence contrary to the contention that individuals cease to be mindful when they know they are being observed and that their words are being recorded (cf. Miller, 1954; Wapner and Alper, 1952).

In order to insure validity of conclusions, results obtained through observational methods were cross-checked with results obtained through sociometric technique, stereotype ratings of in-groups and out-groups, and through data obtained by techniques adapted from the laboratory. Unfortunately, these procedures cannot be elaborated here. The conclusions summarized briefly are based on results cross-checked by two or more techniques.

The production of groups, the production of conflict between them, and the reduction of conflict in successive stages were brought about through the introduction of problem situations that were real and could not be ignored by individuals in the situation. Special "lecture methods" or "discussion methods" were not used. For example, the problem of getting a meal through their own initiative and planning was introduced when participating individuals were hungry.

Facing a problem situation which is immediate and compelling and which embodies a goal that cannot be ignored, group members *do* initiate discussion and *do* plan and carry through these plans until the objective is achieved. In this process the discussion becomes *their* discussion, the plan *their* plan, the action *their* action. In this process discussion, planning, and action have their place, and, when occasion arises, lecture or information has its place, too. The sequence of these related activities need not be the same in all cases.

The subjects were selected by rigorous criteria. They were healthy, normal boys around the age of eleven and twelve, socially well adjusted in school and neighborhood, and academically successful. They came from a homogeneous sociocultural background and from settled, well-adjusted families of middle or lower-middle class and Protestant affiliations. No subject came from a broken home. The mean I.Q. was above average. The subjects were not personally acquainted with one another prior to the experiment. Thus, explanation of results on the basis of background differences, social maladjustment, undue childhood frustrations, or previous interpersonal relations was ruled out at the beginning by the criteria for selecting subjects.

The first stage of the experiments was designed to produce groups with distinct structure (organization) and a set of norms which could be confronted with intergroup problems. The method for producing groups from unacquainted individuals with similar background was to introduce problem situations in which the attainment of the goal depended on the co-ordinated activity of all individuals. After a series of such activities, definite group structures or organizations developed.

The results warrant the following conclusions for the stage of group formation: When individuals interact in a series of situations toward goals which appeal to all and which require that they co-ordinate their activities, group structures arise having hierarchical status arrangements and a set of norms regulating behavior in matters of consequence to the activities of the group.

Once we had groups that satisfied our definition of "group," relations between groups could be studied. Specified conditions conducive to friction or conflict between groups were introduced. This negative aspect was deliberately undertaken because the major problem in intergroup relations today is the reduction of existing intergroup frictions. (Increasing friendly relations between groups is not nearly so great an issue.) The factors conducive to intergroup conflict give us realistic leads for reducing conflict.

A series of situations was introduced in which one group could achieve its goal only at the expense of the other group—through a tournament of competitive events with desirable prizes for the winning group. The results of the stage of intergroup conflict supported our main hypotheses. During interaction between groups in experimentally introduced activities which were competitive and mutually frustrating, members of each group developed hostile attitudes and highly unfavorable stereotypes toward the other group and its members. In fact, attitudes of social distance between the groups became so definite that they wanted to have nothing further to do with each other. This we take as a case of experimentally produced "social distance" in miniature. Conflict was manifested in derogatory name-calling and invectives, flare-ups of physical conflict, and raids on each other's cabins and territory. Over a period of time, negative stereotypes and unfavorable attitudes developed.

At the same time there was an increase in in-group solidarity and co-operativeness. This finding indicates that co-operation and democracy within groups do not necessarily lead to democracy and co-operation with out-groups, if the directions and interests of the groups are conflicting.

Increased solidarity forged in hostile encounters, in rallies from defeat, and in victories over the out-group is one instance of a more general finding: Intergroup relations, both conflicting and harmonious, *affected the nature of relations within the groups involved*. Altered relations between groups produced significant changes in the status arrangements *within* groups, in some instances resulting in shifts at the upper status levels or even a change in leadership. Always, consequential intergroup relations were reflected in new group values or norms which signified changes in practice, word, and deed within the group. Counterparts of this finding are not difficult to see in actual and consequential human relations. Probably many of our major preoccupations, anxieties, and activities in the past decade are incomprehensible without reference to the problems created by the prevailing "cold war" on an international scale.

REDUCTION OF INTERGROUP FRICTION

A number of the measures proposed today for reducing intergroup friction could have been tried in this third stage. A few will be mentioned here, with a brief explanation of why they were discarded or were included in our experimental design.

1. Disseminating favorable information in regard to the out-group was not included. Information that is not related to the goals currently in focus in the activities of groups is relatively ineffective, as many studies on attitude change have shown (cf. Williams, 1947).

2. In small groups it is possible to devise sufficiently attractive rewards to make individual achievement supreme. This may reduce tension between groups by splitting the membership on an "every-man-for-himself" basis. However, this measure has little relevance for actual intergroup tensions, which are in terms of group membership and group alignments.

3. The resolution of conflict through leaders alone was not utilized. Even when group leaders meet apart from their groups around a conference table, they cannot be considered independent of the dominant trends and prevailing attitudes of their membership. If a leader is too much out of step in his negotiations and agreements with out-groups, he will cease to be followed. It seemed more realistic, therefore, to study the influence of leadership within the framework of prevailing trends in the groups involved. Such results will give us leads concerning the conditions under which leadership can be effective in reducing intergroup tensions.

4. The "common-enemy" approach is effective in pulling two or more groups together against another group. This approach was utilized in the 1949 experiment as an expedient measure and yielded effective results. But bringing some groups together against others means larger and more devastating conflicts in the long run. For this reason, the measure was not used in the 1954 experiment.

5. Another measure, advanced both in theoretical and in practical work, centers around social contacts among members of antagonistic

groups in activities which are pleasant in themselves. This measure was tried out in 1954 in the first phase of the integration stage.

6. As the second phase of the integration stage, we introduced a series of superordinate goals which necessitated co-operative interaction between groups.

The social contact situations consisted of activities which were satisfying in themselves—eating together in the same dining room, watching a movie in the same hall, or engaging in an entertainment in close physical proximity. These activities, which were satisfying to each group, but which did not involve a state of interdependence and co-operation for the attainment of goals, were not effective in reducing intergroup tension. On the contrary, such occasions of contact were utilized as opportunities to engage in name-calling and in abuse of each other to the point of physical manifestations of hostility.

The ineffective, even deleterious, results of intergroup contact without superordinate goals have implications for certain contemporary learning theories and for practice in intergroup relations. Contiguity in pleasant activities with members of an out-group does not necessarily lead to a pleasurable image of the out-group if relations between the groups are unfriendly. Intergroup contact without superordinate goals is not likely to produce lasting reduction of intergroup hostility. John Gunther, for instance, in his survey of contemporary Africa, concluded that, when the intergroup relationship is exploitation of one group by a "superior" group, intergroup contact inevitably breeds hostility and conflict (Gunther, 1955).

INTRODUCTION OF SUPERORDINATE GOALS

After establishing the ineffectiveness, even the harm, of intergroup contacts which did not involve superordinate goals, we introduced a series of superordinate goals. Since the characteristics of the problem situations used as superordinate goals are implicit in the two main hypotheses for this stage, we shall present these hypotheses:

1. When groups in a state of conflict are brought into contact under conditions embodying superordinate goals, which are compelling but cannot be achieved by the efforts of one group alone, they will tend to co-operate toward the common goals.

2. Co-operation between groups, necessitated by a series of situations embodying superordinate goals, will have a cumulative effect in the direction of reducing existing conflict between groups.

The problem situations were varied in nature, but all had an essential feature in common—they involved goals that could not be attained by the efforts and energies of one group alone and thus created a state of interdependence between groups: combating a water shortage that affected all and could not help being "compelling"; securing a much-desired film, which could not be obtained by either group alone but required putting their resources together; putting into working shape, when everyone was hungry and the food was some distance away, the only means of transportation available to carry food.

The introduction of a series of such superordinate goals was indeed effective in reducing intergroup conflict: (1) when the groups in a state of friction interacted in conditions involving superordinate goals they did co-operate in activities leading toward the common goal and (2) a series of joint activities leading toward superordinate goals had the cumulative effect of reducing the prevailing friction between groups and unfavorable stereotypes toward the out-group.

These major conclusions were reached on the basis of observational data and were confirmed by sociometric choices and stereotype ratings administered first during intergroup conflict and again after the introduction of a series of superordinate goals. Comparison of the sociometric choices during intergroup conflict and following the series of superordinate goals shows clearly the changed attitudes toward members of the out-group. Friendship preferences shifted from almost exclusive preference for in-group members toward increased inclusion of members from the "antagonists." Since the groups were still intact following co-operative efforts to gain superordinate goals, friends were found largely within one's group. However, choices of out-group members grew, in one group, from practically none during intergroup conflict to 23 per cent. Using chi square, this difference is significant ($P < .05$). In the other group, choices of the out-group increased to 36 per cent, and the difference is significant ($P < .001$). The findings confirm observations that the series of superordinate goals produced increasingly friendly associations and attitudes pertaining to out-group members.

Observations made after several superordinate goals were introduced showed a sharp decrease in the name-calling and derogation of the out-group common during intergroup friction and in the contact situations without superordinate goals. At the same time the blatant glorification and bragging about the in-group, observed during the period of conflict, diminished. These observations were confirmed by comparison of ratings of stereotypes (adjectives) the subjects had actually used in referring to their own group and the out-group during conflict with ratings made after the series of superordinate goals. Ratings of the out-group changed significantly from largely unfavorable ratings to largely favorable ratings. The proportions of the most unfavorable ratings found appropriate for the out-group—that is, the categorical verdicts that "all of them are stinkers" or ". . . smart alecks" or ". . . sneaky"—fell, in one group, from 21 per cent at the end of the friction stage to 1.5 per cent after interaction oriented toward superordinate goals. The corresponding reduction in these highly unfavorable verdicts by the other group was from 36.5 to

6 per cent. The over-all differences between the frequencies of stereo-type ratings made in relation to the out-group during intergroup conflict and following the series of superordinate goals are significant for both groups at the .001 level (using chi-square test).

Ratings of the in-group were not so exclusively favorable, in line with observed decreases in self-glorification. But the differences in ratings of the in-group were not statistically significant, as were the differences in ratings of the out-group.

Our findings demonstrate the effectiveness of a series of super-ordinate goals in the reduction of intergroup conflict, hostility, and their by-products. They also have implications for other measures proposed for reducing intergroup tensions.

It is true that lines of communication between groups must be opened before prevailing hostility can be reduced. But, if contact between hostile groups takes place without superordinate goals, the communica-tion channels serve as media for further accusations and recriminations. When contact situations involve superordinate goals, communication is utilized in the direction of reducing conflict in order to attain the com-mon goals.

Favorable information about a disliked out-group tends to be ignored, rejected or reinterpreted to fit prevailing stereotypes. But, when groups are pulling together toward superordinate goals, true and even favorable information about the out-group is seen in a new light. The probability of information being effective in eliminating unfavorable stereotypes is enormously enhanced.

When groups co-operate in the attainment of superordinate goals, leaders are in a position to take bolder steps toward bringing about un-derstanding and harmonious relations. When groups are directed toward incompatible goals, genuine moves by a leader to reduce intergroup ten-sion may be seen by the membership as out of step and ill advised. The leader may be subjected to severe criticism and even loss of faith and status in his own group. When compelling superordinate goals are intro-duced, the leader can make moves to further co-operative efforts, and his decisions receive support from other group members.

In short, various measures suggested for the reduction of intergroup conflict—disseminating information, increasing social contact, conferences of leaders—acquire new significance and effectiveness when they become part and parcel of interaction processes between groups oriented toward superordinate goals which have real and compelling value for all groups concerned.

TWENTY-FOUR

CREATIVE ALTERNATIVES TO
A DEADLY SHOWDOWN

For some years, the world has lived in the ominous shadow of a deadly showdown. The consequences of such a tragic climax have been vividly described by the creators of weapons themselves. These grim consequences have led many to search for measures to avoid a showdown and to reduce the conflicts which are at its roots.

Among the various measures advocated are the following:

1. Various models of deterrence, that is, up-to-date models of the old "balance of power."

2. Conferences of leaders and their representatives to negotiate differences.

3. Programs of person-to-person contact, such as exchange of persons and conferences of students, scientists, businessmen, artists and teachers.

4. Dissemination of information designed to correct erroneous views of each other held by the parties in conflict.

There is at least one condition necessary if any of these measures are to be effective—the provision of a broad *motivational* basis for contacts, communication, and negotiation. If such a broad motivational basis is created any one of these measures, except the first, permits creative alternatives to a deadly showdown. I will touch on these measures and their variants in context. First, however, I should make it clear why I do not regard the first—namely, deterrence—as a creative solution.

As C. N. Barclay, British military author, stated in the *New York Times Magazine* of May 5, 1963:

The deterrent is the modern version of the balance of power, employed in the past—not very successfully—to keep the peace in Europe. The difference lies in the fact that failure to keep the peace in the days of conventional weapons . . . was not universally fatal. Failure with nuclear weapons, on the other hand, would be catastrophic for all mankind (p. 17).

From *Trans-Action*, 1964, January, pp. 3–7. Reprinted with the permission of *Trans-Action*.

Let us not be misled by new trappings or the use of high speed computers. A rose by any other name smells as sweet, and deterrence smells like a preliminary to war. In contrast, the aim of the other measures is to reduce conflict, not maintain it.

THE RESEARCH BACKGROUND

Whatever a social psychologist such as myself can contribute to the search for alternatives to a headlong plunge into mass destruction must rest on the research and theory in his specialty. I will, therefore, mention briefly the factual basis for my conclusions.

Fifteen years ago, we began a program of research on conflict between human groups and its resolution. Hunches, or hypotheses if you like, were based on existing research and on cases of conflict between groups of all sizes and description. Our hunches concerned conditions *sufficient* for the development of conflict between groups, along with the hostile acts and attitudes that accompany it, and conditions *necessary* for the subsequent reduction of the conflict and change of the participants' attitudes. Three experiments were conducted, each continuing 24 hours a day for nearly a month.

Here, I will not go into details of the experiments, which will be of interest mainly to fellow social psychologists and which are readily available in print. A brief summary, however, may be in order as point of departure for the focus of this paper.

The experiments started with two bunches of unacquainted and very similar individuals, brought to a summer camp. By presenting them with situations where pulling together with one's fellows led to desired ends, we soon had two genuine groups—each with its own recognized leader, name, and local customs. Once the groups formed, a series of events was introduced in which the victory of one group inevitably meant defeat for the other. Over a period of time, as predicted, the two groups became hostile toward each other; they called each other names; they disliked each other intensely, and they began to fight. This unfortunate outcome was a necessary preliminary to the study of various measures in reducing conflict between groups.

There are some similarities between these experiments and real life. First, the entire experience was very natural for the individuals studied, and the problems they faced were very real to them. They cared a great deal about their groups and their vicissitudes. Second, like many groups in real life, behavior toward the other group was not regulated by rules enforced by some superior authority. The groups formulated their own ways of relating to each other.

Being experiments, however, these studies were necessarily in miniature. The groups were small, as they had to be to have experimental control of their habitat. The members were young boys; since then, however, similar results have been obtained by other investigators working with adults. Still, there is a genuine problem of whether or not one is justified in drawing analogies between what happened to these small groups and what happens to large and powerful nations. I leave this to your judgment and, ultimately, to the outcome of future research conducted on a larger scale.

SUPERORDINATE GOALS

I shall now venture to state some things we learned from these experiments about intergroup conflict and its reduction. A variety of measures were proposed for the reduction of conflict and were tried out in the experiments. One of these turned out to be a *necessary* condition for the avoidance of violent alternatives.

This necessary condition is the existence of "superordinate goals." Superordinate goals are those ends greatly desired by all those caught in dispute or conflict, which cannot be attained by the resources and energies of each of the parties separately, but which require the concerted efforts of all parties involved. Even in our miniature experiments, we found that a *series* of superordinate goals was required if concerted effort was to become general, and if hostility was to turn to friendly interchange between groups. Even at this level, the reduction of intergroup conflict is not a one-shot affair. A series of superordinate goals has a cumulative effect, which provides a broad motivational base on which person-to-person contacts, information, and conferences between leaders or representatives can become effective.

Communication must be opened between groups before prevailing hostilities can be reduced. But person-to-person contact and communication without goals which are urgent, compelling, and highly appealing to *all* groups involved frequently serve only as mediums for further accusations and recriminations. The discussion or the negotiation gets bogged down, directly or indirectly, in the fruitless question of "Who's to blame?" for the existing state of affairs.

The experiments revealed a dynamic sequence resulting in a vicious circle, with each side justifying its own actions and casting blame on the other side. For this to happen, it was sufficient to have two groups, each pitted against the other for a goal that can be won only if one group fails. It is also pertinent to note that individual members need not in any way be neurotic or sinful for the vicious circle to occur.

In the experiments, the groups were from the same culture and the members were as similar in background and appearance as possible. Shall we then, attribute their behavior to universal human nature? Since we arranged the conditions which started this vicious circle and since we later successfully altered it, there is no justification for assuming that this is "just the way of human nature."

When the groups in our experiments were in conflict, considering each other as enemies, each adopted a policy of deterrence. In addition to security measures designed to conceal their possessions and locations, weapons were improvised from available resources and were hoarded "in case" they were needed. Banners were destroyed and raids on each other's property were conducted in stealth as a show of power. It may be, therefore, that deterrence is a way of conducting conflict rather than a preserver of the peace, as it is sometimes represented.

GROUP CONFLICTS AND STEREOTYPES

In the course of encounters between the groups, each individual— whether leader or appointed representative or rank-and-file—acted as a loyal, responsible member of his group. Being loyal and responsible, in this case, meant that he directed his energies and efforts against the rival. The unfavorable qualities, the derogatory stereotypes attributed to the other group, as derogatory stereotypes were the *products* of this process, and were not an initial condition for it. One's own group was endowed with favorable qualities which were self-justifying and even self-glorifying. The rival group was assigned stereotyped traits which justified its treatment as an enemy. Since this is a *product* of intergroup conflict, and is not its initial cause, attempts to remove the stereotyped conceptions in and of themselves—through information, pleas for fairmindedness, or justice—are ordinarily rather futile and fruitless.

Once hostile attitudes and unfavorable stereotypes of another group are stabilized, they influence the manner in which individual members see and size up events. Each side sees the actions of the other through the colored glasses of hostility, which filter out the favorable colors in which we see ourselves and our friends. Undoubtedly, this filtering process affects the judgment of *negotiators* and *representatives*. For example, in one experiment, an individual holding a high position in his own group decided, with the best of motives, that the time had come to negotiate peaceful relations with the hostile group. He was received by them as an enemy who sought to mislead them with pretended expressions of reconciliation. His departure was accompanied by a hail of "ammunition" collected by the group "in case" they were attacked—in this case, green apples.

THE LEADER REJECTED

Equally interesting was the fate of this individual, who had made reasonable attempts at reconciliation, when he returned to his own group. Far from being received as a hero, he was chastised for even making the attempt. This is but one of many examples of the fact that leadership, representation, and negotiation between groups are governed primarily by and operate within the bounds acceptable in each group.

If he is to negotiate effectively, a leader or his delegate must remain a part of his own group. In order to do so, he must act in ways that his fellow members regard as acceptable and decent, in terms of their group's definitions. The realistic alternatives that a leader or negotiator can consider, therefore, are limited. Not all possible alternatives that are logically conceivable, or even rational, are realistically available. The realistic alternatives are those that are clearly acceptable to members of his own group at the time. In large groups, where negotiations may be conducted in secret, a leader has somewhat more latitude. But there is not one leader in the world today who could long remain in power after committing his group to a course clearly unacceptable to the members.

How can the binding stereotypes and self-justifications of groups in conflict change, and how can the vicious circle stop, if the groups do not accept the regulation of some still larger body? Many methods are effective in the context of a series of superordinate goals, which are felt as urgent by *all* parties involved.

NEW COMMUNICATION POSSIBLE

When contacts between persons involve superordinate goals, communication is utilized to reduce conflict in order to find means of attaining common goals. True and favorable information about the other group is seen in a new light, and then the probability of this information being effective is enormously enhanced.

When groups cooperate toward superordinate goals, their leaders are in a position to take bolder steps toward greater mutual understanding and trust. Lacking superordinate goals, however, genuine moves by a leader to reduce intergroup conflict may be seen by his own group as out-of-step and ill-advised. He may be subjected to severe criticism and even to a loss of faith. Where there are superordinate goals, however, these encourage a leader to make moves to advance cooperative efforts. He can more freely delegate authority, and negotiation can proceed more effectively. The decisions reached are more likely to receive support from other group members.

Various measures suggested for reducing intergroup conflict acquire new significance and effectiveness when they become part and parcel of joint efforts directed toward goals with real and compelling value for all groups concerned. The development of such superordinate goals provides the necessary motive. It is needed to lift the heavy hand of the past—with its entrenched stereotypes and vicious circle of "Who's to blame?"—and to work out procedures for cooperation.

Over a period of time, the procedures of groups working toward superordinate goals are generalized to new problems and situations. In time, the process should assume organizational forms. If the tasks of building such organizations seem formidable, they are certainly no more formidable than those which a modern war would impose. There can be no doubt that man's potentialities can be realized better in the course of such efforts than in the vicious circle of assigning blame for the present state of affairs, in pursuing old fears, old hostilities, old conflicts—with their awesome possibilities in this present world.

BEYOND THE EXPERIMENTS

In considering the possibility of superordinate goals in international affairs, we must pass beyond our experiments. For in our experiments, superordinate goals emerged in problem situations that involved the deprivation of vital necessities or the achievement of a venture much-desired by all. They were not matters for interpretation, and they did not require experts with different opinions about the "facts" to offer conjectures. The conditions giving rise to superordinate goals in our experimental groups were compelling and immediate—right in front of their eyes, a naked necessity for all to see and feel.

DEBATING HUMAN SURVIVAL

In the thousand-fold complex problems engulfing the people of the world today, there seems to be a debate about one goal which should be overriding—human survival. There is debate among scientists as well as policy-makers about the range of weapons of destruction and their carriers; about the radius of destruction in population centers; about whether 100 million or 500 million people would perish or be mutilated; about which peoples and places would be involved; about how many and what kind of shelters are required for survival as human beings, if they survive; about the effects of radiation on the present and future generations of children. Such debates continue as though we were splitting hairs instead of talking about millions of human lives.

In the midst of these debates, the problem of human survival is obscured; instead of human survival emerging as an all-embracing superordinate goal, its urgency is muffled. Yet human survival is the most inclusive superordinate goal. It provides the needed motivational basis for

—making possible the effective negotiations of leaders toward the abolishment of nuclear warfare as an alternative.

—communication and information to be effective toward abandonment of war as a means of furthering national or ideological policy—*any* national or ideological policy.

—exchange of persons across national lines to be occasions for understanding rather than promoting the vicious circle of "Who's to blame?"

But, for all of these, human survival has to be felt as a necessity—

like the air we breathe, the food we eat, the danger sign that we heed when near high explosives.

A DECLARATION FOR HUMAN SURVIVAL

One effective first step toward the recognition of human survival as a superordinate goal my be a universal *declaration* for human survival and development, including in vivid word and picture, the horrors of nuclear war, its cost in life, its destruction of human civilization and culture, and the ever-present dangers of radiation to those who survive. Some experts on communication conclude that people do not listen to threats, pointing to studies showing that the threat of cancer is not sufficient to cause people to stop smoking. However, we know that when people of a country learn of a genuine threat to the lives and well-being of their country, even in the newspapers, they do have a strong desire for survival and removal of the threat; and all sectors of society pull together for this purpose. Human survival is a positive goal for all peoples, and the common threat to all today has not been presented with comparable urgency.

As we all know, declarations have been made by groups of scientists, by professional bodies, and even by heads of governments and military men of stature. What is intended here is not just another declaration at a single conference, or in a few newspapers, or in an occasional policy statement. What is intended here is an agreement—especially by policy makers of the major powers—that a universal declaration for human survival, which also conveys in understandable terms what nuclear warfare means, has their full support. Of course, even this is not sufficient.

Such a universal declaration for human survival as a recognized superordinate goal needs the support of all religious bodies which ask for prayers for peace, so that the universal declaration for human survival will be part of their daily and weekly exercises. All organizations, boards, and regents directing policies at university, high school, and grade school levels in every country, who profess to have at heart the well-being and development of the younger generation as civilized human beings, should make such a universal declaration an integral part of their educational programs. Owners and directors of the mass media of communication in all countries—who profess public responsibility in enlightening and informing—should feature prominently and repeatedly such a universal declaration for human survival as a cherished goal. At the cost of appearing naive, I also propose that political parties in all countries who profess their concern with peace on earth and the brotherhood of man should include this universal declaration as an integral part of their platforms—even if this be the only plank they share in common.

If through these means, human survival becomes a superordinate goal for the majority of peoples of the world, then nuclear war may be out-of-bounds in their eyes as an alternative in national or ideological policies. Being out-of-bounds in terms of cherished goals of the people for survival and development as human beings, the attempts of demagogues to fish in muddied waters, to dramatize issues and events out of all proportion, will fall on deaf ears. Leaders will be charged with staying within the bounds of the cherished goals of their peoples.

A NEW FRAMEWORK FOR COOPERATION

I do not suggest at all that a universal declaration could settle the problems underlying international conflicts. I do propose it as a *first* step toward eliminating nuclear war as an alternative that any leader could consider. The underlying conflicts, however, can be effected to the extent that the nations of the world and their citizens engage in common enterprises which each sees as being for the benefit of all, regardless of their differences.

The differences between nations may seem so great today that the possibility of common concerns seems slim. I am inclined, however, to find merit in the observation by Eugene Rabinowitch (*Bulletin of the Atomic Scientists,* February, 1963) that there are such areas, and that "the cultural and scientific areas are the least controversial and most suitable for international cooperation" at present (p. 7). The implications of our own research also support his contention that such cooperation should be, not merely an exchange of persons, but "common enterprises" jointly initiated and carried out on a large scale.

In brief, the implication of our research is that when superordinate goals are concretely perceived and emotionally felt by members of groups in conflict, they do tend to cooperate, to pull together their resources and energies to attain them. A series of such efforts over a period of time is effective in reducing their hostilities, changing their unfavorable images of each other, and producing a climate in which creative alternatives to mutual extinction can be explored. The exploration of creative alternatives may be more effective than the prevailing policy of contending parties at present, in which strategists attempt to figure out probabilities of deterrence. This policy of deterrence contains the constant hazard of getting out of hand because of even a small miscalculation or misinformation at this or that particular point.

INTER-NATION UNIVERSITIES

A final word on committing the knowledge, resources, and efforts of major parties in conflict to common, large-scale projects, as part of a process directed toward the superordinate goal of human survival on the level of the cultures attained through centuries. Such common and interdependent projects could include, for example, joint efforts by cosmonauts, technicians, and researchers of nations aimed at the conquest of space. Such projects could include inter-nation universities, in which the faculty consists of scholars and scientists who have outgrown the 19th-century conception of national ways of life and ideological divisions as closed systems. These are only examples already proposed by various authors such as Charles E. Osgood and Eugene Rabinowitch. In joint meetings of scholars and scientists dedicated to human survival, and the survival of human cultures across national and ideological lines, a whole series of such common and interdependent ventures could be imaginatively worked out.

The involvement of talents, resources, and efforts in joint and interdependent *new* projects is less liable to misinterpretations as trickery or propaganda moves. In the more direct political and military areas where parties already have entrenched stands, sometimes fixed as national norms or stereotypes, the likelihood of misinterpreting the motives and moves of the other side is greater. However, once a new series of joint and interdependent projects is under way, active involvement in it is likely to be conducive to an atmosphere of good faith, in which the negotiating parties will not be suspect at every turn and twist of occasion.

TWENTY-FIVE

CONFLICT AND COOPERATION
BETWEEN FUNCTIONALLY RELATED GROUPS

With Carolyn W. Sherif

In our experiments on intergroup relations, two of the major hypotheses tested were the following:

1. Members of a group that is caught in rivalry and conflict with another group will tend to close ranks, thus strengthening their loyalty and solidarity within their own group (Sherif *et al.*, 1961, p. 123).

2. Intergroup relations that are of ongoing concern to groups will produce changes in the pattern of leader-follower relations, in plans and actions within each group (Sherif *et al.*, 1961, p. 126).

To test these hypotheses, groups were formed experimentally under controlled conditions. To study intergroup relations, we have to have groups, with unmistakable organizational boundaries. Otherwise, whatever we are studying, we are not studying intergroup relations.

The data most relevant to the two hypotheses were collected at the period in the experiments when groups were at the height of rivalry and conflict. They were so embroiled in conflict that the state of their rivalry became the dominant theme in plans discussed within each group, in the activities they chose, and the problem situations requiring their decisions. Their intergroup relations became the ongoing concern within each group, almost to the exclusion of other activities that had occupied them in more peaceful times, when each group was functioning as a more or less autonomous, closed system in the absence of the crucial variable of intergroup entanglements.

The salience of the ongoing concern was revealed through a disproportionate frequency of references to the wickedness of the rival group, to how the out-group had started the whole nasty conflict, to their underlying character, which explained the irrationality and sneakiness of their aggression. It was also reevaled through preoccupation

Paper presented to the American Psychiatric Association, New York, 1965. (Translated in *Rivista di Sociologia*, Anno III, 9, Roma, 1966.)

within each group in devising strategies and measures for *deterrence* against the probable aggressive schemes of the other group.

In the process, interpersonal bickering within each group was drastically reduced. In line with the first prediction, each group achieved greater consensus of opinion and purpose, a heightened sense of identity as a group, and stronger loyalty to fellow members.

In line with the second prediction, measurable changes occurred in the status or power pattern within each group. There were upward and downward shifts in the hierarchy of leader-follower relations. In fact, in one group, the leader himself lost his leadership power, even though he had been a resourceful coordinator of peaceful activities. During the stress and strain of repeated encounters with the out-group, he steadily lost ground in the eyes of fellow members of his own group. Finally, he was deposed in favor of one of his lieutenants who became exemplary at this time in devising daring plans and executing them.

I have used these illustrative data from experiments to make the problem of this paper concrete. The problem concerns factors conducive to conflict and cooperation between functionally related groups. *Functional relations* between two or more groups refer to problems that are of ongoing concern to them, whether these are positive or negative in terms of the compatibility or incompatibility of their goals and designs. I do not use the term in the sense of *functional* as opposed to *dysfunctional*. The term *functional relations* means here that the goals, policies and actions of each group have an impact on events within the others, for good or evil. Thus, functionally related groups are parts in an intergroup system. in which events in one constituent part affect the others.

In the rest of this paper, I will mention experiments related to this problem, and share with you the plans for new experiments on the impact of functional relations among groups whose designs and goals are initially compatible or incompatible with one another. In the face of the hundreds of studies conducted in the name of small group research that do not concern groups at all, I am haunted with the criterion of validity. Therefore, I will first discuss briefly the basic rationale which served to guide the formulation of the experiments we envisage. Extended discussion of this rationale is presented in several chapters of my book on these problems (1966).

FRAMEWORK FOR ASSESSING THE ETIOLOGY OF INTERGROUP BEHAVIOR

The most recent surveys of empirical and experimental findings (for example, J. P. Scott, 1958; Berkowitz, 1962) clearly conclude that aggression and conflict are not self-generated, intrapsychic events. These states of *relationship* arising as a consequence of transactions among people in situations that promote or block the goals they are pursuing. Therefore, adequate understanding of the etiology of both conflict and cooperation requires their assessment within the precise framework, or context, of the situations in which they arise.

We cannot extrapolate uncritically from findings about behavioral events that occur within an interpersonal framework to those taking place within the context of an organized group. Neither can we extrapolate from what goes on *within* a group to explain intergroup events. Such extrapolations have proven sterile in the past, and will continue to yield caricatures of conflict and cooperation between groups. They amount to ignoring the *independent variables* that characterize the domain of intergroup relations. The properties of organized group settings and of relationships between groups are independent variables not to be taken lightly.

Conflict and cooperation between groups and between nations take place within the framework of group trends, policy orientations, and decision-making agencies with distinctive organizational arrangements and codes for conduct. This fact was well expressed by the psychiatrist J. D. Frank, one of the most persistent workers in this problem area. In his recent paper on "Group Psychology and the Elimination of War" (1964), Frank concluded: "Individuals fight but they do not wage war. This is reserved for organized groups" (p. 41).

Intergroup trends toward conflict or cooperation are shaped by individuals who act as integral parts of organized frameworks. Those concerned in bringing about changes in intergroup trends are effective to the extent that they succeed in influencing the prevailing organizational agencies. Policy and decision makers are not outside of this framework. The alternative strategies available to them are within the latitude of acceptance of their groups at the given period. All possible alternatives that are rational or appropriate are not realistically available to them. The realistic alternatives they can advance are those clearly acceptable to their group at the time.

If a policy-maker or negotiator goes beyond the acceptable bounds, or fails to prepare the ground for their extension before making commitments to a given strategy, the decisions or the agreements he makes with an adversary are doomed to remain *personal* decisions, unheeded or rejected by his own group. From the many cases substantiating this point, let me mention the fate of a labor negotiator named O'Brien, who spent ten months in a hospital after returning from negotiations with management with an agreement that deviated greatly from the expectations of his union. (This case was reported by Holbrook, 1946, in *A Century of American Ore and Steel.*) Everyone is familiar with the tragic fate of President Woodrow Wilson, whose solemn agreement to have his country in the League of Nations was repudiated by the nation that twice elected him President.

The dependence of negotiators on organizational trends recently received experimental verification by Blake and his associates (1961,

1964) in an interesting series of experiments. The problem concerned the conditions in which a group would picture their representatives as heroes or traitors. Those negotiators who came back with decisions within the bounds of their group's expectations were considered heroes, and those who deviated appreciably from the group's preferred strategies were considered traitors. "Impartial" arbitrators of group differences suffered a similar fate, losing their impartiality in the eyes of group members when they ruled against the group's preferred strategies.

Guided by such considerations, in our research program, the choice of variables to be included in research design and alternatives to be tested are extracted from surveys of actualities of group functioning and trends in their relationship (Sherif and Sherif, 1953). This mode of experimental simulation starts by making a special issue of the *isomorphism*, or correspondence, between the actualities of intergroup relations and the research model. The gap between so many research generalizations and actualities they attempt to predict has been duly noted by more and more investigators as a vexing problem. The gap may be due in part to lack of concern over this isomorphism issue.

In our research, tentative generalizations were extracted from extensive surveys concerning the following: (1) The formation and functioning of groups with their associated power relations and normative codes of conduct that define the bounds of acceptable strategies. (2) The rise of conflict or cooperation between groups with their associated negative or positive attitudes and stereotypes toward out-groups. The prerequisite information on the above two topics suggested realistic measures for the reduction of conflict and change in associated codes of conduct.

Since we have reported the body of evidence and qualifications elsewhere, I will state the major generalizations in the form of short propositions. Then I will discuss experimental extensions on a more complicated level.

INTERACTION ON THE LEVEL OF IN-GROUPS

When individuals interact repeatedly toward compelling goals that they urgently experience in common, the product of their interaction is a human group. The main properties of this unique and characteristically human process are: (1) an organizational pattern for their dealings with one another, and (2) normative yardsticks or codes to regulate their activities towards the common ends. Psychologically, this differentiation into a status hierarchy and rise of common standards during repeated interactions amounts to stabilization of interpersonal expectations. Lack of stabilization in these respects is tension-producing.

The boundaries of the organizational power structure and the normative code of conduct define a sense of "we-ness" for members,

cherished within the group and upheld by members in dealings with
outsiders. In time, the standards shared in their sphere of "we-ness"
become personally binding for individual members who are worthy and
true. Members who are within the fold make judgments, condemn or
justify events related to their "we-ness" in terms of their sense of identification within the group.

Marked deviations from the viewpoints and premises thus stabilized
on the part of less committed or disturbed members bring further loss
in their position and effective power within the group. For the powerful
and good, the group standards define responsibility, personal account-
ability, "do's" and "don'ts" in matters relevant to the group, and thus
become ingredients to the individual conscience. Of course, this is an
ethnocentric code of ethics. Conscience thus constituted is absolutistic
in its evaluations, which proceed only from the premises within the
narrow scope of the in-group in question.

INTERACTION AT THE LEVEL OF FUNCTIONALLY RELATED GROUPS

Groups that were once more or less closed systems come into trans-
action with one another through developments in technology, increased
ease and speed in communication; increased volume of production
and commerce, population movement, and exposure to common threat.
Through such circumstances, groups become functionally related in
positive or negative ways, depending chiefly on the compatibility or
incompatibility of the goals each pursues relative to those of other groups.

If the goals pursued by one group are perceived by another group
(rightly or wrongly) as a threat or block to the pursuit of its goals, the
result is *conflict* between them. Over time, negative attitudes and stereotypes of the out-group are stabilized with the contending parties. Then,
they serve as premises for sizing up the adversary, for predicting his
behavior, and for developing strategies to deal with him. Repeated rivalry in conflict strengthens solidarity within the groups, so that all
members, good and true, proceed from premises defined by the standpoint of their group in the conflict. Strategies designed for deterrence
or destruction of the opponent are "ethically" justified by these premises, which become ingredients in the conscience of members most
devoted or most rewarded by their membership. In this way, each new
encounter between groups bears the heavy hand of past conflicts and
starts a new spiral of circular argument over "who is to blame" for it.

No matter whether the organizational forms within groups are
authoritarian or democratic, no matter what the child-rearing practices
within them, no matter how cooperative or competitive the practices
within the family, intergroup conflict over time produces such a vicious
circle. The sufficient condition for the sequence of events just described
is the mutual incompatibility of goals persistently pursued by two or

more groups. This generalization is based on scientific evidence, both empirical and experimental.

Those who claim to be working rationally in the name of science to devise strategies of deterrence by force, or its threat, are themselves caught in the vicious circle, either by choice of a conscience shaped in the ethnocentric image of one of the contenders, or by their roles in its organization which they do not choose to vacate. They are technicians whose made-to-order projects proceed from assumptions that science cannot take for granted, but should take as the object of investigation, as noted by the physicist Watson-Watt (1961) in discussing the roles of technicians and scientists in modern society. Their rational models proceed from ready-made premises that remain to be scientifically justified.

In modern times, the functional relatedness of groups has resulted in increased dependence of group on group, whether they like it or not. The dependence of group on group has created ever-enlarging inter-group systems, such that the safety, economic livelihood, and plans of groups within them are vitally affected by their transactions with one another. Now, I will present several propositions concerning the rise of organizational forms and binding standards for regulating smaller groups caught in transactions in an intergroup system.

WIDENING CIRCLES OF IDENTIFICATION ON
THE SCOPE OF INTERGROUP SYSTEMS

When groups are prompted by common gains for their livelihood, exposed to common dangers, or otherwise recognize a common predicament among them, they enter into transactions with one another. This tendency is promoted by proximity, but also by advances in technology, which enlarge the spheres of their interdependence.

Over time, groups thus caught tend to band together in matters pertaining to their common predicament, depending upon its urgency and upon the extent to which the predicaments cannot be solved without their joint efforts. Confronted with problem situations or goals which are compelling to each group but require that they pull together—that is, confronted with superordinate goals—the groups band together. Over time they implement their efforts through organizational forms and rules of conduct that bear authority for constituent subunits, at least in spheres of life pertaining to their common predicament.

The formation of a union or federated agency toward one or several superordinate goals enlarges the sense of identity in spheres relevant to the union. In these respects, "we-ness" expands beyond the bounds of the constituent in-groups. Over time, codes of conduct that are established in the larger organization in these particular spheres come to define the individual member's concepts of loyalty and responsibility in these respects. The range of loyalties commanded by the constituent groups, on one hand, or by the larger association, on the other, vary with the scope of the recognized dependencies among the subunits.

Of course, these trends do not occur without resistance by some groups within the intergroup system or their members. Superordinate goals are not necessarily congruent with other goals and established procedures within the groups constituting the system. Therefore, they may disrupt procedures and arrangements already stabilized within smaller constituent's units as the "normal state of affairs."

Even in this country, whose union has followed the trend just described, there are islands of resistance that cling to their prerogatives as closed systems in spheres that they still regard as local and not infringing the terms of the constitution of their union. They assert their pleas for sovereignty in these spheres in terms of "states rights." In newly developing countries today, older tribal organizations, ethnic groups or language groups similarly assert the authority of tribal or local custom despite their commitment to federal authority of the new nation in such spheres as foreign policy, foreign trade, and peace or war.

The growth of organizational forms and codes among groups for dealing with recognized dependence has also occurred on the international level. In the sphere of a common concern, nations have developed organizations and rules across countries and continents. In many cases, the codes thus evolved are not framed within the grooves of habitual practice within the participating nations.

In a recent United Nations publication on *International Law in a Changing World* by Thirteen Experts (1963), the trend toward evolving rules across sovereign nations in particular spheres of life is documented impressively. There are literally one hundred organizations with rules that various nations accept as binding in a variety of activities, such as health, communication, transportation, postal service, weather information, and certain other scientific endeavors. Their subordinate place in the schemes of respective nations can be seen, of course, in the fact that war or its threat relegates the effectiveness of these international agencies to less than the value of the documents on which they are recorded.

The untold sufferings of World War I were required for nations to recognize their interdependence in maintaining peace through a League of Nations. Founded as part of a war settlement, endowed with no genuine power to enforce decisions, and scuttled by powerful countries jealous of their sovereignty even before it got under way, the League of Nation's fate is well known (U Thant, 1964). From the unprecedented destruction and human toll of World War II, the United Nations arose among nations still reluctant to relegate the prerogative of waging war, which they consider to be the privilege of a sovereign nation alone, and still determined to take the law in their own hands should it suit their interests.

Still, the postwar world has seen unprecedented enlargement in the scope of international attempts toward federation in matters of commerce and in foreign dealings. Even as the shadows of nuclear holocaust hang over the world, we are witnessing international and cross-continental attempts to secure peace, as well as organizations of African states, Afro-Asian states, and others, as documented, for example, by the sociologist Etzioni (1962) by Legum (1962) and the leaders of new nations in Africa and Asia.

THE NEEDED RESEARCH

Therefore, the urgent problem for research today lies in the conditions affecting spheres in which groups delegate their sovereign powers to a larger federation or union. We are told by social scientists (such as Rupert Emerson, 1960, and Boyd Shafer, 1955) and even by men in politics (such as Rusk, 1964, and Fulbright, 1964) that the traditional concept of sovereignty is obsolete. Psychologists such as Otto Klineberg (1962) have written that even some matters traditionally considered "internal affairs" of a country now have an impact in intergroup relations. What are the conditions in which groups that consider themselves autonomous consent to relinquish their unbridled right to hostile, aggressive, and warlike actions towards others? When do the affairs within a group become the business of everybody, even those outside the group?

On the basis of the propositions presented about conflict and cooperation between functionally related groups, we are envisaging a series of experiments on these problems. By necessity, these experiments are designed in a series of successive stages over time. The independent variables pertain to conditions in which individuals interact among themselves and then groups interact as units. Here I can only give an abstract without going into details of design and procedure.

As in our earlier experiments, groups will be produced through the introduction of highly appealing goals whose attainment requires coordinated action and division of labor over a period of time. The autonomous groups will then be brought into contact, two or three at a time. Their first encounters will be in situations that embody compelling superordinate goals. We predict that the groups will form a combination or federation of some sort in those particular spheres related to their mutual dependence in attaining these goals. At least in these spheres, procedures and rules will emerge that will be binding for members of all groups in the combination, thus enlarging their identification and code of ethics beyond their in-group ethnocentrism.

The next problem is what will happen when these small combinations are brought together into functional relations with one another. Half of the combinations will transact in situations embodying goals, whose attainment by one combination of groups is incompatible with their attainment by another combination. The other half of the combinations will transact in situations embodying goals that are compatible.

In the case of the combinations who transact around mutually exclusive or conflicting goals, we predict a closing of ranks within each combination, conflict between combinations, the rise of hostile attitudes and stereotypes, and the assertion of sovereign rights to proceed along practices already established within the combination. For those whose initial contact centers around compatible goals, the establishment of still larger organizational units is predicted, in matters pertaining to these goals that affect them all.

Finally, the sphere of dependence between the combinations will be progressively broadened. A graduated series of dependence will be introduced, proceeding from highly specific contacts to increasingly central and pervasive issues.

When will the affairs within the conflicting combinations become a matter of such concern to others that they are no longer seen as internal affairs? How pervasive is the sphere of dependence between groups before they take steps to establish binding rules that transcend those established by constituent combinations? We predict that concern over internal affairs of other combinations and groups will increase as the scope of interdependence among groups increases. We predict an increased tendency to relegate intergroup conduct to a larger body as the sphere of common concern increases in scope, even though each organization maintains its autonomy and prerogatives in other respects.

Experiments that incorporate the major variables of group and intergroup relations enable us to specify the conditions that arouse intense emotions and the strategies they provoke. Of course, experimental simulation cannot claim more than that essential properties of intergroup conflict and cooperation are operating in miniature. At the very best, experimental simulation can be no more than a paradigm in miniature. It is not possible to replicate the content of goals, the activities or the length of time occupied.

Therefore, it would be naive to presume that validation of predictions based on what happens in an experiment occupying three months, such as that described, would be forthcoming in a few years. Groups do not give up their sovereign prerogatives easily, even in the spheres in which they are most interdependent for the survival and preservation of their culture and civilization. Nations resist the relegation of the prerogative to wage peace or war even to an agency in which they themselves are represented, while proclaiming that a deadly showdown will be catastrophic for all. One cannot help noting that it has taken destruction and suffering of great proportions to prompt nations even to consider a superordinate agency with power to prevent their recurrence.

Yet there is an unmistakable trend today toward increasing dependence among nations, acknowledged by almost all. Efforts toward establishing binding rules to prevent nations from taking the law into their own hands in matters of peace and war that affect the survival of all are unprecedented in scope, despite the ups and downs in the immediate picture. But here, a grim question must be asked: Will this trend succeed in taking its course before it is crushed with everything else in the catastrophe of a deadly showdown of worldwide scope?

In this vital issue, we face a dilemma on which serious research effort should be concentrated. On the one hand, the dependence of nations and blocs of nations on each other for avoiding a worldwide showdown is proclaimed by policy makers and scientists of all the great blocs. On the other hand, there are voices from the same blocs asserting that it would be worth sacrificing some millions of their populations for the maintenance of their way of life and the cherished values of their cultures.

Underlying the assertion that even sacrifice of millions and destruction of urban centers might become necessary to preserve a way of life or ideology, there is the assumption that evacuation of cities and bomb and fallout shelters will insure the survival of what is dear and sacred in a new world devoid of malicious aggressors. This assumption needs serious re-examination. Taking even the lowest estimates of the human toll and destruction, it is necessary to ask what kind of human beings would emerge from weeks or months in shelters after the catastrophe, even though they may maintain life and limb as biological organisms. This question goes beyond the domain of competence of physicists, biochemists, and biologists. This problem lies in the domain of human psychology and personality. Already some pertinent questions have been raised by psychologists and sociologists in Arthur Waskow's *The Shelter Centered Society* (1962).

There is an accumulating body of evidence in psychology and social science that provides a realistic basis to predict what kind of creatures the survivors would be. Predictions on this score cannot be based realistically on research that puts people in shelters for this purpose for a couple of weeks or even longer periods. They know that the world is proceeding normally outside and that they will return to it at the end of the experiment. They may even get a thrill from participating in the adventure, coming out to tell their friends with relish about their stamina.

Realistic predictions can be based on research on the consequences of human uncertainty and insecurity, for these would certainly be the lot of survivors, both in shelters and when they emerge. The psychological stability of the human person and the healthy integration of his self-image that supports cherished values of human dignity and integrity depend mainly on the stability of his physical, social, and cultural moorings. They depend on the stability of moorings with other people and with communities providing regularities for their dealings and a dependable world of objects and schedules to which they are accustomed.

Disruption of stable moorings with people dear in their eyes, disruption of anchorages in predictable environments with familiar symbols produce psychological instabilty and insecurity, even for perfectly normal and healthy human individuals. Everything we know about the consequences of human uncertainty and insecurity indicates that those who emerge from their shelters after the major catastrophe, should it descend on the human race, would exhibit in profound form the behavioral characteristics of men caught in uncertainty, insecurity and confusion (Ausubel, 1952; Durkheim, 1951; Merton, 1957; Saintsbury, 1955; Sherif and Cantril, 1947; Sherif and Harvey, 1952; Stouffer et al., 1949). These include erratic and broad fluctuations in behavior from its customary modes, as persons frantically flounder around in search of some stable, dependable moorings. They include heightened proneness to accept and to conform to the guides offered by others, whether they are appropriate or not. Borrowing a phrase from the novelist Faulkner that Silver repeated in *The Closed Society* (1964), we can predict that their questions would include the forlorn cry: Why didn't someone tell us what would happen?

Someone should tell the peoples of the world and their leaders that the best evidence available indicates that survivors will not be the same people after weeks or months in shelters, completely uncertain of what they will find outside and emerging to a world deprived of what is stable, near and dear to them. Further research should concentrate on the consequences of uncertainty and confusion to the human person, and to his capacity to maintain human dignity and integrity in the face of irrevocable destruction of stable ties and moorings, of course in minor spheres that produce no lasting harm. Such research, I am convinced, would serve to guide us out of the dilemma so that people can be told before it is too late.

WORKS CITED

ABT, L. E., and BELLAK, L. (Eds.). *Projective psychology.* New York: Alfred A. Knopf, 1950.

ALLENDOERFER, C. B., and OAKLEY, C. O. *Fundamentals of freshman mathematics.* New York: McGraw-Hill, 1959.

ALLPORT, F. H. *Social psychology.* Boston: Houghton Mifflin, 1924.

————. Psychology in relation to social and political problems. In P. Achilles (Ed.), *Psychology at work.* New York: McGraw-Hill, 1932.

————. Methods in the study of collective action phenomena. *J. soc. Psychol. S.P.S.S.I. Bull.,* 1942, *15,* 165–185.

————, and KATZ, D. *Students' attitudes.* Syracuse: Craftsman, 1931.

ALLPORT, G. W. *Personality: a psychological interpretation.* New York: Holt, 1937.

————. The ego in contemporary psychology. *Psychol. Rev.,* 1943, *50,* 451–478.

————, and KRAMER, B. N. Some roots of prejudice. *J. Psychol.,* 1946, *22,* 9–39

————, and POSTMAN, L. *The psychology of rumor.* New York: Holt, 1947.

ANASTASI, A. Psychological traits and group relations. In M. Sherif and M. O. Wilson (Eds.), *Group relations at the crossroads.* New York: Harper, 1953.

————, and FOLEY, J. P. *Differential psychology.* (Rev. ed.) New York: Macmillan, 1949.

ANDERSON, N. *The hobo: the sociology of the homeless man.* Chicago: University of Chicago Press, 1923.

ANSBACHER, H. L. The history of the leaderless group discussion technique. *Psychol. Bull.,* 1951, *48,* 383–391.

APTER, D. E. Theory and the study of politics. *Amer. polit. Sci. Rev.,* 1957, *51,* 747–762.

ARENSBERG, C. M. Behavior and organization: industrial studies. In J. H. Rohrer and M. Sherif (Eds.), *Social psychology at the crossroads.* New York: Harper, 1951.

ASCH, S. E. *Social psychology.* Englewood Cliffs, N.J.: Prentice-Hall, 1952.

————. Effects of group pressures upon the modification and distortion of judgments. In G. E. Swanson, T. M. Newcomb, and E. L. Hartley (Eds.), *Readings in social psychology.* (2nd ed.) New York: Holt, 1952.

———. Studies of independence and conformity. 1. A minority of one against a unanimous majority. *Psychol. Monogr.*, 1956, 70, No. 9.

AULD, F., JR. Influence of social class on personality test responses. *Psychol. Bull.*, 1952, 49, 318–332.

AUSUBEL, D. P. *Ego development and the personality disorders.* New York: Grune and Stratton, 1952.

———. *Theory and problems of adolescent development.* New York: Grune and Stratton, 1954.

———. Relationships between shame and guilt in the socializing process. *Psychol. Rev.*, 1955, 62, 378–390.

AVIGDOR, R. The development of stereotypes as a result of group interaction. Unpublished doctoral dissertation, New York University, 1952. Summarized in M. Sherif and Carolyn W. Sherif, *Groups in Harmony and Tension.* New York: Harper, 1953.

BALDWIN, J. M. *Mental development in the child and the race.* New York: Macmillan, 1895.

———. *The individual and society.* Boston: Badger, 1911.

BARKER, R. G. On the nature of the environment. Kurt Lewin Memorial Address. *J. soc. Issues*, 1963, 19, 17–38.

BARTLETT, F. C. *Remembering: a study in experimental and social psychology.* New York: Cambridge University Press, 1932.

BARTON, R. F. *The half way sun.* New York: Brewer and Warren, 1930.

BASS, B. M. *Leadership, psychology, and organizational behavior.* New York: Harper, 1960.

BEARD, C. A., and BEARD, MARY R. *The rise of American civilization.* Vol. I. New York: Macmillan, 1930.

BECKER, H. Anthropology and sociology. In J. Gillin (Ed.), *For a science of social man.* New York: Macmillan, 1954.

———. Field work among Scottish shepherds and German peasants: "wholes" and their handicaps. *Soc. Forces*, 1956, 35, 10–15.

BEEBE-CENTER, J. *Pleasantness and unpleasantness.* New York: Van Nostrand, 1932.

BELL, W. The utility of the Shevky typology for the design of urban sub-area field studies. *J. soc. Psychol.*, 1958, 47, 71–83.

BENEDICT, RUTH. Anthropology and the abnormal. *J. Gen. Psychol.*, 1934, 10, 60–64.

BERKOWITZ, L. *Aggression: a social psychological analysis.* New York: McGraw-Hill, 1962.

BERNARD, L. L. Recent discussions regarding social psychology. *Amer. J. Sociol.*, 1942, 48, 13–27.

BERNE, E. V. C. An experimental investigation of social behavior patterns in young children. *Univ. Iowa Stud. Child Welf.*, 1930, 4, No. 3.

BERRY, B. *Race relations.* Boston: Houghton Mifflin, 1951.

BERRY, M. F., and EISENSON, J. *The defective in speech.* New York: Crofts, 1945.

BIDNEY, D. Towards a psychocultural definition of the concept of personality. In S. S. Sargent and M. W. Smith (Eds.), *Culture and personality.* New York: Viking Fund, 1949.

BIRD, C. *Social psychology.* New York: Appleton-Century-Crofts, 1940.

BLAKE, R. R., and BREHM, J. W. The use of tape recording to simulate a group atmosphere. *J. abnorm. soc. Psychol.,* 1954, *49,* 311–313.

———, and MOUTON, JANE S. Loyalty of representatives to ingroup positions during intergroup competition. *Sociometry,* 1961, *24,* 171–183.

———, and RAMSEY, G. V. (Eds.). *Perception: an approach to personality.* New York: Ronald Press, 1951.

———, SHEPARD, H. A., and MOUTON, JANE S. *Managing intergroup conflict in industry.* Houston: Gulf Publishing Co., 1964.

BLAU, P. M., and SCOTT, W. R. *Formal organizations.* San Francisco: Chandler, 1962.

BLUMENFELD, W. Educational psychology in Peru. In "On present-day psychology and education in the Americas." *Inter-Amer. soc. Psychol. Monogr.,* 1956, *I,* 34–41.

BLUMER, H. Collective behavior. In A. M. Lee (Ed.), *New outline of the principles of sociology.* New York: Barnes and Noble, 1946.

BOAS, F. *The mind of primitive man.* New York: Macmillan, 1911.

BOGARDUS, E. S. A social distance scale. *Sociol. and soc. Res.,* 1933, *17,* 265–270.

———. Changes in racial distance. *Int. J. opin. attit. Res.,* 1947, *I,* 55–62.

BONNER, H. *Social psychology.* New York: American Book Co., 1953.

———. *Group dynamics: principles and applications.* New York: Ronald Press, 1959.

BOOKER, E. L. *Flight from China.* New York: Macmillan, 1946.

BORING, E. G. Attribute and sensation. *Amer. J. Psychol.,* 1924, *35,* 301–304.

BOVARD, E. W., JR. Social norms and the individual. *J. abnorm. soc. Psychol.,* 1948, *43,* 62–69.

BRESSLER, J. Judgment in absolute units as a psychophysical method. *Arch. Psychol.,* 1933, No. 152.

BROOM, L., SIEGEL, B. J., VOGT, E. Z., and WATSON, J. B. Acculturation: an exploratory formulation. (The Social Science Research Council summer session on acculturation, 1953.) *Amer. Anthrop.,* 1954, *56,* 973–1000.

BROWN, J. F. *Psychology and the social order.* New York: McGraw-Hill, 1936.

BRUNER, J. S. Social psychology and group processes. *Annu. Rev. Psychol.,* 1950, *1,* 119–150.

———, and GOODMAN, C. C. Value and need as organizing factors in perception. *J. abnorm. soc. Psychol.,* 1947, *42,* 33–44.

———, and KRECH, D. (Eds.). *Perception and personality: a symposium.* Durham, N.C.: Duke University Press, 1949–50.

BUGENTAL, J. F. T., and ZELEN, S. L. Investigations into the "self concept." I. The W-A-Y technique. *J. Personal.,* 1949–1950, *18,* 483–498.

BURGESS, E. W. The influence of Sigmund Freud upon sociology in the United States. *Amer. J. Sociol.,* 1939–40, *45,* 356–374.

CAMPBELL, A., and STOKES, D. E. Partisan attitudes and the presidential vote. In E. Burdick and A. J. Brodbeck (Eds.), *American voting behavior.* Glencoe, Ill.: Free Press, 1959.

CAMPBELL, D. T. The indirect assessment of social attitudes. *Psychol. Bull.,* 1950, *47,* 15–38.

CANTRIL, H. General and specific attitudes. *Psychol. Monogr.,* 1932, No. 192.

———. The social psychology of everyday life. *Psychol. Bull.*, 1934, *31*, 297–330.

———. *The invasion from Mars*. Princeton, N.J.: Princeton University Press, 1940. Summary in T. M. Newcomb and E. L. Hartley (Eds.), *Readings in Social Psychology*. New York: Holt, 1947.

———. The intensity of an attitude. *J. abn. soc. Psychol.*, 1946, *41*, 124–135.

CAPLOW, T. Rumors in war. *Social Forces*, 1947, *25*, 298–302.

CARMICHAEL, L. L., HOGAN, H., and WALTER, A. An experimental study of the effect of language on the reproduction of visually perceived form. *J. exp. Psychol.*, 1932, *15*, 73–86.

CARR, H. A. *Psychology: a study of mental activity*. New York: Longmans, 1925.

CARTER, L. F. Leadership and small group behavior. In M. Sherif and M. O. Wilson (Eds.), *Group relations at the crossroads*. New York: Harper, 1953.

———, and SCHOOLER, K. Value, need and other factors in perception. *Psychol. Rev.*, 1949, *56*, 200–207.

CARTWRIGHT, D. American social psychology and the war. *J. consult. Psychol.*, 1945, *9*, 67–72.

———, and ZANDER, A. F. (Eds.). *Group dynamics: research and theory*. Evanston, Ill.: Row, Peterson, 1953.

CASSIRER, E. *Language and myth*. New York: Dover, 1946.

CENTERS, R. Social class identifications of American youth. *J. Pers.*, 1949–1950, *18*, 209–302.

———. The American class structure: a psychological analysis. In G. E. Swanson, T. M. Newcomb, and E. L. Hartley (Eds.), *Readings in social psychology*. New York: Holt, 1952.

CHAPANIS, A. Men, machines, and models. *Amer. Psychologist*, 1961, *16*, 113–131.

CHAPMAN, D. W. Relative effects of determinate and undeterminate Aufgaben. *Amer. J. Psychol.*, 1932, *44*, 163–174.

———, and VOLKMANN, J. A social determinant of the level of aspiration. *J. abnorm. soc. Psychol.*, 1939, *34*, 225–238.

CHAPMAN, J., and ECKSTEIN, M. A social-psychological study of the alleged visitation of the Virgin Mary in Puerto Rico. *Yearb. Amer. phil. Soc.*, 1954, 203–206.

CHUNN, C. E. (Ed.). *Of rice and men*. Los Angeles: Veterans Publishing Co., 1946.

CLARK, K. B., and CLARK, M. K. The development of consciousness of self and the emergence of racial identification in Negro preschool children. 1939. See T. M. Newcomb and E. L. Hartley (Eds.), *Readings in social psychology*. New York: Holt, 1947.

———, ———. Skin color as a factor in the racial identification of Negro preschool children. *J. soc. Psychol.*, 1940, *11*, 159–169.

———, ———. Racial identification and preference in Negro children. In T. M. Newcomb and E. L. Hartley (Eds.), *Readings in social psychology*. New York: Holt, 1947.

CLEMMER, D. *The prison community*. Boston: Christopher House, 1940.

COFFIN, T. E. Some conditions of suggestion and suggestibility: study of some attitudinal and situational factors influencing the process of suggestion. *Psychol. Monogr.*, 1941, *63*, No. 241.

COHEN, E. Stimulus conditions as factors in social change. *Sociometry*, 1957, *20*, 135–144.

COOLEY, C. H. *Human nature and the social order.* New York: Scribner's, 1902.

———. A study of the early use of self-words by a child. *Psychol. Rev.*, 1908, *15*, 339–357.

COOK, S. W., and HARRIS, R. E. The verbal conditioning of the galvanic skin reflex. *J. exp. Psychol.*, 1937, *21*, 202–210.

COPE, L. Calendars of the Indians North of Mexico. *Calif. Publ. Arch. Ethnol.*, 1919, *16*, 124–137.

COTTRELL, L. S., JR. The analysis of situational fields in social psychology. *Amer. sociol. Rev.*, 1942, 7, 370–382.

———, and GALLAGHER, R. Developments in social psychology, 1930–1940. *Sociometry Monogr.*, 1941, No. 1.

CRUTCHFIELD, R. S., Social psychology and group processes. *Ann. Rev. Psychol.*, 1954, *5*, 171–202.

DARWIN, C. Biographical sketch of an infant. *Mind*, 1877, *2*, 285–294.

DASHIELL, J. F. Experimental studies of the influence of social situations on the behavior of individual human adults. In C. Murchison (Ed.), *Handbook of social psychology.* Worcester, Mass.: Clark University Press, 1935.

DAVIS, K. The sociology of parent-youth conflict. *Amer. sociol. Rev.*, 1940, *5*, 523–535.

DE GRAZIA, A. The process of theory-research interaction. *J. Politics*, 1951, *13*, 88–99.

DE LAGUNA, G. A. *Speech, its function and development.* New Haven: Yale University Press, 1927.

DEUTSCH, M. Guidelines for testing minority group children. *J. soc. Issues*, 1964, 20, No. 2.

DIXON, W. J., and MASSEY, F. J. *Introduction to statistical analysis.* New York: McGraw-Hill, 1951.

DOBY, J. F., SUCHMAN, E. A., MCKINNEY, J. C., FRANCIS, R. G., and DEAN, J. P. *An introduction to social research.* Harrisburg, Pa.: Stackpole Press, 1954.

DOLLARD, J., DOOB, L. W., MILLER, N. E., MOWRER, O. H., and SEARS, R. R. *Frustration and aggression.* New Haven: Yale University Press, 1939.

DOOB, L. W. *Social psychology.* New York: Holt, 1952.

DOW, G. S. *Society and its problems: introduction to the principles of sociology.* New York: Crowell, 1922.

DUNLAP, K. *Social psychology.* Baltimore; Williams and Wilkins, 1925.

DURKHEIM, E. *The elementary forms of religious life.* London: G. Allen, 1915.

———. *The rules of sociological method.* Chicago: University of Chicago Press, 1938.

———. *Suicide: a study in sociology.* Glencoe, Ill.: Free Press, 1951.

ECKSTEIN, H. (Rapporteur). Political theory and the study of politics: a report of a conference. *Amer. polit. Sci. Rev.*, 1956, *50*, 465–487.

EDWARDS, A. L. *The social desirability variable in personality assessment and research*. New York: Dryden Press, 1957.

EDWARDS, W. The theory of decision making. *Psychol. Bull.*, 1954, *51*, 380–417.

ELDERSVELD, S. J., HEARD, A., HUNTINGTON, S. P., JANOWITZ, M., LEISERSON, A., McKEAN, D. D., and TRUMAN, D. B. Research in political behavior. *Amer. polit. Sci. Rev.*, 1952, *46*, 1003–1045.

EMERSON, R. *From empire to nation*. Cambridge, Mass.: Harvard University Press, 1960.

ETZIONI, A. *The hard way to peace: a new strategy*. New York: Collier, 1962.

FARBER, M. L. The study of national character: 1955. *J. soc. Issues*, 1955, *11*, 52–56.

FARIS, E. The beginnings of social psychology. *Amer. J. Sociol.*, 1945, *50*, 422–428.

FARIS, R. E. L. *Social psychology*. New York: Ronald Press, 1952.

————. Development of the small group research movement. In M. Sherif and M. O. Wilson (Eds.), *Group relations at the crossroads*. New York: Harper, 1953.

FARNSWORTH, P. R., and BEAUMONT, H. Suggestion in pictures. *J. Gen. Psychol.*, 1929, *2*, 362–366.

FERNBERGER, S. W. On absolute and relative judgments in lifted weight experiments. *Amer. J. Psychol.*, 1931, *43*, 560–578.

FESTINGER, L. An analysis of compliant behavior. In M. Sherif and M. O. Wilson (Eds.), *Group relations at the crossroads*. New York: Harper, 1953.

————. Laboratory experiments. In L. Festinger and D. Katz (Eds.), *Research methods in the behavioral sciences*. New York: Dryden Press, 1953.

————. Social psychology and group processes. *Ann. Rev. Psychol.*, 1955, *6*, 187–216.

FORD, C. S., and BEACH, F. A. *Patterns of sexual behavior*. New York: Harper, 1951.

FRANK, J. D. Individual differences in certain aspects of the level of aspiration. *Amer. J. Psychol.*, 1935, *47*, 119–128.

————. Group psychology and the elimination of war. *Int. J. Group Psychother.*, 1964, *14*, 41–48.

FRAZIER, F. *Bourgeoisie noire*. Paris: Librairie Plon, 1955.

FREEDMAN, R., HAWLEY, A. H., LANDECKER, W. S., and MINER, H. M. *Principles of sociology*. New York: Holt, 1952.

FRENCH, J. R. P., JR. Experiments in field settings. In L. Festinger and D. Katz (Eds.), *Research methods in the behavioral sciences*. New York: Dryden Press, 1953.

————. A formal theory of social power. *Psychol. Rev.*, 1956, *63*, 181–194.

FRENCH, R. L. Social psychology and group processes. Ann. Rev. Psychol., 1956, 7, 63–94.

FREUD, S. *Group psychology and the analysis of the ego*. London: International Psychology Press, 1922.

————. *The ego and the id*. London: Hogarth, 1927.

————. Totem and taboo. In *The basic writings of Sigmund Freud*. New York: Modern Library, 1938.

FROMM, E. Psychoanalytic characterology and its application to the understanding of culture. In S. S. Sargent and M. W. Smith (Eds.), *Culture and personality*. New York: Viking Fund, 1949.

FULBRIGHT, J. W. *Old myths and new realities*. New York: Random House, 1964.

GARCEAU, O. Research in the political process. *Amer. polit. Sci. Rev.*, 1951, 45, 69–85.

GESELL, A., and ILG, F. L. *Infant and child in the culture of today*. New York: Harper, 1943.

————, and THOMPSON, H. *Infant behavior*. New York: McGraw-Hill, 1934.

————, ————. *The psychology of early growth*. New York: Macmillan, 1938.

GIBB, C. A. Leadership. In G. Lindzey (Ed.), *Handbook of social psychology*. Vol. 2. Reading, Mass.: Addison-Wesley, 1954.

GIBSON, J. J. The reproduction of visually perceived forms. *J. exp. Psychol.*, 1939, 12, 1–39.

GILLIN, J. (Ed.). *For a science of social man*. New York: Macmillan, 1954.

GILLIN, J., and RAIMY, V. Acculturation and personality. *Amer. Sociol. Rev.*, 1940, 5, 371–380.

GLIXMAN, A. R. Categorizing behavior as a function of meaning domain. *J. person. soc. Psychol.*, 1965, 2, 370–377.

GOLDENWEISER, A. A. *Early civilization*. New York: Alfred A. Knopf, 1926.

GOLDSTEIN, N. F. *The roots of prejudice against the Negro in the United States*. Boston: Boston University Press, 1948.

GOODENOUGH, F. L. *Developmental psychology*. (2nd ed.) New York: Appleton-Century-Crofts, 1945.

————, and BRIAN, C. R. Certain factors underlying the acquisition of motor skill by pre-school children. *J. exp. Psychol.*, 1929, 12, 127–155.

————, and HARRIS, D. B. Studies in the psychology of children's drawings: II. 1928–1949. *Psychol. Bull.*, 1950, 47, 394–399.

GOODMAN, MARY ELLEN. *Race awareness in young children*. Reading, Mass.: Addison-Wesley, 1952.

GOTTSCHALK, L. R. *The era of the French revolution, 1715–1815*. Boston: Houghton Mifflin, 1929.

GRAHAM, C. H. Behavior and the psychophysical methods: an analysis of some recent experiments. *Psychol. Rev.*, 1952, 59, 62–70.

GREENBERG, P. J. Competition in children: an experimental study. *Amer. J. Psychol.*, 1932, 44, 221–248.

GRIFFITH, C. R. *General introduction to psychology*. New York: Macmillan, 1923.

GUETZKOW, H. S., and BOWMAN, P. H. *Men and hunger*. Elgin, Ill.: Brethren Publishing House, 1946.

GUILFORD, J. P. Racial preferences of a thousand American university students. *J. soc. Psychol.*, 1931, 2, 179–204.

GUNTHER, J. *Inside Africa*. New York: Harper, 1955.

HALLOWELL, A. I. Psychology and anthropology. In J. Gillin (Ed.), *For a science of social man*. New York: Macmillan, 1954.

482   *Works Cited*

———. The self and its behavioral environment. *Explorations,* 1954, *1,* 108–165.

HARE, A. P., BORGATTA, E. F., and BALES, R. E. *Small groups.* New York: Alfred A. Knopf, 1955.

HART, H. N. *The science of social relations: an introduction to sociology.* New York: Holt, 1927.

HARTLEY, E. L. *Studies in prejudice.* New York: Kings Crown Press, 1945.

———. *Problems of prejudice.* New York: Kings Crown Press, 1946.

———. Psychological problems of multiple group membership. In J. Rohrer and M. Sherif (Eds.), *Social psychology at the crossroads.* New York: Harper, 1951.

———, and HARTLEY, R. E. *Fundamentals of social psychology.* New York: Alfred A. Knopf, 1952.

———, ROSENBAUM, M., and SCHWARTZ, S. Children's use of ethnic frames of reference: an exploratory study of children's conceptualizations of multiple ethnic group membership. *J. Psychol.* 1948, *26,* 267–386; Children's perception of ethnic group membership. *Ibid.,* 387–398; Note on children's role perception. *Ibid.,* 399–405.

HARTLEY, R. E. Personal characteristics and acceptance of secondary groups as reference groups. *J. Indiv. Psychol.,* 1957, *13,* 45–55.

HARTUNG, F. E. Cultural relativity and moral judgments. *Phil. Sci.,* 1954, *21,* 118–126.

HARVEY, O. J. An experimental approach to the study of status relations in informal groups. *Amer. sociol. Rev.,* 1953, *18,* 357–367.

———. An experimental investigation of negative and positive relations between small groups through judgmental indices. *Sociometry,* 1956, *19,* 201–209.

———, and SHERIF, M. Level of aspiration as a case of judgmental activity in which ego-involvements operate as factors. *Sociometry,* 1951, *14,* 121–147.

HEBB, D. O. *A textbook of psychology.* Philadelphia: W. B. Saunders, 1966.

HEIDBREDER, E. Toward a dynamic psychology of cognition. *Psychol. Rev.,* 1945, *52,* 1–22.

HELSON, H. Adaptation level theory. In S. Koch (Ed.), *Psychology: a study of a science. Vol. 1. Sensory, perceptual, and physiological foundations.* New York: McGraw-Hill, 1959.

———. Current trends and issues in adaptation level theory. *Amer. Psychologist,* 1964, *19,* 26.

HENRI, V. Uber die lokalisation der tastempfindungen. Berlin: Reuther, 1897.

———. Recherches sur la localisation des sensations tactiles *L'Ann. psychol.,* 1895, *2,* 168–177.

Herald Tribune. New York. Sunday, May 4, 1947.

HERSKOVITS, M. J. *Man and his works.* New York: Alfred A. Knopf, 1949.

HILGARD, E. R. *Introduction to psychology.* New York: Harcourt, Brace, 1953.

———, CAMPBELL, A. A., and SEARS, W. N. Development of discrimination with and without verbal report. *Amer. J. Psychol.,* 1937, *49,* 564–580.

HILLER, E. T. *The strike.* Chicago: University of Chicago Press, 1928.

———. *Social relations and structure.* New York: Harper, 1947.

HINCKLEY, E. D. The influence of individual opinion on construction of an attitude scale, *J. soc. Psychol.*, 1932, *37*, 283–296.

————, and RETHLINGSCHAFER, D. Value judgments of heights of men by college students. *J. Psychol.*, 1951, *31*, 257–296.

HIROTA, K. Experimental studies of competition. *Jap. J. Psychol.*, 1951, *21*, 70–81. Abstracted in *Psychol. Abstr.*, 1953, *27*, 351.

HOCART, A. M. The psychological interpretation of language. *Brit. J. Psychol.*, 1912, *5*, 267–279.

HOFFMAN, E. L., SWANDER, D. V., BARON, S. H., and ROHRER, J. H. Generalization and exposure time as related to autokinetic movement. *J. exp. Psychol.*, 1953, *46*, 171–177.

HOLBROOK, S. H. *A century of American ore and steel*. New York: Macmillan, 1946.

HOLLINGWORTH, H. L. The central tendency of judgment. *J. Philos.*, 1910, *7*, 461–468.

HOLMAN, G. *Commando attack*. New York: G. P. Putnam, 1942.

HOLMBERG, A. M. The Siriono: a study of the effect of hunger frustration on the culture of a semi-nomadic Bolivian Indian society. Doctoral dissertation, Yale University, July, 1946.

HOLT, R. R. Effects of ego-involvement upon levels of aspiration. *Psychiatry*, 1945, *3*, 299–317.

HOMANS, G. C. *The human group*. New York: Harcourt, Brace, 1950.

HOOD, W. R., and SHERIF, M. Appraisal of personality-oriented approaches to prejudice. *Sociol. soc. Res.*, 1955, *40*, 79–85.

————, ————. Verbal report and judgment of an unstructured stimulus situation. Paper read at Southwestern Psychological Assn., Little Rock, April, 1957; *J. Psychol.*, 1962, *54*, 121–130.

HOPPE, F. Erfolg und Misserfolg. *Psychol. Forsch.*, 1930, *14*, 9.

HOROWITZ, E. L. The development of attitudes toward the Negro. *Arch. Psychol.*, 1936, No. 194.

————. Race attitudes. In O. Klineberg (Ed.), *Characteristics of the American Negro*. Part IV. New York: Harper, 1944.

————, and HOROWITZ, R. Development of social attitudes in children. *Sociometry*, 1937, *1*, 301–338.

HOROWITZ, R. E. Racial aspects of self-identification in nursery school children. *J. Psychol.*, 1939, *7*, 71–99.

HORROCKS, J. E. *The psychology of adolescence*. Boston: Houghton Mifflin, 1951.

HOVLAND, C. I. Changes in attitude through communication. *J. abnorm. soc. Psychol.*, 1951, *46*, 424–437.

————. Effects of the mass media of communication. In G. Lindzey (Ed.), *Handbook of social psychology*. Vol. 2. Reading, Mass.: Addison-Wesley, 1954.

————, HARVEY, O. J., and SHERIF, M. Assimilation and contrast effects in reactions to communication and attitude change. *J. abnorm. soc. Psychol.*, 1957, *55*, 244–252.

————, JANIS, I. L., and KELLEY, H. H. *Communication and persuasion*. New Haven: Yale University Press, 1953.

————, and SHERIF, M. Judgmental phenomena and scales of attitude measurement: item displacement in Thurstone scales. *J. abnorm. soc. Psychol.*, 1952, *47*, 822–832.

HUGHES, E. C. Institutions in process. In A. M. Lee (Ed.), *New outline of the principles of sociology.* New York: Barnes and Noble, 1946.

HULETT, J. E. JR., and STAGNER, R. *Problems in social psychology.* Urbana: University of Illinois Press, 1956.

HUNT, J. L., and PRINGLE, A. G. *Service slang.* London: Faber and Faber, 1943.

HUNT, W. A. Anchoring effects in judgment. *Amer. J. Psychol.*, 1941, *54*, 395–403.

———, and VOLKMANN, J. The anchoring of an effective scale. *Amer. J. Psychol.*, 1937, *49*, 88–92.

HYMAN, H. H. The psychology of status. *Arch. Psychol.*, 1942, No. 269.

INKELES, A., and LEVINSON, D. J. National character: the study of modal personality and sociocultural systems. In G. Lindzey (Ed.), *Handbook of social psychology.* Vol. 2. Reading, Mass.: Addison-Wesley, 1954.

JACKSON, J. M. Structural characteristics of norms. In G. E. Jensen (Ed.), *Dynamics of instructional groups.* Chicago: University of Chicago Press, 1960. (Mimeographed)

JACOBS, R. C., and CAMPBELL, D. T. The perpetuation of an arbitrary tradition through several generations of a laboratory microculture. *J. abnorm. soc. Psychol.*, 1961, *62*, 649–58.

JAHODA, MARIE, DEUTSCH, M., and COOK, S. W. *Research methods in social relations. Part One: Basic processes.* New York: Dryden Press, 1951.

JAMES, W. *Principles of psychology.* New York: Holt, 1890.

JENKINS, W. O. A review of leadership studies with particular reference to military problems. *Psychol. Bull.*, 1947, *44*, 54–87.

JESPERSEN, O. *Language. Its nature, development and origin.* New York: Holt, 1923.

JOHNSON, C. W. *Growing up in the black belt.* Washington: American Council on Education, 1941.

JOHNSON, D. M. The "phantom anesthetist" of Mattoon: a field study of mass hysteria. *J. abnorm. soc. Psychol.*, 1945, *40*, 175–186.

———. *The psychology of thought and judgment.* New York: Harper, 1955.

JOHNSON, R. W. *Human relations in modern business: a guide for action sponsored by American business leaders.* Englewood Cliffs, N.J.: Prentice-Hall, 1949.

JONES, H. E. *Development in adolescence.* New York: Appleton-Century-Crofts, 1943.

JUDD, C. H. *Psychology of social institutions.* New York: Macmillan, 1926.

KANTOR, J. R. *An outline of social psychology.* Chicago: Follett, 1929.

KARDINER, A. The concept of basic personality structure as an operational tool in the social sciences. In R. Linton (Ed.), *The science of man in the world crisis.* New York: Columbia University Press, 1945.

KARPF, FAY B. *American social psychology.* New York: McGraw-Hill, 1932.

KATZ, D. Social psychology and group processes. *Ann. Rev. Psychol.*, 1951, *2*, 137–172.

———. Studies in social psychology in World War II. *Psychol. Bull.*, 1951, *48*, 512–519.

————. Field studies. In L. Festinger and D. Katz (Eds.), *Research methods in the behavioral sciences.* New York: Dryden Press, 1953.

————. Special review. *Psychol. Bull.*, 1955, 52, 346–353.

KELLEY, H. H. Two functions of reference groups. In G. E. Swanson, T. M. Newcomb, and E. L. Hartley (Eds.), *Readings in social psychology.* (Rev. ed.) New York: Holt, 1952.

————, and THIBAUT, J. W. Experimental studies of group problem solving and process. In G. Lindzey (Ed.), *Handbook of social psychology.* Vol. 2. Reading, Mass.: Addison-Wesley, 1954.

KELLOG, W. N., and KELLOG, L. A. *The ape and the child.* New York: Mc-Graw-Hill, 1933.

KELMAN, H. C. Effects of success and failure on "suggestibility" in the auto-kinetic situation. *J. abnorm. soc. Psychol.*, 1950, 45, 267–285.

KEY, V. O., JR. Strategies in research on public affairs. *Items*, 1956, 10, 29–32.

————, and MUNGER, F. Social determinism and electoral decision: the case of Indiana. In E. Burdick and A. J. Brodbeck (Eds.), *American voting behavior.* Glencoe, Ill.: Free Press, 1959.

KLEIN, G. S., and SCHOENFELD, N. The influence of ego-involvement on confidence. *J. abnorm. soc. Psychol.*, 1941, 36, 249–258.

————, and SCHLESINGER, H. J. Perceptual attitudes toward instability: I. Prediction of apparent movement experiences from Rorschach responses. *J. Pers.*, 1951, 19, 289–302.

KLINEBERG, O. *Negro intelligence and selective migration.* New York: Columbia University Press, 1935.

————. *Race differences.* New York: Harper, 1935.

————. Recent studies of national character. In S. S. Sargent and M. W. Smith (Eds.), *Culture and personality.* New York: Viking Fund, 1949.

————. *Social psychology.* (Rev. ed.) New York: Holt, 1954.

————. Intergroup relations and international relations. In M. Sherif (Ed.), *Intergroup relations and leadership.* New York: Wiley, 1962.

KLUCKHOHN, C. Needed refinements in the biographical approach. In S. S. Sargent and M. W. Smith (Eds.), *Culture and personality.* New York: Viking Fund, 1949.

————, and KELLY, W. H. The concepts of culture. In R. Linton (Ed.), *The science of man in the world crisis.* New York: Columbia University Press, 1945.

————, and MURRAY, H. A. (Eds.). *Personality in nature, society, and culture.* New York: Alfred A. Knopf, 1948.

KOCH, S. Behavior as "intrinsically" regulated: work notes toward a pre-theory of phenomena called "motivational." In M. R. Jones (Ed.), *Nebraska symposium on motivation.* Lincoln: University of Nebraska Press, 1956.

KOFFKA, K. Perception. *Psychol. Bull.*, 1922, 19, 566–570.

————. *Principles of gestalt psychology.* New York: Harcourt, Brace, 1935.

KÖHLER, W. *Gestalt psychology.* New York: Liveright, 1929.

————. Some tasks of gestalt psychology. In C. Murchison (Ed.), *Psychologies of 1930.* Worcester, Mass.: Clark University Press, 1930.

KRECH, D., and CRUTCHFIELD, R. S. *Theory and problems of social psychology.* New York: McGraw-Hill, 1948.

KUHLEN, R. G. *The psychology of adolescent development.* New York: Harper, 1951.

KUHN, M. H., and McPARTLAND, T. S. An empirical investigation of self-attitudes. *Am. Sociol. Rev.,* 1954, *19,* 68–76.

KÜLPE, O. Versuche über abstraktion. *Bericht über den I. Kongress für Experimentelle psychologie,* 1904, 56–68.

———. *Outlines of psychology.* London: Allen, Unwin, 1921.

LA FAVE, L., SZEZESIAK, R., YAQUINTO, J., and ADLER, B. Connotation as a supplemental variable to assimilation—contrast principles in psychosocial scales. Paper read at American Psychological Association, Philadelphia, September, 1963. (Mimeographed)

———, and SHERIF, M. Reference scales and placement of items with the own categories technique. Paper read at American Psychological Association, St. Louis. Norman, Oklahoma: Institute of Group Relations, 1962. (Mimeographed)

LANDESCO, J. Organized crime in Chicago. In *The Illinois crime survey.* Illinois Association for Criminal Justice. Chicago: Blakeley, 1929.

LANG, O. *Chinese family and society.* New Haven: Yale University Press, 1946.

LA PIERRE, R. T., and FARNSWORTH, P. R. *Social psychology.* (3rd ed.) New York: McGraw-Hill, 1949.

LASKER, B. *Race attitudes in children.* New York: Holt, 1929.

LAZARSFELD, P. F. The controversy over detailed interviews: an offer for negotiation. *Publ. Opin. Quart.,* 1944, *8,* 38–60.

———, and ROSENBERG, M. (Eds.). *The language of social research.* Glencoe, Ill.: Free Press, 1955.

LEARY, D. B. *Modern psychology. Normal and abnormal. A behaviorism of personality.* New York: Lippincott, 1928.

LE BON, G. *The crowd.* London: T. Fisher Unwin, 1897.

LEGUM, C. *Pan-Africanism.* New York: F. A. Praeger, 1962.

LEISERSON, A. Problems of methodology in political research. *Polit. Sci. Quarterly,* 1953, *68,* 558–584.

———. *Parties and politics: an institutional and behavioral approach.* New York: Alfred A. Knopf, 1958.

LEUBA, C. J. An experimental study of rivalry in young children. *J. comp. Psychol.,* 1933, *16,* 367–378.

LEWIN, K. *Dynamic theory of personality.* New York: McGraw-Hill, 1935.

———. Psychosociological problems of a minority group. *Character and Person.,* 1935, *3,* 175–187.

———. Field theory and experiment in social psychology: concepts and methods. *Amer. J. Sociol.,* 1939, *44,* 868–896.

———. Group decision. In G. E. Swanson, T. M. Newcomb, and E. L. Hartley (Eds.), *Readings in social psychology.* (Rev. ed.) New York: Holt, 1952.

———, DEMBO, T., FESTINGER, L., and SEARS, P. S. Level of aspiration. In J. McV. Hunt (Ed.), *Personality and the behavior disorders.* New York: Ronald Press, 1944.

———, and GRABBE, P. Conduct, knowledge and acceptance of new values. *J. soc. Issues,* 1945, *1,* 53–64.

————, LIPPITT, R., and WHITE, R. K. Patterns of aggressive behavior in experimentally created "social climates." *J. soc. Psychol.*, 1939, *10*, 271–299.

LEWIS, M. M. *Infant speech.* New York: Harcourt, Brace, 1963.

LEWIS, O. Discussion. In J. E. Hulett, Jr., and R. Stagner (Eds.), *Problems in social psychology.* Urbana: University of Illinois Press, 1952.

LINDESMITH, A. R., and STRAUSS, A. L. *Social psychology.* New York: Dryden Press, 1949; Rev. ed., 1956.

————, ————. Critique of culture-personality writings. *Amer. sociol. Rev.*, 1950, *15*, 587–599.

LINDZEY, G. (Ed.). *Handbook of social psychology.* Reading, Mass.: Addison-Wesley, 1954. 2 vols.

LINTON, R. *The cultural background of personality.* New York: Appleton-Century-Crofts, 1945.

LONG, L., and WELCH, L. Reasoning ability of young children. *J. Psychol.*, 1941, *2*, 21–44.

————, ————. Influence of level of abstraction on reasoning ability. *J. Psychol.*, 1942, *13*, 41–59.

LOWIE, R. H. *Primitive society.* New York: Boni and Liveright, 1925.

LUCAS, J. *Combat correspondent.* New York: Reynolds and Hitchcock, 1944.

LUCHINS, A. S. On agreement with another's judgment. *J. abnorm. soc. Psychol.*, 1944, *39*, 97–111.

————. Social influences on perception of complex drawings. *J. soc. Psychol.*, 1945, *21*, 257–273.

LUMLEY, F. E. *Principles of sociology.* New York: McGraw-Hill, 1928.

————. Slogans as a means of social control (1921). *American Sociological Society Papers and proceedings of annual meetings*, 1934, *16*.

LYND, R. S., and LYND, H. M. *Middletown in transition.* New York: Harcourt, Brace, 1937.

McCARTHY, D. Language development in children. In L. Carmichael (Ed.), *Manual of child psychology.* New York: Wiley, 1946.

MACCOBY, E. E., NEWCOMB, T. M., and HARTLEY, E. L. (Eds.), *Readings in social psychology.* (3rd ed.) New York: Holt, 1958.

MACCRONE, I. D. *Race attitudes in South Africa.* New York: Oxford University Press, 1937.

McDOUGALL, W. *An introduction to social psychology.* London: Methuen, 1908.

————. *Outline of psychology.* New York: Scribner's, 1923.

McGARVEY, H. R. Anchoring effects in the absolute judgment of verbal materials. *Arch. Psychol.*, 1943, No. 281.

McGRANAHAN, D. V. The psychology of language. *Psychol. Bull.*, 1936, *33*, 202.

McQUITTY, L. L. A measure of personality integration in relation to the concept of self. *J. Pers.*, 1949–1950, *18*, 461–482.

MALINOWSKI, B. *Argonauts of the Western Pacific.* London: Routledge, 1922.

————. *The father in primitive society.* New York: Norton, 1927.

————. The problem of meaning in primitive languages. Supplement I. In C. K. Ogden and I. A. Richards (Eds.), *The meaning of meaning.* New York: Harcourt, Brace, 1930.

MANDELBAUM, D. G. (Ed.). *Selected writings of Edward Sapir.* Berkeley: University of California Press, 1949.

MANNHEIM, K. *Ideology and Utopia: an introduction to the sociology of knowledge.* New York: Harcourt, Brace, 1936.

MARKS, E. Skin color judgments of Negro college students. *J. abnorm, soc. Psychol.,* 1943, *38,* 370–376.

MARSHALL, S. L. A. *Men against fire.* New York: Morrow, 1947.

MATHIEZ, A. *The French revolution.* New York: Alfred A. Knopf, 1929.

MAUSNER, B. Studies in social interaction. III. Effect of variation of a partner's prestige on the interaction of observer pairs. *J. appl. Psychol.,* 1953, *37,* 391–394.

————. The effect of prior reinforcement on the interaction of observer pairs. *J. abnorm. soc. Psychol.,* 1954, *49,* 65–68.

MAYO, E. *The human problems of an industrial civilization.* New York: Macmillan, 1933.

MEAD, G. H. *Mind, self, and society.* Chicago: University of Chicago Press, 1934.

MEAD, MARGARET. Primitive child. In C. Murchison (Ed.), *Handbook of child psychology.* Worcester, Mass.: Clark University Press, 1933.

MELTON, A. W. Present accomplishments and future trends in problem solving and learning theory. *Amer. Psychologist,* 1956, *11,* 278–281.

MERKER, F. *Die Masai.* Berlin: Dietrich Reimer, 1904.

MEREI, F. Group leadership and institutionalization. *Hum. Relat.,* 1949, *2,* 23–29.

MERRIAM, C. E. *Public and private government.* New Haven: Yale University Press, 1944.

MERTON, R. K. *Social theory and social structure.* Glencoe, Ill.: Free Press, 1957.

————, and KITT, A. S. Contributions to the theory of reference group behavior. In R. K. Merton and P. F. Lazarsfeld (Eds.), *Continuities in social research: studies in the scope and method of the American soldier.* Glencoe, Ill.: Free Press, 1950.

MILLER, F. B. "Resistentialism" in applied social research. *Human Organiz.,* 1954, *12,* 5–8.

MILLER, J. G. (Ed.). *Experiments in social process.* New York: McGraw-Hill, 1950.

MILLER, N. E., and DOLLARD, J. *Social learning and imitation.* New Haven: Yale University Press, 1941.

MILLS, C. W. Two styles of research in current social studies. *Phil. Sci,* 1953, *20,* 266–275.

MOORE, J. S. *The foundations of psychology.* Princeton, N.J.: Princeton University Press, 1922.

MOOREHEAD, A. *Don't blame the generals.* New York: Harper, 1942.

MORENO, J. L. Who shall survive? *Nerv. ment. Dis. Monogr. Series,* No. 58, 1934. (Rev. ed.) New York: Beacon House, 1953.

MORGAN, C. T. *Physiological psychology.* New York: McGraw-Hill, 1943.

MORRIS, C. *Signs, language and behavior.* New York: Prentice-Hall, 1946.

MULLAHY, P. Discussion of H. Mowrer, Pain, punishment, guilt and anxiety.

In P. N. Hoch and J. Zubin (Eds.), *Anxiety*. New York: Grune and Stratton, 1950.

MURCHISON, C. *Social psychology: the psychology of political domination.* Worcester, Mass.: Clark University Press, 1927.

————. *Handbook of social psychology.* Worcester, Mass.: Clark University Press, 1935.

————, and LANGER, S. Tiedemann's observations on the development of the mental faculties of children. *J. Genet. Psychol.*, 1927, *34*, 205–230.

MURDOCK, G. P. Sociology and anthropology. In J. Gillin (Ed.), *For a science of social man.* New York: Macmillan, 1954.

MURPHY, L. B. *Social behavior and child personality.* New York: Columbia University Press, 1937.

MURPHY, G. The freeing of intelligence. *Psychol. Bull.*, 1945, *42*, 1–19.

————. *Personality: a biosocial approach to origins and structure.* New York: Harper, 1947.

————. *Historical introduction to modern psychology.* (Rev. ed.) New York: Harcourt, Brace, 1949.

————. *In the minds of men.* New York: Basic Books, 1953.

————, and LIKERT, R. *Public opinion and the individual.* New York: Harper, 1938.

————, and MURPHY, L. B. *Experimental social psychology.* New York: Harper, 1931.

————, ————, and NEWCOMB, T. M. *Experimental social psychology.* (Rev. ed.) New York: Harper, 1937.

NEWCOMB, T. M. *Personality and social change.* New York: Dryden Press, 1943.

————. Attitude development as a function of reference groups. In M. Sherif, *An outline of social psychology.* New York: Harper, 1948.

————. *Social psychology.* New York: Dryden Press, 1950.

————. Sociology and psychology. In J. Gillin (Ed.), *For a science of social man.* New York: Macmillan, 1954.

NEWSTETTER, W. I., FELDSTEIN, M. J., and NEWCOMB, T. M. *Group adjustment: a study in experimental sociology.* Cleveland: Western Reserve University, School for Applied Social Sciences, 1938.

OLMSTEAD, M. S. *The small group.* New York: Random House, 1959.

ORLANSKY, H. Infant care and personality. *Psychol. Bull.*, 1949, *40*, 1–48.

ORNE, M. T. On the social psychology of the psychological experiment: with particular reference to demand characteristics and their implications. *Amer. Psychologist*, 1962, *17*, 776–783.

O. S. S. Assessment Staff. *Assessment of men.* New York: Holt, 1948.

PARDUCCI, A. Range-frequency compromise in judgment. *Psychol. Monogr.*, 1963, *77*, 2, Whole no. 565.

————, and MARSHALL, L. M. Assimilation vs. contrast in the anchoring of perceptual judgments of weight. *J. exp. Psychol.*, 1962, *63*, 426–437.

PARTEN, M. B. Social participation among pre-school children. *J. abnorm. soc. Psychol.*, 1932, *27*, 243–269.

————. Social play among pre-school children. *J. abnorm. soc. Psychol.*, 1933, *28*, 136–147.

PARSONS, T., and SHILS, E. A. (Eds.). *Toward a general theory of action.* Cambridge, Mass.: Harvard University Press, 1951.

PEAR, T. H. *Psychological factors in peace and war.* New York: Philosophical Library, 1950.

PELHAM, C. Where slogans come from. *Printers Ink,* December 12, 1935, 100–109.

PELZ, D. C. Leadership within a hierarchical organization. *J. soc. Issues,* 1951, 7, 49–55.

PERRIN, F. A. C., and KLEIN, D. B. *Psychology: its methods and principles.* New York: Holt, 1926.

PETERSON, J. Striking illusion of movement. *Amer. J. Psychol.,* 1937, 28, 476–485.

PETTIGREW, T. F. Negro American intelligence: a new look at an old controversy. *J. Negro Educat.,* Winter, 1964, 6–25.

PIAGET, J. *Language and thought of the child.* London: Kegan Paul, 1926.

———. *Judgment and reasoning of the child.* New York: Harcourt, Brace, 1928.

———. *The moral judgment of the child.* London: Kegan Paul, Trench, Trubner, 1932.

PRADO, W. M. Relative ego-involvements of children and adolescents measured by estimates of performance. Unpublished doctoral dissertation, University of Oklahoma, 1958.

PISHKIN, V. Experimenter variable in concept identification feedback of schizophrenics. *Percept. mot. Skills,* 1963, 16, 921–922.

PRATT, C. C. Time errors in the method of single stimulus. *J. exp. Psychol.,* 1933, 6, 798–814.

PREYER, W. *The mind of the child. Part II. The development of the intellect.* New York: Appleton, 1890.

PROSHANSKY, H., and MURPHY, G. The effects of reward and punishment on perception. *J. Psychol.,* 1942, 13, 295–305.

PYLE, E. *Brave men.* New York: Holt, 1943.

PYLES, M. K. Verbalization as a factor in learning. *Child Develpm.,* 1932, 3, 108–113.

QUEENER, E. L. *Introduction to social psychology.* New York: Sloane, 1951.

RADCLIFFE-BROWN, A. *Andaman Islanders.* New York: Cambridge University Press, 1922.

RADIN, P. *Primitive religion, its nature and origin.* New York: Viking Press, 1937.

RAZRAN, G. H. S. Conditioned responses: an experimental study and a theoretical analysis. *Arch. Psychol.,* 1935, No. 191.

REHM, R. Fifty missions over Europe. In D. G. Wright (Ed.), *Observations on combat personnel.* New York: Josiah Macy Foundation, 1945.

REICH, J., and SHERIF, M. Ego-involvement as a factor in attitude assessment by the own categories technique. Norman, Oklahoma: Institute of Group Relations, 1963. (Mimeographed) (Unpublished master's thesis, University of Oklahoma)

REUTER, E. B. Some observations on the status of social psychology. *Amer. J. Sociol.,* 1940, 46, 293–304.

RIECKEN, H. W. (Chairman). Narrowing the gap between field studies and laboratory experiments in social psychology: a statement by the summer seminar. *SSRC Items*, 1954, 8 (4), 37–42.

———, and HOMANS, G. C. Psychological aspects of social structure. In G. Lindzey (Ed.), *Handbook of social psychology*. Vol. 2. Reading, Mass.: Addison-Wesley, 1954.

RIVERS, W. H. R. *History of Melanesian society*. Vol. 1. New York: Cambridge University Press, 1924.

ROBINSON, D. *News of the 45th*. Norman: University of Oklahoma Press, 1944.

ROETHLISBERGER, F. J., and DICKSON, W. J. *Management and the worker*. Cambridge, Mass.: Harvard University Press, 1939.

ROHEIM, G. Psychoanalysis and anthropology. In D. G. Haring (Ed.), *Personal character and cultural milieu*. (Rev. ed.) Syracuse: Syracuse University Press, 1949.

ROHRER, J. H., and SHERIF, M. (Eds.). *Social psychology at the crossroads*. New York: Harper, 1951.

ROSEBOROUGH, M. E. Experimental studies of small groups. *Psychol. Bull.*, 1953, *50*, 275–303.

ROSEN, B. C. Conflicting group membership: a study of parent-peer group cross-pressures. *Am. Sociol. Rev.*, 1955, 155–161.

ROSENTHAL, R. On the social psychology of the psychological experiment: with particular reference to experimenter bias. Paper read at American Psychological Association, New York, September, 1961.

ROSS, E. A. *Social psychology*. New York: Macmillan, 1908.

———. *Outlines of sociology*. New York: Century, 1923.

RUSK, D. Rusk bids nations forego total freedom of action. *New York Times*, May 10, 1964.

SAINTSBURY, P. *Suicide in London: an ecological study*. London: Institute of Psychiatry, 1955.

SAPIR, E. *Language*. New York: Harcourt, Brace, 1921.

———. The unconscious patterning of behavior in society. In E. S. Dummer (Ed.), *The unconscious: a symposium*. New York: Alfred A. Knopf, 1928.

———. *Selected writings of Edward Sapir*. D. C. Mandelbaum (Ed.). Berkeley: University of California Press, 1949.

SARGENT, S. S. *Social psychology*. New York: Ronald Press, 1950.

———, and SMITH, M. W. (Eds.), *Culture and personality*. New York: Viking Fund, 1949.

SCHACHTER, S. Deviation, rejection and communication. In L. Festinger, K. Back, S. Schachter, H. Kelley, and J. Thibaut (Eds.), *Theory and experiment in social communication*. Ann Arbor: Research Center for Group Dynamics, 1952.

SCHAFER, R., and MURPHY, G. The role of autism in a visual figure-ground relationship. *J. exp. Psychol.*, 1943, *32*, 335–343.

SCHNEIRLA, T. C. Problems in the biopsychology of social organization. *J. abnorm. soc. Psychol.*, 1946, *41*, 385–402.

———. Psychology, comparative. *Encyclopedia Britannica*, 1948.

———. The "levels" in the psychological capacities of animals. In J. H. Rohrer and M. Sherif (Eds.), *Social psychology at the crossroads*. New York: Harper, 1951.

————. A consideration of some conceptual trends in comparative psychology. *Psychol. Bull.,* 1952, 49, 559–597.

————. The concept of levels in the study of social phenomena. In M. Sherif and Carolyn W. Sherif, *Groups in harmony and tension.* New York: Harper, 1953.

SCHOTTSTAEDT, W. W., PINSKY, RUTH H., MACKLER, D., and WOLF, S. Sociologic, psychologic and metabolic observations on patients in the community of a metabolic ward. *Amer. J. Medi.,* 1958, 25, 248–257.

SCHUMER, F. C. Some behavioral correlates of Rorschach human movement responses in the autokinetic situation. Unpublished doctoral dissertation, Yale University, 1949.

SCOTT, E. L. *Status expectations and organizational behavior.* Columbus: Ohio State University Research Foundation, 1953.

SCOTT, J. P. *Aggression.* Chicago: University of Chicago Press, 1958.

SEARS, R. R., HOVLAND, C. I., and MILLER, N. E. Minor studies in aggression. I. Measurement of aggressive behavior. *J. Psychol.,* 1940, 9, 277–281.

SEWELL, W. H. Infant training and the personality of the child. *Amer. J. Sociol.,* 1952, 58, 150–159.

SHAFER, B. C. *Nationalism: myth and reality.* New York: Harcourt, Brace, 1955.

SHAW, C. R. *The jack roller.* Chicago: University of Chicago Press, 1930.

————. *The natural history of a delinquent career.* Chicago: University of Chicago Press, 1931.

SHERIF, CAROLYN W. Categorization of valued items as a function of the individual's own reference scale. Paper read at Southwestern Social Science Association, Dallas, April, 1958.

————. Self radius and goals of group members and their age-mates in differentiated urban settings. Paper read at Small Groups session, American Sociological Association, New York, August, 1960. *Southwestern Social Science Quarterly,* 1961, 42, 259–270.

————. Established reference scales and series effects in social judgment. Unpublished doctoral dissertation, University of Texas, 1961.

————. Social categorization as a function of latitude of acceptance and series range. *J. abnorm. soc. Psychol.,* 1963, 67, 148–156.

————, SHERIF, M., and NEBERGALL, R. *Attitude and attitude change.* Philadelphia: W. B. Saunders, 1965.

SHERIF, M. A study of some social factors in perception. *Arch. Psychol.,* 1935, No. 187.

————. *The psychology of social norms.* New York: Harper, 1936.

————. An experimental approach to the study of attitudes. *Sociometry,* 1937, 1, 90–98.

————. *An outline of social psychology.* New York: Harper, 1948a.

————. The necessity of considering current issues as part and parcel of persistent major problems. *Int. J. Opin. Attit. Res.,* 1948b, 2, 63–68.

————. Remarks on socio-cultural influences in small group research. Paper read at symposium entitled Sociological and Anthropological Perspective on Small Group Research at American Psychological Association, Cleveland, September, 1953. (Mimeographed)

————. Integrating field work and laboratory in small group research. *Amer. sociol. Rev.,* 1954, 19, 759–771.

———. Operational report to the Hogg Foundation for Mental Health, The University of Texas. Description of research work on natural groups (1958–1959). (Mimeographed)

———. Social psychology, anthropology, and the "behavioral sciences." *Southwestern Social Science Quarterly*, 1959, *40*, September, 105–112.

———. Individual behavior and group processes in differentiated sociocultural settings. Paper read at Small Groups Session, American Sociological Association, New York, August, 1960.

———. *In common predicament: social psychology of intergroup conflict and cooperation.* Boston: Houghton-Mifflin, 1966.

———, and CANTRIL, H. *The psychology of ego-involvements.* New York: Wiley, 1947.

———, and HARVEY, O. J. A study in ego functioning: elimination of stable anchorages in individual and group situations. *Sociometry*, 1952, *15*, 272–305.

———, ———, WHITE, B. J., HOOD, W. R., and SHERIF, CAROLYN W. *Study of positive and negative intergroup attitudes between experimentally produced groups: Robbers Cave study.* Norman: University of Oklahoma, 1954. (Multilithed)

———, ———, ———, ———, ———. *Intergroup conflict and cooperation: the Robbers Cave experiment.* Norman: University of Oklahoma Book Exchange, 1961.

———, and HOVLAND, C. I. Judgmental phenomena and scales of attitude measurement: placement of items with individual choice of number of categories. *J. abnorm. soc. Psychol.*, 1953, *48*, 135–141.

———, ———. *Social judgment: assimilation and contrast effects in communication and attitude change.* New Haven: Yale University Press, 1961.

———, and KOSLIN, B. The "institutional" vs. "behavioral" controversy in social science, with special reference to political science. Norman: Institute of Group Relations, University of Oklahoma, 1960. (Mimeographed)

———, and SHERIF, CAROLYN W. *Groups in harmony and tension.* New York: Harper, 1953.

———, ———. *An outline of social psychology.* (Rev. ed.) New York: Harper, 1956.

———, ———. Self-radius and goals of group members and their age-mates in differentiated sociocultural settings. Report No. III. Norman: Institute of Group Relations, University of Oklahoma, 1960. (Mimeographed)

———, ———. *Reference groups: exploration into conformity and deviation of adolescents.* New York: Harper, 1964.

———, TAUB, D., and HOVLAND, C. I. Assimilation and contrast effects of anchoring stimuli on judgments. *J. exp. Psychol.*, 1958, *55*, 150–155.

———, WHITE, B. J., and HARVEY, O. J. Status in experimentally produced groups. *Amer. J. Sociol.*, 1955, *60*, 370–379.

———, and WILSON, M. O. (Eds.). *Group relations at the crossroads.* New York: Harper, 1953.

SHEVKY, E., and BELL, W. *Social area analysis.* Stanford: Stanford University Press, 1955.

SHIBUTANI, T. Reference groups as perspectives. *Amer. J. Sociol.*, 1955, *60*, 562–569.

SHILS, E. *The present state of American sociology.* Glencoe, Ill.: Free Press, 1948.

SHINN, M. W. *Notes on the development of a child.* Berkeley: University of California Press, Vol. 1, 1899; Vol. 2, 1907.

SHORT, J. F., TENNYSON, R. A., and HOWARD, K. L. Behavior dimensions of gang delinquency. *Amer. Sociol. Rev.,* 1963, *28,* 411–428.

SIEGEL, A. E., and SIEGEL, S. Reference groups, membership groups, and attitude change. *J. abnorm. soc. Psychol.,* 1957, *55,* 360–364.

SILVER, J. W. *Mississippi: the closed society.* New York: Harcourt, Brace, 1964.

SIMON, H. A. *Administrative behavior.* New York: Macmillan, 1957.

SIMPON, W. *One of our pilots is safe.* New York: Harper, 1943.

SMITH, M. B. Anthropology and psychology. In J. Gillin (Ed.), *For a science of social man.* New York: Macmillan, 1954.

————, BRUNER, J. S., and WHITE, R. W. *Opinions and personality.* New York: Wiley, 1956.

SMITH, M. E. An investigation of the development of the sentence and the extent of vocabulary in young children. *Univ. Iowa Stud. Child Welf.,* 1926, *3,* No. 5.

SMOKE, K. L. Concept formation. In P. L. Harriman (Ed.), *Encyclopedia of psychology.* New York: Philosophical Library, 1946.

SNEDECOR, G. W. *Statistical methods.* Ames: Iowa State College Press, 1950.

SNYDER, R. C., A decision-making approach to the study of political phenomena. In R. Young (Ed.), *Approaches to the study of politics.* Evanston, Ill.: Northwestern University Press, 1958.

————, BRUCK, H. W., and SAPIN, B. *Decision-making as an approach to the study of international politics.* Princeton, N.J.: Princeton University Press, 1954.

SNYGG, D., and COMBS, A. W. *Individual behavior: a new frame of reference for psychology.* New York: Harper, 1949.

SPENCER, B., and GILLEN, F. J. *The Arunta: a study of a stone age people.* New York: Macmillan, 1927.

SPINDLER, G., and GOLDSCHMIDT, W. Experimental design in the study of culture change. *S. W. J. Anthrop.,* 1952, *8,* 68–83.

STEVENS, S. S. On the psychophysical law. *Psychol. Rev.,* 1957, *64,* 153–181.

STEVENSON, H. W., and ALLEN, SARA. Adult performance as a function of sex of experimenter and sex of subject. *J. abnorm. soc. Psychol.,* 1964, *68,* 214–216.

STOGDILL, R. M. Leadership, membership and organization. *Psychol. Bull.,* 1950, *47,* 1–14.

————. *Individual behavior and group achievement.* New York: Oxford University Press, 1959.

STOUFFER, S. A. Some afterthoughts of a contributor to *The American soldier.* In R. K. Merton and P. F. Lazarsfeld (Eds.), *Continuities in social research.* Glencoe, Ill.: Free Press, 1950.

————, LUMSDAINE, A. A., LUMSDAINE, M. H., WILLIAMS, R. M., JR., SMITH, M. B., JANIS, I. L., STAR, S. A., and COTTRELL, L. S., JR. *The American soldier: combat and its aftermath.* Princeton N.J.: Princeton University Press, 1949.

STRAUSS, A. L. (Ed.). *The social psychology of George Herbert Mead.* Chicago: University of Chicago Press (Phoenix Books), 1956.

STRODTBECK, F. L., and HARE, A. P. Bibliography of small group research. *Sociometry,* 1954, *17,* 107–178.

SWANSON, G. E., NEWCOMB, T. M., and HARTLEY, E. L. (Eds.). *Readings in social psychology* (Rev. ed.) New York: Holt, 1952.

SULLIVAN, H. S. *Conceptions of modern psychiatry.* Washington: William Alanson White Psychiatric Foundation, 1947. (2nd ed.)

THIBAUT, J. W., and KELLEY, H. H. *The social psychology of groups.* New York: Wiley, 1959.

THIRTEEN EXPERTS. *International law in a changing world.* New York: Oceana Library for the United Nations, 1963.

THOMAS, W. I., and ZNANIECKI, F. *The Polish peasant in Europe and America.* Chicago: University of Chicago Press, 1918.

THRASHER, F. M. *The gang.* Chicago: University of Chicago Press, 1927.

THRASHER, J. D. Interpersonal relations and gradations of stimulus structure as factors in judgment variations: an experimental approach. *Sociometry,* 1954, *17,* 228–241.

THURNWALD, R. The psychology of acculturation. *Amer. Anthrop.,* 1932, *34,* 557–569.

TITCHENER, E. P. *Systematic psychology: prologomena.* New York: Macmillan, 1929.

TOKI, K. The leader-follower structure in the school class. *Jap. J. Psychol.,* 1935, *10,* 27–56.

TOLMAN, E. C. More concerning the temporal relations of meaning imagery. *Psychol. Rev.,* 1917, *24,* 114–138.

TRESSELT, M. E., and VOLKMANN, J. The production of uniform opinion by nonsocial stimulation: *J. abnorm. soc. Psychol.,* 1942, *37,* 234–243.

TRUMAN, D. B. The impact on political science of the revolution in the behavioral sciences. In *Research frontiers in politics and government.* Washington: The Brookings Institution, 1955, 202–231.

TURNER, R. H. Role-taking, role standpoint and reference group behavior. *Amer. J. Sociol.,* 1956, *61,* 316–328.

U.S. SENATE. *Report of the Committee on the Judiciary.* 87th Congress, 1st Session. Report 169, April 18, 1961.

U THANT. The League of Nations and the United Nations. Address at the University of California. New York: United Nations, 1964.

VAN GENNEP, A. *Les rites de passage.* Paris: E. Noury, 1909.

VAN RIPER, C. *Speech, correction principles and methods.* New York: Prentice-Hall, 1947.

VAUGHAN, E. H. *Community under stress.* Princeton: Princeton University Press, 1947.

VAUGHAN, KATHRYN R. A disguised instrument for the assessment of intergroup attitudes. Unpublished master's thesis, Texas College of Arts and Industries, 1961.

VEBLEN, T. *The theory of the leisure class.* New York: Macmillan, 1899.

VILFROY, D. *War in the West.* Harrisburg, Pa.: Military Service Publishing Co., 1942.

VOLKART, E. (Ed.). *Social behavior and personality, contributions of W. I. Thomas to theory and social research.* New York: Social Science Research Council, 1951.

VOLKMANN, J. The anchoring of absolute scales. *Psychol. Bull.,* 1936, *33,* 742–743.

————. Scales of judgment and their implications for social psychology. In J. H. Rohrer and M. Sherif (Eds.), *Social psychology at the crossroads.* New York: Harper, 1951.

VOTH, A. C. An experimental study of mental patients through the autokinetic phenomenon. *Amer. J. Psychiat.,* 1947, *103,* 793–805.

WALLIS, W. D. *An introduction to anthropology.* New York: Harper, 1926.

WALLON, H. *Les origines du caractere chez l'enfant.* Paris: Presses Universitaire de France, 1933.

WALTER, N. A study of the effects of conflicting suggestions upon judgments in the autokinetic situation. *Sociometry,* 1955, *18,* 138–146. (Unpublished doctoral dissertation, University of Oklahoma, 1952)

WAPNER, S., and ALPER, T. G. The effect of an audience on behavior in a choice situation. *J. abn. soc. Psychol.,* 1952, *47,* 222–229.

WARD, L. F. *Outlines of sociology.* New York: Macmillan, 1928.

WARDEN, C. J. The relative economy of various modes of attack in the mastery of the stylus maze. *J. exp. Psychol.,* 1924, *7,* 243–275.

WARNER, W. L., and LUNT, P. S. *The social life of a modern community.* New Haven: Yale University Press, 1941.

WASKOW, A. I. *The shelter centered society.* Washington: The Peace Research Institute, 1962.

WATSON-WATT, ROBERT. *Man's means to his end.* New York: Clarkson N. Potter, 1961.

WATT, A. F. *The language and mental development of children.* London: Harrop, 1944.

WEBB, W. P. *The Great Plains.* Boston: Houghton Mifflin, 1936.

WEISS, R. S. A structure-function approach to organization. *J. soc. Issues,* 1956, *12,* 66–67.

WELCH, L., and LONG, L. Comparison of the reasoning ability of two age groups. *J. genet. Psychol.,* 1943, *62,* 63–76.

WELLS, F. D. On the variability of individual judgment. In *Essays philosophical and psychological in honor of William James by his colleagues at Columbia University.* New York: Longmans, 1928.

WERTHEIMER, M. *Drei Abhandlungen zur Gestalttheorie.* Berlin: Philosophische Akademie, Erlangen, 1925, 93–99.

————. Laws of perceptual forms. In W. D. Ellis (Ed.), *A sourcebook of gestalt psychology.* New York: Harcourt, Brace, 1939.

WEVER, E. G., and ZENER, K. E. Method of absolute judgment in psychophysics. *Psychol. Rev.,* 1928, *35,* 466–493.

WHITING, J. W. M., and CHILD, I. L. *Child training and personality.* New Haven: Yale University Press, 1953.

WHITTAKER, J. O. Effects of experimentally introduced anchorages upon judgments in the autokinetic situation. Paper read at the International Congress of Psychology, Brussels, June, 1957; unpublished doctoral dissertation, University of Oklahoma, 1958.

WHYTE, W. F. *Street corner society.* Chicago: University of Chicago Press, 1943.

——. Small groups and large organizations. In J. H. Rohrer and M. Sherif (Eds.), *Social psychology at the crossroads.* New York: Harper, 1951.

——. *Money and motivation.* New York: Harper, 1955.

WILLIAMS, J. M. *Principles of social psychology.* New York: Alfred A. Knopf, 1922.

WILLIAMS, R. M., JR. The reduction of intergroup tensions: a survey of research on problems of ethnic, racial and religious group relations. *Soc. sci. Res. Council Bull.,* 1947, 57.

WOODWORTH, R. S., and THORNDIKE, E. L. Judgment of magnitude by comparison with a mental standard. *Psychol. Rev.,* 1900, 7, 344–355.

WORDELL, M. L., and SEILER, E. N. *Wildcats over Casablanca.* Boston: Little, Brown, 1943.

WRIGHT, Q. Modern technology and the world order. In W. F. Ogburn (Ed.), *Technology and international relations.* Chicago: University of Chicago Press, 1949.

YERKES, R. M. *Chimpanzees, a laboratory colony.* New Haven: Yale University Press, 1943.

YOUNG, K. *Social psychology.* (3rd ed.) New York: Appleton-Century-Crofts, 1956.

YOUNG, K. (Ed.). *Sourcebook for social psychology.* New York: Alfred A. Knopf, 1927.

ZETTERBERG, H. L. *Sociology in the United States of America.* Paris: Unesco, 1956.

ZIMBARDO, P. G. Verbal ambiguity and judgmental distortion. *Psychol. Reports,* 1960, 6, 57–58.

ZORBAUGH, H. W. *The Gold Coast and the slum.* Chicago: University of Chicago Press, 1929.

ZURCHER, A. J. State propaganda in Italy. In H. L. Childs (Ed.), *Propaganda and dictatorship.* Princeton, N.J.: Princeton University Press, 1936.

NAME INDEX

Abt., L., 201
Allen, Sara, 254
Allendoerfer, C. B., 35
Alper, T. G., 449
Allport, F. H., 49, 63, 65, 66, 68, 69, 129, 241, 326, 370, 375
Allport, G. W., 78, 195, 344, 372
Anastasi, A., 90
Anderson, N., 69, 374
Ansbacher, H. L., 69
Apter, D. E., 109
Arensberg, C. M., 69, 377
Argonauts, 376
Arunta, 321
Asch, S. E., 50, 62, 75, 84, 88, 173
Ashanti, 128
Auld, F., Jr., 90
Ausubel, D., 75, 76, 77, 83, 92, 196, 200, 226, 474
Avigdor, R., 390, 439, 440

Baldwin, J. M., 16, 66, 76, 77, 225, 226
Barclay, C. N., 455
Barker, R., 248
Baron, S. H., 385
Bartlett, F. C., 3, 34, 36, 37, 43, 84, 190, 317
Barton, R. F., 321
Bass, B. M., 68
Beach, F. A., 80
Beard, C. A., 162, 163
Beard, Mary, 162, 163
Becker, H., 65, 81
Beebe-Center, J., 133, 334, 343
Bell, W., 37, 250, 279, 296
Bellak, L., 201
Benedict, Ruth, 128
Bentham, J., 111
Berkowitz, L., 465
Bernard, L. L., 66, 92
Berne, E. V. C., 78, 227
Bidney, D., 65
Binet, A., 132
Blake, R. R., 190, 386, 466

Blau, P. M., 253
Blumer, H., 55, 88
Boas, F., 89, 127
Bogardus, E. S., 241, 370, 448
Bolivia, 321, 333
Bonner, H., 50, 68
Boring, E. G., 131
Bovard, E. W., 192, 385
Brehm, J. W., 386
Bressler, J., 134
Broom, L., 82
Brown, J. F., 84
Bruner, J. S., 79, 85, 92, 190
Bugental, J. F. T., 229
Burgess, E. W., 67

Calkins, Mary, 224
Campbell, A., 114
Campbell, D. T., 60, 265, 331, 344
Cantril, H., 53, 60, 66, 76, 77, 94, 106, 176, 190, 195, 225, 242, 253, 319, 347, 379, 425, 474
Caplow, T., 195
Carmichael, L. L., 317
Carter, L. F., 70, 73, 85
Cartwright, D., 67, 68, 252
Cassirer, E., 317
Centers, R., 228, 229
Chapanis, A., 251
Chapman, D., 85, 232, 334
Chapman, J., 55, 131
Chicago, University of, 69
Chinese family, 58
Clark, K. B., 78, 227, 242, 371
Clark, Mamie K., 78, 227, 242, 371
Coffin, T. E., 88, 173, 190
Cohen, E., 167
Combs, E. W., 79, 225
Committee on the Judiciary of the U.S. Senate, 271
Cook, S. W., 318
Cooley, C. H., 41, 66, 76, 77, 225, 226
Cope, Leona, 126
Cottrell, L. S., Jr., 49, 68, 85

Crutchfield, R. S., 50, 84, 92, 93

Dahlke, A., 33
Dalton, M., 233
Darwin, C., 225
Dashiell, J. F., 63
Davis, K., 77
De Grazia, A., 101, 109, 110
De Languna, G. A., 317
Deutsch, M., 254
Dewey, J., 66
Dickson, W. J., 69, 70, 232
Dixon, W. J., 209, 212
Doby, J. R., 96
Dollard, J., 67, 317
Doob, L., 50
Douglas, J., 336
Durkheim, E., 3, 38, 40, 44, 45, 52, 53,
    55, 59, 60, 63, 64, 70, 75, 88, 168,
    169, 179, 185, 251, 343, 383, 385,
    397, 474

Eckstein, M. A., 55
Edwards, A. L., 280, 364
Edwards, W., 111
Einstein, A., 36
Elbing, A., 345
Eldersveld, S. J., 110
Emerson, R., 471
Engels, F., 3
Etzioni, A., 471

Farber, M. L., 82
Faris, E., 66
Faris, R. E. L., 50, 68, 84, 176, 374
Farnsworth, P. R., 50
Faulkner, W., 474
Fechner, G., 134
Fernberger, S., 134
Festinger, L., 74, 93
Foley, J. P., 90
Ford, C. S., 80, 321
Frank, J. D., 33, 134, 466
Frazier, F., 74
French, J. R. P., Jr., 92, 94
French, R. L., 66, 92
Freedman, R., 59, 60, 177, 376, 379
Freud, S., 65, 75, 81, 228, 386, 393
Fromm, E., 81, 82, 195
Fulbright, W., 471

Gallagher, R., 49, 68
Garceau, O., 101, 110, 113
Garza, J., 303
Gesell, A., 77, 78, 225, 227, 319
Gibb, C. A., 70, 73

Gibson, J. J., 317
Gillen, F. J., 321
Gillin, J., 61, 82
Glixman, F., 360
Goldenweiser, A. A., 40
Goodenough, F. L., 78, 90, 225, 227, 318
Goodman, C. C., 85
Goodman, Mary Ellen, 78
Graham, C., 167
Great Britain, 446
Greenberg, P. J., 78, 227
Griffith, C. R., 65
Guetzkow, H. S., 399
Guilford, J. P., 370

Hall, G. S., 91
Hallowell, A. I., 48, 67, 81, 82
Hare, A. P., 68, 72
Hartley, E. L., 50, 73, 74, 84, 227, 228,
    241, 242, 245, 326, 328, 330, 370,
    371, 372
Hartley, R. E., 50, 73, 74, 84, 227, 230,
    242, 371
Hartung, F. E., 91
Harvard Business School, 374
Harvey, O. J., 8, 72, 80, 85, 170, 179,
    180, 190–219, 231, 269, 336, 341,
    387, 389, 433, 437, 440, 448, 474
Hawley, A. H., 376, 379
Hebb, D. O., 35
Hecht, Selig, 118
Heidbreder, E., 314
Helson, H., 34, 118, 167, 253, 343, 356
Hendrickson, G., 241
Henri, V., 131, 132
Herskovits, M. J., 56, 82
Hilgard, E. R., 73, 74, 79, 318
Hiller, E. T., 63, 69, 71, 374, 379, 448
Hinckley, E. D., 233, 335, 358
Hirota, K., 78, 227
Hobbes, T., 75
Hoffman, E. L., 385
Holbrook, S., 466
Hollingworth, N., 132
Holmberg, A., 321
Holt, R. R., 78
Homans, G. C., 42, 68, 75, 177, 253
Hood, W. R., 48, 169, 182, 336, 446, 448
Hoppe, T., 134
Horney, Karen, 195
Horrocks, J. E., 77
Hovland, C. I., 70, 179, 180, 238, 239,
    259, 313, 331, 334, 336, 341, 342,
    343, 344, 348, 350, 353, 355, 356,
    357, 358, 364, 399, 400
Hughes, E. C., 55
Hulett, J. E., Jr. 61
Hull, C., 52
Hunt, W. A., 334, 343

Hyman, H. H., 74, 89, 232

Ifugao, 321
Ilg, Frances L., 77, 78, 227, 319
Inkeles, A., 81, 82
International Congress of Applied Psychol., 353

Jackson, J., 179
Jacobs, R. C., 265
Jahoda, Marie, 92, 93, 243
James, W., 3, 16, 76, 225, 350
Jespersen, O., 323
Johnson, C. W., 74
Johnson, D., 167, 195, 336
Johnson, R. W., 69
Jones, H., 77

Kantor, J. R., 49
Kardiner, A., 81, 82
Karpf, Fay B., 66, 76
Katz, D., 67, 91, 92, 94, 97, 370
Kelley, H. H., 63, 68, 74, 90
Kelman, H. C., 192
Key, V. O., 101, 104, 109, 110, 114, 323, 336
Kitt, A. S., 73, 74, 89
Klein, G. S., 78, 192
Klineberg, O., 50, 80, 82, 83, 84, 89, 90, 471
Kluckhohn, C., 44, 48, 54, 65, 81, 82, 85, 317
Koch, S., 48, 50
Koffka, K., 53, 133, 224, 397
Köhler, W., 53, 84, 87, 131, 397
Koslin, B., 98–115, 249
Kramer, B. N., 372
Krech, D., 50, 84, 190
Kuhlen, R. G., 77
Kuhn, M., 229
Kula, 63, 103, 104, 376, 377
Külpe, O., 130, 131, 132

La Fave, L., 48, 336, 345, 362
La Pierre, R. T., 50
Landecker, W. S., 376, 379
Landesco, J., 71, 373
Lang, O., 58, 77
Langer, S., 225
Lazarsfeld, P. F., 93, 97
Le Bon, G., 55
League of Nations, 466, 470
Legum, C., 471
Leiserson, A., 100, 104, 109, 110, 112, 113, 114
Leuba, C. J., 78, 227
Levinson, D. J., 81, 82
Levy-Bruhl, L., 129

Lewin, K., 69, 78, 84, 89, 90, 133, 375, 377, 397, 398
Lewis, M. M., 322
Lewis, O., 65
Likert, R., 241, 372
Lindesmith, A. R., 50, 59, 73, 74, 77, 81, 82, 84
Lindzey, G., 66, 68, 92
Linton, R., 81, 82
Lippit, R., 69
Lowie, R. H., 41
Luchins, A. S., 85, 88, 173
Lumley, F. E., 65, 157
Lunt, P. S., 54
Lynd, Helen M., 44, 54, 185, 325
Lynd, R., 44, 54, 185, 325

McCarthy, D., 315, 322
Maccoby, Eleanor E., 68
MacCrone, I. D., 71
McDougall, W., 49, 65, 75, 80, 225, 229
McGranahan, D. V., 318
Mackler, D., 254
MacLeod, R., 36
McNeil, M. K., 265
McPartland, T. S., 229
McQuitty, L., 231
Malinowski, B., 40, 63, 64, 89, 103, 104, 127, 129, 321, 376
Mandelbaum, D. G., 43
Mannheim, K., 57
Marks, E., 233, 334
Marx, K., 3
Marshall, S. L. A., 192, 193, 194, 195, 356
Massey, F. J., 209, 212
Masai, 321
Mathiez, A., 161
Mausner, B., 173
Mayo, E., 69, 374
Mead, G. H., 3, 16, 41, 52, 59, 66, 75, 76, 77, 81, 84, 86
Mead, Margaret, 89, 128
Melton, A., 34, 52
Meltzer, H., 241
Merei, F., 60, 73
Merriam, C. E., 106, 109
Merton, R. K., 73, 74, 89, 185, 474
Middletown, 325
Milgram, S., 33
Miller, J. G., 61
Miller, N. E., 317, 399
Mills, C. W., 110, 113, 114
Miner, H. M., 376, 379
Moore, J. S., 65
Moorehead, A., 194
Moreno, J. L., 69, 375
Morgan, C. T., 314
Morris, C., 314

Mullahy, P., 195
Munger, F., 114
Murchison, C., 49, 66, 225
Murdock, G. P., 61, 65
Murphy, G., 41, 66, 67, 75, 79, 85, 86, 90, 93, 108, 191, 195, 224, 225, 226, 241, 320, 330, 331, 332, 334, 344, 372, 375, 377, 447
Murphy, Lois B., 66, 93, 227, 331, 344, 375
Murray, H. A., 48, 81, 85

Nebergall, R., 252, 342, 355, 357
New York Academy of Sciences, 223
Newcomb, T. M., 37, 50, 70, 72, 73, 84, 89, 93, 230, 331, 344, 373, 375

Oakley, C. O., 35
Olmstead, M. S., 68
Orlansky, H., 81
Orne, M., 32, 33, 254
O.S.S. Assessment Staff, 69
Osgood, C. E., 463

Paine, T., 163
Parducci, A., 356
Park, R. E., 69
Parsons, T., 44, 54, 86
Parten, M. B., 78, 227
Pasteur, L., 31
Pear, T. H., 446
Pearl, A., 254
Pelham, C., 159
Pelz, D. C., 73
Perrin, F. A. C., 65
Pettigrew, T. F., 254
Piaget, J., 3, 17, 36, 37, 60, 74, 130, 225, 226, 322, 386
Pinsky, Ruth H., 254
Pishkin, V., 254
Pollis, N. P., 258, 259, 272
Postman, L., 195
Potter, E., 401, 405
Prado, W., 231, 261
Pratt, C. C., 134
Preyer, W., 225
Pringle, A. G., 322
Proshansky, H.. 85, 334
Pronko, H., 336
Pyle, E., 193, 194, 195
Pyles, M. K., 318

Queener, E. L., 50

Rabinowitch, E., 462, 463
Radcliffe-Brown, A. A., 40, 77, 126

Radin, P., 77
Raimy, V., 82
Ramsey, G. V., 190
Razran, G., 318
Reed, J., 163
Rehm, R., 194
Reich, J., 345, 361
Rethlingschafer, D., 233
Reuter, E. B., 66
Richardson, L. F., 446
Riecken, H. W., 68, 93
Rivers, W. H. R., 77
Robbers Cave, Oklahoma, 391
Robinson, D., 195
Rockefeller Foundation, 234, 313, 387
Roethlisberger, F. J., 69, 70, 232
Roheim, G., 81
Rohrer, J. H., 61, 385, 433
Roseborough, M. E., 68
Rosen, B. C., 230
Rosenthal, R., 33, 254
Rosenzweig Picture Frustration Test, 401, 404
Ross, E., 49, 55, 65
Rousseau, J. J., 75

Saintsbury, P., 64, 474
Sapir, E., 40, 43, 58, 59, 61, 81, 126, 317
Sargent, S. S., 50, 53, 62, 229
Schachter, S., 379, 438
Schafer, R., 85
Schlesinger, H. J., 192
Schneirla, T. C., 63, 314, 316
Schooler, K., 85
Schottstaedt, W., 254
Schumer, F., 192
Scott, E. L., 73
Scott, J. P., 465
Scott, W. R., 253
Sears, R. R., 399
Seiler, E. N., 194
Sells, S., 120
Sewell, W. H., 81
Shafer, B., 471
Shaw, C. R., 38, 69, 71, 72, 168, 373, 374, 396, 435
Shedd, C., 190
Sherif, Carolyn W., 43, 48, 54, 59, 72f., 78, 85, 89, 94, 96f., 102, 106, 115, 167, 176ff., 190, 223, 231ff., 238, 247, 252, 257, 285ff., 296, 306, 313, 332, 353, 357f., 360, 380, 387, 425, 433, 439, 441, 448, 467
Sherif, M., 4, 43, 50f., 60f., 70ff., 76ff., 80, 85, 88ff., 94ff., 100ff., 115, 139, 167, 169f., 176ff., 182, 190ff., 200f., 225, 231f., 238ff., 242ff., 252f., 257, 265, 285ff., 296, 306, 319, 322, 334, 341f., 348, 353ff., 362, 379f., 382ff., 387, 396, 425, 433, 445ff., 464, 474

Shevky, E., 37, 250, 279, 296
Shibutani, T., 73, 74
Shils, E., 44, 54, 72, 86
Shinn, Millicent W., 77, 225
Short, J., 296
Siegel, Alberta E., 230
Siegel, S., 230
Silver, J. W., 474
Simon, H. A., 110
Siriono of Bolivia, 321, 333
Solomon Islands, 321
Smith, M. B., 81
Smith, M. E., 315
Smoke, K. L., 313
Snyder, L., 190
Snyder, R. C., 111, 112
Snygg, D., 79, 225
Spencer, B., 321
Spencer, H., 251
Spindler, G., 82
Stagner, R., 61
Stanford-Binet, 322
Stern, W., 200, 224
Stevens, S., 167
Stevenson, H. W., 33, 254
Stodtbeck, F. L., 68, 72
Stogdill, R. M., 68, 73
Stouffer, S. A., 74, 94, 193, 194, 199, 474
Strauss, A. L., 50, 59, 73, 74, 76, 77, 81, 82, 84
Sullivan, H. S., 195, 196
Sumner, W. G., 89, 424
Swander, D. V., 190, 201, 385
Swanson, G. E., 68
Swearingen, L., 190

Taine, 161
TAT, 401, 404
Taub, D., 356
Thibaut, J. W., 63, 68, 90
Thirteen Experts, 470
Thomas, W. I., 52, 66, 68, 79, 81, 331, 344
Thorndike, E., 134
Thrasher, F., 38, 60, 63, 69, 71, 168, 322, 373, 374, 396, 435, 448
Thrasher, J. D., 88, 172, 383
Thurnwald, R., 82
Thurstone, L. L., 348, 358
Tiedemann, D., 225
Titchener, E. B., 34, 65, 251
Toki, K., 73
Tolman, E. C., 53
Tresselt, M. E., 88, 167
Trobriand Islands, 103, 104, 127
Truman, D. B., 101
Turner, R., 73, 74

U Thant, 470

Unesco, 377, 447
United Nations, 470

Van Gennep, A., 77
Vaughan, E. H., 193, 195
Vaughan, Kathryn, 364, 365
Veblen, T., 74, 80
Villarreal, E., 285, 306
Volkart, E. H., 81, 180, 336, 355
Volkmann, J., 53, 58, 85, 167, 232, 334, 343
Voth, A. C., 192

Wallis, W., 128
Wallon, H., 77, 225
Walter, N., 172, 190, 317, 386
Wapner, S., 449
Ward, L. F., 65
Warden, C. J., 318
Warner, W. L., 44, 54
Waskow, A., 473
Watson-Watt, R., 469
Watt, A. F., 323
Webb, W. P., 57
Weiss, R. S. A., 90
Welch, L., 318
Welles, O., 195
Wells, F. D., 132, 332
Wertheimer, M., 3, 53, 133, 397
Wever, E. G., 53, 134
White, B. J., 48, 72, 389, 433, 437, 448
White, R. K., 69
White, R. W., 79
Whiting, J. W. M., 81
Whittaker, J. O., 170, 345
Whyte, W. F., 37, 59, 60, 69, 70, 71, 72, 73, 93, 233, 373, 374, 377, 387, 396, 435
Williams, R. M., Jr., 49, 185, 331, 451
Wilson, W., 466
Wittenborn, R., 401, 405
Wolf, S., 254
Woodworth, R., 134
Wright, Q., 58
Wundt, W., 34, 251

Yerkes, R. M., 314
Young, K., 50, 66, 84

Zander, A. F., 68, 252
Zelen, S. L., 229
Zeligs, R., 241
Zener, K. E., 53, 134
Zetterberg, H. L., 48
Znaniecki, F., 79, 331
Zorbaugh, H. W., 69, 168, 269, 373, 374, 396
Zurcher, A., 157

SUBJECT INDEX

Acculturation, 61, 279
Achievement, radius of, 235–37
    See also Goals
"Act," Mead's conception of, 84
Adolescence, reference groups during, 230, 247ff.; studies of, 77
Adolescent behavior, differences according to setting, 296–98; research on, 276f.
Adolescent group, and its setting, 247ff.
Adolescent studies, ethnocentrisms in, 91
Adolescents, estimation of age-mate and parent's performance, 262ff.; similarities across classes, 295f.
Age-mate groups, 276
Aggression. *See* Conflict; Frustration
Aloneness, characterized, 197
American revolution, 160ff.
Analysis, sequence of, 63f.
    See also Levels
Anchorages, of body orientation, 80; and problem of insecurity, 199–201; elimination of, and insecurity, 190ff.; lacking in combat, 199; relative weights of, 88–89
    See also Frame of reference; Reference points
Anthropology, and "behavioral science," 40ff.; and concept of culture, 44f., 53; impact on psychology, 41f., 67
Anthropomorphism, reverse, 314
Anxiety, characterized, 197; criteria differentiating, 195f.; development of, 196f.; neurotic, 198; study of, 190ff.
Applied research, 29ff., 369ff.
Argot, prison, 322
Aspiration-level (*anspruchsniveau*), 134
Assimilation effect, and attitude change, 351f.; determinants of range of, 351ff., in judgment, 238f., 356; in reaction to communication, 341
Assimilation-contrast effects, in categorizing communication, 347ff.
Attitude, and behavior, 14f., 86f., 153, 344f., 382; operational definition of,

344; in patterning perception, 131
Attitude change, 31, 70; through communication, 331; and judgment of communication, 349ff.; toward outgroups, 183f.; predictions of, 350ff.
Attitude measurement, indirect, 7, 334f., 348
Attitudes, as components of self, 78f., 224; inferred from characteristic behavior, 153; measurement of, 18f.; needed concepts in study of, 330ff.; negative (prejudice), 371; of prejudice, 242f.
Aufgabe, experiments on, 131
Authoritarian atmosphere, 241, 262
Autokinetic effect, 2; used in experiments, 138ff., 202
Autokinetic experiments, interpretive summary of, 384f.; summary of results, 144f.
Autokinetic movement, extent of and anxiety, 192ff., 265
Autokinetic situation, in study of insecurity, 191ff.
Autonomy-heteronomy, 74

Basic research, 29ff., 31f.
Battlefield, insecurity on, 192ff.
Behavior, and attitude, 86 (*See also* Attitudes); in groups, valid study of, 269f. (*See also* Group); predictability of, 270ff.
Behavioral analysis, bridging gap with institutional, 109–115
"Behavioral science," 30f., 42f.
Behavioral vs. institutional approaches, 98ff.
Behavioristic schools of psychology and problems of stimulus, 52ff.
Bimodality, in distributions of goals, 299f.
Biogenic motives, 80
    See also Attitudes; Ego attitudes
Block surveys, 278f.

Bodily self, 200
Boomerang effects, 341
 See also Contrast effect

California E-F scale, 230
Car culture, 277
Categories, number of, as index of attitude, 334*ff.*, 348
Categorizing effect, of concepts, 317*ff.*
Categorization, in affective judgment, 133*f.*; of ambiguous stimuli, 334*f.*; of attitude items, 332*f.*; and evaluation, 18*f.*
 See also Judgment
Ceiling effect, 338
Change, and conformity-deviation, 182*ff.*; social, 2, 9, 154*ff.*
 See also Attitude change; Intergroup relations
Cognition, motivational determinants of, 322*f.*, 333, 348
Cognitive dissonance, 342, 350
Cognitive processes, 190*ff.*; frame of reference in, 382*f.*
 See also Perception; Judgment
Cohesiveness. *See* Solidarity
Collective action, properties of, 63
Collective interaction, 55
 See also Slogans
Color pyramid, cultural variations in, 127*f.*
Common enemy, 451
Communication, placement of, 349*ff.*; properties of and judgment, 349*f.*; reaction to, 336*ff.*, 341; in reducing anxiety, 194
Comparison process, 344
 See also Judgment; Categorization
Competition, 227; as cultural norm, 413*f.*; development of, 78
"Comsigns," 314
Concept formation, 313*f.*
Concepts, effects in behavior, 317–24; linguistic, 40*f.* (*See also* Language); in primitive society, 321*f.*; shared, 314
Conceptual development, level of, 227*ff.*
Conceptual functioning, 313*ff.*
Conditioning experiment, 318
Conditions, of varying uncertainty, 203–208
Confidence ratings, and status in groups, 289*f.*
Conflict, experimental conditions for, 438*ff.*; intergroup, 23*f.*, 414*ff.*, 425–29, 446–48, 464*ff.*; psychological, 186, 197*f.*; and superordinate goals, 445*ff.*; theory of, 23, 245*ff.*, 414*ff.*, 425–29, 446*ff.*, 464*ff.*

Conformity, 61; change in, 182*ff.*; to group norms, 257; in group relations, 174*ff.*; and human nature, 166; individual variations in, 181*ff.*; and norm arbitrariness (experiment), 264–68; problem of, 164*ff.*; and stimulus properties, 166–68; studied in laboratory, 166–72
Contact, between groups, 24*f.*, 372, 443; in reducing intergroup tension, 95; in satisfying activities, 451*f.*
Context effects, in judgment, 253*f.*
Consistency, 74; and ego-involved activity, 226; of goal-directed behavior, 76*f.*; in motivational patterns, 82
 See also Self
Contiguity, in intergroup contact, 95
Contrast effect, in judgment, 168, 238*f.*, 356*f.*; in reaction to communication, 341
Convergence of judgments, awareness of, 153; graphs of, 146–47
Cooperation, 227; development of, 78; between groups, 464*ff.*
Creative alternatives, 455*f.*
Crisis, rise of slogans in, 148, 161*ff.*
Cross-cultural comparison, 108; of group discussion method, 377; to minimize ethnocentrism, 91; of self, 77*f.*
Cross-disciplinary checking, of results, 47, 63*ff.*
Cross-pressures, 245
Cross-sectional comparison, 108
Cultural background, in group formation experiments, 413*f.*
Cultural determinism, 62*ff.*
Cultural differences, in reaction to same stimulus, 125*ff.*
Cultural lag, 167
Cultural norms, 40*ff.*; in stabilizing attitudes, 128*f.*
 See also Norms; Values
Cultural products, 54*ff.*
Cultural relativism, 91
Cultural variations, in ego formation, 79
Culture, Freudian interpretation of, 81; non-material, 58*ff.*; as social stimulus, 55*ff.*; study of, 44*f.*
"Culture and Personality" approach, 80–83
"Culture-free" tests, 90
Current issues, and theoretical problems, 369*ff.*

Dark adaptation, 204
Delinquents, interviews with, 254
"Demand character" of research situation, 7, 32
Design, of intergroup experiments, 424*ff.*

Detroit race riot, 243
Deviation, problems of, 164*ff*.; reactions to, 59*f*., 61, 379, 381; sanctions for, 286
Deviate behavior, and intergroup behavior, ·447
Development, of self, 225–27
  See also Ego formation; Self
Differential effects of interaction, 20
Discrepancy, between attitude and communication, 343
  See also Attitude; Communication; Contrast effect
Discussion groups, 255
Disorganization, following defeat, 441
Dominance relations, subhuman, 63

Ecological characteristics, 21
Ecology, 21; of neighborhood and violence, 303*f*.
Education, and concepts, 324*ff*.
Effective initiative, concept of, 285*f*.; as index of leadership, 95; as indicator of power, 256*f*.; ratings of, 287*ff*.; relative frequency of, 176
Ego, definition of, 78*f*.
  See also Self
Ego-attitudes, contradictory, 243*f*.; defined, 79*f*.; disruption of, 197*f*.; in group formation, 398
Ego development, 196*f*.
Ego formation, 77; and language acquisition, 319
Ego functioning, study of, 190*ff*.
Ego-involvement, degree of, 19, 117*f*., 343; and displacement of intermediate items, 362*f*.; as indicated by judgments, 334*f*.; indicator of, 349, 364*f*.; and salience of anchors, 360*f*.; as variable in attitude change, 349*f*.
"Ego structure," 244
Ego tension, 197*f*.
Enculturation, 61; and norms varying in arbitrariness, 266*f*.
End-anchoring, in judgment, 273; perceived by members, 287*ff*.
Equal-appearing intervals, assumption of, 32
Ethnic status, 279
"Ethnic subculture," 278
Ethnocentrism, and absolute norms, 189; checks against, 89–92; in perception, 120
Evaluation, and categorization, 333
Evaluations of performance, as indicator of intergroup relations, 389*f*.
Exchange of persons, for reduction of conflict, 455
Experimental conditions, for group formation, 434*ff*.

Experimental design, of Robbers Cave experiment, 391
Experimental methods, use of, 108
Experimental room, size of, as factor in uncertainty, 204
Experimental setup, in insecurity experiment, 207; in norm formation experiment, 141
Experimentation, in social psychology, 41, 93
Experimenter, role of, 203
Experimenter-subject relationships, 33
Experiments, design of, 24; on intergroup relations, 94*ff*.
Extremity, of attitude, 346*f*.

Faculty psychology, 15
Fascist slogans, 157
Fear, differentiated from anxiety, 195*f*.
Field and laboratory, integration of, 96*ff*.
Field observations, and principles of behavior, 287–91
Field studies, 93*f*.
Field work, in small group research, 374*ff*.
Figure-ground relations, 133
Formal organization, conformity in, 185*ff*.
Frame of reference, concepts as anchors in, 318; of cognitive processes, 382*f*.; diagrammatic representation of, 86; in experiments, 130*ff*.; inner and outer influences in, 14*ff*.; for judgment, 232; of perception, 393
  See also Anchorages; Reference points
"Frame of reference psychophysics" (Helson), 118
French Revolution, 161*ff*.
Frequency of association, 285
Freudian conceptions, 66*f*.
Friendship choices, reversed by group formation, 406, 412
Frustration, 31; collective, 161*f*.; group, 402*ff*., 416*ff*., 438*ff*., 440, 450; individual, 23, 426*f*., 446

Gangs, 21, 271*f*.
  See also Group
Generalization, meaning as, 317
"Generalized other," 77
Gestalt psychology, advent of, 67*f*.
Gift-giving tradition, 236
Goals, adolescent, 280*ff*.; and character of intergroup relations, 399; for education, 299*f*.; setting of, 78
  See also Superordinate goals
Group, defined, 379*f*.; operational definition of, 106; as pattern of reciprocities, 20

Group atmosphere, 69
Group characteristics, in diverse settings, 304ff.
Group conflicts and stereotypes, 458
  See also Conflict
Group decision, 90
Group discussion, in different cultures, 377
Group Dynamics, 375
Group formation, 71, 405–413; during adolescence, 253; hypotheses on, 257, 380, 400, 433ff.; motivations conducive to, 396f.; and psychological consequences, 268f.
Group interaction, differential effects of, 397
Group membership, and conformity, 175ff.; and prejudice, 372
Group organization, 24f.; stabilization of, 257, 405–413
  See also Organization; Status
Group products, reducing to psychological constructs, 248f.
Group psychology (Freud), 393f.
Group relations, conformity-deviation in, 164ff., 174f.
Group situations, vs. togetherness and norm stability, 258–60
Group structure, 71; as property, 379
  See also Organization; Status
Groupness, in degrees, 71f., 255f.
Groups, adolescent, intensive study of, 281–83; compared to togetherness, 177; formal and informal, 378; generality of, 268f.; informally organized, 395f.; not closed systems, 21f.; properties of, and conformity, 175ff.; secretiveness of, 7; as stimulus situations, 55
Guilt, 197

Historical comparisons, to minimize ethnocentrism, 91f.
Homeostatic states, 80, 223
Human nature, assumptions of, 75, 166
"Human relations" approach, 69f.
Human survival, debate on, 460
Hypotheses, on attitude change, 340, 350f.; on distribution of social judgments, 334f.; on group formation and intergroup conflict, 380, 400, 433–44; on group properties, 257; of intergroup experiments, 433–44; on norm formation, 137f.; on relative size of latitudes of acceptance, rejection and noncommitment, 337f.; on situational insecurity, 201

Identifications, widening circles of, 469f.;

with individuals and groups, 191
  See also Reference groups; Self
Ideology, dominant in setting, 22
Imposed categories procedure, 348, 335ff.
In-group, delineation of, 399; relationship with out-group, 372f.
In-group interaction, privacy of, 256
In-group relations, democratic, autocratic, laissez-faire, 398; distinguished from intergroup relations, 446ff.; man in, 19ff.
Inconsistency, due to cross-pressures, 245; in ego-involved behavior, 78; in intergroup behavior, 240ff.
  See also Reference group
Income level, conceptions of, 236
Individual differences, 22; in prejudice and group membership, 373; in reactions to social situations, 125ff.
Individual-society relationship, 74–83
Infant behavior, 226
Insecurity, in crisis situations, 136f.; experimental findings on, 191ff.; and loss of stable anchorages, 46; observations of, 192ff.; problem of, in experiment, 199–201
Institutional analysis, 105; and behavioral, 109–115
Institutional vs. behavioral controversy, 98ff.
Interaction, with common motives, 178; differential effects on behavior, 20, 379; effects on attitudes, 380; human, 1f.; in-group, 467f.; intergroup, 368f., 468f.; theory and research on, 119; voluntary, 176
Interaction episodes, in adolescent groups, 247ff.
Interaction process, importance when stimulus unstructured, 384; "pure," 119
Interactionist position, 66ff.
Interdependence of sociocultural setting and group process, 295f.
Interdisciplinary activities, 42f.
Interdisciplinary approach, methodological necessity of, 11ff.; problems of, 61ff.
Interdisciplinary cooperation, and levels concept, 375
Interdisciplinary efforts, dichotomous approaches in, 99–101; history of, 48ff.
Interdisciplinary problems, 68ff.
Interdisciplinary relations, in training, 36f.
Interdisciplinary task, in small group research, 248f.
Intergroup attitudes, hypotheses on, 400
  See also Prejudice; Social distance
Intergroup behavior, its causes, 465

Intergroup experiments, design and hypotheses of, 424*ff.*
Intergroup conflict, development of, 414*ff.*; its impact on in-group pattern, 464*f.*; measures proposed for reducing, 455; needed research, 471*ff.*; reduction of, 419–21, 445*ff.*, 451*ff.*; theory of, 23, 245*ff.*, 414*ff.*, 425–29, 446*ff.*, 464*ff.*
Intergroup relations, and deterrence policy, 455; experiments on, 388, 391, 392*ff.*; impact on behavior, 446*ff.*; man in, 23*ff.*; method of studying, 94*ff.*; and policy makers, 464*f.*; and role of negotiator, 466*f.*
Intermediate categories, neglected by highly involved subjects, 364*f.*
Internalization, of social values or norms, 59*f.*
International law, in a changing world, 470
Interpersonal relations, 53*f.*; and culture, 41; within group, 273
See also Group formation
Interviews, administrator effect in, 254
Isolates, 405

Judgment, as comparison process, 253; convergence of (graphs), 146–47; distributions of, as index of attitude, 334–36; laboratory experiments on, 115*f.*; of value statements, 31*f.*
See also Social judgment
Judgment experiments, in field settings, 436*f.*
Judgment indicators, of status and role, 72
Judgments of performance, as indicators of group conflict, 440
Judgment variations, as indicator of attitudes, 386*ff.*

Kula exchange system, 63*f.*, 103*f.*

Laboratory, and field approaches, 13; and field research, 93*f.*; limitations of, 172–74; as social situation, 32
Laboratory research, on conformity, 166–72; and field work, 374*ff.*
Language, 41, 59; attainment of, 226*f.*; concepts of, 18*f.*, 314*ff.*; functions of, 317; mastery of, 78
Latitude of acceptable behavior, defined by norm, 178*ff.*, 253
Latitude of acceptance, defined, 345; and importance of activity, 293; as range of conformity, 61; size of, and status, 294

Latitudes of acceptance-rejection and conformity, 291–94
Latitudes of acceptance, rejection, and noncommitment, in attitude research, 336–40; relative sizes of, 181, 343, 346*ff.*
Latitude of noncommitment, defined, 345; as indicator of degree of involvement, 347
Latitude of rejection, defined, 345; as indicator of degree of involvement, 347, 349; size of, 340
Leader-follower relations, 256*f.*
Leaders, of Bull Dogs and Red Devils, 410; limitations on, 451
Leadership, bounds of, 394, 397*f.*; operational index of, 285*f.*
See also Effective initiative
Level of interaction, 468*f.*
Levels of analysis, 50*ff.*, 104–108; concept of, 375*ff.*; in disciplines, 62*ff.*; in social science and psychology, 46*f.*; integration of, 110
Localization, reference points in, 131*f.*
Logical thinking, and norms, 130

Marginality, 231; in groups, 405
Material culture, as social stimuli, 57*ff.*, 167, 384
See also Cultural lag
Member behavior, predictable from group properties, 287*ff.*
Membership character, in perceptual pattern, 133*f.*
Membership groups, and reference groups, 229
Method of single stimuli, in judgment, 134*f.*
Methods, combination of, 8, 34, 97, 256*f.*
"Middle-level" research, 110
Modal personality, 81
Model, selection of, 13, 34
Model building, by analogy, 251*f.*; principle of, 35*f.*
Motivation, human, 17; human and self concept, 223*ff.*; sociological interest in, 65*f.*
Motivational basis, for reduction of intergroup conflict, 455*ff.*
See also Superordinate goals
Motivational concerns, in formation of adolescent groups, 276; salience in various groups, 257
Motivational factors, in social judgment, 348
Motives, for interaction, 379
Multiple groups, and conceptual level, 227–29; and conformity, 185; in complex societies, 82

See also Reference groups

Names, study of stabilization of, 323*f.*
National character studies, 80–83
Natural groups, characterized, 255*f.*; of adolescents, 275*ff.*; three generations of, 305–307
Navaho youth study, 238
Nazi slogans, 156
Neologisms, 322
Nicknames, and roles, 411
Noncommitment, latitude indicating degree of involvement, 347
Norm experiments, procedure of, 139*ff.*
Norm formation, hypotheses, 137*f.*; problem of, 38, 136*ff.*; research on, 169*ff.*
Normative process, in laboratory, 168–72
Normlessness, 2, 186
Norms, arbitrariness of, 257; conflicting, 189; and conformity-deviation problem, 164*ff.*; criteria of, 286; defined, 60; defining latitude of acceptable behavior, 178*ff.*; formation of, in group, 398, in different societies, 125*ff.*; persistence of, 385; psychological basis of, 120*f.*; stability of, in togetherness vs. group situations, 258–60; study of arbitrariness of, 264–68; transmission of, 264–68

Observation, awareness of, 449; of insecurity, 192*ff.*
Observer being observed, 283*f.*
Observer bias, 256*f.*
Observer ratings, checked by independent rater, 286
Occupational goals, level of, 236
Organization, of group, 176*f.*
Own categories, and distribution of judgment, 338*ff.*, 347*ff.*; of individual, 347*ff.*
Own categories procedure, and attitude measurement, 335*ff.*, 348; distribution of judgments in, 338*f.*, 353*ff.*; research using, 357*ff.*; theoretical basis of, 355
Own position, as anchor in evaluation, 357

Paired comparison method, 333*f.*
Panic, in uncertain situations, 194*f.*
Pattern, properties of, 34*f.*
Perception, concepts in, 317*f.*; of similarity, 127; social factors in, 125*ff.*
Perceptual selectivity, 253, 382
  See also Selectivity
Person perception, 283

Personal consistency, 16*f.*
"Personalistic" psychologists, 224
Personality, and ego problems, 219; and self system, 320
Personality structure, 75*f.*
Personality traits, "generality" of, 78
"Phantom anesthetist," 195
Phenomenology, 5*f.*, 342; disciplined, 36
Political opinion, and reference groups, 104
Popularity, 286, 407
Power, in group, 379; indicators of, 256*f.*
Power relations, and popularity, 407; in groups, 176
"Pre-logical stage" (Levy-Bruhl), 129
Prejudice, 5, 23*ff.*, 369*ff.*; development of, 371*f.*; experimental formation of, 419; expressed against nonexistent groups, 328; and social distance scale, 240*ff.*
Prestige effect, in autokinetic study, 151*f.*
Primacy, in judgment, 151
"Primary group," 76
Principles, verified by field observations, 287–91
Problem, choice of, 4
Problems, of interdisciplinary interest, 68*ff.*; persistent and current issues, 369*ff.*
Psychological imperialism, 103*ff.*
Psychophysical experiments, 134
Psychophysical methods, 343
Psychophysical scale, 333; and conformity, 167*ff.*
Psychosocial scale, as baseline in attitude research, 333*ff.*
Public opinion, research on, 30

Racist doctrine, 394
Range of acceptable behavior, 59, 379
  See also Latitude of acceptance
Range of judgment, 208*ff.*
Range of tolerable behavior, defined by values or norms, 45
  See also Latitude of acceptance
Rapport, 270; gauging degree of, 284*f.*
Rate busters, 233
Rate setting, in industry, 232
Rational thought, 111
Reduction of intergroup conflict, sufficient and necessary conditions for, 456*f.*, 462*f.*
  See also Superordinate goals
Reductionism, 44*ff.*, 110*ff.*; in conceptions of social stimuli, 103*ff.*; and culture, 56; in study of cultural setting, 248*ff.*
Reference groups, 16*f.*, 73*f.*; as anchors for self, 232*f.*, 332; and membership

Reference groups (*cont'd*)
group, 185, 229; as psychological
concept, 228; salience of, 260–64;
and self concept, 223*ff*.; shifts in,
230*f*.; use of, 89
Reference group ties, 37; evidence for,
229–32
Reference points, change in, 129*f*.; lack
of, 142*ff*.; review of experiments on,
131*ff*.; in time reckoning, 126*f*.; in
unstructured situations, 140*f*.
See also Anchorage; Frame of reference
Reference scale, 332; source of, 333*f*.
See also Psychophysical scale; Psychosocial scale
Relative weights, of factors, 88*f*.
Reliability, criterion of, 30
Research design, of 1949 intergroup ex-
periment, 401*f*.; on natural groups,
249*f*.; in small group research, 248*f*.
Research methods, choice of, 254–57; in
intergroup experiments, 429–33; as
parts of social situation, 449
Research operations, 5*ff*.
Research program, on intergroup relations
(described), 448–54
Research situation, as social situation,
429–33
Research techniques, as part of situation,
96*f*.; and validity problem, 108*f*.
Research tools, as parts of interaction, 6*f*.
Researcher, role as caretaker, 403
Roles, differentiated by status, 255*f*.; dimensions of, 286; experimenter, dis-
guised, 403; feminine, 198; leadership, 458 (See also Leader); of
professional woman, 243; revealed
in nicknames, 411; and self, 224; in
self development, 226*f*.; sex, 325
See also Group; Organization
Role relationships, 106
Rorschach test, 158; and anxiety, 192
Rules of the game, in moral judgment,
130
Rumor, in crisis situations, 195

S-R theory, 52*f*.
Sanctions, 381; standardized by Bull
Dogs and Red Devils, 411*f*.
See also Deviation
Scientific method, courses in, 326; in
social psychology, 92–97
See also Method; Research
Self (Ego), 16*f*., 18*f*., 78*f*.; aspired, 244;
behavioral evidence of, 223*ff*.; cen-
tral values in, 61; defining problem
area, 224–25; functioning of, 190*ff*.
See also Ego; Ego attitude; Ego-
involvement

Self-awareness, earliest manifestations of,
226
Self-radius and goals, for achievement,
281; and reference groups, 233–39;
of youth, 22
"Self-regarding sentiment," 80
Selectivity, 5*f*.; joint determination of,
87; of mass media, 173; and norms,
126*f*.; of researcher, 97
Semantics, as antidote to stereotyping,
327*ff*.
Shame, 197
Shelter-centered society, 473
Shevky-Bell social area analysis, 250
Similarity, perception of by Trobriand
Islanders, 127
Slogans, 2; defined, 154; and experi-
mental social psychology, 158*f*.; in
presidential elections, 156; psycho-
logical properties of, 160*f*.; psychol-
ogy of, 154*ff*.; rise of, 148
Small group research, critique of, 117*f*.;
field and laboratory, 374*ff*.
Small groups, 68–73; terms characterized,
378*f*.
See also Groups
Social area analysis, 250, 279
Social attitude, properties of, 331–33; as
psychological concept, 60; underly-
ing processes, 149*ff*.
See also Attitude
Social change, and conformity-deviation,
184*ff*.
See also Change; Attitude change
Social context, of behavior, 271*ff*.
Social desirability (Edwards), 250, 280
Social distance, as institution, 240*ff*.;
scale of, 371*f*.
See also Intergroup conflict
Social factors, in perception, 125*ff*.
Social influence, differential, 149*ff*.; tran-
sitory, 174
Social institution, prejudice as, 242
See also Institutional analysis
Social judgment, 347*ff*.
See also Judgment; Psychosocial scales
Social judgment-involvement approach,
to attitudes, 342*ff*.
See also Ego-involvement; Social judg-
ment
Social norm, as sociological concept, 60;
formation of, 136*ff*.
See also Norm; Value
Social organizations, 99*ff*.
See also Group; Organization; Social
institution
Social perception, 68, 85; and cultural
norms, 40
See also Perception; Social judgment
Social products, external reality of, 60*ff*.

Social psychology, converging trends in, 83–97; defined, 50*f.*; definitions of, 49*f.*; development of, 43*f.*; history of, 49*ff.*, 65*ff.*; and psychology, 45*f.*, 102*ff.*, 130*ff.*

"Social psychology of psychological experiment," 12, 32, 254

Social relations, as context for behavior, 253*f.*

Social situation, analysis of, 117*ff.*; sets of factors in, 120*f.*

Social stimulus situation, 12, 51*ff.*; classification of, 54*ff.*; problem of, 102*ff.*; relative weights of factors in, 121

Social values, exteriority of, 45
See also Norm; Value

Socialization, as problem, 56
See also Ego; Self

Society, and individual, 74–83; norms in, 125*ff.*; study of, 44*f.*

Sociocultural settings, and behavior, 278*ff.*; selection of, 234
See also Culture

Socioeconomic class, 278*ff.*

Socioeconomic rank, 279; of setting and values, 298*ff.*

Sociogenic motives, 79, 331
See also Attitude; Ego; Self

Sociograms, of experimental groups, 405, 408*f.*

Sociology, as study of social systems, 44*f.*, 53

Sociometric choices, 24, 69, 405, 408, 436

Solidarity, 23; during group formation, 411; increase during conflict, 450*f.*; indicated by judgments of performance, 389; psychological basis of, 268

Spread of dwellings, as indicator of solidarity, 286

Stanford-Binet test, 322

Status, confidence of observers' ratings, 289*f.*; and conformity, 181*ff.*; in group, 106, 397; and group identification, 415*ff.*; high, and intergroup conflict, 419; hypotheses about judgments, 437; low, and aggressive behavior, 441*f.*; as role dimension, 255
See also Effective initiative

Status hierarchy, 176*f.*; end-anchoring in, 273

Stereotypes, and concept, 325*ff.*; development in intergroup conflict, 416; evidence for rise of, 439*f.*; formation and change of, 182*ff.*; and nature of intergroup relations, 390

Stimulus conditions, in group situations, 107; specification of, 98*ff.*

Stimulus context, of behavior, 118*f.*

Stimulus determinants of behavior, 120

Stimulus factors, relative weights of, 173*f.*

Stimulus field, unstructured, 383

Stimulus properties, and conformity, 166–68

Stimulus situation, conception of, 43*f.*; and conformity, 187*f.*; differential reactions to, 125; structured, 87*f.*

Stimulus structure, gradations in conformity studies, 172

Stress situations, 192*ff.*

Structured stimulus situations, 6, 87*f.*

Study cycle, for natural groups, 282*f.*, 285*ff.*

Subject selection, in intergroup experiments, 400*f.*, 432

Subject-investigator relationship, 6*f.*

"Suggestibility," study of, 192

Suicide, 64

Super-ego, 83, 225
See Ego; Self

Superordinate goals, 95–97, 391; defined for experiment, 443*f.*; and effectiveness of information, 459; introduced in experiments, 452*ff.*; in reduction of intergroup conflict, 445, 457*ff.*; series of, 457

Susceptibility to attitude change, and latitude of rejection, 350

Symbolic behavior, of animals, 316

TAT, 404

Task, in social situation, 118*f.*

Techniques, combination of, 249*f.*, 282*f.*
See also Methods

Technological change, 58

Technology, and attitudes, 167; degree of contact with, 384

Theory and research, interdependence of, 250*ff.*

Thresholds of acceptance-rejection, 335; defined, 348

Trial-and-error learning, 319

Trobriand Islands, 103*f.*

Twins, speech of, 323

Uncertainty, increasing, with fewer anchors, 216; situational, 190*ff.*, 231
See also Insecurity; Unstructured stimulus situations

Units of analysis, in disciplines, 62*ff.*; in psychology, 35; in social psychology, 50*f.*; in social science, 46*f.*, 62*ff.*

Unstructured stimulus situations, 6, 88; in autokinetic setup, 144*ff.*; psychological tendency in, 158*f.*; and uncertainty, 192*ff.*
See also Social situation; Stimulus

Validity, and choice of techniques, 108*f.*;
    of research findings, 30*f.*, 39
Value judgment, expressed in slogan,
    154*ff.*
    See also Evaluation; Social judgment
Values, adolescent, 280*ff.*; homogeneity-
    diversity of, 298*ff.*; similarities across
    classes, 295*f.*
    See also Norms

Variability, individual differences, 229;
    of status ratings, 289
    See also Stimulus conditions
Vocabulary, acquisition, 314*f.*; develop-
    ment, 322
Voting behavior, 114

Win or lose encounters, 95
    See also Conflict

CPSIA information can be obtained at www.ICGtesting.com
Printed in the USA
LVOW061433211111

255937LV00001B/88/P